# PILLARS OF GRACE ENDORSEMENTS

"This book will ignite and impassion your heart for the gospel and the doctrines of grace that undergird it. Dr. Lawson has done something for which we will forever be grateful—he demonstrates conclusively that the truths of Calvinism and the Reformed faith are rooted in the history of the church, from the apostles to the emergence of Martin Luther in the sixteenth century. We have, of course, always suspected this to be true, but few attempts have been made to demonstrate it, and none with such infectious zeal as is to be found in these pages. Few writers can marry church history, exposition, and sound doctrine in such a manner as this. Do not start reading this book unless you are prepared to find that you are unable to put it down. It is that good."

—Dr. Derek W. H. Thomas
*Professor of systematic and practical theology, Reformed Theological Seminary*
*Minister of teaching, First Presbyterian Church, Jackson, Mississippi*

"Reading Steven Lawson's *Pillars of Grace* is like taking a helicopter tour of a mountain range—a breathtaking survey of a series of majestic peaks all pointing upward to heaven. Each chapter offers an informative, fascinating, and accessible look at a significant teacher of God's glorious grace, from Clement to Calvin. Read this book and discover that to be Christian and Reformed is to be rooted in the church through the ages."

—Dr. Joel R. Beeke
*President, Puritan Reformed Theological Seminary,*
*Grand Rapids, Michigan*

"Steve Lawson's research takes us into the controversial and somewhat neglected area regarding the development of the doctrines of grace before John Calvin. Of special value is his large collection of quotations, which show that, yes, there were indeed a few notable TULIP flowers in the church garden before the Reformation blossomed. I especially like his challenge to imitate these heroes. I am pleased to recommend this volume and look forward to the next in the series."

—Dr. Curt Daniel
*Pastor, Faith Bible Church, Springfield, Illinois*
*Author,* The History and Theology of Calvinism

"Bringing witness after witness to the stand, Steve Lawson marshals testimony about the sovereign grace of God from twenty-three specific exemplars, from Clement of Rome to Calvin of Geneva. Following a masterful overview, with the weight of original sources and helpful context from these witnesses, both clarity and unity result. Steve Lawson is to be commended for assembling such a superb cast, arranged in such useful parts—road-tested in a men's group from his own congregation—to sing such a deep and moving chorus. Each study is useful for local church studies and libraries, for pastoral enrichment or officer training, or as fodder for illustrations, gathered by an experienced shepherd. We can rejoice over this excellent work that truly exhibits that which has been believed everywhere in all ages of true and vibrant Christianity. I join Dr. Lawson in praying that this book will cultivate a new generations of pillars."

—Dr. David W. Hall
*Senior pastor, Midway Presbyterian Church,*
*Powder Springs, Georgia*


"Dr. Lawson has produced a veritable *tour de force* with this historical survey of the church's witness to the sweet doctrines of divine sovereignty. Not since the voluminous Dr. Gill has this really been attempted, and Gill's study is seriously dated in many ways. Hence the need for this winsome and judicious work, in which Lawson shows the reader the way these golden threads of grace have wound their way through the church's life in the Patristic, medieval, and Reformation eras. Contrary to popular thought, it can be seen that the eras prior to the Reformation were not devoid of powerful witnesses to these great truths. This is a must read for anyone interested in the way these biblical truths have been received by the church."

—Dr. Michael A. G. Haykin
*Professor of church history and biblical spirituality,*
*The Southern Baptist Theological Seminary, Louisville, Kentucky*
*Director of the Andrew Fuller Center for Baptist Studies*

"Thank you, Dr. Lawson, for your labors in pulling together this rich treasury of biblical teaching on the doctrines of grace over the centuries from faithful men whom Christ appointed and the Spirit endowed for the building up of the saints for the work of service. We are your grateful debtors."

—DR. J. LIGON DUNCAN III
*Senior minister, First Presbyterian Church,*
*Jackson, Mississippi*
*From his Foreword*

"In this important book, Dr. Lawson has documented the teachings of many of the most important theologians, churchmen, and Christian thinkers of these centuries, showing that these men did indeed have much to say about God's saving grace—and much that will be of great encouragement to evangelicals today."

—DR. R. ALBERT MOHLER JR.
*President, The Southern Baptist Theological Seminary,*
*Louisville, Kentucky*
*From his Afterword*

A LONG LINE OF GODLY MEN
VOLUME TWO
AD 100 – 1564

# PILLARS
# OF GRACE

STEVEN J. LAWSON

**R**
*Reformation Trust*
PUBLISHING

A DIVISION OF LIGONIER MINISTRIES · ORLANDO, FLORIDA

*Pillars of Grace*

© 2011 by Steven J. Lawson

Published by Reformation Trust Publishing
a division of Ligonier Ministries
400 Technology Park, Lake Mary, FL 32746

www.ligonier.org    www.reformationtrust.com

Printed in Harrisonburg, Virginia
RR Donnelley and Sons
March 2011
First edition

Cover design: Chris Larson
Interior illustrations: Kent Barton
Interior design and typeset: Katherine Lloyd, The DESK

Unless otherwise indicated, all Scripture quotations are from *The Holy Bible*,
English Standard Version, copyright © 2001 by Crossway Bibles, a division of
Good News Publishers. Used by permission. All rights reserved.

Scripture quotations marked NASB are from the *New American Standard Bible*®,
copyright © 1960, 1962, 1963, 1968, 1971, 1972, 1973, 1975, 1995 by the Lockman
Foundation. Used by permission. (www.lockman.org)

**Library of Congress Cataloging-in-Publication Data**

Lawson, Steven J.
  Pillars of grace : A.D. 100-1564 / Steven J. Lawson.
     p. cm. -- (A long line of godly men ; v. 2)
  Includes bibliographical references and indexes.
  ISBN 978-1-56769-211-2
  1. Grace (Theology)--History of doctrines--Textbooks.  I. Title.
  BT761.3.L39 2010
  234.092′2--dc22

                                                    2010046191

To R.C. Sproul—
formidable theologian, distinguished professor,
prolific author, beloved pastor,
guardian of the gospel.

For the past half-century, Dr. Sproul has brought the profound truths of Reformed theology from the halls of academia to everyday people in the pew. He has been the preeminent figure used by God in this generation to usher in the present resurgence of biblical Calvinism. Having studied under Dr. Sproul, I owe an enormous debt to him in many ways. From systematic theology and expository preaching to pastoral ministry and Christian living, his influence has been indelibly stamped upon me for good. In due time, I believe that history will reveal him to be the Martin Luther of our day.

*"For from Him and through Him and to Him are all things.*
*To Him be the glory forever. Amen."*

(Romans 11:36, NASB)

# CONTENTS

# FROM *FOUNDATIONS* IN THE BIBLE
# TO *PILLARS* IN CHURCH HISTORY

As you pick up this book and begin to become familiar with its purpose, you might be tempted to think that Dr. Steven J. Lawson is simply showing what uninspired men taught over the course of the first fifteen hundred years of church history, but that does not prove that the Bible teaches the sovereignty of God in salvation. If that is the case, here is my advice: Find a copy of Dr. Lawson's *Foundations of Grace*, the first volume in his *A Long Line of Godly Men* series, and read it.

*Foundations* is a *tour de force* of whole-Bible study demonstrating that "God saves sinners." In it, Dr. Lawson piles up 577 pages of Scripture exposition, thoroughly documenting the Bible's teaching on salvation by sovereign grace. He traverses the rich and varied terrain of the Bible to introduce readers to the one true God and His sovereign, saving love from the whole of Scripture. He shows not only that the doctrines of grace are unassailably biblical, but that they are joy-giving, life-changing, Christ-exalting, God-glorifying, missions-motivating, evangelism-encouraging, and discipleship-promoting truths.

J. I. Packer has made the point that all the tenets of Calvinism—that faithfully biblical system of theology that joyfully embraces the rich, comforting, God-exalting, self-abasing, Christ-honoring, scriptural message of the sovereignty of God in salvation and all things—reduce to one overarching claim: "God saves sinners."[1] Each of these words is important for understanding what the Bible teaches about salvation. First, *God* saves sinners. God, not man, saves. We do not save ourselves. Only *God* can save. Second, God *saves* sinners. He does not make us potentially savable. He does not enable us to save ourselves. He saves. Third, God saves *sinners*. He saves a multitude that no man can number out of a world of human beings who are dead in sin and in opposition to His kind and sovereign rule. He saves people who once hated

1

Him, ignored Him, and resisted Him. In salvation, God does not help those who help themselves, because no sinner can help himself. We are not "basically good" and in a position to "get by with a little help" from God. We are "without hope save in his sovereign mercy."[2] Packer concludes: "This is the one point of Calvinistic soteriology which the 'five points' are concerned to establish . . . namely, that sinners do not save themselves in any sense at all, but that salvation, first and last, whole and entire, past, present, and future, is of the Lord, to whom be glory for ever."[3]

In *Foundations of Grace*, Dr. Lawson shows us this truth—"God saves sinners"—from the Old and New Testaments, from the Law and the Prophets, from the Gospels and the Letters, from Genesis to Revelation.

Allow me to give just one example of this Bible truth so amply demonstrated in *Foundations*. In Ephesians 2:8–10, the apostle Paul wants us to understand that God Himself has saved us. He puts this forcefully and strikingly: "For by grace you have been saved through faith. And this is not your own doing; it is the gift of God, not a result of works, so that no one may boast. For we are his workmanship, created in Christ Jesus for good works, which God prepared beforehand, that we should walk in them." In these three verses, Paul manages, in six distinct ways, to tell us that our salvation is not because of us but is all of God. Notice how he does it:

First, he emphasizes that *we are saved by God's grace*. That is, the cause of our salvation is God's free saving favor to us despite our sinfulness, which leaves us deserving of judgment. Notice that Paul juxtaposes "by grace you have been saved" with "not your own doing." This is his way of saying that salvation comes from God, not from us. "Do you want to understand the source, the cause of your salvation?" Paul asks. "Don't look at yourself. Don't look within. Look up to God. Look at the unmerited favor God has shown to you. That is what and who saved you—not something in you, something about you, or something that you did." We do not deserve God's saving mercy. We disqualified ourselves from communion with God by our rebellion against Him, our insurgency against Him, our alienation from Him, our indifference to Him, our walking according to the world, the flesh, and the Devil. And yet, the Lord saves us by grace and lavishes His forgiving favor on us.

Second, Paul says that *we receive our salvation by faith*. "For by grace you have been saved through faith." Salvation is not something we attain by doing; rather, it is something we receive by believing. Paul is emphasizing our passive reception of something from God. We do not get salvation because we pull ourselves up by our bootstraps and grab it. It is not something we accomplish by our own might and main, by staying up late at night and keeping our noses to the grindstone. We simply receive it from God. We receive our salvation by faith rather than by doing something. In other words, we are saved through the instrument of trust. We simply trust God. We have to throw our hands up and say, "Lord God, there is nothing I can do." In the words of the great hymn "Rock of Ages," we have to say, "Nothing in my hands I bring; simply to Thy cross I cling." Simply put, we are saved not by our doing and not by our worthiness, but by God's grace, and we simply, humbly, joyfully receive that salvation *by trust, by faith, by believing God's promise.*

Third, if he has not been clear enough already, Paul next declares that *our salvation is God's gift.* We must understand salvation as a gift from God, not as a right, an obligation, or a payment due us from God for our performance. Look at how he puts this: "For by grace you have been saved through faith. And this is not your own doing; *it is the gift of God. . . .*" Paul's point of emphasis is this: the whole of our salvation is God's gift to us—not our gift to ourselves but God's gift to us; not something we deserve but a free bestowal. He asks, "Do you want to know how you obtained salvation?" He answers, "It was by gift, by grant, by God's grace." So we who by grace trust in Christ need to view our salvation as a free gift from God, one we simply receive by faith.

Fourth—and this is very important for us to note, especially in light of the exegetically unsound and theologically errant views of the so-called new perspective on Paul—the apostle goes on to emphasize that *our salvation is not the effect of works in any way.* It is, he says, "not a result of works, so that no one may boast." Paul is saying, in effect, "By the way, just in case you are missing my point, let me say the same thing again, this time in the negative—your salvation is not due in any way to your works, your doings." In other words, if we want to see how we are saved, we should not look at ourselves, our works. We are not saved by our own efforts, deeds, or actions.

Fifth, Paul says in verse 10, *our salvation is the product of God's workmanship.* "For we are his workmanship, created in Christ Jesus for good works. . . ." What an extraordinary statement. The point is this: Salvation is not the product of our workmanship; rather, it is the product of God's workmanship. We are not saved by what we do, but by what He did. In fact, we not only are not saved *by* our good works, we are saved *in order to do* good works. We are not saved *by* doing what is right in the sight of God, but we are saved *unto* doing, with joy and gladness in gratitude for God's free grace, all that He created us to do originally in paradise. Indeed, the very possibility of our doing anything to be saved is utterly precluded by Paul's language of "creation." We can be created *for* work. But we cannot create ourselves *by* work. Indeed, we cannot create ourselves at all. So by speaking of salvation as a work in which God creates us anew in Christ Jesus, Paul is affirming in the strongest possible way the divine sovereignty and monergistic power at work in our salvation. Our works may and do result from God's saving work, but they do not and cannot cause it. The order of salvation is not "do this and live," but "live and do this."

Sixth, lest we make the erroneous deduction that God looked into the future and foresaw our belief in Christ and our subsequent good works, and thus based His salvation of us on foreseen faith and obedience, Paul tells us that *God saves us by grace and creates us in Christ (not by our works) in order that we should do the works He foreordained for us to do from eternity past.* "For we are his workmanship, created in Christ Jesus for good works, which God prepared beforehand, that we should walk in them." Paul is saying that even the good works we now do were prepared beforehand by our gracious God for us to do. He doesn't save us because He foresees that we will do good works. No, the message is far more glorious and comforting than that. Indeed, it is far more staggering, even mind-boggling, than that. God saves us to "walk" in good works, to do righteousness, to live in godliness, to practice a holiness to which He predestined us from before the world itself ever existed. So our righteousness is not the means, the instrument, or the way of our salvation, it is part of God's goal in His salvation of us. God created us to be His image, to be like Him. That image was marred in our fall into sin. In glorification, that image is fully restored, and so John can say that at the coming of our Lord, "We shall be like him" (1 John 3:2). Thus, these good deeds in which we walk, far from being the cause of our salvation, are instead its goal, its aim. Our doing of good is itself part of God's predestined plan for us. Paul explains this in Ephesians 1:4 by saying that God chose us in Christ "before the foundation of the world, that we should be holy and blameless before him." So Paul emphasizes that our whole salvation is the sovereign, eternal work of God.

There we have it. Six times in three little but hugely important verses, Paul stresses that we are saved by God's grace alone. Our salvation is wholly because of His saving, forgiving, transforming, undeserved, and unearned power and favor. We receive that saving favor through trust (and even that trust is the result of God's Spirit at work in us). We do nothing to earn salvation or merit it; we simply trust God to give us something we do not deserve. It is God's gift given freely to us, not a debt He owes us. Salvation is not accomplished by us, nor does it result from our works. Instead, we ourselves are God's work and are saved by God's work (rather than saved by God because of our works). Even our Christian lives, our walking in good works as saved sinners, are the result of God's workmanship, the consequence (not the cause) of something that God pre-appointed, foreordained, predestined "before the mountains were brought forth" (Ps. 90:2).

Paul's point is that salvation is all of grace. The totality of our salvation is from God. Understanding this is absolutely essential for healthy Christian life, ministry, and experience. This is the truth that Dr. Lawson demonstrates, voluminously, in his earlier book.

What, then, is the purpose of *this* book? What is it about and what is it for? In *Foundations of Grace*, Dr. Lawson shows us how the doctrines of grace are firmly rooted in the teaching of all the Bible. In this volume, *Pillars of Grace*, he begins to walk us through the halls of church history to show us that the church, at its best, has understood that God's grace is sovereign in salvation.

There are at least four benefits of joining Dr. Lawson in this scintillating study. First, there is the simple and obvious opportunity to improve our knowledge of our own Christian family history. Western Christians in our day are not world famous for their grasp of the history of the church. Protestants know little about the history of the church prior to Martin Luther's nailing of his Ninety-five Theses to the door of the Wittenberg church on Oct. 31, 1517. Americans, in particular, lack knowledge of and love for history in general. We are the poorer for this ignorance. But if we will walk with Dr. Lawson through the lives and writings of great Christians from Clement of Rome to John Calvin, we will be enriched with a new appreciation for the treasures that have been bequeathed to us as members of the family of the living God. Dr. Lawson helps us remedy our poverty in this well-written, easy-to-read tour from the second to the sixteenth centuries.

Second, as Dr. Lawson highlights some of the Church Fathers' comments on the sovereignty of God, radical depravity, sovereign election, definite atonement, irresistible calling, preserving grace, and more, and as we see the church's theology of grace develop across the boundaries of time, place, and culture, we gain a greater appreciation that the doctrines of grace are not the invention of the sixteenth, seventeenth, or nineteenth century, or the product of one narrow branch of the Christian tradition. Rather, they are part of a common and catholic (or universal) theological legacy. Yes, they were not always fully understood. Yes, they sometimes were obscured or ignored. But the cumulative testimony of history is a powerful witness to their universality.

Third, studying the doctrines of grace via the writings of the greatest Christian teachers of the ages helps us check and confirm our own understanding of Scripture. Let me explain. Protestants do not believe that any period of church history is finally authoritative for faith and practice, unlike our Roman Catholic friends. We highly value the witness, testimony, and lessons of church history, but we hold, emphatically, that Scripture alone is our supreme rule of faith and life. Nevertheless, the study of church history, or of the church's growth in understanding of the teaching of Scripture (what professionals call "historical theology"), is very helpful and important to us. Why? Not because any writer or era of Christian history is infallible or unerringly authoritative, but because studying historical theology allows us to learn what other Christians in other times thought the Bible taught. This in turn can serve to confirm and test our own understanding of Scripture. I love the way Hughes Oliphant Old (a towering scholar of Christian history and worship) puts this: "We need to be interested in them [the Church Fathers] not in themselves but . . . because of what they point out to us about Scripture."[4]

Fourth, since the formulation of Christian doctrine has always been advanced in controversy, and since theological disputes require the participants to sharpen and clarify their doctrinal articulations and to work out more fully the ramifications of the doctrine under discussion, our study of church history can help us understand Bible doctrine better and more fully appreciate its devotional and practical significance. So, for instance, when we read the writings of Augustine related to the Pelagian controversy, we cannot help but grow in our knowledge of the issues at stake, become more familiar with the questions and categories of the doctrines of grace, and see more clearly the eternal consequences of truth and error in connection with this vital subject.

My brilliant friend Carl Trueman, professor of church history at Westminster Theological Seminary in Philadelphia, sees great value in reading the Church Fathers (what scholars call "Patristics"). In a post on the reformation21 weblog, he offered four reasons why we ought to read the writings of the earliest teachers of the church. Here are his wise words:

1. The doctrines of the Trinity and the Incarnation are basically hammered out in the early church. By tracing the controversies,

we can learn how and why the creedal formulation of these doctrines is important.

2. The pre-Constantinian context of much patristic theology offers a paradigm of how Christians can operate as a minority in a hostile or indifferent society. I am often struck by the difference between the early church apologists' approach to the Roman Empire ("don't persecute us because Christians actually make the best citizens") and the modern approach of "don't mess with us, we're Christians," where Christianity can sometimes look like little more than a cultural idiom for protesting Communism, secularism, etc.

3. The very alien nature of the world in which the Fathers operated challenges us to think more critically about ourselves in our own context. We may not, for example, sympathise much with radically ascetic monasticism; but when we understand it as a fourth-century answer to the age-old question of what a committed Christian looks like at a time when it is starting to be easy and respectable, we can at least use it as an anvil on which to hammer out our own contemporary response to such a question.

4. As Protestants, we cannot claim to understand the historical development of our own tradition unless we come to terms with patristic theology: Luther, Calvin, Owen, and company were deeply read and heavily influenced by patristic writings.[5]

For these reasons and a dozen more, your investment of time and attention in reading through *Pillars of Grace* will be amply repaid.

Let me mention one last point. Dr. Lawson taught through this material with the men's group in his own congregation before he gave it to the larger church for our benefit and edification. As a fellow pastor, that piques my interest. Just think what a blessing it would be to have a congregation whose officers and male leaders are steeped in the knowledge of the truth, the Bible, and church history that Dr. Lawson provides here. Fellow pastors, by all means use this material for your own growth in knowledge and grace. Pillage it for illustrations and content in your preaching. Encourage your women's

Bible studies and small groups to consider using this material for their edification. But do not neglect to teach your men, and especially your officers, the truth contained herein. Your whole congregation will rise up and call you blessed for doing so, for godly men, gripped by grace and truth, will serve their wives, children, parents, and fellow members so well that all will be blessed together with them.

Thank you, Dr. Lawson, for your labors in pulling together this rich treasury of biblical teaching on the doctrines of grace over the centuries from faithful men whom Christ appointed and the Spirit endowed for the building up of the saints for the work of service. We are your grateful debtors. Dear reader, join me now on an epic journey of edification guided by this faithful shepherd of souls.

—*J. Ligon Duncan III*
First Presbyterian Church
Jackson, Mississippi
August 2010

NOTES

1  J. I. Packer, "Introductory Essay," in John Owen, *The Death of Death in the Death of Christ* (London: Banner of Truth, 1959), 4.

2  Presbyterian Church in America, *The Book of Church Order*, 6th Ed., first membership vow (Atlanta: Committee for Christian Education and Publications, 2009), 80.

3  Packer, "Introductory Essay," 4–5.

4  Hughes Oliphant Old, *Worship: Reformed According to Scripture* (Louisville: Westminster John Knox, 2002), 171.

5  Carl R. Trueman, "The Fathers," http://www.reformation21.org/blog/2007/04/the-fathers.php (accessed April 21, 2010).

# UPHOLDING
# THE DOCTRINES OF GRACE

At the height of the Roman Empire, a series of magnificent temples punctuated the landscape of the Mediterranean region. Built prominently atop high hills, these architectural masterpieces were among the wonders of the ancient world. The most prominent feature of these splendid buildings was their pillars, a series of columns carved from beautiful marble, studded with costly jewels, and inlaid with pure gold. Such a colonnade would arrest the attention of Roman citizens and foreign travelers entering one of the temples.

However, the primary purpose of the pillars was not cosmetic but functional. Resting securely on a firm foundation, these sturdy posts supported the whole temple structure. From the overhead beams and stone arches to the high-rising walls, vaulted ceiling, and pitched roof, every part of the temple, in one way or another, was upheld by these cylindrical blocks of marble. The entire edifice was bolstered by their strength. If the columns stood firm, the temple held fast. As a result, these ornate pillars came to be a symbol of stability and strength.

This is precisely the imagery used by the biblical authors to portray the strongest leaders in the early church—these men were *pillars*. The apostle Paul described Peter, James, and John as "pillars" in the church at Jerusalem (Gal. 2:9). These strong men, empowered by God's might, helped stabilize the first-century church by upholding God's Word, thereby strengthening the household of faith. In fact, Paul wrote that the entire church was to be the "pillar and buttress of the truth" (1 Tim. 3:15). This is to say, the mission of the church, like a sturdy colonnade, is to stand for the truth of the Christian faith. Jesus Christ also used this image, saying that all believers are "pillars" in the heavenly temple (Rev. 3:12)—permanent, immoveable, and secure.

9

In keeping with this biblical metaphor, the central thrust of this book—
*Pillars of Grace*—is to show that key leaders of the early church and beyond
acted as pillars, standing firm on the foundation of Scripture and upholding the truth. Specifically, each of these sturdy men upheld the doctrines of
sovereign grace in his hour of history. These stalwarts formed a colonnade,
century by century, in support of the truth of God's supreme authority in
man's salvation. This long line of godly men began with the Church Fathers
and extended through the Monastics, Scholastics, Pre-Reformers, and,
eventually, the Reformers themselves. Among them was a wide variety of
men, including faithful pastors, godly preachers, brilliant apologists, gifted
theologians, prolific writers, and even gallant martyrs. Each pillar was strategically placed by the sovereign Architect and Builder of the church for his
appointed time.

As men saturated with Scripture, these "pillars of grace" supported the living temple of God. They were the most formidable teachers in their day and
the most faithful defenders of Christian orthodoxy against the many heresies
confronting the church. There were many such individuals, but we will focus
on the key figures who took the lead in holding forth the poignant truths of
sovereign grace. Their commitment to this biblical teaching deserves our careful study as we trace the progression of their lives and ministries within the
larger framework of the first sixteen centuries of church history.

This book is the second volume of a set titled *A Long Line of Godly Men*.
It is designed to demonstrate that those figures who were most used in the
early and medieval church, to one degree or another, held to the truths of sovereign grace that were later taught in the Reformation. From the first century
through the sixteenth, the dominant figures in the church were strong men
committed to this strong teaching. That is the witness of history and the central premise of this book.

Who were the key figures who joined this parade of spiritual stalwarts
that marched with the doctrines of grace? Who took their divinely appointed
places immediately after the last authors of Scripture? Who were these early
church leaders? Who were these medieval voices? Who were the Pre-Reformers
and first Reformers? What did they teach regarding the sovereign grace of God
in salvation? This volume is devoted to tracing this triumphant procession of
godly men from AD 30, with the birth of Clement of Rome, to 1564, with the
death of John Calvin in Geneva.

## A Summary of the Biblical Teaching

Before we begin this journey, we need to remind ourselves of what was put forward in Volume One of this series, *Foundations of Grace*. There, the biblical case for the sovereignty of God in salvation was clearly—and, I believe, convincingly—made. From the lawgiver Moses in the first books of the Bible to the apostle John in the last book, we noted that there advanced onto the stage of human history an illustrious procession of faithful men who recorded the teachings of sovereign grace throughout Scripture.

Their names comprise the roll call of a great cloud of witnesses. The long line began with the first leaders of Israel—notables such as Moses, Joshua, and Samuel. It continued with other gallant men, such as Ezra and Nehemiah, and extended to the poets of the Wisdom books, revered authors such as Job, David, and Solomon. To a man, they carefully articulated in the inspired text of Scripture the sovereignty of God in the salvation of men.

This advancing column then was joined by the major prophets of Israel, who also taught the supreme authority of God in the redemption of sinners—Isaiah, Jeremiah, Ezekiel, and Daniel. Each writer heralded the same standard of truth, that is, the eternal purposes of God in His supreme will to save. The minor prophets also were recruited for this cavalcade of biblical authors, notables such as Hosea, Amos, Jonah, Micah, Nahum, Haggai, Zechariah, and Malachi. They, too, held to the determinative will and definite work of God in His saving grace.

The New Testament reveals the same. From Matthew through Revelation, there is a continuation of this succession, each biblical writer recording sovereign grace in salvation. All four of the Gospel writers—Matthew, Mark, Luke, and John—joined this array as they recorded the profound truths that came from the lips of Jesus Christ. His teaching gave unquestionable testimony to the doctrines of grace. Thereafter, the apostles were divinely commissioned to write yet more of the inspired text. Peter, Paul, and John soon found themselves in this parade of sovereign grace teachers. The remaining biblical authors—the author of Hebrews, James, and Jude—also took their God-appointed places in this long line of godly men.

Beginning with Moses in the wilderness and stretching to John on the island of Patmos, Scripture speaks with one voice in trumpeting the sovereignty of God in salvation. It upholds one standard of truth. It teaches one way of salvation. It asserts the one divine operation by which saving grace is applied to spiritually dead sinners. The various aspects of this glorious truth are known collectively as the doctrines of grace, and all of Scripture teaches these unfathomable riches of God's sovereign grace.

## THE BEDROCK DOCTRINE: DIVINE SOVEREIGNTY

The sovereignty of God is not a secondary doctrine that is relegated to an obscure corner in the Bible. Rather, this truth is the very bedrock doctrine of all Scripture. This is the Mount Everest of biblical teaching, the towering truth that transcends all theology. From its opening verse, the Bible asserts in no uncertain terms that God is and that God reigns. In other words, He is *God*—not merely in name, but in full reality. God does as He pleases, when He pleases, where He pleases, how He pleases, and with whom He pleases in saving undeserving sinners. All other doctrines of the Christian faith must be brought into alignment with this keystone truth.

The sovereignty of God is the free exercise of His supreme authority in executing and administrating His eternal purposes. God must be sovereign if He is to be truly God. A god who is not sovereign is not God at all. Such is an imposter, an idol, a mere caricature formed in man's fallen imagination. A god who is less than fully sovereign is not worthy of our worship, much less our witness. But the Bible proclaims for all to hear that "the LORD reigns" (Ps. 93:1). God is exactly who Scripture declares He is. He is the sovereign Lord of heaven and earth, whose supreme authority is over all. This is the main premise of Scripture.

Nowhere is God's sovereignty more clearly demonstrated than in His salvation of the lost. God is free to bestow His saving mercy on whom He pleases. God says, "I will be gracious to whom I will be gracious, and will show mercy on whom I will show mercy" (Ex. 33:19b; Rom. 9:15). He is not obligated to extend His grace to any undeserving sinner. If He were to choose to save none, He would remain perfectly just. He might determine to save a few and still be absolutely holy. Or He could choose to save all. But God is sovereign, and that means He is entirely free to bestow His grace however He will—whether on none, few, or all.

From beginning to end, salvation is of God and, ultimately, for God. The apostle Paul writes, "From him and through him and to him are all things" (Rom. 11:36). In this comprehensive verse, God is declared to be the divine source, the determinative means, and the designated end of all things. This is most true in salvation. According to this text, every aspect of the operation of saving grace is God-initiated, God-directed, and God-glorifying. Every dimension of salvation is from Him, through Him, and to Him. This is to say, salvation originates from His sovereign will, proceeds through His sovereign activity, and leads to His sovereign glory.

## THE SOLIDARITY OF THE TRINITY

Moreover, divine sovereignty in salvation involves each of the three persons of the Godhead—the Father, Son, and Holy Spirit. All three work in perfect unity to rescue the same undeserving sinners. Within the Trinity, there is one saving purpose, one saving plan, and one saving enterprise. Those whom the Father chooses are precisely those whom the Son redeems and those whom the Spirit regenerates. The persons of the Godhead act as one Savior. The Trinity is not fractured in its saving activity. It is not divided in its direction and intent, as if each person of the Godhead seeks to save a different group of sinners. Instead, each member of the Trinity purposes and irresistibly proceeds to save one and the same people—God's chosen people.

Sadly, many believe otherwise. They insist that the Father saves only the few sinners whom He foresees will believe in Christ, thus mistakenly confusing foreknowledge (Acts 2:23; Rom. 8:29–30; 1 Peter 1:2, 20), which means "forelove," with mere foresight. They also imagine that Christ hypothetically died for all sinners—a different group from that which the Father saves—naively assuming there is only one meaning for the scriptural words *world* and *all*. They further claim that the Spirit saves yet another group, that is, some sinners whom He woos. Sadly, they mistake His internal, saving call (1 Cor. 1:2, 9) for a general, non-saving conviction (Heb. 6:4–5). According to this leaky scheme, the three persons of the Godhead are purported to be pursuing three different groups of individuals—*few*, *all*, and *some*. Thus, the persons of the Godhead are sorely divided in Their saving activity. Even worse, the sinner—not God—reigns as determinative in his or her salvation.

But the Bible teaches otherwise. Scripture reveals a perfect unity within the Trinity, a perfect oneness between the Father, Son, and Spirit in Their saving activities. God's Word teaches that the Godhead acts as one Savior in saving one people. The truth is that man is not sovereign in salvation—God is. All three members work together with absolute sovereignty and unwavering resolve to save the very same people for Their own glory. This is accomplished through the free exercise of the supreme authority of all three members of the Trinity. Consider the part that each plays in this cohesive salvation.

## The Sovereignty of the Father

Before the foundation of the world, God chose individuals—undeserving and unworthy though they are—to be the objects of His saving grace (2 Tim. 1:9). The apostle Paul writes, "He chose us in him before the foundation of the world" (Eph. 1:4a). That is to say, He chose His elect by Himself and for Himself—a sovereign choice not based on any foreseen good works or faith on their part. This divine election originated within Himself, by His own gracious choice (Rom. 9:16). For reasons known only to God, He selected whom He would save.

Having chosen His elect, the Father gave them to the Son before time began to be His royal inheritance. This gift was an expression of the Father's love for the Son (John 6:37, 39; 17:2, 6, 9, 24). These chosen ones were selected for the highest purpose—that they would praise the Son forever and be conformed to His image (Rom. 8:29). The Father then, in eternity past, commissioned the Son to enter the world to purchase the salvation of the elect. Further, the Father directed the Holy Spirit to regenerate these same chosen ones. Thus, their salvation was foreordained and predestined by the sovereign will of God before the foundation of the world (Eph. 1:5). The names of the elect were then written in the Lamb's book of life (Rev. 13:8; 17:8). Under the direction of the Father, all three persons of the Godhead irrevocably agreed to execute the salvation of these chosen people. This is the sovereign grace of God the Father in eternity past.

## The Sovereignty of the Son

Having long ago received from the Father the individual names of the elect, Jesus Christ came into this world to purchase their salvation. With a singular intent, Christ purposed to die for His true church—those given to Him by the Father in eternity past. He declared, "I lay down my life for the sheep" (John 10:15). Bound by devotion to His chosen bride, Christ "loved the church and gave himself up for her" (Eph. 5:25b).

With this definite design in the cross, Jesus purchased with His own blood all those who were predestined to believe in Him (Acts 20:28). He did not merely make salvation possible. He did not make a hypothetical redemption. Rather, He actually saved. Christ was not shortchanged at Calvary, but acquired all those for whom He paid. Jesus truly secured eternal life for His sheep. Not one for whom He died will ever perish. This is the sovereign grace of God the Son two thousand years ago in His saving death.

## The Sovereignty of the Spirit

Moreover, the Father and the Son sent the Holy Spirit into this world to apply the saving death of Christ to all the elect. As the gospel is proclaimed, the Spirit issues a special inward call to these chosen ones, those elected by the Father and redeemed by the Son. The Spirit powerfully regenerates their spiritually dead souls, raising them from the grave of sin to saving faith in Christ (Eph. 2:5–6). Jesus asserted, "All that the Father gives me will come to me" (John 6:37a). This saving enterprise is unalterably certain because God "draws" (6:44) all these "given ones" to Christ. The Spirit grants them repentance (2 Tim. 2:25) and authors saving faith within them (Phil. 1:29; 2 Peter 1:1).

In this effectual act, the Spirit opens the spiritually blind eyes of the elect to see the truth (2 Cor. 4:6). He opens their deaf ears to hear His voice (John 10:27). He opens their closed hearts to receive the gospel (Acts 16:14). He activates their dead wills to believe the saving message (John 1:13). The Spirit overcomes all resistance and triumphs in the hearts of the elect. This is the sovereign grace of God the Holy Spirit within time.

## Forever Kept by Sovereignty

Once converted, all the elect are kept by the power of God forever. None of the Father's chosen ones will ever be lost (Titus 1:1–2). None for whom the Son died will ever perish (Rom. 8:33–34). None who are regenerated by the Spirit will ever fall from grace (Titus 3:5–7). All the recipients of the saving grace of God will be ushered into glory forever (Rom. 8:29–30). This broad sweep of salvation reaches back to eternity past and stretches forward into eternity future. Salvation is one indivisible work of grace. Those chosen by God before time began will remain saved forever. All the elect will be preserved throughout the ages to come. God Himself will guard them and cause them to stand faultless before His throne (Jude 24). This view of sovereign grace is breath-taking, awe-inspiring, soul-humbling, and joy-producing.

Above all else, this view is God-glorifying. In each of the doctrines of grace, the glory of God is central. Only a salvation that is from Him and through Him can be to Him. Electing grace redounds "to the praise of his glorious grace" (Eph. 1:6a). Redeeming grace promotes "the praise of his glory" (1:12b). Regenerating grace is "to the praise of his glory" (1:14b). This is because all saving grace is sovereign grace. It is this view of salvation that brings greatest glory to God alone.

Humbled by this lofty truth, Jonathan Edwards wrote, "Those who have received salvation are to attribute it to sovereign grace alone, and to give all the praise to Him, who makes them to differ from others."[1] Should not this be our response as well? May we all fall to our knees and affirm that "salvation and glory and power belong to our God" (Rev. 19:1). May the truth of God's sovereignty in our salvation cause highest praise to be given to Him. "To him be glory forever. Amen" (Rom. 11:36).

## PILLARS RISE FROM STRONG FOUNDATIONS

As stated above, this is a summary of the biblical teaching that was carefully laid out in Volume One, *Foundations of Grace*. The scriptural case was presented that the entire Bible, from Genesis to Revelation, teaches the sovereignty of God in salvation. Virtually every biblical author, as well as Jesus Christ Himself, explicitly teaches these cardinal truths of God's sovereign grace in saving sinners according to His eternal purposes. The Bible speaks with one voice, declaring that "salvation belongs to the LORD" (Ps. 3:8a).

The doctrines of grace—radical depravity, sovereign election, definite atonement, irresistible call, and preserving grace, plus the umbrella doctrine of divine sovereignty and the necessary antithetical doctrine, divine reprobation— are the cornerstone truths of our Christian faith. When forged together, these doctrines form the bedrock of what we have called the "foundations of grace."

Sturdy pillars must rest on a strong foundation. So it is that this volume is titled *Pillars of Grace*. Here we will seek to discover the core convictions of those men, from the Church Fathers to the Reformers, whose message embraced the teaching of the biblical authors. Century by century, these leaders in the church ministered the Word of God and upheld the truth of sovereign grace. It is the intention of this book to demonstrate that the primary leaders of the early and medieval church believed the doctrines of grace in rudimentary but increasingly consistent form. Beginning with the Apostolic Fathers in the first and second centuries and proceeding through the Reformers in the sixteenth century, these men held to these truths and expressed them in their pulpits and with their pens. The dominant figures in the early history of the church were strong men with an understanding of sovereign grace.

Who were the godly men who formed this long line? They were the first pastors and theologians of the Christian era. They were the philosophers and apologists of the embryonic centuries of the church, defenders of the truth who resisted heretical teachings. They were the faithful men who took their stand on the sure foundations of sovereign grace. They were the saints who were most gripped with a high view of God. They were the pillars of grace.

Before we begin this journey, I want to thank many people who have helped make this book a reality. I must express my gratitude to Dr. R. C. Sproul and Ligonier Ministries, who see the importance of this material being put into print; it is to Dr. Sproul that this volume is dedicated. I also want to thank the elders of Christ Fellowship Baptist Church, godly men who have supported me in my book writing and my preaching ministry beyond our church. Greg Bailey, my editor at Reformation Trust, provided excellent counsel and skilled editing. Mark Hassler contributed exceptional research with the quotations and endnotes. Dr. Michael A. G. Haykin and Dr. Curt Daniel read the manuscript, offering invaluable historical and theological input. Kent Barton did a masterful job of rendering sketches of each of these pillars of the faith. John Innabnit, a fellow pastor at Christ Fellowship, also read the manuscript and made many helpful suggestions.

Special recognition must be given to Kay Allen, my executive assistant at Christ Fellowship, who typed the entire manuscript and coordinated the input from others. Further, Keith Phillips, another fellow pastor at Christ Fellowship, deserves special mention for his enormous contributions to the improvement of this book. Without the efforts of these two servants of the Lord, this book would not have been completed. Most of all, I want to thank my wife, Anne, who is a pillar of support for me at home.

Let us now trace the flow of the doctrines of grace through church history, from the first to the sixteenth century. We will see that even in the face of much adversity and opposition, God remains faithful to His cause, establishing the truth of His Word in the hearts of His people.

—*Steven J. Lawson*
Mobile, Alabama
October 2010

NOTE

1 Jonathan Edwards, "The Sovereignty of God in Salvation," in *The Works of Jonathan Edwards, Vol. II* (1834; repr., Edinburgh: Banner of Truth, 1979), 854.

Clement of Rome

Ignatius of Antioch

Justin Martyr

Irenaeus of Lyons

Tertullian of Carthage

Cyprian of Carthage

Athanasius of Alexandria

Basil of Caeserea

Gregory of Nazianzus

Ambrose of Milan

Augustine of Hippo

Isidore of Seville

Gottschalk of Orbais

Anselm of Canterbury

Bernard of Clairvaux

Thomas Bradwardine

John Wycliffe

John Hus

Martin Luther

Ulrich Zwingli

William Tyndale

Heinrich Bullinger

John Calvin

Chapter One

# PILLARS OF
# SOVEREIGN GRACE

## FROM CHURCH FATHERS
## TO PROTESTANT REFORMERS

Whenever one thinks of the doctrines of grace, there is a natural tendency to associate them with the Protestant Reformation, John Calvin, and Calvinism. The common assumption is that the truths of sovereign grace originated in the sixteenth century in an ivory tower in Western Europe. Many suppose that these teachings were invented by the Reformers and then foisted on unsuspecting people recovering from the Dark Ages. Consequently, countless people conclude that prior to the Protestant Reformation, there was virtually no teaching within the church on divine sovereignty in salvation. In fact, some go so far as to say that were it not for the Reformers, there would be almost no advocates today for the doctrine of sovereign election.

But are these assumptions correct? Did the teaching of the doctrines of grace first emerge in the sixteenth century? Did anyone teach Calvinistic truths prior to Calvin? Were total depravity and the bondage of the will asserted before Martin Luther? Did the truths of unconditional election and irresistible calling surface before they were made prominent in Calvin's Geneva? Were the Reformers merely an island unto themselves in the vast ocean of theological history, entirely disconnected from the church leaders who preceded them?

Or, are these assumptions invalid? Could it be that there is a different interpretation of church history, one that is more consistent with the testimony of reliable witnesses? Did Luther and Calvin simply develop and more carefully articulate biblical truths that the Church Fathers and medieval theologians affirmed? Is it possible that the Protestant leaders merely stood on the shoulders of many prominent men before them and taught the same truths? If so, when in church history were the doctrines of grace initially advanced, and who were the men who first grasped and promoted them?

It is my contention that, concerning the doctrines of grace, virtually nothing new was taught during the Reformation era. No teaching of divine sovereignty was proclaimed during the sixteenth century that had not already been developed and taught in previous centuries, to some degree, by the Church Fathers, Monastics, Scholastics, and Pre-Reformers. The renowned Scottish church historian William Cunningham notes, "There was nothing new in substance in the Calvinism of Calvin."[2] Likewise, David F. Wright insists, "The Reformation churches all paid special attention to the early Fathers, not as authorities on par with Scripture but as godly interpreters of the apostolic faith in a united and largely uncorrupted church."[3] Simply put, the message of the Reformers was, essentially, nothing new.

Specifically, the teaching of the Reformers was a climactic point in the development of the church's understanding of the doctrines that testify to God's sovereignty. In the Reformers, the doctrines of grace came to their fullest expression. Hence, the Reformation can be seen as a recovery of doctrines that were taught by the prophets, the apostles, and even Jesus Christ Himself. Furthermore, the Protestant movement was a re-energizing of these ancient truths taught by many of the Church Fathers, especially Augustine, and many medieval theologians. So the Reformation was, in reality, the restoration of these God-exalting doctrines that had been stated with varying degrees of clarity by church leaders throughout the first millennium and a half of church history.

Such continuity in doctrine was the underlying thesis that Calvin set forth in his *Institutes of the Christian Religion.* First published in 1536, this manifesto of the Reformation contended that the Protestant Reformers were not guilty of theological novelty—rather, the Roman Catholic Church was. Calvin maintained that the medieval Roman Catholic Church had vastly departed from the gospel. The Reformation was, he believed, a return to the Scriptures and the theology of the Fathers. Included in this return was the recovery of the doctrines of grace.

Luther made a similar appeal in his *On the Councils and the Church,* written in 1539. The German Reformer stated that the Protestant leaders were merely expositors of Scripture and the rightful heirs of the Church Fathers. The Reformers, he believed, were simply carrying forward the banner of truth that had been passed down to them from the first leaders of the church.

Given the prevailing confusion and the claims of the Reformers, it needs to be made clear that the doctrines of sovereign grace were present in the teaching of the Early Fathers in the church, if only in rudimentary form. The seed of sovereign grace theology was planted by the Church Fathers, though without systematic development. This lack of structure is hardly surprising. In fact, initially, there was no thematic organization of thought as we now know it. G. I. Bray writes: "Although the ancient church admitted the principle of systematization, no ancient divine worked out a complete system of his own. Most theological writing was confined to works in defense of a particular doctrine (e.g., the Trinity), and this pattern remained standard until the thirteenth century."[4] Some argue that the early church simply did not engage in theology.[5] This is overstating the case, but not until medieval Scholasticism would systematic theology as we know it originate. This fact accounts for the delayed development of the doctrines of grace as a body of truth.

Yet progress nevertheless was made long before the sixteenth century. In the fifth century, Augustine connected the cause-and-effect relationships between human inability and divine sovereignty in salvation, specifically in terms of regeneration. This was a revolutionary breakthrough. Over the following centuries, the seedlings of sovereign grace teaching slowly grew and developed, finally coming ready for harvest as a body of divinity in the sixteenth century. Throughout this development, these doctrines were tended and cultivated by Monastics, Scholastics, and Pre-Reformers. When they arrived on the scene, the Reformers simply exegeted Scripture and organized these biblical doctrines into a systematic whole.

This chapter will survey the first fifteen hundred years of church history and trace the development of the doctrines of grace from the Church Fathers to the medieval Monastics, Scholastics, and Pre-Reformers, and, finally, to the Reformers. In this overview, we will witness a gradual unfolding of the church's understanding of these glorious truths. We will see that these doctrines were obscured at times, often hidden behind the controversies of the day. But God ensured their preservation and caused their advancement by raising up faithful men in every generation.

# THE CHURCH FATHERS (AD 100–500)

Standing at the head of the long line of godly men in the church are the Church Fathers, those men who led the church from the end of the New

Testament era through the fifth century. This initial era, also called the Patristic period, was foundational for the establishment of core Christian doctrines. These first teachers and writers were called "Fathers" simply because they came first chronologically in the leadership of the church. As such, they played a pivotal role in the growth and maturation of the church. As godly teachers of Scripture, their major contribution was the formulation of orthodox understandings of Jesus Christ, the Holy Spirit, the Trinity, man, sin, and grace.

## THE APOSTOLIC FATHERS (AD 100–150)

The initial leaders in the early church were the Apostolic Fathers, who served during and immediately after the apostles' ministry. From the end of the first century until the middle of the second century, six men in particular distinguished themselves as leading Apostolic Fathers—Barnabas of Cyprus, Clement of Rome, Ignatius of Antioch, Papias, Polycarp, and Hermas. Some of them actually knew the apostles, while others were considered the firstfruits of the apostolic ministry.[6] These first pillars were the earliest Christian authors, and they formed a vital link between the apostolic era and the second-century church.

In matters of sovereign grace, the Apostolic Fathers simply restated these God-exalting truths as they found them in Scripture, offering almost no further explanation. Louis Berkhof writes, "The Apostolic Fathers . . . are generally in harmony with the truth revealed in the Word of God, and are often represented in the very words of Scripture, but . . . cannot be said to increase or deepen our insight into the truth or to shed light on the inter-relations of the doctrinal teachings of Scripture."[7] The Early Fathers, he adds, were characterized by a lack of "definitiveness" in matters of theology.[8] J. N. D. Kelly writes that the teaching of the Fathers was "more affirmation than explanation."[9] Likewise, Cunningham notes, "The Apostolic Fathers generally use the language of Scripture upon these subjects, while they scarcely make any statements which afford us materials for deciding in what precise sense they understood them."[10] However, Cunningham is quick to add, "There is nothing in the writings of any of the immediate successors of the apostles in the least opposed to them."[11]

The reason for this lack of development is not difficult to discern—the first Fathers had other theological concerns that demanded their attention. Their focus was on the declaration of the gospel in a pagan culture, not resolving the tensions between divine sovereignty and human responsibility.[12]

Thus, there was some confirmation of the doctrines of grace, but little inter-pretation.[13] Not until subsequent generations would these kernels of truth germinate and grow in the fertile minds of godly men.

The first notable Apostolic Father was Clement of Rome, the author of an epistle known as *First Clement*. It has been said that this early letter "makes quite 'Calvinistic' statements."[14] Without hesitation, Clement pointedly refers to Christians as "the elect" and affirms that God will "keep intact the precise number of His elect in all the world."[15] He further identifies believers as God's "chosen portion."[16] It is significant that this first Church Father used these sovereignty-laden terms. Another important Apostolic Father, Ignatius of Antioch, served as bishop of Antioch in Syria and ultimately suffered a martyr's death. As he was being taken to Rome to die, he wrote seven let-ters that are marked by the language of the doctrines of grace. He addressed believers as those who have been "predestined from eternity."[17] Further, he affirmed their final perseverance, saying that Christ is "that life from which we can't be torn."[18] In seed form, these first Fathers alluded to key tenets of sovereign grace.

## THE APOLOGIST FATHERS (150–250)

By the end of the second century, the Christian faith was becoming a com-pelling force within the Roman Empire; as a result, many of Rome's most profound thinkers were becoming followers of Christ. From their ranks arose the next wave of Christian leaders, men known as the Apologists—Justin Mar-tyr, Tatian the Assyrian, Irenaeus of Lyons, Athenagoras of Athens, Aristides of Athens, Theophilus of Antioch, Minucius Felix, and others. These gifted Greek authors sought to present a sound defense of Christianity in the face of intellectual attacks and mounting persecution. As their title suggests, these Apologists were brilliant defenders of the Christian faith, men who wrote against sophisticated philosophical attacks on the gospel. They believed that if they could answer the accusations of the enemies of Christianity, the gospel would gain a stronger hearing in their pagan society. Therefore, they strongly appealed to human reason, constructing a logical defense of the truth that was intended to be intellectually convincing to unbelievers.

As Gnosticism proclaimed a deterministic worldview, it became vital for the Apologists to strongly affirm human responsibility to God. In doing so, they prioritized the moral imperatives of the Bible and emphasized man's free will. Though the Apologists affirmed the sovereignty of God, they did not provide a systematic exposition of this truth as it pertains to salvation. Consequently, any emphasis on sovereign grace lay mostly obscured in the shadows of this controversy. Though they possessed "a 'high view' of the transcendence of God," the Apologists remained somewhat vague concerning the depths to which original sin had plunged the human race into radical corruption.[19] Because Gnostic sects promoted moral laxity, the Apologist Fathers were reluctant to stress divine sovereignty for fear of endorsing any indulgence in sin.

Justin Martyr was the most important of the Apologists. He was the first theologian of note, and his writings displayed more developed thought than those of the Apostolic Fathers. According to John Hannah, Justin had "a fairly developed understanding of sin and grace," though he "had no conception of any debilitating connection or inheritance from the fall of Adam."[20] Justin, in turn, influenced another prominent Apologist Father, Irenaeus of Lyons. A pivotal figure in the development of Christian theology, this early bishop in Gaul was a vigorous defender of the faith who fought valiantly against the heresies of Gnosticism. As he argued for the unity of Scripture, he asserted the truths of divine sovereignty and human freedom, yet without resolving the tension between the two.[21] For Irenaeus, the person and work of Christ were the primary focus, not predestination.[22]

The Apologists, then, mostly affirmed freedom of the will.[23] Consequently, the need for a more precise clarification of the inability of the human will and fallen man's dependence on sovereign grace remained.

## The African Fathers (200–375)

By the third century, the North African coast of the Mediterranean had become a stronghold for the Christian faith. In the thriving Egyptian city of Alexandria, the School of Alexandria developed into a bastion for Christian truth. As the first center for Christian learning, the school taught essential doctrines of the Christian faith along with Hellenistic reasoning, forming what became known as the Alexandrian theology. Another chief city of Roman Africa, Carthage, also became an important center for the teaching of fundamental Christian doctrine. Such teaching was critically needed, as many deviations from the gospel were occurring at this time, including Neoplatonism, Montanism, Manichaeism, and Arianism. These false teachings, directed against the deity of Jesus Christ and the Holy Spirit, required the attention of the ablest minds in the African church. These men, known as the African Fathers, included Clement of Alexandria, Tertullian of Carthage, Cyprian of Carthage, and Athanasius of Alexandria.

At the end of the second century, Tertullian of Carthage, known as "the last of the Greek apologists" and "the first of the Latin fathers," stood as an ardent defender of the faith against the anti-Trinitarian heresy of Monarchianism.[24] Regarding sovereign grace, he made small advances in the doctrine of the total depravity of the human race. He affirmed that every soul is "innately stained with the result of Adam's error" and suffers a debilitating effect.[25] But Tertullian, to an extent, maintained the freedom of the will with a somewhat synergistic view of regeneration.[26] The need remained for clarification of the relationship between the fall of Adam and the sinfulness of man.

In the middle of the third century, Cyprian came to the fore as bishop of Carthage. The writings of this African Father, Berkhof notes, show "an increasing tendency towards the doctrine of the original sinfulness of man, and of a monergistic renewal of the soul."[27] Well-educated and a gifted speaker, Cyprian helped lay the groundwork for the Augustinian view of sin and grace. Cunningham notes, "Cyprian seems to have taken his views of divine truth somewhat more purely and simply from the Scriptures than many of the early writers."[28] Consequently, Cyprian freely ascribed the conversion of sinners to the grace of Christ. He wrote as one standing on the threshold of a clearer understanding of sovereign grace.

A half-century later, Athanasius of Alexandria became the central advocate for the Christian faith in the West. Educated in the School of Alexandria, this heroic figure stood *contra mundum*—"against the world"—in upholding the truth. Athanasius wrote with still deeper insight into the relationships among Adam's fall, the sin of mankind, and the sovereignty of grace. Athanasius did not state the full extent to which the human race participates in Adam's guilt. However, with the Gnostic threat declining in Africa, theologians were finally free to give more thought to the sin of Adam and its deadening effect on the human race. Consequently, this era witnessed some small developments in the doctrines of grace.

## The Cappadocian Fathers (325–400)

Following the death of Athanasius, the focus of the church shifted to the eastern region of the Roman Empire. Three notable men known as the Cappadocian Fathers—Basil of Caesarea, Gregory of Nazianzus, and Gregory of Nyssa—became the chief defenders of Christian orthodoxy.[29] This remarkable trio served the church in the province of Cappadocia, located southeast of Constantinople in Asia Minor. In the face of Arianism, God used these three to further define and defend the church's Trinitarian stance.

Basil of Caesarea was the leading figure of the Cappadocian Fathers, a valiant defender of the faith. He became the principal proponent of the deity of the Son and the Spirit against the Arians and Pneumatomachians. Though weak in his teaching on radical depravity, Basil made strong statements regarding sovereign election. He identified true believers as "the chosen of God"[30] and as "the chosen flock of the Lord,"[31] though without defining the doctrine of election. The chosen ones, he contended, will never see corruption, but will be eternally preserved.

In this same period, Gregory of Nazianzus, known as Gregory the Theologian, used his considerable intellect in resisting the Unitarian teaching of Apollinarius. To this end, he expounded the doctrine of the Trinity with increasing clarity. Gregory held stronger views than the other Cappadocians on original sin and the resulting depravity of the human race. Out of fallen humanity, he stated, God sovereignly chose His "vessels of election."[32] Gregory distinguished between "a certain book of the living" and "a book of them that are not to be saved," implying a reprobation of sorts.[33]

Thus, the church's understanding of the doctrines of grace slowly but steadily advanced. Charles Hodge explains, "It is not maintained that the Greek fathers held the doctrine of original sin in the form in which it was afterwards developed by Augustine, but they nevertheless taught that the race fell in Adam, that they all need redemption, and that redemption can only be obtained through the Lord Jesus Christ."[34] In other words, the Cappadocian Fathers were clear regarding *what* saving grace is and man's need for it. But *how* this grace is applied to fallen man needed deeper insight.[35] At this time, synergistic regeneration still had a foothold in the thinking of many church leaders. The connection between man's inability and God's sovereignty in regeneration would be defined by the next group of theologians—the Latin Fathers, especially Augustine.

## The Latin Fathers (350–500)

The fourth and early fifth centuries witnessed the rise of the Latin Fathers in the West, including Hilary of Poitiers, Ambrose of Milan, Jerome of Rome and Jerusalem, and Augustine of Hippo. These men were called Latin Fathers because their theological works were written primarily in Latin, the language of the Western provinces of the Roman Empire. They were less concerned with the dangers of Gnosticism and more focused on other areas of theology. Specifically, they turned their attention to the deadening effects of Adam's sin on the will of man.

To a much greater degree, these Fathers emphasized the divine initiative of grace in saving faith. Still, they taught a "causative cooperation" between God and man.[36] Berkhof notes: "The doctrine of a sinful, as distinguished from a corrupt nature, is even more clearly asserted in the writings of Ambrose . . . all men have sinned in Adam, and are therefore born in sin. At the same time [the Latin Fathers] do not hold to an entire corruption of the human will, and consequently adhere to the synergistic theory of regeneration, though they appear to be more uncertain and contradictory in this matter than some of the earlier Fathers. All in all we find in them a gradual preparation for the Augustinian view of sin and grace."[37] In short, these Western Fathers remained moderately synergistic in their view of regeneration, though they often spoke in terms of sovereign grace.

One prominent Latin Father was Ambrose, bishop of Milan, another resolute defender of Christianity against the heresy of Arianism. As he wrote, Ambrose articulated more of the doctrine of original sin,[38] but he still affirmed man's free will. Further development was needed to correlate these truths into one consistent body of thought.

Not until the beginning of the fifth century did the early church more carefully address the full depths of the corruption of man and his need for sovereign grace. This doctrinal advancement came through Augustine, bishop of Hippo, the greatest theologian among the Latin Fathers. At this time, the heretical British monk Pelagius espoused that man in his natural state retains the moral ability to achieve salvation on his own. Pelagius asserted that Adam injured only himself by his sin. Thus, men enter this world without the depravity of original sin. Children, he maintained, learn to sin by their bad environments and evil examples. Man possesses a free will, unhindered by sin, that can choose to please God.[39] Thus, Pelagius saw election as based on divine foresight, making salvation entirely dependent on man's choice and ability.

In response, Augustine strongly asserted the inability of unregenerate sinners to merit salvation. Moreover, he said, no one can believe in Christ apart from a sovereign work of God overcoming man's sinful resistance. Augustine refuted the false notion that God merely looks down the proverbial tunnel of time and foresees the free will of man choosing Him. Instead, he developed a full-blown doctrine of predestination. He firmly maintained the biblical teaching on original sin, total depravity, sovereign election, monergistic regeneration, and absolute predestination.[40] He saw man as hopelessly plagued by radical corruption and, therefore, unable to initiate or contribute to his salvation. By necessity, he viewed God as sovereign in the exercise of His saving grace toward elect sinners.

Regarding election, Augustine taught that salvation is a sovereign gift, fixed in eternity past, irrespective of the merit of man. Augustine, Loraine Boettner argues, "went far beyond the earlier theologians, and taught an unconditional election of grace, and restricted the purposes of redemption to the definite circle of the elect."[41] The whole race fell in Adam, Augustine maintained, so that everyone is born totally depraved and spiritually dead. Therefore, the human will is free only to sin, but not free to choose any good toward God.[42] Thus, Augustine was the first theologian to carefully connect the biblical truths of man's moral inability in sin and God's sovereignty in election and regeneration. Augustine's influence would dominate medieval Christianity and provide the chief stimulus for the Reformation.

Though Augustine asserted salvation by grace, he maintained that the irresistible grace of predestination is applied by the sacrament of baptism.[43] He also espoused progressive justification. He even held that some believers are not of the elect and will not persevere. Thus, his theological steps forward did not go far enough.[44] Despite his advances in the areas of sin and grace, further clarity was needed on salvation by faith alone. The Reformation would be the triumph of Augustine's views on sovereign grace, as held by the Protestants, over his views on sacramentalism and the church, as held by the Roman Catholics.

In the fifth century, the Augustinian doctrine of grace immediately faced a stiff challenge in the mediating position known as Semi-Pelagianism. According to this theological camp, mankind is fallen in Adam, but not spiritually dead, merely sick and dying. Thus, man does not suffer from moral inability but only disability. Salvation, then, is a joint effort between God and man. If man is to receive grace, he must cooperate with God. To the contrary, the Augustinians maintained that salvation is all of grace. Even the faith to believe, they claimed, is from God, and this grace is granted to those predestined to believe. Wright notes: "The initial point of difference concerned 'the beginning of faith.' Augustine's critics insisted that this was an act of unaided human freedom, although grace instantly strengthened incipient faith. Augustine held that 'the will is prepared by God' by prevenient grace alone."[45] This was the dividing issue.

John Cassian, the leader of the Semi-Pelagian movement, with Vincent of Lérins and Faustus of Rhegium, argued that Augustine was extreme in his views on radical corruption, unconditional election, and sovereign regeneration. Cassian insisted that grace is necessary, but it is conditional, and sinful man can successfully resist divine grace. This synergistic view made divine grace and human will co-operative factors in regeneration. According to the Semi-Pelagians, election and predestination were "based on what God foresaw the creature would do when presented with a choice."[46] Prosper of Aquitaine countered with a strong Augustinian defense, though with some modifications. The battle for sovereign grace would continue into the medieval era.

# THE MEDIEVAL LEADERS (500–1500)

That period of history extending roughly from the years 500 to 1500 is known as the medieval age.[47] It is with good reason that the first five hundred years of this period have been called the Dark Ages.[48] Boettner describes this era: "Clouds of ignorance blinded the people. The Church became more and more ritualistic and salvation was thought to be through the external Church."[49] At this hour, the church often wavered from a firm Augustinian stance because many considered divine sovereignty to be an excessively harsh truth. As a result, large numbers compromised the truths of divine predestination.

## THE MONASTICS (500–1200)

From the middle of the first millennium, Monasticism emerged as a significant force in Christianity. Monks withdrew from society into monasteries to practice poverty, chastity, and asceticism. Their minds, they believed, must not be detached from their piety. Therefore, they pursued knowledge with a heavy emphasis on meditation and the adoration of God. Their aim in their study of Scripture was not to analyze the text in a literal, precise manner, but to apply the message of salvation to the hearer. It is worth noting that Calvin saw in monastic theology "the preservation of a purer form of Augustinian theology" than would be found in Scholasticism,[50] though the Monastics' "interpretation of Scripture was heavily allegorical."[51]

At this time, the Roman Catholic Church was corrupting the gospel with its insistence on works righteousness. The Pelagian and Semi-Pelagian errors had been condemned in the sixth century at the councils of Orange (529) and Valence (529); nevertheless, they became the popular theological viewpoints in Rome. Thus, most medieval teachers maintained that God willed the salvation of all men, not merely of the elect. Rome increasingly taught that the doctrine of predestination was based on foresight and abandoned any strict Augustinian doctrine of salvation.[52] But during these Dark Ages, God raised up a few isolated lights for sovereign grace, including Isidore of Seville, Gottschalk of Orbais, and Bernard of Clairvaux.

In the seventh century, Isidore, the archbishop of Seville, Spain, became a strong advocate for God's sovereignty in man's salvation. Isidore was known as an encyclopedist, and his *Sententiarum libri tres* was the first manual of Christian doctrine compiled in the Latin church. In this work, Isidore addressed matters of theology, specifically the doctrines of salvation, writing clearly of God's absolute predestination. He wrote that predestination is twofold: a predestination unto salvation and a predestination unto damnation.[53] Isidore died a national hero, leaving no small influence through his works.

Two centuries later, Gottschalk of Orbais, a German monk, appeared on the scene as a strict Augustinian. In the monastery at Orbais, Gottschalk strongly advanced such doctrines as radical corruption, sovereign election, definite atonement, irresistible grace, and reprobation.[54] He insisted that Christ died only for the elect, and he held that fallen man does not possess free will.[55] Though perceived to be harsher than Augustine, he held to the same God-centered system of truth, with some additions. Like Augustine, he maintained that God does not will that all should be saved. Rather, he taught, God foreordains the elect to heaven and the nonelect to hell. Thus, Gottschalk was among the first to teach double predestination, a predestination of the elect unto life and a predestination of the reprobate unto judgment.[56]

In the twelfth century, Bernard of Clairvaux became the most influential and famous monk of his day. Sometimes called "the last of the fathers," he was "the last great representative of the early medieval tradition of monastic theology."[57] Bernard was staunchly Augustinian, though less harsh than Gottschalk.[58] During the Crusades, he gave an unmistakable witness for the doctrines of grace.[59] Though predestination was still considered harsh by many, Bernard remained unwavering in his predestinarian stance as he upheld divine sovereignty in salvation. A brilliant writer, he cast a strong influence on those who followed him and, much later, on the Reformers. In fact, Calvin quotes Bernard in his *Institutes of the Christian Religion* more than any other church leader, with the exception of Augustine.

## THE SCHOLASTICS (1000–1350)

With the new millennium, the Dark Ages came to an end and Scholasticism became the prevailing form of philosophy and theology. This thought process combined Aristotelian philosophy, humanistic logic, and biblical truth.[60] It arose primarily because of a shift in education from the contemplative monasteries to the halls of cathedral schools and then to the universities at Paris, Oxford, Cambridge, and St. Andrews. Scholasticism emphasized the reading and explicating of classical texts. However, the Scholastics often became involved in exaggerated exegesis; like the Monastics, their chief exegetical method was often allegorical interpretation. Also, many Scholastics subscribed to Semi-Pelagianism. However, some Scholastic voices were raised to teach sovereign grace. Those men, steeped in Augustinian doctrine, included Anselm of Canterbury and Thomas Bradwardine of Oxford.

In the eleventh century, Anselm, a Benedictine monk, became archbishop of Canterbury and the first truly great theologian of the medieval Western church.[61] Considered "the pioneer of the new scholastic approach to theology," Anselm strove to use reason in his defense of the Christian faith.[62] In doing so, he reintroduced the teachings of Augustine, stressing that original sin transfers both guilt and pollution to every member of the human race. Consequently, Anselm taught that man's will is free to choose only sin. Until God moves the will, according to Anselm, it is impotent toward spiritual good.[63] As salvation is the unmerited gift of God, he maintained that saving faith must come through sovereign grace. Anselm was thoroughly Augustinian, stressing some of its harsher implications, such as double predestination.

In the first half of the fourteenth century, medieval Scholasticism helped bring about a moderate revival of Augustinianism. The doctrine of predestination again became a more significant part of the theology of many church leaders.[64] While some still subscribed to belief in free will, many Scholastics realized it was an overly simplistic position. Thus, the Scholastics increasingly sought to understand man's responsibility in view of God's sovereignty.[65] Yet Rome continued its descent into its man-centered, works-oriented religion of sacramentalism and sacerdotalism.

At this time, another Scholastic and professor at Oxford, Bradwardine, taught Augustinian truth. Called "Doctor profundus," he affirmed pure sovereign grace in his teaching. In his chief work, *De Causa Dei Contra Pelagium*, Bradwardine strongly asserted the Augustinian themes of the bondage of the will, predestination, and fallen man's desperate need for sovereign grace.[66] Writing from a theocentric standpoint, he stressed that God unchangeably wills and controls all that comes to pass, including the salvation of the elect.[67] Bradwardine served as an important bridge between Augustine and John Wycliffe, and played an important role in preparing the way for the Reformation.[68]

## THE PRE-REFORMERS (1350–1500)

By the latter half of the fourteenth century, a revival in learning known as the Renaissance was under way, restoring a love for classical literature, including the Bible and the writings of the Church Fathers. New influences were impacting the older universities such as Cambridge and Oxford. New universities, such as Wittenberg, stressed the priority of the original languages and careful exegesis. As a result, there was a resurgence in the pursuit of biblically centered theology, and many church leaders began to think along the lines of moderate Augustinianism.[69] A courageous group of men known as the Pre-Reformers, forerunners of the Protestant Reformation, placed an emphasis on the doctrine of divine predestination. Because of their strong biblical convictions, these early advocates of reform—the Waldensians, Gregory of Rimini, John Wycliffe, John Hus, and Girolamo Savonarola, among others—sought to restore the church to her true foundation as set forth in the Scriptures. Their work helped bring about a deeper understanding of the doctrines of grace and a wider acceptance of them.

The most influential of the pre-Reformers was Wycliffe, a professor at Oxford University and a prolific writer. Known as "the Morning Star of the Reformation," he was the first to translate the Bible into the English language. Wycliffe possessed a deep reverence for the Word of God, one that so penetrated his theological beliefs that he became thoroughly Augustinian. He boldly proclaimed the absolute sovereignty of God and the foreordination of all things. He also stressed that the true church is comprised of God's elect. The visible church includes reprobates, Wycliffe insisted, but not the true church, which was formed in eternity past. Predestination, he maintained, is the foundation of the church. Even the pope, he said, may be numbered among the nonelect. Many of Wycliffe's students absorbed his Augustinian views and, through their influence, his sovereign grace teaching spread throughout England and across Europe. His God-centered beliefs were very similar to those that would be held later by Luther and Calvin.[70] L. L. Morris contends, "The interest in Wyclif's theology centers upon its similarity to the thinking of the Protestant Reformers."[71] In Wycliffe, the doctrines of grace had a new champion.

At this time, Oxford had a number of students from Bohemia, many of whom absorbed Wycliffe's teachings. When they returned home, Wycliffe's doctrine soon took root in their homeland. Hus, a scholar and teacher in Prague, embraced these truths and became a preacher of rare power. He proclaimed that the true church is the company of the elect.[72] Further, he asserted that because the true church is the body of Christ, its head is Christ, not the pope. He further maintained that the Roman Catholic Church was a mixed company since many nonelect belonged to it. Echoing Wycliffe, Hus said that perhaps even the pope and cardinals were numbered among the nonelect. This Augustinian view of the church, built squarely on sovereign election, led to his inevitable martyrdom.

With godly men such as Wycliffe and Hus preparing the way, the world stage was set for the greatest hour in church history since the apostolic age. Rome was in complete spiritual bankruptcy. The common people were restless. New worlds were being explored. Learning was advancing. Universities were expanding. The printing press was busy. The light of sovereign grace was soon to burst brightly over the horizon.

# THE PROTESTANT REFORMERS (1483–1575)

The early years of the sixteenth century witnessed the beginning of the Protestant Reformation, that great movement that Philip Schaff calls "the chief propelling force in the history of modern civilization."[73] It has been said that the Reformation was a genuine revival of Augustinian doctrine.[74] At the core of Reformed theology is the primacy and supremacy of God. The Reformation was decidedly marked by its emphasis on the sovereignty of God, especially as it pertains to salvation. Such a theocentric theology radically affected the Reformers' understanding of grace. They saw that from Him and through Him and to Him are all things (Rom. 11:36). This included, they believed, every aspect of grace—election, regeneration, redemption, and preservation. Only in these God-centered truths is all glory given to God.

In their doctrine of salvation, the Protestant leaders sought to hold to the full counsel of God. They combined the teaching of Augustine on monergistic regeneration with the teaching of Wycliffe and Hus on salvation by faith alone. G. W. Bromiley states, "All Reformers stressed the impotence of sinners and God's omnipotence in electing grace and reconciliation."[75] Schaff adds, "All the Reformers were originally strong Augustinian predestinarians and denied the liberty of the human will."[76] Thus, the Reformers taught that saving faith, which alone is necessary for salvation, is sovereignly created by the Holy Spirit. All faith *in* Christ comes *from* Christ, they maintained. Faith alone saves, and this faith is the gift of God to His elect.

## GERMAN REFORMERS

When the Reformation burst forth in Germany, it was led by Luther, Martin Bucer, and Philip Melanchthon. Luther was a former Augustinian monk and, as such, was deeply influenced by the teaching of Augustine. During this pivotal era, Luther wrote *The Bondage of the Will*, a brilliant response to the Dutch humanist Desiderius Erasmus, in which he carefully argued for the biblical teaching on the sovereignty of grace. Luther relied heavily on the writings of the apostles John and Paul, who taught that though man is responsible to believe, he is unable to do so. Thus, Luther said, the will of fallen man is completely enslaved to sin in matters pertaining to God. That means man is not free to choose salvation. Instead, Luther argued, God is absolutely sovereign, and will have mercy upon whom He will have mercy. Those chosen by God to eternal life are drawn by sovereign grace to believe in Christ. With this argument, Luther set Jesus Christ and His saving work at the center of his theology rather than man and his self-righteous works.[77] The Reformation, then, as noted earlier, was the triumph of Augustine's doctrine of salvation over his doctrine of the church.[78]

Through his prolific writings, Luther argued that God elects, predestines, calls, justifies, and glorifies those whom He foreknew in eternity past. Thus, it is God who saves. This was the central tenet of the Reformation. Luther wrote, "No man can be thoroughly humbled until he knows that his salvation is utterly beyond his own powers, devices, endeavors, will, and works, and depends entirely on the choice, will, and work of another, namely, of God alone."[79] Luther landed a devastating blow to the free will of man when he wrote, "We are so weak and uncertain that if it depended on us, not even a single person would be saved."[80] Man, he maintained, cannot be saved apart from the work of God.

## ENGLISH REFORMERS

Through Luther's writings, his doctrine spread across the English Channel to the universities of Oxford and Cambridge. Students began reading, discussing, and embracing the works of the German Reformer with growing interest. Many young English Reformers would eventually carry these truths to martyrs' deaths, including William Tyndale, Hugh Latimer, and John Rogers.

Tyndale made his great impact on the reform movement by translating the Bible from the original languages into English. By providing the Scriptures for the common man to read, Tyndale ignited a fire that burned brightly and expelled a thousand years of darkness. Robert Letham notes, "Tyndale exemplified the Protestant belief that the reform of the church and the salvation of men and women depended upon dispelling spiritual ignorance through a knowledge of the sure word of God."[81] A diligent student of God's Word, Tyndale was distinctly Reformed in his views on salvation, assigning to God every phase of sovereign grace, from election to preservation.

## SWISS REFORMERS

On the Continent, the Reformation made a particularly strong impact in Switzerland, where it was led by a number of gifted men. These included Ulrich Zwingli, Heinrich Bullinger, and John Calvin.

Zwingli, a pastor-theologian in Zurich, steered the northern Swiss churches into staunchly Reformed convictions. He held a strong belief in the sufficiency of Scripture as the sole authority for the church and affirmed that justification is by faith alone. Schaff notes, "Zwingli gives prominence to God's sovereign election as the primary source of salvation."[82] Saving faith, Zwingli maintained, comes from God, the gift of the Holy Spirit to the elect.

After Zwingli died on the battlefield, Bullinger succeeded him in Zurich and continued to proclaim Reformed truth. As the co-author of the First Helvetic Confession and the sole author of the Second Helvetic Confession, Bullinger exerted a considerable influence throughout Europe for sovereign grace theology. Most notably, he understood election within a Christ-centered framework, specifying that the atonement was intended for those chosen by God.

In southern Switzerland, there arose the primary leader and chief architect of Reformation theology—Calvin of Geneva. This faithful pastor became the premier exegete and foremost expositor of the Reformation. Consequently, he became the ablest teacher of sovereign grace. In 1536, Calvin published the first edition of his *Institutes of the Christian Religion*, which became his *magnum opus* and defined the Protestant movement, setting forth the glory of God as primary. This glory, Calvin said, is seen most clearly in His sovereignty over the affairs of providence and the salvation of sinners. From unconditional election in eternity past to glorification in eternity future, Calvin affirmed that saving grace is given by the supreme will of God. Such teaching made Calvin the prime pillar of sovereign grace.

Calvin plainly asserted God's sovereignty in man's salvation. In commenting on Ephesians 1:4, he wrote: "The foundation and first cause, both of our calling and of all the benefits which we receive from God, is here declared to be His eternal election. If the reason is asked, why God has called us to enjoy the gospel, why He daily bestows upon us so many blessings, why He opens to us the gate of heaven,—the answer will be constantly found in this principle, that *He hath chosen us before the foundation of the world.*"[83] What is more, Calvin maintained that God's sovereign choice in election is not based on man's worth or individual merit. To the contrary, he taught, "We were all lost in Adam; and therefore, had not God, through His own election, rescued us from perishing, there was nothing to be foreseen."[84] Simply put, Calvin's explanation of the doctrines of grace, rooted in thorough and careful biblical exegesis, marked the culmination in the development of these glorious truths. Calvin proved so convincing in his teaching that he became a leading influence on Western civilization.

At this critical time, the Reformed, God-centered view of Scripture came clearly into focus, unshackled from human traditions and secular philosophy. The Reformers unashamedly expounded the most foundational truth—that God *is* God. They gladly assigned God His rightful place as sovereign Lord over all. They proclaimed that He sovereignly reigns over the affairs of human history and the eternal destinies of all men. They declared that He is both the Creator and Controller of the universe. Further, they understood that salvation is entirely the gracious work of God. They affirmed the sovereign activity of God in rescuing fallen men, directed by His eternal purpose. The Protestant leaders were emphatic that God has foreordained all that comes to pass. Nowhere was this proclaimed more forcefully than in the salvation of His chosen ones.

That which the Church Fathers first stated in elementary form, that which Augustine enlarged and the medieval theologians expanded, the Reformers exhaustively declared—the doctrines of grace. The Protestant leaders spoke with one voice in boldly asserting the biblical doctrines of God's sovereignty in the salvation of His elect. They believed that the sinfulness of man and the supremacy of God were perfectly unified in one body of truth. The motto of the city of Geneva had come to pass—*Post tenebras lux,* "After darkness, light."

# A COLONNADE OF GODLY MEN

From Clement of Rome in the first century to Calvin of Geneva in the sixteenth, there is a progression in the church's understanding of the doctrines of grace, a gradual maturation in the comprehension of these glorious truths. What began as mere restatements of Scripture grew into fuller descriptions of God's sovereign grace in salvation. This volume in the series *A Long Line of Godly Men* will consider the times, lives, and teachings of the men who provided leadership in the church during these centuries of growth. Specifically, we shall seek to understand how they affirmed the doctrines of grace in their own times. This book will explore what these leading men believed and wrote concerning God's supreme grace in the salvation of His chosen ones.

Admittedly, these stalwarts had feet of clay. Though they helped bring great clarity to the church regarding many essential truths, they were capable of holding views that contradicted their own teachings. For instance, the unbiblical idea of baptismal regeneration was held by several of the Church Fathers.[85] Even the matter of the extent and efficacy of the atonement was largely ambiguous and slow to develop. These pillars of grace also differed on many secondary issues, such as church government, baptism, the Lord's Supper, and eschatology. They were not perfect men possessing infallible understanding. Rather they were flawed figures with fallible minds.

But when it came to the truths about salvation, there was considerable unity in their growing understanding of sovereign grace. Throughout the first sixteen centuries of the church, this long line of godly men increasingly asserted the key aspects of God's sovereignty in saving grace. A growing consensus concerning Scripture's teaching on the doctrines of grace gradually emerged. From mere traces of these biblical truths in the teachings of the early centuries, the church's understanding developed with time and came into greater focus. In spite of their many imperfections, God used these figures, to varying degrees, to document, define, and defend the doctrines of grace.

In no period of history has God left Himself without a witness. In the second through fourth centuries, the Church Fathers spoke these truths, though they needed greater clarification. In the fifth century, God raised up

Augustine, who brought further illumination to these doctrines. In the Dark Ages, this noble procession wore thin. Throughout the late medieval period, stalwarts for sovereign grace were often few. But in the Protestant Reformation, teachers of the doctrines of grace were plentiful and prolific. Through it all, God maintained a line of godly men, those who upheld the pattern of sound words (2 Tim. 1:13).

Throughout the flow of church history, God remains faithful to His cause. As Lord of the church, He guarantees the success of His truth. As the Author of Scripture, He ensures the triumph of His theology. From His throne above, our sovereign Lord sends forth faithful messengers to proclaim His supreme authority. By His Holy Spirit, God prepares the hearts of His people to embrace the teaching of sovereign grace, all in His perfect timing.

As we trace this long line of godly men from the first century to the sixteenth century, may the Lord use these pages to raise up new messengers who will sound the trumpet of His distinguishing grace. In this hour, may He prepare a new generation of renewed minds and passionate hearts to proclaim these glorious truths of Scripture.

Notes

1  Charles H. Spurgeon, *The New Park Street Pulpit: Vol. 4* (Pasadena, Texas: Pilgrim Publications, 1859), 340–341.

2  William Cunningham, *Historical Theology: A Review of the Principal Doctrinal Discussions in the Christian Church since the Apostolic Age, Vol. 1* (1862; repr., Edinburgh: Banner of Truth, 1969), 180.

3  David F. Wright, "Patristic Theology," in *New Dictionary of Theology*, eds. Sinclair B. Ferguson, David F. Wright, and J. I. Packer (Downers Grove, Ill.: InterVarsity, 1988), 495.

4  G. I. Bray, "History of Systematic Theology," in *New Dictionary of Theology*, 672.

5  Hans von Campenhausen, *The Fathers of the Church* (Peabody, Mass.: Hendrickson, 2000), 5.

6  A. Cleveland Coxe, "Preface," *Ante-Nicene Fathers, Vol. I: The Apostolic Fathers with Justin Martyr and Irenaeus*, eds. Alexander Roberts, James Donaldson, and A. Cleveland Coxe (1864; repr., Grand Rapids: Eerdmans, 1973), vii.

7  Louis Berkhof, *The History of Christian Doctrines* (1937; repr., Edinburgh: Banner of Truth, 1969), 40.

8  Berkhof, *The History of Christian Doctrines*, 39.

9  J. N. D. Kelly, *Early Christian Doctrines* (New York: Harper & Row, 1978), 163.

10  Cunningham, *Historical Theology, Vol. 1*, 180.

11  Cunningham, *Historical Theology, Vol. 1*, 180.

12 John Hannah states, "The Church Fathers . . . were not preoccupied with untangling the paradoxes in the proclamation of the gospel that would occupy church leaders in the later centuries." John Hannah, *Our Legacy: The History of Christian Doctrine* (Colorado Springs, Colo.: NavPress, 2001), 203.

13 Cunningham observes, "He who sees Augustinian or Calvinistic doctrines clearly and explicitly taught in the Bible, will have no difficulty in seeing also plain traces of them at least in the works of the Apostolic Fathers; and he who can pervert the statements of Scripture into an anti-Calvinistic sense, may, by the same process, and with equal ease, distort the Apostolic Fathers." Cunningham, *Historical Theology, Vol. 1*, 180.

14 R. K. McGregor Wright, *No Place for Sovereignty: What's Wrong with Freewill Theism* (Downers Grove, Ill.: InterVarsity, 1996), 18–19.

15 Clement of Rome, *First Clement*, 59:2, cited in Wright, *No Place for Sovereignty*, 19.

16 Clement, *First Clement*, 29:1, cited in *Early Christian Fathers*, ed. and trans. Cyril C. Richardson (New York: Touchstone, 1996), 57.

17 Ignatius, *To the Ephesians*, Salutation, cited in Richardson, *Early Christian Fathers*, 87–88.

18 Ignatius, *To the Ephesians*, Salutation, cited in Richardson, *Early Christian Fathers*, 88.

19 T. G. Donner, "Apologists," in *New Dictionary of Theology*, 37.

20 Hannah, *Our Legacy*, 205.

21 Concerning this neglect, D. Martyn Lloyd-Jones explains: "If you look at the long history of the Church, you will find that in different times and in different centuries some doctrines assume a particular importance. The great doctrine in the early centuries of the Church was, of necessity, the doctrine of the person of Christ. It had to be. That was the doctrine that was most attacked, so the Church placed its maximum emphasis upon it." D. Martyn Lloyd-Jones, *God the Father, God the Son, Vol. 1: Great Doctrines of the Bible* (Wheaton, Ill.: Crossway, 1996), 140.

22 William G. T. Shedd comments: "At a time when the truth that man is a responsible agent was being denied by the most subtle opponents which the Christian theologians of the first century were called to meet, it was not to be expected that very much reflection would be expended upon the side of the subject of sin which relates to weakness and bondage of the apostate will." William G. T. Shedd, *A History of Christian Doctrine* (1889; repr., Minneapolis: Klock & Klock, 1978), 2:29.

23 Hannah, *Our Legacy*, 206.

24 R. Kearsley, "Tertullian," in *New Dictionary of Theology*, 675.

25 Hannah, *Our Legacy*, 208.

26 Berkhof, *The History of Christian Doctrines*, 130. Berkhof adds: "Tertullian . . . does not altogether deny the freedom of the will. And though he reduces human efficiency to a minimum, he sometimes uses language that savors of the synergistic theory of regeneration, that is, the theory that God and man work together in regeneration." Berkhof, *The History of Christian Doctrines*, 129–130.

27 Berkhof, *The History of Christian Doctrines*, 130.

28 Cunningham, *Historical Theology, Vol. 1*, 164.

29 Gregory of Nyssa was "The first who sought to establish by rational considerations the whole complex of orthodox doctrines." Philip Schaff and Henry Wace, eds., *Nicene and Post-Nicene Fathers, Second Series, Vol. V: Gregory of Nyssa: Dogmatic Treatises, Etc.* (Grand Rapids: Eerdmans, n.d.), 8.

30 Basil, in *Saint Basil: The Letters, Vol. 4: Letters 259–368*, trans. Roy J. Deferrari and Martin R. P. McGuire (Cambridge, Mass., and London: Harvard University Press and W. Heinemann, 1950–70), 35.

31 Basil, in *Saint Basil: The Letters, Vol. 2: Letters 59–185*, trans. Roy J. Deferrari (Cambridge, Mass., and London: Harvard University Press and W. Heinemann, 1950–62), 93.

32 Gregory, Oration 42, 7–8, cited in *Gregory of Nazianzus*, ed. and trans. Brian E. Daley (London: Routledge, 2006), 144.

33 Gregory, Oration 42, 7–8, cited in *Gregory of Nazianzus*, 144.

34 Charles Hodge, *Systematic Theology, Vol. II* (Grand Rapids: Eerdmans, 1977), 152.

35 Berkhof writes: "On the whole, the main emphasis was on the free will of man rather than on the operation of divine grace. It is not the grace of God, but the free will of man that takes the initiative in the work of regeneration. But though it begins the work, it cannot complete it without divine aid. The power of God co-operates with the human will, and enables it to turn from evil. . . . These Fathers do not always make a clear distinction between the good which the natural man is able to do and that spiritual good which requires the enabling power of the Holy Spirit." Berkhof, *The History of Christian Doctrines*, 128–129. J. N. D. Kelly contends, "The Greek fathers, with their insistence that man's free will remains intact and is the root of actual sinning, have a much more optimistic outlook than the West. It is easy to collect passages from their works which at any rate in the light of later orthodoxy, appear to rule out any doctrine of original sin." Kelly, *Early Christian Doctrines*, 349.

36 Hannah, *Our Legacy*, 211.

37 Berkhof, *The History of Christian Doctrines*, 130.

38 G. A. Keith, "Ambrose," in *New Dictionary of Theology*, 16.

39 These points are summarized by Hodge in *Systematic Theology, Vol. II,* 152–155.

40 Timothy George, *Theology of the Reformers* (Nashville: Broadman, 1988), 73.

41 Loraine Boettner, *The Reformed Doctrine of Predestination* (Phillipsburg, N.J.: P&R, 1932), 365.

42 Summarizing Augustine's position, Boettner writes, "God elects whom He will irrespective of their merits, and . . . saving grace is efficaciously applied to the elect by the Holy Spirit." Boettner, *The Reformed Doctrine of Predestination*, 366.

43 Berkhof, *The History of Christian Doctrines*, 138.

44 Kelly writes, "The student who seeks to understand the soteriology of the fourth and early fifth centuries will be sharply disappointed if he expects to find anything corresponding to the elaborately worked out syntheses which the contemporary theology of the Trinity and the Incarnation presents." Kelly, *Early Christian Doctrines*, 375.

45 David F. Wright, "Semi-Pelagianism," in *New Dictionary of Theology*, 636.

46 Hannah, *Our Legacy*, 215.

47 G. W. Bromiley, "History of Theology," in *New Dictionary of Theology*, 310.

48 Anthony N. S. Lane, "Monastic Theology," in *New Dictionary of Theology*, 441.

49 Boettner, *The Reformed Doctrine of Predestination*, 366–367.

50 Lane, "Monastic Theology," in *New Dictionary of Theology*, 442.

51 Lane, "Monastic Theology," in *New Dictionary of Theology*, 441.

52 Louis Berkhof, *Systematic Theology* (1939; repr., Grand Rapids: Eerdmans, 1976), 110.

53 Berkhof, *The History of Christian Doctrines*, 141.

54 D. E. Nineham, "Gottschalk of Orbais: Reactionary or Precursor to the Reformation?" in *Journal of Ecclesiastical History*, 40 (1989), 12.

55 R. G. Clouse, "Gottschalk," in *New Dictionary of Theology*, 279.

56 Wright, *No Place for Sovereignty*, 22. Berkhof writes: "Augustine had occasionally spoken of a double predestination, and Isidore of Seville still wrote of it as being twofold. But many of the

Augustinians in the seventh, eighth, and ninth centuries lost sight of this double character of predestination, and interpreted it as Gregory had done. Then came Gottschalk, who found rest and peace for his soul only in the Augustinian doctrine of election, and contended earnestly for a double predestination, that is, a predestination of the lost as well as of the saved." Berkhof, *The History of Christian Doctrines*, 141.

57 Anthony N. S. Lane, "Bernard of Clairvaux," in *New Dictionary of Theology*, 91.

58 Tony Lane, *A Concise History of Christian Thought* (Grand Rapids: Baker Academic, 2006), 111.

59 Lane, "Bernard of Clairvaux," in *New Dictionary of Theology*, 90.

60 Anthony N. S. Lane, "Scholasticism," in *New Dictionary of Theology*, 621.

61 Anthony N. S. Lane, "Anselm," in *New Dictionary of Theology*, 26.

62 David F. Wright, "Augustinianism," in *New Dictionary of Theology*, 61.

63 Arthur Custance, *The Sovereignty of Grace* (Grand Rapids: Baker, 1979), 42.

64 Wright, *No Place for Sovereignty*, 22.

65 Wright, *No Place for Sovereignty*, 22.

66 Paul Helm, "Thomas Bradwardine," in *New Dictionary of Theology*, 109.

67 Helm, "Thomas Bradwardine," in *New Dictionary of Theology*, 109.

68 Helm, "Thomas Bradwardine," in *New Dictionary of Theology*, 109.

69 Bromiley, "History of Theology," in *New Dictionary of Theology*, 310.

70 Boettner, *The Reformed Doctrine of Predestination*, 366–367.

71 L. L. Morris, "John Wyclif," in *New Dictionary of Theology*, 733.

72 J. T. Jones, "John Hus," in *New Dictionary of Theology*, 323.

73 Philip Schaff, *History of the Christian Church, Vol. VII: Modern Christianity, The German Reformation* (1910; repr., Grand Rapids: Eerdmans, 1984), 1.

74 William Cunningham, *The Reformers and the Theology of the Reformation* (1862; repr., Edinburgh: Banner of Truth, 1989), 1.

75 Bromiley, "History of Theology," in *New Dictionary of Theology*, 311.

76 Philip Schaff, *History of the Christian Church, Vol. VIII: Modern Christianity: The Swiss Reformation* (1910; repr., Grand Rapids: Eerdmans, 1984), 92.

77 J. Atkinson, "Martin Luther," in *New Dictionary of Theology*, 403.

78 Wright, *No Place for Sovereignty*, 23.

79 Martin Luther, *Luther's Works, Vol. 33*, eds. Jaroslav Jan Pelikan, Hilton C. Oswald, and Helmut T. Lehmann (St. Louis: Concordia, 2002), 62.

80 Martin Luther, *Luther's Works, Vol. 35*, eds. Jaroslav Jan Pelikan, Hilton C. Oswald, and Helmut T. Lehmann (St. Louis: Concordia, 2002), 378.

81 Robert Letham, "English Reformers," in *New Dictionary of Theology*, 572.

82 Philip Schaff, *History of the Christian Church, Vol. VIII*, 91.

83 John Calvin, *Commentaries on the Epistles of Paul to the Galatians and Ephesians*, trans. William Pringle (Grand Rapids: Baker, 2003), 197. Emphasis in original.

84 Calvin, *Commentaries on the Epistles of Paul to the Galatians and Ephesians*, 198.

85 For more information on this subject, see G. W. Bromiley, "Baptismal Regeneration," in *Evangelical Dictionary of Theology*, 2nd Ed., ed. Walter A. Elwell (Grand Rapids: Baker, 2001), 135.

# CHAPTER ONE
## STUDY QUESTIONS

1.  When did the discipline of systematic theology begin? Did it start early or late in church history?

2.  Who were the Church Fathers? Why were they called Fathers?

3.  What was the unique role of the Apostolic Fathers? To what extent did they teach the doctrines of grace?

4.  Explain the role of the Apologist Fathers in the second and third centuries. What was their primary ministry to the church?

5.  When and where did the African Fathers serve? What development did they contribute to the doctrines of grace?

6.  Why were the Cappadocian Fathers so strategic in guarding sound doctrine? To what extent did they hold to free will and original sin?

7.  Who were the key Latin Fathers? Describe the unique place of Augustine in the development of sovereign grace truth. With whom was he embroiled in controversy? How did this crisis serve to clarify sovereign grace?

8.  What was the arena in which leaders in the Dark Ages taught? Who were the key theologians that influenced the church in this era? Did any hold strongly to the doctrines of grace?

9.  What was the role of the Scholastics? What place did the university system play in spreading the doctrines of grace?

10. Describe the unique place of the Pre-Reformers. How did they prepare the way for the Reformation?

11. Why were the Reformers so mightily used by God? Detail their commitment to the doctrines of grace.

*By* His majestic word He established the universe, and by His word He can bring it to an end. "Who shall say to Him, What have You done? Or who shall resist His mighty strength?" He will do everything when He wants to and as He wants to. And not one of the things He has decreed will fail.[1]

–Clement of Rome

Chapter Two

# FIRST AMONG
# THE FATHERS

## APOSTOLIC FATHER:
## CLEMENT OF ROME

Tracing the development of the doctrines of grace from the end of the first century to the sixteenth is like attempting to map the flow of an uncharted river through a dense continent. There are places where the river is clearly in sight, easily followed. But there are other locations where the river meanders through dense forest and the view is obstructed. In a similar way, certain dark, complex, and controversial times in church history are difficult to penetrate, making any attempt to chart the flow of the doctrines of sovereign grace over fifteen hundred years a daunting challenge. Still, that is the goal of this book—to chart the development of theology concerning the sovereignty of God in the salvation of man.

Of this we can be sure—during the church's first millennium and a half, there was a definite progression of understanding in virtually every area of theology. The flow of thought developed, it could be said, from a brook to a stream to a river. However, the church's understanding of the doctrines of grace initially was slow to develop. Grasping the truths of sovereign grace was a "long drawn-out process"[2] because, as a study of church history reveals, there was a "logical order" of progression from one area of theology to the next.[3] The development of the doctrines of grace came only after the church had addressed other areas of theology. For example, the doctrine of predestination was not a focus of the church until the beginning of the fifth century.[4] And it was not until the Protestant Reformation of the sixteenth century that the river of sovereign grace understanding reached its greatest depths.

## CONCERNS OF THE EARLY CHURCH

While traces of the doctrines of grace can be found in the writings of the Apostolic Fathers, these early church leaders, as we have seen, did not provide new theological insights into the truths of sovereign grace, nor did they organize them into a system of thought. There were several reasons why the early church struggled to bring the doctrines of grace into focus.

First, the Church Fathers were engaged in proclaiming the gospel message. As the early church began to penetrate the pagan culture, the believers' primary emphasis was on the preaching of the gospel, not a detailed explanation of the intricacies of sovereign grace. James Orr writes: "The age of Apologetics was the vindication of the fundamental ideas of all religion—of the Christian especially—in conflict with Paganism and with the Gnostics. . . . It was not so much as yet the special doctrines of the Christian faith that were in discussion—though these also were partly drawn in—as rather the broad truths that underlie all religion: the unity, spirituality, and moral government of God, man's freedom and responsibility, the certainty of judgment, the need of repentance, the idea of revelation, the canon of Scripture, [and] the vindication of the primary facts of the Gospel."[5] The Fathers were principally concerned with reaching their pagan culture with the good news of Christ, not with how sovereign grace brings that truth to the heart.

Second, the Church Fathers were focused on refuting heresies. The second through fourth centuries were marked by many theological aberrations, such as Unitarianism, Sabellianism, Monarchianism, Arianism, and Macedonianism. Each of these heresies blatantly attacked the Trinity, the divine nature of Christ, and the deity of the Holy Spirit. The integrity of the saving gospel of the Christian faith was at stake. Thus, the Early Fathers were preoccupied with refuting these false movements.[6] To do so, they constructed well-defined creeds that served to outline and defend the essential truths of the Christian faith. J. N. D. Kelly notes that these "definitions were hammered out against this background of controversy."[7] In other words, controversy helped the church grow in its theological understanding. Until a doctrine was attacked, it remained undeveloped, stated in relatively vague terms.[8] But controversy compelled the early leaders to greater clarification. Only later would controversies over salvation prompt church leaders to greater specificity on sovereign grace.[9]

Third, the Church Fathers were concerned with the canon of Scripture. By the end of the first century, the apostles had passed off the scene, and their authoritative preaching was a thing of the past. There were no Christian libraries at the church's disposal. There were no systematic theologies sitting on shelves. There was no more special revelation from heaven. But there were a number of books written by the apostles and their immediate associates. It was up to the Church Fathers to discover what it meant for the faith to be delivered once and for all to the saints. It was their task to begin to sort through all they had been divinely given.

Fourth, the Church Fathers wanted to distance themselves from fatalism. Manichaeism, Stoicism, and other false religious movements taught a blind, deterministic fatalism. Teaching predestination gave the appearance that the Church Fathers were in agreement with these heresies. Loraine Boettner says the fact that "the doctrine of Predestination received such little attention in this age was no doubt partly due to the tendency to confuse it with the Pagan doctrine of Fatalism which was so prevalent throughout the Roman Empire."[10]

Fifth, the Church Fathers sought to merge Greek philosophy with biblical teaching. From the second century onward, the Fathers made secular philosophy the handmaid of theology. The influence of Platonism and Stoicism, in particular, was widespread. But in attempting to reach the pagan mind, they often failed to distinguish between Greek philosophy and Christian doctrine.[11] Many of the Fathers tried to appeal to natural reason in proclaiming the gospel to pagans. They did so because they wanted to demonstrate to Greek minds that Christianity was rational, reasonable, logical, and philosophically sound. But sovereign grace can be understood only by supernatural revelation. Mere human reason will never grasp the truths of the doctrines of grace.

## EXPANSION OF THE EARLY CHURCH

While the development of the church's understanding of the doctrines of grace was initially slow, the growth of the church itself was explosive. By the end of the first century, the Christian faith was rapidly spreading to the extremities of the Roman Empire. The church had taken the gospel into Judea and Samaria, then into Asia Minor, Europe, North Africa, and even Ethiopia. Though resistance against the early believers was formidable, the faith thrived. Judaism, with its dead religion and empty ritual, could not thwart the progress of the church. The Roman government, with its imperial might and emperor cult, could not impede the advance of the truth. The Greek culture, with its pagan polytheism and secular philosophies, could not halt the march of the gospel.

In spite of mounting pressures, the first believers turned their world upside down with a spiritual explosion that reverberates to this day.

Soon, the church had established itself even in the very capital of the empire—Rome. Peter went there to preach the Word (1 Peter 5:13) and encourage the believers. Paul endured two imprisonments there. Even their brutal martyrdoms could not quench the gospel fires that were burning brightly there and spreading beyond. John, the last living apostle, endured fierce persecution at the end of the century, and his recorded letters to the seven churches of Asia Minor (Rev. 2–3) revealed that the church had spread to all the major cities of that region. Christianity was a rapidly expanding force.

What factors ignited such a dynamic expansion of the church? How did the early believers spread the gospel so successfully? There are two ways to answer these questions—from the divine perspective and from the human perspective. Both are correct.

From the divine perspective, the reason for the rapid expansion of the church lay in the overruling sovereignty of God. Jesus had promised, "I will build my church, and the gates of hell shall not prevail against it" (Matt. 16:18). As the first century unfolded, the invisible hand of God worked providentially in the glove of human circumstances, affecting world events for the advancement of the gospel. The Holy Spirit emboldened the early believers to spread the Word and caused their preaching and teaching to succeed. The hearts of unbelievers were sovereignly opened to receive the gospel (Acts 2:39, 47). For these reasons, the kingdom of God proved to be unstoppable and invincible.

From the human perspective, there were many evident causes for the expansion of the church. Politically, there was the *pax Romana*, "the Roman peace," an official policy that provided an environment in which the early believers could propagate the Christian faith. Linguistically, *koine* ("common") Greek was the standard language of the people throughout the empire and was used in the writing of the New Testament. This unifying language made the Scriptures readily understandable everywhere the disciples went. Travel was relatively easy and safe; Roman roads expedited land travel and Roman fleets swept the Mediterranean of pirates. Thus, the gospel could be taken swiftly and safely from Jerusalem to other lands. Culturally, the first-century world was open-minded to new spiritual and philosophical ideas. Newer secular philosophies were replacing the old strongholds of Greek and Roman polytheism.

The marketplace of ideas was open for business. Religiously, the Jews had a renewed interest in the Scriptures. Finally, there was gifted and godly leadership in the church as the apostles began to depart the scene.

## THE APOSTOLIC FATHERS

As the early church began to grow and advance, God raised up the Apostolic Fathers, a group of faithful men who propagated the Christian faith and provided leadership after the apostles. They comprised the first generation of Church Fathers. The Apostolic Fathers were living even while the last of the apostles served; some actually were discipled by and were appointed by apostles themselves. To a man, the Apostolic Fathers were committed to spreading the Christ-centered gospel.

As their title implies, the doctrine of the Apostolic Fathers was distinctly apostolic. This was to be expected from men who were contemporaries of the apostles. Their writings form an important bridge between the New Testament books and the works of the Apologists, who wrote in the second century.[12] While the Apostolic Fathers were not theological or systematic in what they wrote, they were pastoral and practical.[13] They did not address doctrinal matters per se, but wrote most directly to correct individual churches, helping them overcome internal division or inappropriate conduct, and calling them to submit to the authority of Scripture. Using the Old Testament, the sayings of Jesus, the oral traditions of the apostles, and especially the Pauline epistles, the Apostolic Fathers led the early church in resolving the problems of the day.

In all, six men are regarded as Apostolic Fathers—Barnabas of Cyprus (ca. 5–ca. 61), Clement of Rome (ca. 30–ca. 101), Ignatius of Antioch (ca. 35–ca. 107), Papias (ca. 60–130), Polycarp (ca. 69–ca. 155), and Hermas (second century). Each of these men took a strong stand for biblical truth.

## CLEMENT OF ROME

Clement was one of the early bishops of the church in Rome.[14] Some suggest that Clement was a disciple of Paul and Peter.[15] E. C. Dargan notes that Clement's strong character and position testify to his power as a teacher of the Word.[16] So highly regarded was Clement, David F. Wright notes, that his most famous writing, an epistle known as *First Clement*, enjoyed almost scriptural status in the churches in Egypt and Syria.[17] This letter reveals that Clement built his ministry on the foundation laid by the apostles in their inspired writings.

Nothing is known about Clement's childhood and early adult life. He first stepped into the spotlight of recorded history when, as an adult, he was appointed a bishop of the Roman church.[18] According to the early church historian Eusebius, Clement was the third bishop of Rome.[19] He initially served as a co-bishop with two other men, Linus and Cletus.[20] Later, he functioned as the lead bishop in the church,[21] the first among equals. Eventually, he succeeded them in overseeing the church.[22]

This was an important position of spiritual leadership, for Rome was the capital of the empire and the symbolic center of ancient civilization.[23] By the latter half of the first century, Rome also had become a major center for the Christian faith. Consequently, the bishop of Rome occupied an influential position in the early church. Many doctrinal issues were resolved through his influence. Thus, in the last decade of the first century, Clement not only provided spiritual leadership for one of the most strategic congregations in Christianity, he was responsible for providing spiritual counsel for other churches.

The circumstances surrounding the end of Clement's life are uncertain, though later tradition circulated many accounts about his travels and death.[24] According to various legends, he was banished to the Crimea in the reign of Emperor Trajan and forced to work in the mines.[25] After much hard labor, according to this tradition, he allegedly was bound to an anchor and thrown into the Black Sea.[26]

While this account is questionable, what is certain is the spiritual fidelity that Clement maintained in the service of Christ until the end of his life. Moreover, his commitment to the doctrines of grace is permanently recorded in his letter, *First Clement*, as a testimony to all future generations of the adherence to these truths in the early church.

## CLEMENT'S WRITINGS

During Clement's tenure as bishop in Rome, the congregation at Corinth hastily replaced some senior elders with younger men in a rebellion of young against old, causing a division in the church.[27] Making matters worse, the deposed elders had likely been appointed by the apostles themselves. When

Clement heard of these problems, he wrote an open letter, probably around AD 96,[28] urging the new leadership to restore the older men to their former ministry positions. He urged the quarreling Christians to seek peace for the same reasons Paul had cited in writing to them forty years earlier in the letter of 1 Corinthians. The epistle he wrote is known as *First Clement.*

Apart from possibly the *Didache* (ca. 100), *First Clement* is the earliest Christian writing after the New Testament.[29] It was intended to give pastoral counsel to a wayward church.[30] This oldest non-canonical epistle possesses a noticeable resemblance to various biblical books in its language and truth.[31] Biblical references and quotations are numerous; about one-fourth of the letter comprises quotations from the Old Testament.[32] *First Clement* reads very much like Paul's own letters to the Corinthians.[33] It is clear that Clement knew 1 Corinthians very well.[34]

But what is far more important is the theology revealed in this epistle. It is plainly Pauline in its doctrine and strongly resembles the epistle to the Hebrews. At the same time, it reveals the influence of the writing style and teaching of Peter.[35] Commenting on these influences in Clement's life, Irenaeus noted, "[Clement] had seen the apostles and associated with them, and still had their preaching sounding in his ears and their tradition before his eyes."[36] In short, *First Clement* reveals an author who held firmly to biblical truths, including the truth of sovereign grace.

## CLEMENT'S THEOLOGY

As noted in Chapter 1, the Apostolic Fathers did not engage in deep theology but primarily quoted Scripture to make their points. Speaking to this point, William Cunningham notes that Clement and the other Apostolic Fathers, "generally used the language of the Scriptures upon these subjects, while they scarcely make any statements which afford us materials for deciding in what precise sense they understood them."[37] Berkhof adds that their writings "cannot be said to increase or deepen our insight into the truth or to shed light on the inter-relations of the doctrinal teachings of Scripture."[38] Nevertheless, trace evidences of the doctrines of divine sovereignty, radical depravity, sovereign election, definite atonement, irresistible call, and preserving grace appear in embryonic form in the writings of the Apostolic Fathers, including *First Clement.* R. K. McGregor Wright notes that "ideas later associated with John Calvin . . . already appear quite clearly in this literature."[39] In other words, the

Early Church Fathers' teachings regarding election and predestination were in complete harmony with the truths of Scripture but did not provide penetrating insights. Clement and the men who followed him affirmed individual truths but did not systematize these doctrines or address their cause-and-effect relationships.

Having received the teaching of Paul and Peter, it is not surprising that Clement incorporated elements of the truths of sovereign grace in his writings. In doing so, he faithfully taught what had been recorded by the inspired authors of Scripture and took his place in the long line of godly men who have proclaimed the sovereign grace of God in salvation.

**Doctrine in Focus:**

## DIVINE SOVEREIGNTY

Throughout his letter to the Corinthians, Clement asserts the sovereignty of God over all the affairs of this world: "The heavens move at His direction and peacefully obey Him. Day and night observe the course He has appointed them, without getting in each other's way. . . . By His will and without dissension or altering anything He has decreed, the earth becomes fruitful at the proper seasons."[40] By divine direction, there is harmony in God's creation. Clement states: "All these things the great Creator and Master of the universe ordained to exist in peace and harmony."[41] Here Clement, in a clear statement of divine sovereignty, declared that God directs whatsoever comes to pass.

Clement affirms that God's sovereign will is immutable and irresistible: "By His majestic word He established the universe, and by His word He can bring it to an end. 'Who shall say to Him, What have You done? Or who shall resist His mighty strength?' He will do everything when He wants to and as He wants to. And not one of the things He has decreed will fail. Everything is open to His sight and nothing escapes His will."[42] By this statement, Clement maintained the absolute providence of God over all the works of His hands. All that God has ordered, he believed, surely comes to pass.

**Doctrine in Focus:**

## RADICAL DEPRAVITY

Clement held that fallen man is so ruined in sin that he is incapable of saving himself. Having forfeited his moral ability to do good, man cannot present himself acceptable to God. Clement writes that we are "not justified of ourselves or by our wisdom or insight or religious devotion or the holy deeds we have done from the heart."[43] That is, no man has the innate ability to save himself. What is more, Clement teaches that all people come into this world spiritually dead in sin: "We must take to heart, brothers, from what stuff we were created, what kind of creatures we were when we entered the world, from what a dark grave he who fashioned and created us brought us into his world."[44] Fallen man must be raised to new life by God.

Quoting the prophet Isaiah, Clement writes, "Like sheep we have all gone astray: each one went astray in his own way."[45] He affirmed that all unconverted men by nature are running away from God. In reality, Clement said, none seek for God.

**Doctrine in Focus:**
## Sovereign Election

Given his belief in man's inability to save himself, it is entirely consistent that Clement affirmed sovereign election. He wrote that the "elect" are "chosen of God," using these biblical terms as synonyms for believers in Christ. In the opening sentence of his epistle, Clement states that believers are "those whom God has chosen."[46] He later adds that as the apostles preached the Word of God, "there was joined a great multitude of the elect."[47] He clearly believed the church to be the ingathering of God's chosen ones.

Clement rightly maintained that all believers were chosen by God to be His inheritance. With great reverence, he writes, "We must, then, approach Him with our souls holy, lifting up pure and undefiled hands to Him, loving our kind and compassionate Father, who has made us His chosen portion."[48] Clement understood that salvation originates with God, not man. Therefore, man must come to God in a posture of pride-crushing humility and sin-forsaking purity. The doctrine of election is, in fact, very practical in the daily life of the believer.

This Early Church Father also affirmed the greatest blessing in any Christian's life—forgiveness of sin. This divine blessing can be traced back to God's sovereign choice of that individual in eternity past. Commenting on Psalm 32:1–2, Clement states that forgiveness of sin belongs exclusively to the elect: "Happy is the man whose sin the Lord will not reckon. . . . This is the blessing which was given to those whom God chose through Jesus Christ our Lord. To Him be the glory forever and ever. Amen."[49] His mind illumined by Scripture, Clement saw that election leads to forgiveness.

Urging the Corinthians to put aside their contentions, Clement appealed to the example of the many godly men who trusted God through persecution and mistreatment in the past. He urged the Corinthians to follow their example because, he said, it is only the elect of God who fervently persevere through hard times. He writes: "Let us, then, follow the innocent and the upright. They, it is, who are God's elect."[50] This deep trust in God amid present difficulties gives evidence that a person is among the elect. They alone are worthy of emulation.

**Doctrine in Focus:**
DEFINITE ATONEMENT

Clement spoke of the elect of God in connection with Christ's work on the cross, affirming that believers were chosen "in Him [Christ]" (Eph. 1:4) and that the Father chose Christ to carry out the redemption of these chosen ones. He writes, "And now may the all-seeing God and Master 'of spirits' and Lord 'of all flesh,' who chose the Lord Jesus Christ and us through Him 'to be His own people,' grant to every soul over whom His magnificent and holy name has been invoked, faith, fear, peace, patience, long-suffering, self-control, purity, and sobriety."[51] In this statement, Clement acknowledged the Father's election of both Christ and His elect. From this, it might be understood that Christ was chosen to save the chosen ones.

Clement alluded to the truth that Christ's death was intended for the elect, writing: "By love all God's elect were made perfect. Without love nothing can please God. By love, the Master accepted us. Because of the love He had for us, and in accordance with God's will, Jesus Christ our Lord gave His blood for us, His flesh for our flesh, and His life for ours."[52] With these words, Clement maintained that Christ sacrificially shed His blood for the elect. Whether or not Clement consciously intended this, these words are in line with the truth that Christ died only for the elect.

Elsewhere Clement teaches that the atonement was for all who believe: "It was by the blood of the Lord that redemption was going to come to all who believe in God and hope on him."[53] The free offer of the gospel in the death of Christ is extended to all, but only the elect believe and receive it.

**Doctrine in Focus:**
IRRESISTIBLE CALL

Clement maintained that the Holy Spirit sovereignly brings all those chosen by God to repentance and saving faith. In the first sentence of *First Clement*, he identifies the believers in Corinth as those "who are called . . . by God's will."[54] Clement further writes, "We . . . by His will have been called in Jesus Christ."[55] He recognized that it is by divine initiative and calling that believers exercise faith in Christ.

Clement said that the sovereign will of God is ultimately the determinative factor in repentance. He states: "It is the will of God that all whom He loves should partake of repentance, and so not perish with the unbelieving and impenitent. He has established it by His almighty will."[56] With these words, Clement made a bold distinction between those whom God loves and the unbelieving. It is by God's determinative will that those whom He loves come to repentance. The new birth is the result of His omnipotent will that cannot be resisted.

As Clement exults over the gifts of God, he writes: "How blessed and amazing are God's gifts, dear friends! Life with immortality, splendor with righteousness, truth with confidence, faith with assurance, self-control with holiness!"[57] The gifts in this sequence seem to be related to redemption, indicating that Clement was thinking of saving faith. Thus, he was calling saving faith a supernatural gift of God. Here he asserted divine sovereignty in salvation, that God must give faith before anyone can truly believe. When the gift of faith is given, it always results in conversion.

**Doctrine in Focus:**

Preserving Grace

Finally, Clement asserted that the salvation God gives to His elect is an enduring work of grace, never to be reversed or undone. He says: "But if any of those whom God wills should partake of the grace of repentance, should afterwards perish, where is His almighty will? And how is this matter settled and established by such a will of His?"[58] In other words, God holds His elect eternally secure by His omnipotent will. Elsewhere he writes, "We will beg with earnest prayer and supplication that the Creator of the universe will keep intact the precise number of His elect in the whole world, through his beloved Child Jesus Christ."[59] Likewise, in his salutation to the Corinthian believers, Clement notes that their faith is lasting: "Has anyone, indeed, stayed with you without attesting the excellence and firmness of your faith?"[60] Faith is a sovereign gift of God, Clement believed, and when He gives it, He establishes it forever. Therefore, none of the elect will perish, for God will preserve them.

# RESOLUTE IN CHRIST

In every generation, the strongest pillars in the church are those men who are strongest in the truth. There are no exceptions. Without the truth, men are weak in faith and lack convictions to stand for God. Clement's strong stand for Christ clearly was rooted and grounded in the Word of God. Specifically, he stood on the immoveable rock of divine sovereignty, a matchless truth by which he held fast in the storms through which he passed in his life. In the end, his sturdy beliefs determined how he died—with resolution and dignity. Men like Clement uphold the truths of sovereign grace in every age and are mightily used by God to undergird His work in every hour.

What we believe determines how we live. Further, it dictates how we serve the Lord. Strong doctrinal moorings in the sovereignty of God produce a deep commitment to the Son of God. Theological principles shape how we impact the day in which we live. Moreover, they affect how we live our lives in the cause of Christ. But sad to say, shallow theology always produces shallow convictions. Doctrinal compromise inevitably leads to superficial living.

May we be those who, in this present moment, stand strongest in the doctrines of grace. With such a firm foundation, may we be used by God as strong and sturdy pillars in His church. May we faithfully undergird His work in this uncertain hour of human history.

NOTES

1  Clement of Rome, *First Clement*, 27, cited in *Early Christian Fathers*, ed. and trans. Cyril C. Richardson (New York: Touchstone, 1996), 56.

2  J. N. D. Kelly, *Early Christian Doctrines* (Peabody, Mass.: Prince, 2007), 163.

3  James Orr, *The Progress of Dogma* (Vancouver: Regent College Publishing, 2000), 25.

4  Loraine Boettner, *The Reformed Doctrine of Predestination* (Phillipsburg, N.J.: P&R, 1932), 365.

5  Orr, *The Progress of Dogma*, 24.

6  To this point, Louis Berkhof remarks, "Pressure from without and from within called for a clear statement for defense of the truth, and thus gave birth to theology." Louis Berkhof, *The History of Christian Doctrines* (1937; repr., Edinburgh: Banner of Truth, 1969), 56.

7  Kelly, *Early Christian Doctrines*, 5.

8  Dirk Jellema writes: "In the first centuries of the Christian Church, predestination was not an issue. Theological energy was taken up with definitions of the Trinity and arguments regarding the nature of Christ." Dirk Jellema, "Predestination," in *New International Dictionary of the Christian Church*, gen. ed. J. D. Douglas (Grand Rapids: Zondervan, 1978), 798.

9   William Cunningham remarks: "Calvinists and anti-Calvinists have both appealed to the early church in support of their respective opinions, although we believe it cannot be made out that the fathers of the first three centuries give any very distinct deliverance concerning them. These important topics did not become subjects of controversial discussion during that period; and it holds almost universally in the history of the church, that until a doctrine has been fully discussed in a controversial way by men of talent and learning taking opposite sides, men's opinions regarding it are generally obscure and indefinite, and their language vague and confused, if not contradictory. These doctrines did not become subjects of controversial discussion till what is called the Pelagian controversy, in the beginning of the fifth century." William Cunningham, *Historical Theology: A Review of the Principal Doctrinal Discussions in the Christian Church since the Apostolic Age, Vol. 1* (1862; repr. Edinburgh: Banner of Truth, 1969), 179–180.

10   Boettner, *The Reformed Doctrine of Predestination*, 366.

11   Concerning this period of church history, Berkhof notes, "It must be admitted that they represented Christianity largely in terms of philosophy, that they did not clearly discriminate between philosophy and theology, and that their representations of the truths of revelation . . . suffered from an admixture of Greek philosophical thought." Berkhof, *The History of Christian Doctrines*, 60.

12   Tony Lane, *A Concise History of Christian Thought* (Grand Rapids: Baker Academic, 2006), 8.

13   David F. Wright, "Apostolic Fathers," in *New International Dictionary of the Christian Church*, 59.

14   "Clement of Rome," in *Cyclopedia of Biblical, Theological, and Ecclesiastical Literature, Vol. VIII*, eds. John McClintock and James Strong (Grand Rapids: Baker, 1981), 376.

15   Philip Schaff, *History of the Christian Church, Vol. II: Ante-Nicene Christianity: From the Death of John the Apostle to Constantine the Great, A.D. 100–325* (1910; repr., Grand Rapids: Eerdmans, 1980), 637.

16   Edwin Charles Dargan, *A History of Preaching, Vol. 1: From the Apostolic Fathers to the Great Reformers* (Grand Rapids: Baker, 1974), 45.

17   David F. Wright, "Clement of Rome," in *New International Dictionary of the Christian Church*, 235.

18   N. R. Needham, *2,000 Years of Christ's Power, Part One: The Age of the Early Church Fathers* (London: Grace Publications, 1997), 59.

19   Eusebius, *Ecclesiastical History* (Peabody, Mass.: Hendrickson, 1998), 2.21; 3.34; 5.6.

20   A. Cleveland Coxe, "Introductory Note to the First Epistle of Clement to the Corinthians," in *Ante-Nicene Fathers, Vol. I: The Apostolic Fathers with Justin Martyr and Irenaeus*, eds. Alexander Roberts, James Donaldson, and A. Cleveland Coxe (1864; repr., Grand Rapids: Eerdmans, 1973), 1.

21   Earle E. Cairns, *Christianity Through the Centuries: A History of the Christian Church*, 3rd Ed. (1954; repr., Grand Rapids: Zondervan, 1996), 75.

22   Eusebius, *Church History*, Books 1–5, trans. Roy J. Deferrari (New York: Fathers of the Church, Inc., 1953), 163.

23   Jonathan Hill, *The History of Christian Thought* (Downers Grove, Ill.: InterVarsity, 2003), 18.

24   Wright, "Clement of Rome," in *New International Dictionary of the Christian Church*, 235.

25   "Clement of Rome, St.," in *The Oxford Dictionary of the Christian Church*, ed. E. A. Livingstone (1957; repr., Oxford: Oxford University Press, 1997), 360.

26   "Clement of Rome, St.," in *The Oxford Dictionary of the Christian Church*, 360.

27   Stuart G. Hall, "The Early Idea of the Church," in *The First Christian Theologians: An Introduction to Theology in the Early Church*, ed. G. R. Evans (Oxford: Blackwell, 2006), 45.

28 Lane, *A Concise History of Christian Thought*, 8.

29 Cairns, *Christianity Through the Centuries*, 75.

30 Robert A. Baker, *A Summary of Christian History*, rev. John M. Landers (Nashville: Broadman & Holman, 1994), 27.

31 Alexander Roberts and James Donaldson, "Introductory Note to the First Epistle of Clement to the Corinthians," *Ante-Nicene Fathers, Vol. I*, 3.

32 Joseph T. Lienhard, "Clement of Rome," in *Biographical Dictionary of Christian Theologians* (Peabody, Mass.: Hendrickson, 2000), 129.

33 Roger E. Olson, *The Story of Christian Theology* (Downers Grove, Ill.: InterVarsity, 1999), 42.

34 Lienhard, "Clement of Rome," in *Biographical Dictionary of Christian Theologians*, 130.

35 Philip Schaff, *History of the Christian Church, Vol. 1: Apostolic Christianity: From the Birth of Christ to the Death of St. John, A.D. 1–100* (1910; repr., Grand Rapids: Eerdmans, 1980), 643.

36 Irenaeus, *Against Heresies*, 3.3.3, cited in Richardson, *Early Christian Fathers*, 372–373.

37 Cunningham, *Historical Theology, Vol. 1*, 180.

38 Louis Berkhof, *The History of Christian Doctrines* (1937; repr., Edinburgh: Banner of Truth, 1969), 40.

39 R. K. McGregor Wright, *No Place for Sovereignty: What's Wrong with Freewill Theism* (Downers Grove, Ill.: InterVarsity, 1996), 18–19.

40 Clement, *First Clement*, as cited in *Readings in Christian Ethics: A Historical Sourcebook*, eds. J. Philip Wegaman and Douglas M. Strong (Louisville: John Knox, 1996), 20:1–4.

41 Clement, *First Clement*, as cited in Wegaman and Strong, *Readings in Christian Ethics*, 20:11.

42 Clement, *First Clement*, 27, cited in Richardson, *Early Christian Fathers*, 56.

43 Clement, *First Clement*, 32, cited in Richardson, *Early Christian Fathers*, 58.

44 Clement, *First Clement*, 38, cited in Richardson, *Early Christian Fathers*, 61.

45 Clement, *First Clement*, cited in *The Epistles of St. Clement of Rome and St. Ignatius of Antioch: Ancient Christian Writers*, ed. James A. Kleist (Mahwah, N.J.: Paulist Press, 1978), 16:6.

46 Clement, *First Clement*, cited in Kleist, *The Epistles of St. Clement of Rome and St. Ignatius of Antioch*, 1:1.

47 Clement, *First Clement*, cited in Kleist, *The Epistles of St. Clement of Rome and St. Ignatius of Antioch*, 5:6.

48 Clement, *First Clement*, 29, cited in Richardson, *Early Christian Fathers*, 57.

49 Clement, *First Clement*, 50, cited in Richardson, *Early Christian Fathers*, 67.

50 Clement, *First Clement*, 46, cited in Richardson, *Early Christian Fathers*, 65.

51 Clement, *First Clement*, 64, cited in Richardson, *Early Christian Fathers*, 73.

52 Clement, *First Clement*, 49, cited in Richardson, *Early Christian Fathers*, 66.

53 Clement, *First Clement*, 12, cited in Richardson, *Early Christian Fathers*, 49.

54 Clement, *First Clement*, 1, cited in Richardson, *Early Christian Fathers*, 43.

55 Clement, *First Clement*, 32, cited in Richardson, *Early Christian Fathers*, 58.

56 Clement, *First Clement*, 5.1, cited in Michael Horton, *Putting Amazing Back into Grace: Embracing the Heart of the Gospel*, 2nd Ed. (Grand Rapids: Baker, 2002), 252.

57 Clement, *First Clement*, 35, cited in Richardson, *Early Christian Fathers*, 59.

58 Clement, *First Clement*, 8, cited in Horton, *Putting Amazing Back into Grace*, 252.

59 Clement, *First Clement*, 59, cited in Richardson, *Early Christian Fathers*, 70.

60 Clement, *First Clement*, 1, cited in Richardson, *Early Christian Fathers*, 43.

# CHAPTER TWO
## STUDY QUESTIONS

1.  Describe the development of theology from one era to the next. How long did it take the church to clarify the doctrines of sovereign grace? When did these doctrines first come to the forefront of the church's attention?

2.  Detail the spread of Christianity throughout the first century. What were the causes of its expansion?

3.  Explain the unique role of the Apostolic Fathers. Who were the leading figures in this transitional period? To what authority did they appeal in making their argument with individual churches?

4.  What office did Clement of Rome hold in the church? Was he a singular bishop or did he serve alongside others? What was the significance of this arrangement in the church at Rome?

5.  Describe the cost Clement paid for following Christ. What sacrifice has God called you to make for Him?

6.  What is the unique place of *First Clement* in the body of ancient Christian literature? How and to what extent did the apostle Paul influence this early epistle?

7.  To what extent did Clement allude to the sovereignty of God? What place did he assign to this important truth? How did this view influence his understanding of other doctrines?

8.  Did Clement espouse the doctrine of sovereign election? Did he mention this truth? How readily did he write of it?

$O$ut of the fullness of God the Father
you have been blessed with large numbers
and are predestined from eternity to enjoy
forever continual and unfading glory.
The source of your unity and election is
genuine suffering which you undergo by
the will of the Father and of Jesus Christ
our God.[1]

–Ignatius of Antioch

# Chapter Three

# GOD-BEARER

## APOSTOLIC FATHER:
## IGNATIUS OF ANTIOCH

E ven as the fires of persecution flamed against the church in the early
second century, the long line of godly men continued. At this time, the
church was increasingly colliding with the ideologies of ancient Rome. Initially, the Roman government considered the early believers to be merely a
nonthreatening extension of Judaism. But the ever-increasing Jewish hostility
toward the church and persecution of the Christians eventually distanced the
followers of Christ from Israel in the eyes of Rome. Soon, the church began
to feel the sadistic wrath of the empire as well as the anger of Israel. The well-
being of believers was seriously jeopardized.

Why were the Christians so persecuted? There were several reasons. Many
Christian meetings were held privately at night, which raised concerns about
antigovernment subversion and revolution. Christians were also labeled atheists because they refused to worship the idols in the pantheon of Roman
gods—Jupiter, Juno, Mars, Neptune, Mercury, Venus, and the like. Instead,
they gave exclusive allegiance to an invisible deity. Worse yet, they were falsely
accused of cannibalism because they claimed to eat the body of Christ and
drink His blood. They were rumored to be incestuous because of their love
for one another and the practice of the holy kiss. Most Christians were from
the lower classes, so they already were objects of prejudice on the part of the
Roman elite. The believers taught that all people were equally depraved, causing the aristocrats to fear a class upheaval. Finally, Christians were seen as a
threat to many ancient trades, such as the prostitution businesses associated
with idol worship.

This anti-Christian bias was inflamed whenever a natural disaster struck the empire, such as a volcanic eruption, earthquake, famine, or drought. The Romans feared these catastrophes meant that the gods were displeased because of the Christians' refusal to worship them. Tertullian, a third-century Christian apologist, summarized the endless blame cast on early believers when he wrote, "If the Tiber rises as high as the city walls, if the Nile does not rise to the fields, if the weather will not change, if there is an earthquake, a famine, a plague—straightway the cry is heard: 'Toss the Christians to the lion!'"[2] Many felt that Christians should be exterminated for provoking the wrath of the gods.

## SERVING ONLY ONE GOD

Matters went from bad to worse when Emperor Domitian (AD 81–96) demanded to be lauded as *Dominus et Deus*—"Lord and God." He required Roman citizens to confess "Caesar is Lord" as a public testimony of their allegiance to the empire. The Christians, however, could not compromise their loyalty to Christ as Lord. Any believer saying "Caesar is Lord" would be guilty of an act of sedition against the King of heaven. Therefore, they refused to offer a pinch of incense on the altar to the emperor. Soon it became official Roman law that Christians would be punished if they refused to renounce their exclusive fidelity to Jesus Christ and worship Caesar. In the eyes of Rome, the church became *religio illicita*—an illegal religion. As a result, many disciples at the end of the first century were severely persecuted, even being put to death for their faith in Christ. Moved by their steadfast commitment, Cleveland Coxe writes, "Those were times of heroism, not of words; an age, not of writers, but of soldiers; not of talkers, but of sufferers."[3]

In regard to the persecution launched by Domitian, Philip Schaff, the noted church historian, writes:

[Domitian] became as cruel and bloodthirsty as Nero, and surpassed him in hypocrisy and blasphemous self-deification. He began his letters: "Our Lord and God commands," and required his subjects to address him so. He ordered gold and silver statues of himself to be placed in the holiest place of the temples. . . . He searched for the descendants of David and the kinsmen of Jesus, fearing their aspirations. . . . Many Christians suffered martyrdom under his reign, on the charge of atheism—among them his own cousin, Flavius Clemens, of consular dignity, who was put to death, and his wife Domitilla, who was banished to the island of Pandateria, near Naples.[4]

As the first century ended, Emperor Trajan (98–117) relaxed the persecution of Christians. Under Trajan, Christianity remained an illegal sect, but believers were not sought out. However, disciples who fell into Roman hands were relentlessly punished if they refused to recant their allegiance to Christ. Such was the costly commitment of the early believers. They preferred to resign their lives than renounce Christ. But despite this hostile environment, the early church actually grew in strength. This is not surprising. The church is generally strongest when her opposition is the greatest. Adversity revives the church, while prosperity ruins her.

During this difficult hour, God raised up Ignatius to serve the risen Christ and the church. Great men rarely minister in easy times. Rather, they typically come to the fore in those seasons that are most demanding and dangerous. Such men are usually found standing firmly on the solid rock of sovereign grace. This was the case with Ignatius.

# IGNATIUS OF ANTIOCH

Known also as Theophorus—meaning "one who has God" or "God-bearer"— Ignatius (ca. 35–ca. 107) was bishop of Antioch in Syria, the third-largest city in the Roman Empire at that time.[5] He was the first monarchial bishop, meaning he alone was bishop rather than one among a plurality of elders. Given this position of solitary authority, he gained widespread prominence in the early church.[6] For some forty years, he faithfully pastored the church of Antioch, where he was a bold witness for Christ until he was martyred.[7] Shunning popular approval, Ignatius grew increasingly indifferent to the world and chose to strictly pursue truth and Christian virtue.[8]

Like most at this time, Ignatius was born of pagan parents and raised in a non-Christian home. Under these ungodly influences, he early joined in the persecution of the Christians.[9] But in due time, Ignatius was soundly converted to the Christian faith. It is believed he had the privilege of receiving instruction directly from Peter and Paul[10] and enjoying fellowship with many of the other apostles.[11] John Chrysostom (d. 407) said, "They [the apostles] witnessed every possible human virtue [in Ignatius]."[12]

Over time, Ignatius came to possess a thorough knowledge of Scripture and sound doctrine, great piety, and exceptional gifts.[13] The apostles deemed him fit for spiritual leadership and appointed him bishop of Antioch.[14] Chrysostom maintained that Ignatius was personally ordained by the laying on of hands by the apostles themselves.[15] In this weighty position, Ignatius was responsible for the spiritual oversight of the church in Antioch of Syria, the bustling center of commerce and culture of the region, considered more important than even Alexandria in Egypt.[16] Years earlier, God had planted a thriving church in Antioch (Acts 11:19–21), and it was there that the disciples had first been called Christians (v. 26). In Antioch, Paul first ministered the Word publicly (vv. 25–26) and set out on three missionary journeys (Acts 13:1–3; 15:40; 18:22–23). Ignatius stood in a truly remarkable place to minister.

## Heresies Trouble the Church

During Ignatius' bishopric, dangerous heresies began to brew in Antioch.[17] As a result, the believers grew weak in their faith. Chrysostom writes: "[W]herever one looked, cliffs and pits and wars and battles and dangers; and governors and emperors and peoples and cities and races—both domestic and foreign— were plotting against the believers."[18] Consequently, Antioch devolved into a cesspool of immorality, false teaching, and rank ungodliness. Amid this moral pollution, Ignatius persistently labored, a beacon of light and a stalwart of the faith.

When Trajan passed through Antioch on his way to make war in Armenia and Mesopotamia, he summoned Ignatius to appear before him.[19] He was pressured to blaspheme the name of Christ with threats on his life, but he refused to do so. Trajan pronounced the death sentence on Ignatius and ordered that he be bound in chains, transported to Rome, and thrown to the wild beasts to be devoured. Ignatius prayed: "Suffer me to become food for the wild beasts, through whose instrumentality it will be granted me to attain to God. I am the wheat of God, and let me be ground by the teeth of wild beasts, that I may be found the pure bread of Christ."[20] Only a strong faith in the living God can cause a man to stand like this.

Ignatius thought of his journey to Rome for execution as "a conscious imitation of the Lord's last journey to Jerusalem and the cross."[21] He was taken to Rome in the custody of ten soldiers, to whom he was kept chained. He described this ordeal as being "fastened . . . to ten leopards (I mean to a detachment of soldiers), who only get worse the better you treat them."[22] He probably was also in the company of other condemned prisoners.[23] He was forced along the northerly road across Asia Minor, through Philadelphia, Smyrna, and Troas.

However, along the way, he was allowed to receive visits from the believers in Ephesus, Magnesia, and Tralles, who sought to encourage him.[24] While in Troas, he wrote to the Christians in Philadelphia and Smyrna. From Troas, he was led to Philippi, then Rome. As he approached the imperial capital, the Christians came out to the edge of the city to meet him and encourage him in the Lord. They knew all too well that martyrdom awaited him.

## DEATH IN THE COLOSSEUM

Ignatius reached Rome around AD 107.[25] He was taken to the famous Roman Colosseum, also known as the Flavian Amphitheatre, a large, circular stadium with three tiers that seated in excess of fifty thousand frenzied spectators. This arena represented the godless grandeur of imperial Rome. It was here that the gladiators dueled to the death. But the most gruesome deaths belonged to the early Christians, who were fed for sport to the lions.

As Ignatius entered the Colosseum to face death, the crowd shouted in anticipation of the martyrdom. But Ignatius held fast. Earlier, he had said that "near the sword means near God."[26] In the hour of his death, God was never nearer to him. Martyrdom was to be his crown. Death meant his homecoming, the means by which he would be taken to glory to stand before Christ.

In his letter to the Roman church, Ignatius had written words appropriate to his dying moments: "I want all men to know that I die for God of my own free will. . . . Entice the wild beasts, that they may become my sepulchre and may leave no part of my body behind, so that I may not, when I am fallen asleep, be burdensome to anyone. Then shall I truly be a disciple of Jesus Christ, when the world shall not so much as see my body."[27] He later added, "Come fire, cross, battling with wild beasts, wrenching of bones, mangling of limbs, crushing of my whole body, cruel tortures of the devil—only let me get to Jesus Christ!"[28] And in a separate letter to the Ephesians he wrote, "May I rise again in [my bonds] . . . so that I may be found in the lot apportioned to the Ephesian Christians."[29] With this steadfast confidence in a future resurrection, Ignatius died, bearing witness for Christ.

# IGNATIUS'S WRITINGS

The seven epistles Ignatius wrote while en route to Rome were "the letters of a prisoner on his way to martyrdom."[30] Five were addressed to local churches throughout Asia Minor—Ephesus, Magnesia, Tralles, Philadelphia, and Smyrna—one to the church in Rome, and one to Polycarp. Known as the *Epistles of Ignatius*, these letters reveal that Ignatius possessed a thorough knowledge of the Old Testament, the Gospels, and several letters of Paul.[31] Further, these epistles contain the first written theology of the Christian faith outside the Bible, providing specific definitions of biblical doctrines.

## IGNATIUS'S THEOLOGY

In his epistles, Ignatius gives evidence of holding to the truths of God's sovereignty in salvation. In them, we find trace elements of these God-honoring truths, though, as with the other Early Church Fathers, they lack the precision of later Augustinian writings. Noted church historian Justo L. González observes, "One should not expect that these seven epistles of Ignatius . . . would be a detailed, balanced, and systematic exposition of his theology."[32] Also, it must be taken into consideration that these letters were composed while he was a prisoner, chained to Roman soldiers, en route to his death in Rome. This was hardly a time for writing deep theological treatises. Ignatius wrote these letters to address specific pastoral concerns that were on his mind. As a result, the "religious character" of these writings is "popular rather than deep."[33] Had the circumstances been different, González contends, Ignatius, "quite possibly, would have dealt with other subjects."[34]

Ignatius's epistles showed that he was eager to defend the undiminished deity and full humanity of Christ.[35] He opposed the Docetists, who contended that the incarnation of Christ was not real, but that He only seemed to be a man. In actuality, they contended, He was a mere spirit being.[36] Thus, they denied the physical body and humanity of Christ and rejected His virgin birth and substitutionary death. The result was a Jesus who was not a man and therefore could not die. In response to these heretical teachings, Ignatius boldly affirmed the true humanity of Jesus as a necessary component of the true gospel: "There is only one physician—of flesh yet spiritual, born yet unbegotten, God incarnate, genuine life in the midst of death, sprung from Mary as well as God, first subject to suffering then beyond it—Jesus Christ our Lord."[37] As a result of this stance, Michel Rene Barnes notes that "the center of Ignatius' theology is the reality of Christ's divinity and humanity."[38] Barnes believes that Ignatius's theological formation "had the critical function of supporting his rejection of Docetism, which he sees as robbing Christianity of its grasp of who and what Christ was, as well as robbing it of the promise of the salvation that Christ offered."[39] Simply put, this Early Father was a true defender of the Christian faith, guarding the church against heresy.

He also refuted the heresy of the Judaizers, who insisted that all people, even Gentiles, needed to strictly observe Old Testament rituals, especially circumcision, in order to be justified before God.[40] Paul minced no words in pronouncing a divine curse—*anathema*—on them and their false gospel (Gal. 1:6–10). This false teaching also had been rebuked by the Council of Jerusalem (Acts 15) and by the author of the book of Hebrews. Still, the threat of the Judaizers had continued to spread. Ignatius was uncompromising in his stance that old covenant Jewish practices had no place in Christian living. He wrote, "It is absurd to speak of Jesus Christ with the tongue, and to cherish in the mind a Judaism which has now come to an end."[41] He desired that Christians should maintain a total separation from this former way of life.

**Doctrine in Focus:**
DIVINE SOVEREIGNTY

First and foremost, Ignatius affirmed the absolute sovereignty of God, by which He actively governs all things. Ignatius declares: "[To] the church that is in charge of affairs in Roman quarters and that the Most High Father and Jesus Christ, His only Son, have magnificently embraced in mercy and love. You have been granted light . . . by the will of Him who willed all that is."[42] In this simple statement, Ignatius revealed that he believed nothing occurs outside God's sovereign will, which brings about all that comes to pass. Such a weighty declaration suggests he held a transcendent view of God.

**Doctrine in Focus:**
RADICAL DEPRAVITY

In addition, Ignatius accepted the biblical doctrine of radical corruption. He believed that the fall affected the entirety of man's being—body, mind, emotions, and will. Not only is sinful man unable to save himself, his fallen will must obey sin. Ignatius writes: "Carnal people cannot act spiritually, or spiritual people carnally, just as faith cannot act like unbelief, or unbelief like faith."[43] This is to say, unregenerate sinners are plagued by moral inability and cannot exercise saving faith apart from grace. The natural man cannot please God.

In such a desperate state, lost sinners must be brought to repentance. Ignatius writes: "But I warn you in advance against wild beasts in human shapes.

You must not only refuse to receive them, but if possible, you must avoid meeting them. Just pray for them that they may somehow repent, hard as that is."[44] This Early Father maintained that unconverted people must recognize their depravity or they will never turn from their sin. Ignatius recognized that such repentance is "hard," hinting at the biblical truth that only God can cause a lost sinner to see his helpless estate.

**Doctrine in Focus:**

## SOVEREIGN ELECTION

Moreover, Ignatius hinted at God's election of certain individuals unto eternal life. He believed all grace flows out of the sovereign choice of God to save His elect before time began. In his letter to the Ephesians, Ignatius begins: "Ignatius, the 'God-inspired,' to the church at Ephesus in Asia. Out of the fullness of God the Father you have been blessed with large numbers and are predestined from eternity to enjoy forever continual and unfading glory."[45] By this greeting, Ignatius alluded to the unconditional election of God by which He has chosen and predestined some to salvation from eternity past.

**Doctrine in Focus:**

## PRESERVING GRACE

Finally, Ignatius held that all believers will be forever preserved in grace. No true believer can ever fall away from salvation in Christ. Ignatius writes: "For Jesus Christ—that life from which we cannot be torn—is the Father's mind."[46] Here, Ignatius acknowledged that Christ Himself is the life of believers, and none who possess this life can be "torn" from it. This means that spiritual life from Christ lasts forever. Such a conviction surely gave this future martyr great confidence when facing the lions in Rome.

Ignatius also asserted that the fruit of a changed life inevitably manifests itself in the elect. He states: "No one who professes faith falls into sin, nor does one who has learned to love, hate. 'The tree is known by its fruit.' Similarly, those who profess to be Christ's will be recognized by their actions. For what matters is not a momentary act of professing, but being persistently motivated by faith."[47] In other words, Ignatius held that those who are converted no longer practice sin as a habitual lifestyle. Rather, they give increasing evidence of their salvation by perpetual growth in godliness in their lives.

# ONE WHO BEARS GOD

Throughout his life and especially in his death, Ignatius lived up to his nickname. This Apostolic Father was truly a "God-bearer" in his day. He repeatedly upheld the basic confession that Jesus is Lord. He explicitly referred to Jesus as God more than a dozen times throughout his letters. Moreover, he determinedly labored in defense of the Christian faith against heretical attack and fervently shepherded the church at Antioch. Even in the face of death, Ignatius remained unshakeable in his commitment to Christ, whom he proclaimed at great personal cost.

By this unwavering testimony, Ignatius showed himself to be a strong pillar in the early church. Here was a man of supreme confidence in the overruling sovereignty of God in all of life. God has such heroic leaders in every generation—those who stand strong in His Word, who live out their faith with courage, and who trust fully in His sovereignty, even in their hour of persecution.

Where are such courageous men today? Where are the steady pillars for the contemporary church? We have great need of such stalwarts. May Christ give His church such strong servants in this present day, men who are not driven by opinion polls, who are not swayed by the shifting winds of the times, but who are staunch soldiers of the cross. May these dedicated disciples march with deep convictions in the truth and with high confidence in the Lord Himself.

NOTES

1  Ignatius, *To the Ephesians*, in *Early Christian Fathers*, ed. Cyril C. Richardson (New York: Touchstone, 1996), 87–88.

2  Tertullian, *Apology*, in *Tertullian: Apologetical Works, and Minucius Felix: Octavius*, trans. Rudolph Arbesmann, Sister Emily Joseph Daly, and Edwin A. Quain (New York: Fathers of the Church, Inc., 1950), 102.

3  A. Cleveland Coxe, "Preface," *Ante-Nicene Fathers, Vol. I: The Apostolic Fathers with Justin Martyr and Irenaeus*, eds. Alexander Roberts, James Donaldson, and A. Cleveland Coxe (1864; repr., Grand Rapids: Eerdmans, 1973), vii.

4  Philip Schaff, *History of the Christian Church, Vol. I: Apostolic Christianity: From the Birth of Christ to the Death of St. John, A.D. 1–100* (1910; repr., Grand Rapids: Eerdmans, 1980), 427–428.

5  John MacArthur, *The MacArthur New Testament Commentary: Acts 1–12* (Chicago: Moody, 1994), 313.

6  Paul Woolley, "Antiochene Theology," in *Evangelical Dictionary of Theology*, 2nd Ed., ed. Walter A. Elwell (Grand Rapids: Baker, 2001), 72.

7  Philip Schaff, *History of the Christian Church, Vol. II: Ante-Nicene Christianity: From the Death of John the Apostle to Constantine the Great, A.D. 100–325* (1910; repr., Grand Rapids: Eerdmans, 1980), 657.

8  John Chrysostom, *On the Holy Martyr Ignatius*, in *The Cult of the Saints*, trans. Wendy Mayer with Bronwen Neil (Crestwood, N.Y.: St. Vladimir's Seminary Press, 2006), 104.

9  "St. Ignatius," in *The Oxford Dictionary of the Christian Church*, ed. E. A. Livingstone (1957; repr., Oxford: Oxford University Press, 1997), 817.

10  Richard Newton, *Heroes of the Early Church* (1889; repr., Birmingham, Ala.: Solid Ground Christian Books, 2005), 17.

11  John Chrysostom, *Eulogy of Ignatius*, in *The Cult of the Saints*, 104.

12  Chrysostom, *Eulogy of Ignatius*, in *The Cult of the Saints*, 105.

13  Newton, *Heroes of the Early Church*, 17.

14  Chrysostom, *Eulogy of Ignatius*, in *The Cult of the Saints*, 106.

15  Chrysostom, *Eulogy of Ignatius*, in *The Cult of the Saints*, 105.

16  Roger Olson, *The Story of Christian Theology: Twenty Centuries of Tradition and Reform* (Downers Grove, Ill.: InterVarsity, 1999), 202.

17  Chrysostom, *Eulogy of Ignatius*, in *The Cult of the Saints*, 109.

18  Chrysostom, *Eulogy of Ignatius*, in *The Cult of the Saints*, 107.

19  "Ignatius," in *Cyclopedia of Biblical, Theological, and Ecclesiastical Literature, Vol. IV*, eds. John McClintock and James Strong (Grand Rapids: Baker, 1981), 491.

20  Ignatius, *To the Romans*, chap. 4, cited in Roberts, Donaldson, and Coxe, *Ante-Nicene Fathers, Vol. I*, 75.

21  W. Ward Gasque, "The Challenge to Faith," *Introduction to the History of Christianity*, ed. Tim Dowley (Minneapolis: Fortress, 2002), 92.

22  Ignatius, *To the Romans*, 5, cited in Richardson, *Early Christian Fathers*, 104.

23  Ivor J. Davidson, *The Birth of the Church: From Jesus to Constantine, A.D. 30–312* (Grand Rapids: Baker, 2004), 181.

24  Earle E. Cairns, *Christianity Through the Centuries: A History of the Christian Church*, 3rd Ed. (1954; repr., Grand Rapids: Zondervan, 1996), 76.

25  Davidson, *The Birth of the Church*, 181.

26  Ignatius, *To the Smyrnaeans*, 4, cited in Richardson, *Early Christian Fathers*, 113.

27  Ignatius, *To the Romans*, 4, cited in Tony Lane, *A Concise History of Christian Thought* (Grand Rapids: Baker Academic, 2006), 9.

28  Ignatius, *To the Romans*, 5, cited in Richardson, *Early Christian Fathers*, 105.

29  Ignatius, *To the Ephesians*, 11.2, cited in A. Cleveland Coxe, "Epistle of Ignatius to the Ephesians," *Ante-Nicene Fathers, Vol. I*, 54.

30  Richardson, *Early Christian Fathers*, 74.

31  Richardson, *Early Christian Fathers*, 78.

32  Justo L. González, *A History of Christian Thought, Vol. 1: From the Beginnings to the Council of Chalcedon* (Nashville: Abingdon, 1970), 72.

33 Richardson, *Early Christian Fathers*, 74.

34 González, *A History of Christian Thought, Vol. 1*, 73.

35 Woolley, "Antiochene Theology," in *Evangelical Dictionary of Theology*, 72.

36 Michael A. Smith, "Ignatius of Antioch," in *Introduction to the History of Christianity*, 83.

37 Ignatius, *To the Ephesians*, 7, cited in Richardson, *Early Christian Fathers*, 90.

38 Michel Rene Barnes, "Ignatius of Antioch," in *Biographical Dictionary of Christian Theologians*, eds. Patrick W. Carey and Joseph T. Lienhard (Peabody, Mass.: Hendrickson, 2002), 263.

39 Barnes, "Ignatius of Antioch," in *Biographical Dictionary of Christian Theologians*, 263–264.

40 John MacArthur, *The Truth War: Fighting for Certainty in an Age of Deception* (Nashville: Thomas Nelson, 2007), 85.

41 Ignatius, *To the Magnesians*, 10.3, cited in Laurie Guy, *Introducing Early Christianity: A Topical Survey of Its Life, Beliefs and Practices* (Downers Grove, Ill.: InterVarsity, 2004), 40.

42 Ignatius, *To the Romans*, Salutation, cited in Richardson, *Early Christian Fathers*, 102–3.

43 Ignatius, *To the Ephesians*, 8, cited in Richardson, *Early Christian Fathers*, 90.

44 Ignatius, *To the Smyrnaeans*, 4, cited in Richardson, *Early Christian Fathers*, 113.

45 Ignatius, *To the Ephesians*, Salutation, cited in Richardson, *Early Christian Fathers*, 87–88.

46 Ignatius, *To the Ephesians*, Salutation, cited in Richardson, *Early Christian Fathers*, 88.

47 Ignatius, *To the Ephesians*, 14, cited in Richardson, *Early Christian Fathers*, 92.

# CHAPTER THREE
## STUDY QUESTIONS

1. Explain the anti-Christian bias at the end of the first century and the beginning of the second century. How did the Christians suffer?

2. What was the attitude of the Roman officials toward the early believers? In what ways did they resist the early church?

3. Was Ignatius a single leader in the church of Antioch or did he serve with a team of elders? What does Scripture say concerning this?

4. Detail Ignatius's journey, under custody, from Antioch to Rome. What was his crime? How did he die? What was his final contribution to the church?

5. Describe Ignatius's writings. In what ways are they important for our understanding of the early church? To whom were they written?

6. Explain what we know of Ignatius's theology. How does he give evidence of holding to the truths of the sovereignty of God in salvation?

7. What challenges was Ignatius chiefly concerned with in his day? What can be said of the relationship between his preoccupations with other issues and his view of the doctrines of grace?

8. What was Ignatius's position concerning preserving grace? How did this belief likely help him as he faced martyrdom?

"Do you gentlemen suppose," I went on, "that we could have grasped the meaning of these Scriptural passages without a special grace from Him who willed them?"[1]

–Justin Martyr

Chapter Four

# DEFENDER
# OF THE FAITH

## APOLOGIST FATHER:
## JUSTIN MARTYR

E arly in the second century, Christianity was clashing not only with the
emperor cult of the Roman Empire but with the predominant Greek
philosophies of the day. In the ancient world, the great minds of Athens and
Corinth wrestled with the fundamental issues of life, and the ideas of famous
Greek philosophers, including Socrates, Plato, Aristotle, and Zeno, dominated the worldviews of this hour. So expansive was Greek philosophy that it
dealt with everything from the physical nature of the world—what it is made
of and where it came from[2]—to religious issues such as the existence of God,
the nature of the soul, life after death, suffering, and salvation.[3]

Basically, four philosophies from the classical and Hellenistic periods
competed for the highest thoughts of the Roman citizens—Platonism, Aristotelianism, Stoicism, and Epicureanism. Each philosophical school sought
to construct a complete moral and spiritual outlook on life. The goal of the
Greek thinkers was to experience the most worthy life one could lead, "a life
of enlightenment and contemplation of virtue and striving after the divine."[4]
Their ideas had deeply penetrated the thinking of the Romans, shaping the
empire in profound ways. In many respects, the ideas of these philosophical
schools were far more powerful than the advancing chariots and armed soldiers of Rome. These philosophies energized the passions of the citizens and
moved their spirits.

As Christianity spread, the preaching of the gospel dramatically confronted
these ancient ideologies and impacted the thinking of the Greco-Roman world.

That collision of worldviews led to a backlash against Christianity. As noted in the previous chapter, pagan antagonists raised inflammatory accusations against the followers of Christ. The believers were accused of atheism because they would not worship Caesar; of cannibalism because they spoke of eating the Lord's flesh and drinking His blood; of incest because they addressed one another as brothers and sisters, and gave a holy kiss; and of being anti-social because they refused to participate in the orgies and debaucheries of the day. The goal of this campaign was to discredit Christianity and ultimately stem its success in the marketplace of ideas.

In the face of this intellectual clash, Christianity and the gospel stood in great need of sturdy defenders. If the faith was to continue to spread across the Roman Empire, it needed to give an account of itself to the watching world. In this strategic hour, God raised up a series of trained Christian teachers and writers known as the Apologist Fathers, men who were skilled defenders of the faith.

# THE APOLOGIST FATHERS

As gifted teachers and writers, the Apologists ministered from the early second century to the early third century. Theirs was the discipline of "apologetics," a term derived from the Greek word *apologia*, meaning "a speech for the defense" or "a defense to support the truth."[5] Apologetics is the attempt to render the Christian faith convincing to an unbeliever by defusing attacks against it and presenting the biblical truth as credible.[6] It was the strategic task of the Apologist Fathers to skillfully explain Christianity to the secular culture of their day and earnestly defend it against popular accusations and conflicting heresies. Their chief objective was "to gain a fair hearing for Christianity, to dispel popular slanders and misunderstandings, and sometimes to show that Christians were loyal subjects, and to provide for this purpose some account of Christian belief and practice."[7]

These frontline Christian intellects included Justin Martyr (ca. 100–165), Tatian the Assyrian (ca. 120–180), Theophilus of Antioch (ca. 120–190), Irenaeus of Lyons (ca. 130–200), Athenagoras of Athens (ca. 133–190), Aristides of Athens (second century), Minucius Felix (second or third century), and others.

In their defense of the faith, they sought to show that the movement was not an innovation or novelty, but "quite ancient and respectable."[8] In addressing the Jews, the Apologists defended the full divinity of Jesus Christ and sought to disprove Jewish claims by applying countless Old Testament prophecies to the person and work of Christ, showing that He was the long-awaited Messiah. When they spoke to the pagans, the Apologists argued that Christianity addressed the same subjects as the various secular philosophies, yet with better answers: "Their first concern was to rebut charges of atheism and immorality (Thyestian feasts, Oedipodean intercourse) and the underlying charge of sedition. But they went further and argued that Christianity was a true philosophy, in comparison with which other philosophies were either false, or (as Justin argued) shadows of the truth fulfilled in Christ."[9] The Apologists showed that the wells of man-centered philosophy were dry and unable to satisfy man's thirst for meaning; then they presented the living water of God's Word with vigor.

The Apologists gave special attention to the truth that Jesus Christ is "the *Logos*." This was a technical term used by Greek philosophers for the essence of divine reason in the world. To the Greek philosophers, the *logos* was "the impersonal, abstract principle of reason and order in the universe." In their minds, it was "a creative force, and the source of wisdom."[10] The early Apologists used the word *logos,* but declared that Christ was its fulfillment—precisely as the apostle John had done (John 1:1, 14–18; 1 John 1:1–3). They used "the *Logos*" to refer to Christ as the full revelation and perfect wisdom of God, the divine person of His Son. John MacArthur writes: "John presented Jesus as the personification and embodiment of the *logos*. Unlike the Greek concept, however, Jesus was not an impersonal source, force, principle, or emanation. In Him, the true *logos* was God becoming a man, a concept foreign to Greek thought."[11] With this line of reasoning, these Early Fathers strove to show that "Christ is the culmination and completion of all the partial knowledge of truth in Greek philosophy."[12] Simply put, the Apologists declared Jesus to be "Immanuel, which means, God with us" (Matt. 1:23).

The Apologists, then, made it their primary task to make a reasonable case for Christianity to the religious world of the Jews and the pagan world of the Romans. They were dauntless defenders of the faith and zealous evangelists of the lost, seeking to win the unconverted to Christ. The first of them was Justin Martyr.

# JUSTIN MARTYR

As one of the most important Christian writers of the second century,[13] Justin exercised a strong influence over other early Christian theologians.[14] Scholars consider him the most significant of the Apologists,[15] the most famous,[16] the foremost,[17] and the most outstanding.[18] He was perhaps the best Christian scholar of the time.[19] It has been said that the early church historian Eusebius believed that Justin easily overshadowed all the great men who taught during the second century.[20] Resisting the prevailing pagan philosophies, Justin became the first to write a credible defense of the Christian faith. His surname, "Martyr," refers to the violent death he suffered for the gospel for refusing to sacrifice to Roman gods.[21] He was a valiant warrior for the Christian faith, in life and in death.

Born at the beginning of the second century, Justin was raised in a pagan home[22] of Greek parentage at Flavia Neapolis (modern Nablus), formerly the city of Shechem, in Samaritan Palestine.[23] His father, Priscius,[24] a wealthy Greek, and his grandfather, Bacchius, enjoyed the privileges of Roman citizenship. Their elevated status gave Justin access to better schools, where he became well educated and deeply versed in the empty philosophies of the world.[25] From his youth, Justin seemed to be in a relentless pursuit of the truth, continually seeking intellectual fulfillment. In this quest, he eventually embarked on many travels abroad in order to inquire at the most highly regarded schools of philosophy. Through this exposure, Justin became well versed in the primary ideologies with which the pagans thought about God, life, and morality.

In his pilgrimage from school to school, Justin first studied the philosophy of the Stoics, a school of thought founded at Athens.[26] Derived from the teaching of the Hellenistic philosopher Zeno (ca. 336–264 BC), Stoicism taught that the "divine essence" was in everything. This philosophy of materialistic pantheism claimed that divinity was no less material than a physical object.[27] But Justin found the answers provided by Stoicism unsatisfying.

Next, Justin sought out the followers of the most famous philosopher of the ancient world, Aristotle (384–322 BC). This exceptional thinker had been a student of Plato (ca. 427–347 BC) for twenty years and had gained many followers.[28] Founding his own school in Athens, Aristotle began with assumptions similar to Plato's, but his thinking soon went in different directions. He taught that man is born with the capacity to do good without supernatural intervention. He states: "Nature gives us the capacity of receiving [virtues], and that capacity is perfected by habit."[29] Despite its popularity, Aristotelianism also proved to be intellectually bankrupt for Justin.

Still in pursuit of truth, Justin moved to Ephesus in Asia Minor. There he became a student of Platonism, the system of thought that Plato had developed centuries earlier. Influenced by the great Athenian philosopher Socrates (469–399 BC), Plato was regarded as one of the most important thinkers who had ever lived, a great challenge for Justin. Plato believed that "the material world was transient and imperfect and that only a transcendent realm of 'Ideas' or 'Forms' was permanent and genuinely true."[30] He said that all these Ideas or Forms were encapsulated in one ultimate ideal, known as the principle of the Good—not a personal God, but a supreme Form. However, like the other schools of secular thought, Platonic philosophy was a dead end for Justin.[31]

## "Search the Scriptures"

By this point, Justin had become sadly disillusioned. His search for the truth had seemingly left him further from it than when he had begun. Troubled in spirit, Justin was walking by himself on a beach when he came upon an old man of ragged appearance.[32] They entered into conversation, and the subject soon turned to the search for truth. Justin asked how the truth was to be found. The elderly man, who was a Christian, pointed Justin to the Bible, saying, "Search the Scriptures."[33] The prophets of the Old Testament, the man argued, long preceded the Greek philosophers Justin had been studying. He claimed that the biblical writers spoke with superior wisdom as they addressed the coming Messiah, Jesus Christ, and the future events of history. Ultimately, the elderly man urged Justin to pray that God would lead him into the knowledge of the truth in Christ.

At this insistence, Justin turned to the Bible and began to read the prophets of the Old Testament. As he engaged the Scriptures, divine light shined within him. The Holy Spirit illumined God's Word and gave him a clear understanding of the truth. Justin would later testify: "My spirit was immediately set on fire, and an affection for the prophets, and for those who are friends of Christ, took hold of me."[34] Under the influence of the truth in Jesus Christ, Justin became a Christian in his mid-thirties (ca. 133).

Justin became convinced that the Bible gave the best presentation of the truth concerning God, life, and reality, and that the ultimate enlightenment and the highest path of morality were to be found in the Christian faith.[35] His long, arduous search for the truth was complete. Dramatically changed, Justin became a bold defender of the Christian faith.[36] He spent the next years traveling extensively, teaching the way of salvation in Jesus Christ. After a period in Ephesus, he moved to Rome, where he established a school devoted to the teaching and defense of the gospel of Christ as "the perfect philosophy."[37] As he proclaimed the gospel, he continued to wear a philosopher's robe, an outward sign of his new belief that Jesus Christ was the true wisdom of God. In time, Justin became the foremost Apologist of the second century.

## Standing Firm in a Dangerous Time

Justin spent his last years teaching in Rome, making straightforward claims that Christianity is the true faith. He wrote his *First Apology* and sent it to the Emperor Antoninus Pius (137–161), who received it positively. But when Antoninus Pius died, his son, Marcus Aurelius (161–180), became emperor, and this transition brought a new season of horrific persecution for Christians, the most severe to date. Marcus Aurelius, an intensely religious man, worshiped the Roman gods and aimed to re-establish reverence for them. In this climate, Justin sent his *Second Apology* to the new emperor, but Marcus Aurelius was enraged by it. He arrested Justin and six of his fellow workers, including a woman. When Justin and the other six believers were brought before Rusticus, the prefect of the city of Rome, the only charge brought against them was that of being Christians, members of an illegal religion. Justin and the others were immediately taken away and beaten. Then they were taken to the place of execution, where, according to the prefect's orders, their heads were severed.

After much searching, Justin found the truth of divine Scripture, and once he embraced it, he would not let go. He proved faithful even unto death. At no time was he more committed to the defense of the faith than when his life was on the line. In the face of adversity, Justin was resolute in his commitment to the gospel of Jesus Christ. This pillar of the faith not only believed in the sovereignty of God, he lived it. The doctrines of grace fueled his courage to stand for the truth in the hour of his greatest ordeal. Justin died as he lived—glorifying God.

# JUSTIN'S WRITINGS

In addition to speaking and teaching, Justin wrote apologetic treatises against some of the heresies plaguing the early church. Eusebius writes: "Justin was in his fullest prime in the time of these men, presenting the divine word in the garb of a philosopher, and contending for the faith in his treatises."[38] Possessing the ability to systematize doctrine, he became the first real theologian to appear after the writing of the New Testament.[39] Sadly, only three of his works have survived: the *First Apology*, the *Second Apology*, and the *Dialogue with Trypho the Jew*. Still, these works represent the most substantial body of surviving literature from the Apologist Fathers.[40]

## FIRST APOLOGY

The *First Apology* (ca. 150) defended Christianity before Emperor Antoninus Pius. In it, Justin complained bitterly about "the injustices meted out to Christians" because of their association with Christ.[41] He argued convincingly that the believers were not a threat to the Roman Empire. Justin then asserted that Christianity alone had full truth. He declared that Jesus Christ was the Son of God, but that paganism consisted of fables invented by demons. Moreover, he affirmed the intellectual coherence of Christianity, declaring that it was far more consistent in its theological and philosophical assertions than any other way of thinking. Finally, Justin described the religious practices of Christianity. He refuted the unfounded charges of atheism and immorality raised against the Christian faith, stating that believers were actually more virtuous than the pagans.

## SECOND APOLOGY

Justin wrote the *Second Apology* (ca. 165) to the next Roman emperor, Marcus Aurelius, as well as the Senate, soldiers, and citizens. It was a brief but passionate reissue of the *First Apology*, along with a supplementary text. In it, Justin recounted examples of the unjust and irrational treatment of Christians by the emperor. He argued that the Roman persecution of Christians arose out of "ignorance and prejudice."[42] His protest against such injustice was provoked by the execution of people innocent of any crime except for confessing the name of Christ. It was only for the sake of Christians, Justin wrote, that God refrained from bringing ruin on the world.

## DIALOGUE WITH TRYPHO THE JEW

A third work, the *Dialogue with Trypho the Jew* (ca. 155–167), was a longer treatise written in the form of a conversation between Justin and an educated Jewish philosopher, a Hellenist named Trypho. In it, Justin defended

Christianity against Jewish attacks on the person and work of Christ. Arguing from the Scriptures, he presented "a calm, rational discussion" between Trypho and himself in an effort to present Christianity as the one coherent system of truth.[43] He wrote: "I discovered that His [Christ's] was the only sure and useful philosophy. Thus it is that I am now a philosopher."[44] This long and courteous debate took place at Ephesus, the probable site of Justin's conversion.[45]

In these three works, Justin showed himself to be an able writer with a strong understanding of Scripture and significant powers of logic. He combined the intellect of a scholar with the heart of an evangelist. His writings provide valuable insight into how early Christians interpreted the Bible.

# JUSTIN'S THEOLOGY

Justin did not set out to write theological treatises on the doctrines of grace, but to give a defense of the Christian faith to unbelievers. This he did with great skill—his writings are on a noticeably higher plane than those of other Early Church Fathers, giving a masterful presentation of Christianity's tenets.[46] Nevertheless, his writings do convey a growing recognition of God's sovereignty in man's salvation.

**Doctrine in Focus:**
RADICAL DEPRAVITY

Like many of the Apologist Fathers, Justin often wrote in seemingly contradictory terms. He would speak with a language of sovereign grace while elsewhere speaking in favor of man's free will. On the whole, the Apologist Fathers, Justin included, were "unanimous that man is endowed with free-will."[47] This apparent contradictory stance was likely due to a defective understanding of original sin. William Cunningham notes that "the testimony of the early primitive church is as favourable to the Calvinistic peculiarities, as they are often called, of predestination and perseverance, as to any of the other doctrines commonly designated as evangelical—with the exception perhaps, of the doctrine of original sin."[48] J. N. D. Kelly likewise comments, "It must be admitted that, as compared with the New Testament, [the Early Church Fathers] as a whole are not greatly preoccupied with sin, and that their writings exhibit a marked weakening of the atonement idea. . . . What looms much larger in their imagination is the picture of Christ as the lawgiver, the bestower of knowledge, immortality, and fellowship with God."[49] In other words, the Apologists did not fully connect the fall of Adam with the depraved nature of mankind. Because of this, according to John Hannah, Justin would sometimes assert "that sin has not affected the ability of humankind to freely choose Christ."[50] Justin, Hannah adds, held that "sin is more a behavior or habit of moral life than it is an obstacle to salvation."[51]

Still, Justin regularly contended that mankind is in dire need of redemption because of sin. With the atoning work of Christ in mind, Justin writes: "He did not condescend to be born and to be crucified because He was in need of birth or crucifixion; He did it solely for the sake of man, who from the time of Adam had become subject to death and the deceit of the serpent, each man having sinned by his own fault."[52] Here Justin stated that sin subjects every person to spiritual death and causes them to transgress God's law. No man except Christ is exempt from sin because of the solidarity of the human race in Adam.

Justin also affirmed that God's curse rests on all people, both Jews and Gentiles. He writes: "For the whole human race will be found to be under a curse. For it is written in the law of Moses, 'Cursed is every one that continueth not in all things that are written in the book of the law to do them.' And no one has accurately done all."[53] This is seemingly an affirmation by Justin that the entire race has suffered a radical fall, that "all have sinned and fall short of the glory of God" (Rom. 3:23).

Justin adds that man is not able to understand divine truth by his own sin-corrupted intellect. He comments: "Men cannot naturally perceive such great divine truths through their human faculties."[54] To overcome this inability to understand spiritual truth, man needs God to shine light into his soul. Justin writes: "No one can perceive or understand these truths unless he has been enlightened by God and His Christ."[55] It seems clear that Justin believed that all unconverted men are in spiritual darkness and cannot understand divine truth until God through Christ gives them supernatural understanding.

How are we to understand Justin's statements in regard to free will? He writes: "Neither do we maintain that it is by fate that men do what they do, or suffer what they suffer. Rather, we maintain that each man acts rightly or sins by his free choice."[56] Elsewhere Justin remarks: "He [God] created angels and men free to do that which is righteous. And He appointed periods of time during which He knew it would be good for them to have the exercise of free will."[57] In these statements, Justin contended that man retained the ability to choose to perform righteous acts by his free will.

Why did Justin make these assertions about free will? Hannah writes that "such statements about the ability of humankind, which seem to minimize the effect of sin on moral choices, can be understood in light of the polemic of the church leaders against the Gnostic sects which asserted that the Christian faith denied moral responsibility. In defending themselves, the Apologists affirmed freedom of the will."[58] As noted earlier, fatalism was a popular view among pagan sects of the time. As a result, the Apologists tended to stress man's free will as a means of distinguishing Christianity from such heterodox teachings.

**Doctrine in Focus:**
## SOVEREIGN ELECTION

Justin nonetheless held to the biblical doctrine of sovereign election. The Scriptures affirm that God does not choose everyone for salvation, but has selected a specific people to receive it. Commenting on God's gracious election, Justin writes: "In the beginning God dispersed all men according to nationality and language, and from all these nations He chose for Himself yours—a useless, disobedient, and faithless nation. And He showed that those of every nationality who were chosen have obeyed His will through Christ."[59] Justin taught that God sovereignly chose His elect for Himself based on nothing in them. In this comment from his *Dialogue with Trypho the Jew*, Justin noted that God chose the people of Israel, but it was not the Jews alone who were to be saved—God also elected people from "every nationality." He chose Jews and Gentiles from eternity past to be His redeemed people.

**Doctrine in Focus:**
## DEFINITE ATONEMENT

Justin used the language of a particular atonement, indicating he understood that Christ came into the world to save specific sinners. Justin writes, "For He [Christ] also became man, as we state, and was born in accordance with the will of God the Father for the benefit of believers."[60] Again he notes, "[Christ was] made man of a virgin according to the will of the Father for the salvation of those who believe in Him."[61] Finally, writing of the Lord's Supper, he says, "This prophecy also alludes to the bread which our Christ gave us to offer in remembrance of the Body which He assumed for the sake of those who believe in Him, for whom He also suffered."[62] By these comments, Justin asserted that Christ came into the world for believers, not unbelievers. This

DEFENDER OF THE FAITH    85

conforms with the biblical teaching that Jesus suffered and died for the elect.

In similar terms, Justin declared that Christ's sufferings and His substitutionary death were for those who are purified from all sin. This again is a reference to those who receive the benefit of the cross, the elect. This substitutionary sacrifice is represented in the broken bread of the Lord's Supper, which Christ instituted. Justin writes: "'Likewise,' I continued, 'the offering of flour, my friends, which was ordered to be presented for those cleansed from leprosy, was a prototype of the Eucharistic Bread, which our Lord Jesus Christ commanded us to offer in remembrance of the Passion He endured for all those souls who are cleansed from sin.'"[63] These words certainly imply that Christ came for those who are actually cleansed from sin, not for those who remain unclean.

**Doctrine in Focus:**

IRRESISTIBLE CALL

Justin also acknowledged that all men, being dead in sin, cannot believe until God calls them to Himself. This work of grace is the irresistible call that God extends to His elect.

Justin clearly spoke of the absolute necessity for divine grace if man is to understand the truth of the Scriptures. Remarking on man's dependence on God, Justin writes, "If, therefore, one were not endowed with God's great grace to understand the words and deeds of the Prophets, it would be quite useless for him to relate their words and actions, when he can give no explanation of them."[64] Again, he writes, "Do you gentlemen suppose . . . that we could have grasped the meaning of these Scriptural passages without a special grace from Him who willed them?"[65] Justin maintained that a special grace—a sovereign grace—according to God's will is essential in order for fallen people to grasp the truth.

It is by this special enlightenment that people come to know Christ savingly. Justin says, "He thus revealed to us all that we have learned from the Scriptures by His grace, so that we know Him as the First-begotten of God before all creatures."[66] He also writes: "Knowing this, why don't you stop deceiving yourselves and those around you? Why don't you learn from us who have been taught wisdom by the grace of Christ?"[67] In yet another place, he says: "We, therefore, were endowed with the special grace of hearing and understanding, of being saved by Christ, and of knowing all truths revealed by the Father."[68] This is God's saving grace, which conveys divine wisdom to the sinner, leading to salvation. This enlightenment is God-given insight about man's lost condition and the free grace of God in salvation.

## GUARDING THE TRUTH

Throughout his life, Justin was a true champion of the Christian faith, a staunch guardian of biblical truth. He devoted himself to intellectual interests as a means to bring clarity to the truth in a godless world. In so doing, he became the foremost philosopher and Apologist of his day, confronting pagan criticisms of Christianity. Through his extensive ministry, Justin expounded the clear teachings of Scripture in his God-appointed hour.

The church always stands in need of such men, who, by God's grace, expose the bankruptcy of worldly wisdom and challenge the lies of man-made philosophy. We need men whose hearts are gripped by the truth of Scripture and who can succinctly show how that truth is superior to the lies and vain speculations of modern thought. Above all, we need men who are willing to lay their lives on the line so that God might be glorified in all things, including the administration of His sovereign grace.

May God give us men like Justin Martyr in this day. May He grant to us once again those who will defend the faith at *all* costs.

NOTES

1  Justin, *Dialogue with Trypho*, 119, cited in *Writings of Saint Justin Martyr*, trans. Thomas B. Falls (New York: Christian Heritage, 1948), 331.

2  Jonathan Hill, *The History of Christian Thought* (Downers Grove, Ill.: InterVarsity, 2003), 14.

3  Hill, *The History of Christian Thought*, 14.

4  Hill, *The History of Christian Thought*, 14.

5  Louis Berkhof writes: "Pressure from without and from within called for a clear statement for defense of the truth, and thus gave birth to theology. The earliest Fathers who took up the defense of the truth are for that reason called Apologists." Louis Berkhof, *The History of Christian Doctrines* (1937; repr., Edinburgh: Banner of Truth, 1969), 56.

6  W. G. Phillips, "Apologetics," in *Evangelical Dictionary of Theology*, 2nd Ed., ed. Walter A. Elwell (Grand Rapids: Baker, 2001), 83.

7  "Apologists," in *The Oxford Dictionary of the Christian Church*, 3rd Ed., ed. E. A. Livingstone (1957; repr., Oxford: Oxford University Press, 1997), 87.

8  Robert A. Baker, *A Summary of Christian History*, rev. John M. Landers (Nashville: Broadman & Holman, 1994), 17.

9   "Justin Martyr, St.," in *The Oxford Dictionary of the Christian Church*, 915.

10  John MacArthur, *The MacArthur New Testament Commentary, John 1–11* (Chicago: Moody, 2006), 16.

11  MacArthur, *The MacArthur New Testament Commentary, John 1–11*, 16.

12  C. H. Pinnock, "Apologists," in *New Dictionary of Theology*, eds. Sinclair Ferguson, David F. Wright, and J. I. Packer (Downers Grove, Ill.: InterVarsity, 1988), 38.

13  Steve Jeffery, Michael Ovey, and Andrew Sach, *Pierced for Our Transgressions: Rediscovering the Glory of Penal Substitution* (Wheaton, Ill.: Crossway, 2007), 164.

14  Jeffery, Ovey, and Sach, *Pierced for Our Transgressions*, 164.

15  Ivor J. Davidson, *The Birth of the Church: From Jesus to Constantine, A.D. 30–312* (Grand Rapids: Baker, 2005), 214.

16  Justo L. González, *The Story of Christianity, Vol. 1: The Early Church to the Dawn of the Reformation* (Peabody, Mass: Prince Press, 2004), 52.

17  B. K. Kuiper, *The Church in History* (Grand Rapids: Eerdmans, 1964), 50.

18  "Justin Martyr, St.," in *The Oxford Dictionary of the Christian Church*, 915.

19  González, *The Story of Christianity, Vol. I*, 46.

20  "Justin," in *Cyclopedia of Biblical, Theological, and Ecclesiastical Literature, Vol. IV*, eds. John McClintock and James Strong (Grand Rapids: Baker, 1981), 1104.

21  Jeffery, Ovey, and Sach, *Pierced for Our Transgressions*, 164.

22  "Justin Martyr, St.," in *The Oxford Dictionary of the Christian Church*, 915.

23  "Justin," in *Cyclopedia of Biblical, Theological, and Ecclesiastical Literature, Vol. IV*, 1104.

24  "Justin," in *Cyclopedia of Biblical, Theological, and Ecclesiastical Literature, Vol. IV*, 1104.

25  A. Cleveland Coxe, "Introductory Note to the First Apology of Justin Martyr," in *Ante-Nicene Fathers, Vol. I: The Apostolic Fathers, Justin Martyr, Irenaeus*, eds. Alexander Roberts, James Donaldson, and A. Cleveland Coxe (1885; repr., Peabody, Mass.: Hendrickson, 2004), 160.

26  Hill, *The History of Christian Thought*, 16.

27  Davidson, *The Birth of the Church*, 31.

28  Aristotle is best known for teaching Alexander the Great, who, through his many conquests, spread the Greek language—providentially helping the rapid spread of the gospel. "Every Christian must recognize the career of Alexander, and the history of his empire, as an immediate precursor of the Gospel." *Ante-Nicene Fathers, Vol. II: Fathers of the Second Century: Hermas, Tatian, Athenagoras, Theophilus, and Clement of Alexandria (Entire)*, eds. Alexander Roberts, James Donaldson, and A. Cleveland Coxe (repr., Grand Rapids: Eerdmans, 1971), 166.

29  Aristotle, *The Nicomachean Ethics*, trans. J. E. C. Welldon (Buffalo, N.Y.: Prometheus, 1987), 43.

30  Davidson, *The Birth of the Church*, 30.

31  Some of Plato's ideas *were* compatible with Scripture. For instance, he valued the good of the community/state over the individual; individual rights were seen as counterproductive. He sought the greatest good for the unit as a whole: "The object of our legalization . . . is of society as a whole . . . and its uses to unite all citizens to make them share together the benefits which each individually can confer on the community; and its purpose in fostering this attitude is not to leave everyone to please himself, but to make each man a link in the unity of the whole." Plato, *The Republic*, 2nd Ed., trans. Desmond Lee (London: Penguin, 1987), 263. So it should be in the Christian community, where the focus is on the corporate body rather than the individual.

32  "Justin," in *Cyclopedia of Biblical, Theological, and Ecclesiastical Literature, Vol. IV*, 1105.

33  "Justin," in *Cyclopedia of Biblical, Theological, and Ecclesiastical Literature, Vol. IV*, 1105.

34 Justin, *Dialogue with Trypho*, 8, cited in *The First Apology; The Second Apology; Dialogue with Trypho; Exhortation to the Greeks; The Monarchy, or, The Rule of God*, ed. Thomas B. Falls (New York: Christian Heritage, 1948), 160.

35 Davidson, *The Birth of the Church*, 207.

36 Jeffery, Ovey, and Sach, *Pierced for Our Transgressions*, 164.

37 Jeffery, Ovey, and Sach, *Pierced for Our Transgressions*, 164.

38 Eusebius, *Eusebius: The Ecclesiastical History and the Martyrs of Palestine*, 4.11.8 (London: S.P.C.K., 1927), 113–114.

39 Hill, *The History of Christian Thought*, 15.

40 Davidson, *The Birth of the Church*, 207.

41 Hill, *The History of Christian Thought*, 17.

42 Roger E. Olson, *The Story of Christian Theology: Twenty Centuries of Tradition and Reform* (Downers Grove, Ill.: InterVarsity, 1999), 60.

43 Hill, *The History of Christian Thought*, 18.

44 Justin, *Dialogue with Trypho*, 8, cited in Falls, *The First Apology*, 160.

45 Tony Lane, *A Concise History of Christian Thought* (Grand Rapids: Baker Academic, 2006), 10.

46 Lane, *A Concise History of Christian Thought*, 10.

47 J. N. D. Kelly, *Early Christian Doctrines* (New York: Harper & Row, 1978), 166.

48 William Cunningham, *Historical Theology: A Review of the Principal Doctrinal Discussions in the Christian Church since the Apostolic Age, Vol. 1* (1862; repr. Edinburgh: Banner of Truth, 1969), 179.

49 Kelly, *Early Christian Doctrines*, 165.

50 John Hannah, *Our Legacy: The History of Christian Doctrine* (Colorado Springs, Colo.: NavPress, 2001), 206.

51 Hannah, *Our Legacy*, 206.

52 Justin, *Dialogue with Trypho*, 88, cited in Falls, *The First Apology*, 289.

53 Justin, *Dialogue with Trypho*, chap. XCV, cited in Roberts, Donaldson, and Coxe, *Ante-Nicene Fathers, Vol. I*, 247.

54 Justin, *Justin's Hortatory Address to the Greeks*, 8, cited in Falls, *The First Apology*, 383.

55 Justin, *Dialogue with Trypho*, 7, cited in Falls, *The First Apology*, 161.

56 Justin, *The Second Apology*, chap. VII, cited in Roberts, Donaldson, and Coxe, *Ante-Nicene Fathers, Vol. I*, 190.

57 Justin, *Dialogue with Trypho*, chap. CII, cited in Roberts, Donaldson, and Coxe, *Ante-Nicene Fathers, Vol. I*, 250.

58 Hannah, *Our Legacy*, 206.

59 Justin, *Dialogue with Trypho*, 130, cited in Falls, *The First Apology*, 349–50.

60 Justin, *The Second Apology*, 6, cited in Falls, *The First Apology*, 125.

61 Justin, *The First Apology*, 63, cited in Richardson, *Early Christian Fathers*, 285.

62 Justin, *Dialogue with Trypho*, 70, cited in Falls, *The First Apology*, 262.

63 Justin, *Dialogue with Trypho*, 41, cited in Falls, *The First Apology*, 210.

64 Justin, *Dialogue with Trypho*, 92, cited in Falls, *The First Apology*, 294.

65 Justin, *Dialogue with Trypho*, 119, cited in Falls, *The First Apology*, 331.

66 Justin, *Dialogue with Trypho*, 100, cited in Falls, *The First Apology*, 304.

67 Justin, *Dialogue with Trypho*, 32, cited in Falls, *The First Apology*, 196.

68 Justin, *Dialogue with Trypho*, 121, cited in Falls, *The First Apology*, 336.

# CHAPTER FOUR
# STUDY QUESTIONS

1. Describe the state of the church at the beginning of the second century. What place did philosophy have at this time? What worldviews were competing for the minds of men?

2. What charges were being brought against the believers of the early church? What defense needed to be offered in order to guard the truth?

3. What does the word *apologetics* mean? How was this discipline needed in the early church? How is it needed today? In what ways do you feel that you are equipped to defend the truth?

4. What was the primary objective of the Apologist Fathers? What was their chief ministry? How did they appeal to philosophy in answering the pagans?

5. How did Justin Martyr stand out in the second century? What made him such a vital force for the gospel? What place did philosophy occupy in his life? How did he use it to advance the Christian faith?

6. Describe the writings of Justin Martyr. What was the primary thrust of his works? Why did he compose these works?

7. Describe Justin Martyr's position on radical depravity. Where was it lacking?

8. What did Justin say regarding sovereign election? Did he ever allude to a specific intent of the atonement? If so, what did he say? According to Justin Martyr, is there a special grace that enables faith and that leads to the knowledge of Christ?

*God . . . knows hidden things, . . . knoweth all things before they can come to pass; and for this reason has He said, "Jacob have I loved, but Esau have I hated."*[1]

—Irenaeus of Lyons

Chapter Five

# OPPOSING GNOSTICISM

## APOLOGIST FATHER:
## IRENAEUS OF LYONS

B y the mid-second century, the worship of mythological gods had begun to decline. Apostate Judaism, still reeling from the destruction of Jerusalem in AD 70, was in further regression. Even emperor worship had weakened, depending on which Caesar was on the throne. At this time, only two religions were growing in strength and stature—biblical Christianity and heretical Gnosticism. This latter movement had become the greatest philosophical threat confronting the church. With its roots reaching back into New Testament times, Gnosticism was at its peak of power in the middle of the second century and was inflicting much damage on those under its influence.

Gnosticism drew its name from the Greek word *gnosis*, or "knowledge," for Gnosticism claimed to have a secret knowledge that only a small segment of humanity could attain. Those who supposedly possessed it were considered to be "spiritual" people. Gnosticism took a syncretistic approach to salvation, mixing elements of various religions and secular philosophies. Platonism was mixed with Eastern mysticism and Zoroastrianism, along with elements of Judaism and Christianity. The deadly result, Gnosticism, flourished in the eastern Mediterranean around Alexandria, Egypt, and in Asia Minor before eventually spreading west to Rome and Gaul (France).

Gnosticism arose from the natural human desire to create a theodicy, an explanation for the origin of evil.[2] It taught a sharp dualism, deeming the spiritual realm to be good but matter to be evil.[3] Since God is a spirit, the Gnostics reasoned, He could not have created an evil material world. Thus, a lower god, the demiurge, sometimes identified with the God of the Old

Testament, must have created all matter. Further, Gnosticism taught that a hierarchy of spirit beings formed a "buffer" between God and the physical world. All told, there were some thirty layers of spirit beings. These beings, which were emanations from God, grew increasingly less divine and more physical as they approached the material world, forming a bridge between God and man.

Salvation, according to the Gnostics, was escape from the body, which came through secret knowledge. Since the body was evil, it was to be treated harshly. Strangely, the Gnostics' dualistic thinking also led to extreme licentiousness in the pursuit of sinful pleasures.[4] Since the body was evil, they reasoned, what occurred in it was of little consequence.

The Gnostics rejected the humanity of Jesus Christ. Since God could have nothing to do with matter, they concluded that He could not have assumed a human body. They rejected Christ's incarnation and denied His crucifixion. They maintained that He did not literally give His life as a sacrifice for sin. Plus, they claimed, there was no bodily resurrection of Christ—for He had no body. Thus, Gnosticism attacked the very heart of the gospel: the virgin birth, sinless life, substitutionary death, and bodily resurrection of Jesus. Some Gnostics adopted a doctrine known as Docetism, which insisted that Christ only *seemed* to have had a body and to have died. But for Christ to actually have had a body that died was impossible, they claimed, because He was pure spirit.

Church historian Philip Schaff summed up the tenets of Gnosticism in this way: "The common characteristics of nearly all the Gnostic systems are (1) Dualism; the assumption of an eternal antagonism between God and matter. (2) The demiurgic notion; the separation of the creator of the world or the demiurgos from the proper God. (3) Docetism; the resolution of the human element in the person of the Redeemer into mere deceptive appearance."[5] Such false teaching had to be exposed for what it was—heresy.

As noted in the previous chapter, this crucial task was taken up by the Apologists of the second and early third centuries. These Church Fathers decisively opposed the Gnostics through their writing and teaching. With zeal and determination, they sought to guard the one true way of salvation found in the fully human, yet fully divine, person of Jesus Christ and His finished work.

Irenaeus became the great champion in the battle against the lies of Gnosticism. He was deeply committed to preserving the purity of the gospel of

Christ. What is more, at the heart of his theology was the biblical truth of the sovereign grace of God in man's salvation.

# IRENAEUS OF LYONS

Irenaeus (ca. 130–200) was the first important Christian figure to minister in Western Europe in the second-century church. Considered the first among the Western Fathers,[6] he championed orthodoxy against Gnostic heresy.[7] Trained in Asia Minor in the East, he served in Europe in the West. Irenaeus thus stood as a link between early Greek theology and Western Latin theology.[8] What is more, Theodoret of Cyrrhus (ca. 393–460) called Irenaeus the "Light of the Western Church," claiming that true genius shone from his teachings.[9] His work reveals remarkable theological profundity.[10] It has been said that no post-apostolic Christian writer before Augustine has had as much bearing on modern controversies as Irenaeus.[11]

Irenaeus was born in Asia Minor, in the seaport town of Smyrna. Though the city was a center for emperor worship, Irenaeus was raised in a Christian family[12] and became an early convert to Christianity.[13] As a boy, he was strongly influenced by the teaching of the great Polycarp, who had sat under the teaching of the apostle John.[14] Years later, Irenaeus reflected on Polycarp's profound impact on his life, declaring that he had recorded the truth taught by his revered pastor "not on paper, but in my heart, and by the grace of God I constantly bring it afresh to mind."[15] Thus, Irenaeus's strong orthodoxy and deep convictions can be traced back to these formative years under Polycarp's teaching.

## Sent to Western Europe

By the middle of the second century, Christianity was spreading in the western regions of the Roman Empire. Christian missions had progressed as far west as the Rhone River in Gaul (southern France). A trade route connected the prosperous cities of Smyrna in Asia Minor and Marseilles in Gaul, making Lyons a gateway between the Mediterranean world and the provinces north of the Alps. Polycarp sent an evangelist named Pothinus to Gaul to preach the gospel. He won converts and started a church at Lyons, the second-largest city in Gaul, where the Roman forum sat on a hill overlooking the confluence of the Rhone and Saône rivers.[16] Pothinus became the pastor there and oversaw a vibrant work. In response to growing pastoral needs, Irenaeus was sent to Lyons, where he became a presbyter and helped shepherd the flock.[17]

After Irenaeus's arrival in Lyons, severe persecution broke out against the church under the Emperor Marcus Aurelius (AD 177). Martyrdom soon came to Lyons. Eusebius, the fourth-century historian, recorded the events: "First of all, [the Christians] endured nobly the injuries heaped upon them by the populace; clamors and blows and dragging and robberies and stoning and imprisonments, and all things which an infuriated mob delight in inflicting on enemies and adversaries. Then, being taken to the forum by the tribune and the authorities of the city, they were examined in the presence of the whole multitude, and having confessed, they were imprisoned until the arrival of the governor. . . . Afterwards, they were brought before [the governor], and he treated [them] with the utmost cruelty."[18] The old charges of cannibalism (because the Christians were said to eat Jesus' body and drink His blood in the Lord's Supper) and sexual orgies (because of the closeness of their fellowship and the way they greeted one another with a holy kiss) were raised against the believers again. These were, of course, gross distortions of their Christian beliefs and practices.[19]

As the persecutions intensified, the Galician believers sent Irenaeus to the church at Rome with letters describing the extraordinary heroism of the believers who were suffering in Lyons. Additionally, the correspondence warned against an even greater danger—the spreading heresy of Gnosticism—and appealed for help.

## INTO THE FIGHT

While in the imperial capital, Irenaeus discovered that the bishop of Rome, Eleutherus, had embraced a heretical teaching known as Montanism. This sobering realization further motivated Irenaeus to join the fight against theological errors in the church. Then, while Irenaeus was still in Rome, Pothinus was martyred in Lyons. This loss necessitated that Irenaeus return quickly to Gaul to tend to the flock. Upon arriving, he was immediately thrust into the primary leadership role of the church when he was appointed bishop of Lyons.

As an overseer, Irenaeus faithfully preached the Word, evangelized, and defended his congregation against encroaching heresy. Schaff remarks that he "labored . . . with zeal and success, by tongue and pen, . . . for the spread of Christianity in Gaul, and for the defense and development of its doctrines."[20] Irenaeus became a strong preacher who "connected almost the whole population of Lyon."[21] In other words, his preaching had a wide appeal that galvanized the city. Moreover, he sent missionaries to other parts of Gaul.[22] In short, Irenaeus was a substantial force for the advancement of the gospel of Jesus Christ.

Little is known about the end of Irenaeus's life. He likely lived until the early third century.[23] Some think that he died a natural death, while others believe that he was martyred. He was buried under the altar before the pulpit of the Church of St. John in Lyons. The selection of this resting place so close to the pulpit from which he preached stands as a strong testimony of his deep love for the enduring truth of God's Word.

# IRENAEUS'S WRITINGS

With the danger of Gnosticism escalating, Irenaeus could not sit idly by. Taking pen in hand, he wrote several books to refute this heresy, which had crept in "like locusts, to devour the harvests of the Gospel."[24] His writings guarded and matured the early believers at Lyons. An investigation of Irenaeus's writings reveals that his "main contribution lay in the refutation of heresy and the exposition of apostolic Christianity."[25]

## AGAINST HERESIES

Irenaeus's most notable and important work—and his only major writing that has survived[26]—was titled *On the Detection and Overthrow of the So-Called Gnosis* (ca. 180). This monumental treatise, commonly called *Against Heresies*, is "the most valuable relic of early Christian antiquity."[27] Schaff regarded it as "the polemic theological masterpiece of the ante-Nicene age."[28]

Irenaeus's purpose in the book was twofold: "(1) to render it impossible for any one to confound Gnosticism with Christianity, and (2) to make it impossible for such a monstrous system to survive, or ever to rise again."[29] Irenaeus made use of the four Gospels and all of the Epistles[30] except Philemon, James, 2 Peter, and 3 John.[31]

*Against Heresies* is divided into five books. The first volume contains a detailed description of the heresies of Gnosticism. In it, Irenaeus refutes with Scripture the erroneous writings of the followers of Ptolemaeus, a disciple of the Gnostic theologian Valentinus.[32] The second volume strongly refutes Gnosticism with logic and common sense. Here Irenaeus proves Gnosticism's essential unity with the heathen systems of philosophy.[33] His arguments are based on sound reasoning, proving how incoherent Gnostic teachings were, "to unmask the theosophy of Gnosticism for the rubbish that it was."[34] The final three volumes present the truths of Scripture as being in complete contradiction to Gnosticism. Here Irenaeus shows the solidarity of the Old Testament with the New Testament through a series of expositions of Scripture that establish the sound doctrine of the faith.

### DEMONSTRATION OF APOSTOLIC PREACHING

Another of Irenaeus's works, *Demonstration of Apostolic Preaching*, often called *Epideixis*, is a short treatise addressed to a Christian named Marcianus. He gives a foundational overview of the Christian faith in which he discusses Trinitarian theology and the creation of the universe and humanity, as well as a biblical history to the incarnation of Christ and His saving activity. Irenaeus contrasts Adam's disobedience with Christ's obedience and shows how the promises made to Abraham and David were fulfilled in Christ. This work also discusses salvation by faith, the preexistence of Christ, His incarnation, and the missionary activity of the apostles. It closes with an appeal for preachers of the Word to vehemently defend the truth against heretics.[35]

# IRENAEUS'S THEOLOGY

Irenaeus is revered by many as the first great systematic theologian of the Christian church.[36] His masterful works give evidence of his belief in the sovereign grace of God and demonstrate an ongoing progression in the development of sovereign grace truth. He affirmed that God predetermines all things and rules over the affairs of men, including their eternal destinies, for His own glory. As he wrote against Gnosticism, Irenaeus spoke of divine choice and certainty in salvation. At other times, however, he spoke of man's free will. The task of fully defining the extent of the fall of Adam and the depraved nature of mankind remained for theologians of subsequent centuries.

**Doctrine in Focus:**
### DIVINE SOVEREIGNTY

Irenaeus maintained the biblical truth of God's divine predetermination. He writes, "But He Himself in Himself, after a fashion which we can neither describe nor conceive, predestinating all things, formed them as He pleased."[37] By this statement, Irenaeus declared that just as God created all things, He predetermined all things. He unashamedly used the language of predestination to assert that God decreed all things in a way that exceeds our full comprehension.

Further, Irenaeus taught that God actively governs all things in our world. He writes, "This is the Father of our Lord, by whose providence all things consist, and all are administered by His command; and He confers His free gifts upon those who should [receive them]."[38] God rules His universe, overseeing all individuals, events, and things within it. Irenaeus later writes: "He has regard to all things, and exercises a providence over all, 'making His sun to rise upon the evil and on the good, and sending rain upon the just and unjust.' This providence is over believer and unbeliever alike, over the spiritual and natural realms"[39] In a similar fashion, he declares, "God does . . . exercise a providence over all things . . . and arranges the affairs of our world."[40] Irenaeus believed there are no exceptions to God's sovereign reign. God even rules over Satan, Irenaeus affirmed, so that the Devil has no power except as it is given by God. He writes: "Since God rules over men and [Satan] too, and without the will of our Father in heaven not even a sparrow falls to the ground, it follows that [Satan's] declaration, 'All these things are delivered unto me, and to whomsoever I will I give them,' proceeds from him when puffed up with pride. For the creation is not subjected to his power, since indeed he is himself but one among created things. Nor shall he give away the rule over men to men; but both all other things, and all human affairs, are arranged according to God the Father's disposal."[41] Irenaeus was clear that Satan does not exercise ultimate control over this world. Such authority belongs exclusively to God.

Irenaeus believed that God's creation and providence are inextricably linked with His omniscience. He states: "Not one of the things which have been, or are, or shall be made, escapes the knowledge of God, but . . . through His providence every one of them has obtained its nature, and rank, and number, and special quantity, and . . . nothing whatever either has been or is produced in vain or accidentally, but with exceeding suitability [to the purpose intended], and in the exercise of transcendent knowledge."[42] The all-knowing wisdom of God, according to Irenaeus, strategically governs every class and category of creation.

**Doctrine in Focus:**
## RADICAL DEPRAVITY
Irenaeus acknowledged that Adam's sin had brought about the devastation of the entire human race. Recognizing Adam's role as the representative of all

his descendants, Irenaeus asserted that when the first man sinned, all mankind transgressed with him. He writes: "Indeed we had offended [God] in the first Adam, when he did not perform His commandment. . . . We were debtors to none other but to Him whose commandment we had transgressed at the beginning."[43] This is to say, all human beings are guilty because of Adam's fall.

In this state of depravity, Irenaeus argued, all men are ignorant of God. Concerning man's inherent inability to know God, he states: "Since it was impossible, without God, to come to a knowledge of God, He teaches men, through His Word, to know God. To those, therefore, who are ignorant of these matters, and on this account imagine that they have discovered another Father, justly does one say, 'Ye do err, not knowing the Scriptures, nor the power of God.'"[44] No one can come to a saving knowledge of God apart from being taught by God Himself.

Similarly, Irenaeus affirmed that all men give themselves to the world system and their carnal desires. He writes, "Man . . . shall be justly condemned, because, having been created a rational being, he lost the true rationality, and living irrationally, opposed the righteousness of God, giving himself over to every earthly spirit, and serving all lusts."[45] In short, the spirit of this evil age rules over the rebellious hearts of all unconverted men.

Irenaeus held that the sin of Adam and Eve resulted in the spiritual, physical, and emotional death of all mankind. He says, "Eve . . . having become disobedient, was made the cause of death, both to herself and to the entire human race."[46] The wages of sin is death, rendering man morally unable to please God. Neither does man have the spiritual capacity to come to Him. What can a dead man do? Nothing.

Nevertheless, like other Apologist Fathers, Irenaeus often seemingly contradicted himself by speaking of man's free will. He wrote of fallen man possessing a power to choose whether to obey or disobey God[47] and expressed confidence in human ability and moral freedom.[48] He writes, "But man, being endowed with reason, and in this respect similar to God, having been made free in his will, and with power over himself, is himself his own cause that sometimes he becomes wheat, and sometimes chaff."[49] Similarly, he maintained that "it is in man's power to disobey God and to forfeit what is good."[50] This inconsistency may have stemmed partly from the context in which Irenaeus lived and ministered. Like Justin Martyr, he was constantly embattled by Gnostic attacks. Gnosticism inaccurately "asserted that the Christian faith denied moral responsibility."[51] To counter this idea, the Apologists stressed man's obligation. In so doing, they unfortunately weakened their position concerning man's depravity, as well as God's exclusive role in salvation.

**Doctrine in Focus:**

SOVEREIGN ELECTION

Irenaeus believed in the sovereign choice of God in salvation. He understood that God chooses who will be saved, so that the divine will is the determinative factor in the redemption of spiritually dead sinners. He writes: "[God] saved from the beginning those who are saved."[52] By this, Irenaeus declared that God chose a people in eternity past for salvation.

Predestination, Irenaeus maintained, is according to the determinative foreknowledge of God. He states:

> We were but recently made by Him who is the highest and best, by Him who is able to bestow the gift of incorruptibility, made according to the image which is with Him and predestined according to the foreknowledge of the Father to be what we were not yet. Made the beginning of [His new] creation, we have received [this gift] in times foreknown by the dispensation of the Word, who is perfect in all things, for He is the mighty Word, and true man. Redeeming us by His blood in accordance with His reasonable nature, He gave Himself a ransom for those who had been led into captivity.[53]

Irenaeus affirms this same truth elsewhere when he writes, "But God, foreknowing all things, prepared fit habitations for [the elect], kindly conferring that light which they desire on those who seek after the light of incorruption, and resort to it."[54] Thus, Irenaeus saw salvation as the necessary result of God's eternal foreordination. He understood that foreknowledge does not simply mean that God passively foresaw future events, but that He actively chose His elect to salvation from eternity past.

The root of salvation, Irenaeus asserted, is the electing love of God. Before the foundation of the world, the Father chose those upon whom He would set His love. Irenaeus states: "Our God, one and the same . . . who knows hidden things, . . . knows all things before they can come to pass; and for this reason has He said, 'Jacob have I loved, but Esau have I hated.'"[55] God foreknows all things because He has foreordained all things. This includes His electing love for His chosen ones.

Irenaeus wrote that God's chosen people are not limited to ethnic Israel, but can be found among the Gentiles as well. These chosen ones, he said, are like a beautiful tower for all to see. Irenaeus states, "Wherefore the Lord God did even give [the vineyard] up (no longer hedged around, but thrown open throughout all the world) to other husbandmen, who render the fruits in their seasons,—the beautiful elect tower being also raised everywhere."[56] With this statement, Irenaeus taught the unfailing election by God of people throughout the world unto salvation.

**Doctrine in Focus:**

DEFINITE ATONEMENT

Irenaeus recognized that Christ came into the world to atone for sin. He often stated that Jesus' death was for those who would believe—the true church. He writes: "For it was not merely for those who believed on Him in the time of Tiberius Caesar that Christ came, nor did the Father exercise His providence for the men only who are now alive, but for all men altogether, who from the beginning, according to their capacity, in their generation have both feared and loved God, and practiced justice and piety towards their neighbours, and have earnestly desired to see Christ, and to hear His voice."[57] By this statement, Irenaeus taught that Christ came into this world to save all men, but he identified "all" as those who fear and love God, and who desire to see Christ and hear Him. In other words, Christ came for all who would believe on Him in every generation.

**Doctrine in Focus:**

IRRESISTIBLE CALL

Irenaeus was especially lucid concerning the doctrine of God's irresistible call. He understood that a spiritually dead sinner must be raised and drawn by grace to believe on Christ. God Himself, he reasoned, resurrects His chosen ones so that they may trust in Christ for salvation. This involves the life-giving work of the Holy Spirit, who convicts, illumines, and bestows faith in Christ. Irenaeus writes: "For the Lord taught us that no man is capable of knowing God, unless he be taught of God; that is, that God cannot be known without God."[58] Thus, Irenaeus held that no one can know God unless the Lord Himself inwardly teaches him or her. God must take the initiative to make Himself known to impotent sinners.

Likewise, Irenaeus declared that knowledge of God comes through Christ.

He states: "Him [God], therefore, I have rightly shown to be known by no man, unless by the Son, and to whomsoever the Son shall reveal Him. But the Son reveals the Father to all to whom He wills that He should be known; and neither without the goodwill of the Father nor without the agency of the Son, can any man know God."[59] Irenaeus was speaking here of that sovereign work of Christ toward those to whom He wills to make the Father known, that is, to God's elect.

Irenaeus also acknowledged that Christ must create faith in a sinner before he can believe in Him. He explains, "Now, this Jesus did, drawing us off from the religion of stones, and bringing us over from hard and fruitless cogitations, and establishing in us a faith like to Abraham."[60] That is, Christ creates the faith by which sinners believe in Him. No spiritually dead sinner has the power of choice to believe on Christ apart from divine enabling.

Furthermore, Irenaeus stated that those who are spiritually dead are made to live and bear fruit by the miracle of regeneration. He writes: "For as a compacted lump of dough cannot be formed of dry wheat without fluid matter, nor can a loaf possess unity, so, in like manner, neither could we, being many, be made one in Christ Jesus without the water from heaven. And as dry earth does not bring forth unless it receive moisture, in like manner we also, being originally a dry tree, could never have brought forth fruit unto life without the voluntary rain from above. For our bodies have received unity among themselves by means of that laver which leads to incorruption; but our souls, by means of the Spirit."[61] By this statement, Irenaeus affirmed that the spiritual fruit of eternal life comes only from above, that is, from God.

**Doctrine in Focus:**
## Divine Reprobation

Irenaeus not only held to the truth of sovereign election, he affirmed the corresponding teaching—the doctrine of divine reprobation. He did not shy away from the hard truth that when God elected some individuals to eternal life, He passed over others, leaving them in their sin to face His just judgment. He states: "God, knowing the number of those who will not believe . . . has given them over to unbelief, and turned away His face from men of this stamp, leaving them in the darkness which they have chosen for themselves."[62] This demonstrates, at least in embryonic form, a belief in the doctrine of reprobation. It clearly presents God as having a different attitude toward the reprobate than toward His elect.

Irenaeus points to Pharaoh as an example of every reprobate's stubborn refusal to believe: "[Did not God] also at that time give over to their unbelief, Pharaoh, who never would have believed, along with those who were with him?"[63] Irenaeus understood that the nonelect will never believe. The reprobates whom God passes over cannot escape the hardness of their unbelief.

# IN DEFENSE OF THE GOSPEL

Irenaeus was a true defender of the faith. He lived in a critical hour of church history and, by God's grace, proved to be equal to the challenges of his age. When the winds of error were howling and threatening to impede the life and ministry of the church, the bishop of Lyons took a stand for the purity of the true gospel. This Early Father stood up to the heresy of Gnosticism, helping to preserve the stability of the church. His strong stand was grounded in his strong theology.

As you survey the landscape of this day, where do you see the truth of God's Word under similar attack? Where do you note the walls of orthodoxy crumbling around you? Where do you witness the truths of sovereign grace being undermined? Any observer of the world today must agree that these assaults are steadily occurring, even on the evangelical scene. In many quarters, the person and work of Christ remain under constant attack. Numerous cults deny the deity of Christ. False religions undermine His substitutionary death. Erroneous teachings distort the core of the gospel message. Such teachings are increasingly prevalent in the world and continue to trouble the church. Never has there been a greater need for sound doctrine.

If you are possessed by a holy zeal for God's honor, as was the bishop of Lyons, you will be stirred to guard the truth of Scripture. If you are standing strong for the gospel, you will be committed to advancing transcendent theology. Such fiery passion is enflamed by a firm commitment to the doctrines of grace.

Will you build your life on the truths of the sovereign grace of God? Will you position yourself on this high theological ground in order to defend these biblical truths and fortify the church from heretical attacks? May God strengthen you to defend the truth of His supreme authority over all of human history.

NOTES

1  Irenaeus, *Against Heresies*, IV.21.2, in *Ante-Nicene Fathers, Vol. I: The Apostolic Fathers with Justin Martyr and Irenaeus*, eds. Alexander Roberts, James Donaldson, and A. Cleveland Coxe (1864, repr., Grand Rapids: Eerdmans, 1973), 493.

2  Earle E. Cairns, *Christianity Through the Centuries: A History of the Christian Church*, 3rd Ed. (1954; repr., Grand Rapids: Zondervan, 1996), 96.

3  Edwin M. Yamauchi, "The Gnostics," in *Introduction to the History of Christianity*, ed. Tim Dowley (Minneapolis: Fortress, 2002), 96.

4  Yamauchi, "The Gnostics," in *Introduction to the History of Christianity*, 96.

5  Philip Schaff, *History of the Christian Church, Vol. II: Ante-Nicene Christianity: From the Death of John the Apostle to Constantine the Great, A.D. 100–325* (1910; repr., Grand Rapids: Eerdmans, 1980), 452.

6  Schaff, *History of the Christian Church, Vol. II*, 748.

7  Schaff, *History of the Christian Church, Vol. II*, 748.

8  Tony Lane, *A Concise History of Christian Thought* (Grand Rapids: Baker Academic, 2006), 12.

9  Theodoret of Cyrrhus, cited in "Irenaeus," in *Cyclopedia of Biblical, Theological, and Ecclesiastical Literature, Vol. IV*, eds. John McClintock and James Strong (Grand Rapids: Baker, 1981), 647.

10  Jonathan Hill, *The History of Christian Thought* (Downers Grove, Ill.: InterVarsity, 2003), 26.

11  Cyril C. Richardson, ed., *Early Christian Fathers* (New York: Touchstone, 1996), 343.

12  Lane, *A Concise History of Christian Thought*, 12.

13  Hill, *The History of Christian Thought*, 26.

14  Richardson, *Early Christian Fathers*, 347.

15  Irenaeus, *Fragments from the Lost Writings of Irenaeus*, chap. 2, cited in Schaff, *History of the Christian Church, Vol. II*, 749.

16  Eric Osborn, "Irenaeus of Lyons," in *The First Christian Theologians: An Introduction to Theology in the Early Church*, ed. G. R. Evans (Malden, Mass.: Blackwell, 2004), 121.

17  Lane, *A Concise History of Christian Thought*, 12.

18  Eusebius, *Church History*, 5.1.7–9, cited in *Nicene and Post-Nicene Fathers, Second Series, Vol. I: Eusebius: Church History, Life of Constantine the Great, Oration in Praise of Constantine*, eds. Philip Schaff and Henry Wace (1890; repr. Peabody, Mass.: Hendrickson, 2004), 212.

19  Laurie Guy, *Introducing Early Christianity* (Downers Grove, Ill.: InterVarsity, 2004), 67.

20  Schaff, *History of the Christian Church, Vol. II*, 749.

21  Guy, *Introducing Early Christianity*, 67.

22  Guy, *Introducing Early Christianity*, 67.

23  Lane, *A Concise History of Christian Thought*, 12.

24  Roberts, Donaldson, and Coxe, *Ante-Nicene Fathers, Vol. I*, 309.

25  Lane, *A Concise History of Christian Thought*, 12.

26  Hill, *The History of Christian Thought*, 26.

27  "Irenaeus," in *Cyclopedia of Biblical, Theological, and Ecclesiastical Literature, Vol. IV*, 647.

28  Schaff, *History of the Christian Church, Vol. II*, 753.

29  Irenaeus, *Against Heresies*, introductory notes, cited in Roberts, Donaldson, and Coxe, *Ante-Nicene Fathers, Vol. I*, 310.

30  Schaff, *History of the Christian Church, Vol. II*, 752.

31 John Hannah, *Our Legacy: The History of Christian Doctrine* (Colorado Springs, Colo.: NavPress, 2001), 42.

32 "Valentinus," in *The Oxford Dictionary of the Christian Church*, ed. E. A. Livingstone (1957; repr., Oxford: Oxford University Press, 1997), 1675.

33 Roberts, Donaldson, and Coxe, *Ante-Nicene Fathers, Vol. I*, 310.

34 M. A. Smith, *From Christ to Constantine* (Downers Grove, Ill.: InterVarsity, 1971), 61.

35 Claudio Moreschini and Enrico Norelli, *Early Christian Greek and Latin Literature: A Literary History, Vol. One: From Paul to the Age of Constantine*, trans. Matthew J. O'Connell (Peabody, Mass.: Hendrickson, 2005), 231.

36 Ivor J. Davidson, *The Birth of the Church: From Jesus to Constantine, A.D. 30–312* (Grand Rapids: Baker, 2004), 225.

37 Irenaeus, *Against Heresies*, II.2.4, cited in Roberts, Donaldson, and Coxe, *Ante-Nicene Fathers, Vol. I*, 361.

38 Irenaeus, *Against Heresies*, IV.36.6, cited in Roberts, Donaldson, and Coxe, *Ante-Nicene Fathers, Vol. I*, 517.

39 Irenaeus, *Against Heresies*, V.27.1, cited in Roberts, Donaldson, and Coxe, *Ante-Nicene Fathers, Vol. I*, 556.

40 Irenaeus, *Against Heresies*, III.25.1, cited in Roberts, Donaldson, and Coxe, *Ante-Nicene Fathers, Vol. I*, 459.

41 Irenaeus, *Against Heresies*, V.22.2, cited in Roberts, Donaldson, and Coxe, *Ante-Nicene Fathers, Vol. I*, 551.

42 Irenaeus, *Against Heresies*, II.26.2, cited in Roberts, Donaldson, and Coxe, *Ante-Nicene Fathers, Vol. I*, 397–98.

43 Irenaeus, *Against Heresies*, V.16.3, cited in Roberts, Donaldson, and Coxe, *Ante-Nicene Fathers, Vol. I*, 544.

44 Irenaeus, *Against Heresies*, IV.5.1, cited in Roberts, Donaldson, and Coxe, *Ante-Nicene Fathers, Vol. I*, 466.

45 Irenaeus, *Against Heresies*, IV.4.3, cited in Roberts, Donaldson, and Coxe, *Ante-Nicene Fathers, Vol. I*, 466.

46 Irenaeus, *Against Heresies*, III.22.4, cited in Roberts, Donaldson, and Coxe, *Ante-Nicene Fathers, Vol. I*, 455.

47 Christopher A. Hall, *Learning Theology with the Church Fathers* (Downers Grove, Ill.: IVP Academic, 2002), 124.

48 Hall, *Learning Theology with the Church Fathers*, 124.

49 Irenaeus, *Against Heresies*, IV.4.3, cited in Roberts, Donaldson, and Coxe, *Ante-Nicene Fathers, Vol. I*, 466.

50 Irenaeus, *Against Heresies*, IV.37.4, cited in Roberts, Donaldson, and Coxe, *Ante-Nicene Fathers, Vol. I*, 519.

51 Hannah, *Our Legacy*, 206.

52 Irenaeus, *Against Heresies*, IV.28.2, cited in Roberts, Donaldson, and Coxe, *Ante-Nicene Fathers, Vol. I*, 501.

53 Irenaeus, *Against Heresies*, V.1.1, cited in Richardson, *Early Christian Fathers*, 385.

54 Irenaeus, *Against Heresies*, IV.39.4, cited in Roberts, Donaldson, and Coxe, *Ante-Nicene Fathers, Vol. I*, 523.

55 Irenaeus, *Against Heresies*, IV.21.2, cited in Roberts, Donaldson, and Coxe, *Ante-Nicene Fathers*, *Vol. I*, 493.

56 Irenaeus, *Against Heresies*, IV.36.2, cited in Roberts, Donaldson, and Coxe, *Ante-Nicene Fathers*, *Vol. I*, 515.

57 Irenaeus, *Against Heresies*, IV.22.2, cited in Roberts, Donaldson, and Coxe, *Ante-Nicene Fathers*, *Vol. I*, 494.

58 Irenaeus, *Against Heresies*, IV.6.4, cited in Roberts, Donaldson, and Coxe, *Ante-Nicene Fathers*, *Vol. I*, 468.

59 Irenaeus, *Against Heresies*, IV.7.3, cited in Roberts, Donaldson, and Coxe, *Ante-Nicene Fathers*, *Vol. I*, 470.

60 Irenaeus, *Against Heresies*, IV.7.2, cited in Roberts, Donaldson, and Coxe, *Ante-Nicene Fathers*, *Vol. I*, 470.

61 Irenaeus, *Against Heresies*, III.17.2, cited in Roberts, Donaldson, and Coxe, *Ante-Nicene Fathers*, *Vol. I*, 444–445.

62 Irenaeus, *Against Heresies*, IV.29.2, cited in Roberts, Donaldson, and Coxe, *Ante-Nicene Fathers*, *Vol. I*, 502.

63 Irenaeus, *Against Heresies*, IV.29.2, cited in Roberts, Donaldson, and Coxe, *Ante-Nicene Fathers*, *Vol. I*, 502.

# CHAPTER FIVE
## STUDY QUESTIONS

1.  What challenge did the heretical teaching of Gnosticism pose to the church of the second century? What were the core tenets of Gnosticism? Why was it so threatening?

2.  Describe Irenaeus's background. Where did he grow up? Who were the major influences in his early life?

3.  Where was Irenaeus sent to minister the gospel? What danger confronted him upon his arrival? Where has the Lord placed you to serve Him? What are the chief threats to the gospel in your sphere of influence? How does Irenaeus encourage you?

4.  What were the chief works of Irenaeus? What did he address in his writings? How can these works help to equip you to confront the doctrinal challenges of this day?

5.  Describe Irenaeus's commitment to the doctrines of grace. Explain his stance on divine sovereignty in providence and in salvation. Can you give an explanation of the doctrine of providence?

6.  What was Irenaeus's position on radical depravity? Where was he strong? In what area was he weak?

7.  Did Irenaeus hold to sovereign election? What is the evidence that this was his firm belief? Have you come to the same conviction in your life? If so, how has this doctrine transformed you?

*For, who can know truth without the help of God? Who can know God without Christ? Who has ever discovered Christ without the Holy Spirit? And who has ever received the Holy Spirit without the gift of faith?*[1]

–Tertullian of Carthage

Chapter Six

# FATHER OF
# LATIN THEOLOGY

## AFRICAN FATHER:
## TERTULLIAN OF CARTHAGE

D uring the second and third centuries, a new heresy began to trouble the early church. This false teaching was Monarchianism—also
known as Sabellianism, after one of its leaders, Sabellius—which first emerged
in Asia Minor and flourished in the West. Such error was a frontal assault on
two cardinal doctrines of Christianity, namely, the Trinity and the deity of
Jesus Christ. Rather than holding to the orthodox view of the nature of God,
that there is one God who exists in three persons, Monarchians espoused that
there is one God who exists merely as one person. Only the Father is divine,
they maintained, not the Son or the Holy Spirit. Such a serious departure from
true Christianity laid the axe to the root of the saving gospel of Jesus Christ.
This heterodoxy rejected the nonnegotiable truths concerning Christ's deity
and the atonement He accomplished in His sacrificial death on the cross.

The first deadly form of Monarchianism was known as Adoptionism or
Dynamic Monarchianism. This heresy insinuated that Jesus was only a man
who was energized by the Holy Spirit.[2] More specifically, it maintained that
Jesus was only a man and that God adopted Him at the time of His baptism.[3] Only then, the Monarchians claimed, was Jesus called the Son of God.
In short, Adoptionism sought to explain the relationship between the Father
and the Son by way of a power that came upon Jesus, a force that infused
Him with divinity.[4] This was a clear distortion of Scripture, which teaches
that Christ was the Son of God before and after His baptism. The Christ of

109

the Monarchians was "another Jesus," such as Paul condemned (2 Cor. 11:4), for this heresy flatly denied the equality of the Son with the Father.

A second form of Monarchianism was known as Modalism, which asserted that the Father, the Son, and the Holy Spirit were the same person acting in three different roles. Adherents to this falsehood claimed that God existed in various modes—hence, Modalism—but only in one mode at any one time. Thus, Modalists believed that God was, first, the Creator, and that later He was manifested as God the Redeemer, or the Son. But both Father and Son were the same person. When Jesus was born of Mary, they argued, it was God the Father who was born. During the incarnation, they claimed, there was no Father in heaven. When Christ ascended again to heaven, He supposedly resumed His previous role as God the Father. When the Holy Spirit descended at Pentecost, heaven was emptied once again.[5] Simply put, Modalism taught that only one person is God, not three.

This assault on the tri-unity of God raised the need for doctrinal clarification. Numerous questions arose: What did the Bible teach about the Trinity? Was there one God in one person? Was there one God in three roles? Were there three Gods in three roles? Were the Father and Son the same or distinct? If Jesus was distinct from the Father, how should He be seen? Did Christ have one nature or two? Was He divine and human? If Jesus had two natures, was He half divine and half human? Or was He fully divine and fully human? What is more, why was it necessary to think accurately about the Trinity? Could a person be a Christian and be wrong concerning the Trinity? Could one believe in a Savior who was half divine and half human, and yet be saved?

In this dangerous hour, Tertullian stepped forward to defend the Godhead against the erroneous teachings of Monarchianism. He affirmed the clear biblical teaching that there is one God who exists eternally in three persons. Each person of the Trinity, he asserted, possesses all the divine attributes. Tertullian also upheld the truth that Jesus Christ is fully God *and* fully man. He stated these truths of Scripture in theologically precise terms, some of which were adopted by the Council of Chalcedon in AD 451 in its statements of doctrinal truths.

## THE AFRICAN FATHERS

In the third and fourth centuries, Africa became a fertile field for the progress of the church. The North African coast of the Mediterranean Sea witnessed significant advances in the development of Christian doctrine. Many of the greatest theologians of the early church lived and ministered in cities along this coast. It was there that the first center for Christian learning was established in Alexandria, Egypt. This institution was the School of Alexandria, where Christian doctrine was taught to new converts. In due time, Christian leaders were trained for the African church there. So unique was this school that its doctrine came to be known as Alexandrian theology. This school of thought combined fundamental Christian doctrines with Hellenistic reasoning.

Among the highly esteemed theologians who comprised the body of teachers known as the African Fathers were Clement of Alexandria (ca. 150–ca. 215), Tertullian of Carthage (ca. 160/170–ca. 215/220), Cyprian of Carthage (ca. 200–258), and Athanasius of Alexandria (ca. 298–373). In later years, even the greatest of all theologians of the early church, Augustine of Hippo, would arise from African soil.

Concerning the contribution of the African Fathers to the larger body of Christ, Thomas C. Oden comments:

> These African exegetes powerfully affected the dogmatic formulations of the orthodoxy of the East and the West. Dogmatic definitions [worked] off of textual interpretations hammered out chiefly in Africa, the Maghreb and the Nile Valley. [Later] definitions of Christology and the Trinity were profoundly shaped by definitions and concepts that were defined decades earlier in Africa by Tertullian, Cyprian, Athanasius, Augustine and Cyril. . . . The major battles with heresy were fought out in Africa before they were received ecumenically. Gnosticism, Arianism, Montanism, Marcionism and Manichaeism were all thoroughly argued as problems of biblical interpretation in Africa before these arguments reached clear definitions in the Rhone and Rhine and Orontes Valleys.[6]

This is to say, the African church became, for a time, the center of sound Christian teaching for the body of Christ. The African Fathers who ministered there were strategically used to articulate the truths of the Christian faith and to refute false teachings such as Neoplatonism, Montanism, Manichaeism, and Arianism. The importance of these men in the development of Christian theology would be difficult to overestimate.[7] The first of them to make significant contributions to the doctrines of grace was Tertullian of Carthage.

# TERTULLIAN OF CARTHAGE

Tertullian was a heroic champion of orthodoxy in Africa against every sort of heresy.[8] He is commonly regarded as the first great writer of the church in North Africa.[9] Also, he is known as "the father of Latin theology" because he was the first important Christian to write in Latin, the language of the western half of the Roman Empire.[10] As a result, Tertullian is seen as the founder of Western theology.[11] He is acclaimed as the father of orthodoxy in regard to the doctrines of the Trinity and the person of Jesus Christ.[12] In addition to his accomplishments as a theologian, he is considered the outstanding apologist of the West[13] and, along with Irenaeus, the major opponent of Gnosticism.[14] Through his efforts to establish Christian orthodoxy, Tertullian stamped his astute thinking and unique personality into the character of the Western church with a force few have equaled.[15]

Tertullian's full name was Quintus Septimius Florens Tertullianus.[16] Born in Carthage (in modern-day Tunisia), the foremost city of Roman Africa,[17] he was raised in a pagan home, likely that of a Roman centurion. As a young man, he received a solid education in Greek, Latin, and the classics. He had a fiery nature and a fighting spirit that drove him to throw himself into whatever he did.[18] Little more is known about his early years, except that he followed a lifestyle of willful sin and wanton pleasure.[19]

As a young adult, Tertullian was sent to Rome to study law, a vocation that made good use of his sharp mind and powers of analysis and persuasion. He soon became a proficient and noted public speaker. However, while in Rome, he became impressed by the unflinching courage of Christians in the face of persecution. Many believers were being thrown to the lions or burned publicly, yet without compromise or fear. Their bold witness had a profound effect on Tertullian, exposing his self-righteousness and bringing him under strong conviction.[20] Through the witness of suffering Christians, he was dramatically converted to Christ around the age of forty.[21]

Tertullian immediately rejected his licentious way of life[22] and began to follow Jesus Christ. He used his sharp intellect to absorb the Scriptures and quickly mastered the essentials of the Christian faith. He also began to defend the truth of God, soon becoming a fearless champion against Jews and heretics, especially Gnostics.[23] Returning to Carthage, he openly attacked the false teachings that he considered to be contradictions of the true gospel of grace.

In his latter years, in one of the great mysteries of church history, Tertullian joined a splinter movement known as Montanism. In the previous chapter, we saw that Irenaeus was motivated to join the fight against heresy when Eleutherus, the bishop of Rome, embraced this false teaching. Unlike Irenaeus, Tertullian was seduced by Montanism and joined the movement around AD 207.

The founder of this movement, Montanus, had been a pagan priest, but had converted to Christ in AD 155. Given to fanatical extremes, Montanus believed himself to be an appointed prophet of God and began declaring the imminent appearance of the New Jerusalem.[24] He also taught that the end of the age would be preceded by a new outpouring of the Holy Spirit. As a result, he urged believers to withdraw from the world for the sake of purity. The church must be ready for the coming of Christ, Montanus said, and that required living in seclusion from the world.

Apparently Tertullian's strict moral views influenced him to join the Montanists.[25] Also, Tertullian had grown impatient with the hypocrisy he saw in some quarters of the early church and particularly disliked the half-heartedness of church leaders. Additionally, the Montanists believed that their leaders were receiving new prophecies from the Holy Spirit, a view that appealed to Tertullian's enthusiastic nature. When he embraced Montanism, Tertullian became its most well-known adherent. However, toward the end of his days, Tertullian became disenchanted with Montanism and started another splinter group. This group, which became known as Tertullianism, existed for the next two centuries in Carthage.

Tertullian died toward the close of the first quarter of the third century, somewhat in obscurity. Despite falling prey to fallacies toward the end of his life, he was a pillar used by God.

# TERTULLIAN'S WRITINGS

From AD 196 to 212, Tertullian was the author of a long list of apologetical, theological, controversial, and ascetic works. Employing a writing style that has been described as "brilliant, masterful, and difficult," he devastated his opponents by undermining their reasoning.[26] As noted above, he was especially concerned to clarify the Trinity and the dual natures of Jesus Christ.[27] In these watershed areas, Tertullian made contributions that remain with the church to this day. He showed that the *Logos*—Jesus Christ—is the incarnate

God, equal with the Father yet distinct. In addition, he declared that the Holy Spirit is God, yet distinct from the *Logos* or the Father.[28] To describe the plurality of God, Tertullian was the first to use the Latin term *trinitas*, which we translate as "Trinity."[29]

Further, Tertullian appealed to his legal background and introduced two terms that would be critical in defining the Trinity: *person* and *substance*. The Godhead is comprised of three persons—Father, Son, and Holy Spirit—who possess one substance. By this formulation, Tertullian affirmed the unity of the Father, Son, and Holy Spirit without denying Their distinction.

Tertullian wrote some thirty works in all. The most noteworthy is *Apology*, which addresses the legal and moral absurdity of the persecution directed against Christians. He also wrote *Against Praxeas*, known for its affirmation that Jesus Christ has two natures joined in one person. Here he exposed the unscriptural implications of Modalism and formulated a doctrine of the Trinity. He also set the concepts of the Godhead in new language, much of which became normative. Other works include *To the Martyrs*, *Testimony of the Soul*, *Prescription of Heretics*, *The Soul*, and *Against Marcion*.

## TERTULLIAN'S THEOLOGY

Tertullian was a profound theological thinker, yet there were significant limitations in his doctrine. Louis Berkhof notes that "he sometimes uses language that savours of the synergistic theory of regeneration, that is, the theory that God and man work together in regeneration."[30] Moreover, William Cunningham critiques Tertullian in stating:

> He gives less prominence than any preceding writer to the peculiar principles of evangelical truth, and . . . teaches some things rather more explicitly opposed to them. . . . In regard to the offices and work of Christ, even about the atonement of Christ as the ground of a sinner's forgiveness, there are scarcely any clear, full, and satisfactory statements to be found in Tertullian's voluminous writings. He has asserted the power of man to do the will of God. . . . Although he has made statements on the subject of the justification of a sinner . . . he has also made others which are clearly opposed to it. He has asserted the doctrine of justification by works . . . he may thus be said to have laid the foundations of a mode of teaching—of a system of perverting

Scripture—which, in the hands of the Church of Rome, has contributed so fearfully to the destruction of men's souls. He taught
what may be called the common absurdities and extravagances of the
fathers, in regard to angels, demons, and the souls of men departed.
. . . He mentions and recommends—and he is the first Christian
writer who does so—prayers for the dead, and offerings to them on
the anniversaries of their deaths.[31]

Philip Schaff is less critical of Tertullian's theology. He writes, "Tertullian's theology revolves about the great Pauline antithesis of sin and grace,
and breaks the road to the Latin anthropology and soteriology afterwards
developed by his like-minded, but clearer, calmer, and more considerate
countryman, Augustine."[32] John McClintock and James Strong write that
Tertullian was "the pioneer of orthodox anthropology and soteriology, the
teacher of Cyprian, and forerunner of Augustine."[33]

Despite his controversial teachings, Tertullian touched on matters that
would later become known as the doctrines of grace. His writings evidence
an especially strong grasp of the effects of Adam's sin, a view that would
influence Western theology profoundly.[34] Tertullian emphasized that the
inclination to sin was "transmitted from Adam to successive generations."[35]
In fact, his thoughts "prepared the way for . . . [the] doctrine of the Fall and
Original Sin which came, through Augustine."[36] Berkhof writes: "Tertullian
clearly teach[es] that our sinful condition is the result of Adam's fall. . . . He
regarded original sin as a hereditary sinful taint or corruption."[37] In other
words, Tertullian's works reveal some expansion of understanding in the doctrines of sovereign grace.

**Doctrine in Focus:**
## DIVINE SOVEREIGNTY
Displaying his apologetic abilities, Tertullian argued that God is the sovereign Creator of this world, and that His creative work proves His divinity.
Addressing the Marcionite belief that the God of the Old Testament was a
different and lower being than the God of the New Testament, he states: "[T]
he Marcionites shamelessly turn up their nose and set about the demolition of
the Creator's works. 'A great work, indeed,' they say, 'and worthy of a god, is
this world.' Is then the Creator in no sense a god? Clearly he is a god. Consequently the world is not unworthy of a god. For God has made nothing which

is unworthy of Himself."[38] For Tertullian, the Christian God is the Creator, who brought all things into being by His sovereign will.

Tertullian asserted that God's will is supreme over the circumstances of life, over men, and over eternal destinies. He writes, "We proclaim that there is but one God, called by this name alone, from whom all things come and to whom the universe is subject."[39] By this statement, Tertullian affirmed that all power belongs to God, who determines all things.

**Doctrine in Focus:**

RADICAL DEPRAVITY

Tertullian possessed an especially penetrating view of man's sinfulness. It has been said that he taught that the human inclination to sin was "transmitted from Adam to successive generations of progeny."[40] In other words, he believed that the sin nature in man stems from Adam's fall.

Following the Genesis account, Tertullian declared that Adam was induced by Satan to disobey and rebel against God. When Adam impetuously chose sin over obedience to God, he came under God's wrath. Tertullian writes: "Whence (the origin) of delinquency, arose the first origin of judgment; hence, whence man was induced to offend, God began to be wroth. Whence (came) the first indignation in God, thence (came) His first patience; who, content at that time with malediction only, refrained in the devil's case from the instant infliction of punishment. Else what crime, before this guilt of impatience, is imputed to man? Innocent he was, and in intimate friendship with God, and the husbandman of paradise. But when once he succumbed to impatience, he quite ceased to be of sweet savour to God; he quite ceased to be able to endure things celestial."[41] Here Tertullian was quite specific about the change that came over Adam when he sinned.

But Adam's sin, Tertullian believed, brought not just his own condemnation, but the condemnation of every person throughout history. Since Adam was the representative of the human race, Tertullian states, "Man in the beginning was beguiled to transgress God's command, and on that account was given over to death, and brought it about that the whole race, thus infected from [Adam's] seed, became a sharer in and transmitter of his condemnation."[42] All of mankind is under judgment because of Adam's sin.

The sin nature that men inherit from Adam manifests itself in actual sins. Tertullian writes, "It becomes evident that sins, and the lusts of the flesh, and disbelief, and wrath, are accounted to the common nature of all men."[43]

Tertullian maintained that all unconverted men have lost the power to choose to do good. He writes: "The evil tree will never bear good fruit unless the good branch be grafted onto it, and the good tree will bear evil fruit unless it be cultivated. . . . Such is the power of Divine Grace, stronger than nature itself, that it can even make subject to itself the faculty of free will which is generally said to be master of itself."[44] This is to say, an evil nature can produce only evil choices. Tertullian understood the biblical teaching that all people are born guilty before God and suffer the radical depravity of human nature.

Nevertheless, Tertullian, like many Fathers before him, often contradicted himself by speaking both for and against man's free will. With this fact in mind, John Hannah notes that "in the matter of inability and freedom, Tertullian was inconsistent. He waffled between the two views, first asserting one and then the other without seeking to explain how both might be valid."[45]

On the one hand, Tertullian asserts that the sovereign grace of God has sway over every aspect of man in salvation: "This will be the power of the grace of God—more potent indeed than nature—exercising its sway over the faculty that underlies itself within us: even the freedom of our will."[46] Elsewhere he writes with an opposing language: "I find, then, that man was constituted free by God. He was master of his own will and power. . . . For a law would not be imposed upon one who did not have it in his power to render that obedience which is due to law. Nor again, would the penalty of death be threatened against sin, if a contempt of the law were impossible to man in the liberty of his will. . . . Man is free, with a will either for obedience or resistance."[47] Such remarks are incongruous and could point to the erroneous attacks that Tertullian and other Fathers were facing in their day. Hannah cites John Calvin as suggesting that the "early church leaders stressed freedom 'because a frank confession of man's powerlessness would have brought upon them the jeers of the philosophers with whom they were in conflict,' and because 'they wished to avoid giving fresh occasion for slothfulness to the flesh already indifferent toward good.'"[48] Instead, the Fathers prioritized the moral imperatives of the Bible, stressing man's personal responsibility to God.

**Doctrine in Focus:**
DEFINITE ATONEMENT

As a great Trinitarian mind, Tertullian understood that there is perfect unity within the Godhead. He seems to have grasped that this indivisible solidarity of the Father, the Son, and the Spirit includes a unity of mission in Their saving purposes. Expositing Exodus 32:32, which tells of Moses' offer to sacrifice himself for the Israelites, Tertullian saw a parallel to Christ's sacrifice of Himself on the cross. He writes, "Greatly to be pitied are you, as well as the Israelites, for not realizing that in the person of Moses there is a prefiguring of Christ, who intercedes with the Father, and offers his own soul for the saving of the people."[49] Tertullian may have believed that just as Moses offered to die for the people of Israel, Christ died for a specific group of people.

Tertullian likewise asserted that Christ died for the church, implying a definite atonement for elect sinners. As Tertullian put it, Christ died in His *physical* body for His *spiritual* body, the church. He writes: "[W]e are being reconciled in His body by means of death: and evidently His death took place in that body in which by means of the flesh it was possible for Him to die— not by means of the church, though no doubt for the sake of the church."[50] The intent of the cross was for the church. Later theologians would clarify that the intent of the atonement defines its extent.

**Doctrine in Focus:**

## IRRESISTIBLE CALL

Tertullian believed that if anyone is to believe in Christ, God must overcome his resistance to the gospel. Were it not for the irresistible call of God, no sinner would be able to respond to the free offer of the gospel in Jesus Christ, nor would he even want to. Tertullian writes: "For, who can know truth without the help of God? Who can know God without Christ? Who has ever discovered Christ without the Holy Spirit? And who has ever received the Holy Spirit without the gift of faith?"[51] Saving faith is the gift of God that must be given before sinners can believe in Christ.

Tertullian held that salvation is entirely a divine work. Just as the universe contributed nothing to its creation, man contributes nothing to his salvation. When commenting on Ephesians 2:10, he states: "*We are*, he says, *His own workmanship, created in Christ.* To make is one thing, to create is another. But he has assigned both these acts to one alone. Now man is the Creator's workmanship: and so the same God who made us has also created us in Christ. In respect of our substance, of what we are in ourselves, He made us, but in respect of grace He has created us."[52] Thus, Tertullian maintained that God, who spoke everything into existence out of nothing, does the same in salvation. Man is created in Christ as a divine work of grace.

Only by the working of sovereign grace can spiritually dead sinners become Christians. Tertullian writes: "Christians are made, not born!"[53] God must regenerate sinners if they are to possess salvation. But while asserting that men are not born in a right relationship with God, Tertullian declared they must be born anew in Christ. He writes: "Every soul is considered as having been born in Adam until it has been reborn in Christ. Moreover, it is unclean until it has been thus regenerated."[54] The unconverted heart remains corrupt until it is born again from above. Just as we have no say in our natural birth, we have no say in our spiritual birth.

**Doctrine in Focus:**
PRESERVING GRACE

Tertullian attested that the mark of the true Christian is perseverance in the faith. He states, "No one is wise, no one is faithful, no one worthy of honour unless he is a Christian, and no one is a Christian unless he perseveres to the end."[55] Tertullian did not explicitly state here that perseverance depends on divine preservation, but he grasped the significance of perseverance in the battle against sin and temptation. Later theologians would show that no such perseverance is possible apart from divine grace.

Tertullian certainly understood that God guards His people. Commenting on Jesus' healing of a demon-possessed man in Mark 5, Tertullian made the point that the demons went out of the man and into the herd of swine only because Jesus allowed it. The demons had no inherent power over the swine, and they have even less over God's sheep: "Nor would the devil's legion have had power over the herd of swine unless they had got it from God; so far are they from having power over the sheep of God."[56] In other words, God protects His chosen people against the attacks of the Evil One.

Tertullian affirmed that the Lord knows those who are His. Based on His intimate knowledge of the human heart, He someday will separate the wheat from the chaff, gathering the wheat into His barn but burning the chaff (Matt. 3:12). He states: "You are human, and so you know other people only from the outside. You think as you see, and you see only what your eyes let you see. But 'the eyes of the Lord are lofty.' 'Man looks on the outward appearance, God looks on the heart.' So 'the Lord knows them that are His' and the roots of the plant which He has not planted. He shows the last to be first, He carries a fan in His hand to purge His floor."[57] God is not deceived, because He has sovereignly decreed. Therefore, the one God knows remains forever.

**Doctrine in Focus:**

DIVINE REPROBATION

Tertullian affirmed the doctrine of reprobation, the teaching that God has passed over the nonelect and allowed them to remain in their sins. Discussing his opposition to various heresies, he writes: "These were the inventions of 'spiritual wickedness against which is our wrestling,' brethren, inventions we had to look into, necessary to faith, so that 'they which are elect may be made manifest' and the reprobate be discovered."[58] By juxtaposing the elect and the reprobate in this way, Tertullian showed that he understood that the doctrine of election necessitates the opposite truth, the doctrine of reprobation.

# STANDING ON SCRIPTURE ALONE

What must we learn from this Early Father? We can learn precisely what Tertullian forgot, namely, that the written Word of God is the sole standard by which God's people live. The Bible asserts that the infallible teachings of Christ, the prophets, and the apostles recorded in Scripture are the only true foundation for the church (Eph. 2:20). Further, Christ presents Himself as building His church on the sure foundation of divine revelation, a work that will continue until His return (Matt. 16:18). This foundational truth of biblical authority was affirmed during the sixteenth-century Protestant Reformation in the historic slogan *sola Scriptura*.

With any building, there is only one foundation. This undergirding base is laid only once, at the very beginning of the building's construction. Employing this building metaphor, Scripture teaches that divine revelation was given once at the outset of the church's construction. This was the unique role of the prophets and apostles. Now that the canon of Scripture is closed, believers are to "contend for the faith that was once for all delivered to the saints" (Jude 3). This is a duty that Tertullian fulfilled well for most of his adult ministry. But sadly, this noted Father neglected the unique role of Scripture at the end of his ministry.

Let us give ourselves to the written Word of God, not to ecstatic experiences, dreams, visions, or supposed utterances. Let us be firmly grounded in the inerrant and infallible Word of the living God. Only by devoting ourselves to the Scriptures will we be able to earnestly contend for the faith God has given to His church.

Notes

1  Tertullian, *On the Soul*, 1, in *Tertullian: Apologetical Works, and Minucius Felix: Octavius*, trans. Rudolph Arbesmann, Sister Emily Daly, and Edwin Quin (New York: Fathers of the Church, Inc., 1950), 180.

2  Samuel J. Mikolaski, "Monarchianism," in *New International Dictionary of the Christian Church*, gen. ed. J. D. Douglas (Grand Rapids: Zondervan, 1978), 670.

3  Robert A. Baker, *A Summary of Christian History*, rev. John M. Landers (Nashville: Broadman & Holman, 1994), 35.

4  John Hannah, *Our Legacy: The History of Christian Doctrine* (Colorado Springs, Colo.: NavPress, 2001), 76.

5  Baker, *A Summary of Christian History*, 36.

6  Thomas C. Oden, *How Africa Shaped the Christian Mind* (Downers Grove, Ill.: InterVarsity, 2007), 46–47.

7  To this point, Oden adds: "The Christians to the south of the Mediterranean were teaching the Christians to the north. Africans were informing and instructing and educating the very best of Syriac, Cappadocian and Greco-Roman teachers. . . . In Christian history . . . the flow of intellectual leadership demonstrably moved largely from Africa to Europe—south to north. . . . How profound had been the African influence on every subsequent phase of scriptural interpretation. . . . We learned to trace the path back from Antioch, Jerusalem, Constantinople, Nisibis and Rome to its origins in Africa. This intellectual leadership moved by land from the Nile Valley to the deserts of the Negev, the hills of Judea, and north through Syria and Cappadocia, and by sea to all points north. The core ideas of the monastic movements moved from the Nitrian desert and from the Pharaonic-speaking central Nile Valley north to the lauras and monastic communities of the Jordan, and all the way to the Tigris and Halys Rivers during the fourth and fifth centuries. . . . The Christian leaders in Africa figured out how best to read the law and prophets meaningfully, to think philosophically, and to teach the ecumenical rule of triune faith cohesively, long before these patterns became normative elsewhere." Oden, *How Africa Shaped the Christian Mind*, 28–30.

8  Justo L. González, *The Story of Christianity, Vol. 1: The Early Church to the Dawn of the Reformation* (Peabody, Mass.: Prince, 2004), 77.

9  M. A. Smith, *From Christ to Constantine* (Downers Grove, Ill.: InterVarsity, 1971), 100.

10  Tony Lane, *A Concise History of Christian Thought* (Grand Rapids: Baker Academic, 2006), 15.

11  González, *The Story of Christianity, Vol. 1*, 77.

12  Roger E. Olson, *The Story of Christian Theology: Twenty Centuries of Tradition and Reform* (Downers Grove, Ill.: InterVarsity, 1999), 93.

13  Earle E. Cairns, *Christianity Through the Centuries: A History of the Christian Church*, 3rd Ed. (1954; repr., Grand Rapids: Zondervan, 1996), 106.

14  Lane, *A Concise History of Christian Thought*, 16.

15  Jonathan Hill, *The History of Christian Thought* (Downers Grove, Ill.: InterVarsity, 2003), 32.

16  Hill, *The History of Christian Thought*, 32.

17  Eric Osborn, "Tertullian," in *The First Christian Theologians: An Introduction to Theology in the Early Church*, ed. G. R. Evans (Malden, Mass.: Blackwell, 2004), 143.

18  Cairns, *Christianity Through the Centuries*, 106.

19  Hill, *The History of Christian Thought*, 33.

20 Hill, *The History of Christian Thought*, 33.

21 "Tertullian," in *Cyclopedia of Biblical, Theological, and Ecclesiastical Literature, Vol. X*, eds. John McClintock and James Strong (1867–1887; repr., Grand Rapids: Baker, 1981), 288.

22 R. C. Kroeger and C. C. Kroeger, "Tertullian," in *Evangelical Dictionary of Theology*, 2nd Ed., ed. Walter A. Elwell (Grand Rapids: Baker, 2001), 1176.

23 Kroeger and Kroeger, "Tertullian," in *Evangelical Dictionary of Theology*, 1176.

24 H. D. McDonald, "Montanism," in *New International Dictionary of the Christian Church*, 674.

25 Everett Ferguson, "Tertullian," in *Introduction to the History of Christianity*, ed. Tim Dowley (Minneapolis: Fortress, 2002), 112.

26 "Tertullian," in *The Oxford Dictionary of the Christian Church*, ed. E. A. Livingstone (1957; repr., Oxford: Oxford University Press, 1997), 1592.

27 Kroeger and Kroeger, "Tertullian," in *Evangelical Dictionary of Theology*, 1176.

28 Tertullian, *Against Praxeas*, 2, in *Tertullian's Treatise Against Praxeas*, trans. Ernest Evans (London: Society for Promoting Christian Knowledge, 1948), 132.

29 Hannah, *Our Legacy*, 78.

30 Louis Berkhof, *The History of Christian Doctrines* (1937; repr., Edinburgh: Banner of Truth, 2002), 130.

31 William Cunningham, *Historical Theology: A Review of the Principal Doctrinal Discussions in the Christian Church Since the Apostolic Age, Vol. 1* (Edinburgh: Banner of Truth, 1960), 160.

32 Philip Schaff, *History of the Christian Church, Vol. II: Ante-Nicene Christianity: From the Death of John the Apostle to Constantine the Great, A.D. 100–325* (1910; repr., Grand Rapids: Eerdmans, 1980), 824.

33 "Tertullian," in *Cyclopedia of Biblical, Theological, and Ecclesiastical Literature, Vol. X*, 289.

34 Kroeger and Kroeger, "Tertullian," in *Evangelical Dictionary of Theology*, 1176.

35 Kroeger and Kroeger, "Tertullian," in *Evangelical Dictionary of Theology*, 1176.

36 "Tertullian," in *The Oxford Dictionary of the Christian Church*, 1352.

37 Louis Berkhof, *Systematic Theology* (Grand Rapids: Eerdmans, 1996), 237, 244.

38 Tertullian, *Against Marcion*, I.13, in *Tertullian: Adversus Marcionem*, trans. Ernest Evans (Oxford: Clarendon Press, 1972), 33–35.

39 Tertullian, *Testimony of the Soul*, 2, in *Tertullian: Apologetical Works, and Minucius Felix: Octavius*, 133.

40 Kroeger and Kroeger, "Tertullian," in *Evangelical Dictionary of Theology*, 1176.

41 Tertullian, *Of Patience*, chap. 5, in *Ante-Nicene Fathers, Vol. III: Latin Christianity: Its Founder, Tertullian. I. Apologetic; I. Anti-Marcion; III. Ethical*, eds. Philip Schaff and Henry Wace (1864; repr., Grand Rapids: Eerdmans, 1971), 710.

42 Tertullian, *Testimony of the Soul*, Chap. 3, in *On the Testimony of the Soul and on the "Prescription" of Heretics*, ed. T. Herbert Bindley (London: Society for Promoting Christian Knowledge, 1914), 21-22.

43 Tertullian, *Against Marcion*, V.17, in *Tertullian: Adversus Marcionem*, 619.

44 Tertullian, *On the Soul*, 21, in *Tertullian: Apologetical Works, and Minucius Felix: Octavius*, 229.

45 Hannah, *Our Legacy*, 208.

46 Tertullian, *A Treatise on the Soul*, chap. 21, in *Ante-Nicene Fathers, Vol. III*, 202.

47 Tertullian, *Against Marcion*, chap. 5, in *Ante-Nicene Fathers, Vol. III*, 301.

48 Hannah, *Our Legacy*, 209–210 (citing John Calvin, *The Institutes of the Christian Religion*, II.2.4).

49 Tertullian, *Against Marcion*, II.26, in *Tertullian: Adversus Marcionem*, 159.

50 Tertullian, *Against Marcion*, V.19, in *Tertullian: Adversus Marcionem*, 633.

51 Tertullian, *On the Soul*, 1, in *Tertullian: Apologetical Works, and Minucius Felix: Octavius*, 180.

52 Tertullian, *Against Marcion*, V.17, in *Tertullian: Adversus Marcionem*, 619.

53 Tertullian, *Apology*, 18, in *Tertullian: Apologetical Works, and Minucius Felix: Octavius*, 54.

54 Tertullian, *On the Soul*, 40, in *Tertullian: Apologetical Works, and Minucius Felix: Octavius*, 271.

55 Tertullian, *Prescriptions Against Heretics*, 3, in *Early Latin Theology: Selections from Tertullian, Cyprian, Ambrose, and Jerome*, ed. and trans. S. L. Greenslade (Louisville: Westminster, 1956), 32.

56 Tertullian, *De Fuga in Persecutione*, sec. 2, in *Ante-Nicene Fathers, Vol. IV: Tertullian, Part Fourth; Minucius Felix; Commodian; Origen, Parts First and Second*, eds. Philip Schaff and Henry Wace (1864; repr., Grand Rapids: Eerdmans, 1971), 117.

57 Tertullian, *Prescriptions Against Heretics*, 3, in *Early Latin Theology*, 32–33.

58 Tertullian, *Prescriptions Against Heretics*, 39, in *Early Latin Theology*, 59.

# CHAPTER SIX
## STUDY QUESTIONS

1. Describe the heresy of Monarchianism. What were its forms? How was this heresy contrary to the Christian doctrine of the Trinity? What Scriptures would you appeal to in order to establish your belief?

2. How important is the doctrine of the Trinity to the Christian faith? Why does the gospel depend on this truth concerning the Godhead? Why is the deity of Christ essential to salvation?

3. What important place did Tertullian fulfill in the African church? What training did he receive before entering the ministry? How did this prepare him for future service in articulating theological truths?

4. Detail Tertullian's relationship to Montanism. Why was he susceptible to such a theological novelty? How can you ensure that such a departure will not occur in your life?

5. Compare the writings of Tertullian with those of earlier Fathers. What were the strengths of his theological writings? What unique contributions did Tertullian make to theology?

6. What does it mean that Tertullian is said to have held to a synergistic regeneration? Citing references, explain how Scripture teaches either a monergistic regeneration or synergistic regeneration.

7. How did Tertullian seemingly contradict himself as he spoke to both the depravity and free will of man? How would you explain this tension? Is there really such a thing as free will in man?

8. Define the doctrine of reprobation. What was Tertullian's view of this truth? How does this biblical truth relate to sovereign election?

*B*elieve me, good men cannot leave the Church. The wind does not carry off the grain, the storm does not bring down the tree with strong roots. It is the empty husks that are tossed away by the tempest, the feeble trees that are thrown down by the hurricane. And it is such men that John the Apostle upbraids and smites when he says: "They went out from us, but they were not of us; for if they had been of us, they would have continued with us." . . . In this way the faithful are approved and the faithless detected. Here and now, even before the Day of Judgment, the souls of the just and the unjust are parted and the chaff is separated from the wheat.[1]

–Cyprian of Carthage

# MASTER OF RHETORIC

## AFRICAN FATHER:
## CYPRIAN OF CARTHAGE

With the dawning of the third century, North Africa was becoming a strategic theater for the advancement of the gospel of Jesus Christ. The church south of the Mediterranean Sea was teaching believers to the north, instructing Antioch, Jerusalem, and even Rome. Out of Africa came the first extensive exegesis of the New Testament, a body of work that inevitably shaped even the Cappadocian Fathers—Basil the Great, Gregory of Nazianzus, and Gregory of Nyssa. The African influence on the equipping of church leaders for the proper interpretation of Scripture cannot be overstated.

The African Fathers took the lead in interpreting the Bible in a literal or plain fashion.[2] With this hermeneutic, men such as Tertullian, Cyprian, Athanasius, Augustine, and Cyril carefully articulated Trinitarian and christological theology. At the same time, African leaders confronted and denounced the major heresies—Gnosticism, Arianism, Montanism, Marcionism, and Manichaeism.

From the early ecclesiastical debates in the North African city of Carthage, there arose the basic pattern that future ecumenical councils would follow. A century prior to the First Council of Nicaea (325)—generally regarded as the first ecumenical council—African Fathers were defining, documenting, and defending Christian orthodoxy as they convened together. Moreover, advanced teaching skills, involving rhetorical, exegetical, and polemical devices, were first honed in Africa. Also, it was there that the full canon of Scripture first became normative. The importance of the African church at this early stage was critical.

127

In this time and place, God raised up a man named Cyprian of Carthage, who became a gifted leader and teacher of the Scriptures. He was to be instrumental in the advancement of early Christianity. What is more, Cyprian taught the doctrines of grace with more clarity than any man since the apostles. He was one of the first thinkers to connect the absolute sovereignty of God with the way in which salvation is applied to spiritually dead sinners. In so doing, he was one of the first to promote the tenets of monergistic regeneration. So important was Cyprian in the history of the African church and Western Christianity that he was quoted by John Calvin more than any other Church Father before Augustine.

With the influence of Gnosticism declining in his day, Cyprian was able to turn his attention to the subject of the new birth, discerning the connection between original sin and the human will. He made many definitive statements regarding this pivotal aspect of the doctrines of grace.

# CYPRIAN OF CARTHAGE

Cyprian (ca. 200–258) is regarded as the greatest bishop of the third century.[3] But this African Father made his greatest mark as a theological and biblical scholar and writer.[4] His works were widely circulated, both in antiquity and in the Middle Ages.[5] Augustine acclaimed Cyprian as "the most lauded commentator on the divine declarations,"[6] "that loveliest of teachers,"[7] "so memorable a teacher of the word of truth,"[8] and "the most luminous doctor."[9] In addition, Augustine referred to Cyprian as one who "preached . . . the true grace of God as it should be preached, that is, the grace which no human merits precede,"[10] and he called Cyprian, along with Ambrose, the "most excellent commentators on the words of God."[11] Martin Luther said, "I have a high regard for St. Cyprian's person and faith,"[12] hailing him as among the most outstanding Fathers[13] and greatest theologians.[14]

Born in the North African city of Carthage, Cyprian was raised in an affluent pagan home. His father was one of the principal senators in the Roman administration in Carthage,[15] a position that enabled Cyprian to be educated in the best schools of the day.[16] This education included instruction in the Greek and Roman classics, rhetoric, and law.[17] After completing his studies, he became a professor of rhetoric,[18] an orator,[19] and a lawyer.[20] With these accomplishments, he took his place in the ranks of North African Roman society[21] and the rich upper class.[22]

But despite his worldly successes, Cyprian grew disenchanted with the vanity, corruption, and immorality of the world around him.[23] A spiritual crisis was brewing in his heart. As he grew increasingly aware of evil, Cyprian was left with a confused sense that he was close to the end of the age.[24] Disoriented and disturbed, he searched for relief, but found none. He was experiencing that void in the human heart that only God can fill.

## CONVERSION TO CHRIST

At the age of approximately forty-six, in 246, Cyprian came in contact with a Carthaginian elder named Caecilius. This mature believer presented the gospel to Cyprian, who put his trust in Jesus Christ. He found peace immediately. Of this conversion, Cyprian wrote:

> I myself was held in bonds by the innumerable errors of my previous life, from which I did not believe that I could by possibility be delivered, so I was disposed to acquiesce in my clinging vices; and because I despaired of better things, I used to indulge my sins as if they were actually parts of me, and indigenous to me. But after that, by the help of the water of new birth, the stain of former years had been washed away, and a light from above, serene and pure, had been infused into my reconciled heart,—after that, by the agency of the Spirit breathed from heaven, a second birth had restored me to a new man;—then, in a wondrous manner, doubtful things at once began to assure themselves to me, hidden things to be revealed, dark things to be enlightened, what before had seemed difficult began to suggest a means of accomplishment, what had been thought impossible, to be capable of being achieved; so that I was enabled to acknowledge that what previously, being born of the flesh, had been living in the practice of sins, was of the earth earthly, but had now begun to be of God, and was animated by the Spirit of holiness.[25]

Upon his conversion, Cyprian acknowledged that every blessing is from God and believers should respond to Him in gratitude and faithfulness: "Our power is of God, I say, all of it is of God. From Him we have life; from Him we have prosperity. . . . But let fear be the guardian of innocence, so that the Lord, who of His mercy has flowed into our hearts with the silent approach of celestial tenderness, may be kept in the guest-chamber of a heart that gives delight by its righteous action, lest the security we have received beget carelessness, and the old enemy creep upon us anew."[26]

Cyprian immediately abandoned his lifestyle of worldly pleasures, gave his entire fortune to the poor,[27] and took a vow of chastity. It was written of him: "His house was open to every comer. No widow returned from him with an empty lap; no blind man was unguided by him as a companion; none faltering in step was unsupported by him for a staff; none stripped of help by the hand of the mighty was not protected by him as a defender. Such things ought they to do, he was accustomed to say, who desire to please God. And thus running through the examples of all good men, by always imitating those who were better than others he made himself also worthy of imitation."[28] By his works, Cyprian showed that he was radically converted and sold out for Christ.

In addition, Cyprian devoted himself to the study and practice of Christianity.[29] He laid aside the reading of all literature other than the Bible and distinctly Christian books.[30] He studied the best theologians, including his favorite, Tertullian, who also lived in Carthage and whom Cyprian called "the master."[31] Jerome, writing in the fourth century, said, "Cyprian was accustomed never to pass a day without reading Tertullian."[32] His greatest desire had become to know God and learn His Word.

## Appointed Bishop of Carthage

Within two years of his conversion, Cyprian rose through the ranks of the church. He was inducted into the presbytery and then considered for the bishopric of Carthage.[33] With the unanimous approbation of the bishops of the province, he was elevated to this position, the most important church office in the Roman province of Africa.[34] This post gave him leadership over the surrounding churches. He was to serve as bishop for ten years, from 248 until his death in 258.

But as soon as Cyprian was appointed bishop, he faced unexpected opposition from some of the senior clergy at Carthage. Among them were noted leaders such as Fortunatus and Donatus, who were jealous of this upstart who had been appointed bishop over them.

Worse trouble came a year later in the form of persecution under the Roman Emperor Decius, the first empire-wide attack on Christians since the beginning of the church. On January 3, 250, the emperor performed the annual sacrifice to Jupiter and the Roman gods in the Capitoline temple in

Rome. He demanded that every citizen offer similar sacrifices throughout the empire. If anyone disobeyed, he was to be considered guilty of treason and of offending the gods. At first, the penalty was the confiscation of property, but then it was escalated to the loss of life.

The Decian persecution proved to be the most intense trial the church had ever faced. Many professing Christians buckled and obeyed the emperor's demands. They were known as "the lapsed." Christians who stood fast were known as "the confessors." Thousands of believers lapsed, but most of them still considered themselves genuine followers of Jesus Christ.

## FORCED INTO EXILE

Cyprian refused to obey the imperial edict. However, to save his life, he fled from Carthage. Some scorned his flight from persecution as an act of cowardice, especially since many Christians stayed and suffered. But he kept up an active correspondence with the church as many of his flock faced martyrdom. In his many letters, Cyprian also counseled other bishops who were facing difficult matters.

While Cyprian was away from Carthage, many of the lapsed confessed Christ again and sought restoration to the church. Although Cyprian himself had fled, he opposed easy reconciliation. He believed lapsed believers seeking to return should do penance to prove their faith, a period of sincere sorrowing that should end with their appearance before the congregation in sackcloth and ashes. However, other church leaders allowed many of the lapsed to return with no such penance.

When Cyprian returned to Carthage in 251, he called a council in which he played the lead role in resolving the controversy over the lapsed. The council agreed to his proposal that those who had sacrificed to the gods could be received back into the church only after a period of time in which their repentance could be proven to be real.

In the final years of his life and his service as bishop, Cyprian held other synods at Carthage to settle disputes and doctrinal matters. Throughout the Roman Empire, he became known as a major teacher of Christianity.

In the summer of 257, the Emperor Valerian initiated a new wave of violent persecution against the church.[35] His decree demanded allegiance to Roman gods and forbade Christians from assembling for worship. As the bishop of Carthage, Cyprian was summoned before the Roman authorities and told that he must practice the idolatrous pagan ceremonies. He responded that he could not worship anyone or anything except the one true God. Further, when Cyprian was asked for the names of his presbyters, he refused to give them. So on August 30, 257, Cyprian was banished into exile.

The next summer, Cyprian was allowed to return to Carthage to resume his ministry. But on September 14, 258, the proconsul, Galerius Maximus, summoned Cyprian to appear before him.[36] During the interrogation, Cyprian was ordered to sacrifice to the pagan gods and deny Christ. When Cyprian once again refused to deny his Lord, he was immediately condemned to death by beheading.

# CYPRIAN'S WRITINGS

Cyprian's writings have been recognized as among the best Christian literature of the time.[37] His theological works enjoyed great popularity from the time of their publication[38] and left a profound influence on the church.[39] Though he lacked the brilliance of his mentor, Tertullian, his writings nevertheless showed "sober judgment" and "pastoral instincts."[40] For the most part, his works were written in response to church problems. Two of his larger works—*Concerning the Lapsed* and *On the Unity of the Church*—were highly significant in the life of the early church.

## CONCERNING THE LAPSED
This letter deals with the heated controversy over those who denied Christ during the Decian persecution. After the persecution, were defectors to be received back into the church? If so, how? In *Concerning the Lapsed* (*De lapsis*) (251), Cyprian praised those who had remained in Carthage during the persecution and affirmed those who had gone to prison for their strong witness to Christ. He then stated that the lapsed should be received back, but only after a period of penance. This little book is one of his most passionate and polemical works.[41]

## ON THE UNITY OF THE CHURCH
The views Cyprian expressed in *Concerning the Lapsed* proved unacceptable to many Christians in Carthage. A deacon named Novatus defiantly started a rival church that offered easy admittance for those who had lapsed. They subsequently elected their own bishop, Fortunatus, as a rival to Cyprian. Deeply disturbed, Cyprian responded by writing *On the Unity of the Church* (251).

This was his landmark work. The church, he said, is a divine institution, the bride of Christ, and there can be only one bride. Only in the church is salvation found, while outside is darkness and confusion. Since the church is the exclusive home of the truth, divisions are the work of Satan. The preservation of the church's unity is found in its leaders, who speak with one voice on matters of salvation. Those who refuse this authority, Cyprian argued, call their salvation into question.

## CYPRIAN'S THEOLOGY

Cyprian possessed a simple, literal understanding of the Bible.[42] William Cunningham notes that Cyprian took his views of divine truth "somewhat more purely and simply" from the Scriptures than many of the early writers, with less tendency than many to "mix up scriptural truth with philosophical speculations."[43] His writings, W. G. T. Shedd asserts, exhibit a tendency toward "the doctrine of an original sinfulness, and a monergistic renovation of the human soul."[44] As noted above, the waning of Gnosticism at this time allowed theologians to address other theological issues, such as the effects of sin on the human will. Louis Berkhof writes, "In the writings of Cyprian there is an increasing tendency towards the doctrine of the original sinfulness of man, and of a monergistic renewal of the soul."[45] In short, Cyprian was one of the first to emphasize the absolute sovereignty of grace over the spiritually dead will and, along with others of the African Fathers, served as a "gradual preparation for the Augustinian view of sin and grace."[46]

**Doctrine in Focus:**
DIVINE SOVEREIGNTY
Cyprian affirmed the sovereignty of God over every aspect of life. He writes: "'Thy will be done in heaven as it is on earth,' not that God may do what He wishes, but that we may be able to do what God wishes. For who stands in the way of God's doing what He wishes? But since the devil stands in the way of our mind and action obeying God in all things, we pray and petition that God's will be done in us. That it may be done in us, there is need of God's will, that is, of His help and protection, because no one is strong in his own strength, but is safe by the indulgence and mercy of God."[47] Here Cyprian maintained that God is supreme over the will of man and Satan in all things.

**Doctrine in Focus:**

## RADICAL DEPRAVITY

Cyprian clearly taught the radical corruption of the human soul. Augustine observed that Cyprian confessed original sin.[48] Calvin later repeated Cyprian's words, "Let us glory in nothing, because nothing is ours,"[49] then paraphrased Cyprian with these words: "If there is nothing good in us; if man, from the crown of the head to the sole of the foot, is wholly sin; if it is not even lawful to try how far the power of the will extends,—how can it be lawful to share the merit of a good work between God and man?"[50] This is a summary of Cyprian's position on radical depravity.

In accord with Scripture, Cyprian taught that as a result of Adam's violation of God's command, the entire human race is in a state of sin. When the first man sinned, all mankind was subjected to divine judgment and suffered death. Cyprian writes: "Let us consider the judgment of God which, at the very beginning of the world and of the human race, was passed upon Adam who was unmindful of God's command and a transgressor of the law that was imposed. Then we shall know how patient we ought to be in this world, we who are born under the condition that we must struggle here under trials and conflicts. . . . We are all bound and confined by the bond of this sentence."[51] God's curse, he wrote, is upon all people.

Referencing Job 14:5 and Psalm 51:5, Cyprian affirmed again that total depravity extends to all men. He states, "No one is without filth and without sin."[52] Commenting on 1 John 1:8, he writes, "No one can be without sin, and whoever says that he is without fault is either proud or foolish."[53] Likewise, he teaches that there is none "who cannot be without some wound of conscience."[54] He adds, "Let no one so flatter himself on his pure and immaculate heart that relying on his innocence he thinks that medicine should not be applied to his wounds."[55] Finally, Cyprian writes, "Daily there cannot be lacking some sinning in the sight of God."[56] By these statements, Cyprian forcefully espoused the radical depravity of all men.

Cyprian reasoned that the mere fact that men are told to confess their sins daily is indisputable proof that all sin daily. Referencing 1 John 1:8–9, Cyprian writes: "Moreover, how necessarily, how providently and salutarily, are we admonished that we are sinners, who are compelled to plead for our sins, so that, while indulgence is sought from God, the soul is recalled to a consciousness of its guilt! Lest anyone be pleased with himself, as if innocent, and by exalting himself perish the more, he is instructed and taught that he sins daily, since he is ordered to pray daily for his sins."[57] If we are compelled by Scripture to continually confess, Cyprian argued, it is because we all continually sin.

Cyprian believed that even infants are infected with original sin. He writes: "Even in the case of those who have sinned most grievously, offending many times in their past lives against God, they are granted remission of their sins, subsequently, on becoming believers. No one is denied access to baptism and grace. How much less reason is there then for denying it to an infant who, being newly born, can have committed no sins. The only thing that he has done is that, being born after the flesh as a descendent of Adam, he has contracted from that first birth the ancient contagion of death."[58] Cyprian saw that sinning does not make us sinners, but that we sin because we are sinners. As a result, all people are pulled downward into the pollution of sin by their depraved nature.

**Doctrine in Focus:**
SOVEREIGN ELECTION

Cyprian also asserted the doctrine of sovereign election in the salvation of sinners. He declared that believers are "elected to hope, consecrated to faith, destined to salvation, sons of God, brethren of Christ, associates of the Holy Spirit, owing nothing any longer to the flesh."[59] Election, he maintained, is the root of every spiritual blessing.

So well known was Cyprian's position on this subject that Augustine writes that Cyprian teaches "predestination . . . as preached by the apostles."[60] He adds: "This is what Cyprian saw with complete faith and declared with full confidence, and by it he certainly proclaimed predestination to be most certain."[61]

Quoting the same words of Cyprian cited by Calvin above, Augustine writes: "For, if 'we must boast over nothing, we have nothing of our own,' we must not, then, boast over our obedience either, no matter how persevering it is, nor should we call it ours as if it were not given to us from above. And it is, therefore, a gift of God which He foreknew, as every Christian admits, that He would give to those He called by that calling of which it was said, *The gifts and calling of God are irrevocable* (Rom. 11:29). This is, then, the predestination which we preach with faith and humility."[62] Augustine agreed with Cyprian that sovereign election crushes man's pride and ultimately elevates praise to God.

Augustine also declared that Cyprian "taught without any ambiguity the true grace of God, that is, the grace which is not given in accord with our merits. And since God foreknew that He would give this grace, these words of Cyprian undoubtedly preach predestination."[63] Divine grace, given apart from any merit of men, clearly points to election, as both Cyprian and Augustine understood.

**Doctrine in Focus:**

IRRESISTIBLE CALL

Cyprian further taught that God irresistibly calls His elect to Himself. The new birth comes by divine initiative. Commenting on the Lord's Prayer, in which Jesus instructed His disciples to address God as "Father," Cyprian writes: "A new man, reborn and restored to his God by his grace says in the first place, 'Father,' because he has now begun to be a son . . . 'as many as received Him, He gave to them the power to become the sons of God, to those who believe in His name.'"[64] God's work of regeneration is a spiritual adoption that He instigates.

Augustine wrote that Cyprian taught that faith is God's gift. He summarizes Cyprian's teaching as follows: "Though we say that obedience is a gift of God, we, nonetheless, exhort human beings to obedience. But to those who hear obediently the exhortation of the truth, the gift of God has itself already been given, namely, that they hear it obediently."[65] Cyprian himself concludes, "Our power is of God, I say, all of it is of God."[66] This includes even the ability to believe in Christ.

**Doctrine in Focus:**

PRESERVING GRACE

Finally, Cyprian believed that a true believer can never be separated from Christ. His salvation is eternally secure. Cyprian writes, "Thus there is nothing that can separate the union between Christ and the Church, that is, the people who are established within the Church and who steadfastly and faithfully persevere in their beliefs: Christ and His Church must remain ever attached and joined to each other by indissoluble love."[67] Again, citing Romans 8:35, he writes: "As it is written: *Who shall separate us from the love of Christ? Shall trial or tribulation or persecution or hunger or nakedness or peril or sword?* None of these can separate those who believe, none can prize away those who cling to His body and blood."[68] These are clear affirmations of the eternal security of believers.

Cyprian taught that those who depart from the faith were never truly in Christ. He states: "For it is not possible for a man to perish unless it is plainly evident that perish he must, since the Lord says in His own Gospel: *Every planting which My heavenly father has not planted will be rooted out.* Accordingly, whoever has not been planted in the precepts and counsels of God the Father, will alone be able to depart from the Church. . . . But all the others, through the mercy of God the Father, the compassion of Christ our Lord and our own patience, will be reunited with us."[69] He adds: "Those who withdraw from Christ have only themselves to blame for their own destruction, whereas the Church, which believes in Christ and holds fast to the teachings it has learned, never departs from Him in any way. . . . They are the Church who remain in the house of the Lord."[70] Those who are truly born again cannot leave the fold permanently.

Persecution cannot separate a believer from Christ, Cyprian said. Commenting on Habakkuk 3:17, he states that a true believer "relying on the truth of hope and established in the stability of faith is not moved by the assaults of this world and life."[71] Elsewhere he writes:

The wind does not carry off the grain, the storm does not bring down the tree with strong roots. It is the empty husks that are tossed away by the tempest, the feeble trees that are thrown down by the hurricane. And it is such men that John the Apostle upbraids and smites when he says: "They went out from us, but they were not of us; for if they had been of us, they would have continued with us." . . . But the Lord allows such things out of respect for the freedom of the will, so that, when our hearts and minds are probed by the test of truth, the undamaged faith of such as are approved may shine out in manifest light.[72]

The unregenerate man will defect under pressure, but the faith of the true believer will remain "undamaged."

Likewise, heresy cannot cause a true child of God to lose his salvation. Instead, it reveals unbelievers. Cyprian writes: "The Holy Spirit warns us through the Apostle: 'There must be also heresies among you, that they which are approved may be made manifest among you.' In this way the faithful are approved and the faithless detected. Here and now, even before the Day of Judgment, the souls of the just and the unjust are parted and the chaff is separated from the wheat."[73]

Continuing his use of the metaphor of wheat and chaff, Cyprian writes: "The Lord, who is the protector and guardian of His own people, does not allow His wheat to be plundered from His threshing floor; it is only the chaff that can be separated off from the Church."[74] Elsewhere, he writes of those who leave the church, "They are no seedbed planted by God the Father who, we can see, stand with none of the strength and firmness of true wheat but who are blown about and scattered like so much chaff before the blasts of the Enemy."[75] In the end, apostasy purifies and strengthens the church. Cyprian writes: "But, far more importantly, the majority in the Church do still retain sincerity of heart, integrity of devotion, and souls dedicated exclusively to their Lord and God. So far from the faithlessness of these others crushing and destroying their Christian faith, it rather serves to give that faith fresh spirit and ardour for glory. As the blessed Apostle says in his words of exhortation: What if some of them have fallen from faith? Do you imagine that their faithlessness has made void the faithfulness of God? Far from it. For God is true, but every man a liar."[76] Because God is true, He preserves those He saves.

## BOLDLY CONFESSING THE FAITH

Cyprian's life and ministry were marked by a steadfast commitment to Christ and the teachings of the full counsel of God. Though many would-be professors of Christ succumbed to Roman pressure, he remained unflinching in his devotion to the Head of the church. Perseverance in the midst of adversity is the mark of true faith.

When tested, Cyprian did not lapse from the faith, as many had done. In the hour of his trial, the bishop of Carthage remained true to his convictions. He knew that God alone must be worshiped and Jesus Christ alone must be confessed as Lord. As a result, he sealed his testimony with his blood, a powerful witness to the Savior whom he upheld throughout his Christian life and ministry.

As the world grows increasingly post-Christian, may many strong voices for the truth be raised up and heard. In an hour when the world is increasingly antagonistic toward the gospel message, may there be bold witnesses for Christ who herald the divine truths of Scripture. As many grow in their hostility toward the truths of divine sovereignty in salvation, may heroic champions of the doctrines of grace arise within the church and proclaim these God-exalting, God-honoring truths. May the Lord raise up bold confessors of Christ in this day.

NOTES

1  Cyprian, *Unity of the Catholic Church*, 9–10, in *Early Latin Theology: Selections from Tertullian, Cyprian, Ambrose, and Jerome*, ed. and trans. S. L. Greenslade (Louisville: Westminster, 1956), 130.

2  David F. Wright, "Roman Africa," in *New International Dictionary of the Christian Church*, gen. ed. J. D. Douglas (Grand Rapids: Zondervan, 1978), 16.

3  Philip Schaff, *History of the Christian Church, Vol. II: Ante-Nicene Christianity: From the Death of John the Apostle to Constantine the Great, A.D. 100–325* (1910; repr., Grand Rapids: Eerdmans, 1980), 845.

4  Edwin Charles Dargan, *A History of Preaching, Vol. I: From the Apostolic Fathers to the Great Reformers* (Grand Rapids: Baker, 1974), 59.

5  Claudio Moreschini and Enrico Norelli, *Early Christian Greek and Latin Literature: A Literary History, Vol. One: From Paul to the Age of Constantine*, trans. Matthew J. O'Connell (Peabody, Mass.: Hendrickson, 2005), 364.

6  Augustine, *A Treatise Against Two Letters of the Pelagians*, IV.24, in *Nicene and Post-Nicene Fathers, First Series, Vol. V: Augustin: Anti-Pelagian Writings*, ed. Philip Schaff (1888; repr., Peabody, Mass.: Hendrickson, 2004), 427.

7  Augustine, *On Christian Doctrine*, I.11, cited in *The Works of Saint Augustine: Teaching Christianity*, ed. John E. Rotelle (Hyde Park, N.Y.: New City Press, 1996), 160.

8  Augustine, *Answer to the Two Letters of the Pelagians*, IV.26, in *The Works of Saint Augustine: Answer to the Pelagians, II: Marriage and Desire, Answer to the Two Letters of the Pelagians, Answer to Julian*, ed. John E. Rotelle (Hyde Park, N.Y.: New City Press, 1998), 206.

9  Augustine, *On Perseverance*, chap. 49, in *Nicene and Post-Nicene Fathers, First Series, Vol. V*, 546.

10  Augustine, *The Gift of Perseverance*, I.49, in *The Works of Saint Augustine: Answer to the Pelagians, IV: To the Monks of Hadrumetum and Provence*, ed. John E. Rotelle, trans. Roland J. Teske (Hyde Park, N.Y.: New City Press, 1999), 225.

11  Augustine, *The Gift of Perseverance*, I.49, in *The Works of Saint Augustine: Answer to the Pelagians, IV*, 225.

12  Martin Luther, *Luther's Works, Vol. 41: Church and Ministry III*, eds. Jaroslav Jan Pelikan, Hilton C. Oswald, and Helmut T. Lehmann (1966; repr., Philadelphia: Fortress, 1999), 47.

13  Martin Luther, *Luther's Works, Vol. 48: Letters I*, eds. Jaroslav Jan Pelikan, Hilton C. Oswald, and Helmut T. Lehmann (1963; repr., Philadelphia: Fortress, 1999), 24.

14  Martin Luther, *Luther's Works, Vol. 9: Lectures on Deuteronomy*, eds. Jaroslav Jan Pelikan, Hilton C. Oswald, and Helmut T. Lehmann (1960; repr., St. Louis: Concordia, 1999), 164.

15 "Cyprian," in *Cyclopedia of Biblical, Theological, and Ecclesiastical Literature, Vol. II*, eds. John McClintock and James Strong (Grand Rapids: Baker, 1981), 624.

16 W. Ward Gasque, "The Challenge to Faith," in *Introduction to the History of Christianity*, ed. Tim Dowley (Minneapolis: Fortress, 2002), 95.

17 Earle E. Cairns, *Christianity Through the Centuries: A History of the Christian Church*, 3rd Ed. (1954; repr., Grand Rapids: Zondervan, 1996), 110.

18 Ivor J. Davidson, *The Birth of the Church: From Jesus to Constantine, A.D. 30–312* (Grand Rapids: Baker, 2004), 325.

19 Moreschini and Norelli, *Early Christian Greek and Latin Literature: A Literary History, Vol. One*, 365.

20 N. R. Needham, *2,000 Years of Christ's Power, Part One: The Age of the Early Church Fathers* (London: Grace Publications, 1997), 130.

21 Roger E. Olson, *The Story of Christian Theology: Twenty Centuries of Tradition and Reform* (Downers Grove, Ill.: InterVarsity, 1999), 116.

22 Needham, *2,000 Years of Christ's Power, Part One*, 130.

23 Needham, *2,000 Years of Christ's Power, Part One*, 130.

24 Moreschini and Norelli, *Early Christian Greek and Latin Literature: A Literary History, Vol. One*, 365.

25 Cyprian, *To Donatus*, 4, in *Saint Cyprian: Treatises*, trans. Roy J. Deferrari (New York: Fathers of the Church, Inc., 1958), 9–10.

26 Cyprian, *To Donatus*, 4, in *Saint Cyprian: Treatises*, 10.

27 Needham, *2,000 Years of Christ's Power, Part One*, 130.

28 Pontius the Deacon, *The Life and Passion of Cyprian, Bishop and Martyr*, I.3, in *Ante-Nicene Fathers, Vol. 5: Hippolytus, Cyprian, Caius, Novatian, Appendix*, eds. Alexander Roberts, James Donaldson, and A. Cleveland Coxe (1864; repr., Peabody, Mass.: Hendrickson, 2004), 268.

29 "Introductory Notice to Cyprian," *Ante-Nicene Fathers, Vol. V*, 264.

30 Gasque, "The Challenge to Faith," in *Introduction to the History of Christianity*, 95.

31 Jerome, *Lives of Illustrious Men*, chap. 53, in *Nicene and Post-Nicene Fathers, Second Series, Vol. III: Theodoret, Jerome, Gennadius, Rufinus: Historical Writings, Etc.* (1888; repr., Peabody, Mass.: Hendrickson, 2004), 373

32 Jerome, *Lives of Illustrious Men*, chap. 53, in *Nicene and Post-Nicene Fathers, Second Series, Vol. III*, 373.

33 Jerome, *The Fathers of the Church, Vol. 100: On Illustrious Men*, trans. Thomas P. Halton (Washington: The Catholic University of America Press, 1999), 95.

34 Tony Lane, *A Concise History of Christian Thought* (Grand Rapids: Baker Academic, 2006), 24.

35 Davidson, *The Birth of the Church*, 332.

36 Moreschini and Norelli, *Early Christian Greek and Latin Literature: A Literary History, Vol. One*, 375.

37 Justo L. González, *The Story of Christianity, Vol. 1: The Early Church to the Dawn of the Reformation* (Peabody, Mass.: Hendrickson, 2004), 88.

38 "Cyprian," in *The Oxford Dictionary of the Christian Church*, 3rd Ed., ed. E. A. Livingstone (1957; repr. Oxford: Oxford University Press, 1997), 441.

39 Needham, *2,000 Years of Christ's Power, Part One*, 135.

40 González, *The Story of Christianity, Vol. 1*, 88.

41 Moreschini and Norelli, *Early Christian Greek and Latin Literature: A Literary History, Vol. One*, 370.

42 Needham, *2,000 Years of Christ's Power, Part One*, 130.

43 William Cunningham, *Historical Theology: A Review of the Principal Doctrinal Discussions in the Christian Church Since the Apostolic Age, Vol. 1* (Edinburgh: Banner of Truth, 1996), 164.

44 W. G. T. Shedd, *A History of Christian Doctrine, Vol. Two* (1897; repr., Birmingham, Ala.: Solid Ground, 2006), 47.

45 Berkhof, *The History of Christian Doctrines*, 130.

46 Berkhof, *The History of Christian Doctrines*, 130.

47 Cyprian, *The Lord's Prayer*, 14, in *Saint Cyprian: Treatises*, 138–139.

48 Augustine, *A Treatise Against Two Letters of the Pelagians*, IV.22, in *Nicene and Post-Nicene Fathers, First Series, Vol. V*, 426.

49 John Calvin, *Institutes of the Christian Religion*, trans. Henry Beveridge (Grand Rapids: Eerdmans, 1989), 2.2.9.

50 Calvin, *Institutes of the Christian Religion*, 2.2.9.

51 Cyprian, *The Good of Patience*, 11, in *Saint Cyprian: Treatises*, 273–274.

52 Cyprian, *Testimonies Against the Jews*, III.54, cited in *Ante-Nicene Fathers, Vol. V*, 547. Augustine cites this passage as evidence that Cyprian contended for the pervasive sinfulness of man. Augustine, *A Treatise Against Two Letters of the Pelagians*, IV.27, in *Nicene and Post-Nicene Fathers, First Series, Vol. V*, 430.

53 Cyprian, *Works and Almsgiving*, 3, in *Saint Cyprian: Treatises*, 229.

54 Cyprian, *Works and Almsgiving*, 3, in *Saint Cyprian: Treatises*, 229.

55 Cyprian, *Works and Almsgiving*, 3, in *Saint Cyprian: Treatises*, 229.

56 Cyprian, *Works and Almsgiving*, 18, in *Saint Cyprian: Treatises*, 244. Augustine cites this text to argue that Cyprian maintained radical depravity. Augustine, *A Treatise Against Two Letters of the Pelagians*, IV.27, in *Nicene and Post-Nicene Fathers, First Series, Vol. V*, 429.

57 Cyprian, *The Lord's Prayer*, 22, in *Saint Cyprian: Treatises*, 146. Augustine cites Cyprian here on the depravity of man. Augustine, *A Treatise Against Two Letters of the Pelagians*, IV.27, in *Nicene and Post-Nicene Fathers, First Series, Vol. V*, 429.

58 Cyprian, *Letters 65*, 5.2, in *The Letters of St. Cyprian of Carthage: Letters 55–66*, ed. G. W. Clarke (New York: Newman, 1984), 105.

59 Cyprian, *Of the Discipline and Advantage of Charity*, 2, in *Ante-Nicene Fathers, Vol. 5*, 588.

60 Augustine, *On the Predestination of the Saints*, in *Nicene and Post-Nicene Fathers, First Series, Vol. V*, 546.

61 Augustine, *The Gift of Perseverance*, 36, in *The Works of Saint Augustine: Answer to the Pelagians, IV*, 215.

62 Augustine, *The Gift of Perseverance*, 36, in *The Works of Saint Augustine: Answer to the Pelagians, IV*, 215.

63 Augustine, *The Gift of Perseverance*, 36, in *The Works of Saint Augustine: Answer to the Pelagians, IV*, 215

64 Cyprian, *The Lord's Prayer*, 9, in *Saint Cyprian: Treatises*, 133.

65 Augustine, *The Gift of Perseverance*, 36, in *The Works of Saint Augustine: Answer to the Pelagians, IV*, 215.

66 Cyprian, *To Donatus*, 4, in *Saint Cyprian: Treatises*, 10.

67 Cyprian, *Letter 63*, 8.1, in *The Letters of St. Cyprian of Carthage: Letters 55–66*, 105.

68 Cyprian, *Letter 11*, 5.3, in *The Letters of St. Cyprian of Carthage: Letters 1–27*, ed. G. W. Clarke (New York: Newman, 1984), 79.

69 Cyprian, *Letter 52*, 4.2, *The Letters of St. Cyprian of Carthage: Letters 28–54*, ed. G. W. Clarke (New York: Newman, 1984), 85.

70 Cyprian, *Letter 59*, 7.3, in *The Letters of St. Cyprian of Carthage: Letters 55–66*, 74–75.

71 Cyprian, *To Demetrian*, in *Saint Cyprian: Treatises*, 185.

72 Cyprian, *Unity of the Catholic Church*, 9–10, in *Early Latin Theology*, 130.

73 Cyprian, *Unity of the Catholic Church*, 10, in *Early Latin Theology*, 130.

74 Cyprian, *Letter 66*, 8.1, in *The Letters of St. Cyprian of Carthage: Letters 55–66*, 121.

75 Cyprian, *Letter 59*, 7.3, in *The Letters of St. Cyprian of Carthage: Letters 55–66*, 75.

76 Cyprian, *Letter 67*, in *The Letters of St. Cyprian of Carthage: Letters 67–82*, ed. G. W. Clarke (New York: Newman, 1984), 26–27.

# CHAPTER SEVEN
# STUDY QUESTIONS

1. What were the primary contributions of the African Fathers to the development of the early church? Can you explain their role in the recognition of the canon of Scripture?

2. Describe the recognition that has been given to Cyprian of Carthage. Specifically, what was his unique role in the early church?

3. Explain Cyprian's early upbringing. What influences affected his life as a young man? How did these influences prepare him for future ministry?

4. Describe the conversion of Cyprian. How does it compare with your personal conversion? What is conversion? How is one converted to Jesus Christ?

5. Give an overview of Cyprian's exile. Explain how it impacted his life and ministry. How has adversity affected your Christian walk? Has it made you stronger in the Lord?

6. What was the chief focus of Cyprian's writings? How important is reading good Christian literature? How can you expand your reading of Christian material? Why or why not?

7. Explain Cyprian's views on divine sovereignty and radical depravity. Do you agree with Cyprian's positions?

8. What role does faith play in salvation? Does faith come from God or man? Cite verses to support your position.

Nor let the words "before the world" and "before He made the earth" and "before the mountains were settled" disturb any one. . . . For though the grace which came to us from the Saviour appeared, as the Apostle says, just now, and has come when He sojourned among us; yet this grace had been prepared even before we came into being, nay, before the foundation of the world.[1]

–Athanasius of Alexandria

Chapter Eight

# AGAINST THE WORLD

## AFRICAN FATHER:
## ATHANASIUS OF ALEXANDRIA

E arly in the fourth century, a dubious convert came into the fold of professing Christendom—the Roman Emperor Constantine (ca. 274–337).
By the emperor's own account, as he marched into battle he heard a voice
from heaven saying, "By this sign you will conquer."[2] Looking up, he supposedly saw a cross in the sky. The emperor interpreted this alleged symbol
to mean that God was with him and would grant him victory. Armed with a
new confidence, Constantine devastated his opposition (ca. 312). Afterward,
he attributed his military triumph to the power of the cross and declared himself a Christian.

Immediately, the emperor's newfound allegiance to Christianity changed
the status of believers across the empire. With Constantine openly professing Christ, Christians no longer needed to fear persecution from the Roman
authorities. The Edict of Milan (313) soon granted official tolerance to all
religions in the empire, including Christianity. Furthermore, in light of Constantine's conversion, Christianity gained a prominent standing, becoming the
unofficial faith of the empire. Believers found themselves in an unprecedented
season of peace and popularity. Once opposed and oppressed, Christians were
now acclaimed and admired.

But the official acceptance of Christianity brought with it significant dangers. At this time, hordes of unregenerate Roman citizens came into the church
and were baptized as believers. The sacred thus merged with the secular, and
the immediate result was doctrinal compromise, all for the sake of political
expediency. Such concessions prepared the soil of the church for the corruptions of Roman Catholicism. In future years, such externalized religion would

145

bear bitter fruit. Thus, popularity proved to be a greater threat to Christianity than persecution, and the church was weakened significantly.

## ARIUS: ARCHENEMY OF THE TRINITY

In this compromised condition, the church was vulnerable to doctrinal heresy. A particularly tenacious false teaching came from the mind of Arius (280–336), a presbyter in Alexandria, Egypt, who launched an assault on the deity of Christ and the tri-unity of the Godhead. Arius argued that Jesus, the second person of the Trinity, was no more than a created being, though He was the greatest of God's creatures—an archangel.[3]

When Arianism began to gain a foothold in the churches, a synod convened in Alexandria (321) to hear the matter. The synod judged Arius to be a heretic and stripped him of his pastoral office. Providentially, the official deposition was written by a young assistant to the bishop of Alexandria—Athanasius.

Tragically, this public rebuke did little to restrain Arius, who traveled throughout the empire spreading his theological poison. This forced Constantine to convene a church council in Nicaea, in modern Turkey, to address the controversy. Despite his outward concern for orthodoxy, Constantine actually cared more for political unity than theological accuracy. Nevertheless, the Council of Nicaea was one of the most significant gatherings in church history. From across the empire, 318 bishops came together, including young Athanasius.

## THE SYMBOL OF NICAEA

The Nicene Council, which met in 325, examined Arius's teachings and overwhelmingly condemned him as a heretic. Only two bishops sided with Arius. These three dissenting pastors were exiled and Arius's writings were burned. Then the council drafted a carefully worded statement on the Trinity, known as the Symbol of Nicaea, which affirmed the divine nature of Christ; it became the basis for future creeds and confessions of the Christian faith.[4] The statement adopted at Nicaea also denounced the Arians, declaring them *anathema*—damned.[5]

Despite the Nicene Council's formulation of the Symbol of Nicaea and its condemnation of Arius and his followers, Arianism continued to find adherents. As time passed, many became sympathetic to Arius and even argued for his pastoral reinstatement. Among church leaders, convictions weakened and resolves wavered. In the end, compromises began to seem expedient. As a means of maintaining peace, Constantine's advisers, who were theologically inept, urged him to reinstate Arius. Finally, Constantine caved in and overturned the council's anathema. He ordered Arius to be restored as a presbyter in Alexandria, the home of Athanasius.

However, Arius never returned to his office. He died prior to his restoration ceremony (336). Never one to mince words, Athanasius said that Arius's bowels had burst asunder when he died, like those of the greatest of all apostates, Judas Iscariot. Still, the battle over Arius's erroneous doctrine continued.

In this epochal controversy, Athanasius proved himself to be one of the great defenders of the faith. He became the preeminent guardian of the doctrines of the deity of Christ and of the triune nature of the Godhead. As we will see, his championing of orthodoxy went hand in hand with his steadfast commitment to the doctrines of grace.

# ATHANASIUS OF ALEXANDRIA

In his opposition to Arianism, Athanasius (ca. 298–373) became the principal defender of orthodoxy in his generation.[6] Because of his unyielding stand, he has been labeled the "Father of Orthodoxy"[7] and the "saint of stubbornness."[8] Scholars have judged that he was the most significant bishop ever to occupy the ancient seat of Alexandria, an influential city for early Christianity,[9] and the greatest theologian of his time.[10]

Athanasius's life bears a close resemblance to that of Martin Luther.[11] Like the German Reformer who sparked the Reformation, Athanasius was willing to stand alone for truth against the religious establishment in the face of false teaching. In fact, Luther considered Athanasius to be one of the most illustrious Fathers, along with Augustine.[12] For his singular courage in the face of widespread heresy, it was said that Athanasius stood *contra mundum*— "against the world."

## A Christian Upbringing

Athanasius was born of wealthy parents in Alexandria, the second-largest city in the ancient West, a major port, and an important intellectual and cultural center. Christian scholarship was virtually born in Alexandria. The library at Alexandria boasted its Catechetical School, which became the prototype of the later European university system. As a young man, Athanasius received a strong theological education in the Catechetical School.

Athanasius also had a solid spiritual upbringing. Gregory of Nazianzus (330–389) commented about Athanasius's youth:

> He was brought up, from the first, in religious habits and practices, after a brief study of literature and philosophy, so that he might not be utterly unskilled in such subjects, or ignorant of matters which he had determined to despise. For his generous and eager soul could not brook being occupied in vanities, like unskilled athletes, who beat the air instead of their antagonists and lose the prize. From meditating on every book of the Old and New Testament, with a depth such as none else has applied even to one of them, he grew rich in contemplation, rich in splendor of life.[13]

In his early twenties, Athanasius became the personal assistant to the bishop of Alexandria, a man named Alexander. In this role, Athanasius attended the important synod in Alexandria (321) at which Arius was first condemned, as well as the Council of Nicaea (325). These experiences helped prepare him for the critical theological battles that lay ahead. When Alexander died on April 17, 328, the logical choice to succeed him as bishop was his protégé, Athanasius. He succeeded Alexander at the relatively young age of thirty, overseeing the church in Alexandria and all the bishops in Egypt and Libya. In the following years, Arianism was virtually eradicated from the churches of Egypt under his influence.

When Constantine equivocated on the Nicene Council's conclusions and reinstated Arius as a presbyter in Alexandria (336), he ordered Athanasius to accept Arius back into this position. But true to his convictions, Athanasius refused. He saw Arius as a heretic, not a brother in Christ. To accept him would be to accept false doctrine. Like Luther, his conscience was bound to the Word of God. Because of this defiance, Constantine exiled Athanasius to the outer extremity of the Roman Empire in modern Germany.

## NEW EMPEROR, OLD COMPROMISE

After Constantine's death, the Roman Empire was divided among his three sons. Constantius, the second son, controlled the East. On Nov. 23, 337, after a short time on his throne, Constantius granted Athanasius permission to return to Alexandria to resume his ministry. But Constantius, like his father, sought to keep his empire intact at any price. Thus, he demanded an official revision of the Nicene Creed concerning the deity of Christ, a revision that would reflect Arian beliefs. He wanted the word *homoousios*, meaning "of the same substance," changed to *homoiousios*, "of a similar substance." Tragically, many bishops backed Constantius in this demand.

But once again, Athanasius would not budge. He saw Constantius's revision as nothing less than an accommodation to heresy. The difference between *homoousios* ("same") and *homoiousios* ("similar") was only one small "i," but it was the difference between describing Christ as fully divine or as a created being. Athanasius saw that Christ's full deity and His saving work are inseparably bound. If His substitutionary death was to be of value, Jesus must be fully God. Athanasius understood that only a fully divine Savior can reconcile sinners to God. If Jesus is less than God, His saving work at the cross was less than sufficient. If so, man is still in his sins and under divine wrath.

Athanasius paid a great price for the truth he cherished so deeply. Spanning his tenure as bishop of Alexandria—June 8, 328, until his death on May 2, 373—he was sent into exile five times by the Roman authorities. He spent seventeen of his forty-five years as bishop in exile from Alexandria. But even while he was banished, his flock remained faithful to him and continued to consider him their bishop. More important, the *homoousios* position eventually prevailed in the ongoing debates in the church.

Despite this adversity, Athanasius maintained his firm stance for the Christian faith, especially the doctrine of Christ's deity. For most of his adult life, he fought in the arena of theological debate, warring against Arianism and fighting for the deity of Christ. He died as he began, valiantly displaying "an enormously ruthless strength of character."[14]

Parker Williamson summarizes Athanasius's life in this way:

Athanasius set his name to the creed which expressed his belief [the Athanasian Creed], and for fifty years he stood unswervingly by that confession. Every argument that ingenuity could invent was used to prove it false. Bishops met together in great numbers, condemned his views, and invoked upon him the curse of God. Emperors took sides against him, banished him time and time again, and chased him from place to place, setting a reward on his head. At one time all bishops of the church were persuaded or coerced into pronouncing sentence against him, so that the phrase originated, "Athanasius against the world." But with all this pressure bearing on him, he changed his ground not one inch. His clear eye saw the truth once, and he did not permit his conscience to tamper with temptations to deny it. His loyalty to the truth made him a great power for good, and a great blessing to the churches of his own, and of all times.[15]

# ATHANASIUS'S WRITINGS

Athanasius was a prolific writer, and the deity of Christ was his principal subject. *On the Incarnation of the Word* and *Discourses Against the Arians* are his major works on this issue. The first is a positive presentation of Christ's equality with the Father, while the latter is a polemic against the followers of Arius.

## ON THE INCARNATION OF THE WORD

This treatise (ca. 335) teaches the full deity of Christ, demonstrating that it was His deity that made His saving work efficacious. Athanasius stressed that redemption was accomplished because Christ was fully God, not a mere creature.[16] He argued that Jesus Christ had to come as the God-man in order to die in the place of His people and satisfy God's righteous judgment of their sin. Athanasius understood that, by His death, "Christ restored to humanity what was lost through Adam's disobedience."[17] Christ's sacrificial death, which Athanasius characterized as "substitutionary,"[18] was a complete triumph: "He surrendered it [His body] to death instead of all, and offered it to the Father . . . in order that by dying in Him the law with respect to the corruption of mankind might be abolished. . . . The logos of God, being above all, by offering His own temple and bodily instrument as a substitution for the life of all, satisfied all that was required by His death."[19]

## DISCOURSES AGAINST THE ARIANS

*Discourses Against the Arians* (356–360) is considered Athanasius's polemical masterpiece. This four-volume set was a frontal attack on Arianism. Athanasius mounted his response to Arius by expounding the eternality of the Son. The natures of the Father and of the Son are identical, he said—both are eternal.[20] He then addressed difficult passages that were being skewed by the Arians (Acts 2:36; Col. 1:15; Heb. 1:14). He also provided exegesis of selected texts proving the deity of Christ, such as John 14:10, in which Jesus states,

"I am in the Father and the Father is in me," and John 17:11, in which Jesus prays that the Father will keep His disciples so "that they may be one, even as we are one." This set is truly a treasure in the vault of church history.

# ATHANASIUS'S THEOLOGY

Not only was Athanasius the premier defender of the deity of Christ and the Trinity among the Early Church Fathers, he had a strong understanding of the basic elements of the sovereign grace of God in salvation and helped further develop the church's understanding of the relationship of sin and grace. Throughout Athanasius's writings, trace elements of the doctrines of grace affirm his belief in the sovereignty of God in the salvation of sinners. Furthermore, his strong Trinitarian focus led him to believe in a unified work of salvation by the three persons of the Godhead. He understood that each member of the Trinity is uniquely involved in redemption.

**Doctrine in Focus:**

DIVINE SOVEREIGNTY

The sovereignty of God was the cornerstone of Athanasius's theology. In his view, all truth had to be aligned with this master truth. He writes:

> In like manner, when the Prophets spoke of God as All-ruling, they did not so name Him, as if the Word were included in that All; (for they knew that the Son was other than things originated, and Sovereign over them Himself, according to His likeness to the Father); but because He is Ruler over all things which through the Son He has made, and has given the authority of all things to the Son, and having given it, is Himself once more the Lord of all things through the Word. Again, when they called God, Lord of the powers, they said not this as if the Word was one of those powers, but because while He is Father of the Son, He is Lord of the powers which through the Son have come to be. For again, the Word too, as being in the Father, is Lord of them all, and Sovereign over all; for all things, whatsoever the Father hath, are the Son's.[21]

Athanasius taught that both the Father and the Son reign over the universe. No power can resist the free exercise of Their sovereign will.

Being fully God, Jesus Christ possesses and exercises supreme authority over all things, Athanasius maintained. He writes: "Beloved brethren, I greet you well, calling upon God, Who is the chief witness of my intention, and on the Only-begotten, the Author of our Law, Who is Sovereign over the lives of all men."[22] Christ, he adds, "ever was and is, as Son, so also Lord and Sovereign of all."[23] The Son shares sovereignty with the Father.

Athanasius also affirmed that the sovereign God sustains all creation. He writes: "Why, neither sun, nor moon, nor heaven, nor the stars, nor water, nor air had swerved from their order; but knowing their artificer and sovereign, the Word, they remain as they were made."[24] By His authority, God upholds the works of His hands.

Describing God's dominion over creation, Athanasius writes: "We acknowledge One God, alone Ingenerate, alone Everlasting, alone Unbegun, alone True, alone having Immortality, alone Wise, alone Good, alone Sovereign; Judge, Governor, and Providence of all, unalterable and unchangeable, just and good."[25] Athanasius believed that God's providential reign is exercised with perfect wisdom, justice, and goodness.

**Doctrine in Focus:**

RADICAL DEPRAVITY

Athanasius believed in the radical depravity of the human race. However, Hannah maintains that he "perceived a unity between Adam's first sin and the race of humankind, but he did not understand that humankind participates in Adam's guilt."[26] Thus, Athanasius writes of "original sin, which through Adam passed unto all"[27] and affirms that "when Adam had transgressed, his sin reached unto all men."[28] The teaching of Scripture made it clear to him that Adam's one act of rebellion had spread sin to all mankind.

He also recognized that sin devastated the entirety of God's creation. He says: "Man sinned, and is fallen, and by his fall all things are in confusion: death prevailed from Adam to Moses (cf. Rom. v. 14), the earth was cursed, Hades was opened, Paradise shut, Heaven offended, man, lastly, corrupted and brutalized."[29] Athanasius understood the depth of the tragedy brought about through Adam's sin.

Worse, all of Adam's descendants are under a sentence of spiritual death because of sin. Athanasius writes: "Thus, then, God has made man, and willed that he should abide in incorruption; but men, having despised and rejected the contemplation of God, and devised and contrived evil for themselves (as was said in the former treatise), received the condemnation of death with which they had been threatened; and from thenceforth no longer remained as they were made, but were being corrupted according to their devices; and death had the mastery over them as king."[30] This means man is in a state in which he is unable to save himself. A dead man can do nothing.

Man is so depraved, Athanasius writes, that he is essentially a slave: "We once were subject from the first to the slavery of corruption and the curse of the Law."[31] This slavery means that man is given over to illicit pleasures and has no desire for the truth: "Men nevertheless, overcome by the pleasures of the moment and by the illusions and deceits sent by demons, did not raise their heads toward the truth, but loaded themselves the more with evils and sins, so as no longer to seem rational, but from their ways to be reckoned void of reason."[32] Such is the outworking of original sin in the hearts of men, as Athanasius clearly saw.

Moreover, Athanasius asserted that the fall plunged man into a state of corruption. Man, therefore, is in dire need of restoration. Athanasius says, "None other could restore a corruptible being to incorruption but the Saviour."[33] To this point, J. N. D. Kelly remarks that "the dominant strain in Athanasius' soteriology is the physical theory of Christ, by becoming man, restored the divine image in us."[34] Athanasius clearly saw man's need for Christ to restore him from his corrupt and depraved nature.

**Doctrine in Focus:**
SOVEREIGN ELECTION

In his writings, Athanasius affirmed that God chose an elect people to receive the inheritance of salvation and that the Father designated Christ to secure this blessing for His people. He writes: "How then has He chosen us, before we came into existence, but that, as He says Himself, in Him we were represented beforehand? . . . or how, as the Apostle goes on to say, have we 'an inheritance being predestinated,' but that the Lord Himself . . . had a purpose, for our sakes, to take on Him through the flesh all that inheritance of judgment which lay against us?"[35] He adds, "[We have] the spiritual life and blessing which before these things have been prepared for us in the Word Himself according to election."[36] Athanasius taught that God prepared salvation before the foundation of the world and determined that it would be brought to pass in Christ.

Expanding on Christ's "election" as Savior, he adds: "'Before the world' there had been prepared for us in Christ the hope of life and salvation. . . . The Father's will was in Him before the world, as has been said, and before land was, and before the mountains were settled, and before the fountains burst forth."[37] Not only were the elect chosen before time, but Christ was appointed from the beginning to be the Savior of all those who believe. Athanasius further asserts, "How then, or in whom, was it prepared before we came to be, save in the Lord who 'before the world' was founded for this purpose; that we, as built upon Him, might partake, as well-compacted stones, the life and grace which is from Him?"[38] Every aspect of God's redemptive plan was inscrutably prepared "before the world."

Athanasius addressed the subject of God's election with clarity and power:

> This grace had been prepared even before we came into being, nay, before the foundation of the world, and the reason why is kindly and wonderful. It seemed not that God should counsel concerning us afterwards, lest He should appear ignorant of our fate. The God of all then, creating us by His own Word, and knowing our destinies better than we, and foreseeing that, being made "good," we should in the event be transgressors of the commandment, and be thrust out of paradise for disobedience, being loving and kind, prepared beforehand in His own Word, by whom also He created us, the Economy of our salvation; that though by the serpent's deceit we fell from Him, we might not remain quite dead, but having in the Word the redemption and salvation which was afore prepared for us, we might rise again and abide immortal.[39]

True to Scripture, Athanasius believed that the salvation of the elect was ordained in eternity past. He writes: "How did we receive it 'before the world was,' when we were not yet in being, but afterwards in time, but that in Christ was stored the grace which has reached us?"[40]

**Doctrine in Focus:**
Irresistible Call

Athanasius seems to have understood that sin renders fallen men unable to trust Christ by their own wills. God must intervene and call sinners to Himself if they are to believe. He writes: "Although there be one Son by nature,

True and Only-begotten, we too become sons, not as He in nature and truth, but according to the grace of Him that calls."[41] Here Athanasius affirmed that sinful men are made sons of God by the special grace that summons them unto Him. God's effectual calling of His chosen ones enables them to believe on Christ.

Athanasius affirmed with Scripture that many hear the external call of the gospel message, but only a few are supernaturally enabled to respond to it. Judas Iscariot, Athanasius writes, is a prime example of one who was called but not chosen: "'For many are called, but few chosen.' Judas to wit, though he came to the supper, because he despised it went out from the presence of the Lord, and having abandoned his life, hanged himself. But the disciples who continued with the Redeemer shared in the happiness of the feast."[42] In short, many are called to the blessings of the Lord, but not all are chosen to actually partake of them.

**Doctrine in Focus:**

PRESERVING GRACE

Athanasius was clear that the Lord preserves forever those in whom He initiates salvation. The saving grace that God bestows, he wrote, is irrevocable. Though a believer may fall into sin, grace remains. Commenting on 1 Samuel 16:14a ("Now the Spirit of the LORD departed from Saul"), Athanasius says: "When then a man falls from the Spirit for any wickedness, if he repent upon his fall, the grace remains irrevocably to such as are willing; otherwise he who has fallen is no longer in God (because that Holy Spirit and Paraclete which is in God has deserted him), but the sinner shall be in him to whom he has subjected himself, as took place in Saul's instance; for the Spirit of God departed from him and an evil spirit was afflicting him."[43]

Athanasius made this same point in commenting on 1 John 2:19. He writes: "For that their authors went out from us, it plainly follows, as the blessed John has written, that they never thought nor now think with us. Wherefore, as says the Saviour, in that they gather not with us, they scatter with the devil, and keep an eye on those who slumber, that, by this second sowing of their own mortal poison, they may have companions in death."[44] Athanasius reasoned that those who fall away, like Saul, do so because they were never recipients of saving grace.

By contrast, true believers never utterly fall. Citing Jesus' High Priestly Prayer in John 17, Athanasius writes: "And if He says, 'as we,' this again is only a request that such grace of the Spirit as is given to the disciples may be without failure or revocation. For what the Word has by nature, as I said, in the Father, that He wishes to be given to us through the Spirit irrevocably; which the Apostle knowing, said, 'Who shall separate us from the love of Christ?'"[45] Athanasius saw that a genuine work of divine grace remains forever in the one who receives it.

He also understood that God causes His elect to persevere in their love for God, Christ, and the brethren. He writes: "Therefore it is plain, that in the Name of Father and Son we shall be able, becoming one, to hold firm the bond of charity."[46] Believers persevere in their love for one another by virtue of being positioned in the Father and the Son. Likewise, Athanasius affirms that true Christians cannot fall prey to false prophets: "The faithful Christian and true disciple of the Gospel, having grace to discern spiritual things, and having built the house of his faith upon a rock, stands continually firm and secure from their deceits."[47] The one whose faith is built on the gospel will never be moved. Simply put, endurance is the mark of the elect because God preserves them.

## SOLDIERS OF CHRIST, ARISE

When the cardinal doctrines of the Christian faith were under siege, Athanasius held tenaciously to biblical fidelity in his day. This African Father faithfully guarded the high ground of Christian truth at a time when others retreated amid rising persecution. No matter what, the bishop of Alexandria was willing to stand firm upon Scripture and, whenever necessary, defend Scripture with Scripture.

The need is the same in this hour of history. Nothing has changed. The truth is always under ruthless assault and the stakes are always high. In every generation, men of God must follow in the footsteps of this magnificent Church Father, remaining faithful to the text of Scripture.

We must not shy away from doctrinal disputes that strike against the very heart of the gospel. We must not flinch in the face of divisive attacks. The ever-changing tides of popular fads that are sweeping through the church today must not prevail over God-authored doctrines. We must lift high the person and work of the Lord Jesus Christ. We must hold fast to the sovereign rule of God over all things.

NOTES

1  Athanasius, *Discourses Against the Arians*, II.22.75, cited in *Nicene and Post-Nicene Fathers, Second Series, Vol. IV: Athanasius: Select Works and Letters*, eds. Philip Schaff and Henry Wace (Grand Rapids: Eerdmans, 1971), 389.

2  Philip Schaff, *History of the Christian Church, Vol. III: Nicene and Post-Nicene Christianity* (1910; repr., Grand Rapids: Eerdmans, 1984), 20–25.

3  John MacArthur, *The Truth War* (Nashville: Thomas Nelson, 2007), 104.

4  The Nicene statement reads: "We believe in one God, the Father almighty, Creator of all things visible and invisible; and in one Lord Jesus Christ, the Son of God, begotten of the Father, only-begotten, that is, from the essence of the Father, God from God, and light from light, true God from true God, begotten, not created, of the same essence as the Father, through Whom all things were created both in heaven and on earth; Who for us human beings and for our salvation came down and was incarnate, was made man, suffered and rose again on the third day, ascended into heaven, and is coming again to judge the living and the dead; and [we believe] in the Holy Spirit." Cited in Schaff and Wace, *Nicene and Post-Nicene Fathers, Second Series, Vol. IV*, 75.

5  The document read: "As for those who say, There was a time when He [the *Logos*] was not; and, He was not before He was created; and, He was created out of nothing, or out of another essence or thing; and, The Son of God is created, or changeable, or can alter—the holy, catholic and apostolic Church anathematizes those who say such things." Cited in N. R. Needham, *2,000 Years of Christ's Power, Part One: The Age of the Early Church Fathers* (London: Grace Publications, 1997), 205.

6  "Athanasius," in *Nelson's New Christian Dictionary*, ed. George T. Kurian (Nashville: Thomas Nelson, 2001), 60.

7  Schaff and Wace, *Nicene and Post-Nicene Fathers, Second Series, Vol. IV*, lviii.

8  Roger E. Olson, *The Story of Christian Theology: Twenty Centuries of Tradition and Reform* (Downers Grove, Ill.: InterVarsity, 1999), 161.

9  Olson, *The Story of Christian Theology*, 162.

10  Olson, *The Story of Christian Theology*, 162.

11  Olson, *The Story of Christian Theology*, 162.

12  Martin Luther, *Luther's Works, Vol. 14: Selected Psalms III*, eds. Jaroslav Jan Pelikan, Hilton C. Oswald, and Helmut T. Lehmann (1958; repr., St. Louis: Concordia, 1999), 310.

13  Gregory of Nazianzus, *Oritations, XXI*, cited in Robert Letham, *The Holy Trinity: In Scripture, History, Theology, and Worship* (Phillipsburg, N.J.: P&R, 2004), 145.

14  Jonathan Hill, *The History of Christian Thought* (Downers Grove, Ill.: InterVarsity, 2003), 65.

15  Parker T. Williamson, *Standing Firm: Reclaiming Christian Faith in Times of Controversy* (Springfield, Pa.: PLC Publications, 1996), 38.

16  Claudio Moreschini and Enrico Norelli, *Early Christian Greek and Latin Literature: A Literary History, Vol. Two: From the Council of Nicea to the Beginning of the Medieval Period*, trans. Matthew J. O'Connell (Peabody, Mass.: Hendrickson, 2005), 35.

17  John Hannah, *Our Legacy: The History of Christian Doctrine* (Colorado Springs, Colo.: NavPress, 2001), 157.

18  Hannah, *Our Legacy*, 157.

19  Athanasius, *On the Incarnation of the Word*, section 9, cited in *Documents of the Christian Church*, ed. Henry Bittenson (Oxford: Oxford University Press, 1963), 33.

20 Moreschini and Norelli, *Early Christian Greek and Latin Literature, Vol. Two*, 33.

21 Athanasius, *Defense of the Nicene Definition*, VII.30, cited in Schaff and Wace, *Nicene and Post-Nicene Fathers, Second Series, Vol. IV*, 170–171.

22 Athanasius, *Discourses Against the Arians*, II.5.61, cited in Schaff and Wace, *Nicene and Post-Nicene Fathers, Second Series, Vol. IV*, 132.

23 Athanasius, *Discourses Against the Arians*, II.15.18, cited in Schaff and Wace, *Nicene and Post-Nicene Fathers, Second Series, Vol. IV*, 357.

24 Athanasius, *On the Incarnation of the Word*, 43, cited in *Christology of the Later Fathers*, ed. Edward R. Hardy (Louisville: Westminster John Knox, 2006), 97.

25 Athanasius, *Councils of Ariminum and Seleucia*, II.16, cited in Schaff and Wace, *Nicene and Post-Nicene Fathers, Second Series, Vol. IV*, 458.

26 Hannah, *Our Legacy*, 210.

27 Athanasius, *Councils of Ariminum and Seleucia*, II.16, cited in Schaff and Wace, *Nicene and Post-Nicene Fathers, Second Series, Vol. IV*, 392.

28 Athanasius, *Discourses Against the Arians*, I.12.51, cited in Schaff and Wace, *Nicene and Post-Nicene Fathers, Second Series, Vol. IV*, 336.

29 Athanasius, *On Luke 10:22 (Matthew 11:27)*, section 2, cited in Schaff and Wace, *Nicene and Post-Nicene Fathers, Second Series, Vol. IV*, 87.

30 Athanasius, *On the Incarnation of the Word*, 4, cited in Hardy, *Christology of the Later Fathers*, 59.

31 Athanasius, *Discourses Against the Arians*, II.15.14, cited in Schaff and Wace, *Nicene and Post-Nicene Fathers, Second Series, Vol. IV*, 355.

32 Athanasius, *On the Incarnation of the Word*, 12, cited in Hardy, *Christology of the Later Fathers*, 67.

33 Athanasius, *On the Incarnation of the Word*, 20, cited in J. N. D. Kelly, *Early Christian Doctrines* (New York: Harper & Row, 1978), 377–378.

34 Kelly, *Early Christian Doctrines*, 377.

35 Athanasius, *Discourses Against the Arians*, II.22.76, cited in Schaff and Wace, *Nicene and Post-Nicene Fathers, Second Series, Vol. IV*, 389.

36 Athanasius, *Discourses Against the Arians*, II.22.76, cited in Schaff and Wace, *Nicene and Post-Nicene Fathers, Second Series, Vol. IV*, 390.

37 Athanasius, *Discourses Against the Arians*, II.22.76, cited in Schaff and Wace, *Nicene and Post-Nicene Fathers, Second Series, Vol. IV*, 390.

38 Athanasius, *Discourses Against the Arians*, II.22.76, cited in Schaff and Wace, *Nicene and Post-Nicene Fathers, Second Series, Vol. IV*, 389.

39 Athanasius, *Discourses Against the Arians*, II.22.75, cited in Schaff and Wace, *Nicene and Post-Nicene Fathers, Second Series, Vol. IV*, 389. In his Second Discourse, quoted here in part, Athanasius explained Proverbs 8:22 ("The LORD possessed me at the beginning of His way, before His works of old"), arguing against the "heretics" for the existence of the pre-incarnate Christ and for God's sovereign election of sinners. As seen here, he explained that the reason for election was "kindly and wonderful."

40 Athanasius, *Discourses Against the Arians*, II.22.76, cited in Schaff and Wace, *Nicene and Post-Nicene Fathers, Second Series, Vol. IV*, 389.

41 Athanasius, *Discourses Against the Arians*, III.25.19, cited in Schaff and Wace, *Nicene and Post-Nicene Fathers, Second Series, Vol. IV*, 404.

42 Athanasius, *Festal Letters*, VII.9, cited in Schaff and Wace, *Nicene and Post-Nicene Fathers, Second Series, Vol. IV*, 526.

43 Athanasius, *Discourses Against the Arians*, III.25.25, cited in Schaff and Wace, *Nicene and Post-Nicene Fathers, Second Series, Vol. IV*, 407.

44 Athanasius, *Discourses Against the Arians*, I.1.1, cited in Schaff and Wace, *Nicene and Post-Nicene Fathers, Second Series, Vol. IV*, 306.

45 Athanasius, *Discourses Against the Arians*, III.25.25, cited in Schaff and Wace, *Nicene and Post-Nicene Fathers, Second Series, Vol. IV*, 407.

46 Athanasius, *Discourses Against the Arians*, III.25.21, cited in Schaff and Wace, *Nicene and Post-Nicene Fathers, Second Series, Vol. IV*, 405.

47 Athanasius, *To the Bishops of Egypt*, 1.4, cited in Schaff and Wace, *Nicene and Post-Nicene Fathers, Second Series, Vol. IV*, 225.

# CHAPTER EIGHT
## STUDY QUESTIONS

1. What is the danger of an external religion that is without internal reality? How should Constantine serve as a warning for us? What is to be the nature of the church?

2. What deadly heresy did Arius introduce? What were the unique features of this false teaching? Where do you see traces of Arianism today?

3. Explain the value of Christian creeds and confessions. Describe the role they have played in preserving sound doctrine. What doctrinal standards have helped shape your theological convictions?

4. Describe the early years of Athanasius. How was he trained in Christian truth? How can you train your children in the faith? What catechisms or confessions might you teach them?

5. To what extent did Athanasius suffer persecution? How have you suffered for your faith in Christ? How has God used such adversity to further the gospel through you?

6. Comment on the writings of Athanasius. What is the role of polemical writing in Christian literature? What book have you read recently that is a defense of the Christian faith? How did it prepare you to bear witness for Christ?

7. Why is it important that divine sovereignty undergird our faith? How does this truth affect our lives?

8. Describe Athanasius's view of Christian perseverance. Explain this doctrine in light of Scripture. How is this truth an encouragement to you?

*Now perfect and complete glorying in God is this: not to exult in one's own righteousness, but being aware that one is lacking in true righteousness, to be justified by faith alone in Christ.*[1]

–Basil of Caesarea

# RESISTING ARIANISM

## CAPPADOCIAN FATHER:
## BASIL OF CAESAREA

As the fourth century dawned, the strategic hub of God's activities primarily shifted from North Africa to Asia Minor in the eastern part of the Roman Empire, specifically to the province of Cappadocia in what is modern-day Turkey. At that time, God raised up another group of men, the Cappadocian Fathers, to continue the battle against Arianism and other false teachings. Two core truths of the gospel were under attack in this hour—the humanity and deity of the Son, and the co-equality of the Holy Spirit with the Father and the Son. The Cappadocian Fathers helped the church define and defend biblical understandings of these key doctrines.

As noted in the previous chapter, Arius, a priest in Alexandria, Egypt, taught that Jesus was inferior to the Father in His nature, power, and honor. Such teaching undermined the true message of the gospel by distorting the divine person and saving work of Christ. In response to the controversy over Arius's teachings, the Emperor Constantine convened the Council of Nicaea in 325. More than three hundred bishops examined the charges against Arius and condemned him and his followers as heretics who had deviated from cardinal truths of Christianity. Then the council composed a doctrinal statement that accurately expressed the standard of Christian orthodoxy. In this statement, known as the Symbol of Nicaea, the bishops carefully articulated that Christ is *one* person with *two* natures—one divine and one human. Moreover, the council asserted that God is *one* God who exists eternally in *three* persons—Father, Son, and Holy Spirit—each equal in essence.

Tragically, this statement did not stop the attacks on the Trinity. Years after the council, the church still was battling doctrinal assaults on the co-equality and co-eternality of the three persons of the Godhead. The Semi-Arians staked out a compromise position between Trinitarian orthodoxy and Arianism. In their estimation, the Son was *similar* to the Father in essence (*homoiousios*), but not the *same* as the Father (*homoousios*). Constantius, Constantine's son, took this position and demanded that the wording of the Symbol of Nicaea be altered from *homoousios* to *homoiousios*, a blatant compromise of the truth. The Pneumatomachians, or "Spirit-fighters," taught that God created the Holy Spirit out of nothing. Their leader, Eustathius, contended that the Spirit was not fully divine. Finally, the Eunomians denied the deity of Christ, asserting that He was a mere created being. Eunomius (d. 394) taught that a hierarchy of spirit-beings possessed degrees of deity, but none were fully divine. Both Jesus Christ and the Holy Spirit, he said, were part of this less-than-divine hierarchy.

These heretical views of the Godhead needed to be emphatically refuted. The Cappadocian Fathers answered the call to defend the truth against these grotesque errors. As this trio wrote and preached, they displayed a solid understanding of key aspects of the doctrines of grace.

# THE CAPPADOCIAN FATHERS

When Athanasius died in 373, his role as the leading theologian in the West passed to the trio of men known to history as the Cappadocian Fathers. These notable men were among the most remarkable in the history of early Christianity, and they were used mightily by God during the second half of the fourth century to defend orthodox doctrine. The three of them—Basil of Caesarea (ca. 329–379), Gregory of Nazianzus (330–389), and Gregory of Nyssa (ca. 336–after 394)—were natives of the province of Cappadocia in Asia Minor. Thus, they came to be called the Cappadocian Fathers. They were a close-knit band of spiritual brothers, a homogeneous group of theologians and church leaders. Basil and Gregory of Nyssa, in fact, were biological brothers and lifelong friends of Gregory of Nazianzus.

The Cappadocian Fathers combined classical and biblical learning, intellectual precision, and skilled rhetoric with zeal for the truth. Their prolific writings addressed a wide range of topics in theology, biblical exegesis, and spirituality. Together, they emerged as the main stalwarts in the work of defining and defending the theological distinctives of the tri-unity of God.[2] What is more, they were leading figures in the final defeat of Arianism in the church.[3]

All three Cappadocian Fathers made important contributions to the church's understanding of the Trinity. Basil emphasized what the three persons of the Trinity have in common (*ousia*) and what is particular to each (*hupostasis*). He argued that all three have the same essence. He set down the doctrine of the Trinity in definitive terms, and he used his powers of persuasion and his influence to convince others that Nicene orthodoxy was the correct interpretation. Gregory of Nazianzus then stressed the differences among the persons of the Trinity. Gregory of Nyssa emphasized that each person of the Trinity is involved in every divine action, whether creation, providence, salvation, or judgment. Each was mightily used to uphold the Nicene orthodoxy that was validated at the Council of Constantinople in 381. This was a great victory for Trinitarian truth.

## BASIL OF CAESAREA

Basil of Caesarea was the first of the Cappadocian Fathers to appear on the scene and was the most authoritative and dominant of the three. Armed with a deep knowledge of the Scriptures, he thoroughly exposed the Arian errors. Though he lived only fifty years and died two years before the historic Council of Constantinople, his ministry steered the church through the dangerous waters of Trinitarian heresy to the harbor of biblical orthodoxy.

Basil was one of the most eminent of the Greek Fathers, those Fathers of the church who wrote in the Greek language.[4] A man of many talents, he distinguished himself as a gifted pulpit orator and able theologian.[5] He was regarded as eloquent, learned, and statesmanlike, with an unusual talent for organization.[6] Basil's sermons and treatises have been praised as the clearest, most beautiful Christian Greek writings from the Patristic period.[7] Because of his invaluable contribution to the formulation of the doctrine of the Trinity, he earned the title "Basil the Great."[8] Others called him "the theologian of the Holy Spirit."[9]

Basil was born in Caesarea, in the province of Cappadocia, into a wealthy Christian family. His grandfathers had suffered severe persecution for their faith under Emperor Galerius (306–313), losing their worldly fortunes. Basil was raised by his godly maternal grandmother, Macrina, and his mother, Emmelia, through whom the seed of piety was planted in him.[10] He had four brothers and five sisters. Basil would later appoint two of his brothers as bishops, one of whom, Gregory, became a great theologian in his own right. His oldest sister, also named Macrina, was known for her godliness and proved to be a great spiritual influence on Basil.[11] She took strict care of the Christian education of her brothers. His father, a skilled rhetorician, taught Basil the finer points of logic and presentation.

## EDUCATED IN CONSTANTINOPLE AND ATHENS

Basil pursued formal education, a privilege typically reserved for the wealthy.[12] He left Caesarea in 347 to study in Constantinople, where he was taught by the highly esteemed teacher Libanius. Basil then traveled to Athens, the cradle of European philosophical thought, to attend the famous Platonic academy from 350 to 355.[13] There he received prized instruction in rhetoric, math, and philosophy. At the academy, Basil was surrounded by the brightest prodigies, who came to receive the best education Greek culture offered. One of Basil's classmates—a young man named Julian—was a future emperor of Rome, an indication of the elite nature of the students with whom he associated.

At the academy, Basil renewed an earlier acquaintance with Gregory of Nazianzus, who also was to become a leading Greek Father. The two became devoted friends. Gregory later wrote that Basil worked hard to maintain a pure lifestyle amid the vice and temptations of Athens: "We knew only two streets of the city, the first and the more excellent one to the churches, and to the ministers of the altar; the other, which, however, we did not so highly esteem, to the public schools and to the teachers of the sciences. The streets to the theatres, games, and places of unholy amusements, we left to others. Our holiness was our great concern; our sole aim was to be called and to be Christians. In this we place our whole glory."[14] One writer has compared this friendship to that of Jonathan and David.[15]

## IN PURSUIT OF ASCETICISM

At some point after his return to Caesarea from Athens, Basil made a whole-hearted commitment to Christ, renouncing what he saw as a superficial attachment to Christianity. He writes: "Much time had I spent in vanity, and had wasted nearly all my youth in the vain labour which I underwent in acquiring the wisdom made foolish by God. Then once upon a time, like a man roused from deep sleep, I turned my eyes to the marvellous light of the truth of the Gospel, and I perceived the uselessness of 'the wisdom of the princes of this world, that come to naught.' I wept many tears over my miserable life and I prayed that guidance might be vouchsafed me to admit me to the doctrines of true religion."[16]

While in Athens, Basil had encountered ascetic ideas espoused by Eustathius (later to be the leader of the Pneumatomachians) and he had become curious about this rigid lifestyle of self-denial. Therefore, he embarked on an extended tour of Syria, Mesopotamia, Palestine, and Egypt, visiting Christian hermits who were pursuing holiness in small monasteries. Eventually, he joined a small community in a lonely district in Pontus.[17] There he lived as an ascetic, engaged in personal study, writing, and prayer.

Reflecting on this isolated time, Basil later wrote: "What is more blessed than to imitate on earth the choice of angels, at break of day to rise to prayer, and praise the Creator with anthems and songs; then to go to labor in the clear radiance of the sun, accompanied everywhere by prayer, seasoning work with praise, as if with salt? Silent solitude is the beginning of purification of the soul. For the mind, if it be not disturbed from without, and do not lose itself through the senses in the world, withdraws into itself, and rises to thoughts of God."[18]

Basil invited Gregory of Nazianzus to join him in the solitary forests of Pontus near the Iris River. During this time, the companions composed a consolidation of Origen's teachings known as the *Philocalia*. Basil also excelled in helping others with monastic rule and administration, providing structure and efficiency for communal life.[19]

## To the Front Line of Christianity

But Basil's giftedness would not allow him to remain in isolation long. He was summoned by the bishop of Caesarea to attend the Synod of Constantinople (360). At this gathering, Basil influenced the other leaders to uphold the orthodox teaching of the Trinity as stated by the Symbol of Nicaea. Even though he was only thirty years old, Basil played an active role in debating the Arians on the biblical teaching of the Godhead and defeating them.

When the bishop of Caesarea, Dianius, died in 362, Eusebius—known as "the Father of Church History"—succeeded him.[20] Eusebius asked Basil to be his assistant; he accepted and was ordained as a presbyter in 364. Basil excelled in management, a gift the bishop did not possess, sparking his jealousy. Not wanting to create conflict, Basil withdrew again into seclusion. There he devoted himself to further intense study and completed an important work, a defense of the Trinity titled *Against Eunomius* (364). Soon, however, Gregory of Nazianzus reconciled Basil and Eusebius, and Basil returned to his post as Eusebius's assistant.

When Eusebius died (370), Basil was appointed bishop of Caesarea, which was one of the most important Christian cities in Asia Minor. This appointment also gave him the oversight of fifty bishops in Cappadocia. Basil immediately began to use this elevated position to fight the great enemy of the truth in his day, Arianism. He systematically appointed to the various churches orthodox bishops who were sound in Trinitarian doctrine. To bolster this line of defense, he installed his trusted friend Gregory of Nazianzus as bishop of Sasima, his younger brother Gregory as bishop of Nyssa, and his younger brother Peter as bishop of Sabaste.

## Confrontation with the Emperor

The reigning emperor in the East was Valens, who supported Arianism. When Valens announced that he would visit Caesarea, it was understood that the emperor would use this appearance to promote the heretical teachings of Arius. Imperial officers arrived beforehand to prepare for Valens's visit by seeking to influence Basil through imperial promises and threats.

But unlike other bishops, Basil could not be controlled by such tactics. A heated exchange ensued, with the praetorian prefect threatening Basil. But Basil replied: "Nothing more! Not one of these things touches me. His property cannot be forfeited, who has none; banishment I know not, for I am restricted to no place, and am the guest of God, to whom the whole earth belongs; for martyrdom I am unfit, but death is a benefactor to me, for it sends me more quickly to God, to whom I live and move; I am also in great part already dead, and have been for a long time hastening to the grave."[21] The prefect was taken aback. No one had ever spoken to him like this, he declared. Basil answered, "Perhaps that is because you have never met a true bishop."[22]

Basil was under danger of banishment. However, Valens's six-year-old son became ill, then recovered when the emperor sent for Basil. The emperor attributed this recovery from sickness to Basil's prayers. This providence turned the imperial antipathy away from Basil and he was spared exile.

Basil lived a taxing life in which he faced many difficulties, perplexities, and divisions.[23] Furthermore, he was poor, with only a single, worn-out garment, and was almost always sickly. He ate almost nothing but bread, salt, and herbs for most of his life.[24] The wear on Basil's body through his rigorous self-discipline eventually took its toll, and he died at the relatively young age of forty-nine.

# BASIL'S WRITINGS

One chief weapon Basil used in his battle against Arianism was his pen. In his doctrinally pointed writings, he launched scathing attacks on Arian error. However, he left a substantial body of writings that addressed many key issues besides Arianism. His writings comprise dogmatic treatises on the Trinity and the Holy Spirit, exegetical commentaries on Psalms and Isaiah, sermons, works about monasticism, an essay on the benefits of a classical education, and more than three hundred letters.

## AGAINST EUNOMIUS

While in seclusion following his falling-out with Eusebius, Basil wrote *Against Eunomius* (364), his celebrated defense of the Trinity.[25] Eunomius was one of the most radical Arians, claiming that Christ was a mere created being. In this polemic response, Basil affirmed that all three persons of the Trinity have one substance and are fully divine. Although Basil was only thirty-four years old at the time, he brilliantly explicated this cornerstone doctrine of the Christian faith. Through this work, Basil showed himself to be a capable theologian.[26] This writing gave notice that he was destined to play a part of first importance as an opponent of the Arians.[27]

## ON THE HOLY SPIRIT

Basil's primary contribution to Christian theology was his writing concerning the person of the Holy Spirit. His *On the Holy Spirit* (ca. 375) was the first major treatise by the Church Fathers on the Spirit. He argued convincingly for the full deity of the Spirit, saying that the Spirit had been "ignored if not forgotten" at the Council of Nicaea (325), with the Father and Son receiving the attention.[28] The Symbol of Nicaea did not address the idea that there is a hierarchy within the Trinity, so Basil undertook this cause. This work was also intended to refute Eustathius, the leader of the Pneumatomachians, who had denied the Spirit's deity.

It has been said that in *On the Holy Spirit*, "The whole of Trinitarian theology, thus reorganized with genius, is set forth by Basil in language that is at once limpid and precise, accurate, and clear. Consequently this work, though that of a young man, makes a basic contribution to the definition of the Christian dogma."[29] This is a staggering assessment of Basil's ability in the theological arena.

# BASIL'S THEOLOGY

Like other ancients before him, Basil did not write in a systematized fashion and did not produce a systematic theology in the modern sense.[30] But his works nevertheless reveal his theological understandings in many important areas, demonstrating continuing doctrinal development within the church. As Basil defended the deity of the Holy Spirit, he affirmed the fall of the human race in Adam and the sovereignty of God in the election of a people for Himself.

**Doctrine in Focus:**
## DIVINE SOVEREIGNTY

Basil saw God's sovereignty demonstrated in Scripture from the earliest verses. This Father maintained that God exercised His supreme authority in creation when He commanded that the waters should be gathered into one place and the dry land should appear (Gen. 1:9). He writes: "Give your attention to the meaning of the Scripture, that not only the excess water flowed away from the earth, but also whatever was mixed with it throughout its depths, obedient to the inexorable command of the Lord, also withdrew. 'And so it was.'"[31] The mighty waters of the primal earth rolled back at God's voice, a picture of His command of the flow of world events.

Likewise, Basil stated, God controls the distribution of all good things for the blessing of His people. He writes: "I now say that I ought to give thanks to God when He gives benefits . . . surely He administers our affairs better than we should if the choice were ours."[32] Basil was right—God oversees the affairs of history infinitely better than any man could.

Basil was confident that nothing lies outside God's eternal purpose and sovereign rule. As he states: "Do not say, 'This happened by chance' and 'That occurred accidentally.' Nothing is casual, nothing indeterminate, nothing happens at random, nothing among things that exist is caused by chance."[33]

**Doctrine in Focus:**
## RADICAL DEPRAVITY

Although Basil, like the other Cappadocian Fathers, did not hold to the full-orbed doctrine of radical depravity that Augustine would later develop, he understood that Adam's sin had debilitated all people. Regarding the universality of sin, he states, "Every human soul is subject to the evil yoke of bondage of the common enemy of all, and being deprived of the liberty it had from its Creator, is led captive by sin."[34] Likewise, "No man has the power with respect to God to make atonement for a sinner, since he himself is liable for sin."[35] Basil clearly understood that all men are enslaved to sin.

Basil also affirmed that Adam's sin brought God's curse on all creation, not just humanity. He writes: "[Before the fall,] the rose bush was without thorns; later, the thorn was added to the beauty of the flower so that we might keep pain closely associated with the enjoyment of pleasure and remind ourselves of the sin for which the earth was condemned to bring forth thorns and thistles for us."[36] Basil saw that the natural world was not spared the effects of the disobedience of the first man.

**Doctrine in Focus:**
SOVEREIGN ELECTION

Basil was committed to the biblical doctrine of election. He affirmed that God sovereignly chose a people for Himself unto salvation. Expounding on Jesus' words in John 10:16 ("I have other sheep that are not of this fold"), Basil states that Jesus was speaking of elect individuals, those who "from among the Gentiles, are predestined to salvation." These chosen ones are "the sheep of Christ." They will be brought into the one fold, the church, "the one holy court of God," where they can offer the Lord adoration.[37]

Two years before his death, Basil wrote a letter to some monks who were being harassed by the Arians. In this correspondence, he writes: "Remember that it is not the many who are being saved, but the chosen of God. Therefore never let the multitude of the crowd daunt you, for they are swayed by the winds as is the water of the sea. For even if but one be saved, as was Lot at Sodom, he ought to abide in right judgment, keeping his hope in Christ unshaken, because the Lord will not abandon His holy ones."[38] In this communication, he affirmed that it is the elect who are saved.

Similarly, in a letter to a fellow bishop, Basil identified believers as "the chosen flock of the Lord."[39] The elect of God, he wrote elsewhere, will "inherit the kingdom." Basil maintained that this blessing has been ordered by God from before time began, just as Jesus explained in Matthew 25:34: "Foretelling by means of the parable of the shepherd the blessing that will be given [to the elect] in the time of retribution, Christ said: 'Come, blessed of my Father, inherit the kingdom prepared for you from the beginning of the world.'"[40] In short, the elect of God are those who will inherit the kingdom.

172 PILLARS OF GRACE

**Doctrine in Focus:**

IRRESISTIBLE CALL

Given man's depravity, Basil understood that salvation must be a sovereign work of grace. If the elect are to be saved, God must irresistibly call them to Himself. Basil writes: "Persuasions of falsely called knowledge provide a cause of death to those who receive them. But, this death he will not see who was redeemed by Him who was pleased to save those trusting in the foolishness of preaching."[41] This is to say, the redeemed believe not because they are humanly persuaded, but by divine power. He adds: "The proclamation of the gospel has great power in leading and drawing to salvation, and every soul who is held fast by its immoveable doctrines is confirmed, by grace, in the unshakeable faith in Christ."[42] Thus, Basil believed that a sinner comes to faith in Christ through the power of the Spirit's effectual calling.

Regeneration, Basil believed, brings the end of one's former life and ushers in the beginning of a new life. He states: "[It] is necessary that the old way of life be terminated, and this is impossible unless a man is born again, as the Lord has said. Regeneration, as its very name reveals, is a beginning of a second life. Before beginning a second life, one must put an end to the first."[43] The new birth is essential, but given man's fallen condition, he cannot effect that new birth for himself. God must create a second life within spiritually dead sinners, which He does in the new birth.

Likewise, the saving faith that accompanies the new birth, Basil maintained, does not originate within man but is granted by God. Basil teaches: "Faith does not come into being by mathematical certainties, but by the work of the Spirit."[44] Basil saw that faith is the result of the sovereign operation of divine regeneration. Regarding Basil's view of saving faith, the noted Baptist theologian John Gill writes, "Faith is the work of God, and he [Basil] means not what God requires of us, but what He works in us."[45]

Basil clearly taught that sinful man does not apprehend Christ by his own efforts. Salvation is by divine initiative. Basil writes: "Nothing is left for you, O man, to boast about, since your glorying and hope should lie in this, that you put to death your entire self, and seek the life to come in Christ. We already have a foretaste of this life, and living entirely as we do by the grace and gift of God. . . . Why then, tell me, do you glory in what you have as your own instead of giving thanks to the Giver for his gifts?"[46] There is nothing about which man can boast when it comes to the salvation of his soul.

**Doctrine in Focus:**

## Preserving Grace

Basil held that sovereign grace stretches from eternity past to eternity future. Those whom God chose before the foundation of the world and predestined to be saved will be ushered safely into glory and will not experience eternal destruction. He writes: "He who chose the narrow and wearisome way instead of the smooth and easy one . . . will not see everlasting corruption, namely, the misery that will last for ever."[47] In other words, those who are saved by grace will remain on the way of grace forever.

God-given faith, Basil maintained, cannot be moved away from Him. Such trust involves a full assurance of the truth. Basil writes: "What is the mark of faith? An unwavering conviction of the truth of the words breathed out by God, not to be shaken by any process of reasoning, or the introduction of the law of nature, or a counterfeit piety."[48] True faith, Basil declares, does not falter.

Basil wrote that all who place their trust in Christ have built on a foundation that is all of grace. As he says with regard to Psalm 116:1: "These words [I have loved because the Lord hath heard the voice of my prayer] seem to be equivalent to the words of the apostle, and to be said with the same affection by the prophet as by the apostle, 'Who shall separate us from the love of Christ? Shall tribulation, or distress, or persecution, or hunger, or nakedness, or danger, or the sword?' Therefore I have loved all those things, knowing that I endure these dangers for the sake of godliness."[49] He adds: "Eternal rest lies before these who have struggled through the present life . . . a rest not given in payment for a debt owed for their works, but provided as a grace of the munificent God for those who have hoped in him."[50] Nothing can separate those who trust in the Savior from the love of God in Christ (Rom. 8:39); their rest shall be eternal.

# FAITHFUL TO THE END

Despite his many hardships, Basil remained steadfast and faithful to the truth. This guardian of the gospel determined to study God's Word and fought to preserve the truth in his generation. He longed to use every breath to uphold the standard of sound words. His dying words, fittingly, were the prayer of David in Psalm 31:5: "Into Your hands, O Lord, I commit my spirit; You have redeemed me, O Lord, God of truth."[51] It is entirely appropriate that such an ardent defender of the faith died with Scripture on his tongue. Basil died as he had lived, speaking the truth of God's Word.

The church today has a dire need for Bible-believing men such as the bishop of Caesarea. This hour of church history must have men who courageously defend the sacred truth of the Word, faithfully guard the doctrinal precision of the church, and fearlessly refute those who would contradict it. Such valiant men are forged upon the anvil of sovereign grace truth by the persistent hammerings of the Spirit.

What is more, men who mark their eras are those who are gripped by a high view of God. They have been brought low in meek humility under divine sovereignty, but they have the deep imprint of particular grace upon them. As a result, these heralds of sovereign grace truth are noble stalwarts of the Christian faith.

May God raise up and bestow such faithful leaders on His church in the twenty-first century. May God give to His church today men who live for the glory of their triune God.

NOTES

1   Basil, *Of Humility*, in *Patrologiae cursus completus, Series graeca* (henceforth PG), ed. J. P. Migne, (Paris: Petit-Montrouge Excudebatur et venit apud J.P. Migne editorem, 1857), 31.529. Trans. Michael A. G. Haykin.

2   Roger E. Olson, *The Story of Christian Theology: Twenty Centuries of Tradition and Reform* (Downers Grove, Ill.: InterVarsity, 1999), 176.

3   "Cappadocian Fathers," in *New International Dictionary of the Christian Church*, gen. ed. J. D. Douglas (Grand Rapids: Zondervan, 1978), 191.

4   "Basil," in *Cyclopedia of Biblical, Theological, and Ecclesiastical Literature, Vol. I*, eds. John McClintock and James Strong (Grand Rapids: Baker, 1981), 682.

5   Philip Schaff, *History of the Christian Church, Vol. III: Nicene and Post-Nicene Christianity: From Constantine the Great to Gregory the Great, A.D. 311–590* (1910; repr., Grand Rapids: Eerdmans, 1979), 902.

6   "Basil," in *The Oxford Dictionary of the Christian Church*, 3rd Ed., ed. E. A. Livingstone (1957; repr., Oxford: Oxford University Press, 1997), 166.

7   N. R. Needham, *2,000 Years of Christ's Power, Part One: The Age of the Early Church Fathers* (London: Grace Publications, 1997), 218.

8   V. L. Walter, "Cappadocian Fathers," in *Evangelical Dictionary of Theology*, 2nd Ed., ed. Walter A. Elwell (Grand Rapids: Baker, 2001), 208.

9   Olson, *The Story of Christian Theology*, 177.

10  Schaff, *History of the Christian Church, Vol. III*, 895.

11 Basil also became known for his godly character.

12 Morwenna Ludlow, "The Cappadocians," in *The First Christian Theologians: An Introduction to Theology in the Early Church*, ed. G. R. Evans (Malden, Mass.: Blackwell, 2004), 168.

13 Needham, *2,000 Years of Christ's Power, Part One*, 218.

14 Gregory of Nazianzus, cited in Schaff, *History of the Christian Church, Vol. III*, 895.

15 Needham, *2,000 Years of Christ's Power, Part One*, 218.

16 Basil, *Epistle 223*, 2, in *Nicene and Post-Nicene Fathers, Series 2, Vol. VIII: Saint Basil: Letters and Select Works*, eds. Philip Schaff and Henry Wace (Grand Rapids: Eerdmans, 2002), 263.

17 Schaff, *History of the Christian Church, Vol. III*, 899.

18 Basil, cited in Schaff, *History of the Christian Church, Vol. III*, 900.

19 Walter, "Cappadocian Fathers," in *Evangelical Dictionary of Theology*, 207.

20 J. G. G. Norman, "Eusebius of Caesarea," in *New International Dictionary of the Christian Church*, 356.

21 Basil, cited in Schaff, *History of the Christian Church, Vol. III*, 901.

22 Basil, cited in Justo L. González, *The Story of Christianity, Vol. 1: The Early Church to the Dawn of the Reformation* (Peabody, Mass.: Prince Press, 2004), 185.

23 Schaff, *History of the Christian Church, Vol. III*, 902.

24 Schaff, *History of the Christian Church, Vol. III*, 902.

25 Ludlow, "The Cappadocians," in *The First Christian Theologians*, 171.

26 Claudio Moreschini and Eurico Norelli, *Early Christian Greek and Latin Literature: A Literary History, Vol. Two: From the Council of Nicea to the Beginning of the Medieval Period* (Peabody, Mass.: Hendrickson, 2005), 88.

27 Moreschini and Norelli, *Early Christian Greek and Latin Literature: A Literary History, Vol. Two*, 88.

28 Olson, *The Story of Christian Theology*, 177.

29 Moreschini and Norelli, *Early Christian Greek and Latin Literature: A Literary History, Vol. Two*, 88.

30 Olson, *The Story of Christian Theology*, 175.

31 Basil, *On The Hexaemeron*, 4.5, in *Saint Basil: Exegetic Homilies*, trans. Agnes Clare Way (Washington, D.C.: The Catholic University of America, 1963), 61–62.

32 Basil, *Epistle 1*, in *Saint Basil, the Letters, Vol. 1: Letters 1–58*, trans. Roy J. Deferrari (Cambridge, Mass., and London: Harvard University Press and W. Heinemann, 1962–72), 7.

33 Basil, *Homily on Psalm 32*, in *Saint Basil: Exegetic Homilies*, 232.

34 Basil, *Homily on Psalm 48*, in *Saint Basil: Exegetic Homilies*, 317.

35 Basil, *Homily on Psalm 48*, in *Saint Basil: Exegetic Homilies*, 317.

36 Basil, *On the Hexaemeron*, 5.6, in *Saint Basil: Exegetic Homilies*, 74–75.

37 Basil, *Homily on Psalm 28*, 3, in PG 29.288. Trans. Michael A. G. Haykin.

38 Basil, *Epistle 257*, in *Saint Basil: The Letters, Vol. 4: Letters 259–368*, trans. Roy J. Deferrari and Martin R. P. McGuire (Cambridge, Mass., and London: Harvard University Press and W. Heinemann, 1950–70), 35.

39 Basil, *Epistle 81*, in *Saint Basil: The Letters, Vol. 2: Letters 59–185*, trans. Roy J. Deferrari (Cambridge, Mass., and London: Harvard University Press and W. Heinemann, 1950–62), 93.

40 Basil, *On Baptism*, 1.2.2, cited in Jeanne Ducatillon, *Basile de Césarée: Sur le Baptême*, Sources Chrétiennes, No. 357 (Paris: Les Éditions du Cerf, 1989), 108. Trans. Michael A. G. Haykin.

41 Basil, *Homily on Psalm 48*, 5, in *Saint Basil: Exegetic Homilies*, 321.

42 Basil, *Homily on Psalm 44*, 4, in PG 29.397. Trans. Michael A. G. Haykin.

43 Basil, *On the Holy Spirit*, 15.35, in *On the Holy Spirit*, trans. David Anderson (Crestwood, N.Y.: St. Vladimir's Seminary Press, 1980), 57–58.

44 Basil, *On Psalm 115*, 1, in PG 30.104B. Trans. Michael A. G. Haykin.

45 John Gill, *The Cause of God and Truth* (Paris, Ark.: The Baptist Standard Bearer, 2000), 235.

46 Basil, *Of Humility*, in PG 31.529–532. Trans. Michael A. G. Haykin.

47 Basil, *Homily on Psalm 48*, 5, in PG 29.444. Trans. Michael A. G. Haykin.

48 Basil, *The Morals*, 79.22, in PG 31.868. Trans. Michael A. G. Haykin.

49 Basil, *Homily on Psalm 114*, in *Saint Basil: Exegetic Homilies*, 317.

50 Basil, *Homily on Psalm 114*, in *Saint Basil: Exegetic Homilies*, 321.

51 Basil, cited in Schaff, *History of the Christian Church, Vol. III*, 902.

# CHAPTER NINE
## STUDY QUESTIONS

1. Who were the Cappadocian Fathers? What contribution did they make in the battle for the truth? How can you earnestly contend for the Christian faith? Which doctrines are battlefields for the church today?

2. Define the doctrine of the Trinity. What doctrines are compromised when the truth of the Godhead is weakened? Where do you see it under attack today?

3. What spiritual gifts and abilities did Basil have? How were they employed in the Lord's work? How has God gifted you to serve Him? How are you using these God-given abilities?

4. Describe the practice of asceticism. What spiritual disciplines can Christians borrow from this ancient practice? What are the dangers in pursuing asceticism?

5. What potential compromises confronted Basil in his day? How did he respond? How is he an example for you in this?

6. Why is the Holy Spirit important in Christian theology? How did God use Basil to articulate the doctrine of the Holy Spirit? How can you better understand the Holy Spirit? How would a better understanding of Him prepare you for Christian living?

7. How did Basil describe the doctrine of sovereign election? What biblical allusions and passages did he use? What passages of Scripture speak to this doctrine?

8. In what way did Basil understand the ministry of the Holy Spirit in man's salvation? What is the role of the Holy Spirit in regeneration? What is the relationship of the new birth to saving faith?

*The Spirit of God . . . is the author of spiritual regeneration. Here is your proof–None can see or enter into the Kingdom, except he be born again of the Spirit, and be cleansed from the first birth.*[1]

*–Gregory of Nazianzus*

Chapter Ten

# EXPOSITOR
# OF THE TRINITY

## CAPPADOCIAN FATHER:
## GREGORY OF NAZIANZUS

I n the years after the Council of Nicaea, the heresy of Arianism and similar errors continued to plague the church. Although the bishops who had
gathered at Nicaea in 325 had decisively agreed that God is of one essence
yet three in person, and that Jesus Christ is one person in two natures, divine
and human, these essential truths concerning the Godhead remained under
siege. The very heart of the gospel was still in jeopardy. Furthermore, a new
theological firestorm began to gather strength—false views regarding the deity
and saving work of the Holy Spirit, a foundational truth that the Council of
Nicaea did not address.

As unorthodox views of the Spirit's divinity flourished, it became impera-
tive for the church to confront these heretical teachings, championing the
cause of Trinitarian orthodoxy. Therefore, the Roman Emperor Theodosius I
(379–395), a strong adherent of Nicene Christianity, summoned the Council
of Constantinople in 381. This council, second in importance only to Nicaea,
was convened specifically to denounce Arianism and similar heresies. Furthermore, it was tasked with writing a theological statement regarding the Trinity.

Some 150 bishops, including thirty-six who held heretical positions,
debated for three months over this matter. When the dust settled, Constantinople upheld the doctrinal stance of Nicaea. In addition, it overruled lesser
councils that had been sympathetic to the deviations of Arianism. Finally,
Constantinople specifically addressed the deity of the Holy Spirit, asserting
that the Spirit is equal with the Father and the Son.[2]

The Council of Constantinople summarized its work in a creed known as the Constantinople Creed or, technically, the "Niceno-Constantinopolitan Creed." This creed became the definitive statement of the Christian faith during the fourth and fifth centuries. Regarding Jesus Christ and the Spirit, it reads:

> We believe in one Lord, Jesus Christ, the only Son of God, eternally begotten of the Father, God from God, Light from Light, true God from true God, begotten, not made, of one Being with the Father. Through Him all things were made. For us men and for our salvation He came down from heaven; by the power of the Holy Spirit He became incarnate from the Virgin Mary, and was made man. For our sake He was crucified under Pontius Pilate; He suffered death and was buried. On the third day He rose again in accordance with the Scriptures; He ascended into heaven and is seated at the right hand of the Father. He will come again in glory to judge the living and the dead, and His kingdom will have no end. We believe in the Holy Spirit, the Lord, the giver of life, who proceeds from the Father (and the Son). With the Father and the Son He is worshipped and glorified. He has spoken through the Prophets.[3]

The council also condemned a number of unorthodox groups. These included: the Semi-Arians, who tried to steer a middle course between Nicene orthodoxy and Arianism,[4] saying that Jesus Christ had a similar substance (*homoiousios*) to that of the Father, but was not coeternal, co-essential, or coequal with the Father;[5] the Pneumatomachians, or the "Spirit-fighters," who assigned a non-divine status to the Holy Spirit;[6] the Eudoxians, who declared that Christ possessed a different substance (*heteroousios*) than the Father, making Him not coeternal, co-essential, or coequal with the Father; the Apollinarians, who denied the humanity of Christ, saying that the *Logos* replaced the human soul and mind in the incarnate Christ;[7] and the Sabellians, Marcellians, and Photinians, who all asserted one God in one person.

The monumental achievements of Constantinople were the result chiefly of the leadership provided by Gregory of Nazianzus, the most prominent theologian in the East and the leading defender of Nicene orthodoxy. In the absence of Basil of Caesarea, who had died two years earlier (379), Gregory's presence at the Council of Constantinople stabilized the defense of sound doctrine that was under attack. As he addressed Scripture to defend the core truths of Nicene Christianity, Gregory affirmed, in principle, essential elements of the doctrines of grace.

# GREGORY OF NAZIANZUS

Gregory (330–389) is recognized as the most gifted and astute theologian of the three Cappadocian Fathers.[8] His intellectual prowess earned him the revered title "the Theologian."[9] Gregory confronted Arianism and its attendant heresies, and so gained a reputation as one of the main guardians of Christian truth in his time.[10] In an hour when the truth was under assault, this Greek Father proved himself to be the great defender and explainer of Trinitarian orthodoxy in his time.[11]

Born near Nazianzus in the province of Cappadocia in Asia Minor, Gregory was the son of wealthy Christian parents. Both exerted a strong spiritual influence on his life. His father, also named Gregory, served as the bishop of the church of Nazianzus and provided an example of Christian virtue for his son. The elder Gregory had been a heretic, but through the witness of his Christian wife, Nonna, he had been converted to Christ. This godly woman also was influential in the conversion of her son. Gregory would later reflect on his mother's godliness:

She was a wife according to the mind of Solomon; in all things subject to her husband according to the laws of marriage, not ashamed to be his teacher and his leader in true religion. She solved the difficult problem of uniting a higher culture, especially in knowledge of divine things and strict exercise of devotion, with the practical care of her household. If she was active in her house, she seemed to know nothing of the exercises of religion; if she occupied herself with God and His worship, she seemed to be a stranger to every earthly occupation: she was whole in everything. Experiences had instilled into her unbounded confidence in the effects of believing prayer; therefore she was most diligent in supplications, and by prayer overcame even the deepest feelings of grief over her own and others' sufferings. She had by this means attained such control over her spirit, that in every sorrow she encountered, she never uttered a plaintive tone before she had thanked God.[12]

In this Christian home, Gregory was instructed in the Scriptures from an early age. He also was taught the basics of science and other subjects, including rhetoric and oratory. Blessed with an inquisitive and intelligent mind, Gregory spent much of his youth studying classical literature and logic. These disciplines would be foundational for the ministry that lay ahead.

## Educated in Caesarea and Athens

Gregory received a formal education in Caesarea in Cappadocia, where he studied advanced rhetoric. It was there that he met Basil, his future co-worker, with whom he built a lasting friendship. Subsequently, Gregory traveled abroad to pursue further education, a privilege restricted to elite families. He went first to Caesarea in Palestine, where he studied in one of the distinguished schools of eloquence.[13] Gregory's school boasted the personal library of the theologian Origen. He studied under the rhetorician Thespesius, a renowned debater. Gregory then went to Alexandria for additional study, where he probably met the great theologian Athanasius.

At age twenty, Gregory journeyed to Athens, a city famed for its schools of Greek philosophy. He attended the Platonic academy, which was esteemed above all institutions in the ancient world as the highest seat of Grecian learning.[14] In this renowned school, Gregory received a first-class education in rhetoric, logic, and philosophy. He studied under the celebrated rhetoricians Himerius and Prohaeresius, the latter a Christian scholar, and competed academically with the brightest students of the region. His friend Basil was also a student at the academy, and Gregory and Basil became so close that it was said they were one soul animating two bodies.[15]

Following a decade of study in Athens, Gregory, age thirty, was invited to teach in the celebrated academy, a great recognition for one so young. But he chose to return to Nazianzus for a quieter life. Soon, at Basil's insistence, the two friends took up the monastic life in Pontus. This season of seclusion proved to be immensely profitable for the pursuit of spiritual disciplines, such as prayer, study, meditation, and writing. In this cloistered environment, Gregory and Basil coauthored a book titled *Philocalia*, which contained selections from the writings of Origen.

Gregory later wrote of this season of simplicity: "Who will transport me, back to those former days, in which I reveled with thee [Basil] in privations? For voluntary poverty is after all far more honorable than enforced enjoyment. Who will give me back those songs and vigils? who, those risings to God in prayer, that unearthly, incorporeal life, that fellowship and that spiritual harmony of brothers raised by thee to a God-like life? who, the ardent searching of the Holy Scriptures, and the light which, under the guidance of the Spirit, we found therein?"[16]

## THRUST INTO THE PASTORATE

Following this sequestered season, Gregory visited his parents' home in Nazianzus. Unexpectedly, his father ordained him as a presbyter in his home church against his will (361). Such sudden ordinations to ministry were common during that time. Other early church leaders, such as Athanasius, Basil, Ambrose, and Augustine, had their ministries thrust upon them in similar dramatic fashion. Reeling from shock, Gregory immediately withdrew into monastic seclusion at Pontus to seek Basil's counsel. Only reluctantly, with his friend's encouragement, did he return to Nazianzus to accept a pastoral role under his father (362).

When Gregory stepped before the congregation to deliver his first sermon, he humbly explained his hesitancy to assume public ministry: "It has its advantage to hold back a little from the call of God, as Moses, and after him Jeremiah, did on account of their age; but it has also its advantage to come forward readily, when God calls, like Aaron and Isaiah; provided both be done with a devout spirit, the one on account of inherent weakness, the other in reliance upon the strength of him who calls."[17] Gregory's reluctance to seek the pastoral ministry revealed his true humility.

During this time, the lethal lies of Arianism and its related heresies continued to trouble the churches in the East. Basil, who had been appointed bishop of Caesarea and archbishop over fifty churches of Cappadocia (370), felt compelled to refute the false teaching of Arius. He established new pastorates in the small towns of Cappadocia, where he could place trusted men of unwavering orthodox convictions. As part of this effort, Basil strategically appointed Gregory to be bishop of Sasima. This commission, like his ordination, was made against his will, and it is possible he never actually took up his office. This reluctance resulted in a temporary rift with Basil.

Gregory retreated to isolation for another time of quiet meditation. But it soon became necessary for him to return home to help his ailing father in the pastorate. From the pulpit, he openly revealed his struggle between his preference for privacy and the demands of public ministry:

> I am almost torn asunder by my inward longing and by the Spirit. The longing urges me to flight, to solitude in the mountains, to quietude of soul and body, to withdrawal of spirit from all sensuous things, and to retirement into myself, that I may commune undisturbed with God, and be wholly penetrated by the rays of His Spirit. . . . But the other, the Spirit, would lead me into the midst of life, to serve the common weal, and by furthering others to further myself, to spread light, and to present to God a people for His possession, a holy people, a royal priesthood.[18]

Ultimately, the Spirit prevailed, and Gregory remained a faithful helper at his father's side.[19] He assumed the role of an auxiliary bishop until the elder Gregory died at age one hundred (ca. 373).[20] Then he was pressed by the congregation to take up his father's ministerial position, which he did for a brief time.

## BACK INTO QUIET SECLUSION

At the age of forty-five, Gregory retreated into solitude yet again, to the convent of St. Thecla in modern-day Turkey (375). There he remained for about four years. When news reached him that his beloved friend Basil had died (379), he was devastated. He wrote in a letter: "You ask, how it fares with me. Very badly. I no longer have Basil; I no longer have Caesarius; my spiritual brother, and my bodily brother. I can say with David, my father and my mother have forsaken me. My body is sickly, age is coming over my head, cares become more and more complicated, duties overwhelm me, friends are unfaithful, the church is without capable pastors, good declines, evil stalks naked."[21]

But Gregory's public service was not over. He was appointed archbishop of Constantinople (380), but immediately found himself embroiled in ecclesiastical and political in-fighting.[22] Then, with the Arian controversy raging, Emperor Theodosius I called the Council of Constantinople in 381, and Gregory was elected president, his theological abilities making him the obvious choice. But controversy soon flared up over his appointment as archbishop of Constantinople. Alexandrian and Macedonian bishops insisted that canon law prevented him from being the archbishop of Constantinople while simultaneously holding the bishopric at Sasima.[23] Further, Arian bishops falsely accused him of illegal acts. He even received death threats. Weakening under these relentless attacks, he became tired, ill, and frustrated. Unexpectedly, Gregory resigned and delivered his farewell address in Constantinople before withdrawing to Nazianzus.

After Gregory stepped down from the leadership of the Council of Constantinople, the assembled bishops wrote a bold statement, the Constantinople Creed, which affirmed the full deity of the Son and the Spirit. This creedal confession asserted the Spirit to be the "Lord" and "the giver of life," who "with the Father and the Son . . . is together worshipped and glorified." The council confessed the cardinal truth that the three persons of the Godhead are an "uncreated, consubstantial, and coeternal Trinity."[24] This declaration was largely the result of the work of Gregory of Nazianzus.

Gregory returned to his homeland, where he lived quietly, composing hymns and devoting himself to pastoral ministry. Eventually, Emperor Theodosius decided to convene another ecclesiastical council and asked Gregory to preside over the assembly. But Gregory's desire for solitude caused him to decline. He died in obscurity on the family estate where he had been born. Having spent many years in monastic isolation, it was fitting that he ended his days in contemplation, seeking and loving God.

# GREGORY'S WRITINGS

Gregory left behind a vast body of work. Included in his corpus are many orations, over two hundred and forty letters, three hundred poems, and a long autobiography that has been called one of the most transparent in antiquity, exceeded only by Augustine's *Confessions*. A series of sermons he preached on theology was collected and titled *Theological Orations* (380). These sermons are considered classics of ancient literature.

## THEOLOGICAL ORATIONS

This is Gregory's best-known work. It is composed of five lengthy sermons on the Trinity and the deity of the Holy Spirit. These expositions cited more than 750 biblical passages and, it has been said, made more sense of more Scripture than anything preached or written by his Arian opponents.[25] He demonstrated adherence to rules of proper exegesis in grasping the true meaning of the biblical texts.[26] A bold defender of the tri-unity of God, Gregory wrote sharply against the many foes of Trinitarian orthodoxy. He admitted, "I cannot think of the One [God], but I am immediately surrounded with the splendor of the Three; nor can I clearly discover the Three, but I am suddenly carried back to the One."[27]

Throughout this work, Gregory fought both Arians and Sabellians in the matter of the full deity of Christ and the Holy Spirit. He also soundly refuted the Apollinarians, who insisted that Christ was without a human mind and soul. He declared that Christ did, in fact, have both, but avoided the heretical position that there are two separate natures in Christ, which would make Him two persons. Instead, he insisted that the two natures of Christ, one divine and one human, are united in one person, the God-man. Jesus Christ, he asserted, is fully God and fully man.

# GREGORY'S THEOLOGY

The many theological controversies of the fourth century forced Gregory to focus on the biblical truth of the Trinity as much as any of the ancient Fathers. In his defenses, Gregory gained a command of the Word that inevitably led him to address the truths of sovereign grace. Anyone who teaches the Bible and gives careful attention to its truths must weigh in on this subject. Gregory was no exception. It must be admitted that Gregory's comments reveal an embryonic understanding of the doctrines; like others of his time, he did not grasp them in a systematic way. Nevertheless, when Gregory addressed God's sovereignty in man's salvation, he spoke with great clarity.

**Doctrine in Focus:**
DIVINE SOVEREIGNTY

Gregory was a strong believer in God's absolute sovereignty over the affairs of men, world events, and eternal destinies. In affirming the doctrine of providence, he writes, "Believe that the whole universe, all that is visible and all that is invisible, was brought into being out of nothing by God and is governed by the Providence of its Creator, and will receive a change to a better condition."[28] Here he asserted that God controls all that He created. In a prayer in his eulogy for his brother Caesarius, he likewise addressed God with these words: "O Lord and Maker of all things, and specially of this our frame! O God and Father and Pilot of men who are Yours! O Lord of life and death!

O Judge and Benefactor of our souls! O Maker and Transformer in due time of all things by Your designing Word, according to the knowledge of the depth of Your wisdom and providence!"[29] These statements affirm the truth of God's supreme reign over the world.

Gregory held that Christ is enthroned in heaven and will rule until He brings history to its appointed end. In countering Eunomian arguments that Christ will not rule eternally, Gregory cites Luke 1:33 when he writes: "What is to happen afterwards? Will He stop ruling as King or be thrust out of heaven? Who is to make Him stop or what grounds would He have for doing so? What a bold expositor you are, how very independent of royal government! And yet you hear that 'there is no end of His royal rule.'"[30] Gregory would not tolerate the suggestion that Christ's reign is not unending.

**Doctrine in Focus:**
RADICAL DEPRAVITY

Gregory possessed a clear understanding of the radical depravity of mankind. In accord with Scripture, he maintained that when Adam sinned, he was banished from the garden of Eden. In Gregory's words: "[Adam] forgot the commandment given him and yielded to the bitter taste. And at once he came to be banished from the tree of life and from paradise."[31] This banishment led to the separation of the entire human race from God and spiritual life. Gregory states, "Adam caused [heaven] to be closed . . . for himself and those who came after him, just as paradise was closed by a flaming sword."[32] Adam's sin resulted in his expulsion from the presence of God. This same dismissal is suffered by all his descendants.

Gregory had more to say regarding the effect of the fall. He plainly asserted that the entire human race was ruined by the rebellion of the first man. Gregory writes, "[All] partake of the same Adam, and were led astray by the serpent and slain by sin."[33] This is to say, Adam was the representative of the entire human race; when he sinned in the garden, all people were immediately condemned. Gregory further states: "For we believe that since we had fallen due to sin from the beginning and had been led away by pleasure as far as idolatry and lawless bloodshed, we needed to be called back again and restored to our original state, through the heartfelt compassion of God our Father."[34] Thus, he affirmed that Adam's sin caused humanity to fall into a state of rebellion against God. Only by grace is recovery possible.

Gregory believed that the minds of fallen men are imprisoned in sin, a spiritual state that prevents them from understanding divine truth. Concerning this bondage, Gregory states, "For in no other way does the coarseness of a material body and a captive mind come to comprehension of God except by being helped."[35] Fallen men's minds are so enslaved they cannot know God by their own initiative or intellect.

**Doctrine in Focus:**
## SOVEREIGN ELECTION

Gregory understood that believers were chosen by God before time began. Looking beyond the large numbers of people merely attending church, he affirms that salvation belongs to a chosen remnant: "God does not delight in numbers! 'You count your tens of thousands, but God counts those who will be saved; you the immeasurable grains of sand but, I the vessels of election."[36] The "vessels of election" are those who are saved out of the mass of fallen humanity.

Gregory taught that the names of believers in Christ were recorded before they believed. He writes: "Perhaps you have heard . . . of a certain book of the living, and of a book of them that are not to be saved, where we shall all be written, or rather are already written."[37] This book of life (Phil. 4:3; Rev. 3:5; 20:12) contains the names of all the saved; their names were written there long ago. Thus, election precedes faith.

**Doctrine in Focus:**
## IRRESISTIBLE CALL

Gregory saw that salvation is all of God—thus, all of grace. That anyone knows God is entirely of Him. He writes: "We call it gift, grace, baptism, illumination, anointing, robe of incorruption, bath of rebirth, seal, everything honorable. It is a gift because no offering is given for it beforehand; and grace, as given even to debtors."[38] Salvation is a gift of God, based on nothing deserving in the sinner.

Gregory also spoke glowingly of the Spirit's work of illumination, the spiritual enlightenment that is essential for conversion. He says: "This illumination is radiance of souls, transformation of life, engagement of the conscience toward God. Illumination is help for our weakness, illumination is renunciation of the flesh, following of the Spirit, communion in the Word, setting right of the creature, a flood overwhelming sin, participation in light, dissolution of darkness. Illumination is a vehicle leading toward God, departure with Christ, the support of faith, perfection of mind, key of the kingdom of heaven, change of life, deliverance from slavery, release from bonds, transformation of our composite nature. Illumination—what more need I add?—is the most beautiful and most magnificent of the gifts of God."[39]

No unconverted person, Gregory affirmed, can see or enter God's kingdom apart from the new birth. Furthermore, it is the Holy Spirit who works this regeneration; no human being can cause himself to be born again. Gregory writes: "The divine Spirit created me, and the breath of the Almighty taught me; and again, 'You will send forth Your Spirit and they will be created, and you will renew the face of the earth.' He also fashions the spiritual rebirth. Be persuaded by the text: 'Nobody can see the kingdom or receive it unless he has been born from above by the Spirit, unless he has been purified from his earlier birth.'"[40] Gregory was clear that the Spirit is the sole Author of regeneration.

In addition, Gregory affirmed that the Holy Spirit moves among hearts like the wind, sovereignly and independently. He comments: "The Spirit it is who knows all things, who teaches all things, who blows where, and as strongly as, He wills, who leads, speaks, sends out, separates. . . . He reveals, illumines, gives life—or, rather, is absolutely Light and Life."[41] By these words, Gregory affirmed that the Spirit is absolutely free in His working of regeneration. God reveals truth, illumines minds, and quickens spiritually dead sinners as He pleases.

Commenting on Romans 9:16, Gregory argued that no man can choose what is right apart from the gift of the mercy of God. In other words, apart from sovereign grace, man cannot exercise his will to believe on Christ. He writes:

For when you hear, Not of him that wills, nor of him that runs, but of God that shows mercy, I counsel you to think the same. For since there are some who are so proud of their successes that they attribute all to themselves and nothing to Him that made them and gave them wisdom and supplied them with good; such are taught by this word that even to wish well needs help from God; or rather that even to choose what is right is divine and a gift of the mercy of God. For it is necessary both that we should be our own masters and also that our salvation should be of God. This is why He says not of him that wills; that is, not of him that wills only, nor of him that runs only, but also of God. . . . Next; since to will also is from God, he has attributed the whole to God with reason. However much you may run, however much you may wrestle, yet you need one to give the crown.[42]

This statement gives the proper prominence to the priority of the divine will in the regeneration of elect sinners.

# NEVER OUT OF SEASON

Gregory was a true pillar in the early church. In a time when the truth was under vicious attack, he faithfully upheld the standard of Christian orthodoxy. His strong Trinitarian doctrine caused him to be mightily used by the Lord. Though he repeatedly withdrew from the public spotlight, God nevertheless raised him up for his appointed moment in history to champion the cause of the truth.

The church today has great need of servants like Gregory of Nazianzus, men who are meticulous in their doctrinal precision and tenacious in their stand for biblical truth. But the church also needs men, like Gregory, who are meek in their piety, passionate in their pursuit of God, and disinterested in achieving great things for themselves. We desperately need men who will recapture the high ground of Trinitarian orthodoxy and testify to the effectual work of the Holy Spirit in man's salvation.

Such men are never out of season in the church. These timeless virtues are as much in demand today as they were nearly seventeen centuries ago. Such men are gifts to the church from the ascended Christ, its sovereign Head. The Lord bestows them by His abundant grace upon His body. The Lord will grant them to His church in due time, for the Father entrusted them to Him in eternity past.

May the Lord supply this generation with such faithful men. May He give again to His church leaders who will handle accurately the precious Word of truth. Like Gregory, may they be men who do not crave the attention of people, but who seek the glory of God.

NOTES

1 Gregory, *Oration 41*, 14, in *Nicene and Post-Nicene Fathers, Second Series, Vol. VII: Cyril of Jerusalem, Gregory Nazianzen* (1894; repr., Peabody, Mass.: Hendrickson, 2004), 384.

2 B. K. Kuiper, *The Church in History* (Grand Rapids: Eerdmans, 1964), 32.

3 Gerald Bray, *Creeds, Councils & Christ* (Downers Grove, Ill.: InterVarsity, 1984), 206–207.

4 Craig A. Blaising, "First Council of Constantinople," in *Evangelical Dictionary of Theology*, 2nd Ed., ed. Walter A. Elwell (Grand Rapids: Baker, 2001), 291.

5 Blaising, "First Council of Constantinople," in *Evangelical Dictionary of Theology*, 291.

6 Blaising, "First Council of Constantinople," in *Evangelical Dictionary of Theology*, 291.

7 Blaising, "First Council of Constantinople," in *Evangelical Dictionary of Theology*, 291.

8 V. L. Walter, "Cappadocian Fathers," in *Evangelical Dictionary of Theology*, 207.

9 Roger E. Olson, *The Story of Christian Theology: Twenty Centuries of Tradition and Reform* (Downers Grove, Ill.: InterVarsity, 1999), 178.

10 Philip Schaff, *History of the Christian Church, Vol. III: Nicene and Post-Nicene Christianity: From Constantine the Great to Gregory the Great, A.D. 311–590* (1910; repr., Grand Rapids: Eerdmans, 1979), 909.

11 Olson, *The Story of Christian Theology*, 178.

12 Gregory, cited in Schaff, *History of the Christian Church, Vol. III*, 910.

13 Schaff, *History of the Christian Church, Vol. III*, 911.

14 Schaff, *History of the Christian Church, Vol. III*, 911.

15 Schaff, *History of the Christian Church, Vol. III*, 912.

16 Gregory, cited in Schaff, *History of the Christian Church, Vol. III*, 913.

17 Gregory, cited in Schaff, *History of the Christian Church, Vol. III*, 914.

18 Gregory, *Oration 12*, in *Patrologia Graeca*, ed. J. P. Migne (Paris: 1857–1866), 4, 847, cited in Schaff, *History of the Christian Church, Vol. III*, 915–916.

19 Schaff, *History of the Christian Church, Vol. III*, 916.

20 Fredrick W. Norris, "Gregory of Nazianzus," in *Biographical Dictionary of Christian Theologians*, eds. Patrick W. Carey and Joseph T. Lienhard (Westport, Conn.: Greenwood, 2000), 219.

21 Gregory, cited in Schaff, *History of the Christian Church, Vol. III*, 917.

22 Morwenna Ludlow, "The Cappadocians," in *The First Christian Theologians: An Introduction to Theology in the Early Church*, ed. G. R. Evans (Malden, Mass.: Blackwell, 2006), 173.

23 Ludlow, "The Cappadocians," in *The First Christian Theologians*, 173.

24 Blaising, "First Council of Constantinople," in *Evangelical Dictionary of Theology*, 291.

25 Norris, "Gregory of Nazianzus," in *Biographical Dictionary of Christian Theologians*, 220.

26 Norris, "Gregory of Nazianzus," in *Biographical Dictionary of Christian Theologians*, 220.

27 Gregory, *Oration 12*, 36, in *Patrologia Graeca*, 417, cited in Robert L. Reymond, *A New Systematic Theology of the Christian Faith* (Nashville: Thomas Nelson, 1998), 315.

28 Gregory, *Festal Orations: St. Gregory of Nazianzus*, trans. Nonna Verna Harrison (Crestwood, N.Y.: St. Vladimir's Seminary Press, 2008), 140.

29 Gregory, *Oration 7*, 24, in *Nicene and Post-Nicene Fathers, Second Series, Vol. VII*, 238.

30 Gregory, *Oration 30*, 4, in *On God and Christ: The Five Theological Orations and Two Letters to Cledonius*, eds. Frederick Williams and Lionel R. Wickham (Crestwood, N.Y.: St. Vladimir's Seminary Press, 2002), 95.

31 Gregory, *Festal Orations: St. Gregory of Nazianzus*, 167–168.

32 Gregory, *Oration 39*, 16, in G*regory of Nazianzus*, ed. and trans. Brian E. Daley (London: Routledge, 2006), 136.

33 Gregory, *Oration 33*, 9, in *Nicene and Post-Nicene Fathers, Second Series, Vol. VII*, 331.

34 Gregory, *Festal Orations: St. Gregory of Nazianzus*, 171.

35 Gregory, *Festal Orations: St. Gregory of Nazianzus*, 171.

36 Gregory, *Oration 42*, 7–8, in *Gregory of Nazianzus*, 144.

37 Gregory, *Oration 9*, 52, cited in *Fathers of the Church, Vol. 22: Funeral Orations by Saint Gregory of Nazianzen and Saint Ambrose*, ed. Roy Deferrari, trans. Leo P. McCauley (New York: Fathers of the Church, Inc., 1953), 16.

38 Gregory, *Festal Orations: St. Gregory of Nazianzus*, 101.

39 Gregory, *Festal Orations: St. Gregory of Nazianzus*, 100.

40 Gregory, *Festal Orations: St. Gregory of Nazianzus*, 156.

41 Gregory, *Oration 31*, 29, in *On God and Christ*, 140.

42 Gregory, *Oration 37*, 13, in *Nicene and Post-Nicene Fathers, Second Series, Vol. VII*, 341–342.

# CHAPTER TEN
# STUDY QUESTIONS

1. Explain the significance of the Council of Constantinople in the early church. What truths were affirmed in the creed produced by the council? Compare this statement with earlier confessions and creeds. What are the similarities? What are the differences?

2. How has God used controversy to sharpen the doctrinal focus of the church? What specific controversy drove the formulation of the Constantinople Creed?

3. Describe the godly influence of Gregory's mother in his developmental years. What positive spiritual influences were brought to bear on your earlier years? Why is this important? Can you provide references in Scripture to support your view?

4. Detail Gregory's call to the ministry. What characteristics qualified him for such service? What are the scriptural qualifications for a pastor/elder? How should these qualifications guide you in your life?

5. What is the value of times of solitude in our spiritual lives? What place did this practice have in Gregory's spiritual growth? Do you need to seek similar times of seclusion with the Lord?

6. Describe Gregory's commitment to the Scriptures. How did it uniquely equip him for effective ministry? How did it influence his doctrinal convictions? What role does Scripture play in the formation of your theological stance?

7. What was Gregory's understanding of the fall of Adam and its effect on the human race? Describe the doctrine of original sin. What key passages support your position?

8. Explain the importance of the illuminating work of the Holy Spirit in Gregory's theology. What biblical metaphors and analogies did he appeal to? What others can you add?

$G$od has concluded all in unbelief, that He
may have mercy on all, so that the Grace
would not be of him that wills, or of him that
runs, but of God that shows mercy, that you
should not justify yourself, but attribute all
to God who has called you.[1]

–Ambrose of Milan

# IMPERIAL CONSCIENCE

## LATIN FATHER:
## AMBROSE OF MILAN

T he conversion of the Roman Emperor Constantine, as noted in chapter 8, had far-reaching implications for the church. Most directly, it led to the relaxation of the empire's official opposition to the Christian faith. By this action, the church gained a new status in the empire, one that gave it acceptance and even appeal among many who were not true believers. However, these changes led to doctrinal compromises in the name of politics, bringing increased state interference in the affairs of the church. This is to say, civil authorities began to impose official decisions on church leaders. Thus, there arose a need for the church to assert its God-given authority in spiritual matters.

Soon after his profession of faith, Constantine decreed the legal toleration of all religions, including Christianity. While he never made Christianity the official religion of the empire, he felt his position as emperor gave him primacy in the church; he considered himself the "bishop of all bishops" and the "thirteenth apostle."[2] As such, he issued further edicts that restored property to persecuted Christians. However, Constantine remained the *pontifex maximus* (literally, "the greatest bridge-maker"), the high priest of Rome's official pagan religion, a position held by all emperors since Augustus.

Constantine showed his true colors in the controversy over Arianism, which denied the Trinity and the full deity of Christ. Fearing that this theological dispute would disrupt the political unity of the empire, he convened the Council of Nicaea (325) to settle the matter. Constantine himself chaired the opening session. The council defined the orthodox doctrine of the Trinity and anathematized the heretical views of Arianism. This outcome gave Constantine the theological unity he needed to maintain the political stability of his empire.

Tragically, many leaders who signed the statement produced by the council, known as the Symbol of Nicaea, did so merely as an outward show of support for the emperor. In reality, these signees did not hold to the orthodox understanding of the Christian faith. Not surprisingly, the thin facade of doctrinal unity achieved at Nicaea soon vanished. Eusebius, the first church historian, and a few other bishops extended communion to the Arian heretics. This rebellious action outraged Constantine, who ordered those bishops into exile. But Arius and the banished bishops soon appealed to Constantine for reinstatement. At the recommendation of his advisers, the emperor reversed the decision of Nicaea and ordered Arius readmitted to his pastoral post.

Constantine had clearly gone too far in this matter. Acting unilaterally, the emperor had asserted himself over the church. The headship of Jesus Christ in the church had been jeopardized by the emperor's meddling in divine matters. Constantine's action set a dangerous precedent that other emperors would follow. The essential distinction between the church and the state had been compromised.

Establishing this separation was to be the role of Ambrose of Milan.[3] In one of the great confrontations of church history, he stood before the Emperor Theodosius I and declared that in matters pertaining to the church, the emperor's authority was subservient to that of Christ. This was the first time a bishop used his spiritual authority to humble an emperor.[4] The message was clear: The church of Jesus Christ has only one Head—the sovereign Lord of heaven and earth, Jesus Christ, the King of kings.

# THE LATIN FATHERS

In the fourth century, God brought to the forefront in the Western church a group of church leaders known as the Latin Fathers.[5] These men are so named because they wrote in Latin, the language of the Western Roman Empire, as opposed to the Cappadocian Fathers, who wrote in Greek and thus were also known as Greek Fathers. The men most widely recognized as Latin Fathers are Hilary of Poitiers (ca. 315–367/368), Ambrose of Milan (ca. 339–397), Jerome of Rome (ca. 345–ca. 419), and Augustine of Hippo (354–430). These men were mostly trained in pagan schools of rhetoric, but used their skills in the ministry of the gospel and the defense of the Christian faith.

The Latin Fathers defended the supremacy of Christ over the church, placing even the emperor under the sovereignty of the Lord Jesus. They also continued to wrestle with the main heresies of their day, Arianism and Manichaeism. Further, they helped finalize the church's recognition of the canon of Scripture and advanced theology to a new level of sophistication. Of the Latin Fathers, Ambrose and Augustine specifically addressed the doctrines of grace.

## AMBROSE OF MILAN

At the end of the fourth century, Ambrose of Milan became the most prominent figure in Western Christianity.[6] He is considered the supreme defender of the Christian faith in his time.[7] Certainly he was a leading foe of Arianism;[8] in fact, it has been said that Ambrose, more than any other individual, was responsible for the ultimate defeat of this heresy in the West.[9] He was unquestionably Italy's greatest preacher and bishop.[10] Scholars have characterized him as a magnificent minister,[11] a powerful preacher,[12] and a man of great dignity, spiritual force, and unction.[13] He introduced Eastern theology into the Western church,[14] establishing Nicene orthodoxy in the West.[15] He also wrote hymns and was instrumental in establishing sacred singing in public worship. Augustine was converted under Ambrose's preaching and hailed him as "a faithful teacher of the church."[16] Likewise, Jerome spoke of him as "a pillar of the church."[17] Apart from Augustine, the fourth century produced no one more substantial than Ambrose of Milan.

Born in the town of Trier in Gaul, Ambrose was raised in an aristocratic Christian family. His father, Aurelius Ambrosius, had reached the high rank of prefect of Gaul. This gave him oversight of the northwest portion of the Roman Empire, a vast territory that included what is now Spain, Britain, Germany, and France. But Ambrosius died soon after Ambrose's birth. This loss prompted his mother to move to Rome, where his family had originated, to start a new life. There Ambrose attended the best schools, where he received the finest education in the classics, including Latin and Greek. This linguistic training later enabled Ambrose to study the Nicene Creed and the writings of the Cappadocian Fathers.

Following in his father's footsteps, Ambrose devoted himself to legal studies for a public career in law or government. His skills in law soon became evident, and he was appointed a consul (advocate) by the governor of Italy. He was assigned to practice law at Sirmium, near Belgrade, in present-day Serbia, where he carried out his duties with justice and kindness. Ambrose came to be esteemed as a highly principled man, one who protected the innocent and pursued equity on their behalf. He was soon named the imperial governor of Aemillia-Liguria in northern Italy. The principal city of this province was Milan, the capital of the Western empire in the fourth century. As the residence of the emperor and his court, Milan was the site of the highest level of civil authority. This concentration of authority meant that the church of Milan also had increased importance. Ambrose would spend the rest of his life in the city.

## Appointed Bishop of Milan

At the time, the bishop of Milan was Auxentius, an Arian. His influence had enabled the poison of Arianism to gain a stronghold in that part of Europe. When Auxentius died in 373, there was unrest in Milan over the future of the church. Would Arianism continue to enjoy support or would the church turn to orthodox Christianity? It was feared that the choice of the next bishop might provoke a riot.

As governor, Ambrose attended the meetings that were held in Milan to choose the new bishop. Stepping forward at this potentially explosive moment, he addressed the crowd, calming the tension. Unexpectedly, a cry went up from the people: "Ambrose, bishop." He initially resisted the people and tried repeatedly to escape from the city, but was unsuccessful. Finally, after eight days of resistance, Ambrose accepted this appointment as the call of God on his life. He stepped down as governor on December 7, 374, and distributed his money to the poor. Though he was not theologically trained or experienced in ministry, he was unanimously appointed the bishop of the city.

With a local minister, Ambrose began an intensive study of Scripture and theology. He also launched a careful study of selected Church Fathers. His keen intellect helped him grasp many intricacies of sound doctrine. Further, his fluency in Greek helped him study the New Testament properly and understand pro-Nicene (Trinitarian) apologetics.[18] Drawing on this study, Ambrose preached every Sunday throughout the year and daily in selected seasons. He developed into a very capable expositor, displaying noticeable ability in interpreting the Word. His sermons revealed his vast reading and profound insight. Soon, Ambrose distinguished himself as one of the greatest bishops of ancient Christendom.[19]

Many Arians were in the church of Milan when Ambrose became bishop.[20] As a staunch defender of the Christian faith, he openly opposed this false teaching in every way possible. However, Arianism would not die easily. The empress of the Roman Empire, Justina, the wife of the Emperor Valentinian I, demanded that the church teach Arian doctrine. But Ambrose resolutely declared that the state cannot dictate what the church believes or teaches. The head of the church, Ambrose insisted, is the ascended Christ, not the emperor or empress of Rome. In spiritual matters, even an emperor is subservient to the higher authority of Scripture.

## CONFRONTATION WITH THE EMPEROR

In the year 390, Ambrose's loyalty to Christ was severely tested in a famous confrontation with the next emperor, Theodosius I. This contest began when a rioting mob in the city of Thessalonica murdered the governor of Illyria and his officials. When Theodosius received the news, he burst into a rage. Knowing his volcanic temper, Ambrose went to the emperor to urge self-control, but to no avail. Theodosius ordered his army to massacre the Thessalonians. After the emperor regained his composure, he realized he had acted irrationally and tried to stop his soldiers. But it was too late. The army had already murdered some seven thousand people in Thessalonica.

Ambrose respected Theodosius because the emperor was a Nicene Christian who had called the Council of Constantinople (381), which decisively rejected Arianism. Nevertheless, when Ambrose heard of the slaughter in Thessalonica, he wrote a bold letter, calling the emperor to repentance. He wrote:

> I cannot deny that you are zealous for the faith and that you fear God. But you have a naturally passionate spirit; and while you easily yield to love when that spirit is subdued, yet when it is stirred up you become a raging beast. I would gladly have left you to the workings of your own heart, but I dare not remain silent or gloss over your sin. No-one in all human history has ever before heard of such a bloody scene as the one at Thessalonica! I warned you against it, I pleaded with you; you yourself realized its horror and tried to cancel your decree. And now I call you to repent.[21]

This letter was a harbinger of the confrontation that would follow. Theodosius came to church, pretending that he had not received the letter. But Ambrose courageously barred his entrance to the church. When the emperor claimed he had repented, Ambrose responded that mere words were not enough—his contrition of heart must be demonstrated publicly before he could receive the Lord's Supper. Ambrose challenged the emperor with these words: "How will you lift up in prayer the hands still dripping with the blood of the murdered? How will you receive with such hands the most holy body of the Lord? How will you bring to your mouth His precious blood? Go away, and dare not to heap crime upon crime."[22] In response, Theodosius pointed out that King David had been guilty of murder, but that he had been forgiven. Without hesitation, the bishop answered, "Well, if you have imitated David in sin, imitate him also in repentance."[23]

The emperor humbled himself, demonstrating the genuineness of his repentance by walking through the streets of Milan while confessing his sin. Ambrose nevertheless banned Theodosius from attending church for the next eight months. When the probation period was complete, the emperor was required to kneel before the congregation and publicly ask for God's forgiveness. Theodosius complied.

This was the first time a bishop had used his spiritual authority with an emperor. As Ambrose asserted: "The Church belongs to God, therefore it cannot be assigned to Caesar. The emperor is *within* the Church, not *above* it."[24] The point was clear. No emperor, no king, no president is the ruler of the church—Christ is. Like all believers, even the highest civil authority, in matters pertaining to the church, is subject to the Lord Jesus Christ.

Faithful to his calling, Ambrose remained the bishop of the church in Milan even after his confrontation with the emperor. The Lord called him home on April 4, 397, at the age of fifty-seven, after more than twenty-two years as a Christian and a bishop. Before his death, he spent several hours, with his hands crossed, in uninterrupted prayer.[25] His passing was a cause for much lamenting, even by pagans, who recognized the excellence of his life.

# AMBROSE'S WRITINGS

Ambrose wrote numerous theological and ethical works, as well as exegetical commentaries. He also composed sermons, addresses, letters, and hymns. These many works comprise a rich legacy for the church.

### OF THE FAITH

Gratian, an emperor of the Western Roman Empire (375–383), requested that Ambrose write for him a treatise on the deity of Jesus Christ. The emperor desired to resist the corrupting influence of Arianism,[26] which was gaining the upper hand in the eastern provinces of his realm. In response, Ambrose wrote the treatise *De Fide*, or *Of the Faith* (379/380), in which he distinguished true and false Christianity.

## ON THE HOLY SPIRIT

As a sequel to *Of the Faith*, Ambrose wrote a treatise on the deity of the Holy Spirit titled *De Spiritu Sancto*, or *On the Holy Spirit*. This work is comprised of three books. The first is an allegory based on the story of Gideon, comparing episodes in his life with the ministry of the Spirit. The second demonstrates the deity of the Holy Spirit. Ambrose shows that the Spirit's power is the same as that of the Father and the Son, with all three persons working together in creating the world and regenerating man. The third book shows that the Spirit is one in mission with the Father and Son, demonstrating His coequality with the first two persons of the Godhead.

## AMBROSE'S HYMNS

Ambrose helped change the face of public worship in the early church by introducing the antiphonal singing of hymns as opposed to the customary chanting of the psalms. Under this practice, half the congregation sang one stanza of a hymn, then the other half sang the next stanza. Because of Ambrose's influence, this practice spread throughout Europe. Ambrose also wrote hymns to teach the flock in Milan the doctrine of Christ during the Arian controversy. His compositions showed that he was a gifted poet.

# AMBROSE'S THEOLOGY

Ambrose's bold forcefulness and audacity for the truth can, "in the fourth century, only be compared with that of Athanasius."[27] He contended earnestly for the faith against Arian attack, arguing for the deity of Jesus Christ and the Holy Spirit. For all this, Ambrose has rightly earned his place among the giants of early Christianity.[28]

Specifically, Ambrose was sound in Trinitarian doctrine, and this orthodoxy extended to his understanding of the triune nature of salvation. He saw all three persons of the Godhead working perfectly together for the salvation of one people. Those predestined by the Father were purchased by the Son and are regenerated by the Spirit. This salvation is carried out entirely by divine initiative. God's grace must be sovereign because the radical depravity of fallen man causes him to turn away from God. Ambrose maintained that God's work of grace began in eternity past with the election of His chosen ones and will continue throughout eternity future as He gives them glorified bodies. He recognized that God is the pursuer and provider in every aspect of man's salvation.

**Doctrine in Focus:**

## DIVINE SOVEREIGNTY

In defending the deity of Jesus Christ, Ambrose asserted the sovereignty of God. He presented Christ as the Creator and Ruler of the universe, the King over all men. The eternality of the Son, Ambrose states, demands that He must be the sovereign Lord over all He has created: "The Son is the Ruler and Creator of time. He cannot have begun to exist after His own work. You, therefore, must allow Him to be the Ruler and Maker of His work."[29] The eternal Son, Ambrose maintained, governs all the works of His hands.

Without hesitation, Ambrose contended that the Father and the Son are equal in power. Since they are of one substance, they both possess divine omnipotence. He states: "If, then, they are of one Substance, surely they are also of one sovereign Power. Whereas, if the Son is begotten of another substance, how can the Father be Almighty, and the Son not Almighty? For what advantage has God, if He have made His Son of another substance, when confessedly the Son, on His part, has of another substance made us sons of God?"[30] Ambrose was clear that the Father and the Son are one, equally omnipotent and equally sovereign. Elsewhere he writes that the Son exercises "sovereign Power in Himself."[31] That is to say, Christ uses the power He possesses as He pleases, when and where He pleases, and toward whom He pleases.

Further, Ambrose strongly opposed the Arian denial of the preeminence of the Son. He argued from Scripture that Christ as Creator is the power of God in making and managing all things. He writes: "Who then doubts that all things are 'in' Him, when another Scripture says: 'For in Him are all things founded, that are in the heavens, and in Him they were created, and He is before all things, and all things consist in Him'? (Col. 1:16). Of Him, then, you have grace; Himself you have for your Creator; in Him you find the foundation of all things."[32] In Ambrose's thinking, saving grace proceeds from the sovereignty of God in Christ.

**Doctrine in Focus:**

RADICAL DEPRAVITY

Ambrose affirmed the biblical teaching that Adam, the first man, fell into sin. He writes, "The ancient sin of Adam . . . caused him to fall into contempt and neglect of the heavenly commandments."[33] Furthermore, he understood that Adam was the representative of the human race, so that when he sinned, all were condemned. He states, "We were all under sin; in Adam's fall we all had fallen."[34] He adds, "With Adam, the whole race fell."[35] The result, Ambrose concludes, is that "everyone is a sinner"[36] and "all men are under sin."[37] This means Adam's fallen condition was passed on to the entire human race, resulting in guilt: "This inheritance of sin he has transmitted to us, with the result that so long as we are situated in this body we do not want to leave it and to be present with the Lord."[38] This is the ruin of the entire human race.

Expanding on this point, Ambrose asserted that all people are conceived in wickedness and enter this world in a state of sin. Citing David's words in Psalm 51:5, he writes, "We men are all born under sin, and our very origin is in evil, as we read in the words of David: 'For lo, I was conceived in wickedness, and in sin did my mother bring me forth.'"[39] By this statement, he affirmed again that all mankind is born with a sinful nature inherited from Adam.

Adam's sin, Ambrose wrote, spread spiritual death to all men, and in that spiritual death mankind incurred an insurmountable debt to God. He states: "In Adam I fell, in Adam I was cast out of paradise, in Adam I died. . . . I am guilty of sin and owe a debt to death."[40] He adds, "Adam, by his ruin, left us void and empty."[41] Ambrose saw that human beings are spiritually dead and hopelessly in debt to God for their violations of His law.

Ambrose provides a graphic description of mankind's plight when he writes, "We are shut up in a sort of prison; we are caught in a kind of whirlpool of vice; we are wrapped, as it were, in the darkness of sin."[42] Fallen man is in spiritual bondage, enslaved to sin.

**Doctrine in Focus:**

SOVEREIGN ELECTION

Ambrose affirmed that God intended His grace for a chosen people. He writes: "The Law was given to the Jews, but grace was reserved for the elect. The Law was given that, through fear of punishment, it might recall those who were wandering beyond the limits of nature, to their observance, but grace to incite the elect both by the desire of good things, and also by the promised rewards."[43] The saving favor of God was not intended for all men generally, but for a select group determined by God Himself—the elect.

Ambrose also spoke of the elect as those who were chosen by God for salvation. He says: "Everyone can hear, but not everyone can take in what they hear with their ears. Only God's chosen can do this. This is why the Savior says: 'Let those who have ears to hear, hear.'"[44] Only those predestined for salvation are enabled by God to hear His voice in the invitation of the gospel. They were chosen to believe unto salvation.

**Doctrine in Focus:**

DEFINITE ATONEMENT

Ambrose seems to have affirmed, at different times, both a particular and general atonement. With regard to the former, he maintained that Christ died for the sake of His people, the elect. He writes: "The Son of God, who, by reason of His Godhead, was the Creator of all, did in after time, for the salvation of His people, submit to the taking on of the flesh and the suffering of death."[45] These words indicate that Ambrose believed the incarnation and crucifixion of Christ were specifically designed for the benefit of a particular people. In a similar vein, he writes, "He came down, that you may believe; if you believe not, He has not come down for you, has not suffered for you."[46] Here he affirmed that a person's failure to believe indicates he is not among the elect. Both of these comments point toward a belief in particular redemption.

Furthermore, Ambrose emphasizes the exclusivity of Christ's death for those who believe: "Even as the Child, then, is born not unto all, but unto the faithful: so the Son is given to the faithful and not to the unbelieving. He is given to us, not to the Photinians; for they affirm that the Son of God was not given unto us, but was born and first began to exist among us. To us is He given, not to the Sabellians, who will not hear of a Son being given, maintaining that Father and Son are one and the same. Unto us is He given, not unto the Arians, in whose judgment the Son was not given for salvation."[47] These words declare that Christ's death was exclusively for believers.

Nevertheless, Ambrose more often spoke of the cross in terms of a universal atonement. He states: "Christ is the propitiation of all people. He is everyone's redemption. Is any man's blood suitable and sufficient for his own propitiation, seeing that Christ has shed his blood for all? . . . He, and He only, reconciled the world through His blood. . . . Could there be a better advocate than He who made himself a living prayer for the sins of all, and laid down His life for our redemption? This means there is no need to seek propitiation or redemption for individuals, because the precious blood of Christ belongs to all and the Lord Jesus has ransomed every one of us."[48] Elsewhere he writes that the cross was "for the salvation of the whole world."[49]

It appears that, in Ambrose's thinking, the universal offer of the gospel requires a universal atonement of Christ: "He promises redemption to all. No one is to tremble, no one is to fear, no one is to despair. All, without exception, are invited to grace. Without having to pay any ransom money they are redeemed from sin and they grasp the fruit of eternal life."[50] Ambrose also writes, "He would die, and by His blood would cleanse the whole human race."[51] With these words, it seems clear that Ambrose held to the idea of a general atonement.

**Doctrine in Focus:**

IRRESISTIBLE CALL

Ambrose understood that if any person is to receive salvation, the Holy Spirit must sovereignly apply saving grace. In other words, God must impart faith in Christ to the heart of a sinner before he can believe the gospel. Ambrose states, "God has concluded all in unbelief, that He may have mercy on all, so that the Grace would not be of him that wills, or of him that runs, but of God that shows mercy, that you should not justify yourself, but attribute all to God who has called you."[52] Ambrose declared that God calls certain people to Himself, that He may show mercy to them.

Further, it is the Holy Spirit who causes the new birth, not men themselves: "Therefore, it is clear that the Holy Spirit is also the Author of spiritual generation, because we are created according to God, to be the sons of God. . . . He has made us heirs of supernatural regeneration."[53] God sovereignly births individuals into His kingdom as regeneration imparts new life to those who are spiritually dead.

**Doctrine in Focus:**

PRESERVING GRACE

Ambrose clearly believed that once a person is regenerated, saving grace endures forever. Perseverance, Ambrose wrote, is of God, not man. Commenting on Romans 9:16, he states, "Perseverance does not consist in wishing or in running, for it is God's mercy and not man's power that enables you to complete what you have begun."[54] Elsewhere he notes: "Man's steps are directed by the Lord, for 'it is not of him that wills, nor of him that runs, but of God that shows mercy.' It is only by God's mercy that he runs without falling. Those who plant and those who water are nothing; it is God alone that gives the increase. Therefore, to him alone is rightly due the glory."[55] By God's preserving power, the believer finishes the Christian life that he begins.

Ambrose maintained that the Lord pledges continuing grace in the believer's life. He writes, "For it is of the Lord to vouch for a continuance of heavenly sacraments, and to promise that the grace of spiritual joy shall not fail, to grant the defenses of life, the seals of faith, the gifts of virtues."[56] Simply put, God never will withdraw His saving grace from His children. Ambrose further states that a believer "may look upon the shipwrecks of others while himself free from danger; he may behold others driven here and there on the sea of this world, those who are borne about by every wind of doctrine, while himself persevering on the ground of an immoveable faith. . . . The most holy Church is grounded and founded in faith, as she beholds the tempests of heretics and the shipwrecks of Jews, because they refused the pilot whom they had had."[57] The soul that is converted by God will never be destroyed, because God preserves His own to the end.

Commenting on Ephesians 1:13–14, Ambrose revealed that he understood that the gift of the Spirit is a guarantee from God the Father that He will complete the process of salvation in His people. He writes: "Recall, then, that you received a spiritual seal, 'the Spirit.' . . . God the Father sealed you and Christ the Lord confirmed you, placing the Spirit in your hearts."[58] The Spirit is given to all believers as an earnest, or down payment, securing the final transaction of glorification.

Further, Ambrose saw in John 10:27–30 the truth that God the Father and God the Son hold all believers eternally secure in Their saving hands. He states: "His [a believer's] soul perishes not forever, and no one snatches him from the hand of the almighty Father or the Son. For God's hand that made the heavens firm does not lose those whom it has held."[59] Ambrose clearly affirmed that none of the Lord's sheep will slip from His hands and suffer eternal destruction.

**Doctrine in Focus:**

DIVINE REPROBATION

Ambrose was consistent in his teaching on divine sovereignty by asserting the doctrine of divine reprobation. He held that God not only chose a people for Himself, He passed over the nonelect, leaving them in their sin and subject to His just punishment. He writes: "The Lord considered and knew those that were His, and drew His saints to Himself; and those whom He chose not, He did not draw to Himself."[60] Elsewhere he remarks: "People who sin and get off scot free are really being handed over to their own evil passions. There are people who think God is not cognizant of their sins, and who live as though there were no judge and no law. Of them the Bible says: 'God has left them to their own irrational ideas.' For they chose the way of iniquity, while rejecting the way of truth."[61]

# SINGULAR ALLEGIANCE TO CHRIST

Ambrose left a rich legacy for the church and civilization.[62] Specifically, the bishop of Milan bequeathed a proper theological framework on which to build a relationship between the church and the state.[63] His commitment to the authority of Scripture over the authority of the state caused him to be mightily used by the Lord. With great boldness, he affirmed that in matters of faith and conscience, the church of Jesus Christ is not subject to human rulers, not even to an emperor. All are subject to Christ.

We live in a time when the state is again encroaching upon the church. In the name of tolerance, believers are told to refrain from praying in Jesus' name publicly. In the name of separation of church and state, the Ten Commandments are removed from the public arena. More ominously, Christians are told that those who hold public office must not allow their beliefs to influence their decisions. In these and many other ways, the state is claiming a right to dictate what the church may say and do. In such times, there is a deep need for faithful men, much like Ambrose, to take their places in the leadership of Christ's church.

The church is once again in need of men who possess a singular allegiance to Christ. It has need of spiritual leaders who will stand up to the rulers of this world without compromise. The church must have shepherds who will "speak of your testimonies before kings" (Ps. 119:46).

May God give such men who will call into account even the mightiest rulers of this world—men who will take a bold stance before kings and emperors, and there proclaim the exclusivity of Christ's headship of His church. May He give us soldiers of sovereign truth who will fight the good fight and earnestly contend for the faith once for all delivered to the saints. May they be men of rock-solid convictions regarding God's sovereign grace. For such men, the church does wait.

NOTES

1  Ambrose, *On Abraham*, trans. by Theodosia Tomkinson (Etna, Calif.: Center for Traditionalist Orthodox Studies, 2000), 93.
2  Roger E. Olson, *The Story of Christian Theology: Twenty Centuries of Tradition and Reform* (Downers Grove, Ill.: InterVarsity, 1999), 138.
3  N. R. Needham, *2,000 Years of Christ's Power, Part One: The Age of the Early Church Fathers* (London: Grace Publications, 1997), 170.
4  Needham, *2,000 Years of Christ's Power, Part One*, 170.
5  B. K. Kuiper, *The Church in History* (Grand Rapids: Eerdmans, 1964), 33.
6  Geoffrey Hanks, *70 Great Christians: The Story of the Christian Church* (Ross-shire, Scotland: Christian Focus, 2004), 48.
7  Hanks, *70 Great Christians*, 43.
8  V. L. Walter, "Ambrose," in *Evangelical Dictionary of Theology*, 2nd Ed., ed. Walter A. Elwell (Grand Rapids: Baker, 2001), 50.
9  Ivor J. Davidson, *A Public Faith: From Constantine to the Medieval World, A.D. 312–600* (Grand Rapids: Baker, 2005), 101.
10 Olson, *The Story of Christian Theology*, 257.
11 Needham, *2,000 Years of Christ's Power, Part One*, 172.
12 "Ambrose," in *Nelson's New Christian Dictionary*, ed. George T. Kurian (Nashville: Thomas Nelson, 2001), 23.
13 Philip Schaff, *History of the Christian Church, Vol. III: Nicene and Post-Nicene Christianity: From Constantine the Great to Gregory the Great, A.D. 311–590* (1910; repr., Grand Rapids: Eerdmans, 1979), 60.
14 "Ambrose, St.," in *The Oxford Dictionary of the Christian Church*, ed. E. A. Livingstone (Oxford: Oxford University Press, 1997), 49.
15 Tony Lane, *A Concise History of Christian Thought* (Grand Rapids: Baker Academic, 2006), 42.
16 Augustine, *Contra Julianum Pelagianum*, II.32, cited in *Nicene and Post-Nicene Fathers, Second Series, Vol. X: Ambrose: Select Works and Letters*, eds. Philip Schaff and Henry Wace (Grand Rapids: Eerdmans, 1973), xiv.
17 Jerome, *Against Rufin*, I.2, cited in *Nicene and Post-Nicene Fathers, Second Series, Vol. X*, xiv.
18 Davidson, *A Public Faith*, 103.

19 Schaff, *History of the Christian Church, Vol. III*, 962.

20 Kuiper, *The Church in History*, 33.

21 Ambrose, "Letter to Emperor Theodosius," cited in Needham, *2,000 Years of Christ's Power, Part One*, 194–95.

22 Ambrose, cited in Schaff, *History of the Christian Church, Vol. III*, 964.

23 Ambrose, "Sermon Against Auxentius on the Giving Up of the Basilicas," cited in Schaff, *History of the Christian Church, Vol. III*, 964.

24 Ambrose, cited in Needham, *2,000 Years of Christ's Power, Part One*, 172.

25 Schaff, *History of the Christian Church, Vol. III*, 965.

26 Needham, *2,000 Years of Christ's Power, Part One*, 199.

27 Boniface Ramsey, "Ambrose," in *The First Christian Theologians: An Introduction to Theology in the Early Church*, ed. G. R. Evans (Malden, Mass.: Blackwell, 2006), 232.

28 Ramsey, "Ambrose," in *The First Christian Theologians*, 232.

29 Ambrose, *Exposition of the Christian Faith*, 1.9.58, cited in *Nicene and Post-Nicene Fathers, Second Series, Vol. X*, 210.

30 Ambrose, *Exposition of the Christian Faith*, 4.8.94, in *Nicene and Post-Nicene Fathers, Second Series, Vol. X*, 274.

31 Ambrose, *Exposition of the Christian Faith*, 4.5.56, in *Nicene and Post-Nicene Fathers, Second Series, Vol. X*, 269.

32 Ambrose, *Exposition of the Christian Faith*, 4.11.157, in *Nicene and Post-Nicene Fathers, Second Series, Vol. X*, 282.

33 Ambrose, *Commentary on Psalm 48*, Ps. 48:6, in *Commentary of Saint Ambrose on Twelve Psalms*, trans. Íde M. Ní Riain (Dublin: Halcyon, 2000), 289.

34 Ambrose, *Commentary on Psalm 48*, Ps. 48:8–10, in *Commentary of Saint Ambrose on Twelve Psalms*, 291.

35 Ambrose, *Commentary on Psalm 48*, Ps. 48:6, in *Commentary of Saint Ambrose on Twelve Psalms*, 290.

36 Ambrose, *Commentary on Psalm 1*, Ps. 1:1, in *Commentary of Saint Ambrose on Twelve Psalms*, 12.

37 Ambrose, *Commentary on Psalm 43*, Ps. 43:18–20, in *Commentary of Saint Ambrose on Twelve Psalms*, 248.

38 Ambrose, *Commentary on Psalm 43*, Ps. 43:18–20, in *Commentary of Saint Ambrose on Twelve Psalms*, 247–248.

39 Ambrose, *Repentance*, 1.3.13, in *Nicene and Post-Nicene Fathers, Second Series, Vol. X*, 331.

40 Ambrose, "On the Death of His Brother Satyrus," II.6, cited in *The Fathers of the Church, Vol. 22: Saint Gregory Nazianzen and Saint Ambrose Funeral Orations*, trans. Leo P. McCauley, John J. Sullivan, Martin R. P. McGuire, and Roy J. Deferrari (Washington: The Catholic University of America Press, 1953), 199–200.

41 Ambrose, *Commentary on Psalm 48*, Ps. 48:17–18, in *Commentary of Saint Ambrose on Twelve Psalms*, 298.

42 Ambrose, *Commentary on Psalm 118*, Ps. 118:25, in *Homilies of Saint Ambrose on Psalm 118 (119)* trans. Íde M. Ní Riain (Dublin: Halcyon, 1998), 45.

43 Ambrose, *Concerning Widows*, 12.72, in *Nicene and Post-Nicene Fathers, Second Series, Vol. X*, 403.

44 Ambrose, *Commentary on Psalm 48*, Ps. 48:2, in *Commentary of Saint Ambrose on Twelve Psalms*, 286.

45 Ambrose, *Exposition of the Christian Faith*, 3.7.47, in *Nicene and Post-Nicene Fathers, Second Series*, *Vol. X*, 249.

46 Ambrose, *Exposition of the Christian Faith*, 4.2.27, in *Nicene and Post-Nicene Fathers, Second Series*, *Vol. X*, 265.

47 Ambrose, *Exposition of the Christian Faith*, 3.8.58, in *Nicene and Post-Nicene Fathers, Second Series*, *Vol. X*, 251.

48 Ambrose, *Commentary on Psalm 48*, Ps. 48:8–10, in *Commentary of Saint Ambrose on Twelve Psalms*, 292.

49 Ambrose, *Exposition of the Christian Faith*, 4.6.70, in *Nicene and Post-Nicene Fathers, Second Series*, *Vol. X*, 271.

50 Ambrose, *Commentary on Psalm 48*, Ps. 48:2, in *Commentary of Saint Ambrose on Twelve Psalms*, 287.

51 Ambrose, *Commentary on Psalm 43*, Ps. 43:15, in *Commentary of Saint Ambrose on Twelve Psalms*, 237.

52 Ambrose, *On Abraham*, 93.

53 Ambrose, *The Holy Spirit*, Book Two, 7.64, in *Fathers of the Church, Vol. 44: Saint Ambrose: Theological and Dogmatic Works*, trans. Roy J. Deferrari (Washington: Catholic University of America Press, 1963), 118.

54 Ambrose, *Commentary on Psalm 118*, Ps. 118:76, in *Homilies of Saint Ambrose on Psalm 118 (119)*, 143.

55 Ambrose, *Commentary on Psalm 36*, Ps. 36:23, in *Commentary of Saint Ambrose on Twelve Psalms*, 84.

56 Ambrose, *Concerning Widows*, 3.17, in *Nicene and Post-Nicene Fathers, Second Series, Vol. X*, 394.

57 Ambrose, *The Patriarchs*, 5.26, in *Seven Exegetical Works*, trans. Michael P. McHugh (Washington: The Catholic University of America Press, 1972), 257.

58 Boniface Ramsey, *The Early Church Fathers: Ambrose* (London: Routledge, 1997), 155.

59 Ambrose, *Commentary on Psalm 118*, Ps. 118:109, in *Homilies of Saint Ambrose on Psalm 118 (119)*, 204.

60 Ambrose, *Epistle 63*, 53, in *Nicene and Post-Nicene Fathers, Second Series, Vol. X*, 464.

61 Ambrose, *Commentary on Psalm 118*, Ps. 118:29, in *Homilies of Saint Ambrose on Psalm 118 (119)*, 51.

62 Ramsey, "Ambrose," in *The First Christian Theologians*, 232.

63 Ramsey, "Ambrose," in *The First Christian Theologians*, 232.

# CHAPTER ELEVEN
## STUDY QUESTIONS

1. Does Christianity thrive better in times of prosperity or in seasons of persecution? Can you give evidence for your answer from the example of the fourth-century church? What biblical passages support your position? What encouragement can you glean from these texts?

2. Who were the Latin Fathers? What was their unique place in the story of church history? How have they benefited the church?

3. What was Ambrose's unique contribution to the stability of the early church? What spiritual foe did he war against? What spiritual warfare do you find yourself currently engaged in? How has this conflict driven you closer to Christ and His Word?

4. How was Ambrose unexpectedly thrust into the ministry? How did he respond? How do you respond when you find yourself unexpectedly called upon to minister for Christ?

5. Describe Ambrose's confrontation with the emperor. How did Ambrose respond to this challenge? In what ways do you need to step forward and speak up for the Lord Jesus Christ? How can you become bolder in your faith? What is the source of this boldness?

6. How did Ambrose view the role of each member of the Godhead in the work of salvation? What biblical passages mention all three persons of the Trinity in their saving work?

7. How does the doctrine of sovereign election affect our understanding of the role of God the Son and God the Holy Spirit in Their saving ministries?

8. Explain Ambrose's teaching on the doctrine of preserving grace. What were the major biblical passages to which he referred in establishing this position?

*God* "chose us in" Him "before the foundation of the world, predestining us unto the
adoption of children," not because we were
going to be holy and spotless through ourselves, but He chose and predestined us that
we might become so.[1]

—Augustine of Hippo

Chapter Twelve

# GUARDIAN OF GRACE

## LATIN FATHER:
## AUGUSTINE OF HIPPO

N o theologian of the first fifteen hundred years of the church stands
taller than Augustine of Hippo. Historians regard him as the greatest man in the church between the apostle Paul and the Reformer Martin
Luther.[2] He is revered as an intellectual giant, one of the monumental theologians of all time. What is more, virtually all who study his works regard
him as a master rhetorician,[3] one whose writings rank with the timeless literature of the ages.[4] Augustine further distinguished himself as an apologist
and polemicist in his opposition to the heretic Pelagius. In this dispute, he
became the first theologian to adequately expound the inseparable relationship between the doctrines of radical depravity and sovereign grace in the
salvation of God's elect.

One church historian, Roger E. Olson, notes: "Augustine is the end of one
era as well as the beginning of another. He is the last of the ancient writers,
and the forerunner of medieval theology. The main currents of ancient theology converged in him, and from him flow the rivers, not only of medieval
scholasticism, but also of sixteenth-century Protestant theology."[5] Another historian, Jonathan Hill, writes, "The whole history of the Western Church for
the last 1,500 years is the story of Augustine's influence."[6] Hill adds, "[Augus-
tine's] influence over Western thought—religious and otherwise—is total; he
remains inescapable even over fifteen centuries after his death."[7]

In short, it is virtually impossible to overstate the importance of Augustine and his work. His influence echoes down the halls of church history,
as virtually all theological movements claiming orthodoxy take their stand
in the Augustinian tradition.[8] In fact, some of the greatest theologians of

church history, notably Luther and John Calvin, have regarded themselves as his disciples.[9]

## THE FIRST SYSTEMATIC THEOLOGIAN

Augustine's greatest legacy is his groundbreaking work in beginning to meld the doctrines of grace into a cohesive theological system. He was the first to document the cause-and-effect relationships that exist between the truths of sovereign grace and to pull them together into a system of thought that set forth the glory of God. Augustine repeatedly declared that God's majesty is the *summum bonum*—the highest good. This is to say, God's magnification of His own infinite worth stands behind His saving purposes. Thus, Augustine sought to declare the primacy of God—and the praise that must be ascribed to Him—in the grand scheme of salvation. With this goal in mind, he emphasized the sovereignty of divine grace that God might be glorified.

William Cunningham, the distinguished Scottish theologian and church historian, recognized Augustine's monumental contribution in systematizing the doctrines of grace: "It was in the early part of the fifth century that the doctrines of grace were, for the first time, subjected to a full investigation, error being then more openly and explicitly taught, and the truth being more satisfactorily defended and illustrated, developed and systematized, than ever before."[10] Cunningham concluded:

> Augustine has had the peculiar honour assigned to him, by the great Head of the church, of having been the first to develop, in a systematic order, and in their right connection with each other, the great doctrines taught in the word of God concerning man's lost and ruined condition by nature; the gracious agency of God in the conversion and sanctification of sinners; and the true cause or source of all the effects thus produced. . . . No inconsiderable portion of the piety that existed in the church from the time when he flourished till the Reformation—a period of above one thousand years—was instrumentally connected, more or less directly, with his influence and writings.[11]

Theologian Loraine Boettner likewise acknowledges Augustine's impact on theology: "Prior to Augustine's day, the time had been largely taken up in correcting heresies within the Church and in refuting attacks from the pagan world in which it found itself. Consequently but little emphasis had been placed on the systematic development of doctrine. . . . [I]n the fourth century a more settled time had been reached, a new era in theology had dawned, and the theologians came to place more emphasis on the doctrinal content of their message."[12] In other words, the early church first hammered out the foundational truths of the Trinity, the deity and humanity of Christ, the deity of the Spirit, and the canon of Scripture, often in response to deviant teachings. But with the dawning of the fifth century, the church stood ready to ascend the Mount Everest of theology—the sovereignty of God in salvation.

Two factors led to Augustine's theological contributions. Boettner writes, "Augustine was led to develop his doctrines of sin and grace partly through his own personal experience in being converted to Christianity from a worldly life, and partly through the necessity of refuting the teaching of Pelagius."[13] Augustine went through a condemning self-analysis, recalling his former carnality and licentious lifestyle, which came about as a result of his fervent examination of Scripture. As he did so, Augustine realized that man, in and of himself, is radically depraved and therefore completely reliant on God for salvation. In reference to Pelagius's teaching, Boettner notes: "[Pelagius] taught that man in his natural state had full ability to work out his own salvation, that Adam's fall had but little effect on the race except that it set a bad example which is perpetuated, that Christ's life is of value to men mainly by way of example, that in His death Christ was little more than the first Christian martyr, and that we are not under any special providence of God."[14] Augustine was compelled to refute these heretical teachings and, in so doing, he earnestly defended the sovereign grace of God.

## THE FIRST TRUE INTERPRETER OF PAUL

Against Pelagius's views, Augustine developed a God-centered, grace-exalting theological framework. Some of his contemporaries accused him of theological innovation. But as we have seen, many pillars in the church before him had spoken of sovereign grace. Augustine was simply the first to articulate these truths in a systematic fashion. As Luther observed, "Nothing in Augustine is of his own wisdom but is rather that of the most outstanding Fathers, such as Cyprian, [Gregory of] Nazianzus, Rheticus, Irenaeus, Hilary, Olympius, Innocent, and Ambrose."[15]

But Augustine's true light was a predecessor of even the Church Fathers. Boettner writes that he "became the first true interpreter of Paul and was successful in securing the acceptance of his doctrine by the Church."[16] Similarly,

Presbyterian theologian Benjamin B. Warfield notes that Augustine's doctrine "was not new in the sense that it was Augustine's invention; it was the doctrine of Paul, for example, before it was the doctrine of Augustine, and was only recovered for the Church by Augustine."[17] As Augustine himself noted, "I . . . have not been without some whose footsteps I follow [Ambrose and Cyprian] . . . but it is to the canonical Scriptures alone that I am bound to yield."[18] Augustine was simply standing on the shoulders of the godly men who had gone before him. In so doing, he expanded on the teachings of Scripture and unveiled deeper layers of biblical truth.

So important was Augustine's work that many have argued that he was the true father of the Protestant Reformation, even though he lived eleven hundred years before that great movement. The Reformation, R. C. Sproul writes, was "the ultimate triumph of Augustine's doctrine of grace over the legacy of the Pelagian view of man."[19] One measure of Augustine's influence on the Reformation is the fact that both Luther and Calvin relied heavily on his writings. Luther, an Augustinian monk, had much exposure to his works. Calvin quoted Augustine more than any other theologian. When the Genevan Reformer was accused by the Roman Catholic Church of theological innovation, he pointed back to Augustine and declared, "Augustine is so completely of our persuasion that if I should have to make written profession, it would be quite enough to present a composition made up entirely of excerpts from his writings."[20] In other words, Calvin's message was an echo of Augustine's. Augustine's doctrine was the Reformer's doctrine.

To this point, Warfield remarks, "It is Augustine who gave us the Reformation."[21] Augustine, he writes, not only created "an epoch in the history of the Church . . . [he] determined the course of its history in the West up to the present day."[22] Warfield adds, "The whole development of Western life, in all its phases, was powerfully affected by his teaching."[23] In other words, the church today stands downstream from Augustine. The believers of his own day drank deeply from his teaching, but so has every subsequent generation. Any serious student of theology must wrestle with Augustine.

# AUGUSTINE OF HIPPO

Augustine (354–430) entered the world on Sunday, November 13, 354, in the small town of Thagaste near Carthage in North Africa, now Algeria. His father, Patricius, was a middle-class Roman official and a typical pagan. With no interest in Christianity, his chief desire was to see his son advance in Roman culture. But Augustine's mother, Monica, was a Christian of great piety. It has been said that she ranks as "one of the famous mothers of history."[24] This fervent woman wielded a strong spiritual influence on Augustine's life, though it seemingly had no effect for many years.

Augustine's father worked hard to provide his son with the best education. Augustine was taught the rudiments of grammar at Thagaste, then was sent to Madura, twenty miles away, for further education. Augustine studied there from age eleven to fifteen, falling in love with literature and poetry. However, Madura was pagan to the core.[25] This presented young Augustine with abundant opportunities to indulge his raging lusts.[26] As Augustine later wrote in his *Confessions*: "I dared to grow wild again with various and shadowy loves . . . I became corrupt in Your eyes, pleasing myself . . . unholy desire . . . boiled confusedly within me, and dragged away my unstable youth into the rough places of unchaste desires, and plunged me into a gulf of infamy. . . . I wandered farther from You, and You did 'suffer' me; and I was tossed to and fro, and wasted, and poured out, and boiled over in my fornications."[27]

When Augustine was sixteen, his father died. A distinguished citizen of Thagaste stepped in to send Augustine to Carthage to study. Carthage was the largest city of North Africa and possessed the best schools on the continent. For centuries, it had been "the political, economic, and cultural center of Latin-speaking Africa."[28] But as in Madura, opportunities for sexual sin were readily accessible in Carthage. Augustine studied hard, but he fell into immorality. Later, he said of his time in Carthage, "I came to Carthage, where a cauldron of unholy loves was seething and bubbling all around me."[29] He added, "The mists of passion steamed up out of the puddly concupiscence of the flesh, and the hot imagination of puberty."[30] In the midst of this wickedness, Augustine began a fifteen-year live-in relationship with a woman with whom he would have a son.

## Seduced into Manichaeism

Augustine was lured into the heretical movement of Manichaeism. Founded by Mani, a third-century Persian and self-proclaimed apostle, Manichaeism had become widespread throughout the Roman Empire and Asia. It would survive the Middle Ages through various sects such as the Paulicans, Bogomils, Patarenes, and Cathari. W. A. Hoffecker explains the intricate ideas of Manichaeism thusly:

The main features of Manichaeism were enunciated in an elabo-
rate cosmogonical myth of two absolute and eternal principles that
manifest themselves in three eras or "moments." The first moment
describes a radical primordial dualism. Light and darkness (good and
evil) [are] personified in the Father of Lights and the Prince of Darkness. . . . This resulted in . . . the imprisonment of Light particles in
plant, animal, and human life. Adam was a microcosm of the universe—entrapped within his corrupt body was a soul that could be
awakened through gnosis. Redemption of Light occurs by a cosmic
mechanism in the heavens by which particles of Light (souls) are
drawn up and fill the moon for fifteen days. In the last phases of the
moon Light is transferred to the sun and finally to paradise. . . . Mani
was the greatest prophet who, as the paraclete, proclaimed a salvation
by knowledge (gnosis) consisting of strict ascetic practices. In the
last days of the second moment a great war is to be concluded with
judgment and a global conflagration lasting 1,468 years. Light will
be saved and everything material destroyed. The second coming of
Christ initiates the third moment in which Light and Darkness will
be separated forever as in the primordial division.[31]

The movement had intellectual appeal for Augustine, especially because it
addressed the origin of evil. He soon found its answers to life's ultimate questions superior to those of Christianity and base paganism. Thus, he became a
Manichaean proselyte.

His education complete, Augustine returned to Thagaste to teach rhetoric. But his mother, wholly devoted to Jesus Christ, refused to allow him to
move back home because he was an idolater. So Augustine moved in with the
rich benefactor who had funded his schooling and began to tutor the man's
son. He also dabbled with astrology and continued to pursue the world's pleasures without restraint.

Augustine's world was rocked by the unexpected death of his closest friend.
Shocked, he plunged into grief. Augustine reflects: "This darkness fell upon
my heart and wherever I looked there was only death. My country became a
torture, my father's house pure melancholy. All the pleasures I had shared with
[his deceased friend] turned into hideous agony now that he was gone. My eyes
sought for him everywhere, found him not. I hated all familiar sights because
he was not there."[32] Augustine was in despair and had no anchor for his soul.

Because of this personal crisis, Augustine began wrestling with important life questions: What lies beyond death? What is truth? He found no peace, no meaning, no sense of purpose, only a growing dissatisfaction. He was disturbed by his inability to control his unruly will.[33] And he was growing weary of the disordered lives of his students in Thagaste.

## LEAVING FOR ROME

Amid this restlessness, Augustine left North Africa for Rome to teach rhetoric and practice law. His mother clung to him, begging him to stay, but he refused to listen and set off for Rome in 383 with his mistress and son. His mother despaired because of his rebellion. But she was comforted by a Christian friend, who said to her, "A son of so many prayers cannot be lost."[34]

In Rome, Augustine lived with the Manichaeans. But his inner struggle raged stronger and he grew increasingly disillusioned with life. He began to question Manichaean beliefs, especially as he witnessed the unproductive life of ease these cultists led. He was troubled to see that the Manichaeans were grossly materialistic. He also found that the students in Rome were as undisciplined as those in Thagaste. Despite these struggles, Augustine distinguished himself as one of the most gifted young disputants in Rome. When the opportunity arose to teach rhetoric at the imperial court in Milan, Augustine sought and won the job.

Arriving at Milan, Augustine came under two life-changing influences. The first was Neo-Platonic books. Neo-Platonism was a philosophy that advocated the possibility of an infinite spiritual reality. It particularly provoked Augustine's thinking about evil, defining it as the absence of good. Augustine had felt that Scripture failed to answer the problem of evil. But now he was not so certain. Did the presence of evil in the world necessitate that God is the Author of evil? Or could it be that evil is the absence of good? Strangely, it was the pagan philosophy of Neo-Platonism that caused a crack in the door of his thinking. He began to wonder whether his mother's Christian faith might be right.

Moreover, Augustine began to sit under the preaching of the greatest teacher of Italy, Ambrose. This preacher and theologian was known for his peerless oratorical skills, so Augustine came to observe a master at work. Ambrose's rhetorical style and homiletical abilities impressed Augustine, who recounted: "I was trying to discover whether his eloquence came up to his reputation, and whether it flowed fuller or thinner than others said it did.

And thus I hung on his words intently, but, as to his subject matter, I was only a careless and contemptuous listener. I was delighted with the charm of his speech."[35]

However, as Augustine sat in the great cathedral where Ambrose preached, he soon came under deep conviction. He began to question whether he had been wrong about Christianity. Perhaps he had too quickly dismissed it as an anti-intellectual religion for the weak and culturally unpolished. He recalled: "For, although I took no trouble to learn what he said, but only to hear how he said it—for this empty concern remained foremost with me as long as I despaired of finding a clear path from man to thee—yet, along with the eloquence I prized, there also came into my mind the ideas which I ignored; for I could not separate them. And, while I opened my heart to acknowledge how skillfully he spoke, there also came an awareness of how *truly* he spoke—but only gradually."[36]

### Seeking Truth as a Catechumen

As Augustine listened to Ambrose preach, he heard one who was intellectual, articulate, and courageous.[37] Thus, he discovered that Christianity could be erudite and eloquent.[38] As a result, he became a *catechumen*—one who sought instruction in a catechism class—and heard the gospel carefully explained. This exposure to Christianity left his mind in turmoil over the issues of life. He wrestled with the being of God, the origin of evil, the nature of immorality, and the person of Christ.[39] Augustine wrote: "I trembled with love and fear. I realized that I was far away from thee. . . . And thou didst cry to me from afar, 'I am that I am.' And I heard this, as things are heard in the heart, and there was no room for doubt."[40] Augustine clearly was under the convicting work of the Holy Spirit.

Augustine eventually became convinced of the gospel. But while he now hated his sin, he could not forsake it. Finally, in August 386, Augustine sat in the garden of his rented villa, overcome with misery. In his own words:

I flung myself down under a fig tree—how I know not—and gave free course to my tears. The streams of my eyes gushed out an acceptable sacrifice to You. And, not indeed in these words, but to this effect, I cried to You: "And thou, O Lord, how long? How long, O Lord? Will You be angry forever? Oh, remember not against us our former iniquities." For I felt that I was still enthralled by them. I sent up these sorrowful cries: "How long, how long? Tomorrow and tomorrow? Why not now? Why not this very hour make an end to my uncleanness?"[41]

At that moment, he heard the voice of a child playing nearby. The young voice was chanting, "*Tolle, lege, tolle, lege*," meaning, "Take up and read, take up and read." Augustine took this playful voice as the divine direction for which he was searching. He explains: "So, damming the torrent of my tears, I got to my feet, for I could not but think that this was a divine command to open the Bible and read the first passage I should light upon."[41]

Augustine ran to his copy of Paul's epistle to the Romans, opened it, and read the first passage he saw—Romans 13:13–14. He recalled: "I snatched it up, opened it, and in silence read the paragraph on which my eyes first fell: 'Not in rioting and drunkenness, not in chambering and wantonness, not in strife and envying, but put on the Lord Jesus Christ, and make no provision for the flesh to fulfill the lusts thereof.' I wanted to read no further, nor did I need to. For instantly, as the sentence ended, there was infused in my heart something like the light of full certainty and all the gloom of doubt vanished away."[43] At that defining moment, the light of salvation flooded Augustine's soul and he was dramatically converted.

## CONVERTED BY SOVEREIGN GRACE

Released from the bondage of sin, Augustine turned to the Savior: "I sought, therefore, some way to acquire the strength sufficient to enjoy thee; but I did not find it until I embraced that 'Mediator between God and man, the man Christ Jesus,' 'who is over all, God blessed forever,' who came calling and saying, 'I am the way, the truth, and the life.'"[44]

Augustine at once went in to his mother, who had come to Milan from North Africa in hopes of winning her son to Christ, to tell her what had happened: "We explained to her how it had occurred—and she leaped for joy triumphant; and she blessed thee, who art 'able to do exceedingly abundantly above all that we ask or think.'"[45]

He immediately began to read the Scriptures, beginning with the Psalms, which became his first love. Ambrose baptized him soon after, on Easter in 387. In *Confessions*, he recounted his joy: "Nor was I satiated in those days with the wondrous sweetness of considering the depth of Thy counsels concerning the salvation of the human race. How greatly did I weep in

Thy hymns and canticles, deeply moved by the voices of Thy sweet-speaking Church! The voices flowed into mine ears, and the truth was poured forth into my heart, whence the agitation of my piety overflowed, and my tears ran over, and blessed was I therein."[46]

Augustine decided to return to North Africa. He took with him a small group of relatives and associates to found a small community of "servants of God." Sadly, as they prepared to depart from the seaport of Ostia, his mother fell ill and soon died. Augustine was too overcome with grief to sail and remained in Rome for several more months, finally departing in 388. He settled in Cassicacum, where he wrote his first Christian works, and he soon became known for his great intellectual and rhetorical skills.

The church in North Africa was distressed by various movements, especially Donatism and Manichaeism, and the people looked to Augustine for help. He attempted to avoid being recruited for church leadership and moved to the town of Hippo. But the congregation at Hippo forced Augustine into the ministry. In the midst of a worship service, he was apprehended, brought before the church, and ordained by the laying on of hands in 391. Soon thereafter, he was appointed co-bishop of Hippo, serving beside the aged Valerius. Five years later, Valerius died and the forty-two-year-old Augustine became the sole bishop, a position he would hold until his death (430).

## CONTROVERSY WITH HERETICS

Having been a Manichaean before he was converted to Christianity, Augustine was uniquely equipped to dispute with the Manichaeans over the origin of evil and the soul. This strange mixture of heathen and Christian thoughts was continuing to spread.[47] Seeing the threat to the church, Augustine took a stand against this false teaching, rejecting Mani's claims to apostleship and asserting the authority of Scripture. Unleashing his theological genius, Augustine dismantled the arguments of the Manichaeans. He insisted that there is only one God, whose goodness is infinite.[48] The origin of evil, he argued, is found in the sinful decisions of God's creatures. But God is not the Author of evil. Thus, Augustine affirmed both the reality of evil and the creation of all things by a good God.[49]

Augustine also took on the followers of Donatus (d. 355). The Donatists were not heretics, being orthodox in Trinitarian doctrine, but were a schismatic sect in North Africa.[50] They held that the church should reject all cooperation with the state. The true church, they said, should always be persecuted and its martyrs should be its greatest leaders. To the Donatists, the church was the visible society of the elect, entirely separate from the world. Anyone who betrayed the church—perhaps by pouring a libation to the emperor or surrendering a Bible to Roman persecutors to be burned—was branded a traitor by the Donatists and excommunicated. To be accepted back, the Donatists claimed, one had to be rebaptized.

Augustine became the chief spokesman against the extremism of the Donatists. In refuting them, he advanced the concept of an invisible church within the visible church—the true believers within the broader spectrum of church membership. And he insisted that a traitor should be welcomed back into communion upon repentance.

The supreme crisis for Augustine was his conflict with Pelagius. The major doctrines of God, man, sin, Christ, and salvation were all at issue in this dispute. Adolf von Harnack, the noted German church historian, speaks to the watershed significance of the debate between Augustine and Pelagius when he writes: "There has never, perhaps, been another crisis of equal importance in Church history in which the opponents have expressed the principles or issues so clearly and abstractly. The Arian dispute before the Nicene Council can alone be compared with it."[51] This controversy was the defining issue of Augustine's ministry.

The dispute over Pelagius's teaching affects the church to this day. Louis Berkhof notes: "In general the Greek Church Fathers of the third and fourth centuries showed an inclination to discount the connection between the sin of Adam and those of his descendants, while the Latin Church Fathers taught with ever-increasing clearness that the present sinful condition of man finds its explanation in the first transgression of Adam in paradise. The teachings of the Eastern Church finally culminated in Pelagianism, which denied that there was any vital connection between the two, while those of the Western Church reached their culmination in Augustinianism, which stressed the fact that we are both guilty and polluted in Adam."[52] Thus, this controversy was a Continental Divide in the theology of the church, one that separated a God-centered approach to truth from one that is man-centered.

## PELAGIUS: HUMANISTIC MORALIST

Pelagius (ca. 354–after 418) was a well-educated Briton, trained in law,[53] who became a popular teacher late in the fourth century. An eminently moral person, he was a zealous ascetic and was drawn to the reclusive monastic life.[54]

He supposedly became a monk, although he never belonged to an identifiable religious community and never joined the priesthood. He wrote against the Arians and, subsequently, against the Manichaeans, whose fatalism infuriated him. This resistance would later bias him against Augustine and his teaching on the sovereign grace of God.

At the beginning of the fifth century, Pelagius arrived in Rome to assume a teaching position within aristocratic circles. He was shocked by the undisciplined and indulgent lives of the Roman Christians. At the same time, he was studying Augustine's anti-Manichaean writing *On Free Will* and his *Confessions*, in which Pelagius discovered a strong emphasis on grace. He concluded that this teaching on grace was to blame for the moral passivity of the church. Pelagius reasoned that if Christians are told that God forgives all sin, they will sin without restraint.

One particular statement in *Confessions* provoked Pelagius. Augustine said: "My whole hope is in Your exceeding great mercy and that alone. Give what You command and command what You will. You command continuance from us, and when I knew, as it is said, that no one could be content unless God gave it to him, even this was a point of wisdom to know whose gift it was."[55] Augustine's prayer—"Give what You command and command what You will"—acknowledged man's need for sovereign grace. He saw that God must do *in* man what He requires *from* him. God must give enabling grace if man is to fulfill God's commands. Pelagius simply could not accept this. How, he asked, could God require from man what he cannot produce? For Pelagius, a divine command implies human ability.

This was the heart of the dispute between Augustine and Pelagius. Augustine taught that man lost all ability to obey God in the fall of Adam. Because of original sin, human beings cannot perform what God requires. Pelagius, relying on human reason rather than divine revelation, concluded that accountability necessitates ability. Despite the teaching of Scripture, he insisted on the natural ability of fallen man to keep God's law. The main facets of Pelagius's teaching were an exalted view of human responsibility and a weakened view of divine sovereignty.[56]

## PELAGIUS'S SYSTEM OF DOCTRINE

As Pelagius began to teach against what he perceived to be Augustine's error, several doctrinal distinctives surfaced. Pelagius taught that the human soul does not come into the world soiled by original sin transmitted from Adam.[57]

He rejected the idea that a person's will has any bias in favor of wrongdoing as a result of the fall.[58] He stated: "All good and evil, by which we are praise-worthy or blame-worthy, does not originate with us, but is acted by us. We are born capable of either: we are not born full [of character]; we are procreated without holiness and also without sin; before the action of his own individual will, there is nothing in man but what God has created."[59]

Further, Pelagius preached that God commands nothing impossible. Unregenerate man, he said, possesses the power to do good. Pelagius even believed that a person could live a sinless life. He claimed that in Old Testament times, several men actually lived without sin. Infants, he maintained, are born without sin. They learn to sin by observing bad examples around them: "A man can be without sin and keep the commandments of God, if he wishes."[60] Pelagius believed that man's problem is not within him but around him—in his environment and the examples he sees.

The cornerstone of Pelagius's faulty thinking was the idea of uncondi-tional free will.[61] He writes: "All therefore have a free will to sin and not to sin. It is not free will if it requires the aid of God; because every one has it within the power of his own will to do anything or not to do it. Our victory over sin and Satan proceeds not from the help which God affords but is owing to our own free will. . . . Whether we will or whether we will not, we have the capac-ity of not sinning."[62] Pelagius held that God assigned to fallen man the moral ability of "accomplishing the divine will by choice."[63]

Pelagius considered grace merely an external aid provided by God. He writes: "We have a free will, either to sin, or to forbear sinning; and in all good works it is aided by the Divine assistance. We maintain that free will exists generally in all mankind, in Christians, Jews and Gentiles; they have all equally received it by nature, but in Christians only it is assisted with grace."[64] Following this logic, Pelagius believed that God only externally entices men to Christ, but does not internally draw them by the power of the Holy Spirit. He left no room for any special action by God on the soul.[65]

## A MAN-CENTERED THEOLOGY

Von Harnack summarized Pelagian theology in his *History of Dogma* under eighteen main tenets. Sproul has reduced these tenets to bite-sized statements: (1) God's highest attributes are His righteousness and justice. (2) Everything God creates is good. (3) As created, nature cannot be changed essentially. (4) Human nature is indestructibly good. (5) Evil is an act that we can avoid.

(6) Sin comes via satanic snares and sensuous lust. (7) There can be sinless men. (8) Adam was created with free will and natural holiness. (9) Adam sinned through free will. (10) Adam's progeny did not inherit natural death from him. (11) Neither Adam's sin nor his guilt was transmitted. (12) All men are created as Adam was before the fall. (13) The habit of sinning weakens the will. (14) The grace of God facilitates goodness but is not necessary to achieve it. (15) The grace of creation yields perfect men. (16) The grace of God's law illumines and instructs. (17) Christ works chiefly by His example. (18) Grace is given according to justice and merit.[66]

How did Pelagius arrive at these positions? The answer stems partly from his asceticism. Pelagius strove to earn salvation through extreme self-denial of food, comfort, and pleasures. This was pure legalism, the same trap of self-righteousness into which Luther fell before he was converted. It was an overreaction against antinomianism, that attitude toward God's law that permits free license to sin. So opposed was Pelagius to any excuse to sin that he swung to the other end of the spectrum and demanded that man work his way to heaven.

Philip Schaff points to the differences between Augustine and Pelagius:

> The Pelagian controversy turns upon the mighty antithesis of sin and grace. It embraces the whole cycle of doctrine respecting the ethical and religious relation of man to God, and includes, therefore, the doctrines of human freedom, of the primitive state, of the fall, of regeneration and conversion, of the eternal purpose of redemption, and of the nature and operation of the grace of God. It comes at last to the question, whether redemption is chiefly a work of God or of man; whether man needs to be born anew, or merely improved. The soul of the Pelagian system is human freedom; the soul of the Augustinian is divine grace. . . . Pelagianism begins with self-exaltation and ends with the sense of self-deception and impotency. Augustinianism casts man first into the dust of humiliation and despair, in order to lift him on the wings of grace to supernatural strength, and leads him through the hell of self-knowledge up to the heaven of the knowledge of God.[67]

No differences have ever been greater.

## The Condemnation of Pelagius

The Goths attacked Rome in 410/411, forcing Pelagius and his supporters to seek refuge in North Africa, where Augustine ministered. Pelagius avoided Augustine and eventually moved to Jerusalem. But one of Pelagius's followers, a lawyer named Coelestius, remained in Carthage and taught that unredeemed man is free to do good, which, in effect, made salvation by Christ superfluous.[68] The church leaders in Carthage charged him with heresy.

Augustine commissioned a young Spanish presbyter named Paulus Orosius to travel to Jerusalem in order to lay charges against Pelagius (415). But most of the leaders in the Jerusalem church failed to see the seriousness of Pelagius's teaching. They dismissed the controversy as nothing more than a clash of strong personalities over trivial matters and cleared Pelagius. One exception was the fiery Jerome, who, from his retreat in Bethlehem, "rained fire and brimstone" on the head of Pelagius.[69]

Without support from the church in Jerusalem, the African leaders appealed to the church in Rome to condemn this new heresy. But the Roman church was also divided over the issue and refused to take action. Therefore, two North African synods were held in 416, both of which condemned Pelagian teaching. Eventually, he was denounced as a heretic.[70]

However, the controversy refused to die, so the North African church convened a general council at Carthage (418), which was attended by more than two hundred bishops. The council issued several canons against Pelagianism, including the following: "Whosoever says, that Adam was created mortal, and would, even without sin, have died by natural necessity, let him be anathema. Whoever rejects infant baptism, or denies original sin in children, so that the baptismal formula, 'for the remission of sins,' would have to be taken not in a strict, but in a loose sense, let him be anathema."[71] The denial of Pelagian teaching could not have been stronger.

The church also condemned Pelagius's doctrine at the Council of Ephesus in 431, one year after Augustine died. This was the third ecumenical council, following Nicaea in 325 and Constantinople in 381. But this rejection of Pelagianism did not mean the acceptance of everything in the Augustinian system.[72] Semi-Pelagianism—a compromise view that rejected both Pelagius's and Augustine's teachings—was beginning to emerge. Augustinianism won the day at the Council of Ephesus, but Pelagianism was by no means stamped out and Semi-Pelagianism was not addressed.

## Semi-Pelagianism: A Poor Halfway House

Over the next century, those who rejected the views of Pelagius and Augustine, spearheaded by John Cassian (360–433), advanced the mediating position of Semi-Pelagianism. The pivotal tenet of this view is the priority of the human will over the will of God in the work of salvation. The grace of God, it claims, always cooperates with the human will for its advantage. Fallen humanity possesses "some seeds of goodness" that can be "quickened by the assistance of God."[73] In reality, however, this halfway position is nothing more than a sad compromise of truth.

The proponents of Semi-Pelagianism resisted the teaching of the bondage of the human will, the priority and irresistibility of grace, and the predestination of God. They agreed in principle with Augustine regarding the devastation of sin, but not in its full extent. They saw Augustine's emphasis on sovereign election as dangerous.

In subsequent centuries, the dispute over Augustinianism, Pelagianism, and Semi-Pelagianism was repeated again and again in the church. Different leaders in the church have echoed the same arguments in their own times, adding their own emphases and unique perspectives. The names Augustine, Pelagius, and Cassian have been replaced by Luther and Erasmus, Calvin and Arminius, Particular Baptists and General Baptists, Whitefield and Wesley, Warfield and Finney, and many more. But the debate always has focused on original sin, the nature of man's will, sovereign election, foreknowledge, divine calling, regeneration, and perseverance.

The theological conflict in the contemporary evangelical church is primarily between Semi-Pelagianism and Augustinianism. The crux of the issue is the extent to which Adam's sin affected the human race. Semi-Pelagianism says that Adam and the human race merely stumbled. But Augustinianism says that the first man and his posterity fell and are entirely unable to come to God. Semi-Pelagianism diagnoses the human race as being merely sick in sin, but Augustinianism says that man is spiritually dead. Semi-Pelagianism says that man starts toward God and that God helps him; Augustinianism says that God must bring man to Christ, for man cannot take one step toward Him on his own.

## Augustine's Final Days

Through the early years of the fifth century, the Roman Empire was troubled by vicious attacks from a Germanic tribe known as the Vandals. These invaders eventually penetrated into North Africa, where Augustine ministered. Since Augustine's city of Hippo was one of the few fortified towns, many citizens took refuge there. Ultimately, the Vandals laid siege to Hippo, and during this attack Augustine took ill with a fever and died on August 28, 430.

The Vandals finally overcame the defenses of Hippo and destroyed the city, except for Augustine's cathedral and his library. By God's wonderful providence, the bishop's writings were preserved. These works, in which he so ably expounded the Scriptures and defended the doctrines of sovereign grace in salvation, were his greatest legacy. Not until the Reformation of the sixteenth century would the writings of one man prove so valuable in helping the church to come to a fuller understanding of the biblical truths of man's sin and God's sovereign grace.

Commenting on Augustine's rightful place in the annals of church history, Earle E. Cairns writes, "Between Paul and Luther the church had no one of greater moral and spiritual stature than Augustine."[74] Cairns is not alone in this estimation. It is widely agreed that Augustine was a monumental figure in church history, a beacon of biblical truth. It should be noted, however, that Augustine held that sovereign grace was bestowed through the church and its sacraments. To be outside the church, Augustine believed, was to be outside redeeming grace. This emphasis in Augustinian doctrine endured in the church in the West.

Over one thousand years later, the Reformers affirmed Augustine's doctrine of man and sin—*sola fide, sola gratia, solus Christus*—but rejected his doctrine of the church. Luther, Calvin, and the other Reformers taught that the Holy Spirit bestows His grace directly on the elect by creating "personal faith in the sinner for the Gospel."[75] Thus, the Protestant Reformation can be explained as "the triumph of Augustine's doctrine of grace over Augustine's doctrine of the Church."[76]

Summing up Augustine's enduring value for the church, Iain Murray states: "The old world of Augustine's day has passed away, but the errors he fought have not."[77] The distortions of the truth that Augustine warred against sixteen hundred years ago—Pelagianism and Semi-Pelagianism—are still with us us today, though masked with new names. Though the labels have changed, the poison remains deadly. Today more than ever, we need to acquaint ourselves with Augustine and learn from his handling of Scripture in order to combat attacks on the divine Word of God.

# AUGUSTINE'S WRITINGS

Augustine's writing ministry spanned forty-four years. He wrote more than one thousand works, including 242 books, of which a hundred were major undertakings. They form a vast treasury of Christian knowledge and experience that abounds in "lofty ideas, noble sentiments, devout effusions, clear statements of truth, strong arguments against error, and passages of fervid eloquence and undying beauty."[78] So well received were Augustine's works that, while he was still alive, enthusiasts in Gaul began a movement to canonize his writings, putting them on a par with Scripture. His most important works included:

## CONFESSIONS

One of Augustine's first works after becoming bishop of Hippo was *Confessions* (397). Easily one of the most popular and profound works of all time, it is the oldest existing autobiography. This work is cherished for its love for the truth, its honesty, and its edifying reflections. Written in the form of a prayer, it combines spiritual musings with doctrinal teachings. The book traces Augustine's spiritual journey, sin and all. He recounts his life before Christ, his conversion, and his return to Africa, concluding at age thirty-four. Of all his writings, this piece was the most published and most read during his lifetime.

## GRACE AND FREE WILL

In *Grace and Free Will* (426 or 427), Augustine affirmed God's grace and man's free will, and warned that one can be denied only at the expense of the other. Contrary to the Pelagians, Augustine argued that God moves the hearts of men to do good (according to His mercy) or evil (according to what they deserve). Pelagius maintained that man's will is unaffected by original sin and that an unconverted person is neutral, without a bias toward sin. But Augustine denounced this view, insisting that Adam's sin plunged mankind into spiritual death. Thus, man's will is dead toward the things of God. Man can do what pleases God only by grace. Moreover, apart from grace, man is unable to trust Christ. It is by grace—by divine initiative and divine enablement—that the sinner believes.

## ON THE TRINITY

The cornerstone of Western Trinitarian doctrine, *On the Trinity* is a compilation of fifteen books written over a twenty-year period (ca. 399–ca. 419).

While Eastern authors had addressed the Trinity, this was the first substantial treatise on the doctrine in the West, and it became the most influential exposition on the subject among the Latin Fathers. In it, Augustine refuted the heresies of the Arians and Sabellians. Although Arianism had been condemned at the Council of Constantinople (381), it remained popular in the West, particularly in Carthage. Augustine addressed the inter-Trinitarian relationships and convincingly defended the equality of the Son and the Spirit with the Father. Most important, he demonstrated that the three persons of the Trinity are one in essence (*essentia*) and in operation. Augustine asserted the orthodox position that there is only one God but three persons who are united in essence, coequal and coeternal.

## THE CITY OF GOD

The Goths, led by Alaric, defeated Rome in 410. Though it would be another sixty-six years before the last emperor was deposed, this defeat marked the fall of the Roman Empire. Because the empire had been nominally Christian for the previous century, people were quick to blame the Christians for its demise. In response, Augustine attempted to strengthen the faith of believers by writing *The City of God*. The work was started in 413 and appeared in installments over the next thirteen years. It became a classic that contrasts "the city of God"—the church of the saints—with "the city of man"—the unconverted world. Augustine addressed creation, time, the origin of evil, human freedom, divine knowledge of the future, the resurrection of the body, the final judgment, happiness, the incarnation, sin, grace, forgiveness, and other topics.[79]

## ON CHRISTIAN DOCTRINE

Perhaps Augustine's best-known theological treatise is *On Christian Doctrine*, which presents his views on Scripture, hermeneutics, and preaching. So important was this work that when the great European universities were formed in the twelfth century, the curriculum they adopted was essentially the one Augustine had outlined eight centuries earlier in this book. He began *On Christian Doctrine* in 396, around the time he became bishop of Hippo, some ten years after his conversion. The book took more than thirty years to write, being completed in 427. In this work, Augustine outlined the preparations that equip the interpreter of Scripture to rightly understand and explain the Christian message. The book articulates his approach to biblical exposition and catechetical instruction. It is composed of four books, the first three addressing the discovery of the proper meaning of Scripture and the fourth dealing with the teaching of the truth discovered.

### THE PREDESTINATION OF THE SAINTS

*The Predestination of the Saints* addressed election unto salvation, a subject of much debate. Predestination seemed like a new teaching to many in Augustine's day, despite the clear words of the Scriptures. In this book, which he wrote in 428, Augustine carefully articulated the sovereignty of God in His saving grace. Warfield summarized Augustine's view:

> If, peering into God's inscrutable judgments, we go farther, and ask why, from the mass of Adam, all of which undoubtedly has fallen from one into condemnation, this vessel is made for honor, that for dishonor,—we can only say that we do not know more than the fact; and God's reasons are hidden, but His acts are just. Certain it is that Paul teaches that all die in Adam; and that God freely chooses, by a sovereign election, some out of that sinful mass, to eternal life; and that He knew from the beginning to whom He would give this grace, and so the number of the saints has always been fixed, to whom he gives in due time the Holy Ghost. Others, no doubt, are called; but no others are elect, or "called according to his purpose."[80]

This work would prove to be a defining effort in Augustine's presentation of sovereign grace.

## AUGUSTINE'S THEOLOGY

Augustine's soteriology flowed from his beliefs in the total depravity of man after the fall and the sovereignty of God in salvation. He affirmed that sin corrupts every aspect of man, material and immaterial. Though man is not as sinful as he could be, all humans are guilty, spiritually dead, and condemned on account of Adam's sin. Whereas Pelagius elevated the ability of fallen man, Augustine rightly opposed it, assigning fallen man to his proper place. He also held that Scripture teaches that saving grace is activated and received by divine initiative. Whereas Pelagius minimized and compromised divine sovereignty, Augustine magnified the supreme authority and irresistible grace of God in salvation. He taught that God's saving grace abounds far beyond the pervasive effects of sin.

## Doctrine in Focus:
### DIVINE SOVEREIGNTY

Augustine contended that God is sovereign in the free exercise of His will. He writes, "The true God created the world, and by His providence rules all He has created."[81] By this statement, Augustine affirmed that God controls all that He has created, which means that His authority extends to every realm.

Augustine emphatically asserted that God leaves nothing to chance or fate. The invisible hand of providence rules all. He writes, "Nor shall we think that human affairs, in the case of infants, are governed, not by divine providence but by chance, when these are rational souls which are to be saved or condemned, and yet not a sparrow falls to the ground without the will of our Father in heaven."[82] Elsewhere he adds: "In a word, human kingdoms are established by divine providence. And if any one attributes their existence to fate, because he calls the will or the power of God itself by the name of fate, let him keep his opinion, but correct his language."[83] By these statements, Augustine renounced the myths of chance and fate. He saw clearly that the world is governed by divine sovereignty working through providence.

Augustine was forceful in affirming that God rules over even the Devil and his followers. The kingdom of darkness works only as God permits for His higher purposes. He states that demons "do harm by bestowing pretended benefits,—harm all the greater for the deception,—or else openly and undisguisedly doing evil to men. They cannot, however, do anything of this kind unless where they are permitted by the deep and secret providence of God, and then only so far as they are permitted."[84] In another place he writes: "The sins of men and angels do nothing to impede the 'great works of the Lord which accomplish His will.' He who by His providence and omnipotence distributes to every one his own portion, is able to make good use not only of the good, but also of the wicked."[85] By divine sovereignty, God uses even sin to accomplish His purposes.

Augustine further taught that God's sovereignty extends to the realm of salvation and the eternal destinies of men. By His supreme will, He declares that the souls of men rise to the heights of heaven or fall to the depths of hell. Augustine says: "From Adam has sprung one mass of sinners and godless men, in which both Jews and Gentiles belong to one lump, apart from the grace of God. If the potter out of one lump of clay makes one vessel unto honour and another unto dishonour, it is manifest that God has made of the Jews some vessels unto honour and others unto dishonour, and similarly of the Gentiles."[86] With these words, Augustine affirmed the right of the Potter to use the clay as He wishes. God has sovereignly chosen to make some vessels for honor and others for dishonor—in other words, to save some people and not save others.

## Doctrine in Focus:
### Radical Depravity

For Augustine, a clear understanding of the doctrines of grace begins with the study of man and the study of sin. These two disciplines, when practiced in light of biblical truth, point to one inescapable theological truth—the radical depravity of the human race. One cannot talk about man without talking about sin. Augustine emphasized the link between Adam and his posterity, demonstrating that though the first man was created holy, he chose to sin, and his one act of disobedience caused sin to infect every human being. After Adam sinned, man became spiritually darkened, depraved, and dead. He no longer had good motives toward God and could not perform any good deeds that would commend him to God. Thus, man cannot earn any favor from God, only condemnation.

Adam, Augustine said, was created in the image of God and endowed with a disposition toward holiness. He writes, "Man's nature, indeed, was created at first faultless and without any sin."[87] This moral innocence was a finite or relative holiness, as Adam did have the capacity to sin. Sproul explains, "In creation, said Augustine, man had the *posse peccare* (the ability to sin) and the *posse non peccare* (the ability not to sin)."[88] However, Adam was commanded not to choose sin. Augustine writes: "Thus it was fitting that man should be created, in the first place, so that he could will both good and evil—not without reward, if he willed the good; not without punishment, if he willed the evil."[89] He understood that among mankind, Adam alone had freedom of will. He says: "The will, therefore, is then truly free, when it is not the slave of vices and sins. Such was it given us by God."[90] Thus, he argued that Adam, before the fall, was in a state of finite holiness, with the freedom to choose either good or evil.

Augustine next asserted that God placed Adam in the garden for a probationary period to test his allegiance. His test consisted of a simple prohibition against eating of the tree of the knowledge of good and evil. Augustine believed God would have granted absolute perfection to Adam if he had passed this test. He writes: "He made man with free will . . . if he had willed by his own free will to continue in this state of uprightness and freedom from sin, assuredly without any experience of death and of unhappiness he would have received by the merit of that continuance the fullness of blessing with which the holy angels also are blessed; that is, the impossibility of falling any more, and the knowledge of this with absolute certainty."[91] Elsewhere he adds: "If Adam had not sinned, he would not have been divested of his body, but would have been clothed upon with immortality and incorruption, that 'mortality might have been swallowed up of life'; that is, that he might have passed from the natural body into the spiritual body."[92]

Augustine maintained that Adam was seduced to disobey God. But before he committed the sinful act, he first became inclined in his heart to disobey. He states:

> Our first parents fell into open disobedience because already they were secretly corrupted; for the evil act had never been done had not an evil will preceded it. And what is the origin of our evil will but pride? For "pride is the beginning of sin." And what is pride but the craving for undue exaltation? And this is undue exaltation, when the soul abandons Him to whom it ought to cleave as its end, and becomes a kind of end to itself. The wicked desire to please himself secretly existed in Adam, and the open sin was but its consequence. This happens when it becomes its own satisfaction.[93]

In short, Augustine believed that sin entered Adam's heart, and this inclined him toward disobedience.

Augustine further held that when Adam sinned, guilt fell on all men who would ever live. Adam was the representative of the human race, but more than that, because all men would be his descendants, those descendants actually sinned in him. He writes, "Through the bad will of that one man all sinned in him, when all were that one man, and on that account each individual contracted from him original sin."[94] Adam's sinful act condemned all people. Augustine says, "Through his sin he subjected his descendants to the punishment of sin and damnation, for he had radically corrupted them, in himself, by his sinning."[95] In short, the sin of one was the sin of all.

As a result of their inheritance of original sin, all people rebel against God's commands, Augustine said. After the fall, he writes, "the whole mass of the human race stood condemned, lying ruined and wallowing in evil, being plunged from evil into evil and, having joined causes with the angels who had sinned, it was paying the fully deserved penalty for impious desertion."[96] God's condemnation left humans able only to sin. Augustine also observed that Adam's sin brought death—physical, spiritual, and eternal. He says: "For all die in the sin [of Adam] . . . when sin precedes, death follows—not when death precedes, sin follows. Because sin is the sting of death—that is, the sting by whose stroke death occurs, not the sting with which death strikes."[97] Through Adam's disobedience, death entered the world and spread to all.

Further asserting the bondage of the human will, Augustine states that when Adam sinned, he and all his descendants became enslaved to sin: "For it was in the evil use of his free will that man destroyed himself and his will at the same time. For as a man who kills himself is still alive when he kills himself, but having killed himself is then no longer alive and cannot resuscitate himself after he has destroyed his own life—so also sin which arises from the action of the free will turns out to be victor over the will and the free will is destroyed."[98] The will of man became bound to sin, unable to please God. To this point, Sproul remarks: "After the fall, Augustine said the will, or the faculty, of choosing remained intact; that is, human beings are still free in the sense that they can choose what they want to choose. However, their choices are deeply influenced by the bondage of sin that holds them in a corrupt state."[99] In short, unregenerate human beings cannot choose *not* to sin. Augustine adds, "Free choice alone, if the way of truth is hidden, avails for nothing but sin."[100]

Augustine aptly described the sinful state of fallen man when he wrote in his *Confessions* that he was entirely enslaved by sin—mind, emotion, and will. He says: "I was bound by the iron chain of my own will. The enemy held fast my will, and had made of it a chain, and had bound me tight with it. For out of the perverse will came lust, and the service of lust ended in habit, and habit, not resisted, became necessity. By these links, as it were, forged together—which is why I called it 'a chain'—a hard bondage held me in slavery."[101] In other words, original sin reduced man to a spiritual state of total inability, leaving him unable to obey, please, or come to God.

**Doctrine in Focus:**

## SOVEREIGN ELECTION

It was a natural progression of thought for Augustine to teach that, out of fallen humanity, God chose to save a people for Himself. Because sinners are unable to believe on Christ, God must initiate salvation. Furthermore, the pervasiveness of sin means there is no possibility that God elects on the basis of foreseen faith on man's part. He must take the first step, which, as Scripture makes clear, is His election in eternity past. Sinners are saved because God chooses them, not because they choose God. Likewise, they are not elected because they believe; they believe because they are elected. Augustine writes: "Let us, then, understand the calling by which they become the chosen, not those who are chosen because they believed, but those who are chosen in order that they may believe. 'You have not chosen me, but I have chosen you' (Jn. 15:16). For, if they were chosen because they believed, they would, of course, have first chosen Him by believing in Him in order that they might merit to be chosen."[102] The divine initiative in grace, he says, begins with the sovereign election of God, by which He chooses those who will believe and be saved.

Augustine distanced himself from the Pelagians, who believed that divine foreknowledge is merely foresight by God, a passive observance of what man will do by his own ability. He states:

> For the Pelagians think, "We can, through our own power, once we have received God's commandments, become, by the choice of our free will, holy and spotless in His sight in love. And," they say, "since God foreknew that this would be the case, He chose and predestined us in Christ before the foundation of the world." Yet the Apostle says that God did not elect us because He foreknew that we would be such, but in order that we might be such through that very election of "His grace, in which He has graced us in His beloved Son." Therefore, when He predestined us, He foreknew His own work, by which He makes us holy and spotless.[103]

Elsewhere Augustine writes: "Pelagians say that God's grace is given according to our merits. . . . And what else is this but a complete denial of grace?"[104] Augustine purposefully stood with the writers of Scripture, not the human reasoning of Pelagius.

Throughout his writings, Augustine explains that grace precedes both faith and good works. He says: "This is the election of grace, that is, the election by which men are chosen through the grace of God. This is, I say, the election of grace by which one advances beyond all good, human merits. If it is given for any outstanding merits, it is no longer a gratuitous gift, but is rendered as due. For this reason, one cannot use the term 'grace' in its true sense when 'the reward,' as the same Apostle says, 'is not credited as a favor but as something due.'"[105] Divine election, for Augustine, is all of grace.

Augustine clearly affirmed that God's choice of individual sinners is not based on anything in them. He writes: "This is the calling which he means when he says, 'Not of works, but of Him who calls, was it said to her, "The elder shall serve the younger."' Did the Apostle say, 'Not of works but of him who believes'? No, for he took this entirely away from man, so that he might give it all to God. Hence he said, 'But of Him who calls,' not by any kind of call but by that call whereby one becomes a believer."[106] The divine choice is not conditioned by anything deserving within man, such as foreseen faith or good works. Election is graciously directed toward undeserving sinners, apart from any merit.

Furthermore, Augustine maintained that God's choice of individual sinners to salvation was made in eternity past. He writes, "He knew all the names of His own saints, whom He predestinated before the foundation of the world."[107] He adds: "They were chosen before the foundation of the world by that predestination by which God foreknew His future actions, but they were chosen out of the world by that calling, by which God fulfilled that which He predestined. 'For those He predestined, He also called,' that is, with that calling which is according to His purpose."[108]

That which causes one person to believe the gospel and another to reject it, Augustine reasoned, is the sovereignty of God. He says: "'Many hear the word of truth, but some believe and others speak against it. Therefore the former will to believe, but the latter do not will.' Who would not know this? Who would deny it? But since in some persons the will is prepared by God and in others it is not, we must indeed distinguish what comes from his mercy and what comes from his judgment."[109] If salvation were accomplished as a result of man's choice, man would share in the glory of it; thus, election preserves God's glory. Augustine writes: "This He has done 'according to the pleasure of His will,' so that no one might take glory in his own will, but because of the will of God toward him."[110] Since salvation comes to man entirely as a result of God's choice, Augustine said, all glory goes to God.

The reasons for God's choice in election, Augustine declared, are incomprehensible to men. He writes: "As to why God delivers this person rather than that one, 'How incomprehensible are His judgments, and how unsearchable His ways.' For it is better for us here to listen or to say, 'O man, who are you that replies against God?' than to dare to explain, as if we knew, what God has chosen to keep a secret—God who in any event could not will anything unjust."[111] The reasons behind God's election are known only to Him.

Augustine did not see divine election as a harsh truth, but as a display of the unconditional love of God. He strongly denied that it diminishes or weakens God's divine love in any respect. Rather, Augustine knew that election is a glorious display of God's love in light of man's corrupt and depraved nature. It is no wonder that he thus remarks, "He [God] loved us also before the foundation of the world, and then foreordained what He was to do in the end of the world."[112] Though nothing in sinful man elicited such love, God chose to set His favor on His elect.

Augustine believed that God intentionally chose to set His love on a broad cross-section of sinners. He writes: "What is written, that 'He wills all men to be saved,' while yet all men are not saved, may be understood in many ways, some of which I have mentioned in other writings of mine; but here I will say one thing: 'He wills all men to be saved,' is so said that all the predestinated may be understood by it, because every kind of men is among them."[113] Here Augustine affirmed the biblical teaching that the elect include those from every tribe, tongue, and nation.

Likewise, God demonstrates His eternal love in election throughout every era of human history. Augustine explains: "This same Lord denies his saving medicine during no age of the human race prior to the last judgment, which is still to come, to those He predestined by His certain foreknowledge and just beneficence to reign with Him for eternal life."[114] Thus, God is never without a people, but is always bringing His elect to Himself. He will do so until the end of time.

What God chose to do in eternity past, Augustine said, shall never be altered or amended. He emphatically states: "Let us not imagine that God puts down any man in His book, and then erases him: for if Pilate could say 'What I have written, I have written,' how can it be thought that the great God would write a person's name in the book of life and then blot it out again?"[115] The names He has recorded in the book of life are written there permanently: "If anyone of these [predestined ones] perishes, God has falsely sworn; but no one of them does perish, because God does not swear falsely."[116] What God determined before time shall never be changed within time.

**Doctrine in Focus:**
## Definite Atonement

Augustine observed that Scripture presents more than one theme for the atonement, though the idea of substitution is predominant in his writings. With all the richness of the full counsel of God, Augustine addressed the sacrifice of Christ as a sin-bearing, punishment-canceling death. Admittedly, Augustine did not give as much attention to the extent of the atonement as he did to its accomplishment, and scholars disagree whether he ultimately taught limited or universal atonement. However, he did occasionally speak of the cross as having particular intent.

Christ purchased the flock of God with the price of His blood (John 10:11, 15), Augustine said. He writes that the portion of the universal church composed of saved men "has been redeemed from all sin by the blood of the sinless Mediator."[117] Conversely, Augustine affirms that those whom Christ said were not His sheep were not purchased by His atonement: "He saw them predestined to everlasting destruction, not purchased by the price of His blood unto eternal life."[118] Only the elect were purchased by Christ; none for whom He died will suffer destruction.

Augustine also stated that Christ died for those who are foreknown, predestined, and elected before the foundation of the world. Noting that Christ's work on the cross delivered believers from eternal death, he says, "Those who belong to the grace of Christ, foreknown and predestined and chosen before the foundation of the world, . . . simply die as Christ Himself had died for them, that is to say with the death of the flesh alone and not of the spirit."[119] Because Christ died for those chosen and given to Him by the Father, they do not die a spiritual death.

In perhaps his clearest comment on this doctrine, Augustine said that Scripture does not teach a universal salvation, but that Christ's atonement was limited. Augustine argued that when Jesus says in John 12:32, "And I, when I am lifted up from the earth, will draw all people to myself," He is not saying that all of mankind will be drawn to Him; rather, He is saying that all kinds of men will be drawn. Augustine writes: "All is limited by the context to mean 'all sorts of people, all the predestinate. . . . All men either means men of all sorts or is to be taken with an implied limitation in justification."[120] These and similar texts of Scripture, Augustine affirmed, speak of a limited atonement designed for the salvation of God's elect.

**Doctrine in Focus:**
### IRRESISTIBLE CALL

Augustine understood that God must regenerate and give faith to those whom He has chosen for salvation before they can believe. Those who are spiritually dead in their sin are helpless to choose Him. The Holy Spirit must draw the elect to faith in Christ. Augustine writes, "Therefore, God works in the hearts of men, by that calling which is according to his purpose . . . so that they would not hear the gospel in vain, but having heard it, they would be converted and believe, receiving it not as the word of men, but, as it truly is, the word of God."[121] By grace, God works in His chosen ones to bring them to salvation.

Augustine was careful to distinguish the general call of the gospel from the special saving call of the Holy Spirit. The first, he acknowledged, may be resisted, but not the latter. He says:

> God calls His many predestined children to make them members of His predestined only Son, and not with that call by which those who did not wish to come to the wedding were called, for with that call the Jews also were called, to whom Christ crucified is a scandal, and the gentiles were called, for whom Christ crucified is foolishness. Rather, He calls the predestined by that call which the Apostle distinguished when he declared that he preached Christ, the Wisdom and the Power of God, to those who were called, Jews as well as Greeks. For he speaks thus: "But unto those who were called," to show that those others were not called, for he knows that there is a special and certain call reserved for those who are called according to God's purpose, "whom He foreknew and predestined to be conformable to the image of His Son."[122]

In short, the general call of the gospel goes forth to all people, but only those who also receive the inward call of the Spirit are able to respond.

Commenting on John 6:65, Augustine affirmed that no men, not even those who are elect, can come to Christ by their own abilities. He writes: "When speaking of those who do not believe, [Jesus] said, *I told you that no one can come to Me, unless this gift has been given to him by My Father.* This is the grace that Pelagius ought to admit, if he wants not merely to be called a Christian, but to be one."[123] No one can come to Christ unless his will is renewed, but once the Spirit accomplishes His work of regeneration, that person inevitably turns to Christ in belief and trust.

Acknowledging that the interplay of divine sovereignty and human free will is difficult to understand, Augustine writes: "If I were to propose to you the question how God the Father draws men to the Son, when He has left them to themselves in freedom of action, you would perhaps find it difficult of solution. For how does He draw them to Him if He leaves them to themselves, so that each should choose what he pleases? And yet both these facts are true; but this is a truth which few have intellect enough to penetrate. As therefore it is possible that, after leaving men to themselves in free will, the Father should yet draw them to the Son."[124] In the end, God must draw sinners to Christ, for their wills are predisposed to reject Him.

According to Augustine, God powerfully works on human wills. He writes: "For who is 'drawn,' if he was already willing? And yet no man comes unless he is willing. Therefore he is drawn in wondrous ways to will, by Him who knows how to work within the very hearts of men. Not that men who are unwilling should believe, which cannot be, but that they should be made willing from being unwilling."[125] Thus, as a Potter having right over the clay, God conforms the wills of His elect to His. In essence, God takes an unwilling vessel and makes him into a willing vessel ready for use.

The faith by which the elect believe on Christ, Augustine said, does not originate within them. Rather, saving faith is a gift that God bestows on His elect. He writes, "To be drawn to Christ by the Father, and to hear and learn of the Father in order to come to Christ, is nothing else than to receive from the Father the gift by which to believe in Christ."[126] Elsewhere he notes: "He is drawn to Christ to whom it is given to believe on Christ. Therefore the power is given that they who believe on Him should become the sons of God, since this very thing is given, that they believe on Him."[127] Augustine adds, "This grace is thus spoken of in the Gospel. 'No man can come to Me, except the Father which hath sent Me draw him;' . . . in order to show, that the very faith by which the soul believes, and springs into fresh life from the death of its former affections, is given us by God."[128] Faith, quite simply, is a gift of God.

Augustine had no doubt that when God calls one of His elect to Christ, that individual comes. Conversely, if a person never comes to Christ, it is because God never called him. He says: "What does 'Everyone that has heard from the Father, and has learned, comes to me,' mean except that there is no one who hears from the Father, and learns, and does not come to me? For if everyone who has heard from the Father and has learned comes, it follows that everyone who does not come has not heard from the Father and learned, for if he had heard and learned and yet does not come, but, as the Truth says, 'Everyone who has heard from the Father, and has learned, comes.'"[129] Here lies the monumental truth concerning the irresistible call of God.

**Doctrine in Focus:**

PRESERVING GRACE

Augustine unquestionably maintained that God sustains every believer and ultimately brings them safely into glory. He preserves those who receive His saving grace so that they persevere to the very end. No believer will ever fall away from the faith but will endure. Augustine writes, "The grace of God, which both begins a man's faith and which enables it to persevere unto the end, is not given according to our merits, but is given according to His own most secret and at the same time most righteous, wise, and benevolent will."[130] He adds, "He makes us to live, He makes us to persevere even unto the end, in order that for everlasting we may live."[131] Augustine recognized that it is God who enables His people to persevere in their walks with Him, for man does not naturally possess the ability to keep himself in the faith.

Augustine declared that perseverance, like sovereign election and regeneration, is a gift of God given specifically to the elect. He says, "Who could be ordained to eternal life save by the gift of perseverance?"[132] He also comments, "From Him, therefore, is given also perseverance in good even to the end."[133] And he says elsewhere, "These gifts, therefore, of God . . . are given to the elect who are called according to God's purpose, among which gifts is both the beginning of belief and perseverance in the faith to the termination of this life."[134] Augustine saw that perseverance in the faith comes from God, a gift bestowed on the elect.

If perseverance were in the ability of man, Augustine argued, men would have reason to glory in their strength. But this is not the case. He says: "Clearly, then, even in the matter of perseverance in good, God did not want His saints to take pride in their own strength, but in Him; for He not only gives them an aid of the kind given to the first man, without which they are not able to persevere, if they will; but He also effects in them the will itself. The result is that, since there is no perseverance without the power and the will to persevere, both the possibility and the will to persevere are given them by the bounty of divine grace."[135] Perseverance is entirely of God, that no man may boast.

Spiritual endurance, according to Augustine, continues because Jesus Christ intercedes on behalf of His people, asking God that their faith should not fail. He says: "Let us, then, understand the words of Christ: 'I have prayed for you, that your faith may not fail,' as spoken to him who was built upon a rock. So it is that the man of God who takes pride is to take pride in the Lord, not only because he has obtained mercy, with the result that he has faith, but also because his faith does not fail."[136] Elsewhere he writes: "Consequently, with Christ interceding for them, that their faith may not fail, it will most certainly not fail ever. It will, then, persevere unto the end, and the end of this life will find it abiding in them."[137] In these comments, Augustine addressed the fact that the apostle Peter weakened in his faith and failed miserably. But the intercession of Christ ensured that he did not completely fall away from his Lord. Likewise, Christ now intercedes for all His people (Rom. 8:34), ensuring that they will not fall away from Him.

Augustine understood that even though a true believer may fall away from the church, it is merely temporary. He writes: "If he was predestinated, he strayed temporarily, he was not lost forever; he returns to hear what he has neglected, to do what he heard. For, if he is of those who have been predestinated, God foreknew both his straying and his future conversion. If he has gone astray, he returns to hear that voice of the Shepherd and to follow Him."[138] Like Peter, those who are predestined may stumble and fall, but Christ restores them in their faith.

On the other hand, Augustine recognized that counterfeit believers who fall away from the church remain in apostasy. He says: "They were not 'of' them, because they had not been 'called according to His purpose,' they had not been elected 'in Christ before the foundation of the world,' they had not 'obtained their lot' in Him, they had not been 'predestined according to the purpose of Him who works all things.' For if they had had been all this, they would have been 'of' them, and they would no doubt have remained with them."[139] Those who fall away were never true believers.

All of God's people, Augustine said, will persevere to the end. He writes: "The number of the saints predestined by the grace of God to the kingdom of God, to whom perseverance unto the end is likewise given, will be filled up to completeness, and in its full completeness will be kept blessed without end. The mercy of their Savior will cleave to them all, alike when they are converted, and when they are in the strife, and when they are crowned."[140] Having bestowed the gift of faith on His chosen ones, God will guide them through their earthly pilgrimages to the ultimate blessing.

**Doctrine in Focus:**

## DIVINE REPROBATION

Augustine was more explicit in his teaching on election than he was on reprobation. Nevertheless, he acknowledged that while the elect are predestined for heaven, the reprobate are left in their sins and consigned to hell. Augustine illustrated this truth by pointing to the example of Esau. God chose Jacob to receive eternal life, but He passed over Jacob's twin brother. He writes, "Rebecca bare those two, Jacob and Esau: one of them is chosen, the other is reprobated; one succeeds to the inheritance, the other is disinherited."[141] The eternal destinies of both Jacob and Esau were sealed by God's choice.

The reprobate resist the truth, Augustine said, due to the stubbornness of their hearts. Those who are passed over stand pridefully against God's revealed will. Citing 2 Timothy 3:8, he says: "'As Jannes and Jambres withstood Moses, so do these also resist the truth; men of corrupt minds, reprobate concerning the faith.' But how is it that they resist the truth, except by the vain inflation of their swelling pride, while they raise themselves up on high, as if great and righteous persons, though on the point of passing away into empty air?"[142] The fault for the damnation of the reprobate lies with themselves, not with God.

Commenting on Jesus' parable of the dragnet (Matt. 13:47–50), Augustine said that spiritual imposters will be "separated" at the final judgment and will have no place in glory. He writes: "'The kingdom of heaven is like a net cast into the sea and gathering together of every kind.' And there he wishes both the good and the evil to be understood whom he says are to be separated on the shore, that is, at the end of the world . . . that he might show that these least, who by speaking teach good things which they destroy by living evilly, are reprobates and will not even be the least, as it were, in eternal life, but will not at all be there."[143] In the end, despite present appearances, God Himself will separate the elect from the nonelect.

Augustine believed it is a divine mystery why God chooses some to inherit eternal life but passes over others, leaving them in their sins. The answer lies in the secret counsels of God's will. He writes: "Whom he draws and whom he does not draw, why he draws one and does not draw another, do not wish to judge unless you wish to be wrong."[144] We should not speculate as to why God chooses as He does. The reason lies in God alone.

## GOD'S GLORY AT THE CENTER

In Augustine's day, the accepted belief of science was that the earth was the center of the universe. But one thousand years later, the Polish astronomer Nicolaus Copernicus (1473–1543) made an amazing discovery—the earth is *not* the center of the universe. It is not even the center of the solar system. To the astonishment of the scientific world, Copernicus found that the earth revolves around the sun, not the sun around the earth. The earth—and man who lives on it—is not the center of God's creation.

This was essentially the debate between Augustine and Pelagius. The entire controversy centered around this question: Who is at the center of the universe? Is it man? Or is it God in the splendor of His glory? Pelagius claimed that everything in salvation revolves around man. Each person must be his own savior. Even Semi-Pelagians argued somewhat the same, maintaining that man and God must combine efforts—man must contribute faith to God's grace, a form of self-salvation for man.

But the center of Augustine's theology was radically different. He established a God-centered view of salvation. The biblical teaching of sovereign grace uniquely sees God at the center of all things. The radiant beaming of God's supreme glory must be at the center of any theological system, with all lesser truths concerning man revolving around it.

May such a lofty and transcendent view be reclaimed in this day. May the teachings of Augustine boldly resound in the church once more. May this hour of history witness the dawning of a new day of God-centered thinking in the minds of God's people. And may every doctrine revolve solely around the preeminence of the glory of the Son, Jesus Christ, who is brighter than ten thousand suns.

NOTES

1  Augustine, *On the Predestination of the Saints*, 37, cited in *Saint Augustine: Four Anti-Pelagian Writings*, trans. John A. Mourant and William J. Collinge (Washington: The Catholic University of America Press, 1992), 263.

2  Adolf von Harnack, *Monasticism: Its Ideals and History; and The Confessions of St. Augustine* (London: Williams & Norgate, 1913), 123; Benjamin B. Warfield, *Calvin and Augustine*, ed. Samuel G. Craig (Philadelphia: P&R, 1956), 306.

3  B. J. Gundlach, "Augustine of Hippo," in *Evangelical Dictionary of Theology*, 2nd Ed., ed. Walter A. Elwell (Grand Rapids: Baker, 2001), 121.

4  Jonathan Hill, *The History of Christian Thought* (Downers Grove, Ill.: InterVarsity, 2003), 79.

5  Roger E. Olson, *The Story of Christian Theology: Twenty Centuries of Tradition and Reform* (Downers Grove, Ill.: InterVarsity, 1999), 255

6  Hill, *The History of Christian Thought*, 91.

7  Hill, *The History of Christian Thought*, 79.

8  Gundlach, "Augustine of Hippo," in *Evangelical Dictionary of Theology*, 121.

9  Hill, *The History of Christian Thought*, 91.

10  William Cunningham, *Historical Theology: A Review of the Principal Doctrinal Discussions in the Christian Church since the Apostolic Age, Vol. 1* (Edinburgh: Banner of Truth, 1994), 326.

11  Cunningham, *Historical Theology, Vol. 1*, 331.

12  Loraine Boettner, *The Reformed Doctrine of Predestination* (Phillipsburg, N.J.: P&R, 1932), 366.

13  Boettner, *The Reformed Doctrine of Predestination*, 366.

14  Boettner, *The Reformed Doctrine of Predestination*, 366.

15  Martin Luther, *Luther's Works, Vol. 48: Letters I*, eds. Jaroslav Jan Pelikan, Hilton C. Oswald, and Helmut T. Lehmann (1963; repr., Philadelphia: Fortress, 1999), 24.

16  Boettner, *The Reformed Doctrine of Predestination*, 366.

17  Warfield, "Augustine," in *Calvin and Augustine*, 321.

18  Augustine, *Letter 82*, 3, in *Nicene and Post-Nicene Fathers, First Series, Vol. I: The Confessions and Letters of Augustin, with a Sketch of His Life and Work* (1889; repr., Peabody, Mass.: Hendrickson, 2004), 358.

19  R. C. Sproul, "Augustine and Pelagius," *Tabletalk*, June 1996, 11.

20  John Calvin, *Aeterna Dei praedestinatione*, in *Corpus Reformatorum*, 8:266; as cited in Roger E. Olson, "Influencing the Influencers," *Christian History*, Issue 67 Vol. XIX, No. 3, 31.

21  Benjamin B. Warfield, cited in Sproul, "Augustine and Pelagius," 11.

22  Warfield, "Augustine," in *Calvin and Augustine*, 306.

23  Warfield, "Augustine," in *Calvin and Augustine*, 310.

24  B. K. Kuiper, *The Church in History* (Grand Rapids: Eerdmans, 1964), 35.

25  Robert Payne, "The Dark Heart Filled with Light," *Christian History*, Issue 67, Vol. XIX, No. 3, 13.

26  Payne, "The Dark Heart Filled with Light," 13.

27  Augustine, *Confessions*, 2.2.1–2, cited in *Nicene and Post-Nicene Fathers, First Series, Vol. I*, 54.

28  Justo L. González, *The Story of Christianity: The Early Church to the Present Day* (1984; repr., Peabody, Mass.: Prince, 2006), 208.

29  Augustine, *Confessions*, 3.1, cited in *Augustine: Confessions and Enchiridion*, ed. Albert C. Outler (London: S. C. M. Press, 1955), 61.

30 Augustine, *Confessions*, 2.2, cited in *Augustine: Confessions and Enchiridion*, 50.

31 W. A. Hoffecker, "Manichaeism," in *Evangelical Dictionary of Theology*, 729.

32 Augustine, *Confessions*, 4.4, cited in Payne, "The Dark Heart Filled with Light," 14–15.

33 Arthur C. Custance, *The Sovereignty of Grace* (Grand Rapids: Baker, 1979), 15.

34 Kuiper, *The Church in History*, 35.

35 Augustine, *Confessions*, 5.13, cited in *Augustine: Confessions and Enchiridion*, 111.

36 Augustine, *Confessions*, 5.14, cited in *Augustine: Confessions and Enchiridion*, 111.

37 Olson, *The Story of Christian Theology*, 258.

38 Gundlach, "Augustine of Hippo," in *Evangelical Dictionary of Theology*, 122.

39 John D. Legg, *The Church That Christ Built* (Faverdale North, Darlington, England: Evangelical Press, 1986), 43–44.

40 Augustine, *Confessions*, 7.10, cited in *Augustine: Confessions and Enchiridion*, 147.

41 Augustine, *Confessions*, 8.12, cited in *Augustine: Confessions and Enchiridion*, 175.

42 Augustine, *Confessions*, 8.12, cited in *Augustine: Confessions and Enchiridion*, 176.

43 Augustine, *Confessions*, 8.12, cited in *Augustine: Confessions and Enchiridion*, 176.

44 Augustine, *Confessions*, 7.18, cited in *Augustine: Confessions and Enchiridion*, 152.

45 Augustine, *Confessions*, 8.12, cited in *Augustine: Confessions and Enchiridion*, 176–177.

46 Augustine, *Confessions*, 9.16.14, cited in *Nicene and Post-Nicene Fathers, First Series, Vol. I*, 134.

47 Kuiper, *The Church in History*, 36.

48 Justo L. González, *A History of Christian Thought, Vol. 1 From the Beginnings to the Council of Chalcedon* (Nashville: Abingdon, 1992), 213.

49 González, *A History of Christian Thought, Vol. 1*, 213.

50 Hill, *The History of Christian Thought*, 84.

51 Adolf von Harnack, *History of Dogma, Part 2, Book 2*, trans. James Millar (1898; repr., New York: Dover, 1961), 174.

52 Louis Berkhof, *Systematic Theology* (Grand Rapids: Eerdmans, 1976), 219–220.

53 David F. Wright, "Pelagianism," in *New International Dictionary of the Christian Church*, gen. ed. J. D. Douglas (Grand Rapids: Zondervan, 1978), 760.

54 B. L. Shelley, "Pelagius, Pelagianism," in *Evangelical Dictionary of Theology*, 897.

55 Augustine, *Confessions*, 10.29, cited in *Augustine: Confessions and Enchiridion*, 225.

56 Curt Daniel, *The History and Theology of Calvinism* (Dallas: Scholarly Reprints, 1993), 13.

57 Shelley, "Pelagius, Pelagianism," in *Evangelical Dictionary of Theology*, 897.

58 Shelley, "Pelagius, Pelagianism," in *Evangelical Dictionary of Theology*, 897.

59 Pelagius, *Augustinus: De peccato originis*, c.xiii, cited in William G. T. Shedd, *A History of Christian Doctrine, Vol. Two* (1897; repr., Birmingham, Ala.: Solid Ground Christian Books, 2006), 94.

60 Pelagius, cited in Augustine, *The Proceedings of Pelagius*, 54, in *Nicene and Post-Nicene Fathers, First Series, Vol. V*, ed. Philip Schaff (1887, repr., Peabody, Mass.: Hendrickson, 2004), 207.

61 Shelley, "Pelagius, Pelagianism," in *Evangelical Dictionary of Theology*, 879.

62 Pelagius, cited in Daniel, *The History and Theology of Calvinism*, 13.

63 Shelley, "Pelagius, Pelagianism," in *Evangelical Dictionary of Theology*, 897.

64 Pelagius, *Augustinus: De gratia Christi*, xxxi, cited in Shedd, *A History of Christian Doctrine, Vol. Two*, 99–100.

65 Shelley, "Pelagius, Pelagianism," in *Evangelical Dictionary of Theology*, 897.

66 R. C. Sproul, *Willing to Believe: The Controversy Over Free Will* (Grand Rapids: Baker, 1997), 41–42. Adapted from Von Harnack, *History of Dogma, Part 2, Book 2*, 174.

67 Philip Schaff, ed., *History of the Christian Church, Vol. III: Nicene and Post-Nicene Christianity: From Constantine the Great to Gregory the Great, A.D. 311–590* (1910; repr., Grand Rapids: Eerdmans, 1970), 787–788.

68 Shelley, "Pelagius, Pelagianism," in *Evangelical Dictionary of Theology*, 897.

69 Justo L. González, *A History of Christian Thought, Vol. 2: From Augustine to the Eve of the Reformation* (Nashville: Abingdon, 1971), 28.

70 Ivor J. Davidson, *A Public Faith: From Constantine to the Medieval World, A.D. 312–600* (Grand Rapids: Baker, 2005), 181.

71 Cited in Schaff, *History of the Christian Church, Vol. III*, 799.

72 Richard Kyle, "Semi-Pelagianism," in *Evangelical Dictionary of Theology*, 1,089.

73 David Allen, "Semi-Augustinians," *Christian History*, Issue 67, Vol. XIX, No. 3, 32.

74 Earle E. Cairns, *Christianity Through The Centuries: A History of the Christian Church* (1954; repr., Grand Rapids: Zondervan, 1996), 142.

75 N. R. Needham, *2,000 Years of Christ's Power, Part One: The Age of the Early Church Fathers* (London: Grace Publications, 1997), 252.

76 Needham, *2,000 Years of Christ's Power, Part One*, 252.

77 Iain Murray, "Augustine, Bishop of Hippo," *The Banner of Truth Magazine: Issues 1–16* (Edinburgh: Banner of Truth, 2005), 60.

78 Schaff, *History of the Christian Church, Vol. III*, 1,003.

79 Keith Yandell, "The City of God: Augustine's Timeless Classic About the Timeless City," *Christian History*, Vol. VI, No. 3, 22.

80 B. B. Warfield, "Introductory Essay on Augustin and the Pelagian Controversy," in *Nicene and Post-Nicene Fathers, First Series, Vol. V: Augustin: Anti-Pelagian Writings*, ed. Philip Schaff (1888, repr., Peabody, Mass.: Hendrickson, 2004), xl.

81 Augustine. *The City of God*, 1.36 (New York: Modern Library, 2000), 39.

82 Augustine, *On the Gift of Perseverance*, 31, in *Saint Augustine: Four Anti-Pelagian Writings*, 298–299.

83 Augustine, *The City of God*, 5.1, 142–143.

84 Augustine, *The City of God*, 8.24, 275.

85 Augustine, *The City of God*, 14.27, 476.

86 Augustine, *To Simplician*, 1.20, cited in *Augustine: Earlier Writings*, ed. J. H. S. Burleigh (Louisville: Westminster John Knox, 1953), 402.

87 Augustine, *On Nature and Grace*, 3.3, cited in *Nicene and Post-Nicene Fathers, First Series, Vol. V*, 122.

88 Sproul, *Willing to Believe*, 52.

89 Augustine, *Enchiridion*, 28.105, cited in *Augustine: Confessions and Enchiridion*, 402.

90 Augustine. *The City of God*, 14.11, 458.

91 Augustine, *Rebuke and Grace*, 28, cited in *Nicene and Post-Nicene Fathers, First Series, Vol. V*, 483.

92 Augustine, *Merits and Forgiveness of Sins*, 1.2, cited in *Nicene and Post-Nicene Fathers, First Series, Vol. V*, 16.

93 Augustine, *The City of God*, 14.13, 460.

94 Augustine, *Marriage and Desire*, 2.15, in *The Works of Saint Augustine: Answer to the Pelagians II: Marriage and Desire, Answer to the Two Letters of the Pelagians, Answer to Julian*, ed. John E. Rotelle, trans. Roland J. Teske (Hyde Park, N.Y.: New City Press, 1998), 61.

95 Augustine, *Enchiridion*, 8.26, cited in *Augustine: Confessions and Enchiridion*, 354.

96 Augustine, *Enchiridion*, 8.27, cited in *Augustine: Confessions and Enchiridion*, 355.

97 Augustine, *Against the Pelagians*, 4.7, cited in *Nicene and Post-Nicene Fathers, First Series, Vol. V*, 419.

98 Augustine, *Enchiridion*, 9.30, cited in *Augustine: Confessions and Enchiridion*, 356.

99 R. C. Sproul, "The Pelagian Controversy," *Tabletalk*, August 2005, 7.

100 Augustine, *The Spirit and the Letter*, 5, in *Augustine: Later Works*, ed. John Burnaby (Philadelphia: Westminster, 1955), 197.

101 Augustine, *Confessions*, 8.5, cited in *Augustine: Confessions and Enchiridion*, 164.

102 Augustine, *The Predestination of the Saints*, 17.34, in *The Works of Saint Augustine: Answer to the Pelagians IV: To the Monks of Hadrumetum and Provence*, ed. John E. Rotelle, trans. Roland J. Teske (Hyde Park, N.Y.: New City Press, 1999), 177–178.

103 Augustine, *On the Predestination of the Saints*, 38, in *Saint Augustine: Four Anti-Pelagian Writings*, 264.

104 Augustine, *On the Gift of Perseverance*, 53, in *Saint Augustine: Four Anti-Pelagian Writings*, 324.

105 Augustine, *Patience*, 20.17, in *Saint Augustine: Treatises on Various Subjects* (New York: Fathers of the Church, Inc., 1952), 254–255.

106 Augustine, *On the Predestination of the Saints*, 32, in *Saint Augustine: Four Anti-Pelagian Writings*, 256.

107 Augustine, *John*, 7.14, cited in *Nicene and Post-Nicene Fathers, First Series, Vol. VII: Augustin: Homilies on the Gospel of John, Homilies on the First Epistle of John, Soliloquies*, ed. Philip Schaff (1889; repr., Peabody, Mass.: Hendrickson, 2004), 53.

108 Augustine, *On the Predestination of the Saints*, 34, in *Saint Augustine: Four Anti-Pelagian Writings*, 260.

109 Augustine, *On the Predestination of the Saints*, 11, in *Saint Augustine: Four Anti-Pelagian Writings*, 231.

110 Augustine, *On the Predestination of the Saints*, 37, in *Saint Augustine: Four Anti-Pelagian Writings*, 263.

111 Augustine, *On the Predestination of the Saints*, 16, in *Saint Augustine: Four Anti-Pelagian Writings*, 238.

112 Augustine, *John*, 111.4, cited in *Nicene and Post-Nicene Fathers, First Series, Vol. VII*, 415.

113 Augustine, *Rebuke and Grace*, 44, cited in *Nicene and Post-Nicene Fathers, First Series, Vol. V*, 489.

114 Augustine, *The Punishment and Forgiveness of Sins and the Baptism of Little Ones*, 2.47, in *The Works of Saint Augustine: Answer to the Pelagians II*, 110–111.

115 Augustine, cited in William G. T. Shedd, *Dogmatic Theology* (Phillipsburg, N. J.: P&R, 2003), 331.

116 Augustine, *Admonition and Grace*, 7.14, cited in *Writings of Saint Augustine, Vol. 4*, ed. John Courtney Murray (New York: Cima, 1947), 262.

117 Augustine, *Enchiridion*, 16.61, cited in *Augustine: Confessions and Enchiridion*, 375.

118 Augustine, *John*, 48.4, in *St. Augustine: Tractates on the Gospel of John, 28–54*, trans. John W. Rettig (Washington: The Catholic University of America Press, 1993), 639.

119 Augustine, *On the Trinity*, 13.19, in *The Works of Saint Augustine: The Trinity*, ed. John E. Rotelle, trans. Edmund Hill (Brooklyn, N.Y.: New City Press, 1991), 359.

120 Augustine, *John*, 47.2, in *St. Augustine: Tractates on the Gospel of John, 28–54*, 1240

121 Augustine, *On the Predestination of the Saints*, 39, in *Saint Augustine: Four Anti-Pelagian Writings*, 266.

122 Augustine, *On the Predestination of the Saints*, 32, in *Saint Augustine: Four Anti-Pelagian Writings*, 256.

123 Augustine, *The Grace of Christ and Original Sin*, 1.11, in *The Works of Saint Augustine: Answer to the Pelagians II*, 409.

124 Augustine, *Answer to Petilian*, 2.85.186, cited in *Nicene and Post-Nicene Fathers, First Series, Vol. IV: The Writings Against the Manichaeans, and Against the Donatists*, ed. Philip Schaff (1889; repr., Peabody, Mass.: Hendrickson, 2004), 574.

125 Augustine, *Against the Pelagians*, 1.37, cited in *Nicene and Post-Nicene Fathers, First Series, Vol. V*, 389.

126 Augustine, *Predestination*, 15, cited in *Nicene and Post-Nicene Fathers, First Series, Vol. V*, 506.

127 Augustine, *Against the Pelagians*, 1.6, cited in *Nicene and Post-Nicene Fathers, First Series, Vol. V*, 379.

128 Augustine, *Psalms*, Ps. 88:10, cited in *Nicene and Post-Nicene Fathers, First Series, Vol. VIII: Augustin: Expositions on the Book of Psalms*, ed. Philip Schaff (1889; repr., Peabody, Mass.: Hendrickson, 2004), 428.

129 Augustine, *On the Predestination of the Saints*, 13, in *Saint Augustine: Four Anti-Pelagian Writings*, 233–234.

130 Augustine, *Perseverance*, 33, cited in *Nicene and Post-Nicene Fathers, First Series, Vol. V*, 538.

131 Augustine, *Expositions on the Book of Psalms, Vol. III* (Oxford, John Henry Parker, 1849), 287.

132 Augustine, *Rebuke and Grace*, 10, cited in *Nicene and Post-Nicene Fathers, First Series, Vol. V*, 476.

133 Augustine, *Rebuke and Grace*, 23, cited in *Nicene and Post-Nicene Fathers, First Series, Vol. V*, 481.

134 Augustine, *Perseverance*, 47, cited in *Nicene and Post-Nicene Fathers, First Series, Vol. V*, 544.

135 Augustine, *Admonition and Grace*, 12.38, cited in *Writings of Saint Augustine, Vol. 4*, 291.

136 Augustine, *Admonition and Grace*, 12.38, cited in *Writings of Saint Augustine, Vol. 4*, 292–293.

137 Augustine, *Admonition and Grace*, 12.34, cited in *Writings of Saint Augustine, Vol. 4*, 287.

138 Augustine, *St. Augustine: Tractates on the Gospel of John, 28–54*, 45.13, 199.

139 Augustine, *On the Gift of Perseverance*, 21, cited in *Saint Augustine: Four Anti-Pelagian Writings*, 287.

140 Augustine, *Admonition and Grace*, 13.40, cited in *Writings of Saint Augustine, Vol. 4*, 295.

141 Augustine, *John*, 11.10, cited in *Nicene and Post-Nicene Fathers, First Series, Vol. VII*, 78.

142 Augustine, *Psalms*, Ps 37:20, cited in *Nicene and Post-Nicene Fathers, First Series, Vol. VIII*, 96.

143 Augustine, *John*, 122.9, in *St. Augustine: Tractates on the Gospel of John, 112–24*, trans. John W. Rettig (Washington: The Catholic University of America Press, 1995), 260.

144 Augustine, *John*, 26.2, in *St. Augustine: Tractates on the Gospel of John, 11–27*, trans. John W. Rettig (Washington: The Catholic University of America Press, 1988), 260.

# CHAPTER TWELVE
# STUDY QUESTIONS

1. Augustine is widely considered to be the greatest man in church history between the apostle Paul and the Reformer Martin Luther. What characteristics made him such an influential figure? How would you account, humanly speaking, for his greatness?

2. Describe the impact of Augustine on those who followed him. What was the influence of Augustine on the Protestant Reformers? In what area(s) of theology was he most significant?

3. Comment on the pre-conversion days of Augustine. What hope should his deliverance from such a lifestyle give to us in our witness to those who are lost and deeply entrenched in immorality? What did God use to bring Augustine to Himself?

4. List the main false teachings that Augustine confronted in his ministry. Explain how each of these heresies departed from the truth of Scripture. Where do you see these theological aberrations encroaching against the truth today?

5. Comment on the differences between Augustine's and Pelagius's theologies. How did the core ideas of these doctrinal systems (man-centered vs. God-centered) influence other areas of their theologies, either positively or negatively?

6. Summarize Pelagius's theological point of view. How did his view of Adam and his sin affect the whole of his theology? In what ways did this position lead to the teaching on free will?

7. By contrast, how did Augustine understand the fall of Adam and its effect on the human race? What did he see as the state of fallen man's will? Is man's will free or in total bondage?

8. What was Augustine's unique contribution to the doctrine of regeneration? Define monergistic regeneration. What must God do in order for spiritually dead sinners to believe?

*Some are predestined to His most gracious mercy . . . and made vessels of mercy; others, however, who are considered reprobate and predestined to punishment, {are} condemned, and are made vessels of His wrath . . . just as through the prophet God Himself says: "Jacob I have loved, and Esau I have hated."*[1]

*–Isidore of Seville*

Chapter Thirteen

# SPANISH SCHOLAR

## EARLY MONASTIC:
## ISIDORE OF SEVILLE

Throughout the fifth century and into the sixth, the heretical teachings of Pelagius continued to trouble the church. Despite the official condemnation of Pelagianism by church councils in Carthage (418) and Ephesus (431), and notwithstanding the theological work of Augustine, the dispute between adherents of monergistic and synergistic regeneration escalated. In the century between Augustine's death (430) and the Synod of Orange (529), many doctrinal battles were waged over the nature of God's grace in salvation.[2] Amid these controversies, a mediating view emerged, one that attempted to steer away from what many perceived to be the extreme views of both Pelagius and Augustine. This view, as noted in the previous chapter, was Semi-Pelagianism.

This halfway position refused Pelagius's man-centered doctrine that denied original sin and universal guilt. But Semi-Pelagianism also rejected Augustine's God-centered stance on sovereign election and predestination. In short, Semi-Pelagianism insisted that the work of salvation is not exclusive to God. Rather, its adherents argued, man contributes to his salvation. In the view of the Semi-Pelagians, both divine grace and human free will are necessary in salvation.

Ironically, both the Semi-Pelagians and the Augustinians appealed to Augustine's teaching. The Semi-Pelagians pointed to the earlier writings of Augustine, particularly those works he penned against the Manichaeans, in which he defended the place of man's free will in conversion. The Augustinians appealed to the later writings of Augustine, specifically those composed in opposition to the Pelagians, in which he affirmed God's sovereignty in election and predestination. Thus, the debate between Semi-Pelagianism and Augustinianism was, in reality, a dispute between early and later Augustinianism.

Semi-Pelagianism was unwilling to accept the conclusions that Augustine's theology demanded. As a result, this compromising stance mixed human ability with divine grace, producing a synergistic view of salvation.[3] The Semi-Pelagians' minds were more preoccupied with avoiding the inevitable consequences of Augustinianism than with preaching the full counsel of God. That bias drove them to avoid the exposition of such biblical truths as predestination. They produced a hybrid stance that misled many minds.[4]

## THE SEMI-PELAGIAN MOVEMENT

Historically, Semi-Pelagianism is considered to have emerged in southern Gaul (France),[5] where it was spearheaded by John Cassian (360–433), one of the founding fathers of Western monasticism. Other notable monks—Hilary of Arles (401–449), Vincent of Lérins (d. before 450), and Faustus of Rhegium (d. ca. 490/500)—also threw their support behind the theological concessions of Semi-Pelagianism.

Although the Semi-Pelagians affirmed with Augustine that the whole human race fell in Adam and that sinners cannot believe in Christ without God's grace, they resisted Augustine's assertion of the total bondage of the human will. Instead, they maintained that Adam's sin merely resulted in a moral sickness in the human race, not a spiritual death. They further insisted that although a sinner could not save himself, he retained the moral ability to believe in Christ. Consequently, they taught that man, though weakened by sin, still possesses a free will with moral ability. Conversion, they argued, is a joint venture in which God and man must cooperate.

At its core, Semi-Pelagianism contended that the human will can resist the effectual call of God. This being so, predestination is nothing more than passive foresight by God. The Semi-Pelagians believed that predestination involved God merely looking down the tunnel of time to see who would choose Him, then, in turn, He chose them. Election, they claimed, was God's response to man's initial step of faith. This same system of thought would arise again in opposition to the doctrines of grace during the Protestant Reformation in the form of Arminianism.

In opposition to Semi-Pelagianism, there arose a champion of Augustinian doctrine known as Prosper of Aquitaine (ca. 390–ca. 463). This French scholar upheld Augustine's view that all of mankind is enslaved to sin, suffering the bondage of the will. What is more, he taught God's sovereign predestination of His chosen ones to salvation. In so doing, he advocated a monergistic view of regeneration, which held that the Holy Spirit alone effects the new birth of the elect. Prosper published several works in defense of Augustine's views on total depravity and distinguishing grace. Unfortunately, Prosper later began to weaken some of Augustine's strong teachings on sovereign grace. To this point, historian Justo L. González writes, "Prosper's own defense shows a tendency to mitigate some of Augustine's most extreme doctrines."[6] Toward the end of his life, he softened his stance on theological truths such as election.

## THE SYNOD OF ORANGE (529)

The dispute between these two schools of thought came to a head in 529 at the Synod of Orange (Arausio) in what is now southern France. This gathering produced a series of canons based largely on extracts from Augustine's writings. The Augustinian doctrines of original sin and sovereign grace were approved. However, the doctrine of double predestination—the teaching that predestination is dual, both to life and to destruction—was condemned.[7] Jaroslav J. Pelikan writes that this council "vindicated Augustine's essential teaching on grace."[8] Thus, the Council of Orange ensured the victory of Augustinian theology.

Following the Synod of Orange, the church in the West broadly accepted Augustine's monergistic doctrines of sin and salvation. However, the church in the East followed the Semi-Pelagian view. As Louis Berkhof writes:

> Augustine's doctrine of sin and grace was adopted as the anthropology of the Western Church, though its acceptance was never general even there. Influential men, like Leo and Gregory, Bede and Alcuin, adhered to it, though they were not as strong as Augustine in asserting the preterition and reprobation of the lost. They placed great emphasis on the enslavement of the human will, and on the absolute need of divine grace in renewal. It may be said that the most important leaders of the Church remained true to the most practical part of Augustinian anthropology for two or three centuries after Augustine.[9]

Leading Augustinian voices at the time were the African bishop Fulgentius of Ruspe (468–533) and two distinguished bishops of France, Avitus of Vienne (d. 519) and Caesarius of Arles (470–543), who presided over the Synod of Orange. In the centuries that followed, numerous great Western theologians were staunchly Augustinian in their basic understanding of human depravity and sovereign grace. Many of these leading Augustinians were men who pursued the monastic life.[10]

# MEDIEVAL MONASTICS

The period in Western European history from the fall of Rome in the fifth century to the beginning of the Renaissance in the fourteenth century is known as the medieval era.[11] Roughly the first half of this period is called the Dark Ages because it was marked by intellectual, cultural, and religious darkness. Radical political, social, and economic change swept across the western Mediterranean world. Trade dwindled. Money all but went out of use. The middle class disappeared. Wealthy landowners ruled. Cities were abandoned. Education was no longer valued. Illiteracy reigned. Knowledge of ancient cultures disappeared. Myths and fables were accepted as truth. This era came to signify an eclipse in scholarship and achievement. It also was an age of significant spiritual decline.

As the Dark Ages began, however, there were a few lights that shined forth with the doctrines of grace. J. V. Fesko writes, "As the sun began to set on the Patristic age, the theology of Augustine was not eclipsed by the night."[12] A few isolated figures found their places in history as teachers of sovereign grace, for even amid dark times, God always has men who remain committed to the doctrines of grace. Many of these men were monks or, more formally, Monastics.

To a large degree, the heart and soul of the medieval church was found within the monasteries. In these insular communities, monks—from the Greek *monos*, meaning "alone"—gave themselves to the disciplines of the Christian life. They purposely cut themselves off from the world so that they might dedicate themselves to prayer and praise to God throughout the day and night.[13] Monks participated each day in various worship services. They also pursued personal sanctification.[14] To this end, some took vows of poverty and chastity.

In addition to their spiritual pursuits, monks performed physical labor, provided charitable services, and kept learning alive.[15] They cleared forests, cultivated fields, built roads, raised buildings, and taught students. Also, they studied and copied the Scriptures and the writings of the Church Fathers, as well as classical works of philosophy and literature. Thus, the monasteries were the centers of education until the evolution of the cathedral schools and the universities.[16]

For all these reasons, monks often were the leading figures of Christendom during the medieval centuries—chief teachers, promoters of the Crusades, and builders of cathedrals. In a period that was enveloped by darkness, these men upheld the light of knowledge, advancing the understanding and comprehension of Scripture, and with it, the doctrines of grace. Among them were Isidore of Seville (ca. 560–636), Gottschalk of Orbais (805–869), and Bernard of Clairvaux (1090–1153).

# ISIDORE OF SEVILLE

In the sixth and seventh centuries, God raised up an acute mind in Spain to champion the truth of His sovereign grace in man's salvation. Isidore of Seville was an outstanding churchman and an encyclopedic writer who held forth the bright light of the doctrines of grace in this dark period. In many ways, Isidore was a theological bridge from Augustine to Gottschalk of Orbais.

A man of great intellectual power and scholastic ability, Isidore proved to be the outstanding scholar, educator, and ecclesiastical organizer of his age in the West.[17] His many writings established a storehouse of knowledge that was used by countless medieval authors.[18] He was well studied in Latin, Greek, and Hebrew, and well read in biblical, classical, and Patristic writings. He was called the most learned man of his day by the eighth Council of Toledo (653).[19] Others hailed him as "the Schoolmaster of the Middle Ages."[20] Simply put, Isidore excelled in virtually all branches of knowledge[21] and was one of the most distinguished church leaders of the seventh century.[22] Thus, he exerted an immense influence on the later medieval world.[23]

Isidore was the youngest child of an honored Roman family from among the nobility of Cartagena, Spain. When he was a young child, his family fled to Seville during the fighting between the Visigoths and the Byzantine Empire.[24] His father, Severianus, and his mother, Theodora, were both orthodox Christians. Three of his siblings would serve the church in notable ways. One brother, Fulgentius, became the respected bishop of Astigi, and Isidore's sister, Florentina, formed a religious community near Astigi with forty convents and one thousand adherents. But his eldest brother, Leander (ca. 540–600), was considered "a man of perhaps greater [spiritual] force than Isidore himself."[25]

Leander began his career in the church as a Benedictine monk. After founding the Cathedral School in Seville, he became archbishop of Seville (ca. 577) and the chief leader of the orthodox party in its ongoing struggle against the Arian heresy. He spent the years 580 to 585 in Constantinople, where he became the close friend of the future Gregory the Great, the leader of the church in the West.[26] Upon returning to Spain, he was appointed by King Reccared to preside over the Council of Toledo (587). Leander was so strong in the faith that many Visigoths and Suevi—peoples of Germanic origin who had migrated into Spain—were converted from Arianism to Christianity under his influence. Both theological scholars and church historians are in wide agreement that Leander was the foremost churchman of his time in Spain.[27]

## RAISED BY HIS LEARNED BROTHER

While he was still a young man, Isidore's parents died. He received his elementary education at the Cathedral School under the supervision of Leander, mastering Latin, Greek, and Hebrew. Little else is known about the formative years of his life. Years later, upon the death of Leander, Isidore was appointed to follow in his footsteps as archbishop of Seville, a position of primacy among the Spanish bishops.[28]

Isidore's appointment as archbishop came at a difficult time to lead the church. All of Europe was in a state of consternation. The invading Goths had ruled Spain for a century and a half, dominating the Spaniards' way of life. The lands of northern and western Europe were cloaked in moral darkness. Germany was occupied by foreign tribes and was given to idolatry. Sweden, Norway, Denmark, and Scotland were virtually unknown realms. Gaul (France) was divided by competing monarchs. The East was on the precipice of being invaded by the Muslims, with their religion of violence. Isidore faced all these challenges as he ascended to the office of archbishop around the year 600.

The top priority for Isidore was the establishment of schools to educate young people. He also was much concerned with issues such as monastic discipline, clerical education, liturgical uniformity, and the conversion of the Jews.[29] His spiritual leadership brought about a new day of learning in the Scriptures, and his influence promoted a new breadth of education. Through this resurgence, he had a profound impact on the educational practice of medieval Western Europe and the broader culture.[30] Thanks to these successful efforts to educate the people, Isidore is considered one of the "brightest ornaments" of the church of Spain.[31]

## THE COUNCILS OF SEVILLE (619) AND TOLEDO (633)

As the archbishop of Seville, Isidore presided over one of the historic councils of the time—the Second Council of Seville (619). This ecclesiastical gathering was yet another attempt to counter the anti-Trinitarian advances of Arianism. In this meeting, Isidore showed great zeal for doctrinal orthodoxy, strongly opposing the heretical manifestations of Arianism.[32] Under his leadership, the council affirmed that Christ had two natures united in one person.[33] This declaration specifically stood against the adherents of Acephalism, a dangerous strand of Arianism, and helped preserve the purity of the truth about Jesus Christ.

Isidore also presided over the Fourth Council of Toledo (633), the largest official religious gathering ever held in Spain. The council was called by King Sisenand and attended by fifty-six bishops, seven bishop deputies, and six metropolitans. The king himself attended the council, where he solemnly presented himself before the bishops, requested their prayers, and urged them to address abuses in the church. In response, the council issued seventy-five canons under Isidore's direction. They included a decree that bishops must establish seminaries in their cathedral cities for the training of God's servants in the church.

Eventually, the canons adopted at these two councils came to serve as the basis for the constitutional law of the Spanish kingdom. These laws endured to the fifteenth century.[34] Great was Isidore's influence on Spain.

## ISIDORE'S FINAL DAYS

More is known about Isidore's doctrinal beliefs than his personal life or public ministry. However, we know that six months before he passed away, Isidore received from his physicians the sobering news of the certainty of his death. He accepted this report with grace. For the final months of his life, he devoted himself to giving alms to the poor.

As the end approached, Isidore requested that he be carried to the church of St. Vincent the Martyr. There he was surrounded by the bishops who had served in the church at his side and under his direction. In their presence, he publicly confessed his sins and asked for God's forgiveness. He then requested the prayers of those gathered. He died four days later, on April 4, 636. After his death, he came to be considered the national hero of the Spanish church.[35]

# ISIDORE'S WRITINGS

Isidore has been lauded as "one of the most popular authors of the Middle Ages."[36] He takes his place alongside such notables as Jerome, Augustine, Boethius, and Cassiodorus. The body of Isidore's literary work indicates that he was a man of extensive and profound thought. His writings addressed virtually every area of general knowledge and biblical truth known in his day. Few writers of any period cover the intellectual breadth of their time so completely.[37] So significant were his works that it has been said he surpassed all the writers of his own and the immediately preceding periods. His books circulated widely with the migration of Spanish Christians into surrounding realms. Because of his extraordinary ability to synthesize biblical and secular learning, his influence on medieval clerical and monastic education is unsurpassed.[38] It has been said, "This bishop of Seville has enjoyed a long life in his writings, a life that in Europe lasted till the Reformation and in Spain in some ways into modern times."[39]

## BIBLICAL AND THEOLOGICAL WORKS

First, Isidore wrote books that attempted to give a precise explanation of the Scriptures. These expository works included *Scripture Allegories*, short explanations of some 340 biblical names and passages, and *Lives and Deaths of Biblical Saints*, which contained eighty-five biographies of biblical characters. *Introductions in the Old and New Testaments* was an edited compilation of works by various authors that gave general introductions to the entire Bible. *Scripture Numbers* looked into the meanings of numbers in the Bible. *Questions on the Old and New Testaments* was a catechism of forty-one questions and answers about the Bible. And *Expositions of Holy Mysteries* compiled biblical and theological writings from Church Fathers such as Origen, Ambrose, Jerome, Augustine, and others.

## DOGMATIC AND APOLOGETIC WORKS

Further, Isidore wrote works designed to give a defense of orthodox Christianity. *Sentences* compiled works from Augustine and Gregory the Great, and proved to be his most important work, the first manual of Christian doctrine in the Latin church. Its influence has been said to be "incalculable."[40] *The Catholic Faith Defended against the Jews*, a treatise that presented the biblical prophecies and teachings about Christ to a Jewish audience, is regarded as the ablest and most logical of all the early attempts to present Christ to Jews.[41] It gained popularity in the Middle Ages, being translated into several languages. *Synonyms* contained an imaginary dialogue in which the Logos counseled a sinful man in the ways of God. *The Order of Creation* presented a defense of basic biblical doctrines.

## ECCLESIASTICAL AND EDUCATIONAL WORKS

Isidore also addressed ecclesiastical and monastic subjects. *The Ecclesiastical Offices* addressed the worship of the church and the origin of the ministry. *A Monastic Rule* was compiled to govern life within Spanish monasteries. Isidore also dealt with a wide range of educational and philosophical matters. *The Difference* was a dictionary of synonyms, treating the differences between words, and served as a dictionary of theology. *On the Nature of Things* was a natural philosophy that addressed the divisions of time and the earth. *Etymologies* was a twenty-volume encyclopedia that distilled knowledge in many fields— grammar, rhetoric, dialectic, mathematics, geometry, music, astronomy, medicine, jurisprudence, history, theology, geography, geology, architecture, agriculture, anthropology, and other subjects.

*Etymologies* has been hailed as nothing less than "astonishing."[42] It was "a virtual encyclopedia of what was known at that time."[43] In it, Isidore "summarizes all the knowledge of his times"[44] in what has been called "the basic book of the entire Middle Ages."[45] Written at the request of King Sisebut, *Etymologies* reveals Isidore's wide range of research and reading. This work was widely used, copied, and spread through Europe for centuries. Its popularity is attested to by the fact that there are a thousand extant manuscripts, second only to the number of extant manuscripts of the Bible from this time.[46]

## HISTORICAL AND MISCELLANEOUS WORKS

Finally, Isidore wrote historical books. *A Chronicle* is a historical chronology from creation to the year 615, recording the primary events of world history to Isidore's day.[47] Following the pattern of the six days of creation, Isidore divided human history into six ages, an arrangement drawn from Augustine. *History of the Goths, Vandals, and Suevi* contains some historical information found nowhere else. *Famous Men* contained sketches of forty-six key men in history. These works, it has been said, are "the principal source for the history of the Goths."[48] Another such book was *Letters*, thirteen brief pieces of correspondence.

# ISIDORE'S THEOLOGY

Isidore was one of the first medieval theologians to put forth strong Augustinian teaching.[49] His many writings "witness to Augustine's predominant influence and authority."[50] His teaching "bears a striking resemblance to that of Augustine's, but it is not an exact reproduction."[51] Beyond dispute, Isidore firmly believed at least several of the truths of sovereign grace, maintaining that "grace precedes all acts of merit and is an entirely gratuitous gift from God."[52] Isidore clearly saw the root of saving grace to be the sovereign will of God.

**Doctrine in Focus:**
## DIVINE SOVEREIGNTY

The foundation of Isidore's theology was his belief in the sovereignty of God. He acknowledged that everything that exists and comes to pass is a part of the master purpose of God. He writes: "There are many forces, *virtues*, in the arrangement of this world, angels, archangels, princes, powers, and every rank of the heavenly army; and He [God] is the Lord, *Dominus* of them. All are under Him and subject to His sovereignty."[53] By this statement, Isidore espoused that God rules over all things in the spiritual realm. But he believed God's sovereignty extended to the physical realm as well: "Adonai . . . is generally translated Lord, because He rules all creation and because every creature is subject to His domination."[54] Isidore affirmed the high theology that God ordains and directs all things.

Moreover, Isidore maintained that God is all-powerful and therefore can accomplish all that He desires to do. He writes: "Shaddai . . . is 'Omnipotent,' because He can do all things, *omnia potent*; doing what He wished, but not undergoing what He does not want. If anything could happen to Him, He would by no means be omnipotent. He does whatever He wants, and thus He is omnipotent."[55] God always does what He pleases, as He pleases, when He pleases, where He pleases, and with whom He pleases. No resistance can thwart His purposes.

Further, Isidore taught that God alone is sovereign. Only God controls all that He has created. Isidore says: "Again, He is omnipotent because all things everywhere are His, for He alone has the rule of the whole world. Concerning the substance of God, certain other names are spoken, as: Immortal, Incorruptible, Immutable, Eternal. Whence He rightly has charge over all creation."[56] Isidore saw that there is only one supreme will that exercises dominion over all.

**Doctrine in Focus:**
## SOVEREIGN ELECTION

Because of his strong commitment to Scripture, Isidore was convinced of the Augustinian doctrine of sovereign election, the biblical teaching that God freely chooses some to be His own. He writes, "In a wonderful way, the Creator who is just to all, predestines some to life."[57] Here Isidore distinguished between "all" and "some." He taught that only some are predestined to salvation. However, he also contended that God is just to all. This is because God does not owe grace to any sinful creature. Consequently, God is absolutely free to bestow unmerited favor on whomever He chooses.

Further, Isidore said the elect have been predestined to mercy and others to wrath. In commenting on Romans 9, he writes, "Some are predestined to His most gracious mercy . . . and made vessels of mercy; others, however, are considered reprobate and predestined to punishment, condemned, and are made vessels of His wrath . . . just as through the prophet God Himself says: 'Jacob I have loved, and Esau I have hated.'"[58] This is a clear distinction between God's predestinating mercy and His sovereign wrath. Not all sinners, Isidore taught, are treated the same. The elect are granted undeserved mercy and the nonelect receive deserved punishment, as determined by the supreme will of God.

**Doctrine in Focus:**
## IRRESISTIBLE CALL

Isidore did not explicitly address the doctrine of irresistible call, but some hints in his writings suggest he may have accepted this biblical teaching. He says: "[The Holy Spirit] imparts the gift of prophecy to whom He wishes, and sends away sins from whom He wishes. For sins are not forgiven without the Holy Spirit."[59] Although this verse is addressing spiritual gifts, Isidore nevertheless declared the fundamental truth that the Holy Spirit works as He pleases, giving what He sovereignly desires. The will of the Spirit works in perfect union with the sovereign will of the Father. Elsewhere, he writes that the grace of God is given not according to merit. If such were the case, none would receive divine favor. He writes, "It is also grace given not for our merits, but freely by the divine will."[60] In other words, saving grace is sovereignly applied by the Holy Spirit.

**Doctrine in Focus:**

PRESERVING GRACE

Isidore also was less than explicit on the doctrine of God's preservation of believers, but one comment strongly suggests he believed that Christians cannot fall from grace. He spoke of the Holy Spirit as a gift from God that is given to those who love God, that is, Christians. He writes: "So far as [the Holy Spirit] is a gift from God, it is given to those who, through it, love God. In itself, it is God; with us, it is a gift. The Holy Spirit is an everlasting gift, distributing to each person, as it wishes, its gracious gifts."[61] The Bible is clear that the Spirit's abiding presence guarantees that believers are secure in Christ. The fact that Isidore here spoke of the Spirit as an "everlasting gift" may indicate that he believed that those who trust Christ cannot fall away from Him.

**Doctrine in Focus:**

DIVINE REPROBATION

As noted above, Isidore's theological work, particularly his doctrine of election, bears a striking resemblance to that of the great Latin father Augustine. However, Augustine taught a single predestination, the view that God predestines a people to eternal life, while Isidore went further and taught a double predestination, the view that God not only predestines the elect unto eternal life but likewise predestines the nonelect, the reprobate, unto eternal damnation.[62] Augustine argued that predestination is *ad vitam*, meaning God predestines the elect "unto life" or "immortality," while the nonelect are left to condemnation.[63] Isidore professed belief in a twofold predestination, which holds, according to Philip Schaff, that "God [has] from eternity predestinated His elect by free grace to eternal life, and quite similarly all reprobates, by a just judgment for their evil deserts, to eternal death."[64] Going further than Augustine, Isidore declared that predestination is *gemina*: predestination to life and predestination to death.[65] This is to say, he maintained that the active will of God is involved in the reprobation of sinners. Thus, Isidore is said to be "the patriarch of *predestinatio gemina*."[66] As Pelikan writes, "The classic statement of dual predestination . . . [was] formulated by Isidore."[67]

Isidore writes: "Predestination is double, whether of the elect to peace, or of the reprobate to death."[68] Both salvation and condemnation, according to Isidore, can be traced to God's sovereign choice. Again he states: "There is a double predestination, whether of the elect to rest or of the damned to

death. Both are caused by divine judgment."[69] Isidore states that in reprobation, God passes over and abandons the nonelect. The reprobate are thus left
to suffer their deserved judgment from God: "Others He abandons in their
wicked ways to their rightful judgment."[70] Isidore maintained that the reprobate are subject to eternal condemnation. They are, he writes, "predestined
to punishment and had been damned."[71] Simply put, God has prepared for
the reprobate the punishment they deserve for their sins. Pelikan summarizes
Isidore's position: "God's granted to the elect what they did not merit and . . .
granted to the damned what they did deserve."[72]

Isidore was careful to make a distinction in the manner by which God
deals with the reprobate versus His elect. Whereas God works righteousness
in the elect, Isidore said, the eyes of the nonelect are left blind and their hearts
are left hardened. Thus, Isidore viewed reprobation not in terms of God's
positive, active will, but in terms of His permissive will. This is the infralap-
sarian view of God's decrees. To this end, Isidore writes, "God is said also to
blind some; not that He Himself causes the blindness but that, in accordance
with their worthless merits, He does not remove from them their blindness."[73]
To those who would argue against the teaching that God has freely chosen
some and not others, Isidore replied, "In an obscurity so great as this it is of
no avail for man to investigate the divine dispensation and examine the secret
arrangements of predestination."[74] He spoke of God's decrees as "the hidden
order of predestination."[75] The mystery of reprobation, Isidore argued, is to
be left with God.

# LIGHT FOR A NEW DARK AGE

It is not a stretch to say that the state of modern evangelicalism often resembles Europe during the Dark Ages. As in the days of the prophet Amos, there
is a famine in the land for the hearing of the word of the Lord (Amos 8:11).
Faithful preachers are few. Teachers of sovereign grace are rare. A doctrinal
eclipse has left most churches in darkness. True spiritual learning is in steep
decline. Semi-Pelagian doctrine is rampant. The free will of man is touted
over the supreme will of God. From pulpit to pew, the sovereignty of God is
vehemently opposed. Truly, these are dark and difficult days. In such a time,
the church needs vibrant spiritual leaders, men like Isidore, who hold to a
robust Reformed faith.

Amid the prevailing biblical illiteracy and spiritual ignorance, let us pray that the sovereign Head of the church, the Lord Jesus Christ, will once again give men who will carefully teach the timeless truths of the Word of God. May He grant us shepherd-leaders who will faithfully minister His Word. May our exalted Lord give to His church in this hour stalwarts of the faith who will uphold the full counsel of God. May He continue in this time the long line of godly men who have proclaimed the transcendent doctrines of sovereign grace.

Even in this dark day, when many seek to suppress the truth of God's Word, let us draw hope from the unshakeable certainty that Christ is building His church. The sovereign Lord is undergirding and upholding His kingdom work. In all things, the unrivaled King is ensuring its success. As N. R. Needham states, "Christ's spiritual kingdom is indestructible and perpetual: He has always had, and will always have, an uninterrupted succession of believing people on earth, as His Church continually renews its life from each generation to the next—or rather, as Christ Himself continually renews His Church by His Word and Spirit in every age."[76] In every generation, God remains committed to His cause. Thus, in every hour of human history, He providentially raises up faithful standard-bearers of sovereign grace.

NOTES

1  Isidore, *Differentiarum*, 2.32.117–118, in *Patrologia Latina, Vol. 83*, col. 88, ed. J. P. Migne (Paris: 1862), trans. and cited in J. V. Fesko, *Diversity within the Reformed Tradition: Supra- and Infralapsarianism in Calvin, Dort, and Westminster* (Greenville, S.C.: Reformed Academic, 2001), 23.

2  Justo L. González, *A History of Christian Thought, Vol. 2: From Augustine to the Eve of the Reformation* (Nashville: Abingdon, 1971), 55.

3  Ivor J. Davidson, *A Public Faith: From Constantine to the Medieval World, A.D. 312–600* (Grand Rapids: Baker, 2005), 339.

4  William G. T. Shedd, *A History of Christian Doctrine, Vol. Two* (1897; repr., Birmingham, Ala.: Solid Ground, 2006), 107.

5  González, *A History of Christian Thought, Vol. 2*, 56.

6  González, *A History of Christian Thought, Vol. 2*, 59.

7  Philip Schaff, *History of the Christian Church, Vol. III: Nicene and Post-Nicene Christianity: From Constantine the Great to Gregory the Great, A.D. 311–590* (1858; repr., Peabody, Mass.: Hendrickson, 2006), 866.

8  Jaroslav Pelikan, *The Christian Tradition, Vol. 3: The Growth of Medieval Theology (600–1300)* (Chicago: University of Chicago Press, 1978), 81.

9  Louis Berkhof, *The History of Christian Doctrines* (1937; repr., Edinburgh: Banner of Truth, 2002), 138.

10  N. R. Needham, *2,000 Years of Christ's Power, Part One: The Age of the Early Church Fathers* (London: Grace Publications, 1997), 252.

11  The word *medieval* is drawn from two Latin words, *medium* (middle) and *aenum* (age).

12  Fesko, *Diversity within the Reformed Tradition*, 22.

13  C. T. Marshall, "Monasticism," in *Evangelical Dictionary of Theology*, 2nd Ed., ed. Walter A. Elwell (Grand Rapids: Baker, 2001), 786.

14  M. E. Rogers, "Monastery," in *New International Dictionary of the Christian Church*, gen. ed. J. D. Douglas (Grand Rapids: Zondervan, 1978), 71.

15  Marshall, "Monasticism," in *Evangelical Dictionary of Theology*, 786.

16  Marshall, "Monasticism," in *Evangelical Dictionary of Theology*, 786.

17  Davidson, *A Public Faith*, 339.

18  "St. Isidore," in *The Oxford Dictionary of the Christian Church*, 3rd Ed., ed. E. A. Livingstone (1957; repr., Oxford: Oxford University Press, 1997), 851.

19  "Introduction," Isidore, *Isidore of Seville's Etymologies, Vol. One, Books I–X*, trans. Priscilla Throop (Charlotte, Vt.: Medieval MS, 2005), xi.

20  "Introduction," Isidore, *Isidore of Seville's Etymologies, Vol. One*, xi.

21  "St. Isidore of Seville," in *Nelson's New Christian Dictionary*, ed. George T. Kurian (Nashville: Thomas Nelson, 2001), 399.

22  "Isidore of Seville, or Isidorus Hispaliensis," in *Cyclopedia of Biblical, Theological, and Ecclesiastical Literature, Vol. IV*, eds. John McClintock and James Strong (Grand Rapids: Baker, 1981), 688.

23  Davidson, *A Public Faith*, 339.

24  "St. Isidore," in *The Oxford Dictionary of the Christian Church*, 851.

25  Ernest Brehaut, *An Encyclopedist of the Dark Ages: Isidore of Seville* (New York: Columbia University, 1912), 20.

26  "Leander," in *The Oxford Dictionary of the Christian Church*, 961.

27  Brehaut, *An Encyclopedist of the Dark Ages*, 21.

28  Brehaut, *An Encyclopedist of the Dark Ages*, 22.

29  "St. Isidore," in *The Oxford Dictionary of the Christian Church*, 851.

30  "St. Isidore," in *The Oxford Dictionary of the Christian Church*, 851.

31  "Isidore of Seville, or Isidorus Hispaliensis," in *Cyclopedia of Biblical, Theological, and Ecclesiastical Literature, Vol. IV*, 688.

32  "Isidore of Seville, or Isidorus Hispaliensis," in *Cyclopedia of Biblical, Theological, and Ecclesiastical Literature, Vol. IV*, 688.

33  "Seville," in *Cyclopedia of Biblical, Theological, and Ecclesiastical Literature, Vol. IX*, 604.

34  "Isidore of Seville, or Isidorus Hispaliensis," in *Cyclopedia of Biblical, Theological, and Ecclesiastical Literature, Vol. IV*, 688.

35  Peter Toon, "Isidore of Seville," in *New International Dictionary of the Christian Church*, 519.

36  F. Donald Logan, *A History of the Church in the Middle Ages* (London and New York: Routledge, 2002, 2006), 22.

37  Brehaut, *An Encyclopedist of the Dark Ages*, 16.

38 "Introduction," Isidore, *Isidore of Seville's Etymologies, Vol. One*, xii.

39 Logan, *A History of the Church in the Middle Ages*, 22.

40 Philip Schaff, *History of the Christian Church, Vol. IV: Mediaeval Christianity From Gregory I to Gregory VII, A.D. 590–1073* (1885; repr., Peabody, Mass.: Hendrickson, 2006), 666.

41 Schaff, *History of the Christian Church, Vol. IV*, 14.155.

42 Schaff, *History of the Christian Church, Vol. IV*, 14.155.

43 Logan, *A History of the Church in the Middle Ages*, 22.

44 González, *A History of Christian Thought, Vol. 2*, 73.

45 Logan, *A History of the Church in the Middle Ages*, 22.

46 "Introduction," Isidore, *Isidore of Seville's Etymologies, Vol. One*, xii.

47 "St. Isidore of Seville," in *Nelson's New Christian Dictionary*, 399.

48 "St. Isidore of Seville," in *Nelson's New Christian Dictionary*, 399.

49 Fesko, *Diversity within the Reformed Tradition*, 22.

50 Gordon Left, *Medieval Thought: St. Augustine to Ockham* (Hammondsworth: Penguin, 1958), 51.

51 Fesko, *Diversity within the Reformed Tradition*, 22.

52 Brehaut, *An Encyclopedist of the Dark Ages*, 51.

53 Isidore, *Isidore of Seville's Etymologies, Vol. One*, VII.1.8.

54 Isidore, *Isidore of Seville's Etymologies, Vol. One*, VII.1.8.

55 Isidore, *Isidore of Seville's Etymologies, Vol. One*, VII.1.15.

56 Isidore, *Isidore of Seville's Etymologies, Vol. One*, VII.1.15.

57 Isidore, *Isidore of Seville's Etymologies, Vol. One*, VII.1.15.

58 Isidore, *Differentiarum*, 2.32.117–118, in *Patrologia Latina, Vol. 83*, col. 88, trans. and cited in Fesko, *Diversity within the Reformed Tradition*, 23.

59 Isidore, *Isidore of Seville's Etymologies, Vol. One*, VII.3.16.

60 Isidore, *Isidore of Seville's Etymologies, Vol. One*, VII.3.16.

61 Isidore, *Isidore of Seville's Etymologies, Vol. One*, VII.3.16.

62 Alister E. McGrath, *Iustitia Dei: A History of the Christian Doctrine of Justification* (Cambridge: Cambridge University Press, 2005), 161.

63 Fesko, *Diversity within the Reformed Tradition*, 23.

64 Schaff, *History of the Christian Church, Vol. IV*, 527.

65 Fesko, *Diversity within the Reformed Tradition*, 23.

66 Fesko, *Diversity within the Reformed Tradition*, 23.

67 Pelikan, *The Christian Tradition, Vol. 3*, 88.

68 Isidore, *Sententiae*, 2.6, in *Patrologia Latina, Vol. 83*, col. 606, trans. and cited in Fesko, *Diversity within the Reformed Tradition*, 22.

69 Isidore, *Sententiae*, 2.6.1, cited in Pelikan, *The Christian Tradition, Vol. 3*, 88.

70 Isidore, *Differentiarum*, 2.32.117–118, in *Patrologia Latina, Vol. 83*, col. 88, trans. and cited in Fesko, *Diversity within the Reformed Tradition*, 23.

71 Isidore, *Differentiarum*, 2.32.117–118, in *Patrologia Latina, Vol. 83*, col. 88, trans. and cited in Fesko, *Diversity within the Reformed Tradition*, 23.

72 Pelikan, *The Christian Tradition, Vol. 3*, 89.

73 Isidore, *Sententiae*, 2.5.13, in *Patrologia Latina, Vol. 83*, col. 605, trans. and cited in Fesko, *Diversity within the Reformed Tradition*, 24.

74 Isidore, *Sententiae*, in *Patrologia Latina, Vol. 83*, col. 606 cited in Reginald Garrigou-Lagrange, *Predestination: The Meaning of Predestination in Scripture and the Church* (Charlotte, N.C.: Tan, 1998), 54.

75 Isidore, *Sententiae*, 2.6.6, cited in Jaroslav Pelikan, *The Christian Tradition, Vol. 1: A History of the Development of the Doctrine (100–600)* (Chicago: University of Chicago Press, 1973), 88.

76 N. R. Needham, *2,000 Years of Christ's Power, Part Two: The Middle Ages* (London: Grace Publications, 2005), 9.

# CHAPTER THIRTEEN
## STUDY QUESTIONS

1. What is Semi-Pelagianism? How does it differ from Pelagianism? How does it differ from Augustinianism? Historically, how was this doctrinal divergence settled?

2. Why is Semi-Pelagian teaching so devastating to the church? Where do you see this teaching today? How has it affected contemporary preaching? Evangelism? Worship? Ministry methodology?

3. Describe the Dark Ages. Why is this period known by this description? What was the effect of this darkness on the church? How did it affect the development of theology?

4. Describe Isidore's place in church history. What were his strengths and gifts? How are such abilities needed in the church today?

5. How did Isidore's writings contribute to the general learning of the church? Do books play an important role in your spiritual development?

6. Isidore firmly believed in God's absolute sovereignty. Why is this such a pivotal doctrine? How does this doctrine affect one's overall theology and worldview? What is your understanding of divine sovereignty? What are its ramifications for all of life?

7. Describe Isidore's understanding of sovereign election. Where does this understanding place him in regard to Augustine? What does it mean that Isidore held to double predestination?

8. Can you identify elements within Isidore's theological statements that indicate a developing understanding of the doctrines of grace? List these advancements. How has your understanding of the doctrines of grace developed? What has been most influential in bringing about this progression?

$\mathcal{G}$od the immutable, immutably predestined
before the foundation of the world all His elect
by His free grace to eternal life.[1]

–Gottschalk of Orbais

Chapter Fourteen

# CHAMPION FOR PREDESTINATION

## EARLY MONASTIC: GOTTSCHALK OF ORBAIS

E very generation that comes onto the scene of human history must wrestle with the crucial issue of God's sovereignty in salvation. Sadly, some eras have remained superficial in their treatment of God's Word and, thus, have failed to grapple with this core doctrine. Rather than plunging into the depths of Scripture to gather inestimable pearls from the ocean's floor, they have been content merely to wade in the shallows and tidal pools, failing to immerse themselves in the biblical texts regarding this vast subject. They are satisfied to pick up the seashells and driftwood that wash ashore.

Nevertheless, in every era, God has providentially raised up poised and able preachers who proclaimed His sovereignty in man's salvation. Moreover, our Lord, the sovereign Head of the church, guaranteed the success of these spiritual stalwarts who served His purposes. He appointed the time in history when each man would further His work and where on the globe he would be placed. Having immersed themselves in Scripture, these men found priceless treasure. They embraced and upheld the powerful and provocative truths that are the doctrines of grace.

Yet for this reason, they suffered greatly. History records that those who have proclaimed the doctrines of grace have been among the most persecuted saints in the history of the church. These priceless gems have caused many to undergo great tribulation and even martyrdom. The doctrines of grace are antithetical to the natural mind, offending unbelievers to such a degree that proponents often pay a great price for their faith. Numbered among this persecuted lot would be the French Huguenots, the Scottish Covenanters, the Marian Martyrs, and the English Puritans. Heroic individuals—such as John Hus, Martin Luther, and John Calvin—suffered greatly for their biblical convictions. And standing near the head of this list of courageous proponents for the doctrines of grace is a lonely figure from the ninth century—Gottschalk of Orbais.

## A Rebirth of Roman Culture

The ninth century witnessed a resurgence of learning and a revival of culture. After four hundred years of darkness under the Goths, the Mediterranean world was seemingly reborn intellectually and socially. This renewal began on December 25, 800, when Pope Leo III unexpectedly crowned the Frankish (French) king, Charles the Great (742–814)—better known as Charlemagne— as "Emperor of the Romans," a title that was a precursor to that of "Holy Roman emperor." Using his invested power, Charlemagne launched the first attempt at a unified government since the collapse of the Roman Empire (410).[2] As the chosen ruler of the Western world, Charlemagne—who owed his authority to the pope—became one of the colossal figures of European history.[3]

This attempt to revive the Roman Empire led to a reawakening of Christian culture in Europe, a period known as the Carolingian Renaissance (800–900). This renaissance—a term drawn from the French word for "rebirth"—was marked by a revival of interest in European art, literature, education, scholarship, the Latin language, and the ancient classics. New schools were established that taught the seven liberal arts of the *trivium*—grammar, rhetoric, logic—and the *quadrivium*—arithmetic, astronomy, geometry, and music. Learning was alive again.

With this resurgence of education, Charlemagne brought the world's best scholars to the Roman Empire. From Italy, he summoned the grammarian Peter of Pisa and the historian Paul the Deacon. From Spain, the emperor recruited Theodulf, a renowned poet and man of letters, to be bishop of Orléans. From York, he brought in Alcuin to become head of the palace school and chief organizer of the renaissance.[4] This revived awareness in classical styles of European literature and the arts rescued a dying culture from near extinction during the Dark Ages. Moreover, the foundation stones for the Renaissance of the fourteenth through sixteenth centuries were firmly laid.

## A Century of Theological Controversies

However, the ninth century also proved to be a season of great theological controversy. The renewal of learning brought debates, especially doctrinal disputes. Heated arguments arose over a variety of subjects. Some of these arguments centered around images or icons, the role of the saints in worship, the Trinity, the procession of the Holy Spirit, the nature of the soul, the virginity of Mary, the Eucharist, and adoptionism. But the greatest controversy by far surrounded the sovereignty of God in salvation.

"The revival of theological science in the ninth century," the noted nineteenth-century German scholar Adolf von Harnack observed, "led to a thorough study of Augustine."[5] This study reignited interest in the relationship between divine sovereignty and human responsibility. This controversy has appeared in virtually every century, pitting such foes as Augustine and Pelagius, Martin Luther and Desiderius Erasmus,[6] John Calvin and Jacopo Sadoleto,[7] the delegates to the Synod of Dort and the students of Jacobus Arminius, George Whitefield and John Wesley, and Benjamin B. Warfield and Charles Finney. Regardless of the names, the debate remains the same.

In the late Dark Ages, this controversy surfaced when an obscure German monk named Gottschalk of Orbais (805–869) began to revisit the writings of Augustine. The more he read, the more he became convinced of human depravity and the sovereign grace of God in salvation. Soon, Gottschalk became a staunch advocate of the Augustinian position. "A renewal of the controversy," Von Harnack notes, "would hardly have taken place had not the monk Gottschalk of Orbais asserted the doctrine of predestination with as much energy as Augustine had done."[8] However, two Semi-Pelagians opposed Gottschalk—Rabanus Maurus (ca. 780–856) and the Archbishop Hincmar of Reims (ca. 806–882). These powerful men ridiculed and eventually imprisoned Gottschalk for his strict views. That, in turn, outraged other prominent church leaders. This monk, they reasoned, had merely taught the same basic theology as Augustine. Thus, the controversy came to the boiling point.

## The Center of the Crisis

The debate revolved around probing questions: Is the divine will ultimately determinative in man's salvation or is it subservient to the human will? Is salvation the result of divine foreordination or mere foresight? Is salvation entirely of the Lord or does man contribute to it? Does God supply the faith with which the elect believe or does saving trust in Christ originate within fallen man?

In an effort to settle these questions, a series of synods was held in the mid-ninth century. First, the Synod of Chiersy (853) adopted a Semi-Pelagian position, affirming the teaching of Maurus and Hincmar. But the Synod of Valence (855) and the Synod of Langress (859) took a strong Augustinian stand. Finally, in an attempt to find unity, the conflicting parties met at Toucy in France in 860. This synod resulted in a devastating defeat for predestinarianism in France. In short, the doctrines of sovereign grace suffered a major setback and the notion of human free will prevailed. The only concession was that Hincmar's official letter of the synod was not sanctioned by the men in attendance. Also, Nicholas I, the sitting pope, supposedly approved the strongly Augustinian canons of the synods of Valence and Langress, although his decree is lost. To this point, Philip Schaff comments, "The door was left open within the Catholic church itself for a revival of strict Augustinianism, and this took place on a grand scale in the sixteenth century."[9]

The church usually downplays the role of God in salvation and exalts the role of man. The inevitable result is Semi-Pelagianism. But in every period of history, a few faithful voices magnify the divine will and keep the biblical truth of sovereign grace burning brightly. God always has men who uphold the truth of His sovereign will in salvation. At times, this long line of godly men has grown thin. It certainly did in medieval times. But from age to age, it has remained intact, a chain of faithful witnesses. In the ninth century, Gottschalk took his stance on the stage of world history as part of this long line.

## GOTTSCHALK OF ORBAIS

Gottschalk showed himself to be a man of strong convictions and heroic courage.[10] Deeply influenced by Augustine of Hippo, he sought to revive Augustinian theology in the ninth century.[11] D. E. Nineham writes, "Virtually everything Gottschalk wrote could claim the authority of the master, a reference to his mentor, Augustine."[12] His teaching of predestination "was not different, either in matter or form, from that of Augustine . . . and Isidore."[13] Like Augustine before him, and Luther and Calvin after, Gottschalk had an overriding sense of the sovereignty of God.[14]

Born at Mentz, in what is now Germany, Gottschalk was the son of a respected nobleman, Count Berno of Saxony. At an early age, his father sent him to the famous Hessian convent at Fulda that he might take up the monastic life.[15] At this time, the Fulda monastery was the greatest center of religious and secular education in Germany.[16] Gottschalk studied Latin, the Bible, the Church Fathers, and classical literature under the head of the monastery school, Maurus, a noted commentator, theologian, and hymn writer.

Gottschalk's father insisted that his son take monastic vows. Though not fully understanding what this would mean for his life, young Gottschalk did so. But upon reaching the age of maturity, he sought to undo his vows and leave the monastery. He reasoned that vows he took as a child should not be binding. However, Maurus did not want his astute young pupil to leave, so he denied the request. The case was eventually brought to the Synod of Mainz (829), where Gottschalk requested and received an official release from his vows.

But Maurus, who had been appointed abbot of Fulda, appealed to the emperor. To support his case, Maurus wrote a book, *De Oblatione Puerorum* ("Concerning the Offering of Boys"), which argued that the contract entered into by Gottschalk's parents in presenting their son for vows could not be annulled.[17] The book convinced the emperor, who reversed the decision of the Synod of Mainz. The emperor's verdict meant Gottschalk must remain a monk for the rest of his life.

## A Diligent Student of Augustine

Maurus made one concession—he allowed Gottschalk to move from the monastery at Fulda to the monastery at Orbais, in northeast France. In this new environment, Gottschalk became a devoted student of two major theologians, Augustine and Fulgentius of Ruspe (d. 533). Both of these men had been outspoken adherents of the biblical teaching of sovereign grace. Augustine was the strongest voice for divine sovereignty in the early church, and Fulgentius taught double predestination.[18] The writings of these two figures convinced Gottschalk of the doctrines of grace. God's sovereignty over all things, including man's salvation, became "the strength and support of his being."[19]

In his enthusiasm, Gottschalk began to preach and teach the biblical views of Augustine and Fulgentius. His influence grew, and he was able to convince fellow monks of these God-exalting truths. In Gottschalk, the doctrines of grace were revived. Augustinianism had a new champion.

Yet, as is always the case, this resurgence of sovereign grace was not without conflict. Gottschalk's teaching of these grand truths brought him into direct conflict with Maurus.[20] In an attempt to defame and discredit Gottschalk, Maurus wrote two letters against him. The letters restated the arguments and views held centuries before by Augustine's opponents.[21] In response, Gottschalk accused Maurus of Semi-Pelagianism for equivocating on the sovereignty of God in saving grace. This exchange ignited a firestorm over the God-centeredness of salvation.

Gottschalk set out with a few companions on a pilgrimage to Rome, and throughout this journey he propagated Augustinian theology. His travels took him through Italy, the Balkans, and Bulgaria, where he preached and taught extensively.[22] Though his teaching was often rejected, Gottschalk would not be deterred. He also corresponded with several noted scholars about his Augustinian stance. Soon he attracted a significant following.

On his return to Orbais around 847, Gottschalk spent considerable time with Count Eberhard of Friuli, a son-in-law of the Emperor Louis, as well as with Noting, the bishop of Verona, who had received one of the condemning letters from Maurus against Gottschalk. Gottschalk and Noting discussed the doctrines of grace extensively. Alarmed by Gottschalk's deep convictions, Noting urged him to recant, but Gottschalk refused. In frustration, Noting informed Maurus, now the archbishop of Mentz, and urged him to refute Gottschalk's views. Enraged, Maurus wrote a tract denying predestination on the grounds that God's foreordination is conditioned by His foreknowledge. Here, Maurus set forth the conditional view of election, which makes man's will ultimately determinative in human salvation, not the choice of God.

## Before the Synod of Mainz

The archbishop summoned Gottschalk to appear before the Synod of Mainz (848). Before the king and other officials, he was required to give an account of his teaching on the doctrines of grace. Boldly confessing his belief in divine sovereignty in salvation, Gottschalk stated that this doctrine was true to the Scriptures and consistent with Augustine. Not only did God predestine His elect to eternal life from eternity past, Gottschalk maintained, He also foreordained all reprobates to eternal death—double predestination.[23] He insisted that a precise number of people have been predestined to destruction by God's active reprobation. Rather than merely passing over the nonelect, he contended, God actively chose to damn them.

Gottschalk said he was not promoting a view of two predestinations, but of one predestination that pertains either to the gift of grace to the elect or to the execution of justice on the nonelect. Gillian R. Evans summarizes Gottschalk's argument: "To say that predestination is twofold is not to say that there are two predestinations . . . it is like saying that a man is twofold and yet one. His body (exterior) and his soul (interior) are not two men but one. In a similar way the predestination of God is the mercy by which the elect are freed and saved and the truth by which the wicked are justly judged and condemned is twofold, but still one."[24] He was teaching, Evans says, that there was one decree of election to life and to destruction.

Moreover, Gottschalk asserted that the redeeming work of Christ was intended only for those who would believe. This is the biblical doctrine known as definite atonement. Von Harnack notes, "Gottschalk frequently maintained that Christ did not die for the *reprobi* [reprobate]."[25] Rather, the Lord gave Himself at the cross only for the elect.

The synod decided against Gottschalk and ordered him to be delivered to the most powerful bishop in France, Hincmar. At the time of this transfer, Maurus wrote to Hincmar, "We send to you this vagabond monk, in order that you may shut him up in his convent, and prevent him from propagating his false, heretical, and scandalous doctrine."[26] Hincmar, a learned man with a fiery disposition—he has been described as "proud and intolerant"[27]— was easily drawn into this controversy. Relishing the opportunity to publicly refute and personally ruin Gottschalk, he treated the monk without mercy.[28]

## THE FIRST SYNOD OF CHIERSY

Hincmar ordered Gottschalk to appear before the Synod of Chiersy (849) for interrogation. There, Gottschalk affirmed double predestination. In response, the archbishop leveled the charge of heresy, castigating Gottschalk as an "irreconcilable enemy."[29] When Gottschalk refused to recant, Hincmar further accused him of being a "wandering monk" who had spread his "false teaching" throughout Italy.[30] Hincmar said: "He [Gottschalk] has undertaken to proclaim that before all worlds and before whatever God did from the beginning, He foreordained to the kingdom whom He willed and He foreordained to death whom He willed; that those who have been foreordained to death cannot be saved, and those who have been foreordained to the kingdom cannot perish."[31] With this attack, Hincmar became Gottschalk's greatest accuser.[32]

Despite Hincmar's accusations, Gottschalk was unwavering in his resolve for the doctrines of grace and refused to recant his biblical convictions. With great boldness, he rejected every attempt to sway his beliefs. Thus, the synod condemned Gottschalk as a heretic. Hincmar had him publicly flogged, burned his books, and imprisoned him in the monastery at Hautvilliers, near Reims. R. K. McGregor Wright writes:

> Hincmar's treatment of Gottschalk is a classic example of what hatred can accomplish when supported by the power to persecute. He stripped the helpless monk of his priesthood, had him imprisoned for life in a monastery and repeatedly tortured him with floggings in an attempt to force him to abandon his views. It is amazing that Gottschalk endured twelve years of this treatment before he died insane, still convinced that an omniscient God cannot logically choose some for salvation without at the same time choosing to reject others, even though they are no more sinful. This, of course, is the doctrine of reprobation taught today by all consistent Calvinists and found in chapter III of the Westminster Confession. Gottschalk seems to have been among the first to see that Augustine's views required some kind of "double" predestination."[33]

During his imprisonment, Gottschalk wrote two confessions, one shorter and the other longer. In these works, he reasserted his views on double predestination. Because of these convictions, he remained in bitter dispute with Hincmar.

## GOTTSCHALK'S FINAL DAYS

While imprisoned at Hautvilliers, Gottschalk appealed to Pope Nicholas I for a reinvestigation of his case. So sure was Gottschalk that he would be cleared of all charges of heresy that he offered "to step successively into four cauldrons of boiling water, oil, fat, and pitch, and then to walk through a blazing pile."[34] Nicholas agreed to reopen the case, but Gottschalk suddenly became sick. When it appeared he was close to death, the monks who were caring for him notified Archbishop Hincmar and asked him how they were to treat Gottschalk. Hincmar responded by sending a Semi-Pelagian confession of faith and ordering Gottschalk to sign it. He was told he would be denied a Christian burial unless he made a full recantation of his predestinarian beliefs. But Gottschalk did not flinch from his convictions. Without hesitation, he "rejected [the confession] with indignation."[35] Hincmar responded with a severe condemnation and ordered Gottschalk to be censured by the clergy of France.

Gottschalk died before Nicholas could hear his case. The battered monk passed away on October 30, 869, with "unshaken faith."[36] Sadly, he had had a nervous breakdown from which he never recovered. In a final insult, Hincmar made good on his threat to deny Gottschalk a Christian burial. He was laid to rest in "unconsecrated soil."

To the very end, Gottschalk maintained a deep conviction as to God's sovereignty in man's salvation. The truths of sovereign grace were both the cause of his suffering and his comfort in suffering. Many joined with Gottschalk in testifying to those truths, but "he alone was persecuted as a heretical teacher, because the opposition felt that he alone was dangerous to their church system."[37] But though his enemies assailed him, Gottschalk has been regarded by champions of the faith as a martyr to the truth.[38]

# GOTTSCHALK'S WRITINGS

Gottschalk was inflamed with a passion for God and His supreme glory. For him, the doctrines of grace were not a mere intellectual pursuit, but truths that transformed his life and produced high doxology within him. Sovereign grace made him "a religious poet of high order."[39] His hymns revealed a soul of "deep feeling, sensitivity and piety, keenly aware of its own shortcomings and need of God's mercy and grace."[40] His verse, it has been said, was the "most musical" in Europe for centuries.[41] Further, his prose writings were often in the form of sustained prayers, revealing the depths of his devotional life.

Chief among his surviving works are *Shorter Confession* and *Larger Confession*, written while he was imprisoned at Hautvilliers for his predestinarian beliefs. Another work, *On Predestination*, asserted his ardent Augustinian stance. Gottschalk did not waver from his convictions, despite his sufferings. Instead, he used his pen to strongly assert his doctrine of divine sovereignty in man's salvation.

## SHORTER CONFESSION

In Gottschalk's *Shorter Confession*, his zeal for Augustinianism shone forth, especially his deep conviction regarding predestination. Here, the doctrine of absolute predestination is seen to be the sturdy cornerstone of Gottschalk's high theology.

*LARGER CONFESSION*

In the *Larger Confession*, Gottschalk wrote in the form of a prayer and softened his theological stance. He denied that God predestines reprobates to sin, but affirmed that He passes over them, leaving them in their sin. Also in this confession, he demonstrated that he firmly believed that men are incapable of coming to God apart from God's grace first being applied to their wills. Gottschalk saw that men cannot do anything good in God's sight apart from God first doing a work in their hearts.

*ON PREDESTINATION*

In this work, Gottschalk identified divine foreknowledge completely with predestination. Further, he saw predestination as directed toward both the saved and the lost. God chooses those who will receive eternal life, but the reprobate are divinely chosen to continue in their sins. The precise number of elect and nonelect are determined by the eternal decree of God, a predestination to life and a predestination to death.

# GOTTSCHALK'S THEOLOGY

Gottschalk was so committed to the teachings of Augustine—that is to say, the teachings of Scripture—that he forsook his own well-being and often found himself embroiled in bitter theological controversy. For this reason, the citations we have from Gottschalk are limited in number, as most of his works were burned, condemned as heretical teachings. Yet, as the following excerpts reveal, Gottschalk boldly upheld the truths of Scripture, and his heart was gripped by the doctrines of grace. Jaroslav J. Pelikan writes that "in setting forth his doctrine of predestination, Gottschalk believed that he was confessing the universal faith and that it was not he, but his opponents, who were the heretics."[42] He was a stalwart of predestination.

**Doctrine in Focus:**
RADICAL DEPRAVITY

Gottschalk accepted Scripture's depiction of the ruined nature of the human race because of the sin of Adam. Natural man, Gottschalk believed, does not have free will to choose the good, but possesses only the capacity to sin. He says: "After the first man fell by free will, none of us is able to use free will to do good, but only to do evil."[43] In other words, apart from grace, man can pursue only evil.

Gottschalk made this point repeatedly. He writes: "Every rational creature, not only the human but also the angelic, must be acknowledged as always in need of divine grace in order to be pleasing to God."[44] Elsewhere he states, "Without God's grace and help, the free will [of man] cannot do anything good."[45] Moreover, he declares, "For, truly no one, not any one of Your elect, have ever been able to please You from themselves even for a moment, but rather all of Your people have pleased, do please, and will please You always from You, through Your free grace."[46] In short, according to Arthur Custance, Gottschalk believed that "little or no importance could be attached to the natural goodness of man or to any supposed works of merit performed before conversion."[47]

**Doctrine in Focus:**
## Sovereign Election

As an ardent follower of Augustine and Scripture, Gottschalk heralded the doctrine of unconditional election, the truth that God sovereignly chose a people for Himself unto salvation before the foundation of the world. He writes, "He [God] predestined all of the elect to life through the gratuity of the free grace of His kindness, as the pages of the Old and New Testaments very clearly, skillfully, and soberly show those seeking wisdom on this matter."[48] Elsewhere he says that God "elected a world from out of the world."[49] Though God created all people, He did not choose to redeem them all.

Gottschalk saw a connection between the omnipotence and unchangeable character of God and His eternal plan. Because God Himself is immutable, His eternal election is unchangeable, Gottschalk contended. He writes: "God the immutable, immutably predestined before the foundation of the world all His elect by His free grace to eternal life."[50] Just as God is unchanging in His being and character, He is also immutable in His plan of salvation. What God determined in eternity past cannot be changed within time.

Gottschalk dealt with the hard passages of the Bible concerning unconditional election. Commenting on 1 Timothy 2:3–4, which affirms that God desires all people to be saved, Gottschalk explained that the word *all* must mean all who are saved, not all men in general.[51] He says, "Truly God has not in any way desired to save with eternal salvation those whom, as Scripture testifies, He hardens."[52] God's act of election indicates that some are chosen to be saved, but not all.

**Doctrine in Focus:**
## DEFINITE ATONEMENT

Some seven hundred years prior to Calvin's *Institutes of the Christian Religion*, Gottschalk provided the first clear statement of a definite atonement in church history.[53] His statement marks a major development in the church's understanding of the extent of the atonement.

In one of his few surviving statements regarding this doctrine, he succinctly writes, "Our God and master Jesus Christ [was] crucified only for the elect."[54] This statement testifies to Gottschalk's belief in particular redemption for those chosen for salvation. Although previous men had made similar declarations concerning the basic aspects of this doctrine, Gottschalk was the first to demonstrate the strong relationship between predestination and the atonement.[55] For Gottschalk, the doctrine of the atonement was a direct corollary of predestination.[56]

Gottschalk left no doubt that he believed no one can come to new life in Christ unless God wills it to happen. This means that those who do believe on Christ were predestined to do so. He affirms: "All those whom God wills to be saved without doubt are saved. They cannot be saved unless God wills them to be saved; and there is no one whom God wills to be saved, who will not be saved, since our God did all things whatsoever He willed."[57] He adds, "All those impious persons and sinners for whom the Son of God came to redeem by shedding His own blood, those the omnipotent goodness of God predestined to life and irrevocably willed only those to be saved."[58] Christ's atoning work was particular to the elect.

Gottschalk repeatedly turned to God's Word to support this teaching. Commenting on Romans 5:8–9, he logically reasons, "If Christ died even for the reprobate, then the reprobate too, having been justified in His blood, will be saved from wrath through Him. But the reprobate will not be saved from wrath through Him. Therefore, Christ did not die for the reprobate."[59] With these words, Gottschalk resolutely affirmed that Christ died exclusively for the elect.

**Doctrine in Focus:**
## IRRESISTIBLE CALL

Gottschalk emphasized that regeneration is by sovereign grace rather than human initiative or good works. He held that God must effectually work in a sinner's heart before he or she will believe on Christ. This happens, he said, when the Holy Spirit imparts eternal life to spiritually dead sinners. These affirmations appear in a hymn Gottschalk wrote titled "A Hymn to God the Life-Giver," a magnificent declaration of monergistic regeneration. Gottschalk writes:

> Freely You created me by Your goodness;
> Freely create me afresh, I pray, and restore me to life!
> Freely You bestow Your gifts, which is why we say they are grace.
> O Holy Spirit, You bring instant life to those You breathe into;
> Together with the Father and His Son, You thunder forth, govern and give light;
> You increase and You quicken the faith
> Which You grant to whomever You choose.
> Even more, You make clean those polluted by leprosy,
> You make the ungodly righteous;
> Together with the Father and the Son, You recreate Your elect souls,
> And when they are recreated, You also glorify them.[60]

**Doctrine in Focus:**

## Divine Reprobation

In stressing the biblical truth of sovereign grace, Gottschalk was as committed to the teaching of divine reprobation as he was to that of sovereign election. He was convinced that God, before all time, predestined the reprobate to punishment. Schaff notes, "He held a two-fold predestination of the elect to salvation, and of the reprobate to perdition."[61]

Gottschalk's writings are very clear on this point. He says, "Predestination, whether of the elect to life or of the reprobate to death, is twin,"[62] a reference to divine predestination both to life and to death. He adds, "God Himself by His righteous judgment immutably predestined to everlasting death all the reprobate, who on the day of the judgment will be condemned on account of their own evil deserts."[63] In perhaps his most direct statement on this matter, Gottschalk writes: "I believe and confess the omnipotent and immutable God to have foreknown and predestined holy angels, and chosen men free to eternal life, and to have equally predestined the devil himself, prince of all demons with all his apostates, and also with the same reprobate men, evidently his members by His righteous judgment to deserved eternal death on account of their own future evil conduct and deserts, which He most surely foreknew: because thus the Lord Himself says in His Gospel: the ruler of this world has already been judged."[64] The doctrine of double predestination was a teaching that Gottschalk emphasized.

## PAYING A HIGH PRICE

There is extraordinary value for the modern church in knowing the price that those who have gone before have paid to advance the doctrines of grace—men like Gottschalk of Orbais. In his day of theological decline, He stood out as one particularly committed to the teaching of Augustine. His life shows that these precious truths have come down to us at a great price. Heroic men and women stood as the minority in order to uphold the truths of the sovereign grace of God. When we understand how they stood up and were counted faithful, we see that we cannot remain silent.

Like so many of those saints before us, we live in a time when Reformed theology is the minority position. But like those men and women of the past, we must be faithful. As long as we are here, we must lift high the blazing torch of truth. If we suffer for our proclamation of the doctrines of grace, so be it. We will have the comfort of knowing that we stand in a long line of godly men.

Let us pray that God will bring about a resurgence of God-centered doctrine in His church. This remains the need of the hour. It will come at a price, but the gain received will always outweigh the pain required.

NOTES

1   Gottschalk, cited in Hincmar of Reims, *De Praedestinatione Dei et Libero Arbitrio*, 4, in *Patrologia Latina*, Vol. 125, cols. 89–90, ed. J. P. Minge (Paris: 1852), trans. and cited in J. V. Fesko, *Diversity within the Reformed Tradition: Supra- and Infralapsarianism in Calvin, Dort, and Westminster* (Greenville, S.C.: Reformed Academic, 2001), 27.

2   J. G. G. Norman, "Carolingian Renaissance," in *New International Dictionary of the Christian Church*, gen. ed. J. D. Douglas (Grand Rapids: Zondervan, 1978), 195.

3   N. R. Needham, *2,000 Years of Christ's Power, Part Two: The Middle Ages* (London: Grace Publications, 2005), 51.

4   Norman, "Carolingian Renaissance," in *New International Dictionary of the Christian Church*, 195.

5   Adolf von Harnack, *History of Dogma, Vol. 5* (Eugene, Ore: Wipf & Stock, 1997), 292–293.

6   For further study, see Martin Luther, *The Bondage of the Will* (Grand Rapids: Revell, 2000).

7   For further study, see John Calvin and Jacopo Sadoleto, *A Reformation Debate*, ed. John C. Olin (Grand Rapids: Baker, 1976).

8   Von Harnack, *History of Dogma, Vol. 5*, 293.

9   Philip Schaff, *History of the Christian Church, Vol. IV: Medieval Christianity: From Gregory I to Gregory VII, A.D. 590–1073* (1910; repr., Grand Rapids: Eerdmans, 1980), 537.

10  Schaff, *History of the Christian Church, Vol. IV*, 523.

11  William G. T. Shedd, *A History of Christian Doctrine, Vol. Two* (1897; repr., Birmingham, Ala.: Solid Ground, 2006), 113.

12  D. E. Nineham, "Gottschalk of Orbais: Reactionary or Precursor to the Reformation?" *Journal of Ecclesiastical History*, 40 (1989), 11.

13  Von Harnack, *History of Dogma, Vol. 5*, 293.

14  Nineham, "Gottschalk of Orbais," *Journal of Ecclesiastical History*, 12.

15  Schaff, *History of the Christian Church, Vol. IV*, 525.

16  Needham, *2,000 Years of Christ's Power, Part Two*, 65.

17  "Gottschalk," in *Cyclopedia of Biblical, Theological, and Ecclesiastical Literature, Vol. III*, eds. John McClintock and James Strong (1867–1887; repr., Grand Rapids: Baker, 1981), 950.

18  Schaff, *History of the Christian Church, Vol. IV*, 524.

19  Von Harnack, *History of Dogma, Vol. 5*, 293.

20  Needham, *2,000 Years of Christ's Power, Part Two*, 65.

21  Justo L. González, *A History of Christian Thought, Vol. 2: From Augustine to the Eve of the Reformation* (Nashville: Abingdon, 1971), 112.

22  John C. Cavadini, "Gottschalk of Orbais," in *Dictionary of Christian Biography*, ed. Michael Walsh (Collegeville, Minn.: The Liturgical Press, 2001), 541.

23  Willemien Otten, "Carolingian Theology," in *The Medieval Theologians: An Introduction to Theology in the Medieval Period*, ed. G. R. Evans (Malden, Mass.: Blackwell, 2001), 77.

24  Gillian R. Evans, "The Grammar of Predestination in the Ninth Century," *Journal of Theological Studies*, 33 (1982), 141.

25  Von Harnack, *History of Dogma, Vol. 5*, 296.

26  Rabanus Maurus, cited in "Gottschalk," in *Cyclopedia of Biblical, Theological, and Ecclesiastical Literature, Vol. III*, 950.

27  Schaff, *History of the Christian Church, Vol. IV*, 528.

28  Schaff, *History of the Christian Church, Vol. IV*, 528.

29  González, *A History of Christian Thought, Vol. 2*, 111.

30  González, *A History of Christian Thought, Vol. 2*, 111.

31  Hincmar, quoted in Remigius, *A Reply to the Three Letters (Selections)*, in *Early Medieval Theology, Library of Christian Classics, Vol. 9*, eds. John Baillie et al, trans. George E. McCraken (London: SCM, 1958), 155–156.

32  González, *A History of Christian Thought, Vol. 2*, 112.

33  R. K. McGregor Wright, *No Place for Sovereignty: What's Wrong with Freewill Theism* (Downers Grove, Ill.: InterVarsity, 1996), 21–22.

34  Schaff, *History of the Christian Church, Vol. IV*, 529.

35  "Gottschalk," in *Cyclopedia of Biblical, Theological, and Ecclesiastical Literature, Vol. III*, 950.

36 Schaff, *History of the Christian Church, Vol. IV*, 529.

37 Adolf von Harnack, *History of Dogma, Vol. 3* (Gloucester, Mass.: Peter Smith, 1976), 293.

38 González, *The Story of Christianity, Vol. 1* (Peabody, Mass.: Prince, 2004), 529.

39 "Gottschalk," in *The Oxford Dictionary of the Christian Church*, 3rd Ed., ed. E. A. Livingstone (1957; repr., Oxford: Oxford University Press, 1997), 696.

40 Nineham, "Gottschalk of Orbais," *Journal of Ecclesiastical History*, 13.

41 Helen Waddel, *The Wandering Scholars*, 7th Ed. (London: Constable, 1934), 57.

42 Cited in Jaroslav J. Pelikan, *The Christian Tradition, Vol. 3: The Growth of Medieval Theology (600–1300)* (Chicago: University of Chicago Press, 1978), 85.

43 Gottschalk, *On Predestination*, 15, cited in *Ouevres theologiques et grammaticales de Godescalc d' Orbais*, ed. Cyrille Lambot (Louvain, 1945), 242, trans. and cited in Pelikan, *The Christian Tradition, Vol. 3*, 83.

44 Gottschalk, *On Predestination*, 13, cited in *Ouevres theologiques et grammaticales de Godescalc d' Orbais*, 234, trans. and cited in Pelikan, *The Christian Tradition, Vol. 3*, 82.

45 Gottschalk, *Larger Confession*, n.p., cited in *Ouevres theologiques et grammaticales de Godescalc d'Orbais*, 152–153, trans. Victor Genke, cited in Francis X. Gumerlock, "Gottschalk of Orbais: A Medieval Predestinarian," *Kerux* 22:3 (December 2007): 17–34.

46 Gottschalk, *Larger Confession*, n.p., cited in *Ouevres theologiques et grammaticales de Godescalc d'Orbais*, 76, cited in "Gottschalk of Orbais: A Medieval Predestinarian," 17–34.

47 Arthur Custance, *The Sovereignty of Grace* (Grand Rapids: Baker, 1979), 38.

48 Gottschalk, *Larger Confession*, n.p., cited in *Ouevres theologiques et grammaticales de Godescalc d'Orbais*, 39, cited in "Gottschalk of Orbais: A Medieval Predestinarian," 17–34.

49 Gottschalk, *On Predestination*, 9.3, cited in *Ouevres theologiques et grammaticales de Godescalc d' Orbais*, 204, trans. and cited in Pelikan, *The Christian Tradition, Vol. 3*, 92.

50 Gottschalk, cited in Hincmar of Reims, *De Praedestinatione Dei et Libero Arbitrio*, 4, in *Patrologia Latina, Vol. 125*, cols. 89–90, trans. and cited in Fesko, *Diversity within the Reformed Tradition*, 27.

51 Pelikan, *The Christian Tradition, Vol. 3*, 90.

52 Gottschalk. *On Predestination*, 14, cited in *Ouevres theologiques et grammaticales de Godescalc d' Orbais*, 238, trans. and cited in Pelikan, *The Christian Tradition, Vol. 3*, 90.

53 Fesko, *Diversity within the Reformed Tradition*, 32.

54 Gottschalk, cited in George H. Tavard, *Trina Deitas: The Controversy between Hincmar and Gottschalk* (Milwaukee: Marquette University Press, 1996), 125.

55 Tavard, *Trina Deitas*, 32.

56 Pelikan, *The Christian Tradition, Vol. 3*, 94.

57 Gottschalk, cited in Hincmar of Reims, *De Praedestinatione Dei et Libero Arbitrio*, in *Ouevres theologiques et grammaticales de Godescalc d'Orbais*, 40, cited in "Gottschalk of Orbais: A Medieval Predestinarian," 17–34.

58 Gottschalk, cited in Hincmar of Reims, *De Praedestinatione Dei et Libero Arbitrio*, in *Ouevres theologiques et grammaticales de Godescalc d'Orbais*, 40, cited in "Gottschalk of Orbais: A Medieval Predestinarian," 17–34.

59 Gottschalk, cited in *Ouevres theologiques et grammaticales de Godescalc d'Orbais*, 157–158, cited in "Gottschalk of Orbais: A Medieval Predestinarian," 17–34.

60 Gottschalk, cited in Needham, *2,000 Years of Christ's Power, Part Two*, 82.

61 Schaff, *History of the Christian Church, Vol. IV*, 531.

62 Gottschalk, cited in Hincmar of Reims, *De Praedestinatione Dei et Libero Arbitrio*, 4, in *Patrologia Latina, Vol. 125*, cols. 89–90, trans. and cited in Schaff, *History of the Christian Church, Vol. IV*, 531.

63 Gottschalk, cited in Hincmar of Reims, *De Praedestinatione Dei et Libero Arbitrio*, 4, in *Patrologia Latina, Vol. 125*, cols. 89–90, trans. and cited in Fesko, *Diversity within the Reformed Tradition*, 27.

64 Gottschalk, *Confessio Gotteschalci Monachi: Post Haeresim Damnatam*, in *Patrologia Latina, Vol. 121*, col. 347, ed. J. P. Migne (Paris, 1852), trans. and cited in Fesko, *Diversity within the Reformed Tradition*, 34.

# CHAPTER FOURTEEN
# STUDY QUESTIONS

1. Summarize the Carolingian Renaissance. What were its major contributions? What advancements were witnessed at this time?

2. Describe the main theological controversies of the ninth century. What were the driving issues? Who were the main participants? How were these disputes resolved?

3. Explain Gottschalk's early development. What role did the monastery play in his growing understanding of theology? Who became his primary teachers and what impact did their writings have upon his thinking?

4. What is the eternal decree of God? What is the relationship between this decree and the doctrines of election and reprobation? What sacrifice did Gottschalk make for holding these views? How have these views been costly in your life?

5. To what extent did Gottschalk believe in man's free will? In light of the fall of Adam, what moral ability does man have? What capacity does fallen man have to please God?

6. Explain the relationship between God's foreknowledge, predestination, and election. How does God's immutability relate to the doctrine of election? What was there in man that would have prompted God's choice of sinful individuals?

7. How did Gottschalk see the relationship between sovereign election and the extent of the atonement? In Gottschalk's understanding of the cross, for whom did Christ die?

8. Describe Gottschalk's understanding of the new birth. What decisive role must the Holy Spirit play in regeneration? Does sinful man believe before he is regenerated, or does he undergo regeneration and then believe?

*For in whose power is hell, or the devil? Or whose is the kingdom of heaven, if it be not His who created all things? Whatever things, therefore, you dread or hope for, all lie subject to His will, whom nothing can oppose.*[1]

–Anselm of Canterbury

# Chapter Fifteen

# PHILOSOPHER-THEOLOGIAN

## ENGLISH SCHOLASTIC: ANSELM OF CANTERBURY

With the arrival of the eleventh century, four major developments began to unfold that would greatly shape the flow of church history throughout Europe, Asia Minor, and the surrounding regions. The convergence of these four realities marked the eleventh century as a decisive era for generations to come, deeply affected the lives of a number of the men who were to serve in the long line of godly men, and began to lay the groundwork for the great recovery of the doctrines of divine sovereignty in man's salvation that would come in the Protestant Reformation.

What were these history-altering developments? First, there was the rise of the pope as the undisputed head of the Roman Catholic Church. Throughout the Early Middle Ages (ca. 410–1000), the claims of the bishopric of Rome were lofty but its power remained weak because of the fall of the Roman Empire. During this period, the church in the East rarely consulted the pope, and church leaders in the West approached the East only when it was expedient. In fact, councils of bishops—working directly with kings, not the pope—most often presided over the affairs of the church. But all of this changed early in the second millennium, as a series of strong popes, notably Gregory VII (1073–1085) and Innocent III (1198–1216), carried the papacy to a position of unrivaled leadership in Western Christendom. Popes in successive centuries would lead the Roman Catholic Church into some of the teachings that the Reformers would find most objectionable.

Second, the increase in papal authority contributed to a rift between the

Western (Catholic) and Eastern (Orthodox) churches. Beginning in the seventh century, the Eastern church had been greatly weakened because of the rise of Islam. From that point, it went into a steady decline, gradually losing both people and land to the Muslims. Along with those losses went its once-strong influence. Soon the bishop of Rome began to make autocratic demands on Eastern bishops, which Easterners found intolerable. In a backlash, the East refused to recognize some of the decisions of Western ecumenical church councils. Further, the Eastern leaders differed from their Western counterparts on several points, permitting lower ranks of clergy to marry, venerating icons, and insisting that the Father alone sent the Holy Spirit. These divergences eventually led to the East-West schism of 1054, making the East an isolated entity and a relative nonfactor in the flow of church history.

Third, the High Middle Ages (ca. 1000–1300) were the time of the Crusades—four military "holy wars" launched against Muslims and Jews by the Western church (1095–1291), which sought to recapture the Holy Land in order to ensure access to Jerusalem for Christian pilgrims. In the First Crusade (1096–1099), five thousand men marched to Constantinople, Antioch, and Jerusalem, and though they did not free the Middle East from Muslim control, they secured access for Christian pilgrims to the Holy City. In the Second Crusade (1147–1149), Muslims defeated the Christians at Damascus. Forty years later, the Muslims reconquered Jerusalem (1187), sparking the Third Crusade (1189–1192), which resulted in a three-year truce and reestablishment of free access to Jerusalem. Finally, the Fourth Crusade (1202–1204) attacked Constantinople and there set up a new Christian kingdom. Bernard of Clairvaux would play a significant role in these wars.

The Crusades left lasting effects on the church in Europe and the Middle East, not the least of which was the further empowerment of the papacy.[2] For almost two centuries, crusaders fought at the pleasure of the pope, who emerged as the champion of Christianity. What is more, these Crusades set a dangerous precedent for "holy war" against the enemies of the church. Opposition to the pope's authority would be met with the strong arm of Rome itself. Such would be the case just a few centuries later, as papal power would be wielded with deadly effect against the Albigensians in France and Hussites in Bohemia, as well as the Huguenots in France—conflicts that would affect the ministries of John Hus and John Calvin. Moreover, the Crusades fueled the selling of indulgences, that is, the payment of money in exchange for the pardon of sins. Indulgence sales were a primary means of funding the enormous cost of these campaigns and would be a major source of disagreement between Martin Luther and Rome.

Fourth, the seeds were sown during the eleventh century for the Scholastic movement to sprout and flower in the twelfth century. Scholasticism—from the Latin *scholae*, meaning "of the schools"—refers to a return to or revival of classical education. In the centuries between the Islamic capture of Jerusalem (638) and its recapture by the Christian crusaders (1099), theology had been largely the work of monks who studied the Bible, the writings of the Church Fathers, and classical literature. But the magnificent church structures that were being erected throughout Europe became gathering points for independent scholars to teach students. Although these instructors initially taught monks, the monks, in turn, began teaching laypeople. Over time, these teachers formed guilds and collaborated in order to educate numerous students. The result was the birth of the great universities of Europe in places such as Paris, Oxford, and St. Andrews. The men who taught in these schools were known as the Scholastics.

# MEDIEVAL SCHOLASTICS

The birth of the university in the twelfth century gave rise to a new type of education known as Scholasticism. This term came from the Latin word *scholae* ("school") and referred to the theology taught in the schools or the universities during the Middle Ages. The Scholastic theologians, who also were known as "Schoolmen," sought to discover ways to prove the "reasonableness" of the biblical truths of Christianity. They also wanted to compile a systematic account of Christian doctrine and to give a comprehensive account of all truth. To this end, they relied heavily on the philosophy of one of the greatest of the ancient Greek philosophers, Aristotle. Thus, the chief sources of their thought were Scripture, Augustine, and Aristotle, as they sought to show the agreement between revelation and reason, faith and science, theology and philosophy.[3]

The leading Scholastics included Anselm of Canterbury (1033–1109); Peter Abelard (1079–1143); Albertus Magnus (ca. 1193–1280); Bonaventure (1221–1274); Thomas Aquinas (1225–1274), who taught theology in Paris and is considered the greatest of the Scholastics and one of the master

theologians of church history; John Duns Scotus (1265–1308); William of
Ockham (ca. 1288–ca. 1348); and Thomas Bradwardine (ca. 1290–1349).
Some of these scholars were greatly used of God to advance the church's
understanding of the doctrines of grace.

# ANSELM OF CANTERBURY

Anselm is revered as one of the greatest of all medieval theologians.[4] Some even
laud him as the greatest theologian of his time.[5] Endowed with superlative
powers of original thought, he is considered the first of the great philoso-
pher-theologians of the Middle Ages, the man who took Christianity to new
heights of theological insight and thought.[6] For this reason, he has been called
"the summit of the early scholastic genius and the ripest fruit of the monastic schools."[7] Historian Philip Schaff regards Anselm as one of the ablest and
purest men of the medieval church.[8] Likewise, historian Justo L. González
writes that Anselm's scholarship paved the way for the great Scholastics of
the thirteenth century and that his influence led to a new era in the history
of Christian thought.[9] Simply put, Anselm was the most original thinker the
church had seen since Augustine.[10]

Anselm was born in northern Italy, in the town of Aosta, nestled at the
foot of St. Bernard Mountain, a towering peak that divides Italy and Switzerland. He grew up under a godly mother, Ermenberga, who influenced him
toward the things of God from a young age. But Anselm's father, Gundulf,
was an abrasive, rude, and cruel figure. As a youth, Anselm studied with the
Benedictine monks, where he received an excellent primary education. Before
age fifteen, Anselm was persuaded to become a monk. But when he presented
himself to the local abbey, he was refused—a rejection that, along with the
untimely death of his mother, left him despondent.

After a sharp quarrel with his father, Anselm left home in 1056, never to
return. He crossed the Alps into France, and after a period of wandering, he
arrived at the revered Benedictine monastery of Le Bec at Normandy in 1059.
There, he sat under the instruction of the prior, Lanfranc, one of the most
noted teachers of his day. Lanfranc influenced Anselm to begin to teach at Le
Bec. On the advice of his mentor, he again presented himself to be a monk,
and this time he was accepted. With renewed vigor, Anselm gave himself to
the service of the Lord, saturating himself in the study of the Scriptures and
the Church Fathers. He became absorbed in Patristic theology, especially the

intellectual problems it presented. His devotion and intellectual abilities soon gained him a high reputation as a teacher and spiritual leader.[11]

## SUDDENLY CONVERTED TO CHRIST

Anselm did not document the time of his conversion, but he did record his testimony. He became convicted of his lost condition and convinced of the certainty of divine judgment. As a result, Anselm began to seek the Lord until, at last, he repented of his sin and entrusted his life to Christ. Writing about this act of faith, he declared that God had removed the condemnation of his soul and included him among the redeemed. Anselm testified:

> I was on slippery footing because I was weak and prone to sin. I was on the downward road to the chaos of hell because in our first parents I had descended from justice [righteousness] to injustice . . . the unbearable burden of God's judgment was pushing me down. . . . Being thus destitute of all help, I was illumined by You and shown my condition. You taught all these things to others on my behalf, and later You taught these same things to me even before I inquired. . . . You removed the sin in which I had been conceived and born. You also removed the condemnation of my soul. . . . You gave me the name Christian, which derives from Your own name; through Your name I confess, and You acknowledge, that I am among the redeemed. You stood me upright. . . . You made me confident of my soul's salvation, for which You gave Your life. . . . You who cause me to ask [for reception "into the inner chamber of Your love"], cause me also to receive.[12]

Some three years after Anselm's arrival at Le Bec, Lanfranc was promoted to the convent of St. Stephen in Caen. Anselm, age thirty, was made prior of Le Bec in 1063. (He eventually would be promoted, against his will, to be abbot of the monastery.) Anselm soon began writing, and it has been said that the Renaissance of the twelfth century actually began in the eleventh century when Anselm started his vast theological production.[13] His most notable books from this period included *Monologion* (1076), meaning "monologue," which consisted of prayers and letters addressed to Norman monks, and *Proslogion* (1078), or "discourse." The latter, one of his most famous works, contains an advanced version of his ontological argument for the existence of God.

## Made Archbishop of Canterbury

Meanwhile, Lanfranc had become archbishop of Canterbury. After Lanfranc died (1089), the archbishopric lay vacant for four years amid the squabbling of political rivals. During this interim, Anselm was persuaded to come to England to stabilize the English church. After he arrived, King William II (ca. 1056–1100) named Anselm to be the archbishop of Canterbury (1093). Though he initially refused the position, he eventually consented and was carried to the church and consecrated as archbishop.

Anselm foresaw a struggle with the worldly minded William II. Anselm compared himself to an old, feeble sheep and the king to a young, wild bull.[14] Yoked to his new duty, he saw himself drawing the plow of the church in England with the prospect of "being torn to pieces by the ferocity of the bull."[15]

Anselm and William were soon embroiled in a controversy over the independence of the English church from the king.[16] From the days of William the Conqueror (ca. 1028–1087), monarchs of England had exercised control over the church by appointing its bishops. But Anselm refused this royal control over the spiritual leadership of the church. The determinative question was: Would Anselm's highest loyalty be to the monarch or would he answer to the Lord for His church? For Anselm, the answer was the latter. His ultimate allegiance must be to the higher court of heaven. The archbishop gave further offense to William by sending noticeably smaller-than-expected sums of the church's money to the royal treasury, underfunding the king's war. Adding insult to injury, he supposedly sent ill-trained knights to fight the king's battles.[17]

In the face of mounting conflict, Anselm sensed that a voluntary exile on his part was prudent. Seeking relief, the archbishop left for the Continent in 1097. While in exile, Anselm produced his most mature writings. He completed his famous work on the atonement, *Cur Deus Homo*, or "Why God Became Man," in Champagne (France). This is regarded as his most ambitious work.[18] From Champagne, Anselm moved on to Lyons for further biblical study and theological writing.

Upon the death of William II (1100), Henry I assumed the throne of England, creating a new climate for the church. The new king immediately summoned Anselm from exile. The archbishop was received honorably, but the old controversy once again arose: Where should Anselm's highest loyalty be? True to his convictions, Anselm chose allegiance to God and His church rather than to the king and his court. Once more, he fell under the displeasure of the throne. This rift led to a second exile for Anselm. He first traveled to Rome to seek a papal relaxation regarding lay investiture, which is the king's right to name bishops and abbots to office. Anselm then retired to the abbey at Le Bec (1103–1106). Eventually, Henry agreed to relinquish the privilege of investiture to the archbishop and invited Anselm back to England. Anselm returned to a warm welcome in 1107.

## ANSELM'S FINAL DAYS

After his return from his second exile, Anselm experienced two years that were quieter than his earlier days.[19] During King Henry's absence on the Continent in 1108, Anselm was entrusted with the care of the royal family.[20] In this calm season, Anselm turned his attention to the matter of the human will, giving careful thought to the relationship between human freedom of choice, divine foreknowledge, predestination, and the saving grace of God.[21]

Anselm's life ended at the age of seventy-six. As death approached, Anselm requested that he be lifted from his bed and placed in ashes on the floor. In this position of humility, Anselm passed away on April 21, 1109. He was buried in Canterbury Cathedral. Fittingly, he was laid to rest at the side of Lanfranc, his beloved mentor and predecessor.

A commitment to the truth of the Word of God was primary in Anselm's life and ministry. He was dedicated to giving proper explanations of Scripture. What is more, Anselm gave profound treatments of such theological subjects as the existence of God, the necessity of the incarnation, and the fall of the Devil.[22] His influence on his own time was far-reaching and significant, and it was even greater on later generations. History remembers him as a biblical thinker who faithfully served God to advance the truth.

# ANSELM'S WRITINGS

A gifted church leader and administrator, Anselm also excelled in his writing on theology and intellectual problems. His approach consisted of posing a theological problem and then solving it, not so much on the authority of Scripture or the Church Fathers, but through the use of reason.[23] His theological method was purely Scholastic, seeking a balance between faith and reason and between grace and nature.[24] He often raised the objection of an imaginary heretical opponent, using presuppositions that an unbeliever would hold. He then reasoned toward the orthodox position of Scripture.

This approach might suggest that Anselm was an extreme rationalist.[25] But his arguments were based on biblical truth, even if chapter and verse were not stated. His chief works included:

## MONOLOGION

*Monologion* (1076), the first book of its kind, attempted to prove the existence of God solely on rational grounds. Countering Muslim and Jewish world-views, Anselm sought to provide a systematic explanation and defense of Christian belief that did not rely on Christian sources alone.[26] The thrust of his argument was that man possesses the idea of an absolutely perfect being.[27] This idea implies the necessity of existence. The being of God is necessary, Anselm argued, because the idea of perfection is within man and there are degrees of goodness in creation. This has come to be known as the ontological argument for the existence of God.

## PROSLOGION

*Proslogion* (1078) was an advanced ontological argument for the existence of God. Anselm here maintained that the power to think of the being of God implies the existence of such a being. He stated the following proposition: "Truly there is a God, although the fool has said in his heart, there is no God."[28] He then explained why this proposition is true. God has given under-standing to faith and then insisted that men must believe that He is a being far greater than can be conceived.

## CUR DEUS HOMO

Later, Anselm wrote *Cur Deus Homo*, "Why God Became Man." Robert Culver states that *Cur Deus Homo* is a "rationally organized and supported view of the Person and work of Christ that was in full harmony with the author-ity of Scripture and ancient dogma as well. . . . [It] has not been superseded to the present."[29] William G. T. Shedd remarks that this book "exhibits a depth, breadth, and vigor of thinking not surpassed by any production of the same extent in theological literature."[30] Likewise, the noted church historian Jaroslav Pelikan comments that this work "was a virtuoso performance with few rivals in the history of Christian thought."[31] Anselm succeeded in setting forth the doctrine of the atonement from the standpoint of man's need for salvation and its provision through Jesus Christ.[32]

In this work, Anselm uses a fictitious monk, Boso, as a literary foil by which to pose questions and provide rational proofs. The book presents the person and work of Christ and, in so doing, shows how reasonable faith is. Anselm rejected the traditional atonement view, that Christ's death was a ransom paid to Satan, which had been widely held since the Church Fathers. Instead, he unequivocally stated that the Devil has no rights over the human race, but is a robber who has taken sinners unlawfully. It is therefore illogical, he argued, to claim that Christ's atoning work is a means of rescuing us from the Devil. Anselm writes: "I cannot see what force this argument has. If the devil or man belonged to himself or to anyone but God, or remained in some power other than God's, perhaps it would be a sound argument. But the devil and man belong to God alone, and neither one stands outside God's power; what case, then, did God have to plead with His own creature?"[33] Man, he asserted, is God's own creation and therefore God's possession, not Satan's.

Anselm further remarks, "As God owed nothing to the devil but punishment, so . . . whatever was demanded of man, he owed to God and not to the devil."[34] Christ's death was indeed a ransom paid, but to God, not to Satan. Sin outraged God's honor, Anselm reasoned, so man had to suffer punishment or offer compensation to God. However, sin is such an infinite violation that only God Himself could provide a perfect satisfaction for man's sin—which He did in the infinitely perfect life of the God-man, Jesus Christ.

## OTHER WRITINGS

Anselm wrote other great works, including *The Incarnation of the Word*, *The Virgin Conception*, *Original Sin*, *The Procession of the Holy Spirit* (which defended the Western view of the Spirit against the Eastern view), *On Truth*, and *On the Fall of Satan*. His main theological work during the last years of his life was *The Compatibility of God's Foreknowledge, Predestination and Grace with Human Freedom*, which expounded his views on predestination, sin and evil, justification, election, and the idea of merit, while maintaining consistency with the Augustinian view.[35]

# ANSELM'S THEOLOGY

Although Anselm was mentored by Lanfranc, his primary teacher was the great fifth-century theologian Augustine. It was Augustine who taught Anselm how to approach and assimilate the various doctrines of Scripture into one cohesive system of theology. Schaff writes, "Anselm had a profound veneration for the great African teacher, Augustine, and his agreement with him in spirit and method secured for him the titles 'the second Augustine' and the 'Tongue of Augustine.'"[36] R. W. Southern notes that "while Anselm rarely quoted anyone in his writings and though he diverged from some of Augustine's positions, his basic theological system is Augustinian."[37] Still others call Anselm "the Augustine of the twelfth century."[38] Gordon R. Payne makes an interesting connection when he links Augustine to the great theological systematizer John Calvin. He writes: "Where, then, is Calvin to be located theologically and philosophically? The answer is that he is the heir and follower of the Augustinian tradition flowing from Augustine *through Anselm of Canterbury*."[39] These comments indicate that Anselm, like Augustine before him, took a strong stand on the doctrines of grace.

**Doctrine in Focus:**
DIVINE SOVEREIGNTY

Like Augustine, Anselm had a high view of the sovereignty of God. He affirmed God's right and ability to rule His created universe. Anselm writes: "If God chooses that it should rain, it is right that it should rain; and if He desires that any man should die, then is it right that he should die. Wherefore, if it be not fitting for God to do anything unjustly, or out of course, it does not belong to His liberty or compassion or will to let the sinner go unpunished who makes no return to God of what the sinner has defrauded Him."[40] God sovereignly determines everything that comes to pass. Whether rain falls or a man dies, it occurs by divine command.

Anselm held that nothing coerces or compels God—He can do as He pleases. He says: "God does nothing by necessity, since he is not compelled or restrained in anything."[41] He adds, "If He has a fixed determination to do anything, though His design must be destined to an accomplishment before it comes to pass, yet there is no coercion as far as He is concerned, either to do it or not to do it, for His will is the sole agent in the case."[42] Simply put, God is sovereign in the exercise of His will, and none can resist Him.

Anselm also understood that God's absolute rule is unrestricted, extending over all things. He asserts: "For, in whose power is hell, or the devil? Or, whose is the kingdom of heaven, if it be not His who created all things? Whatever things, therefore, you dread or hope for, all lie subject to His will, whom nothing can oppose."[43] Elsewhere he writes, "Nothing contains You, but You contain all things."[44] God is over all things in the heavens or on earth.

Moreover, Anselm maintained that God is all-sufficient within Himself. He writes: "But You are life, and light, and wisdom, and blessedness, and many goods of this nature. And yet You are only one supreme good; You are all-sufficient to Yourself, and need none; and You are He whom all things need for their existence and wellbeing."[45] All things are entirely dependent upon Him for their existence, but God is not dependent on anyone or anything.

Nothing, Anselm writes, can escape God's will. He says:

> If those things which are held together in the circuit of the heavens should desire to be elsewhere than under the heavens or to be further removed from the heavens, there is no place where they can be but under the heavens; nor can they fly from the heavens without also approaching them. For whence and whither and in what way they go, they still are under the heavens; and if they are at a greater distance from one part of them, they are only so much nearer to the opposite part. And so, though man or evil angel refuses to submit to the divine will and appointment, yet he cannot escape it; for if he wishes to fly from a will that commands, he falls into the power of a will that punishes.[46]

All things in creation must submit to God or face eternal condemnation.

**Doctrine in Focus:**
RADICAL DEPRAVITY

Anselm also asserted the radical corruption of the human race. "There was one great thinker during the Middle Ages," Louis Berkhof writes, "who not only reproduced Augustinian anthropology, but also made a positive contribution to it."[47] That one, he argued, was Anselm. Moreover, the noted Princeton theologian Charles Hodge remarks: "Anselm in the eleventh century was essentially Augustinian in his views of sin and grace. He held that man is born in a state of sin, with a will enslaved to evil, free only in sinning. From this state of helplessness, he can be freed only by the grace of the Holy Spirit, not by his own power, and not by an influence which owes its success to the cooperation of an enslaved will."[48] Schaff writes: "Following Augustine, Anselm called the [human] race a sinning mass—*peccatrix massa*. By the Fall, man's body, or flesh, was made, like the beast, subject to carnal appetites, and the mind, in turn, became infected with these appetites."[49] Anselm reiterated the biblical truths of original sin, total depravity, and the bondage of the will.

Regarding the extent of man's fall, Anselm clearly taught that all people sinned in Adam and, consequently, fell in him: "Truly, in him [Adam] we all fell, in whom we all sinned. In him we all lost, who kept easily, and wickedly lost to himself and to us that which when we wish to seek it, we do not know; when we seek it, we do not find; when we find, it is not that which we seek."[50] Anselm understood that, in the garden, Adam represented all of his descendants. Therefore, when Adam sinned, God imputed his guilt and sinfulness to the entire human race.

In advancing this argument, Anselm relied on the plain teachings of Scripture. In agreement with Romans 5:12—"sin came into the world through one man, and death through sin, and so death spread to all men because all sinned"—he writes, "Death came upon the human race by the disobedience of [one] man."[51] However, he asserts that every human being is equally responsible for the devastating effects of the fall: "Each and every child of Adam is responsible for original sin because he is Adam. Yet not merely and simply because he is Adam, but because he is fallen Adam."[52] Adam alone is not to blame for the lostness, deadness, and rebelliousness of the human heart—*all* men are equally guilty.

Similarly, in commenting on Psalm 51:5, Anselm echoes David's words, "I was brought forth in iniquity, and in sin did my mother conceive me." With full awareness of his fallenness, Anselm writes, "Truly, in darkness I was conceived, and in the cover of darkness I was born."[53] Being born with a sin nature, no one can refrain from sinning against the holy God. Anselm declares, "No man passes this life without sin."[54] The universal tendency among men of every nation, tribe, and tongue to violate God's commands testifies to the biblical truth that all are infected with original sin.

Anselm contended that man's sin was so serious, he deserved to be annihilated, but God in His wisdom allowed the human race to continue. He says: "He [man] deserved, by his sin, to lose his existence together with its design; though he never has wholly lost this, viz., that he should be one capable of being punished, or of receiving God's compassion. For neither of these things could take effect if he were annihilated. Therefore God's restoring man is more wonderful than his creating man, inasmuch as it is done for the sinner contrary to his deserts."[55]

Ultimately, Anselm argued, all men, despite being fallen in sin and therefore lacking the moral ability to fulfill what God requires of them, remain responsible to keep God's commands. He writes, "Man's inability to restore what he owes to God, an inability brought upon himself, does not excuse man from paying the satisfaction due to justice; for the result of sin cannot excuse the sin itself."[56] Man is answerable to God even in his fallen condition.

## Doctrine in Focus:
## SOVEREIGN ELECTION

Anselm was thoroughly Augustinian in regard to the doctrine of election. He affirmed God's sovereign prerogative in electing out of all humanity a people for Himself before the foundation of the world. Anselm writes: "We may say that God hath appointed the bounds of the people according to the number of elect men, because men will exist and there will be a natural increase among them, until the number of elect men is accomplished."[57] Like Augustine, Anselm contended that God has sovereignly set the number of the elect, whose redemption is sure. Elsewhere he writes: "We believe that the material substance of the world must be renewed, and that this will not take place until the number of the elect is accomplished, and that happy kingdom made perfect, and that after its completion there will be no change."[58] Time will go on until all of God's elect are redeemed.

In various other places, Anselm made comments that indicate that God's election of certain people was a settled point in his thinking. For instance, Anselm writes, "It is, of course, beyond question that God's foreknowledge and predestination do not conflict, rather even as God foreknows, so he predestines."[59] He adds, "To say that God predestines means that he pre-ordains, that is to bring about that something happen in the future."[60] These statements strongly suggest that Anselm saw no salvation apart from the electing grace of God.

## Doctrine in Focus:
## DEFINITE ATONEMENT

Although the doctrine of Christ's atonement was clearly derived from Scripture and stated by many Early Church Fathers such as Augustine, Anselm is said to have put a "rather special slant on the doctrine of substitutionary-propitiatory atonement."[61] He established the satisfaction theory of the atonement, the view that Christ died a substitutionary death for His elect in order to bring infinite honor to God.[62] Sinners, Anselm argued, have dishonored God and robbed Him of inherent glory, amassing an enormous debt that must be paid. He writes:

> Sin is nothing else than not to render to God His due. . . . He who does not render to God this honor which is due to Him, robs God of what is His own, and dishonours God; and this is what it is to sin. . . . Every one who sins [is] bound to pay back the honour of which he has robbed God; and this is the satisfaction which every sinner is bound to pay to God. . . . Nothing is less tolerable in the order of things than that a creature should rob his Creator of the honour due to Him and not repay Him that of which he robs Him. . . . This is the debt which men owe to God.[63]

This is the backbone of Anselm's theory of the atonement—the idea that God's honor has been injured by man's sin. Therefore, God could vindicate His honor either by punishing the sinner or by accepting a suitable payment for man's egregious sin.[64]

However, Anselm saw sin as a debt so colossal it is utterly impossible for any person to pay it back. He writes: "And this debt was so great that, while it was man alone who owed it, none but God was able to pay it. So he who paid had to be both God and man . . . so that man, who in his own nature owed the debt but could not pay, might be able to do so in the person of God."[65] In other words, Anselm said, it was Jesus Christ, the God-man, who made restitution for man's debt.[66] He asserted that Christ, as the representative Man as well as God, rendered complete satisfaction to God as a voluntary, substitute sacrifice on the cross. Christ, though under no obligation to pay this debt, freely offered Himself as a ransom to God.

Moreover, Anselm taught that Christ's substitutionary sacrifice made atonement for all true believers, in every time and place. He writes, "Since all who are to be saved cannot be present at the sacrifice of Christ, yet such virtue is there in His death that its power is extended even to those far remote in place or time."[67] It was for those the Father chose to be His children that Christ suffered and died. Without question, Christ's atoning work was for a particular people, those "who are to be saved."

Anselm contributed greatly to the advancement of a biblical understanding of the doctrine of the atonement. His writings are logically arranged so that they show the reasonable nature of faith. Nevertheless, there are weaknesses to his understanding of the atonement. Scholars have criticized him on several points, namely, his heavy reliance on medieval justice theory, his emphasis on God's honor rather than His justice, and his failure to mention any penalty for man's sin.[68]

Although Anselm emphasized sin's infinite debt rather than God's justice, and though he said nothing of the lifelong obedience of Christ as an aspect of vicarious satisfaction, the Reformers did not reject his thoughts on the subject, but complemented them.[69] Berkhof notes: "There is substantial agreement between the Reformers and Anselm. Both maintain the objective nature of the atonement and both regard it as a necessity."[70] Likewise, John Hannah remarks: "Sixteenth-century Reformers, such as Luther and Calvin, sought to clarify Anselm's view in light of their own biblical studies . . . while Anselm argued that God must be satisfied for offenses against Him or else wrath awaits us, the Reformers stressed the satisfaction of God through punishment. That is, Anselm stressed the alternatives of payment or judgment; the Reformers saw clearly the biblical concept that a penal judgment had to be rendered."[71] The Reformers would see that Christ made a perfect satisfaction for the sins of those who would believe.

**Doctrine in Focus:**

IRRESISTIBLE CALL

Anselm clearly believed that God effectually calls all whom He elects to salvation. This summons causes them to believe on Christ. In commenting on John 6:44, Anselm declared that the Father irresistibly moves the sinner to come to faith in Christ. He writes: "As the Father is said to draw by imparting an inclination, so there is nothing improper in asserting that he moves man. For as the Son says of the Father: 'No man cometh to Me except the Father draw him,' he might as well have said, except he move him."[72] Anselm rightly understood that God initiates conversion. Unregenerate men cannot come to Christ until they are drawn by the Father.

In this divine initiative, God gives man a new will to believe. Anselm writes: "Since a man is drawn or moved, by his will, to that which he invariably chooses, it is not improper to say, that God draws or moves him, when he gives him this will. And in this drawing or impelling it is not to be understood that there is any constraint, but a free and grateful clinging to the holy will which has been given."[73] Here Anselm taught that when God calls a sinner to Himself, there is no constraint, meaning undue coercion; when the Holy

Spirit works in the heart, the sinner then believes because he wants to do so. No one believes against his will. Rather, God changes the will so that the sinner freely believes.

Likewise, Anselm asserted that God graciously gives grace and faith to man in order to bring about salvation. Without grace, he argued, one can achieve nothing toward salvation. Anselm boldly asserts: "It must all be attributed to grace, because 'it is not of the one who wills, nor of the one who runs, but of God who shows mercy' (Rom. 9:16). For to all, except God alone, it is said: 'What do you have that you have not received? And if you have received it all, why do you boast as though you had not received it?' (1 Cor. 4:7)."[74] Convinced by Scripture, Anselm was clear in his belief that man's salvation is exclusively the result of God's sovereign, saving grace.

**Doctrine in Focus:**
PRESERVING GRACE

Comprehensive in his theology, Anselm also believed that God forever preserves in grace all whom He has chosen, redeemed, and drawn to Himself. He writes: "The whole work which God does for man is of grace . . . it is necessary for God, on account of His unchangeable goodness, to complete the work which He has begun."[75] He also says, "By God's prevenient grace, I consider myself to hold the faith of our redemption, so that even were I totally unable to understand it, nothing could shake the constancy of my belief."[76] God gives saving faith to His elect and preserves it through all trials until their glorification.

# WITH ALL OUR MINDS

We live in a mindless age marked by entertainment that appeals to the emotions of a numb audience. Unfortunately, this deficiency has invaded the evangelical church and captured the minds of many Christian leaders. As a result, ministries are content to spread superficial thoughts drawn from the base thinking of the world.

This hour calls for men to step forward and give themselves to the disciplined study of Scripture in the manner of Anselm. Now is the time for a new generation of Anselms to seize the moment, men who, in an age of spiritual darkness, will serve as beacons to light the true path. As in any age, God has guaranteed the success of His church and ensured that the light of

His gospel will never be extinguished. Therefore, the time is now for us to put away empty thinking that reduces authentic Christianity to a cheap imitation of worldly trivialities. Now is the time to bring forth the great truths of the Word. Whatever is to be the impact of Christianity in this day, it can be no greater than its search for, discovery of, and commitment to the grand doctrines of Scripture. At the top of that ascent are the doctrines of grace.

Will you apply your mind to the quest for this truth? Will you rivet your gaze on the pages of Scripture? Will you wrestle with the biblical text until it yields its one, true, God-intended meaning? Will you set your mind to pull these doctrines together into one system of truth until they all speak with one voice? Where are the truly profound thinkers of this day? Where, I say, are they?

## NOTES

1 Anselm, *Cur Deus Homo*, 1.6, cited in *Proslogium; Monologium: An Appendix, In Behalf of the Fool, by Gaunilon; and Cur Deus Homo*, trans. S. N. Deane (LaSalle, Ill.: Open Court, 1903), 184.

2 N. R. Needham, *2,000 Years of Christ's Power, Part Two: The Middle Ages* (London: Grace Publications, 2005), 205.

3 Philip Schaff and David S. Schaff, *History of the Christian Church, Vol. V: The Middle Ages: From Gregory VII to Boniface VIII, 1049–1294* (1907; repr., Grand Rapids: Eerdmans, 1984), 553, 563.

4 J. Van Engen, "Anselm of Canterbury," in *Evangelical Dictionary of Theology*, 2nd Ed., ed. Walter A. Elwell (Grand Rapids: Baker, 2001), 66.

5 Justo L. González, *A History of Christian Thought, Vol. 2: From Augustine to the Eve of the Reformation* (Nashville: Abingdon, 1987), 167.

6 Jonathan Hill, *The History of Christian Thought* (Downers Grove, Ill.: InterVarsity, 2003), 131.

7 David Knowles, *The Evolution of Medieval Thought* (New York: Random House, 1962), 98.

8 Schaff and Schaff, *History of the Christian Church, Vol. V*, 598.

9 González, *A History of Christian Thought, Vol. 2*, 167.

10 Schaff and Schaff, *History of the Christian Church, Vol. V*, 598.

11 "St. Anselm," in *The Oxford Dictionary of the Christian Church*, 3rd Ed., ed. E. A. Livingstone (1957; repr., Oxford, England: Oxford University Press, 1997), 73.

12 Anselm, *Meditation on Human Redemption*, in *Monologion, Proslogion, Debate with Janielo*, trans. J. Hopkins and H. Richardson (Toronto and New York: The Edwin Mellen Press, 1974–1976), 143, 145.

13 González, *A History of Christian Thought, Vol. 2*, 157.

14 Schaff and Schaff, *History of the Christian Church, Vol. V*, 89.

15 Schaff and Schaff, *History of the Christian Church, Vol. V*, 89.

16 Tony Lane, *A Concise History of Christian Thought* (Grand Rapids: Baker Academic, 2006), 105.

17 Schaff and Schaff, *History of the Christian Church, Vol. V*, 89.

18 Lane, *A Concise History of Christian Thought*, 106.

19 Schaff and Schaff, *History of the Christian Church, Vol. V*, 599.

20 Schaff and Schaff, *History of the Christian Church, Vol. V*, 92.

21 G. R. Evans, "Anselm of Canterbury," in *The Medieval Theologians: An Introduction to Theology in the Medieval Period*, ed. G. R. Evans (Malden, Mass.: Blackwell, 2001), 100.

22 Schaff and Schaff, *History of the Christian Church, Vol. V*, 588.

23 González, *A History of Christian Thought, Vol. 2*, 157.

24 Timothy George, *Theology of the Reformers* (Nashville: Broadman, 1988), 41.

25 George, *Theology of the Reformers*, 157.

26 Roger E. Olson, *The Story of Christian Theology: Twenty Centuries of Tradition and Reform* (Downers Grove, Ill.: InterVarsity, 1999), 310.

27 Alan Cairns, *Dictionary of Theological Terms: A Ready Reference of Over 800 Theological and Doctrinal Terms*, Expanded 3rd Ed. (Belfast, Northern Ireland, and Greenville, S.C.: Ambassador, 2002), 39.

28 Anselm, *Proslogium*, 2, cited in *Proslogium; Monologium: An Appendix, In Behalf of the Fool, by Gaunilon; and Cur Deus Homo*, 6.

29 Robert Duncan Culver, *Systematic Theology: Biblical and Historical* (Ross-shire, Scotland: Mentor, 2005), 600.

30 William G. T. Shedd, *A History of Christian Doctrine, Vol. Two* (Eugene, Ore.: Wipf & Stock, 1998), 283.

31 Jaroslav J. Pelikan, "The Plan of Salvation," *The Christian Tradition, Vol. 3: The Growth of Medieval Theology (600–1300)* (Chicago and London: University of Chicago Press, 1978), 107.

32 Olson, *The Story of Christian Theology*, 319.

33 Anselm, *Cur Deus Homo*, 1.7, in *Saint Anselm: Basic Writings*, translated by S. N. Deane (LaSalle, Ill.: Open Court, 1962), 187.

34 Anselm. *Cur Deus Homo*, 2.19, trans. S. N. Deane (LaSalle, Ill.: Open Court, 1959), 285–286.

35 Needham, *2,000 Years of Christ's Power, Part Two*, 254.

36 Schaff and Schaff, *History of the Christian Church, Vol. V*, 601.

37 R. W. Southern, *Saint Anselm and His Biographer* (Cambridge: Cambridge University Press, 1966), 32.

38 "Anselm of Canterbury," in *Cyclopedia of Biblical, Theological, and Ecclesiastical Literature, Vol. I*, eds. John McClintock and James Strong (Grand Rapids: Baker, 1981), 243.

39 Gordon R. Payne, "Augustinianism in Calvin and Bonaventure," in *Westminster Theological Journal*, Vol. 44:1 (Westminster Theological Seminary, 1982; 2002): 2, emphasis added.

40 Anselm, *Cur Deus Homo*, 1.12, in *Proslogium; Monologium: An Appendix, In Behalf of the Fool, by Gaunilon; and Cur Deus Homo*, 202–203.

41 Anselm, *Cur Deus Homo*, 1.5, in *Proslogium; Monologium: An Appendix, In Behalf of the Fool, by Gaunilon; and Cur Deus Homo*, 241.

42 Anselm, *Cur Deus Homo*, 2.18, in *Proslogium; Monologium: An Appendix, In Behalf of the Fool, by Gaunilon; and Cur Deus Homo*, 270.

43 Anselm, *Cur Deus Homo*, 1.6, *Proslogium; Monologium: An Appendix, In Behalf of the Fool, by Gaunilon; and Cur Deus Homo*, 184.

44 Anselm, *Proslogium*, 19, cited in William G. T. Shedd and Alan W. Gomes, *Dogmatic Theology*, 3rd Ed. (Phillipsburg, N.J.: P&R, 2003), 278.

45 Anselm, *Proslogium*, 22, in *Proslogium; Monologium: An Appendix, In Behalf of the Fool, by Gaunilon; and Cur Deus Homo*, 27.

46 Anselm, *Cur Deus Homo*, 1.15, in *Proslogium; Monologium: An Appendix, In Behalf of the Fool, by Gaunilon; and Cur Deus Homo*, 206.

47 Louis Berkhof, *The History of Christian Doctrines* (1937; repr., Edinburgh: Banner of Truth, 2002), 142.

48 Charles Hodge, *Systematic Theology, Vol. II* (Peabody, Mass.: Hendrickson, 1999), 715.

49 Schaff and Schaff, *History of the Christian Church, Vol. V*, 749.

50 Anselm, *Proslogium*, 18, in *Proslogium; Monologium: An Appendix, In Behalf of the Fool, by Gaunilon; and Cur Deus Homo*, 23.

51 Anselm, *Cur Deus Homo*, 1.3, in *Proslogium; Monologium: An Appendix, In Behalf of the Fool, by Gaunilon; and Cur Deus Homo*, 181.

52 Anselm, *Concerning the Virginal Conception*, 10, cited in Shedd and Gomes, *Dogmatic Theology*, 445. Shedd notes, "Anselm here uses 'Adam' to designate the 'human nature' created in Adam and Eve."

53 Anselm, *Proslogium*, 18, in *Proslogium; Monologium: An Appendix, In Behalf of the Fool, by Gaunilon; and Cur Deus Homo*, 23.

54 Anselm, *Cur Deus Homo*, 1.10, in *Proslogium; Monologium: An Appendix, In Behalf of the Fool, by Gaunilon; and Cur Deus Homo*, 198.

55 Anselm, *Cur Deus Homo*, 2.16, in *Proslogium; Monologium: An Appendix, In Behalf of the Fool, by Gaunilon; and Cur Deus Homo*, 262.

56 Anselm, *Cur Deus Homo*, 1.24, in *Proslogium; Monologium: An Appendix, In Behalf of the Fool, by Gaunilon; and Cur Deus Homo*, 231.

57 Anselm, *Cur Deus Homo*, 1.18, in *Proslogium; Monologium: An Appendix, In Behalf of the Fool, by Gaunilon; and Cur Deus Homo*, 218.

58 Anselm, *Cur Deus Homo*, 1.18, in *Proslogium; Monologium: An Appendix, In Behalf of the Fool, by Gaunilon; and Cur Deus Homo*, 214.

59 Anselm, *De Concordia: The Compatibility of God's Foreknowledge, Predestination, and Grace with Human Freedom*, trans. Thomas Bermingham, in *Anselm of Canterbury: The Major Works*, eds. Brian Davies and G. R. Evans (Oxford: Oxford University Press, 1998), 450–451.

60 Anselm, *De Concordia*, in *Anselm of Canterbury: The Major Works*, 449.

61 Culver, *Systematic Theology*, 555.

62 See Arnold R. Whately, "Anselm's Doctrine of the Atonement," in *The Atonement in History and in Life*, ed. L. W. Grensted (1929; repr., New York: MacMillan, 1936), 205.

63 Anselm, *Cur Deus Homo*, 1.11, cited in Louis Sperry Chafer, "Soteriology," *Bibliotheca Sacra*, Vol. 104 (Dallas: Dallas Theological Seminary, 1947; 2002), S. 104:146–147.

64 George C. Foley, *Anselm's Theory of the Atonement* (Cambridge, Mass.: Cambridge University Press, 1908), 125.

65 Anselm, *Cur Deus Homo*, 2.18, in *Proslogium; Monologium: An Appendix, In Behalf of the Fool, by Gaunilon; and Cur Deus Homo*, 2.18.

66 Louis Berkhof, *Systematic Theology* (Grand Rapids: Eerdmans, 1939), 385.

67 Anselm, *Cur Deus Homo*, 2.16, in *Proslogium; Monologium: An Appendix, In Behalf of the Fool, by Gaunilon; and Cur Deus Homo*, 263.

68 Berkhof notes: "[Anselm's] theory really has no place for the idea that Christ by suffering endured the *penalty* of sin, and that His suffering was strictly vicarious. The death of Christ is merely a tribute offered voluntarily to the honor of the Father." Berkhof, *Systematic Theology*, 386.

69 Culver, *Systematic Theology*, 563.

70 Berkhof, *The History of Christian Doctrines*, 182.

71 John Hannah, *Our Legacy: The History of Christian Doctrine* (Colorado Springs, Colo.: NavPress, 2001), 163.

72 Anselm, *Cur Deus Homo*, 1.10, in *Proslogium; Monologium: An Appendix, In Behalf of the Fool, by Gaunilon; and Cur Deus Homo*, 183.

73 Anselm, *Cur Deus Homo*, 1.10, in *Proslogium; Monologium: An Appendix, In Behalf of the Fool, by Gaunilon; and Cur Deus Homo*, 183.

74 Anselm, *De Concordia*, in *Anselm of Canterbury: The Major Works*, 455.

75 Anselm, *Cur Deus Homo*, 1.5, in *Proslogium; Monologium: An Appendix, In Behalf of the Fool, by Gaunilon; and Cur Deus Homo*, 241.

76 Anselm, *Cur Deus Homo*, 1.2, in *Proslogium; Monologium: An Appendix, In Behalf of the Fool, by Gaunilon; and Cur Deus Homo*, 1.2.

# CHAPTER FIFTEEN
# STUDY QUESTIONS

1. List the major developments of the eleventh century that would alter the flow of church history. What effect did each have on Christendom?

2. What was the Scholastic movement? What were its distinctives? What were the chief sources of the Scholastics' thought? Who were some of the leading Scholastics?

3. Describe the pivotal role of Anselm of Canterbury. What were the leading influences on his early years? Comment on Anselm's conversion experience. How does this compare with your own conversion?

4. What price did Anselm pay for holding firm to the Christian faith? What were the issues behind his exiles? What sacrifices have you paid for holding to the truth? Give specific examples.

5. Summarize the argument of Anselm's primary work, *Cur Deus Homo* ("Why God Became Man"). What new emphasis did this work make regarding the atonement? Explain the difference between the ransom and satisfaction theories of the atonement.

6. Describe the doctrine of radical corruption in terms of Anselm's thinking. What relationship did he see between the fall of Adam and the depravity of the human race? What biblical metaphors did he appeal to in stating his case?

7. According to Anselm, what must God do in order for man to believe in Christ? What does it mean to be drawn by the Father to Christ? Does anyone believe on Christ against his or her will?

*For you have not chosen Me, but I have chosen you {John 15:16}; not for any merits that I found in you did I choose you, but I went before you. Thus have I betrothed you to Myself in faith, not in the works of the law.*[1]

–Bernard of Clairvaux

Chapter Sixteen

# MONASTIC REFORMER

## LATTER MONASTIC:
## BERNARD OF CLAIRVAUX

I n the twelfth century, the church lapsed into a season of formality that
caused the once-flowing wells of religion to run dry. During this spiritual drought, the external trappings of Christendom became the primary
focus rather than internal matters of the heart. Rituals crowded out reality
and symbols took precedence over substance. Scholasticism contributed to
this barrenness by emphasizing intellectual pursuits over heart affections for
Christ, while the expanding power of the papacy added to the bureaucracy
and politicization of the church. As a result, the church was largely stripped
of its spiritual power.

Consequently, some inside the church began to seek a more substantive
experience of Christ. This movement was known as mysticism, as it emphasized the desire of the human heart to enjoy direct communion with God and
have a more personal relationship with Him.[2] Writing in the fifth century,
Augustine had furnished the supreme rationale for mysticism when he said to
God, "You have made us for Yourself and the heart is restless till it finds its rest
in You."[3] As historian Philip Schaff explains, mysticism "aims at the immediate personal communion of the soul with the [living God], through inward
devotions and spiritual aspirations."[4] The goal of the mystics was personal
contact with God, not through rituals or ceremonies.[5]

Though the word *mysticism* would later take on different connotations, it
was used in the twelfth century to describe the spiritual experience of contemplation.[6] In this pursuit, the supreme object of contemplation was the triune
God in the beauty of His holiness. The mystics sought to know and love
Him with their entire being. The leading mystics spoke of the active life and

the contemplative life as two members of the same family, dwelling together as did Mary and Martha.[7] Thus, the mystics of the twelfth century avoided being caught up in emotional excesses and ecstatic experiences.[8] Instead, they "sought after the complete and placid composure of soul under the influence of love for Christ and the pure contemplation of spiritual things."[9] In short, mystics sought to savor the Lord Jesus Christ through personal communion with Him.

## THE RISE OF MONASTIC REFORM

The rise of mysticism coincided with a movement to reform the monasteries. Monasteries were not all they should have been; wealth and worldliness had crept in. A revival began in the tenth century at the monastery of Cluny, in southeastern France. At the heart of this movement was the vision of a pure monastic life.[10] As this reform spread to other monasteries, a renewal of Christian values in society took place.[11] By 1100, one thousand Cluniac monasteries had been established or reformed throughout France and Germany.

During this time of reform, a monk named Robert, who desired to correct the lack of discipline in contemporary Monasticism, founded the Cistercian order in Citeaux, France, in 1098.[12] Motivated by a deep zeal for God and for personal holiness, Robert devoted himself to rigorous self-denial. The Cistercians' reforming efforts made such an impact that the order expanded to 530 houses by the end of the twelfth century. This movement also brought a fresh zeal to decadent Monasticism.[13]

The pious ideals of the Cistercian monastic life were soon embraced by a young man named Bernard. In his lifetime, Bernard distinguished himself as an author, preacher, hymn writer, and crusader, but above all else, he was a monk.[14] Much of the Monastic reform during the twelfth century was the result of his efforts. To his credit, he embraced and expounded God's sovereign grace in man's salvation.

# BERNARD OF CLAIRVAUX

Scholars agree that Bernard of Clairvaux (1090–1153) was the dominant figure in twelfth-century Western Christendom[15] and one of the brightest spiritual stars of the Middle Ages.[16] John Calvin saw Bernard as the major witness to the truth between the sixth and sixteenth centuries.[17] Martin Luther hailed Bernard as a man of admirable holiness[18] and considered him to be one of the best of the medieval saints.[19] He also credited Bernard with writing in the same vein as Augustine.[20] Charles Spurgeon concurred with Luther, saying, "Saint Bernard was a man whom I admire to the last degree, and I count him to be one of the Lord's choice ones."[21] He went on to say that Bernard was "one of the holiest and humblest of men,"[22] one who "seems to go into a delirium of love when he talks about his divine Master!"[23]

Schaff considered Bernard to be "the most imposing figure of his time, and one of the best men of all Christian centuries."[24] This monk, he wrote, was "not equaled by any of his contemporaries in services for the Church and man."[25] Bernard, he said, possessed "intellectual genius . . . [and] magnetic personality," as well as "a heart glowing with love for God and man."[26] Bernard, quite simply, was the best-known and most widely acclaimed man of his day.[27]

Bernard was born of noble parents at the chateau of Fontaines, on the outskirts of Dijon in Burgundy, in east-central France. His father, Tescelin Sorrel, was a crusading knight, known for his honor, justice, and bravery. He took part in the First Crusade, which captured Jerusalem in 1099, and died in a later crusade. His six sons were trained as knights, with the exception of Bernard. Bernard's mother, Aleth, was a deeply pious woman and a model of spiritual virtue. Bernard was her special object of loving attention, as she took a direct part in his early education. Tragically, she died when he was only thirteen years old.

Bernard's early schooling planted within him a great interest in learning. He was sent to the highly regarded school of Saint-Vorles in Chatillon, France, a theological college. There he was instructed in the rudiments of grammar, logic, rhetoric, the Scriptures, and the authors of the great Latin classics, such as Virgil, Terence, Ovid, and Boëthius. These studies shaped Bernard's mind for his later study of God-centered theology.

## THE MONASTERY AT CITEAUX

Bernard early found himself faced with a major life decision. Should he pursue military and civil service as had his father and brothers? Or should he seek the monastic life? After agonizing over this life-defining choice, Bernard—despite the protests of his uncle, Villian d'Aigremont—chose to become a monk. Bernard, age twenty-two, joined the new monastery at Citeaux in 1112, the first abbey of the Cistercian order. It was also the poorest, the most remote, and the most Spartan of the Cistercians' abbeys. This decision was monumental for Bernard, as he later referred to it as the time of his conversion to Christ.

In an early indication of his influence on others, Bernard persuaded thirty young noblemen of Burgundy to join the Cistercian order with him. Among them were two of his brothers and two uncles. In 1113, the rest of his brothers also joined.

In the monastery, Bernard submitted to the severest asceticism—poverty, plainness, and simplicity. But his time at Citeaux was one of intensive learning. Among many subjects, Bernard studied the Scriptures, the Church Fathers, and classical authors such as Seneca, Ovid, Horace, and others.[28] With a growing obsession to learn, he regarded time given to sleep as time lost. Becoming something of a mystic, he also studied nature, which supplied him with many devotional lessons for the spiritual life.

After three years at the abbey of Citeaux, Bernard had distinguished himself by his exemplary scholarship and piety. As a result, he was commissioned to build a new monastery in the remote county of Champagne (1115). The chosen site was a rugged place, filled with so many difficulties and dangers it was known as "the valley of Wormwood." When Bernard arrived with twelve monks to found this monastery, he renamed the site Clairvaux, meaning "Clear Valley" or "Valley of Light." When the monastery was built, Bernard was appointed its first abbot. His aim was to establish a strict pattern of monastic life, including poverty and hard work. In his new capacity, Bernard read diligently, meditated, studied, preached, and wrote, pushing his body to the brink of collapse.

Bernard's immense giftedness quickly became apparent—he was considered to be of the first order of genius.[29] Under his guidance, the monastery in Clairvaux grew rapidly, soon outshining even the mother community in Citeaux.[30] A steady stream of young men journeyed to Clairvaux in order to be received into the monastery, and the number of monks living there soon reached a staggering seven hundred. Other church leaders and even princes began traveling to this isolated retreat to sit under Bernard's biblical teaching and counsel.

## An Expanding Influence

Despite dwelling in this remote place, Bernard exercised immense influence in ecclesiastical and political affairs.[31] Indicative of his humility, Bernard refused all outside efforts to elevate him to a higher office, but he traveled throughout

Europe to take part in important affairs of the church. He became one of the most widely traveled and most active leaders of the twelfth-century church.[32] Among his many accomplishments, Bernard served as secretary to the Synod of Troyes (1129), where the role of the Knights Templars was expanded. This order, so named because its headquarters was near the temple site in Jerusalem, was brought under the oversight of the Cistercians (1130). Bernard then drafted the rule of order for this military-religious organization, which directed its knights to protect the Holy Land from the onslaughts of the Muslims.

Bernard also became one of the greatest preachers of the Middle Ages and, arguably, one of the greatest of all time.[33] The sermons he preached to the monks formed much of his literary output.[34] In these Scripture-based, Christ-exalting expositions, Bernard sought to explain the biblical text and to reach the hearts of his listeners.[35] As he focused chiefly on Christ's person and work, Bernard spoke with an eloquence that was said to be captivating and compelling. In his *Commentary on Galatians*, Luther remarked, "In his sermons Bernard is superior to all teachers, even to Augustine himself, because he preaches Christ so excellently."[36] In one representative sermon, he pleaded with his listeners to be saved:

Wherefore, exclaiming vehemently with the Prophet, "Enter not into judgment with Your servant, O Lord!" let us flee, with all humility, to Mercy, which alone can save our souls. . . . Whosoever, feeling compunction for his sins, hungers and thirsts after righteousness, let him believe in You, who "justifies the ungodly"; and thus, being justified by faith alone, he shall have peace with God. . . . Your Passion is the last refuge, the alone remedy. When wisdom fails, when righteousness is insufficient, when the merits of holiness succumb, it succours us. For who, either from his own wisdom, or from his own righteousness, or from his own holiness, shall presume on a sufficiency for salvation? Oh, he alone is truly blessed to whom the Lord imputes not sin; for there is no one who has not sin. "All have sinned, and come short of the glory of God." Yet "who shall lay anything to the charge of God's elect?" To me, it is sufficient, only to have Him propitiated, against whom only I have sinned. . . . The Apostle says, "If one died for all, then were all dead," meaning thereby to intimate, that the satisfaction made by One should be imputed to all, even as One conversely bore the "sin of all."[37]

Bernard's influence also can be seen in the expansion of the Cistercian order. During his time as abbot of Clairvaux, Bernard founded some seventy other Cistercian monasteries throughout Europe. Extending the offshoots from these monasteries, some 170 abbeys were established throughout France, Italy, Germany, England, Spain, and other parts of Western Europe during the twelfth century. He also had the pleasure of seeing many of his students advance to places of great influence in the church.

## A WATCHDOG OF ORTHODOXY

The twelfth century was not without false teachings, which drove Bernard to assume the role of a watchdog of orthodoxy.[38] In 1140, he became engaged in a prolonged controversy with Peter Abelard (1079–1143), possibly the most brilliant thinker of the twelfth century.[39] Abelard had become well-known as a Scholastic teacher of philosophy and theology in Paris.[40] Sadly, he compromised the gospel, teaching that the death of Christ did not pay a judicial penalty to God on behalf of sinners, but merely provided an example of the love of God.[41] He declared that anyone who considered Christ's death would be inspired by love to be a better person.[42] In saying this, Abelard undermined the cross, viewing it in primarily ethical terms.[43]

Bernard saw Abelard's teaching as an attack on the purity of the gospel. In response, he became an aggressive polemicist, defending the truth with all his powers.[44] Bernard accused Abelard of joining with Arius in his views on the Trinity, with Nestorius in his views on Christ, and with Pelagius in his views on grace and free will.[45] He declared that Christ did far more than merely show God's love. Rather, the One who died on the cross, Bernard maintained, was the divine Savior, who provided a sin-bearing, substitutionary atonement that delivers hell-bound sinners from God's wrath.

Bernard arranged for Abelard to be summoned before the Council of Sens. There, he charged Abelard with heresy, presenting a list of his theological errors. He charged Abelard with teaching that Christ did not assume human flesh in order to free sinners from the yoke of the Devil. Moreover, as historian Justo L. González writes, Bernard indicted Abelard with teaching that "free will of itself suffices to do some good . . . [and] that we have not received the guilt of Adam, but only the penalty."[46] He then called on his adversary to recant his teaching, but Abelard refused. The council was left with no choice but to condemn him as a heretic. Abelard appealed to Rome, but the conviction was upheld. He was condemned to perpetual silence and confinement for his heterodoxy. Abelard retired to the monastery of Cluny, where he died in 1143.

## BERNARD'S FINAL DAYS

Given his increasing fame, Bernard was asked to be the official preacher for the Second Crusade. In this role, he was charged with increasing public support throughout Europe for an expedition to break the Muslim occupation of Palestine. Bernard willingly accepted this assignment and began to travel throughout the European continent. His passionate preaching helped to raise money and an army of relief for the kingdom of Jerusalem.[47] A force of almost two thousand Crusaders departed for the Holy Land in 1147, but they were repeatedly defeated by the Turks.

Bernard continued in his role as a guardian of the truth, becoming known as the "hammer of heretics."[48] In his defense of Christian orthodoxy, he attacked the deviant doctrines of numerous teachers. He refuted Gilbert de la Porree, bishop of Poitiers, at the Council of Paris for his perverse teaching on the Trinity (1147). Bernard's compelling presentation secured De la Porree's condemnation the following year at the Council of Reims. Bernard also opposed such popular preachers of the day as Peter de Bruys, Henry of Lausanne, and Arnold of Brescia. Through this work, Bernard showed himself to be a fearless champion of Christian truth.

One year before his death, Bernard felt compelled to address the errors, corruptions, and defilements of the church.[49] He especially spoke against the perceived abuses of the ecclesiastical courts.[50] In his final writings, *Libri de Consideratione* ("Considerations"), Bernard directly warned the pope against overstepping his bounds.[51] He also called on the pope to repress the abuses of church leaders and reprimanded him for the carnal advisers with whom he had surrounded himself. Bernard chided the pope: "You are not a sovereign lord over the other bishops, but only one among them."[52] In other words, there is only one Sovereign Lord, and it is not the pope.

To the end of his life, Bernard retained his hope in the gospel. Shortly before his death, he said: "There are three things on which I base my hopes for eternity: the love of God for His children, the certainty of His promises, and the power by which He will make these promises come true."[53] He died on August 20, 1153.

# BERNARD'S WRITINGS

Bernard wrote voluminous mystical, theological, and devotional works, and he carried on an extensive personal correspondence with emperors, popes, wayward monks, and theologians.[54] Among writers of devotional literature, Bernard occupies a place in the front rank.[55] His writings reveal a highly polished literary form[56] that features a formal beauty and a richness of imagery that identify him with the twelfth-century rebirth of letters.[57] This eloquence earned him the title "the honey-tongued doctor."[58] Much of his writing focused on prayer and other spiritual subjects as he sought to foster devotion to the person of Christ.[59]

## ON GRACE AND FREE CHOICE

*On Grace and Free Choice* (1128) proved to be the most profound and influential of Bernard's dogmatic works.[60] This treatise has been called Bernard's commentary on Romans, as he addresses the essential problems of the relation of grace and freedom.[61] Augustine's treatises against the Pelagians and Semi-Pelagians are similar to this work. In it, Bernard asserted that, left to themselves, fallen human beings will only sin.[62] Man's power to do good, he claimed, was lost through sin. For this reason, Bernard saw grace as necessary to incline the will to God and holiness. "Grace," he says, "changes the will from evil to good—not by destroying its freedom but by transferring its allegiance."[63] He adds: "What was begun by grace alone is completed by grace and free will together. This happens in such a way that they contribute to each achievement not singly but jointly, not in turns but simultaneously. It is not that grace does part of the work and free will the rest. But each does the whole work, according to its peculiar contribution. Grace does it all and so does free will—except that while all is done in free will, all is done out of [or "by"] grace."[64] In other words, Bernard contended that God's grace transforms the nature of man's will to good.

## SERMONS ON THE SONG OF SOLOMON

Bernard's most famous work is a series of eighty-six sermons on the Song of Solomon. These messages became a book, *Sermons on the Song of Solomon* (1135–1153), "recognized as the masterpiece of the genre."[65] In these sermons, Bernard interpreted the Song of Solomon as an allegory of the spiritual love between Christ the Bridegroom and His bride, the church. This book urges believers to take steps toward mystical union with God through Christ.

## HYMNS

A number of hymns are attributed to the abbot of Clairvaux. Some of these enduring works are "Jesus, the Very Thought of Thee," "O Sacred Head Now Wounded," and "Jesus, Thou Joy of Loving Hearts,"[66] in which Bernard wrote:

> Jesus, Thou Joy of loving hearts,
> Thou Fount of life, Thou Light of men,
> From the best bliss which earth imparts
> We turn unfilled to Thee again.[67]

# BERNARD'S THEOLOGY

Bernard's theological works closely hold to the truths of sovereign grace in salvation. This is not surprising, as his theology followed a strict Augustinian line.[68] Because of this theological affinity and Bernard's far-reaching influence, many scholars have contended that the Augustinian tradition, after the middle of the twelfth century, might more accurately be called the Bernardine tradition.[69]

For this reason, Bernard's teaching was deeply appreciated by Luther and Calvin.[70] Luther called Bernard "the greatest doctor of the church."[71] Calvin quoted Bernard in his *Institutes of the Christian Religion* more frequently than any previous nonbiblical author except Augustine, citing his works to support the doctrines of the bondage of the will, divine grace, justification by faith, and predestination.[72] So immersed was Calvin in Bernard's writings that "the French genius of Geneva may well have written his greatest works feeling the presence of the French genius of Clairvaux peering over his shoulder."[73] The Protestant Reformers merely brought to fruition that which Bernard had set out to accomplish in his own day.[74]

**Doctrine in Focus:**
## DIVINE SOVEREIGNTY

Bernard held to the sovereignty of God over every realm, and he maintained that the distribution of saving grace is inextricably linked to God's supreme authority. He affirms that God, being under no obligation to create human beings, spoke them into being as an expression of His grace: "It was God's creative grace that out of nothingness raised us to the dignity of manhood; and from this appears our duty to love Him, and the justice of His claim to that love."[75] Bernard recognized that mankind failed in that duty to love God, but he taught that God had sovereignly extended His saving love to His people. He writes: "O indulgent bounty of Divine love towards the sons of Adam, which does not cease to load us with benefits, not only where no merit was found, but often even where entire demerit was seen."[76] In other words, God sovereignly chose to bestow His grace and mercy where it was least deserved.

## Doctrine in Focus:
### Radical Depravity

Bernard plainly affirmed that the Scriptures teach the depravity of human nature. He especially acknowledged the bondage of the human will. Summarizing Bernard's teaching, Anthony Lane writes: "The human will is always free in the sense that we will voluntarily and spontaneously. But left to themselves, fallen human beings will only to sin."[77] In this vein, Bernard describes man's will as being "deteriorated by sin" and "under a yoke."[78] Moreover, he writes that the will is "inexcusable, because the will, when it was free, made itself the slave of sin. . . . Thus the soul, in some strange and evil way, is held under this kind of voluntary, yet sadly free necessity, both bond and free; bond in respect of necessity, free in respect of will: and what is still more strange, and still more miserable, it is guilty because free, and enslaved because guilty, and therefore enslaved because free."[79] In other words, man's will is in bondage because of his own sin. Bernard adds, "We are free in the sense that we sin willingly, without anyone forcing us to sin—but not in the sense that we can do otherwise."[80] In short, man's will is free only to sin.

Bernard properly attributed this bondage to the original sin all human beings inherit from Adam. He writes, "It should be known that when it is said, Original sin is in infants, this is spoken of the penalty, temporal and eternal, which is incurred by them through the fault of their first parent."[81] This penalty is upon all men, even the godliest, such as the prophets Jeremiah and John the Baptist: "These holy persons whom God has sanctified, and brought forth from the womb . . . [have] the taint of original sin which they contracted in conception."[82] Adam's one act of disobedience defiled the entire human race. As a result, divine condemnation is levied against all of mankind.

Bernard agreed with Augustine's view that, by sin, man has come under the domination and rule of Satan.[83] He held that every person is a slave of sin and can do nothing of his own accord to return to the state of righteousness Adam experienced before his fall. He writes:

Man therefore was lawfully delivered up, but mercifully set free. Yet mercy was shown in such a way that a kind of justice was not lacking even in his liberation, since, as was most fitting for man's recovery, it was part of the mercy of the liberator to employ justice rather than power against man's enemy. What could man, the slave of sin, fast bound by the devil, do of himself to recover that righteousness which he had formerly lost? Therefore he who lacked righteousness had another's imputed to him, and in this way: The prince of this world came and found nothing in the Saviour; and because he notwithstanding laid hands on the Innocent he lost most justly those whom he held captive; since He who owed nothing to death, lawfully freed him who was subject to it, both from the debt of death, and the dominion of the devil, by accepting the injustice of death; for with what justice could that be exacted from man a second time? It was man who owed the debt, it was man who paid it.[84]

With these words, Bernard stressed the fact that righteousness is found exclusively through Christ, and that although He had no guilt, He accepted the form of a servant in order that He might pay the penalty owed by men.[85] Whatever righteousness human beings may have, Bernard asserted, is as nothing in light of the holiness of God. He says: "What can all our righteousness be before God? Shall it not, according to the prophet, be viewed as 'a filthy rag;' and if it is strictly judged, shall not all our righteousness turn out to be mere unrighteousness and deficiency? What, then, shall it be concerning our sins, when not even our righteousness can answer for itself?"[86] All human righteousness is actually unrighteousness. This means man cannot accomplish any good, and certainly not the greatest good, namely, choosing to receive God's offer of salvation in Christ. He is totally unable to come to Christ apart from the saving grace of God. Bernard states: "Man is not able to do anything good by himself . . . he is incapable of raising himself up in any way whatever by his free will for the reception of Divine grace, without the help of that grace."[87]

Bernard strongly rejected the heretical teaching of the fifth-century opponent of Augustine, Pelagius, who denied the doctrine of original sin. He writes: "We rest in the Christian faith, and not in the heresy of Pelagius, and confess that by generation and not by example was the sin of Adam imparted to us, and by sin death."[88] The problem, Bernard saw, is not that man merely imitates the bad example of Adam and others. Rather, it is that man is conceived with a sinful heart that is solely inclined to disobey God's righteous commands. With this biblical understanding, Bernard "sought to answer those who desired to tone down or weaken the idea of man's corruption in order to give more room to the freedom of man's will."[89]

**Doctrine in Focus:**
### SOVEREIGN ELECTION

As a champion of biblical truth, Bernard argued that because of man's sin and the subsequent bondage of the will, salvation is entirely of God's grace. Those who receive the kingdom of God, he said, are those whom God previously foreknew and foreordained for salvation. Bernard says: "He says: Fear not, little flock, for it is your Father's good pleasure to give you the kingdom (S. Luke xii. 32). Who are these? These are they whom He foreknew and foreordained to be conformed to the image of His Son, that He might be the first born among many brethren."[90] God chose a set number of people before the foundation of the world to become His "little flock." The sovereign God determined to conform them to the image of Christ, that is, to redeem them and glorify them.

This determinative choice was the beginning of an immutable process by which spiritually dead sinners are brought to eternal life. Bernard writes: "The mystery, hidden from eternity, concerning souls that have been predestinated and are to be glorified, begins in some degree to emerge from the depths of eternity, as each soul, called by fear and justified by love, becomes assured that it, too, is of the number of the blessed, knowing well that whom He justified, them also He glorified (Rom. viii. 30)."[91] Those whom God chose before time began are saved within time and will be glorified for all time.

Further, Bernard understood that sovereign election is rooted in the eternal decree of God. He states, "The decree of the Lord stands firm; His purpose of peace stands firm upon those who fear Him."[92] Elsewhere he adds: "He has made known his great and secret counsel. The Lord knoweth them that are his, but that which was known to God was manifested to men; nor, indeed, does he deign to give a participation in this great mystery to any but those whom he foreknew and predestinated to be his own."[93] God's decree, His "great and secret counsel," concerns those who are His for eternity.

Citing John 15:16, Bernard declares that man is saved by God's sovereign will: "For you have not chosen Me, but I have chosen you [John 15:16]; not for any merits that I found in you did I choose you, but I went before you. Thus have I betrothed you to Myself in faith, not in the works of the law."[94] It is through divine election that Christ receives His chosen people to Himself, not by their works. Bernard affirmed this truth in his own experience of grace. He writes, "Therefore my beginning is solely of grace, and I have nothing which I can attribute to myself in predestination or in calling."[95] Election was not dependent on man's merits, but on God's sovereign grace.

Bernard took the apostle Paul's teaching in Romans 9:16 at face value, accepting that salvation flows from the mercy of God, not from anything man can do: "We believe that it pleases the reader that we nowhere depart from the teaching of the Apostle; and wherever the argument may have wandered, we have often made use of his very words. For what else do we mean than what he says: 'It is therefore neither of him that wills, nor of him that runs, but of God that shows mercy'?"[96] God exercises His saving favor through the election of a people, bestowing divine mercy on whom He pleases.

**Doctrine in Focus:**
IRRESISTIBLE CALL

Bernard held that God draws to Himself all whom He has foreordained to eternal life. The sovereign call of the elect into union with Christ is issued by the Holy Spirit, who gives the gift of saving faith. By His irresistible call, God applies the benefits of Christ's saving work to those whom He foreordained to eternal life. Bernard writes, "Christ, not considering it robbery to draw to Himself those whom He has made and redeemed with His own blood, has done when they came to Him, what He had before promised, Him who cometh unto Me, I will in no wise cast out (John vi. 37)."[97] He adds, "He, yes, He Himself draws you, who loves you as His own flesh, as the most precious fruit of His cross, as the most worthy recompense of the blood He shed."[98] Those who trust Christ do so because the Spirit draws them to Him.

Looking at this subject from another perspective, Bernard maintained that regeneration is the sovereign working of God. A person is born again when God calls him or her, giving the gift of faith in Christ. He writes: "He [God] said 'let there be light' and there was light. He said 'be converted' and the children of men were converted. Clearly, then, the conversion of souls is the working of the divine, not the human, voice."[99] The God who brought creation into existence with a word also causes salvation to happen by a mere command.

Bernard contended that man has nothing that merits salvation. Rather, forgiveness is a divine gift. He writes, "First of all, it is necessary to believe that you cannot have forgiveness of sins apart from God's mercy . . . you cannot merit eternal life by any works unless that it is freely given."[100] Making the same point elsewhere, he says: "It [conversion] is the finger of God, clearly a change due to the right hand of the Most High. Your conversion is a good gift and a perfect gift, without doubt descending from the Father of lights. And so to Him we rightly bring every voice of praise who only doeth marvellous things, who hath caused that plenteous redemption that is in Him to be no longer without effect in you."[101] Salvation is God's work, a gift from Him, not a reward for human merit.

When God saves, He graciously changes the disposition of an individual to cause Him to want Christ. Bernard says, "It is grace which arouses our free choice, by sowing the seed of the good thought; it is grace which heals our free choice, by changing its disposition; it is grace which strengthens it so as to lead it to action; it is grace which saves it from experiencing a fall."[102] By grace, lost sinners are so changed as to want Christ for the first time.

In one of his clearest statements on the connection between election and salvation, Bernard explained that God initiates salvation for those whose names He previously wrote in the book of life. In His appointed time, He extends saving grace to these elect ones. Bernard writes, "God, therefore, worketh their salvation, 'whose names are in the book of life,' sometimes by means of the creature without itself, at other times by means of the creature against itself, at other times by means of the creature with itself."[103] Therefore, he adds, "He that wills and runs ought to glory, not in himself, but in Him from Whom he has received the power to will and to run."[104] The believer trusts Christ only because he has been given the ability from God to place his faith in Christ's saving work.

**Doctrine in Focus:**
## DIVINE REPROBATION

Following Augustine, Isidore, and Gottschalk, Bernard held to the doctrine of divine reprobation. He affirmed that just as God elects some to salvation,

He passes over others and leaves them in their sin. While the elect receive what they do not deserve, mercy, the reprobate suffer what they justly deserve, divine judgment. He notes, "Indeed, to saints and the elect tribulation worketh patience, patience experience, experience hope, and hope maketh not ashamed; to the condemnable and reprobate, on the contrary, tribulation causes discouragement, and discouragement confusion, and confusion despair, which destroys them."[105] Bernard clearly recognized that there are two categories of people in God's sight—those He intends to save (the elect) and those He intends to abandon to His judgment (the reprobate). Tribulation, he wrote, reveals the elect from the reprobate in that it works for the good of the first group but not of the second.

Reaffirming this teaching in Romans 1, Bernard taught that the reprobate will inevitably fall into vanity: "The love of vanity is the contempt of truth, and the contempt of truth the cause of our blindness. And because they did not like, he says, to retain God in their knowledge, He gave them over unto a reprobate mind" (Rom.1:28).[106] Though salvation is freely offered to the reprobate, they remain lost and entangled in their sins. As a result, God gives their minds over to think increasingly evil thoughts. They will discover their wretched state when life ends.

# INFLAMED BY SOVEREIGN GRACE

The truths of sovereign grace generate awe toward God in the hearts of those who accept them. This wonder over God's electing love and redeeming grace, in turn, fires these saints with passionate zeal for Him. Far from merely instructing minds, these doctrines inflame souls and activate wills. We see this dynamic at work in the long line of godly men who have upheld the sovereignty of God in salvation, for this grand theology fueled a spiritual fire in these men, igniting their spirits with affection for the glory of God and causing them to live for Him with intensity. Perhaps no one exhibited more passion for Christ and zeal for the glory of God than Bernard of Clairvaux.

In this way, Bernard represents the powerful effect that the doctrines of grace should have on every believer. These teachings are not given merely as fodder for theological arguments. These doctrines should never produce dogmatism without devotion, convictions without compassion, allegiance without affections, or fanaticism without fervor. A cold, clinical Calvinism should be an oxymoron, a contradiction in terms.

Instead, this high theology should ignite a blazing doxology. In other words, an exalted view of God and His sovereign grace should lead inevitably to heartfelt worship. J. Ligon Duncan describes the doctrines of grace as "joy-giving, life-changing, Christ-exalting, [and] God-glorifying . . . truths."[107] When genuinely understood and embraced, he says, the truth of God's sovereignty in the salvation of sinners is "soul-transforming, heart-animating, and life-altering," bringing joy to sinners who have been found by the amazing grace of God.[108] It was true of Bernard, and it should be true of us. The doctrines of grace should produce hearts bursting with love and devotion for the triune God who alone saves.

Has God opened your eyes to behold the precious truths of sovereign grace found in His Word? If so, has not your heart been overwhelmed as you consider that He has chosen to have mercy on you? Do you not say, "Why *me*, Lord?" Do you not see how God has chosen to love you from eternity past? Do you not understand how He sovereignly determined to crown you with His grace? Does not your heart burst to sing of His electing mercy? Are you not awed by His favor?

Then come and join with the long line of godly men in giving praise to God. Come and ascribe power and glory to Him. Lift up your voice and sing to His name. Offer to Him the sacrifice of praise. He chose you for Himself. He selected you from among many to be the bride for His only Son. He redeemed you at an infinite price, sending His Son to suffer an intentional, substitutionary death to rescue you. He pursued you until He found you in the pit of sin. He then sovereignly adopted you into His family. And He preserves you forever in His lovingkindness.

Come now and give praise to God. Magnify His name forever and ever.

NOTES

1  Bernard, *Sermons on the Song of Songs*, 67.11, cited in *The Two-Fold Knowledge: Readings on the Knowledge of Self & the Knowledge of God*, ed. and trans. Franz Posset (Milwaukee: Marquette University Press, 2004), 121.

2  Earle E. Cairns, *Christianity Through the Centuries: A History of the Church*, 3rd Ed. (1954; repr., Grand Rapids: Zondervan, 1996), 242.

3  Augustine, *Confessions*, 1.1.1, cited in Alister E. McGrath, ed., *The Christian Theology Reader* (Oxford, Blackwell, 2007), 433.

4 Philip Schaff and David S. Schaff, *History of the Christian Church, Vol. V: The Middle Ages: From Gregory VII to Boniface VIII, 1049–1294* (1907; repr., Grand Rapids: Eerdmans, 1984), 637.

5 Schaff and Schaff, *History of the Christian Church, Vol. V,* 637.

6 Dennis D. Martin, "Mysticism," in *Evangelical Dictionary of Theology,* 2nd Ed., ed. Walter A. Elwell (Grand Rapids: Baker, 2001), 806.

7 Schaff and Schaff, *History of the Christian Church, Vol. V,* 639.

8 Schaff and Schaff, *History of the Christian Church, Vol. V,* 637.

9 Schaff and Schaff, *History of the Christian Church, Vol. V,* 637–638.

10 N. R. Needham, *2,000 Years of Christ's Power, Part Two: The Middle Ages* (London: Grace Publications, 2005), 151.

11 Needham, *2,000 Years of Christ's Power, Part Two,* 151.

12 Cairns, *Christianity Through the Centuries,* 218.

13 Cairns, *Christianity Through the Centuries,* 218.

14 "St. Bernard," in *The Oxford Dictionary of the Christian Church,* 3rd Ed., ed. E. A. Livingstone (1957; repr., Oxford: Oxford University Press, 1997), 193.

15 Richard V. Pierard, "Bernard of Clairvaux," in *New International Dictionary of the Christian Church,* gen. ed. J. D. Douglas (Grand Rapids: Zondervan, 1978), 123.

16 Needham, *2,000 Years of Christ's Power, Part Two,* 192.

17 Tony Lane, "A Twelfth Century Man for All Seasons," *Christian History,* Issue 24, Vol. VIII, No. 4, 6.

18 Martin Luther, *Luther's Works, Vol. 15: Ecclesiastes, Song of Solomon, Last Words of David, 2 Samuel 23:1–7,* eds. Jaroslav Jan Pelikan, Hilton C. Oswald, and Helmut T. Lehmann (St. Louis: Concordia, 1972), 335.

19 Martin Luther, *A Commentary on St. Paul's Epistle to the Galatians,* 4th Ed., trans. Theodore Graebner (Grand Rapids: Zondervan, n.d.), 192.

20 Martin Luther, *Luther's Works, Vol. 41: Church and Ministry III,* eds. Jaroslav Jan Pelikan, Hilton C. Oswald, and Helmut T. Lehmann (Philadelphia: Fortress, 1999), 27.

21 Charles H. Spurgeon, *Spurgeon's Sermons: Vol. 29* (Pasadena, Texas: Pilgrim, 1985), 165.

22 Charles H. Spurgeon, *Spurgeon's Sermons: Vol. 40* (Pasadena, Texas: Pilgrim, 1985), 192.

23 Charles H. Spurgeon, *Spurgeon's Sermons: Vol. 33* (Pasadena, Texas: Pilgrim, 1985), 562.

24 Schaff and Schaff, *History of the Christian Church, Vol. V,* 343.

25 Schaff and Schaff, *History of the Christian Church, Vol. V,* 343.

26 Schaff and Schaff, *History of the Christian Church, Vol. V,* 343.

27 C. F. Allison, "Bernard of Clairvaux," in *Evangelical Dictionary of Theology,* 151.

28 Schaff and Schaff, *History of the Christian Church, Vol. V,* 346.

29 Schaff and Schaff, *History of the Christian Church, Vol. V,* 343.

30 Needham, *2,000 Years of Christ's Power, Part Two,* 194.

31 "St. Bernard," in *The Oxford Dictionary of the Christian Church,* 192.

32 Tony Lane, *A Concise History of Christian Thought* (Grand Rapids: Baker Academic, 2006), 111.

33 Needham, *2,000 Years of Christ's Power, Part Two,* 194.

34 Emero Stiegman, "Bernard of Clairvaux, William of St. Thierry, the Victorines," in *The Medieval Theologians: An Introduction to Theology in the Medieval Period,* ed. G. R. Evans (Madden, Mass.: Blackwell, 2006), 131.

35 Needham, *2,000 Years of Christ's Power, Part Two,* 194.

36 Martin Luther, cited in Schaff and Schaff, *History of the Christian Church, Vol. V*, 351.

37 Bernard, *Opera*, 6:285, 601, 630, 1556, as cited in James Buchanan, *The Doctrine of Justification: An Outline of its History in the Church and of its Exposition from Scripture* (Edinburgh: Banner of Truth, 1984), 96–97.

38 Stiegman, "Bernard of Clairvaux, William of St. Thierry, the Victorines," in *The Medieval Theologians*, 131.

39 Lane, "A Twelfth Century Man for All Seasons," 9.

40 Justo L. González, *A History of Christian Thought, Vol. 2: From Augustine to the Eve of the Reformation* (Nashville: Abingdon, 1987), 167.

41 González, *A History of Christian Thought, Vol. II*, 170.

42 Jonathan Hill, *The History of Christian Thought* (Downers Grove, Ill.: InterVarsity, 2003), 146.

43 Hill, *The History of Christian Thought*, 146.

44 Stiegman, "Bernard of Clairvaux, William of St. Thierry, the Victorines," in *The Medieval Theologians*, 131.

45 Needham, *2,000 Years of Christ's Power, Part Two*, 196.

46 González, *A History of Christian Thought, Vol. 2*, 172.

47 Justo L. González, *The Story of Christianity, Vol. 1: The Early Church to the Dawn of the Reformation* (Peabody, Mass.: Prince, 2004), 297.

48 Allison, "Bernard of Clairvaux," in *Evangelical Dictionary of Theology*, 151.

49 "Bernard of Clairvaux," in *Cyclopedia of Biblical, Theological, and Ecclesiastical Literature, Vol. I*, eds. John McClintock and James Strong (Grand Rapids: Baker, 1981), 762.

50 "Bernard of Clairvaux," in *Cyclopedia of Biblical, Theological, and Ecclesiastical Literature, Vol. I*, 762.

51 Bernard, cited in "Bernard of Clairvaux," in *Cyclopedia of Biblical, Theological, and Ecclesiastical Literature, Vol. I*, 762.

52 Bernard, cited in "Bernard of Clairvaux," in *Cyclopedia of Biblical, Theological, and Ecclesiastical Literature, Vol. I*, 763.

53 Bernard, cited in S. M. Houghton, *Sketches from Church History* (Edinburgh: Banner of Truth, 1980, 2001), 59.

54 Allison, "Bernard of Clairvaux," in *Evangelical Dictionary of Theology*, 151.

55 Schaff and Schaff, *History of the Christian Church, Vol. V*, 344.

56 Lane, *A Concise History of Christian Thought*, 111.

57 "St. Bernard," in *The Oxford Dictionary of the Christian Church*, 193.

58 Schaff and Schaff, *History of the Christian Church, Vol. V*, 344.

59 "Bernard of Clairvaux," in *Dictionary of Christian Biography*, ed. Michael J. Walsh (Collegeville, Minn.: The Liturgical Press, 2001), 173.

60 Bernard McGinn, "Introduction," in Bernard, *Treatises, Vol. 3: On Grace and Free Choice, in Praise of the New Knighthood*, trans. Daniel O'Donovan (Kalamazoo, Mich.: Cistercian Publications, 1988), 3.

61 McGinn, "Introduction," in Bernard, *Treatises, Vol. 3*, 5.

62 Lane, *A Concise History of Christian Thought*, 111.

63 Bernard, *On Grace and Free Choice*, 14.47, cited in Lane, *A Concise History of Christian Thought*, 111.

64 Bernard, *On Grace and Free Choice*, 14.47, cited in *Treatises, Vol. 3*, 106.

65 Stiegman, "Bernard of Clairvaux, William of St. Thierry, the Victorines," in *The Medieval Theologians*, 131.

66 Pierard, "Bernard of Clairvaux," in *New International Dictionary of the Christian Church*, 123.

67 Bernard, "Jesus, Thou Joy of Loving Hearts," as cited in Schaff and Schaff, *History of the Christian Church, Vol. V*, 357.

68 Lane, *A Concise History of Christian Thought*, 111.

69 W. Stanford Reid, "Bernard of Clairvaux in the Thought of John Calvin," *Westminster Theological Journal*, Vol. 41 (Westminster Theological Seminary, 1979; 2002), 128.

70 Allison, "Bernard of Clairvaux," in *Evangelical Dictionary of Theology*, 151.

71 Martin Luther, cited in Adolf von Harnack, "Bernard van Clairvaux," *Christelijke Encyclopedie. Vol. IV* (Kampen, 1956), 183.

72 Anthony N. S. Lane, *John Calvin: Student of the Church Fathers* (Grand Rapids: Baker, 1999), 97.

73 W. Stanford Reid, "The Reformer Saint and the Saintly Reformer," *Christian History and Biography*, Issue 24, Vol. VIII, No. 4, 28.

74 Reid, "Bernard of Clairvaux in the Thought of John Calvin," *Westminster Theological Journal*, 131.

75 Bernard, *On Loving God*, V, in *On Loving God* (Cistercian Fathers Series), ed. Emero Steigman (Kalamazoo, Mich.: Cistercian Publications, 1995), 6.

76 Bernard, Letter 24.6, in *Some Letters of Saint Bernard, Abbot of Clairvaux*, ed. Francis Aidan Gasquet (London: J. Hodges, 1904), 101.

77 Lane, *A Concise History of Christian Thought*, 111.

78 Bernard, *Sermons on the Song of Songs*, 81, cited in John Calvin, *Institutes of the Christian Religion*, trans. Henry Beveridge (Peabody, Mass.: Hendrickson, 2008), 2.3.5.

79 Bernard, *Sermons on the Song of Songs*, 81, cited in Calvin, *Institutes of the Christian Religion*, 2.3.5.

80 Bernard, *Grace and Free Choice*, cited in Lane, *A Concise History of Christian Thought*, 111.

81 Bernard, Letter 40.8, in *Some Letters of Saint Bernard, Abbot of Clairvaux*, 254–55.

82 Bernard, Letter 65.3, in *Some Letters of Saint Bernard, Abbot of Clairvaux*, 303.

83 Reid, "The Reformer Saint and the Saintly Reformer," *Christian History and Biography*, 29.

84 Bernard, Letter 60.15, in *Some Letters of Saint Bernard, Abbot of Clairvaux*, 279.

85 R. Seeberg, *A Textbook of the History of Doctrine* (Philadelphia: Wipf & Stock, 1997), 72.

86 Bernard, *Opera*, 6:285, as cited in Buchanan, *The Doctrine of Justification*, 96.

87 Bernard, Letter 60.6, in *Some Letters of Saint Bernard, Abbot of Clairvaux*, 252.

88 Bernard, Letter 60.23, in *Some Letters of Saint Bernard, Abbot of Clairvaux*, 291.

89 Reid, "Bernard of Clairvaux in the Thought of John Calvin," *Westminster Theological Journal*, 138.

90 Bernard, Letter 40.4, in *Some Letters of Saint Bernard, Abbot of Clairvaux*, 151.

91 Bernard, Letter 107.5, in *Life and Works of Saint Bernard, Abbot of Clairvaux, Vol. 1*, ed. John Mabillon (London, John Hodges, 1889), 358.

92 Bernard, *Sermons on the Song of Songs*, 14, as cited in Calvin, *Institutes of the Christian Religion*, 3.24.4.

93 Bernard, Letter 107.4, cited in Calvin, *Institutes of the Christian Religion*, 3.12.10.

94 Bernard, *Sermons on the Song of Songs*, 67.11, in *The Two-Fold Knowledge*, 121.

336 PILLARS OF GRACE

95 Bernard, *Pro Dominica I Novembris*, 183:353, cited in Reid, "Bernard of Clairvaux in the Thought of John Calvin," *Westminster Theological Journal*, 142.

96 Bernard, *Of Grace and Free Choice*, in *The Treatise of St. Bernard, Abbot of Clairvaux, Concerning Grace and Free Will, Addressed to William, Abbot of St. Thierry. Translations of Christian Literature, Series II: Latin Texts*, ed. Watkin Wynn Williams (London and New York: Society for Promoting Christian Knowledge; The Macmillan Co., 1920), 83.

97 Bernard, Letter 45.4, in *Some Letters of Saint Bernard, Abbot of Clairvaux*, 181.

98 Bernard, Letter 42.1, in *Some Letters of Saint Bernard, Abbot of Clairvaux*, 165.

99 Bernard, *Sermon to Clerics on Conversion*, in *Sermons of Conversion* (Cistercian Fathers Series) (Kalamazoo, Mich.: Cistercian Publications, 1981), 32.

100 Bernard, *De Gratia*, Letter 190, cited in Calvin, *Institutes of the Christian Religion*, 3:12:3.

101 Bernard, Letter 42.1, in *Some Letters of Saint Bernard, Abbot of Clairvaux*, 166.

102 Bernard, *Of Grace and Free-will*, 14, cited in Needham, *2,000 Years of Christ's Power, Part Two*, 213.

103 Bernard, *The Treatise of St. Bernard, Abbot of Clairvaux, Concerning Grace and Free Will*, 74–75.

104 Bernard, *The Treatise of St. Bernard, Abbot of Clairvaux, Concerning Grace and Free Will*, 83.

105 Bernard, Letter 11.1, in *Some Letters of Saint Bernard, Abbot of Clairvaux*, 47–48.

106 Bernard, Letter 6.1, in *Some Letters of Saint Bernard, Abbot of Clairvaux*, 36.

107 J. Ligon Duncan, endorsement in *Foundations of Grace* (Orlando, Fla.: Reformation Trust, 2006).

108 Duncan, endorsement in *Foundations of Grace*.

# CHAPTER SIXTEEN
## STUDY QUESTIONS

1. Explain mysticism as it was understood in the twelfth century. What were the strengths of this movement? What did it seek to counterbalance? How is mysticism frequently misunderstood today?

2. Why did Monasticism need to be reformed in the twelfth century? What elements of reform were needed? Who did God raise up to launch this reform?

3. Describe the upbringing of Bernard. What factors shaped his early life? What role did asceticism have in his formative years? What influence did he bring to bear on the monastery?

4. Why is preaching central to one's theological convictions? In what ways is preaching today similar to or different from that of Bernard's? What effect does preaching today have on the theology of the church, either positively or negatively?

5. Summarize Bernard's numerous writings. Comment on his hymns. What is the relationship between theology and doxology? How should the former affect the latter?

6. What effect did Bernard have on the Reformers who followed him? What did they see in his writings that elevated their understanding of sovereign grace?

7. Detail Bernard's position on original sin and its effect on the human will. To what extent did Adam's fall subject the human race to the dominion of Satan?

8. Compare the creation of light on the first day of the created order with the new birth and the miracle of illumination. Describe Bernard's position regarding the inward change of regeneration that reverses the affections of the human heart.

When we act we are the ones who act, but
He acts so that we may act.[1]

The will of God is the efficient cause of anything whatever that is done.[2]

–Thomas Bradwardine

# DOCTOR PROFUNDUS

## ENGLISH SCHOLASTIC:
## THOMAS BRADWARDINE

I n the twelfth century, there emerged in Europe a new institution of education—the university. To this point, monasteries and cathedrals had been the central places where students went to receive a higher education. But the university—from the Latin *universitas*, meaning "the whole," as in the whole of knowledge—emerged to facilitate the pursuit of knowledge in all major areas of study. The time had come for specialized study of the arts, law, medicine, and especially theology. The appearance of the universities to answer this need constituted one of the most significant developments in the advancement of Western thought.

Between 1200 and 1500, some eighty educational institutions sprang up in Europe. The first of these arose in Italy, at Salerno and Bologna. Soon, there followed the University of Paris (ca. 1160) and other French universities. Shortly thereafter, English universities were established at Oxford (1167) and Cambridge (1209). In Germany, universities appeared in Vienna (1365), Erfurt (1379), Heidelberg (1385), and eventually Wittenberg (1502), the last medieval university to open its doors.[3] In addition, three major universities were founded in Scotland in the fifteenth century: St. Andrews (1413), Glasgow (1451), and Aberdeen (1495). These centers for higher learning were dedicated to preserving and teaching the *summa*, that is, the sum total of human knowledge.

Many of these universities helped to give birth to the Protestant Reformation. The fires of reform were ignited in the university lecture halls. John Wycliffe (ca. 1330–1384), an English Pre-Reformer, taught at the University of Oxford and spread his Augustinian doctrine to his students. John Hus (ca. 1372–1415), a Bohemian Pre-Reformer, lectured at the University of Prague. Martin Luther (1483–1546), the great German Reformer, was professor of Bible at the University of Wittenberg throughout his adult life. Ulrich Zwingli (1484–1531), a noted Swiss Reformer, received the learning he would later apply to the cause of the Reformation at the universities of Vienna and Basel. John Calvin (1509–1564), the Genevan Reformer, was given the intellectual tools to be a commanding commentator, author, and expositor at the universities of Paris, Bourges, and Orléans.

The University of Oxford was founded only seven years after the University of Paris. It began when France expelled foreign scholars in 1167.[4] This school soon became known for its exceptional theological faculty. John Duns Scotus (1265–1308), a Scottish lecturer at Oxford, is called "the last of the scholastic thinkers of first rank."[5] William of Ockham (1285–1349), a noted English theologian, lectured at Oxford with great influence. Later, Oxford grew into an important religious center in the time of the Reformation and the Restoration. John Owen (1616–1683), the great English theologian, served as vice chancellor at Oxford. John Wesley (1703–1791), Charles Wesley (1707–1788), and George Whitefield (1714–1770) were educated there. Further, Methodism was born at Oxford through the Holy Club (1729).

The fourteenth century proved to be a pivotal period at Oxford. Though many of the great Scholastics at the school had been followers of Augustinian thought, William of Ockham was influential in reviving Pelagianism through his lectures. He implied that fallen man could earn God's grace, meriting salvation through his moral abilities. While scholars who write about Ockham refer to his views as Semi-Pelagianism, his theological system was actually more closely akin to Pelagianism, with its emphasis on the power of the human will to achieve grace. Eventually, Pope John XXII summoned William to Avignon in southern France to answer heresy charges.

Amid this Pelagian revival, God raised up a stalwart of Augustinism to champion the cause of sovereign grace. His name was Thomas Bradwardine (1290–1349). As both a student and professor at Oxford, he confronted the teaching of William of Ockham's Pelagian views at the school. As a result, a revival of Augustinism burst forth in the third decade of the fourteenth century.[6]

# THOMAS BRADWARDINE

Thomas Bradwardine is known to history as *Doctor Profundus*, meaning "The Profound Doctor."[7] He was an Oxford professor of theology and later its chancellor. He went on to serve as the chancellor of St. Paul's Cathedral in London, as chaplain to the king of England, and as the archbishop of Canterbury, the leading ecclesiastical position in England. More important, Bradwardine is regarded as an important influence in preparing the way for the Reformation. He played a critical role in the theological continuity between the medieval church and the Reformation.[8]

Bradwardine was born at Hartfield, on the southern coast of England.[9] Little is known about his early upbringing. The Bradwardine family belonged to the smaller gentry or burgher class. This indicates that they were a family of some means. They must have possessed some standing, because they were able to send young Thomas to Balliol College at Oxford. It is not certain how old Bradwardine was upon his enrollment at Balliol, but the average age of admission to the college at that time was fourteen. He soon displayed strong scholastic abilities and acquired a reputation as a profound thinker and eventually a gifted scholar. Thomas came to be known as both a skilled mathematician and able theologian. He was also a brilliant logician who developed original theories on the subject.

After earning a degree in divinity from Balliol, Bradwardine entered Merton College at Oxford on a fellowship. Here he again achieved great distinction in mathematics and theology. J. H. Merle d'Aubigné notes that Bradwardine "occupied the first rank among astronomers, philosophers, and mathematicians."[10] Unfortunately, his accomplishments bred an intellectual pride that kept him from the humility necessary to receive the gospel of Jesus Christ.[11]

## CONVERTED TO CHRIST

In his student days, Bradwardine came under the teaching of William of Ockham and interacted with his disciples in school. As noted above, Ockham was a strong Pelagian whose theology stated that sinners can, by their natural power, merit the gift of God's grace. This teaching drove Bradwardine to search out the truth. Amid this pursuit, he was struck by the apostle Paul's teaching in Romans 9:16. He came to see that salvation does not depend on man who wills or runs, but on God who shows mercy. He grasped that God's saving grace is a gift that cannot be earned.

However, as Bradwardine surveyed the situation at Merton College, he saw Pelagianism on every side. He writes:

> As in the times of old four hundred and fifty prophets of Baal strove against a single prophet of God; so now, O Lord, the number of those who strive with Pelagius against Thy free grace cannot be counted. They pretend not to receive grace freely, but to buy it. The will of men (they say) should precede, and Thine should follow: theirs is the mistress, and Thine the servant. . . . Alas! Nearly the whole world is walking in error in the steps of Pelagius. Arise, O Lord, and judge Thy cause.[12]

## Teaching and Writing

Bradwardine's new understanding led him to begin writing his greatest work, *The Cause of God Against the Pelagians*. This piece would not be completed until years later, in 1344. Also, D'Aubigné writes, Bradwardine boldly began to teach and proclaim the doctrines of grace at Merton, becoming a formidable foe of Pelagianism.[13] D'Aubigné notes, "He had drunk so deep at the fountain of Scripture that the traditions of men concerned him but little, and he was so absorbed in adoration in spirit and in truth, that he remarked not outward superstitions."[14] He adds: "[Bradwardine's] lectures were eagerly listened to and circulated through all Europe. The grace of God was their very essence, as it was of the Reformation. With sorrow, Bradwardine beheld Pelagianism everywhere substituting a mere religion of externals for inward Christianity, and on his knees he struggled for the salvation of the church."[15]

After earning a number of degrees, Bradwardine entered the theological faculty at Merton. He became professor of theology and taught a strong Augustinianism. Bradwardine soon became a proctor, or a president, of Merton. He also served as chancellor of Oxford, which gave him the authority to issue licenses to teach and to confer degrees.[16]

Bradwardine was scarcely less eminent as a scientist than as a theologian.[17] During this time, he wrote an influential work on physics, *De proportionilus* (ca. 1328). It held sway in European theories of mechanics for almost a century. He also wrote a controversial treatise on future contingents (ca. 1333).

He made influential contributions in the areas of continuity, infinity, proportions, and motion in physics, and he wrote extensively on mathematical subjects and made original contributions to a number of theoretical problems in geometry.

## Bradwardine's Final Days

In 1335, Bradwardine became chaplain to Richard of Bury, bishop of Durham. He then moved to London two years later and assumed the position of chancellor of St. Paul's Cathedral on September 19, 1337. He retained this post until 1348. Soon after this, Bradwardine was made royal chaplain and confessor to King Edward III of England. He sometimes accompanied the king on his travels to the European continent during the wars with France.

In 1349, Bradwardine was chosen to be archbishop of Canterbury. However, King Edward refused to confirm the appointment. But after Edward's preferred candidate died, Bradwardine was chosen for the archbishopric a second time, and this time there was no objection from the king. Bradwardine was consecrated at Avignon on July 10, 1349. But within a few weeks, he contracted the Black Plague, the deadly disease that had ravaged England and France. Bradwardine died after only thirty-eight days in office.

# BRADWARDINE'S WRITINGS

Bradwardine was, as D'Aubigné writes, "one of the greatest geniuses of his time."[18] His genius can be seen in his many writings. As noted above, he wrote on a vast array of subjects in the field of mathematics and physics, but his primary literary contribution was in the area of theology. Specifically, it was a work that refuted Pelagianism and upheld divine sovereignty.

## *The Cause of God Against the Pelagians*

It was *De Causa Dei Contra Pelagium* (*The Cause of God Against the Pelagians*) that earned him the title *Doctor Profundus*. This book is a massive and profound metaphysical polemic against the central and core doctrines of Pelagianism. It was edited in 1618 by Sir Henry Savile, with the help of William Twisse (1575–1646), the presiding officer of the Westminster Assembly. In it, Bradwardine laid out the biblical case for the bondage of the will, predestination, and man's need of grace. This case is consistent with Augustinian theology. The book has been commended for its "unrivalled subtlety and precision."[19] Bradwardine presented God, in eternity, willing all that comes to pass. In all this, he argued, God is not the author of evil.

Historical theologian Jaroslav Pelikan assesses the book's strong Augustinian stance:

> As is not surprising in an author whose chief theological work bore the title *The Cause of God Against the Pelagians*, Bradwardine sought to align himself unequivocally on Augustine's side in the conflict over grace. He marshaled an array of quotations on the priority of grace from Augustine's books, not only from the books specifically directed against Pelagius but from other treatises also, as well as from the *Sentences* of Prosper of Aquitaine. He saw Augustine as one who had "uniquely imitated the apostle" Paul by moving from a hostility toward the doctrine of divine grace to a position as "a herald of grace and a magnificent and vigorous champion of grace."[20]

# BRADWARDINE'S THEOLOGY

Bradwardine was one of the two most influential Augustinians in the first half of the fourteenth century, along with Gregory of Rimini (ca. 1300–1358).[21] He studied and expounded the teachings of Augustine, with his strong emphasis on predestination. By doing so, Bradwardine "revived a rigid Augustinian view, stressing predestination as basic to an ordered universe."[22] As he battled the Pelagianism of the day, his high Augustinianism had an enormous influence.

**Doctrine in Focus:**
DIVINE SOVEREIGNTY

Bradwardine asserted a high view of God's sovereignty as the foundation of his theology. He described God with these words: "God is omnipotent, [the] completely free Lord of His whole creation, whose will alone is the most righteous law for all creation."[23] He saw God as having absolute authority over His creation. He alone is free to act as He pleases.

This lofty view of God is seen most clearly in Bradwardine's strong defense of God's sovereignty in salvation. Again and again Bradwardine insisted that God has every right to administer His grace to His creatures as He sees fit. Following the words quoted above, he cites Romans 9:21 as he writes: "If

[God] should eternally punish the innocent, particularly since He does it for the perfection of the universe, for the profit of others, and for the honor of God Himself, who would presume to dispute with Him, to contradict Him, or ask, 'Why do you do this?' I firmly believe, no one! 'Has the potter no right over the clay to make of the same lump one vessel for honor and another for menial use'?"[24] In Bradwardine's view, God is free to save or judge, and no man has the right to question Him.

Bradwardine knew that he would suffer for teaching this high view of divine sovereignty. He says, "I burn with ardour for God's cause, knowing that I thrust my hand into a terrible flame, for I am not unaware how the pestilential Pelagians are wont to harass an agitated mind with tumult and abuse, and how they will strive to tear this small treatise with their savage teeth."[25] The world does not enjoy hearing that God is sovereign, but Bradwardine would not compromise this essential doctrine.

## Doctrine in Focus:
### RADICAL DEPRAVITY

Bradwardine did not emphasize the doctrine of original sin.[26] This is a surprising omission given the influence of Augustine on his thinking. Regarding Bradwardine's theology, Alister McGrath notes that the fall is "not viewed as a watershed in the economy of salvation."[27] However, this does not mean Bradwardine did not believe in human depravity. His opposition to Pelagianism, with its emphasis on man's ability to contribute to his salvation, shows that Bradwardine understood the plight of the human race. Rudolph Heinze states: "Bradwardine . . . held a bleaker view of human potential than [his] opponents. [He] believed that without God's direct help humans were totally lost in their sin and could not even respond to God."[28] Peter Lillback adds, "Bradwardine's commitment to a renewed Augustinianism is seen in his efforts to refute the capability of human nature to merit grace."[29] Though he may not have emphasized depravity, he nevertheless affirmed it.

Bradwardine agreed with Augustine's comments on John 1:12–13. He writes: "And Augustine, commenting on John asks, 'Why were all born in sin?' That we are children of Adam implies damnation by necessity. But to be children of Christ is man's act through His will and through grace, since men are not forced to become children of Christ. Even though they did not choose to be born children of Adam, all of them are sinners in the true sense of the word. All those who are children of Christ are justified and are just, not because of themselves but because of Christ."[30] Bradwardine affirmed that all men are "children of Adam" and therefore under divine condemnation.

**Doctrine in Focus:**

## Sovereign Election

Bradwardine came to a strong predestinarian position through his reading of Scripture and the writings of Augustine, and through his doctrine of divine omnipotence.[31] In *The Cause of God*, he compiled a large list of quotes on the priority of grace from Augustine's books.[32] Defending his reliance on Augustine's teachings, Bradwardine asked rhetorically, "On this issue who among all authors after Holy Scripture is more reliable than Augustine?"[33] It is indisputable that Bradwardine was strongly committed to sovereign grace, just as Augustine was.

Sovereign election is taught throughout the Bible, Bradwardine said. He writes: "Authorities on divine election obviously introduce predestination into both testaments with many similar references. This is also universally confessed by all teachers, yes also equally by Catholics, learned and unlearned."[34] He went on to cite many biblical references to election, including Exodus 32:31–32; Psalms 68:29; 138:16; Daniel 12:1; Romans 1:4, 8; Ephesians 1:4; Matthew 20:20–23, 25; and Acts 10 and 13.[35] Even those with little training in the Scriptures, he maintained, can see the prominent place of sovereign election in the Bible.

Bradwardine straightforwardly declared that God has elected some to receive salvation. He writes: "Also, that all to be saved or condemned, rewarded or punished in whatever degree, He willed from all eternity to be saved or condemned; and likewise to be rewarded or punished in precisely the same degree; and this by no means through His conditional or underdetermined will, but by His absolute and determined will, just as He wills at the present or final judgment, or will do hereafter."[36] Election is a divine choice made in eternity past. It is not conditional but is absolute. By God's eternal choice, men's destinies are "determined" for all time.

Bradwardine held that predestination and foreknowledge are virtually identical. He writes, "To arrange [God's] future works in His infallible and immutable foreknowledge is nothing other than to predestinate."[37] In other words, he flatly refused the notion that foreknowledge is mere foresight on the part of God. In doing so, he rejected the view that foreknowledge is God's looking into the future to see what men will do in regard to Christ. Bradwardine understood that, in biblical terms, foreknowledge is equivalent to foreordination.

Pelikan confirms that Bradwardine equated predestination with foreknowledge. Quoting Heiko Oberman in regard to motifs in Bradwardine's theology, Pelikan writes:

> Bradwardine sometimes made predestination and the foreknowledge of God identical. . . . Another passage from Augustine served as the basis for teaching, on the authority of the biblical statement that "before the universe was created it was known to Him," that the divine foreknowledge of things was the cause of their coming into being. Bradwardine's treatment of Esau and Jacob as types of predestination to salvation and reprobation owed its inspiration to Augustine's exegesis of the biblical words, "Jacob have I loved, but Esau have I hated." All of this was directed against the neo-Pelagians and was intended to reinforce "the main motif of his doctrine of predestination: predestination does not happen on account of human works, but on account of the gracious will of God," together with its corollary and "the leitmotif in Bradwardine's doctrine of God: the absolute sovereignty of God."[38]

With these words, Bradwardine stood firmly by the authority of God in the distribution of His grace.

Regarding Bradwardine's conviction about the absolute rights of God over mankind, Lillback comments, "For Bradwardine, then, the promise of God's grace is only for the vessels of honor predestinated to such honor by the Potter."[39] In simple terms, Bradwardine believed only the elect are saved. Further, nothing man does influences God's electing decree. Lillback sums up Bradwardine's view succinctly: "God's decree of election has no point of reference with human activity."[40]

**Doctrine in Focus:**
IRRESISTIBLE CALL

Bradwardine admitted that he once held to the Pelagian idea of human ability. He writes:

Idle and a fool in God's wisdom, I was misled by an unorthodox error
at a time when I was still pursuing philosophical studies. Sometimes
I went to listen to the theologians discussing this matter [of Grace
and free will], and the school of Pelagius seemed to me nearest truth.
. . . In the philosophical faculty I seldom heard a reference to Grace,
except for some ambiguous remarks. What I heard day in and day
out was that we are masters of our own free acts, that ours are the
choice to act well or badly, to have virtues or sins and much more
along this line.[41]

In time, however, Bradwardine came to see that fallen man has no moral
ability and therefore cannot save himself. He finally understood that salvation
is of God, from first to last. He writes:

And when I heard now and then in Church a passage read from
the apostles which exalted grace and humbled free will, such as, for
instance, that word in Romans 9:16, *"Therefore it is not in him that
wills, nor in him that runs, but in God that shows mercy,"* I had no lik-
ing for such teaching, for towards grace I was still graceless . . . but
afterwards, and before I had become a student of theology, the truth
before mentioned struck upon me like a beam of grace. It seemed to
me as if I beheld in the distance, under a transparent image of truth,
the grace of God as it is prevenient both in time and nature to all good
works—that is to say, the gracious will of God which precedently
wills that he who merits salvation shall be saved, and precedently
works this merit in him—God in truth, being in all movements the
primary Mover.[42]

Armed with this new, biblical understanding, Bradwardine was quick to
oppose the Pelagians. He says, "[It is the] damnable error of the Pelagians to
apportion faith or grace, with a reference to its beginning in growth, namely
by assigning the former to God, and a latter to us, when in fact the totality
of faith and grace is to be wholly assigning to God."[43] Bradwardine clearly
understood the biblical teaching on man's ability and the cause of salvation.

No one, Bradwardine said, can make himself a son of God by his own
efforts. Only the elect will be adopted. He says: "Now when they bring forward
the quotation from the Gospel of John, 'He gave them power to become sons

of God,' they seemed to wish to conclude from this that some became, or can become the elect sons of God in the course of their life. . . . He did not say, 'He gave them power to make themselves sons of God,' but 'to be made sons of God.' But by whom? Not by themselves. Not out of their own will. . . . Therefore they do not make themselves sons of God. God does this."[44] God's election is the determining factor in salvation.

Bradwardine asserted that God must act in grace on man before any individual can act in faith toward Him. He writes, "When we act we are the ones who act, but He acts so that we may act."[45] God must work on the mind and heart before anyone who is spiritually dead can believe in Christ. Thus, the will of God is the determining cause in regeneration. Bradwardine adds, "The will of God is the efficient cause of anything whatever that is done."[46] Elsewhere he writes, "In every action of the created will God's will is the necessary co-effector."[47] In sum, God's will determines what man's will chooses.

**Doctrine in Focus:**
## PRESERVING GRACE

Bradwardine was fully convinced that those who enter into salvation by faith will never fall from grace. He affirms, "No one can lose his salvation because it is not based on the unchanging winds of human decision but founded upon the bedrock of the eternal will of God."[48] The believer's eternal security, he held, rests on the eternal will of God in salvation. Man cannot negate what God chose to bring about in eternity past.

Moreover, Bradwardine recognized sovereign grace as the undivided effort by God to save His elect. Pelikan writes, "Bradwardine . . . identified the divine assistance of grace, together with justification, merit, perseverance to the end, and eternal blessedness, all as effects of predestination; and he took all of these to be implied in Augustine's definition of predestination as 'the preparation of grace.'"[49] The God who elects and justifies is the One who grants perseverance to the end. Because this is so, sovereign grace irrevocably leads to eternal blessedness. From everlasting to everlasting, salvation is all of grace.

**Doctrine in Focus:**
## DIVINE REPROBATION

Just as God's will is the determinative factor in the eternal destination of the elect, so it is for the reprobate, Bradwardine contended. He writes: "Neither prayers nor any merits, whether good or bad, can turn or change the divine will in the least, either this way or that; but whatever is to be saved or damned, rewarded or punished, in whatever degree, this He willed from eternity to be saved or damned."[50] What God willed from eternity past, whether the salvation or damnation of individuals, is what comes to pass.

Echoing this thought, Bradwardine said that nothing in man can influence God's choice. He writes: "Can it be possible for man's own capacity to be the cause of predestination or reprobation when sometimes, between two of equal capacity, one is chosen and one is abandoned or, at other times, the one of lesser capacity is chosen while the one of the greater is abandoned?"[51] The implied answer to this rhetorical question is no. Man can never be the cause of predestination to salvation or of reprobation to damnation. Such decisions belong to God.

Additionally, Bradwardine concluded that the ultimate reason for reprobation was not in Adam's sin. Rather, it lies with God and the sin of each individual. He says: "It is by no means clear that if Adam had not sinned no one would have been reprobated. It seems possible that even if Adam had not sinned, all his descendents would not necessarily have been made sinless and confirmed until the end. Rather, they would have the freedom to choose or accept good or evil. . . . Therefore, the sin of Adam is not the primary cause of reprobation, but rather, as cited above, if Adam had not sinned, God would have ordained differently."[52] God is sovereign, but man is responsible.

Bradwardine taught that the nonelect remain entirely responsible for their sinful choices. He writes, "In the case of what is good, He is said especially to foreknow and to predestine it; in the case of what is wicked, He brings about only that they exist, not that they are evil."[53] Though God is absolutely sovereign, man remains accountable for his sins. God does not cause anyone to sin, but He passes over some of those who sin and leaves them to face His wrath.

## PASSING ON A LEGACY

Bradwardine served a strategic role in church history. His life paved the way for the resurgence of the doctrine of predestination in the years leading up to the Reformation.[54] He helped shape the convictions of John Wycliffe, the man considered to be the first Pre-Reformer. Justo L. González notes, "On the doctrine of predestination, Wycliffe seems to have read Augustine through the eyes of Bradwardine."[55] Thus, the reformational preaching of Wycliffe can be directly traced back to Bradwardine, who received his teaching from

Augustine. Wycliffe directly influenced John Hus, who impacted Martin Luther, who launched the Reformation. In this sense, Bradwardine has been regarded as a forerunner of the Reformation.[56] Adolf von Harnack, church historian, writes: "Bradwardine . . . placed the *entire* Augustine, together with the predestination doctrine, in strong opposition to the Pelagian tendency of the period. On him Wyclif was dependent as a theologian, and as Huss took all his theological thoughts from Wyclif, and introduced them into Bohemia and Germany, Bradwardine is really to be signalized as the theologian who gave the impulse to the Augustinian reactions that accompanied the history of the Church till the time of Staupitz and Luther, and that prepared the way for the Reformation."[57] Some have even argued that Bradwardine's work influenced Calvin himself.[58]

There *is* a long line of godly men that spans the centuries. From Augustine in the fifth century, through Bradwardine in the fourteenth, to Wycliffe in the fourteenth, to Hus in the fifteenth, and to Luther in the sixteenth, there is a clear sequential effect. When Wycliffe and Hus defined the church as the congregation of the predestined, they were drawing from Augustine by way of Bradwardine. Such is the powerful influence of one individual upon another.

As we stand for "the cause of God" in the twenty-first century, may this sequence continue through our lives to future generations. Whose influence from the past is shaping your convictions? Whom from days long ago are you reading? How is your life being impacted? How is your mind being renewed? And, in turn, whom will you influence?

NOTES

1  Thomas Bradwardine, *The Cause of God*, 2.20, cited in Jaroslav Jan Pelikan, *The Christian Tradition, Vol. 4: Reformation of Church and Dogma (1300–1700)* (Chicago: University of Chicago Press, 1983), 18.

2  Bradwardine, *The Cause of God Against the Pelagians*, 1.9, cited in Pelikan, *The Christian Tradition, Vol. 4*, 25.

3  Philip Schaff and David S. Schaff, *History of the Christian Church, Vol. V: The Middle Ages: From Gregory VII to Boniface VIII, 1049–1294* (1907; repr., Grand Rapids: Eerdmans, 1984), 553, 563.

4  Schaff and Schaff, *History of the Christian Church, Vol. V*, 575.

5  Schaff and Schaff, *History of the Christian Church, Vol. V*, 683.

6  J. V. Fesko, *Diversity within the Reformed Tradition: Supra- and Infralapsarianism in Calvin, Dort, and Westminster* (Greenville, S.C.: Reformed Academic Press, 2001), 40.

7   "Thomas Bradwardine," in *The Oxford Dictionary of the Christian Church*, 3rd Ed., ed. E. A. Livingstone (1957; repr., Oxford: Oxford University Press, 1997), 231.

8   Paul Helm, "Thomas Bradwardine," in *New Dictionary of Theology*, eds. Sinclair B. Ferguson, David F. Wright, and J. I. Packer (Downers Grove, Ill.: InterVarsity, 1988), 109.

9   "Thomas Bradwardine," in *The Oxford Dictionary of the Christian Church*, 231.

10  J. H. Merle d'Aubigné, *The Reformation in England, Vol. 1* (Edinburgh: Banner of Truth, 1994), 76.

11  D'Aubigné, *The Reformation in England, Vol. 1*, 76.

12  Bradwardine, *The Cause of God Against the Pelagians*, cited in D'Aubigné, *The Reformation in England, Vol. 1*, 76.

13  D'Aubigné, *The Reformation in England, Vol. 1*, 76.

14  D'Aubigné, *The Reformation in England, Vol. 1*, 76.

15  D'Aubigné, *The Reformation in England, Vol. 1*, 76.

16  Schaff and Schaff, *History of the Christian Church, Vol. V*, 558.

17  "Thomas Bradwardine," in *Cyclopedia of Biblical, Theological, and Ecclesiastical Literature, Vol. I*, eds. John McClintock and James Strong (Grand Rapids: Baker, 1981), 873.

18  D'Aubigné, *The Reformation in England, Vol 1*, 76.

19  Helm, "Thomas Bradwardine," in *New Dictionary of Theology*, 109.

20  Pelikan, *The Christian Tradition, Vol. 4*, 18.

21  Pelikan, *The Christian Tradition, Vol. 4*, 18.

22  Dirk Jellema, "Predestination," in *New International Dictionary of the Christian Church*, gen. ed. J. D. Douglas (Grand Rapids: Zondervan, 1978), 798.

23  Bradwardine, *The Cause of God Against the Pelagians*, 1.62, cited in Fesko, *Diversity within the Reformed Tradition*, 53–54.

24  Bradwardine, *The Cause of God Against the Pelagians*, 1.62, cited in Fesko, *Diversity within the Reformed Tradition*, 53–54.

25  Bradwardine, *The Cause of God Against the Pelagians*, preface (i), cited in Gordon Leff, *Bradwardine and the Pelagians* (Cambridge: Cambridge University Press, 1957), 14.

26  Fesko, *Diversity within the Reformed Tradition*, 42.

27  Alister McGrath, *The Intellectual Origins of the European Reformation* (Oxford: Basil Blackwell, 1987), 91.

28  Rudolph W. Heinze, *Reform and Conflict: From the Medieval World to the Wars of Religion, A.D. 1350–1648* (Grand Rapids: Baker, 2005), 37.

29  Peter A. Lillback, *The Binding of God* (Grand Rapids: Baker Academic, 2001), 51.

30  Bradwardine, *The Cause of God Against the Pelagians*, in Lillback, *The Binding of God*, 51.

31  McGrath, *The Intellectual Origins of the European Reformation*, 91.

32  Bradwardine, *The Cause of God Against the Pelagians*, 1.23, cited in Pelikan, *The Christian Tradition, Vol. 4*, 18.

33  Bradwardine, *The Cause of God Against the Pelagians*, 2.31, cited in Pelikan, *The Christian Tradition, Vol. 4*, 18.

34  Bradwardine, *The Cause of God Against the Pelagians*, 1.45, cited in Fesko, *Diversity within the Reformed Tradition*, 43–44.

35  Fesko, *Diversity within the Reformed Tradition*, 43.

36  Bradwardine, *The Cause of God Against the Pelagians*, 1.23, cited in Fesko, *Diversity within the Reformed Tradition*, 42.

37 Bradwardine, *The Cause of God Against the Pelagians*, 2.14, cited in Pelikan, *The Christian Tradition, Vol. 4*, 31.

38 Pelikan, *The Christian Tradition, Vol. 4*, 31–32.

39 Lillback, *The Binding of God*, 53.

40 Lillback, *The Binding of God*, 52.

41 Bradwardine, *The Cause of God Against the Pelagians*, in *Forerunner of the Reformation: The Shape of Late Medieval Thought*, ed. Heiko Oberman, trans. Paul L. Nyhus (London: Lutterworth, 1967), 135.

42 Bradwardine, *The Cause of God Against the Pelagians*, 1.85, cited in Gordon Leff, *Bradwardine and the Pelagians: A Study of His 'De Causa Dei' and its Opponent* (Oxford: Cambridge University Press, 2009), 5:14.

43 Bradwardine, *The Cause of God Against the Pelagians*, 1.46, cited in Fesko, *Diversity within the Reformed Tradition*, 47.

44 Bradwardine, *The Cause of God Against the Pelagians*, 1.54, cited in Fesko, *Diversity within the Reformed Tradition*, 43.

45 Bradwardine, *The Cause of God Against the Pelagians*, 2.20, cited in Pelikan, *The Christian Tradition, Vol. 4*, 18.

46 Bradwardine, *The Cause of God Against the Pelagians*, 1.9, cited in Pelikan, *The Christian Tradition, Vol. 4*, 25.

47 Bradwardine, *The Cause of God Against the Pelagians*, 1.3–4, cited in Gordon Leff, "Thomas Bradwardine's De Causa Dei," *Journal of Ecclesiastical History* 7 (1956): 22.

48 Bradwardine, cited in Heiko A. Oberman, *Bradwardine, Archbishop Thomas Bradwardine, A Fourteenth Century Augustinian: A Study of His Theology In Its Historical Context* (Utrecht: Drukkerijen en Uitgevers-Maatschappj v/h Kemink & Zoon N.V., 1957), 115, as cited in Fesko, *Diversity within the Reformed Tradition*, 43.

49 Pelikan, *The Christian Tradition, Vol. 4*, 31.

50 Bradwardine, *The Cause of God Against the Pelagians*, 1.23, cited in Pelikan, *The Christian Tradition, Vol. 4*, 26.

51 Bradwardine, *The Cause of God Against the Pelagians*, 153, cited in Fesko, *Diversity within the Reformed Tradition*, 44.

52 Bradwardine, *The Cause of God Against the Pelagians*, 1.60, cited in Fesko, *Diversity within the Reformed Tradition*, 45.

53 Bradwardine, *The Cause of God Against the Pelagians*, 1.45, cited in Fesko, *Diversity within the Reformed Tradition*, 46.

54 R. E. D. Clark, "Thomas Bradwardine," in *New International Dictionary of the Christian Church*, 151.

55 Justo L. González, *A History of Christian Thought, Vol. 2: From Augustine to the Eve of the Reformation* (Nashville: Abingdon, 1971), 326.

56 "Thomas Bradwardine," in *Cyclopedia of Biblical, Theological, and Ecclesiastical Literature, Vol. I*, 873.

57 Adolf von Harnack, *History of Dogma, Vol. 6* (Eugene, Ore.: Wipf and Stock, 1997), 169–170.

58 Anthony N. S. Lane, *John Calvin: Student of the Church Fathers* (Grand Rapids: Baker, 1999), 17, 24.

# CHAPTER SEVENTEEN
## STUDY QUESTIONS

1. Explain the significance of the rise of universities during the twelfth century on the development of Western thought. How did the universities create an environment in which sovereign grace thought would develop?

2. Describe the lingering effects of Pelagianism and Semi-Pelagianism on the church in the twelfth century. How has such man-centered thinking continued to plague the church?

3. Comment on the Pelagianism that Bradwardine witnessed at Merton College. How did such teaching ultimately shape his theological thinking? Did it drive him closer to the truth or away from it? How are we to react to such theological deviations in our day?

4. Describe the centrality of the Word of God in Bradwardine's thinking. Why is this crucial in the formation of doctrinal convictions? How has Scripture helped you to better understand the doctrines of salvation? What book of the Bible has been most influential in shaping your theological thinking about sovereign grace?

5. How did Bradwardine become known as *Doctor Profundus*? What place should polemics have in the role of the Christian faith? How should you earnestly contend for the faith in this day?

6. What was the bedrock of Bradwardine's theology? Describe the freedom of God to do as He pleases. Expand on the biblical metaphor that God is the Potter and we are the clay.

7. Did Bradwardine believe that God merely foresees and chooses those who will choose Him? Or does sovereign election precede and lead to saving faith? Cite verses that teach your understanding of Scripture regarding this point.

8. Where did Bradwardine begin his theological journey regarding sovereign grace? Describe the transformation by which he was redirected from Pelagianism to an Augustinian view of sovereign election and monergistic regeneration. What is your understanding of Scripture regarding these truths?

*We are predestined, that we may obtain divine acceptance, and become holy; having received that grace through Christ's taking human nature, whereby we are rendered finally pleasing to God. And it appears that this grace, which is called the grace of predestination, with the charity of final perseverance, cannot by any means fail.*[1]

–John Wycliffe

# Chapter Eighteen

# MORNING STAR OF THE REFORMATION

## ENGLISH PRE-REFORMER: JOHN WYCLIFFE

W herever there is an increased knowledge of biblical truth, the doctrines of grace are soon to follow. This is to say, the more people are immersed in the Bible, the more likely they are to grasp the awe-inspiring profundities of God's sovereignty in salvation. Naturally, open access to the Bible in one's own language is instrumental in the advancement of such doctrinal depth.

The first steps toward such ready access to biblical truth in England occurred in the fourteenth century. First, the English language came into general use. Prior to this time, the wealthy of England spoke French and used English only when addressing inferiors. But in 1362, English replaced French as the language of the courts. At the same time, the English people began to escape the illiteracy that had held back much of the populace. Grammar schools sprang up and a focus on academics increased. By this time, Oxford University had become arguably the leading university in Europe. With such changes, the English-speaking peoples were ready as never before for the Bible in their own tongue.

Sadly, the primary obstacle to such access was the Roman Catholic Church. Catholicism dominated life in medieval Europe, and the leadership in Rome did not want to see the Bible translated into vernacular languages lest its interpretations be challenged from below. Furthermore, friars had become corrupt and bishops had become "men of the world." Thus, the unvarnished truths of Scripture were not taught. Far from providing hope and light, the medieval pulpit was shallow, filled with stories, myths, fables, and traditions, with few if any biblical references. In the minds of listeners, there was little difference between Bible narratives and fairy tales. The people were kept in a state of confusion, exploitation, and, worse, lostness.

Gregory of Rimini, a Parisian philosopher-theologian of the Middle Ages, recounts the man-centered teaching that flowed from the churches during this time: "It is the opinion of many moderns that man, by his natural powers alone, with the general concurrence of God, can perform a morally good act in the present state of fallen nature, as for example to love God above all things, to be sorry for and to detest one's sins. . . . They depart from the definitions of the church and favor the condemned error of Pelagius."[2] In short, many in the medieval church held that salvation was a cooperative effort, a combination of God's grace and human free will. Michael Horton comments, "The popular medieval phrase was, 'God will not deny His grace to those who do what they can.'"[3] The modern idea that "God helps those who help themselves" was already in vogue.

John Foxe, author of *Foxe's Christian Book of Martyrs*, further describes the spiritual darkness of those days:

> At this time Christianity was in a sad state. Although everyone knew the name of Christ, few if any understood His doctrine. . . . Instead, the Church was solely concerned with outward ceremony and human traditions. People spent their entire lives heaping up one ceremony after another in hopes of salvation, not knowing it was theirs for the asking. Simple, uneducated people who had no knowledge of Scripture were content to know only what their pastors told them, and these pastors took care to only teach what came from Rome—most of which was for the profit of their own orders, not for the glory of Christ.[4]

Amid this spiritual darkness, some courageous men began to push for reform. These like-minded stalwarts have become known to history as the Pre-Reformers.

## PRE-REFORMERS

In the fourteenth century, the rebirth of classical culture known as the Renaissance was beginning to flower. At its core, the Renaissance emphasized confidence in the powers of man's intellect. In this context, humanism emerged as an intellectual movement in reaction to the traditional academic curriculum of the Scholastic period. Humanism signaled a new approach to education, one built on the study of languages, history, rhetoric, philosophy, poetry, and ethics. Drawing on the ideals of the Greco-Roman civilization, the humanists sought cultural, intellectual, and sociopolitical advancements across Europe.

It was in the soil of this intellectual movement that the seed of church reform was planted by valiant spiritual leaders who were strongly committed to the Word of God. These heroic men were known as "the Forerunners of the Reformation" or simply the Pre-Reformers. Like the prophets of old, these Pre-Reformers proclaimed their message with divine thunder, for they were committed to the authority of God's Word in opposition to the traditions of the Roman Catholic Church. Alister McGrath notes that there was an increasing conviction in this time that Scripture was "the sole material base of Christian theology."[5] There was a deepening certainty that "Scripture contained all that is necessary for salvation."[6] With this growing commitment to *sola Scriptura*, it was inevitable that the doctrines of grace would soon receive new attention. Indeed, the Pre-Reformers helped bring about an Augustinian resurgence that paved the way for the Reformation.

The most notable of these leaders were Gregory of Rimini (ca. 1300–1358), John Wycliffe (ca. 1330–1384), John Hus (ca. 1372–1415), and Girolamo Savonarola (1452–1492). Among these men, Wycliffe had such a great influence on the Reformation, which arose about a century after his death, he has been called the first Reformer[7] and, more famously, "the Morning Star of the Reformation."[8] By his teachings and by his challenge to the church's opposition to translation of the Bible into the English language, he did much to advance the understanding of the doctrines of grace in England and across the European continent.

# JOHN WYCLIFFE

Wycliffe was an English scholar and theologian who did more to change the course of his nation's history than perhaps any other person.[9] He was the leading scholar of his time,[10] for which he is known as the Evangelical Doctor.[11] He was largely responsible for the early reputation of Oxford, where he studied and taught for almost forty years.[12] He possessed a brilliant mind, undaunted courage, and a silver tongue.[13] He was also gifted with great skill with the pen.[14] Because of his work of spreading the gospel in England, Wycliffe was called the fifth evangelist.[15] Historian J. H. Merle d'Aubigné writes that he was "the greatest of the English Reformers: he was in truth the first Reformer of Christendom. . . . If Luther and Calvin are the fathers of the Reformation, Wycliffe is its grandfather."[16] Wycliffe was the leading figure of his generation for the evangelical cause and for the doctrines of grace.

Wycliffe was born into a propertied English family of some means.[17] They owned land near Richmond in Yorkshire, where Wycliffe was raised.[18] The family surname is thought to have been originally Wye-cliffe, referring to a rocky cliff on the banks of the Tees River, eleven miles north of Richmond in North Yorks.[19] Little is known about Wycliffe's early years other than that he lived in a secluded country area and probably was educated by a village priest.[20] In 1342, Wycliffe's family village came under the lordship of John of Gaunt, the duke of Lancaster. John was the third son of the future King Edward III. In later years, when Wycliffe rose to national prominence, this nobleman became his patron and protector.

## EDUCATED AT OXFORD

Wycliffe left home for Oxford University in 1346, when he was about sixteen years of age. This was the common age for entry into the university system. Oxford had been established more than a century prior to his arrival, in 1167, and had become one of the leading universities of Europe. It was a demanding institution; it was especially known for its oral examinations, which were intended to develop the students' skills in debate. There were six colleges in Oxford, and Wycliffe became a student at Balliol College.

The following year, 1347, the Black Plague swept through Europe. An astonishing one-third of the population was killed. Within a year, the plague reached England, where one hundred thousand people died in London alone. In Wycliffe's native country, more than two-thirds of the population died. The devastation of the plague left a deep impression on young Wycliffe, confronting him with the shortness of life and the certainty of death. This led to his conversion to Jesus Christ while attending Balliol.

In 1356, Wycliffe transferred to Merton College at Oxford, which was distinguished by two of its former professors, William of Ockham and John Duns Scotus. Also, the revered Thomas Bradwardine, a noted theologian and scholar, and a strong proponent of the doctrines of sovereign grace, had taught there.

## Teaching and Further Study

After earning a bachelor's degree from Merton, Wycliffe resumed his studies at Balliol in 1360, first as a fellow and then as a master (professor). Wycliffe developed into an accomplished professor of philosophy, mastering the late Scholastic tradition.[21] He so distinguished himself that King Edward III took notice. Wycliffe had written a pamphlet in which he argued that the pope had no right to require tribute from the king and the church. The king made Wycliffe one of his chaplains, and Wycliffe appeared before Parliament to argue that the pope did not possess authority over the church in England or the English government. In response to Wycliffe's arguments, Parliament refused tribute to the pope.

Wycliffe received his bachelor of divinity degree in 1369. After a brief stay at New Canterbury Hall as warden, Wycliffe went to Queen's College. He was soon recognized as the leading theologian and philosopher in Europe. As a result, when John of Gaunt assumed a position of power in 1371 as King of Castille, he sought Wycliffe's help in persuading Parliament in matters of national importance.

After sixteen years of preparation, Wycliffe received the doctorate of theology in 1372. During this year, Pope Gregory XI taxed the English clergy, which Edward III forbade. To this point, Wycliffe had not entered into any conflict with Rome. But that was soon to change.

## Conflict with Rome

Wycliffe represented the king of England at a meeting with papal officers in Bruges, France, in 1374. His task was to negotiate peace with France while seeking to influence the pope's appointments in England. Upon his return to England, Wycliffe began to speak out against the abuses he saw in the church. Specifically, he questioned abuses of power by the pope. Wycliffe wrote a tract attacking the pope as the Antichrist. As a result, he was summoned to London to answer charges of heresy in 1377. He was accompanied by John of Gaunt, who went to protect him from the ecclesiastical authorities. He maintained that the Bible is the sole criterion of doctrine and no ecclesiastical council can add to its teaching. Further, he stated that the authority of the pope has no basis in Scripture.

That same year, 1377, an enraged Pope Gregory XI issued a bull (decree) against Wycliffe. It cited nineteen errors from his writings in *On Civil Dominion*. The pope called Wycliffe "the master of errors" and demanded that he be handed over to Rome. Wycliffe consented to a temporary house arrest, but he refused to appear in London again. Instead, he agreed to stand trial before the archbishop of Canterbury in Lambeth, where he suffered only a reprimand.

By 1378, Wycliffe returned to Oxford, where he began to speak out as a doctrinal reformer. Specifically, Wycliffe began to attack the Roman doctrine of transubstantiation, the false belief that the bread and wine in the Eucharist miraculously change into the body and blood of Christ when blessed by the priest. Wycliffe called this doctrine religious superstition. He sought to overthrow this teaching, which he regarded as the heart of the clergy's claim to superiority. But this attack against the Mass aroused great opposition. Even the king withdrew his support from Wycliffe, and the University of Oxford followed suit. However, Wycliffe remained true to the Scriptures, even though he had the support of only a small group of scholars.

## WYCLIFFE'S VIEWS CONDEMNED

Because of the controversy, the English Parliament insisted that the archbishop of Canterbury convene a special council to examine Wycliffe's doctrine. The council condemned Wycliffe and ordered him to appear before the pope. But Wycliffe refused to go and escaped persecution by withdrawing to Lutterworth in Leicestershire. There, in isolation, he revised his works and produced a series of pamphlets attacking his enemies.

During this time, Wycliffe was putting the finishing touches on his translation of the Bible into English. This heroic effort was the result of his deep convictions about the divine inspiration of Scripture and the need of the English people to read it in their native tongue. Wycliffe said: "It is impossible for any part of the Holy Scripture to be wrong. In Holy Scripture is all the truth. One part of Scripture explains another."[22] Further, Wycliffe said the Bible is superior to all other books because its Author is Christ: "As the person of one author is to another, so is the merit of one book compared to another; now it is a doctrine of the faith that Christ is infinitely superior to every other man, and therefore His book, or Holy Scripture, which is His law, stands in a similar relation to every other writing which can be named."[23]

Wycliffe spent the last two years of his life as the rector at Lutterworth. Much of his time was spent writing. In 1382, he was summoned to appear in Rome to give an account for his doctrine, but a stroke left him partly immobilized and unable to travel. Two years later, in 1384, he suffered a second, more severe stroke. He died on December 31, 1384.

# WYCLIFFE'S WRITINGS

Wycliffe was a prolific author of extensive theological works. Among his books are *Summa de Ente* ("Summa on Being," ca. 1365–1372), *De Civili Dominio* ("On Civil Dominion," 1375–1376), *De Ecclesia* ("On the Church"), *De Veritate Sacrae Scripturae* ("On the Truth of Sacred Scripture"), *De Potestate Papae* ("On the Power of the Pope," 1377–1378), *Confessio* ("Confession," 1381), and *De Apostasia* ("On Apostasy," ca. 1382).

## ON CIVIL DOMINION

In *De Civili Dominio*, Wycliffe insisted that if clergymen were not in a state of grace, they could have their endowments removed from them by the civil power. By taking this position, Wycliffe hoped to reform the Roman church by stripping it of its property, which he believed was a source of its corruption.[24] God gave property to the church, he said, but its leaders were not the owners of that property, only stewards. If these leaders failed to fulfill their spiritual duties, Wycliffe argued, the civil authorities had the right to take the property from them and redistribute it to others who would serve God properly. The rich nobles, including John of Gaunt, supported Wycliffe in this. However, the last portion of this book caused Pope Gregory XI to condemn Wycliffe, as it directly challenged the authority of the pope's office.[25]

## THE PASTORAL OFFICE

In this work, Wycliffe addressed the duties of the faithful minister, such as preaching. He argued from the ministry of Jesus that preaching is the minister's highest service. The preaching of the Word, he said, is more important than even administering the sacraments, for when the Word is preached, the church grows. Wycliffe said: "A priest should live holily, in prayer, in desires and thought, in godly conversation and honest teaching, having God's commandments and His Gospel ever on his lips. And let his deeds be so righteous that no man may be able with cause to find fault with them, and so open his acts that he may be a true book to all sinful and wicked men to serve God. For the example of a good life stirreth men more than true preaching with only the naked word."[26]

## WYCLIFFE'S BIBLE

Wycliffe's greatest work proved to be his translation of the Bible into English. The Roman Catholic Church used Jerome's Latin Vulgate and refused to translate it into the language of the people. Wycliffe undertook this massive effort so that the English people could read the Bible for themselves. Wycliffe did not know the biblical languages and was forced to translate from the Latin version. In all probability, he received help in this ambitious project. It is possible that his disciples did the work, though he inspired the project.

Two versions of the English Bible were associated with Wycliffe. The earlier Wycliffe version was begun about 1383 or 1384 and was a literal rendering of the Latin Vulgate. The later Wycliffe version was a thorough revision of the earlier one with idiomatic English. It was produced a few years after Wycliffe's death by his close colleague John Purvey (ca. 1353–ca. 1428) between 1388 and 1395.

Not all were pleased to see an English translation appear. The angry complaint of Knighton, a canon of Leicester, is as follows:

> Christ delivered his gospel to the clergy and doctors of the church, that they might administer to the laity and to weaker persons, according to the state of the times, and the wants of man. But this master John Wickliffe translated it out of Latin into English, and thus laid it more open to the laity, and to women who can read, than it formerly had been to the most learned of the clergy, even to those of them who had the best understanding. . . . And in this way the gospel pearl is cast abroad, and trodden under foot of swine, and that which was before precious both to clergy and laity, is rendered as it were the common jest in both! The jewel of the church is turned into this sport of the people, and what was hitherto the principal gift of the clergy and divines, is made for ever common.[27]

However, the prologue to the later version defended the right of the common people to have access to God's Word in a translation they could understand,[28] based on "the same assertion 'that every layman may in every place preach and teach the gospel' for 'every good man, though he be unlearned, is a priest.'"[29]

## WYCLIFFE'S THEOLOGY

Wycliffe was sound in the gospel in all its parts. It has been said of Wycliffe, "In an age when all sides of the debate equated novelty with heresy, Wycliffe presented some very old ideas in new, even radical, ways."[30] These ancient truths, Wycliffe said, were centered in the evangelical gospel, by which "we may enter into that straight gate, as Christ our Savior and all that follow Him have done."[31] Loraine Boettner adds: "Wycliffe was a reformer of the Calvinistic type, proclaiming the absolute sovereignty of God and the Foreordination of all things. His system of belief was very similar to that which was later taught by Luther and Calvin."[32] Like the Reformers, Wycliffe ardently held to the doctrines of grace.

## Doctrine in Focus:
### DIVINE SOVEREIGNTY

Wycliffe affirmed that God brought all things into being by His infinite power. He writes, "We should believe that God the Father, being almighty, without beginning and ending, made heaven, and earth, and all creatures, of naught, through His word."[33] Moreover, Christ rules over all things by the Father's appointment: "Christ is the supreme Lord, while the pope is a man, and liable to mortal sin, and who while in mortal sin, according to divines, is unfitted for dominion."[34] The God who created all that exists continues to rule over all.

What is more, Wycliffe taught that nothing can hinder the decrees of the sovereign God. He writes: "Let it be certain, that God has predetermined an event, and the result is beyond all accident, it must follow. Now what could hinder this preordination of events on the part of God? His knowledge is perfect. His will unvarying. And all creature-impediments opposed to Him are futile. From these facts, it follows that whatsoever is future, must necessarily come."[35] Whatever God has predestined must, by necessity, become reality.

Wycliffe affirmed that all that Christ prophesied must come to pass. He says:

> If Christ prophesied of certain events, certainly to come, such events have been or will be. The antecedent, namely that Christ has thus prophesied, is necessary, and the consequence is also necessary. The consequence is not in the power of any man, or of any creature; nor are the sayings of Christ, or the elections of his mind to be affected by accident. And therefore as it is necessary that Christ has foretold certain things, so it is necessary they should come to pass. By arguments of this kind also, we shew other events to be necessary, the coming

of which has been determined by God. Nor will it matter, after what manner God may chose to inform us, that he had actually so determined before the foundation of the world.[36]

The Word of God is sure. All that He has ordained will certainly become reality.

**Doctrine in Focus:**

## RADICAL DEPRAVITY

Wycliffe held to the doctrine of total depravity, correctly tracing the problem of man's sin to the sin of Adam. The first man, Wycliffe said, was without excuse when he sinned. He writes: "God bade Adam not to eat of the apple; but he broke God's command; and he was not excused therein, neither by his own folly, (or weakness,) or by Eve, nor by the serpent. And thus by the righteousness of God, this sin must always be punished."[37] By his sin, Adam fell into a state of death. Wycliffe writes, "Adam indulged pride so as to bring death upon himself voluntarily."[38] But Adam's sin was imputed to all men, so that his penalty fell on all his descendants. When the first man sinned, the entire human race suffered death. Wycliffe succinctly states, "by Adam all die."[39] The act of the one man brought death to the many.

Furthermore, Wycliffe saw that Adam's sin resulted in the depravity that infects all people. He explains, "We are all originally sinners, as Adam, and in Adam; his leprosy cleaves to us faster than Naaman's did to Gehazi."[40] He adds, "Man was ruined by the forbidden fruit of a tree."[41] This ruin, Wycliffe taught, affects every faculty of man—mind, emotion, and will. Regarding the mind, Wycliffe writes, "We are all sinners, not only from our birth, but before, so that we cannot so much as think a good thought."[42] Regarding the heart, or affections, Wycliffe says man is subject to "the threefold lust of the world, that is, from the love of possessions and riches, from the love of highness and vain worship, and from fleshy lusts."[43] Also, he maintains that man's will is held captive: "Wicked men are called the kingdom of the devil, for he reigns in them, and they do his will."[44] The sum of all this, Wycliffe teaches, is that "man is the most fallen of creatures, and the unkindest of all creatures that ever God made!"[45] Man is in a depraved state.

However, Wycliffe's understanding of the extent of original sin must be considered somewhat limited. Philip Schaff observes: "[Wycliffe] seems to have endeavored to shun the determinism of Bradwardine and declared that the doctrine of necessity does not do away with the freedom of the will, which is so free that it cannot be compelled."[46] Thus, Wycliffe affirmed total depravity, but he was somewhat ambiguous about the extent to which the will is in bondage to sin.

**Doctrine in Focus:**

## Sovereign Election

Wycliffe understood that the true church of God consists of those predestined to eternal life, not necessarily those who claim membership in the visible church.[47] Concerning election and predestination, it is said that he "stressed election as a key theological concept and viewed the church as the community of the elect."[48] This emphasis on the church as the body of elect believers appears in his writings. He states, "For no one except for the predestined and the sanctified, those without stain or wrinkle at the proper time, is a member of the Church."[49] He adds, "Although the Church is spoken of in many ways throughout Scripture, I think that we can conceive of it in its best known sense, namely the congregation of all the predestined."[50] Those chosen by God constitute the true church of God.

Wycliffe affirmed that election is unmerited, not based on any foreseen goodness in the one chosen. He writes: "Predestination is God's chief gift most freely given, since no one can merit his own predestination."[51] Elsewhere he writes: "God makes sinful man and unkind man, a good man; and all the goodness of this comes of the goodness of God."[52] One writer underscores this aspect of election: "Wycliffe insists that believers ought to believe that they are predestinate because they must hope and believe with fear in God's grace."[53] Election is entirely by grace, Wycliffe insisted, not of any good works.

Wycliffe believed that election is unconditional. H. B. Workman, a Wycliffe biographer, explains the Oxford professor's position: "The Church, as the mystical body of the predestinated, is a unity that knows nothing of papal primacies and hierarchies, and of the 'sects' of monks, friars, and priests; nor can the salvation of the elect be conditioned by masses, indulgences, penance, or other devices of sacerdotalism."[54] There are no conditions that the elect must meet in order to be chosen by God; indeed, they are incapable of meeting any conditions.

**Doctrine in Focus:**

IRRESISTIBLE CALL

Wycliffe made known the sovereign regeneration of God, which gives life to the elect, causing them to believe in Jesus Christ. Regarding the new birth, he states: "God Himself is certainly the first cause and the only cause of pre-destination."[55] He asserted that God must overcome man's resistance in order for salvation to be received. Wycliffe writes: "Lord Jesus, turn us to You, and we shall be turned! Heal us and then we shall be verily holy; for without grace and help from You, may no man be truly turned or healed."[56] No man can turn *to* Christ until he is turned *by* Him. Wycliffe adds, "It is impossible for a creature to know anything unless it knows it through grounding from the authority of God teaching and moving to assent."[57] Wycliffe explains: "The prophet speaks . . . of souls perfectly turning to God, saying . . . He shall draw my feet, that is my soul and my affections, out of the snare, and the net of the love of this world."[58] God's work of regeneration is irresistible.

What is more, Wycliffe taught that regeneration is entirely of grace. He writes: "For all things are of grace . . . God's goodness is the first cause which gives men these good things. And so it may not be that God does good, unless he does these good things freely by His grace."[59] He adds that even saving faith is the gift of God: "Faith is a gift of God; and so God gives it not to man, unless he gives it graciously. And thus all good things that men have are gifts of God. And thus, when God rewards a good work of man, He crowns His own gift. And this is of grace."[60] Wycliffe maintained that God gives saving faith through grace. He writes: "The ground of all goodness is steadfast faith, or belief. This, through grace and mercy, is obtained of God."[61] Finally, he insisted that love *for* God comes *from* Him. He says, "No man can . . . love God, or be chaste, unless God give it to him."[62] All these comments clearly show that Wycliffe believed God is the sole Author of saving faith and the love for Him that accompanies it.

**Doctrine in Focus:**

PRESERVING GRACE

Wycliffe also understood that if salvation is entirely of God, then grace can never be lost. Saving grace is preserving grace—God will keep those He predestined before the foundation of the world secure throughout the ages to come. Wycliffe writes: "We are predestined, that we may obtain divine acceptance. . . . And it appears that this grace, which is called the grace of predestination, with the charity of final perseverance, cannot by any means fail."[63] He adds: "Predestination . . . cannot be lost, since it is the foundation of glorification or beatitude, which cannot be lost either."[64] Wycliffe was clear about the immutable nature of grace.

# A LIGHT SHINING IN DARKNESS

Thirty-one years after Wycliffe died, in 1415, the Council of Constance condemned him on 260 counts of heresy. The council ordered that his writings be burned and that his bones be exhumed and put out of consecrated ground. Finally, in 1428, the pope ordered that Wycliffe's remains be dug up and burned, and his ashes scattered into the Swift River.

But Wycliffe's bones were more easily rejected than his lasting influence. As one observer notes: "They burnt his bones to ashes and cast them into the Swift, a neighboring brook running hard by. Thus the brook has conveyed his ashes into the Avon; Avon into the Severn; Servern into the narrow seas; and they into the main ocean. And thus the ashes of Wycliffe are the emblem of his doctrine which now is dispersed the world over."[65] Wycliffe's impact was felt throughout England and the European continent.

One of the main ways in which Wycliffe impacted his world was through the Lollards, a wave of men who followed his example in preaching. A powerful preacher himself, Wycliffe commissioned men to preach throughout England. He called them the Order of Poor Priests, but Wycliffe's enemies scorned them as "Lollards," a derisive term probably meaning "a mumbler" or "an idler." They preached obedience to God, reliance on the Bible as the guide to Christian living, and simplicity of worship. They rejected the Mass and the supremacy of the pope. They also denied that an organized church was necessary for salvation.

Following Wycliffe's death, the Lollards continued his work of bringing the Scriptures to the people. But they faced great opposition and their efforts were suppressed. Thus, these men carried his writings abroad, some to Bohemia in central Europe. There, his works enormously impacted another Pre-Reformer, John Hus.

Wycliffe, the Morning Star of the Protestant Reformation, shines as a gleaming light against the dark backdrop of the Roman Catholic Church in the fourteenth century. It is often said that the light shines brightest when the night is darkest. Wycliffe proved the truth of this adage.

As it was in Wycliffe's day, so it is in this hour of history. The contemporary church is once again shrouded in darkness. May the Lord raise up a generation of men who stand out as bright lights for the glory of the Lord Jesus Christ.

NOTES

1 John Wycliffe, *Writings of the Reverend and Learned John Wickliff* (London: Religious Tract Society, 1831), 41.

2 Gregory of Rimini, cited in John Hannah, *Our Legacy: The History of Christian Doctrine* (Colorado Springs, Colo.: NavPress, 2001), 222.

3 Michael Horton, "The Crisis of Evangelical Christianity," *Modern Reformation* (January–February 1994), 17.

4 John Foxe, *Foxe's Christian Martyrs of the World* (Uhrichsville, Ohio: Barbour, 1989), 31.

5 Alister McGrath, *The Intellectual Origins of the European Reformation* (Oxford: Blackwell, 1987), 140.

6 McGrath, *The Intellectual Origins of the European Reformation*, 140.

7 David Fountain, "John Wycliffe: The Evangelical Doctor," in *Puritan Papers, Vol. Five: 1968–1969*, ed. J. I. Packer (Phillipsburg, N.J.: P&R, 2005), 43.

8 Phillip Schaff and David S. Schaff, *History of the Christian Church, Vol. VI: The Middle Ages: From Boniface VIII to the Protestant Reformation, 1294–1517* (1910; repr., Grand Rapids: Eerdmans, 1984), 315.

9 David Fountain, *John Wycliffe: The Dawn of the Reformation* (Asheville, N.C.: Revival Literature, 1984), 1.

10 A. Kenneth Curtis, J. Stephen Lang, and Randy Petersen, *The 100 Most Important Events in Christian History* (Grand Rapids: Revell, 2000), 86.

11 Fountain, "John Wycliffe: The Evangelical Doctor," in *Puritan Papers, Vol. Five*, 43.

12 Curtis, Lang, and Petersen, *The 100 Most Important Events in Christian History*, 86.

13 S. M. Houghton, *Sketches From Church History* (Edinburgh: Banner of Truth, 2001), 65.

14 Houghton, *Sketches From Church History*, 65.

15 Schaff and Schaff, *History of the Christian Church, Vol. VI*, 358.

16 J. H. Merle d'Aubigné, *History of the Reformation of the Sixteenth Century* (Grand Rapids: Baker, 1976), 710.

17 Tony Lane, *A Concise History of Christian Thought* (Grand Rapids: Baker Academic, 2006), 135.

18 "Wycliffe, John," in *The Oxford Dictionary of the Christian Church*, 3rd Ed., ed. E. A. Livingstone (Oxford: Oxford University Press, 1997), 1769.

19 "Wycliffe," in *Cyclopedia of Biblical, Theological, and Ecclesiastical Literature, Vol. II*, eds. John McClintock and James Strong (Grand Rapids: Baker, 1981), 1041.

20 Donald L. Roberts, "John Wycliffe and the Dawn of the Reformation," *Christian History*, Vol. II, No. 2, Issue 3, 10.

21 Robert G. Clouse, "Wycliffe, John," in *New International Dictionary of the Christian Church*, gen. ed. J. D. Douglas (Grand Rapids: Zondervan, 1978), 1064.

22 Wycliffe, cited in Fountain, *John Wycliffe: The Dawn of the Reformation*, 48.

23 Wycliffe, *Trialogus*, B.III, cited in Professor Gotthard Victor Lechler, *John Wycliffe and His English Precursors*, trans. Dr. Lorimer, rev. Dr. Green, popular edition (London: The Religious Tract Society, 1904), 260.

24 Earle E. Cairns, *Christianity Through the Centuries: A History of the Christian Church*, 3rd Ed. (1954; repr., Grand Rapids: Zondervan, 1996), 244.

25 Schaff and Schaff, *History of the Christian Church, Vol. VI*, 328.

26 Wycliffe, cited in Schaff and Schaff, *History of the Christian Church, Vol. VI*, 329.

27 Knighton, cited in Wycliffe, *Writings of the Reverend and Learned John Wickliff*, 25.

28 F. F. Bruce, "Bible (English Versions)," in *New International Dictionary of the Christian Church*, 126.

29 Wycliffe, cited in Herbert B. Workman, *The Dawn of the Reformation: Vol. 1: The Age of Wycliffe* (London: The Epworth Press, 1933), 277.

30 Ian Christopher Levy, "Conclusion," in *A Companion to John Wyclif: Late Medieval Theologian, Vol. 4*, ed. Ian Christopher Levy (Leiden and Boston: Brill, 2006), 461.

31 Robert Vaughan, "Life of Wycliffe," Vol. I, 303, cited in John Wycliffe, *Writings of the Reverend and Learned John Wickliff*, 54.

32 Loraine Boettner, *The Reformed Doctrine of Predestination* (Phillipsburg, N.J.: P&R, 1932), 367.

33 Wycliffe, *Writings of the Reverend and Learned John Wickliff*, 53.

34 Wycliffe, *Writings of the Reverend and Learned John Wickliff*, 14.

35 Wycliffe, *Trialogus*, III.9, cited in Robert Vaughan, *The Life and Opinions of John De Wycliffe, Vol. 2* (London: B. J. Holdsworth, Hatchard and Son, 1828), 354.

36 Wycliffe, *Trialogus*, III.9, cited in Vaughan, *The Life and Opinions of John De Wycliffe, Vol. 2*, 353–354.

37 Wycliffe, *Writings of the Reverend and Learned John Wickliff*, 186.

38 Wycliffe, *Writings of the Reverend and Learned John Wickliff*, 181.

39 Wycliffe, *Writings of the Reverend and Learned John Wickliff*, 159.

40 Wycliffe, *Writings of the Reverend and Learned John Wickliff*, 42.

41 Wycliffe, *Writings of the Reverend and Learned John Wickliff*, 181.

42 Wycliffe, *Writings of the Reverend and Learned John Wickliff*, 42.

43 Wycliffe, *Writings of the Reverend and Learned John Wickliff*, 65.

44 Wycliffe, *Writings of the Reverend and Learned John Wickliff*, 89.

45 Wycliffe, *Writings of the Reverend and Learned John Wickliff*, 17.

46 Schaff and Schaff, *History of the Christian Church, Vol. VI*, 326.

47 R. Tudor Jones, *The Great Reformation* (Bryntirion, Wales: Bryntirion Press, 1985), 17.

48 Dirk Jellema, "Predestination," in *New International Dictionary of the Christian Church*, 798.

49 Wycliffe, *De Ecclesia*, 4, 84/29–85/3, cited in Takashi Shogimen, "Wyclif's Ecclesiology and Political Thought," in *A Companion to John Wyclif*, 224.

50 Wycliffe, *De Ecclesia*, 2/25–28, cited in Shogimen, "Wyclif's Ecclesiology and Political Thought," in *A Companion to John Wyclif*, 216.

51 Wycliffe, *De Ecclesia*, 6, 139/4–14, cited in Shogimen, "Wyclif's Ecclesiology and Political Thought," in *A Companion to John Wyclif*, 223.

52 Wycliffe, *Writings of the Reverend and Learned John Wickliff,* 190.

53 Shogimen, "Wyclif's Ecclesiology and Political Thought," in *A Companion to John Wyclif,* 224.

54 Workman, *The Dawn of the Reformation, Vol. 1,* 176.

55 Wycliffe, *Hom. Bib. Reg.,* 104, cited in Vaughan, *The Life and Opinions of John De Wycliffe, Vol. 2,* 357.

56 Wycliffe, *Of Perfect Life,* cited in Vaughan, *The Life and Opinions of John De Wycliffe, Vol. 2,* 361.

57 Wycliffe, *De Trinitate,* ed. Allen duPont Breck (Colorado, 1962), 2, 19, cited in Stephen Lahey, "Wyclif's Trinitarian and Christological Theology," in *A Companion to John Wyclif,* 144.

58 Wycliffe, *Writings of the Reverend and Learned John Wickliff,* 98.

59 Wycliffe, *Writings of the Reverend and Learned John Wickliff,* 193.

60 Wycliffe, *Writings of the Reverend and Learned John Wickliff,* 193.

61 Wycliffe, *Writings of the Reverend and Learned John Wickliff,* 51.

62 Wycliffe, *Writings of the Reverend and Learned John Wickliff,* 119.

63 Wycliffe, *Writings of the Reverend and Learned John Wickliff,* 41.

64 Wycliffe, *De Ecclesia,* 6, 139/4–14, cited in Shogimen, "Wyclif's Ecclesiology and Political Thought," in *A Companion to John Wyclif,* 223.

65 Schaff and Schaff, *History of the Christian Church, Vol. VI,* 325.

# CHAPTER EIGHTEEN
# STUDY QUESTIONS

1. Comment on the state of the church in the fourteenth century. What was the pervasive theology of the day? In what ways did the translation of Scripture into the vernacular language correct the errors within the church?

2. Describe the Pre-Reformers. Summarize the period in which they lived. List the most notable of these spiritual leaders. What role did these men play in advancing the church's understanding of the doctrines of grace?

3. Comment on John Wycliffe's education. Where did he study? Who were his primary teachers? Explain the significance of his education under doctrinally sound, biblical teaching. How should this affect your pursuit of education today?

4. Explain Wycliffe's views regarding the Roman Catholic Church, particularly the pope. In what ways did these views influence his writings? What was the result of his doctrinal convictions? In light of Wycliffe's strong stance, how are we to act in the face of biblical and ecclesiastical error?

5. Why did the translation of the Bible into English in the fourteenth century have such a powerful and lasting effect in igniting reformation flames? What obstacles did this translation face? Why?

6. In what way was Wycliffe a "forerunner" of the Protestant Reformers? To what extent did his belief in the absolute sovereignty of God shape his doctrinal convictions? How should this truth shape our theological beliefs?

7. Summarize Wycliffe's view of the fall and its effect on the human race, especially the freedom of man's will. What Scripture passages come to mind concerning man's will? Does Scripture affirm the freedom of the will or the bondage of the will? Cite several verses.

8. Explain Wycliffe's view of faith in salvation. What is the relationship between faith and grace? In what way did his view affirm monergistic regeneration?

*H*ence neither is the pope the head nor are the cardinals the whole body of the holy, universal, catholic church. For Christ alone is the head of that church, and His predestinate are the body and each is a member.[1]

–John Hus

# FIERY
# FORERUNNER

## BOHEMIAN PRE-REFORMER:
## JOHN HUS

W ith the dawning of the fifteenth century, seeds of reform had been planted in England and were making their way onto the European continent. At this time, the city of Prague in Bohemia had come under the influence of powerful biblical preaching. Hence, religious reform was already taking root there. This initial awakening came as a result of godly men such as Conrad of Waldhausen, who preached there from 1360 to 1369. He was followed by Jan Milic, who boldly proclaimed the Word of God until 1374. Then Matthew of Janow kept this movement alive until his death in 1394.[2] These prolific preachers plowed the soil in preparation for the fuller harvest of reform that would come with the Protestant Reformers.[3]

The flames of reform in England began to feed the movement in Bohemia after 1383, when Anne of Luxembourg, the sister of the king of Bohemia, married King Richard II of England, strengthening the political allegiance between the two nations. As a result of this alliance, students soon began traveling between the universities of Oxford and Prague, studying abroad. These exchanges facilitated the transmission of intellectual ideas.

In England, Czech students studying at Oxford became captivated by the Reformed teachings that had been handed down by John Wycliffe. In time, these inflamed students carried these God-centered truths back home to Bohemia, where Wycliffe's theological and philosophical views were widely adopted almost immediately.[4] The impact of Wycliffism upon the theological landscape of Prague was monumental and long lasting.[5] At the heart of this emerging movement was a return to Scripture and a renewed pursuit of doctrinal integrity and personal purity. Countless students in central Europe soon embraced this doctrinal system. Suddenly, reformation fires were burning brightly on the Continent—and at the martyr's stake.

Amid this theological firestorm, Wycliffe's teachings caught fire in the heart of one Czech student in particular—John Hus. So consumed was Hus with Wycliffe's views that, years later, when the Bohemian Reformer was called upon to give a defense of his doctrinal convictions, he simply stated that he had been reading Wycliffe's writings for twenty-plus years. The truths Wycliffe taught had come to be Hus's own beliefs.[6] In Hus, the movement to reform the Bohemian church had found its champion.

This religious reform in Bohemia brought a renewed emphasis on the doctrines of grace. In this pivotal hour, the truths of sovereign grace were elevated to the forefront of the life of the church once again. The torch of biblical truth was lit and gospel light was kindled to extinguish the darkness.

# JOHN HUS

Hus (ca. 1372–1415) easily ranks as the most outstanding of the Bohemian reformers.[7] A gifted preacher, Hus achieved "proto-reformation status"[8] as the leading popular exponent of the Bohemian reform movement.[9] After his death, he was regarded as a national hero.[10] Hus was solid in the Scriptures and well-acquainted with Wycliffe's writings. He held to the sole authority of Scripture, wrote against papal authority, proposed a Bible translation into the Czech language, and introduced congregational singing to the Bohemian church.[11] For his doctrinal convictions, he was condemned and martyred a century before Martin Luther took his historic stand for the same truths.

Hus was born in Husinec (or Husinetz), a small market town in southern Bohemia, in the modern-day Czech Republic, and was raised of peasant stock. The name *Hus* means "goose." His mother desired that he become a priest, so he entered the elementary school in nearby Prachatice at about thirteen years of age.[12] However, he received only an average education;[13] the shortcomings of this early training would later be seen in the limited scholarship of his adult ministry.[14]

In 1390, Hus enrolled at the University of Prague, beginning what would be a long relationship with this institution. During his student days, Hus was first exposed to Wycliffe's writings when he earned money copying his works.

Five copies of the complete works of Wycliffe in Hus's handwriting remain in the Stockholm Royal Library today. Through this rigorous discipline, Hus absorbed Wycliffe's teaching.[15]

He graduated with a bachelor's degree in 1393, ranking sixth in his class of twenty-two.[16] He then completed the master of arts degree in 1396. He immediately began teaching philosophy in the faculty of arts, an honor for such a young man. Hus was appointed a professor of theology at the University of Prague in 1398 and became dean of the theological faculty in 1401. He also took priestly vows, largely motivated by a desire for prestige, financial security, and the acceptance of the academic community.[17]

During these years, something unexpected occurred—Hus was dramatically converted to Christ. Though the historical details are not clear, the personal transformation was radical.[18] He adopted a simpler lifestyle and showed great interest in spiritual growth.

## CAPTURED BY WYCLIFFE'S TEACHINGS

In 1401, Jerome of Prague (ca. 1379–1416) returned from Oxford with more copies of Wycliffe's writings. These theological works greatly impacted Hus and the others who read them. Especially captivating were those concerning the spirituality of the church. These ideas birthed a theological movement in Bohemia that would influence eastern Europe's Christianity into the seventeenth century.[19]

Hus especially agreed with Wycliffe's stance against clerical corruption and with his opposition to the sale of indulgences.[20] Most important, Hus agreed with the Oxford professor that the true church is comprised of genuine believers within the institutional church. This means, Hus believed, that the true church is made up of the elect who are predestined to grace and glory. This position led Hus to reject, from the pope down, the leadership of the Roman Catholic Church. He even concluded that the Catholic hierarchy was among the nonelect, meaning they were false shepherds of the flock.

In 1402, Hus was appointed the rector and preacher of the enormous Bethlehem Chapel in Prague.[21] The sanctuary of this influential church was capable of seating three thousand worshipers. The church had been founded a decade earlier by a wealthy merchant to be a center for Reformed preaching.[22] Two sermons a day were preached there in the language of the common people. The building often could not contain the swelling congregation.[23] Hus was a careful student of the Scriptures, and his fiery sermons fanned widespread popular support for Reformed thinking.[24] This was especially true among the university students, who were appalled by the dead religion of Rome.[25] As a result, student riots erupted in support of Wycliffism and in opposition to the erroneous, extrabiblical teachings of the Roman Catholic Church.[26] Regarding Hus's fearless preaching, J. H. Merle d'Aubigné comments:

> With a freedom, and in an evangelical spirit, which reminds us of Luther, he testified against the vices of the clergy and the nobility, and did not spare even the Pope and his court. Kindness and severity were both tried for the sake of silencing this voice, but in vain. Many of his sermons are so eloquent, so penetrating and powerful, that they would scarcely be allowed, even in the present day, to appear in Austria without alteration. With him Gospel truth was everything, and in publishing this he cared little for persons and rank. He thought with the Apostles, "If I yet please men, I should not be the servant of Christ" (Gal. 1:10).[27]

In the pulpit, Hus stressed the authoritative role of Scripture in the church. He elevated biblical preaching to a central place in the worship service.[28] His sermons were not ornate, but simple, lucid, fervent, and, above all, thoroughly biblical. His preaching left an indelible impression on the minds of the people. From the pulpit, he set forth the truth with sufficient force, it was said, to make Rome tremble.[29]

## Papal Defiance

On May 28, 1403, Johann Hubner, a German master (teacher) at the University of Prague, selected forty-five theses from Wycliffe's writings and secured from the faculty the charge of heresy.[30] This condemnation caused a split in the school between the German and Czech professors, the former opposing the English Reformer and the latter defending his ideas. However, the new archbishop of Prague, Zbynek Zajic, favored Wycliffe's ecclesiastical reforms, so Wycliffe's writings were accepted. As a result, the reform movement grew initially.[31] But in 1408, the adversaries of reform persuaded Zajic to reinstate the old doctrines of Rome.

The following year, the Council of Pisa met to attempt to resolve a dispute over the papacy between Benedict XIII and Gregory XII. Instead of resolving the issue, however, the council elected yet another claimant, Alexander

V. Which of the men should be recognized as the pope? Hus, along with King Wenceslaus IV and the Czech teachers, sided with Alexander. The German teachers sided with Gregory. King Wenceslaus forced the archbishop to acknowledge the new pope. Zajic then secured from Alexander a papal bull (decree) prohibiting preaching in private chapels, including Bethlehem Chapel. When Hus received this order, he immediately rejected it. Thus, Zajic excommunicated him and had Wycliffe's books burned in Prague. Still, with the government's support, Hus continued to preach at Bethlehem Chapel.

The defiant Hus was summoned to appear in Rome. He refused and instead sent representatives. Hus was excommunicated again, this time for willful contempt of papal authority.

When the king changed the university's constitution, the German teachers and students left the school. Hus was elected rector of the university, which was growing in its sympathy for Wycliffe. However, the conflict between Rome and Hus was escalating. Alexander's successor, Pope John XXIII, promoted the sale of indulgences for the forgiveness of sins. Hus could not be silent on this issue and condemned indulgences as heresy, a hideous corruption of the true gospel. In response, he was excommunicated a third time.

In 1412, public demonstrations broke out in Prague, aroused by the Reformed truths Hus was teaching. A simulated papal bull was burned publicly by reform-minded students. But in the uprising, three young men were beheaded for opposing the sale of indulgences. As a mounting threat to Rome, Hus was excommunicated a fourth time. Prague, largely siding with Hus, threatened violence against the papacy. To prevent that, Hus went into voluntary exile in southern Bohemia, where he remained during much of the conflict (1413–1414). There he wrote some of his finest works, among them *Exposition of the Faith*, *The Ten Commandments*, and *The Lord's Prayer*.

## Arrested and Imprisoned

In the fall of 1414, Pope John XXIII convened the ecumenical Council of Constance at Constance, Germany, to address two escalating problems: the papal schism and the rising heresy in the Western church, especially in Bohemia. Hus stood squarely in the center of this latter controversy. He was summoned to attend the council as a delegate, but his friends warned him not to accept. They suspected an ambush awaited him. But Hus received an assurance of safety from the Holy Roman emperor, Sigismund. With high hopes of presenting his views to the assembled authorities,[32] Hus accepted the invitation to the council.

Hus arrived in Constance on November 3, 1414. Despite the repeated government promises of safety, he was immediately arrested for heresy. He was thrown into prison, where he languished for eight months while the council addressed other matters. In the terrible conditions of the prison, Hus's health declined significantly. Only a visit from the pope's physician and relocation to a better cell spared his life.[33]

Stephen Palecz, a detractor, came to see Hus in prison when he grew very ill. Later, Hus recorded the venomous words with which Palecz greeted him before the council: "Since the birth of Christ, there hath not arisen a more dangerous heretic than yourself, excepting Wycliffe."[34] But Hus remained steadfast. Later, he recorded an exchange with one of the Roman Catholic authorities: "One of the doctors said to me that, whatever I did, I should submit to the Council, though my whole case was good and in order, and added, 'If the Council told you, "You have only one eye," although you have two, you ought to agree with the Council that it is so.' To which I replied, 'If the whole world told me so, as long as I have the use of my reason, I could not say so without resisting my conscience.'"[35] Like Luther at the Diet of Worms, Hus's conscience was captive to the Word of God.

## TRIED FOR WYCLIFFISM

In July 1415, Hus was placed on trial for "Wycliffism." He was ordered to condemn Wycliffe's works. Hus responded that he would yield to the church when instructed by Scripture. He stated that he supported Wycliffe, but would condemn any of the English Reformer's teachings if they were proven wrong by the Bible. Hus firmly held to the teachings set forth by Wycliffe; although they had been deemed heresy by the Roman Catholic Church, Scripture had confirmed them to Hus's conscience.

Hus was then urged to recant his own teachings. He later said: "I have not recanted nor abjured a single article. The Council desired me to declare the falsity of all of my books and each article taken from them. I refused to do so, unless they should be proved false by Scripture."[36] Elsewhere he wrote: "I refuse to be the enemy of the truth and will resist to the death all agreement with falsehood. . . . It is better to die well than to live badly."[37]

In a letter to the University of Prague as his execution approached, he said: "I, Master John Hus, in chains and in prison, now standing on the shore of this present life and expecting on the morrow a dreadful death, which will,

I hope, purge away my sins, find no heresy in myself, and accept with all my heart any truth whatsoever that is worthy of belief."[38]

## CONDEMNED AS A HERETIC

On July 6, 1415, the Council of Constance declared the teachings of Wycliffe to be heretical.[39] The council then solemnly condemned Hus as the leading exponent of Wycliffe's views.[40] In a humiliating ceremony, six bishops stripped him of his priestly garments and shaved his head. They put on his head a paper hat covered with red demons and the word *heretic*. Finally, the bishops committed his soul to the Devil, but in response, Hus said, "And I commit myself to my most gracious Lord Jesus."[41]

In the face of death, Hus then boldly told his executioners, "Today, you are burning a goose [the meaning of his name in Czech]; however, a hundred years from now, you will be able to hear a swan sing; you will not burn it, you will have to listen to him."[42] No one could foresee how these words would be fulfilled one hundred years later in Germany through Luther, who saw himself as the fulfillment of Hus's prediction.

The council handed Hus over to Emperor Sigismund, who was sitting on an imperial throne in full regalia. Hus, bound in chains, was ordered to recant or die. He refused to deny his writings, so the soldiers led him away to be burned at the stake. When asked to recant one last time, Hus replied: "God is my witness that the things charged against me I never preached. In the same truth of the gospel which I have written, taught, and preached, drawing upon the sayings and positions of the holy doctors, I am ready to die to-day."[43]

That very afternoon at the execution site, commonly known as the Devil's Place,[44] Hus was burned at the stake, a martyr for the truth he had preached so fearlessly. It is recorded that he died singing, "Jesus, son of the living God, have mercy on me."[45]

Though Hus was dead, the reform movement lived on. The truth of Scripture was, once again, restored in that day.

# HUS'S WRITINGS

Hus did not leave a large body of writing, yet what he wrote was profound and often provocative. He was mightily used to shape his day and subsequent generations. His writings especially bear the fingerprints of his mentor,

Wycliffe—some of them reproduce Wycliffe almost thought for thought.[46] However, Hus criticized the Roman Catholic Church less than Wycliffe.

### ON THE CHURCH

During his exile, Hus produced his most significant book, *On the Church*, which he finished in July 1413.[47] In it, Hus directly attacked the pope's plenary authority.[48] It proved to be, next to Wycliffe's works, the most famous treatment on the church since Cyprian's *De Ecclesia* and Augustine's writings against the Donatists.[49] His main argument was that the Christian church is the universal body of those predestined to life.[50] The pope and the cardinals, he stressed, are not the church because they give no evidence of being numbered among the elect. Further, Hus insisted that Peter never was the head of the Roman Catholic Church, but only an equal with the other bishops. This work became the chief document of the Hussite revolution in fifteenth-century Bohemia. It even played an important role in Luther's eventual break with the papacy.[51]

### LETTERS

At the end of his life, as Hus lay in prison in Constance, he wrote many passionate letters. His letters during his last month rank among the greatest in Christian literature.[52] For example, Hus writes: "O most holy Christ draw me, weak as I am, after Thyself, for if Thou dost not draw us we cannot follow Thee. Strengthen my spirit, that it may be willing. If the flesh is weak, let Thy grace precede us; come between and follow, for without Thee we cannot go for Thy sake to cruel death. Give me a fearless heart, a right faith, a firm hope, a perfect love, that for Thy sake I may lay down my life with patience and joy. Amen."[53] If Hus had added nothing to the intellectual heritage of the church, he would still have enriched its moral outlook through these letters.

## HUS'S THEOLOGY

Hus was not an original theologian, but was a skilled popularizer of Wycliffe's theology.[54] Most of what he wrote was little more than a paraphrase of Wycliffe's works into the vernacular of the Bohemians.[55] This work made Reformed truth accessible to the common people, which accounts for Hus's popularity. Like Wycliffe, he saw Scripture as the chief authority in the church, but his theology was a mixture of evangelical and traditional Roman Catholic doctrines.[56] However, he was strongly predestinarian in matters of soteriology.

**Doctrine in Focus:**

DIVINE SOVEREIGNTY

Hus strongly affirmed the sovereignty of God. He writes that God alone has "the power to kill and make alive, to destroy and to save, and to preserve His faithful ones in divers sore perils, and to grant unto them the eternal life with joy unspeakable."[57] In other words, sovereignty resides exclusively with God, and this comprehensive authority extends to every aspect of salvation.

Most of Hus's affirmations of God's sovereignty appear in the context of his appeals against the authority of the Roman Catholic Church. The pope cannot be the head of the church, Hus reasoned, because there can be only one Sovereign. He writes, "Any Christian cannot be the head of the universal church with Christ (for the church cannot be a monster having two heads)."[58] To the contrary, he asserts, "Christ alone is the head of the universal church."[59] Along these lines, Hus says: "Neither is the pope the head nor are the cardinals the whole body of the holy, universal, catholic church. For Christ alone is the head of the church, and His predestinate are the body and each one is a member, because His bride is one person with Jesus Christ."[60] Mere human leaders die, he writes, but Christ is "a King that cannot die . . . a King of glory Who has the gift of eternal life."[61] All these statements exalt the authority of God over His church.

**Doctrine in Focus:**

RADICAL DEPRAVITY

Hus was clear about the state of human nature. Natural man, he writes, is prone to "greed, simony, pride, luxury, the forsaking and despising of God's word."[62] Furthermore, he says, people are ensnared by "the world, the flesh, and the devil," especially "the vanities of this world."[63] As a result, all men are subject to judgment. Hus states, "There is at hand the judgment of a Judge most awful, at Whose bidding necessity will be laid upon all men to publish their evil deeds to the whole world, and by Whose will their souls and bodies will be burned in everlasting fire."[64] It is clear that Hus held to the radical corruption of the human race in sin.

**Doctrine in Focus:**

SOVEREIGN ELECTION

Hus frequently asserted the unconditional election of God. He writes, "Predestination is the election of the divine will through grace; or, as it is commonly said, predestination is the preparation of grace—making ready—in the present time, and of glory in the future."[65] Having chosen His elect in eternity past, the Father gave them to the Son as a love gift to be His cherished possession. Hus writes, "No one belongs to Christ's kingdom, which is the church, except the Son whom the Father gave to Him."[66] Therefore, merely being in the visible church, Hus wrote, is not a guarantee of salvation. A right standing in grace belongs only to the elect. Hus asserts: "No place, or human election, makes a person a member of the holy universal church, but divine predestination does in the case of every one who persists in following Christ in love."[67] The sovereign will of God is the ultimate determiner of who comprises the church.

Hus even maintained that the unity of the church is based on sovereign election. He writes, "The unity of the catholic [universal] church consists in the unity of predestination, inasmuch as her separate members are one by predestination and in the unity of blessedness, and inasmuch as her separate sons are finally united in bliss."[68] A common election by God establishes and undergirds the unity of all believers.

However, Hus underscored that those chosen by God must come to faith in Christ. He says: "This distinction between predestination and present grace deserves to be strongly emphasized, for some are sheep by predestination and ravening wolves according to present righteousness, as Augustine deduces . . . 'some are sons by predestination and not yet by present grace.'"[69] Many of the elect, he insisted, are yet to be called by God into His kingdom and live in the present as "ravening wolves."

On the other hand, the elect already within the church can be identified by their persistent holy living. Hus says: "If anyone is predestined to eternal life, it necessarily follows that he is predestinated unto righteousness, and, if he follows life eternal, he has also followed righteousness. But the converse is not true. For many are made partakers of present righteousness but, from want of perseverance, are not partakers of eternal life."[70] Only the elect have a true righteousness that endures. Others may give the appearance of being saved through a superficial righteousness, but in reality, they are not numbered among the elect.

Speaking of these religious hypocrites, Hus acknowledged that many in the visible church confess Christ falsely. He writes: "How clearly does not he [Augustine] show that many are in the church who are nominally called 'sons' by men, who nevertheless are not of the church, for they are not truly sons of

God predestinated unto the life of glory."[71] Only those predestined to eternal life are in the true church.

## Doctrine in Focus:
### DEFINITE ATONEMENT

As Hus railed against the veneration of the pope, he proclaimed the vicarious, sin-bearing sacrifice of Jesus Christ on the cross. He writes: "He redeemed us from everlasting damnation. Such, then, is the mercy that comes to you from God the Father and the Lord Jesus Christ our Saviour."[72] Hus firmly asserted the substitutionary death of God's Son as the exclusive sacrifice for sin.

Regarding the extent of the atonement, Hus spoke sparingly but clearly. The Son of God, he writes, is "that most patient and brave Soldier . . . [who] knew He would rise again on the third day and overcome His foes by His death and redeem the elect from damnation."[73] These words show that Hus understood that the cross was intended for those chosen by the Father. What is more, concerning the saving mission of our Lord, he writes, "He [Christ] came not to destroy the elect, but to save them . . . it is My elect—not the proud, the fornicators, the greedy, the wrathful, the envious, the world-sick, the foes of My word and My life—but it is My elect that hear and keep My word and suffer with Me in grace."[74] Hus saw that Christ's saving death was for those chosen and predestined by the Father.

## Doctrine in Focus:
### PRESERVING GRACE

Hus had no doubts that the elect who comprise the church cannot lose their salvation. In agreement with John 10:28–29, he writes: "Christ, the best of teachers, proves by the greatness of God's gift, which is the Holy Spirit, that no one is able [to fall away from grace], because his Father is almighty, and from his hand no one is able to pluck anything. . . . Because Christ and his Father are one with the Holy Spirit—who is Christ's gift, by whom the church is knit together with Him—therefore, no one is able to pluck His sheep out of His hand."[75] The Good Shepherd loses none of His sheep. None who receive the gift of the Holy Spirit will ever fall away from Christ.

Elsewhere in his writings, Hus was equally firm. He says, "The grace of predestination unto eternal life, from which a person foreordained cannot finally fall away . . . bestows an infinite good to be enjoyed forever . . . [and] makes sons of an eternal heritage."[76] Hus adds, "The predestinate . . . have radical and abiding grace, from which they cannot fall away."[77] The saving grace God gives is an eternal possession, never to be revoked.

Hus saw that preservation is a work of God. He writes, "God Almighty will strengthen the hearts of His faithful one whom He hath chosen before the foundation of the world that they may receive an incorruptible crown."[78] Hus further states, "And He [Christ] gathers His members together gently, for the love of predestination does not fail, 1 Cor. 13."[79] God will not abandon those predestined to be part of the bride of Christ. Hus writes: "He himself from eternity has chosen every member of his church into the bridal relation. Therefore he will desert no such member."[80] Thus, the elect are kept inseparably connected to Christ. Hus says: "The grace of predestination, is the chain by which the body of the church and every member of it are joined to Christ."[81]

**Doctrine in Focus:**

## DIVINE REPROBATION

Hus distinguished the true church from the visible church by differentiating between reprobate unbelievers and predestined believers. He writes, "All are divided into the reprobate and the predestinate, the former being ultimately the members of the devil and the others members of the mystical body which is the holy church, the bride of our Lord Jesus Christ."[82] Although there may be nonelected individuals within the church, it will not always be so. Hus says, "[The church] is the mystical body of Christ, that is now hidden to us, of which body the damned do not really have part, but they are like dung which in the day of judgment are to be separated from the body of Christ."[83] Though they may attend the visible church and even join its membership, the reprobate are always outside the true church.

Hus bolstered this point through his explanation of Jesus' kingdom parables. In explaining the parable of the fish caught in the net (Matt. 13:47–50), Hus says, "The predestinate are represented by the good fish, and the reprobate by the bad fish which are cast out."[84] He finds the same distinction in the parable of the marriage feast (Matt. 22:1–14): "[In] the marriage supper . . . are gathered . . . the good and the bad, who are mingled in holy church. But the bad are not true sons, just as those are not true friends, because they lack the marriage garment, which is predestinating love."[85] Those who enter the marriage feast with the proper garments are the elect, but those without such attire are the reprobate.

Hus pointed to Judas Iscariot as an example of one who was within the visible body of Christ but who was yet reprobate. He writes, "That reprobate [Judas] never was Christ's disciple, as Augustine shows, but a wolf clad in sheep's clothing."[86] Thus, Hus saw that one may be in the church, even in the ministry, as was the case with Judas, and still be reprobate.

In agreement with Augustine, Hus declared that the reprobate are followers of Satan. He writes: "He [Augustine] says: 'Christ spoke truly in regard to certain shepherds, for He holds all good shepherds in Himself, when He said: "I am the chief Shepherd and all ye are one in Me." But the reprobate, who is a member of the devil, is not duly joined together in the same structure with his head.'"[87] The reprobate may seem to believe the gospel, but their "faith" cannot save them—they will fall away. Hus says: "So many according to common fame are called heads or members of the church, although according to God's foreknowledge they are members of the devil, who for a time believe and afterwards fall away or are now and always were unbelievers."[88] The nonelect may start with an outward confession of Christ, but they will fall away from Him in time, revealing their unbelief. In short, Hus says, "It is evident that no reprobate is truly a part of holy mother church."[89]

## INFLUENCING FUTURE GENERATIONS

The compelling story of John Hus reads like a dress rehearsal for what would follow a century later with Martin Luther.[90] When writing to Spalatin in February 1520, Luther said, "Without knowing it I both taught and held the teaching of Hus: in short, we were all Hussites without knowing it."[91] Luther saw himself as a fulfillment of Hus's prediction of a coming swan, writing in 1531: "John Hus prophesied of me when he wrote from his prison in Bohemia: They will now roast a goose (for Hus means a goose), but after a hundred years they will hear a swan sing; him they will have to tolerate. And so it shall continue, if it please God."[92] Such was Hus's enduring influence on Luther and the other Reformers. Charles Spurgeon said: "They burnt John Hus, and Jerome of Prague; but Hus foretold, as he died, that another would arise after him, whom they should not be able to put down; and in due time he more than lived again in Luther. Is Luther dead? Is Calvin dead today? That last man the moderns have tried to bury in . . . misrepresentation; but he lives, and will live, and the truths that he taught will survive all the calumniators that have sought to poison it."[93]

By God's grace, the truths Hus proclaimed in his day live on in our generation. Hus's gospel is our gospel. And that which thundered in Prague during the fifteenth century must thunder again in this present hour. May the Bohemian Reformer exert a lasting influence on a new generation of believers in this day. May all those predestined by God be strong in this hour of history—for God's glory and the good of His people. And may we pass the inheritance of the doctrines of grace to generations yet to come.

## Notes

1   John Hus, *The Church*, trans. David Schaff (1915; repr., Westport, Conn.: Greenwood Press, 1974), 66.

2   R. Tudor Jones, *The Great Reformation* (Bryntirion, Wales: Bryntirion Press, 1985), 18.

3   Stephen Lahey, "Wyclif and Lollardy," in *The Medieval Theologians: An Introduction to Theology in the Medieval Period*, ed. G. R. Evans (Malden, Mass.: Blackwell, 2001), 351.

4   Phillip Schaff and David S. Schaff, *History of the Christian Church, Vol. VI: The Middle Ages: From Boniface VIII to the Protestant Reformation, 1294–1517* (1910; repr., Grand Rapids: Eerdmans, 1984), 359–360.

5   Lahey, "Wyclif and Lollardy," in *The Medieval Theologians*, 351.

6   Schaff and Schaff, *History of the Christian Church, Vol. VI: The Middle Ages*, 360.

7   N. R. Needham, *2,000 Years of Christ's Power, Part Two: The Middle Ages* (London: Grace Publications, 2005), 391.

8   Lahey, "Wyclif and Lollardy," in *The Medieval Theologians*, 352.

9   Matthew Spinka, "Hus, Jan (1373–1415)," in *New International Dictionary of the Christian Church*, gen. ed. J. D. Douglas (Grand Rapids: Zondervan, 1978), 492.

10  N. R. Needham, *2,000 Years of Christ's Power, Part Two*, 393.

11  Stephen Nichols, *The Reformation* (Wheaton: Crossway, 2007), 19.

12  Spinka, "Hus, Jan (1373–1415)," in *New International Dictionary of the Christian Church*, 492.

13  Edwin Charles Dargan, *A History of Preaching, Vol. I: From the Apostolic Fathers to the Great Reformers* (Grand Rapids: Baker, 1974), 346.

14  Dargan, *A History of Preaching, Vol. I*, 346.

15  Howard Kaminsky, *A History of the Hussite Revolution* (Eugene, Ore.: Wipf & Stock, 1967), 24.

16  Dargan, *A History of Preaching, Vol. I*, 346.

17  Paul Kubricht, "Hus, Jan," in *Evangelical Dictionary of Theology*, 2nd Ed., ed. Walter A. Elwell (Grand Rapids: Baker, 2001), 582.

18  Kubricht, "Hus, Jan," in *Evangelical Dictionary of Theology*, 582.

19  Lahey, "Wyclif and Lollardy," in *The Medieval Theologians*, 351.

20  Thomas A. Fudge, "To Build a Fire," *Christian History*, Issue 68, Vol. XIX, No. 4, 11.

21  Jones, *The Great Reformation*, 19.

22  Tony Lane, *A Concise History of Christian Thought* (Grand Rapids: Baker Academic, 2006), 138.

23 J. H. Merle d'Aubigné, *History of the Protestant Church in Hungary from the Beginning of the Reformation to 1850*, trans. J. Craig (1854; repr., Harrisonburg, Va.: Sprinkle, 2001), 20.

24 Robert A. Baker, *A Summary of Church History* (Nashville: B&H Academic, 2005), 169.

25 Bruce L. Shelley, *Church History in Plain Language*, 2nd Ed. (Nashville: Thomas Nelson, 1995), 231.

26 Shelley, *Church History in Plain Language*, 231.

27 D'Aubigné, *History of the Protestant Church in Hungary from the Beginning of the Reformation to 1850*, 20.

28 Caroline T. Marshall, "Jan Hus," in *Introduction to the History of Christianity*, ed. Tim Dowley (Minneapolis: Fortress, 2002), 336.

29 "Hus," in *Cyclopedia of Biblical, Theological, and Ecclesiastical Literature, Vol. IV*, eds. John McClintock and James Strong (Grand Rapids: Baker, 1981), 419.

30 Spinka, "Hus, Jan (1373–1415)," in *New International Dictionary of the Christian Church*, 492.

31 Spinka, "Hus, Jan (1373–1415)," in *New International Dictionary of the Christian Church*, 492.

32 Shelley, *Church History in Plain Language*, 231.

33 Fudge, "To Build a Fire," *Christian History, Vol. XIX*, No. 4, 16.

34 Hus, Letter 59, in *The Letters of John Hus*, eds. R. Martin Pope and Herbert B. Workman (London: Hodder and Stoughton, 1904), 222.

35 Hus, Letter 60, in *The Letters of John Hus*, 226.

36 Hus, Letter 78, "To the University of Prague (June 27, 1415)," in *The Letters of John Hus*, 268.

37 Hus, Letter 27, in *The Letters of John Hus*, 120.

38 Hus, Letter 78, "To the University of Prague (June 27, 1415)," in *The Letters of John Hus*, 268.

39 Timothy George, *Theology of the Reformers* (Nashville: Broadman, 1988), 35.

40 George, *Theology of the Reformers*, 35.

41 Hus, as cited in Needham, *2,000 Years of Christ's Power, Part Two*, 393.

42 Erwin Weber, "Luther with the Swan," *The Lutheran Journal*, Vol. 65, no. 2, 1996, 10, cited in John Piper, *The Legacy of Sovereign Joy: God's Triumphant Grace in the Lives of Augustine, Luther, and Calvin* (Wheaton: Crossway, 2000), 10.

43 John Hus, cited in David S. Schaff, *John Hus: His Life, Teachings and Death After Five Hundred Years* (Eugene, Ore.: Wipf and Stock, 2001), 257.

44 Shelley, *Church History in Plain Language*, 232.

45 Rudolph W. Heinze, *Reform and Conflict: From the Medieval World to the Wars of Religion, A.D. 1350–1648* (Grand Rapids: Baker, 2005), 66.

46 Schaff and Schaff, *History of the Christian Church, Vol. VI*, 44.

47 Schaff and Schaff, *History of the Christian Church, Vol. VI*, 44.

48 Schaff and Schaff, *History of the Christian Church, Vol. VI*, 44.

49 Schaff and Schaff, *History of the Christian Church, Vol. VI*, 44.

50 Lahey, "Wyclif and Lollardy," in *The Medieval Theologians*, 351.

51 George, *Theology of the Reformers*, 35.

52 Shelley, *Church History in Plain Language*, 231.

53 Hus, Letter 73, in *The Letters of John Hus*, 253.

54 Jonathan Hill, *The History of Christian Thought* (Downers Grove, Ill.: InterVarsity, 2003), 175.

55 Hill, *The History of Christian Thought*, 175.

56 Kubricht, "Hus, Jan," in *Evangelical Dictionary of Theology*, 582.

57 Hus, Letter 17, in *The Letters of John Hus*, 90.

58 Hus, *The Church*, 27.

59 Hus, *The Church*, 27.

60 Hus, *The Church*, 66.

61 Hus, Letter 56, in *The Letters of John Hus*, 221.

62 Hus, Letter 17, in *The Letters of John Hus*, 92–93.

63 Hus, Letter 18, in *The Letters of John Hus*, 97.

64 Hus, Letter 20, in *The Letters of John Hus*, 105.

65 Hus, *The Church*, 22–23, citing Augustine, *On the Predestination of the Saints*, in *Nicene and Post-Nicene Fathers, First Series, Vol. V; Augustin: Anti-Pelagian Writings* (1888; repr., Peabody, Mass.: Hendrickson, 2004), 498.

66 Hus, *The Church*, 33.

67 Hus, *The Church*, 22.

68 Hus, *The Church*, 14.

69 Hus, *The Church*, 25.

70 Hus, *The Church*, 23.

71 Hus, *The Church*, 34.

72 Hus, Letter 24, in *The Letters of John Hus*, 113–114.

73 Hus, Letter 73, in *The Letters of John Hus*, 252.

74 Hus, Letter 20, in *The Letters of John Hus*, 104.

75 Hus, *The Church*, 34.

76 Hus, *The Church*, 24.

77 Hus, *The Church*, 35–36.

78 Hus, Letter 73, in *The Letters of John Hus.* 251.

79 Hus, *The Church*, 35.

80 Hus, *The Church*, 35.

81 Hus, *The Church*, 14, fn2.

82 Hus, *The Church*, 40.

83 Hus, *The Church*, 10, fn2.

84 Hus, *The Church*, 40.

85 Hus, *The Church*, 41.

86 Hus, *The Church*, 48.

87 Hus, *The Church*, 32.

88 Hus, *The Church*, 51.

89 Hus, *The Church*, 37.

90 Hill, *The History of Christian Thought*, 176.

91 Martin Luther, Letter to Melanchthon, June 27, 1530, cited in Jones, *The Great Reformation*, 19.

92 Martin Luther, cited in Ewald M. Plass, *What Luther Says: An Anthology, Vol. 3* (St. Louis: Concordia, 1959), 1175, cited in Piper, *The Legacy of Sovereign Joy*, 10–11.

93 Charles H. Spurgeon, *The Metropolitan Tabernacle Pulpit: Sermons Preached by C. H. Spurgeon, Vol. 38* (Pasadena, Texas.: Pilgrim, 1892), 10–11.

# CHAPTER NINETEEN
## STUDY QUESTIONS

1. Describe the cultural and political climate of early fifteenth-century Prague. What seminal events preceded John Hus? In what ways were these affairs central to reform in Bohemia?

2. Comment on Hus's preaching. Who influenced him? What role did preaching play in reforming the church at Prague? What role must preaching play if there is to be a reformation in this day?

3. Summarize the conflict between Hus and the papacy. What issues were central to the dispute? What was the result of their disagreements?

4. Explain the influence of John Wycliffe's writings on Hus's doctrinal development. How were Hus's writings similar to Wycliffe's? How were they different? According to both Pre-Reformers, what is central to the church?

5. Define the sovereignty of God. Explain how God is sovereign in all of creation and in man's salvation. What effect has this truth had on your worldview?

6. According to Hus, what is the relationship between predestination and the elect? Between predestination and the reprobate? What scriptural passages can you cite as proof for God's absolute predestination?

7. Why did Hus believe that those who comprise the true church of God can never lose their salvation? What scriptural metaphors did he draw on to support the doctrine of God's preserving grace? What role does predestination play in the perseverance of the saints?

8. Although Hus preceded Martin Luther by more than a century, Hus has been compared with the great German Reformer. In what ways were the lives and ministries of the two alike? Cite several similarities.

$N$o man can be thoroughly humbled until he knows that his salvation is utterly beyond his own powers, devices, endeavors, will, and works, and depends entirely on the choice, will, and work of another, namely, of God alone. For as long as he is persuaded that he himself can do even the least thing toward his salvation, he retains some self-confidence and does not altogether despair of himself, and therefore he is not humbled before God, but presumes that there is—or at least hopes or desires that there may be—some place, time, and work for him, by which he may at length attain to salvation. But when a man has no doubt that everything depends on the will of God, then he completely despairs of himself and chooses nothing for himself, but waits for God to work; then he has come close to grace, and can be saved.[1]

–Martin Luther

# Chapter Twenty

# FORTRESS
# FOR TRUTH

## GERMAN REFORMER:
## MARTIN LUTHER

The Protestant Reformation stands as the most far-reaching, world-changing display of God's grace since the birth and early expansion of the church. It was not a single act, nor was it led by one man. This history-altering movement played out on different stages over many decades. Its cumulative impact, however, was enormous. Philip Schaff, a noted church historian, writes: "The Reformation of the sixteenth century is, next to the introduction of Christianity, the greatest event in history. It marks the end of the Middle Ages and the beginning of modern times. Starting from religion, it gave, directly or indirectly, a mighty impulse to every forward movement, and made Protestantism the chief propelling force in the history of modern civilization."[2] The Reformation was, at its heart, a recovery of the true gospel of Jesus Christ, and this restoration had an unparalleled influence on churches, nations, and the flow of Western civilization.

Under the guiding hand of God, the world scene had been uniquely prepared for the Reformation. The church was greatly in need of reform. Spiritual darkness personified the Roman Catholic Church. The Bible was a closed book. Spiritual ignorance ruled the minds of the people. The gospel was perverted. Church tradition trumped divine truth. Personal holiness was abandoned. The rotten stench of manmade traditions covered pope and priest. The corruption of ungodliness contaminated both dogma and practice.

On the other hand, a new day was dawning. Feudal states were giving way to nation-states. Exploration was expanding. Christopher Columbus discovered

393

the New World in 1492. Trade routes were opening. A middle class was rising. Opportunities for learning were increasing. Knowledge was multiplying. Johannes Gutenberg's invention of the printing press (1454) had vastly improved the dissemination of ideas. Under all of these influences, the Renaissance was at high noon. Moreover, a further alteration in the world scene was soon to be ushered in by the Protestant Reformation of the sixteenth century, bringing great changes especially in the church of Jesus Christ.

In light of such dramatic upheaval, certain questions beg to be asked: What factors led to the Protestant Reformation? Where was the Reformation born? How did this powerful movement come about? Where did it spread? Who were the key leaders who stoked its flames? What biblical truths were unleashed on the world at this time? To begin to answer these questions, we must focus in on those giants of the faith who led the Reformation.

# THE MAGISTERIAL REFORMERS

At the beginning of the sixteenth century, God began to raise up a series of strong-willed figures known to history as the Reformers. There had been earlier reformers in the church, but those who came to prominence in this period were the best-educated, most godly, and most faithful reform leaders the church had ever seen.[3] These men were steeped in Scripture and marked by audacious courage in the face of opposition. They were emboldened by deep convictions as to the truth and a love for Christ's church that drove them to attempt to bring it back to its timeless standard. In the simplest terms, they longed to see God's people worship Him according to Scripture.[4] These men were shining lights in a dark day.

"The Reformers did not see themselves as inventers, discoverers, or creators," according to historian Stephen Nichols. "Instead, they saw their efforts as rediscovery. They weren't making something from scratch but were reviving what had become dead. They looked back to the Bible and to the apostolic era, as well as to early church fathers such as Augustine (354–430) for the mold by which they could shape the church and re-form it. The Reformers had a saying, '*Ecclesia reformata, semper reformanda*,' meaning 'the church reformed, always reforming.'"[5]

The Magisterial Reformers are so called because their reform efforts were supported by at least some ruling authorities, or magistrates, and because they believed the civil magistrates ought to enforce the true faith. This term is used to distinguish them from the radical reformers (Anabaptists), whose efforts had no magisterial support. The Reformers are also called "magisterial" because the word *magister* can mean "teacher," and the Magisterial Reformation strongly emphasized the authority of teachers.

## SCRIPTURE ALONE

In time, the message of the Reformers became encapsulated in five slogans known as the *solas* of the Reformation: *sola Scriptura* ("Scripture alone"), *solus Christus* ("Christ alone"), *sola gratia* ("grace alone"), *sola fide* ("faith alone"), and *soli Deo gloria* ("the glory of God alone"). The first of these, *sola Scriptura*, was the defining benchmark of the movement.

There are only three possible forms of spiritual authority. First, there is the authority of the Lord and His written revelation. Second, there is the authority of the church and its leaders. Third, there is the authority of human reason.[6] When the Reformers cried "Scripture alone," they were expressing their commitment to the authority of God as expressed through the Bible. James Montgomery Boice states their core belief: "The Bible alone is our ultimate authority—not the pope, not the church, not the traditions of the church or church councils, still less personal intimations or subjective feelings, but Scripture only."[7] The Reformation was essentially a crisis over which authority should have primacy. Rome claimed the church's authority lay with Scripture *and* tradition, Scripture *and* the pope, Scripture *and* church councils. But the Reformers believed that the authority belonged to Scripture *alone.* Schaff writes:

> While the Humanists went back to the ancient classics and revived the spirit of Greek and Roman paganism, the Reformers went back to the sacred Scriptures in the original languages and revived the spirit of apostolic Christianity. They were fired by an enthusiasm for the gospel, such as had never been known since the days of Paul. Christ rose from the tomb of human traditions and preached again His words of life and power. The Bible, heretofore a book of priests only, was now translated anew and better than ever into the vernacular tongues of Europe, and made a book of the people. Every Christian man could henceforth go to the fountain-head of inspiration, and sit at the feet of the Divine Teacher, without priestly permission and intervention.[8]

## THE FOUNTAIN OF SOVEREIGN GRACE

This commitment to Scripture alone led to the rediscovery of the doctrines of grace. Any return to the Bible inevitably leads to the truth of God's sovereignty in saving grace. The other four solas—*solus Christus, sola gratia, sola fide,* and *soli Deo gloria*—flow from *sola Scriptura.*

The first Reformer was an Augustinian monk who nailed Ninety-five Theses against the Roman Catholic practice of selling indulgences to the door of the Castle Church in Wittenberg, Germany, on October 31, 1517. His name was Martin Luther (1483–1546). This bold act by a monk with a mallet launched the Reformation.[9] Other Reformers would follow, such as Ulrich Zwingli (1484–1531), Hugh Latimer (1487–1555), Martin Bucer (1491–1551), William Tyndale (ca. 1494–1536), Philip Melanchthon (1497–1560), John Rogers (1500–1555), Heinrich Bullinger (1504–1575), and John Calvin (1509–1564). To a man, they were firmly committed to the truths of Scripture and sovereign grace.

# MARTIN LUTHER

Luther was a giant of history;[10] he was so significant he was once described as an "ocean."[11] Some believe he was the most significant European figure of the second millennium.[12] Luther was the pioneer Reformer, the one whom God first used to spark a transformation of Christianity and the Western world.[13] He was the undisputed leader of the German Reformation.[14] In a day of ecclesiastical corruptions and apostasies, he was a valiant champion of the truth; his powerful preaching and pen helped to restore the pure gospel.[15] More books have been written about him than any other man of history except Jesus Christ and possibly Augustine.[16]

Luther came from hard-working stock. He was born in the little town of Eisleben, Germany, on November 10, 1483. His father, Hans, was a copper miner who eventually gained some wealth from a shared interest in mines, smelters, and other business ventures. His mother was pious but religiously superstitious. Luther was raised under the strict disciplines of the Roman Catholic Church and was groomed by his industrious father to be a successful lawyer. To this end, he pursued an education at Eisenach (1498–1501) and then at the University of Erfurt in philosophy. At the latter, he received a bachelor of arts degree in 1502 and a master of arts degree in 1505.

Luther's life took an unexpected turn in July 1505, when he was twenty-one. He was caught in a severe thunderstorm and knocked to the ground by a nearby lightning strike. Terrified, he cried out to the Catholic patroness of miners, "Help me, St. Anna, and I will become a monk."[17] Luther survived the storm and made good on his dramatic vow. Two weeks later, he entered the Augustinian monastery in Erfurt. His father was furious over Luther's apparent wasted education, but Luther was determined to follow through on his vow.

## Lost in Self-Righteousness

In the monastery, Luther was driven to find acceptance with God through works. He wrote: "I tortured myself with prayer, fasting, vigils and freezing; the frost alone might have killed me. . . . What else did I seek by doing this but God, who was supposed to note my strict observance of the monastic order and my austere life? I constantly walked in a dream and lived in real idolatry, for I did not believe in Christ: I regarded Him only as a severe and terrible Judge portrayed as seated on a rainbow."[18] Elsewhere he recalled: "When I was a monk, I wearied myself greatly for almost fifteen years with the daily sacrifice, tortured myself with fastings, vigils, prayers, and other very rigorous works. I earnestly thought to acquire righteousness by my works."[19]

In 1507, Luther was ordained to the priesthood. When he celebrated his first Mass, as he held the bread and cup for the first time, he was so awestruck at the thought of transubstantiation that he almost fainted. "I was utterly stupefied and terror-stricken," he confessed. "I thought to myself, 'Who am I that I should lift up mine eyes or raise my hands to the divine majesty? For I am dust and ashes and full of sin, and I am speaking to the living, eternal and true God.'"[20] Fear only compounded his personal struggle for acceptance with God.

In 1510, Luther was sent to Rome, where he witnessed the corruption of the Roman church. He climbed the *Scala Sancta* ("The Holy Stairs"), supposedly the same stairs Jesus ascended when He appeared before Pilate. According to fables, the steps had been moved from Jerusalem to Rome, and the priests claimed that God forgave sins for those who climbed the stairs on their knees. Luther did so, repeating the Lord's Prayer, kissing each step, and seeking peace with God. But when he reached the top step, he looked back and thought, "Who knows whether this is true?"[21] He felt no closer to God.

Luther received his doctor of theology degree from the University of Wittenberg in 1512 and was named professor of Bible there. Remarkably, Luther kept this teaching position for the next thirty-four years, until his death in 1546. In the classroom, Luther first lectured on Psalms (1513–1515), Romans (1515–1517), and Galatians and Hebrews (1517–1519). But the more Luther studied, the more perplexed he became. One question consumed him: How is a sinful man made right before a holy God?

## Tetzel and the Indulgence Controversy

In 1517, a Dominican itinerant named John Tetzel began to sell indulgences near Wittenberg with the offer of the forgiveness of sins. This crass practice had been inaugurated during the Crusades to raise money for the church. Commoners could purchase from the church a letter that allegedly freed a dead loved one from purgatory. Rome profited enormously from this sham. In this case, the proceeds were intended to help Pope Leo X pay for a new St. Peter's Basilica in Rome. Tetzel's famous line was, "As soon as the coin in the coffer rings, the soul from purgatory springs."[22]

This horrible abuse enraged Luther. He determined that there must be a public debate on the matter. On October 31, 1517, he nailed a list of Ninety-five Theses regarding indulgences to the front door of the Castle Church in Wittenberg. A few of the theses are as follows:

1. When our Lord and Master Jesus Christ said, "Repent" [Matt. 4:17], He willed the entire life of believers to be one of repentance.

2. This word cannot be understood as referring to the sacrament of penance, that is, confession and satisfaction, as administered by the clergy.

21. Thus those indulgence preachers are in error who say that a man is absolved from every penalty and saved by the papal indulgences.

27. They preach only human doctrines who say that as soon as the money clinks into the money chest, the soul flies out of purgatory.

32. Those who believe that they can be certain of their salvation because they have indulgence letters will be eternally damned, together with their teachers.

36. Any truly repentant Christian has a right to full remission of penalty and guilt, even without indulgence letters.

62. The true treasure of the church is the most holy gospel of the glory and grace of God.[23]

Nailing such theses to the church door was a common practice in the scholarly debates of the time. Luther hoped to provoke calm discussion among the faculty, not a popular revolution. But a copy fell into the hands of a printer, who saw that the Ninety-five Theses were printed and "spread as on angel's wings" throughout Germany and Europe in a few weeks.[24] Luther became an overnight hero. With that, the Reformation essentially was born.

## LUTHER'S CONVERSION: THE TOWER EXPERIENCE

It is possible Luther was still not yet converted. In the midst of his spiritual struggles, Luther had become obsessed with Romans 1:17: "For in it the righteousness of God is revealed from faith for faith, as it is written, 'The righteous shall live by faith.'" Luther had understood the righteousness of God to mean His active righteousness, His avenging justice by which He punishes sin. On those terms, he admitted that he hated the righteousness of God. But while sitting in the tower of the Castle Church in Wittenberg, Luther meditated on this text and wrestled with its meaning. It is worth letting him tell the story in his own words. He writes:

> Though I lived as a monk without reproach, I felt that I was a sinner before God with an extremely disturbed conscience. I could not believe that he was placated by my satisfaction. I did not love, yes, I hated the righteous God who punishes sinners, and secretly, if not blasphemously, certainly murmuring greatly, I was angry with God, and said, "As if, indeed, it is not enough, that miserable sinners, eternally lost through original sin, are crushed by every kind of calamity by the law of the Decalogue, without having God add pain to pain by the gospel and also by the gospel threatening us with his righteousness and wrath!" Thus I raged with a fierce and troubled conscience. Nevertheless, I beat importunately upon Paul at that place, most ardently desiring to know what St. Paul wanted.
>
> At last, by the mercy of God, meditating day and night, I gave heed to the context of the words, namely, "In it the righteousness of God is revealed, as it is written, 'He who through faith is righteous shall live.'" There I began to understand that the righteousness of God is that by

which the righteous lives by a gift of God, namely by faith. And this is the meaning: the righteousness of God is revealed by the gospel, namely, the passive righteousness with which merciful God justifies us by faith, as it is written, "He who through faith is righteous shall live." Here I felt that I was altogether born again and had entered paradise itself through open gates. There a totally other face of the entire Scripture showed itself to me. Thereupon I ran through the Scriptures from memory. I also found in other terms an analogy, as, the work of God, that is, what God does in us, the power of God, with which he makes us strong, the wisdom of God, with which he makes us wise, the strength of God, the salvation of God, the glory of God.[25]

The time of Luther's conversion is debated.[26] Some think it took place as early as 1508, but Luther himself wrote that it happened in 1519, two years *after* he posted his Ninety-five Theses.[27] More important is the reality of his conversion. Luther came to realize that salvation was a gift for the guilty, not a reward for the righteous. Man is not saved by his good works but by trusting the finished work of Christ. Thus, justification by faith alone became the central tenet of the Reformation. The righteousness of God imputed to believing sinners is, Luther declared, a "foreign righteousness." That is to say, the righteousness man needs to possess is alien to his experience. It comes from outside of him. It must be given by God—the very righteousness of Jesus Christ.

## ATTACKING PAPAL AUTHORITY

Justification by faith alone clashed with Rome's teaching of justification by faith and works. Thus, the pope denounced Luther for preaching "dangerous doctrines" and summoned him to Rome. When Luther refused, he was called to Leipzig in 1519 for a public debate with John Eck, a leading Catholic theologian. In this dispute, Luther affirmed that a church council could err, a point that had been made by John Wycliffe and John Hus. Luther said: "I assert that a council has sometimes erred and may sometimes err. Nor has a council authority to establish new articles of faith. A council cannot make divine right out of that which by nature is not divine right. Councils have contradicted each other. . . . A simple layman armed with Scripture is to be believed above a pope or council. . . . Neither the Church nor the pope can establish articles of faith. These must come from Scripture. For the sake of Scripture we should reject pope and council."[28]

Luther went on to say that the authority of the pope was a recent contrivance. Such religious superstition, he exclaimed, opposed the Council of Nicaea and church history. Worse, it contradicted Scripture. By taking this stand, Luther irritated the major nerve of Rome—papal authority.

In the summer of 1520, the pope issued a bull, an edict sealed with a *bulla,* or red seal. The document began by saying: "Arise, O Lord, and judge Your cause. A wild boar has invaded Your vineyard."[29] With these words, the pope was referring to Luther as an unrestrained animal causing havoc. Forty-one of Luther's teachings were deemed to be "heretical, or scandalous, or false."[30] Luther's beliefs were found to be "offensive to pious ears, or seductive of simple minds, or repugnant to Catholic truth."[31] With that, Luther had sixty days to repent or suffer excommunication. Luther responded by publicly burning the papal bull. This was nothing short of open defiance. Thomas Lindsay writes, "It is scarcely possible for us in the twentieth century to imagine the thrill that went through Germany, and indeed through all Europe, when the news spread that a poor monk had burnt the Pope's Bull."[32] But though he was hailed by many, Luther was a marked man in the eyes of the church.

## THE DIET OF WORMS: LUTHER'S STAND

In 1521, the young Holy Roman emperor, Charles V, summoned Luther to appear at the Diet of Worms in Worms, Germany, in order to officially recant. The renegade monk was shown his books on a table in full view. Then Luther was asked whether he would retract the teachings in the books. The next day, Luther replied with his now-famous words: "Unless I am convinced by the testimony of the Scriptures or by clear reason (for I do not trust either in the pope or in councils alone, since it is well known that they have often erred and contradicted themselves), I am bound by the Scriptures I have quoted and my conscience is captive to the Word of God. I cannot and I will not recant anything, since it is neither safe nor right to go against conscience. I cannot do otherwise, here I stand, may God help me, Amen."[33] These defiant words became a Reformation battle cry.

Charles V condemned Luther as a heretic and placed a hefty price on his head. When Luther left Worms, he had twenty-one days for safe passage to Wittenberg before the sentence fell. While he was en route, some of his supporters, fearing for his life, kidnapped him and took him to the Wartburg Castle. There, he was hidden from public sight for eight months. During this time of confinement, Luther began his translation of the Bible into German, the language of the commoners. Through this work, Reformation flames would spread even swifter.

On March 10, 1522, Luther explained the mounting success of the Reformation in a sermon. With strong confidence in God's Word, he declared: "I simply taught, preached, and wrote God's Word; otherwise I did nothing. And while I slept . . . the Word so greatly weakened the papacy that no prince or emperor ever inflicted such losses upon it. I did nothing; the Word did everything."[34] Luther saw that God had used him as a mouthpiece for truth. The Reformation was founded not on him and his teachings, but on the unshakeable footing of Scripture alone.

## THE BONDAGE OF THE WILL

In 1524, Desiderius Erasmus of Rotterdam, the great humanist scholar, wrote a book titled *Diatribe on the Freedom of the Will*, opposing Luther's denial of man's free will. Luther answered the following year with *The Bondage of the Will*. This theological masterpiece would become his *magnum opus*. Luther's manifesto is a masterful reaffirmation of the Augustinian position on sovereign grace. Luther argues convincingly from Scripture that the fall of Adam plunged the human race into sin. Thus, all men are morally unable to exercise their fallen wills to believe the gospel. In the book, Luther thanks Erasmus for going to the root of the controversy instead of addressing peripheral issues: "I praise and commend you highly for this also, that unlike all the rest you alone have attacked the real issue."[35]

In the book, Luther represents the human will as a horse or donkey that goes just as the rider directs it: "The human will is placed between the two [riders] like a beast of burden. If God rides it, it wills and goes where God wills. . . . If Satan rides it, it wills and goes where Satan wills; nor can it choose to run to either of the two riders or to seek him out, but the riders themselves contend for the possession and control of it."[36] The Devil is the rider of the unconverted man, Luther contends, controlling his will and attempting to restrain it from believing in Christ. God, on the other hand, is the rider of the will of the one in a state of grace. To bolster his case, Luther states that he has many generals he can send into this debate. But, he says, only two are needed—the apostles John and Paul. This duo, he argues, would soundly defeat the vain notion of free will and would uphold the freedom of God's will to save whom He pleases.

The next year, 1525, Luther married Katherine von Bora. This amazing woman was an escaped nun committed to the Reformation cause. The two repudiated their monastic vows in order to marry. Luther was forty-two and Katie was twenty-six. Luther states that he married to upset the pope and to "make the angels laugh and the devils weep."[37] Their union produced six children and much joy.

Luther had an extremely happy family life, which eased the demands of his ministry. The Luther home was a place of busy activity, with their own children and eleven nephews, nieces, and orphans. The Luthers opened their home to visitors and travelers, adding to the chaos. Because of their large family, Elector John the Steadfast gave Luther a former monastery in which to live. This three-story building had forty rooms on just the first floor. In these spacious accommodations, Luther lived and hosted a growing number of students and visitors. His dinner dialogues with guests in this home were compiled into his famous *Table Talk*. In many ways, Luther's home represented his life—busy, bustling, and boisterous.

## REFORM BRINGS CONTROVERSY

By 1528, the Reformation had swept across Germany. The major cities that had embraced the new cause were Erfurt, Magdeburg, Nuremberg, Strasbourg, and Bremen. Broader regions followed suit: Hesse, Brandenburg, Brunswick-Lüneburg, Schleswig-Holstein, and Silesia.[38] Through his many writings, Luther's influence also expanded to surrounding countries. Students came from all over Europe to learn from this great Reformer.

After enjoying an initial unity of doctrine, the German and Swiss Reformers found themselves in a major disagreement over the nature of the Lord's Supper. The Reformers unanimously rejected the Roman Catholic doctrine of transubstantiation, the teaching that the bread and wine are transformed into the body and blood of Jesus Christ when they are blessed by a priest in the Mass. Luther affirmed consubstantiation, the teaching that the body and blood of Christ are present and combine with the elements. Zwingli in Zurich maintained that the elements are simply a memorial of Christ's body and blood. Later, Calvin in Geneva insisted upon the spiritual presence of Christ in Communion. Luther wrote against Zwingli, and the division threatened the Reformed movement.

In 1529, the Marburg Colloquy was called in order to resolve the dispute. The two Reformers faced each other across a table and argued their positions, but agreement could not be reached. Sadly, Luther refused to shake Zwingli's hand. The issue remained unresolved.

Till the end of his life, Luther maintained a heavy workload of lecturing, preaching, teaching, writing, and debating. This work for reform came at a high physical and emotional price. Each battle extracted something from him and left him weaker. He soon became subject to illnesses. In 1537, he became so ill that his friends feared he would die. In 1541, he again became seriously ill, and this time he himself thought he would pass from this world. He recovered yet again, but he was plagued by various ailments throughout his final fourteen years. Among other illnesses, he suffered from gallstones and even lost sight in one eye.

### FAITHFUL TO THE END

In early 1546, Luther traveled to Eisleben, his hometown. He preached there and then traveled on to Mansfeld. Two brothers, the counts of Mansfeld, had asked him to arbitrate a family difference. Luther had the great satisfaction of seeing the two reconciled.

That same evening, Luther fell ill. As the night passed, Luther's three sons—Jonas, Martin, and Paul—and some friends watched by his side. They pressed him: "Reverend father, do you stand by Christ and the doctrine you have preached?" The Reformer gave a distinct "yes" in reply. He died in the early hours of February 18, 1546, within sight of the font where he was baptized as an infant.[39]

Luther's body was carried to Wittenberg as thousands of mourners lined the route and church bells tolled. Luther was buried in front of the pulpit in the Castle Church of Wittenberg, the very church where, twenty-nine years earlier, he had nailed his famous Ninety-five Theses to the door. Upon his death, his wife, Katherine, wrote concerning his lasting influence and monumental impact upon Christendom: "For who would not be sad and afflicted at the loss of such a precious man as my dear lord was. He did great things not just for a city or a single land, but for the whole world."[40] She was right. Luther's voice sounded throughout the European continent in his own day and has echoed around the world through the centuries since.

# LUTHER'S WRITINGS

Luther was one of the most prolific writers of all time, easily among the top five Christian writers in output.[41] He wrote 544 works that eventually were bound in fifty-four thick volumes in English. In the great Weimar edition in German, this enormous literary output comprises more than one hundred folio volumes. But more important by far than the volume of Luther's writings is its "powerful originality and unnerving profundity."[42] Luther was a biblical theologian who battled against the ecclesiastical tradition and Scholastic philosophy of his day. He wrote, "Theology is heaven, yes even the kingdom of heaven; man however is earth and his speculations are smoke."[43] For Luther, nothing compared with the study of biblical theology. His most important titles include:

## THE BONDAGE OF THE WILL

In 1525, Luther wrote *The Bondage of the Will*, a masterful attack on the freedom of the human will. This is one of the most important books ever written. J. I. Packer calls it "the greatest piece of theological writing that ever came from Luther's pen. In its fertility of thought, its vigor of language, its profound theological grasp, its sustained strength of argument and the grand sweep of its exposition, it stands unsurpassed among Luther's writings. It is the worthiest representative of his mature thought that he has left us."[44] In the book, Luther declares: "We must produce our forces against free choice. But we shall not produce all of them; for who could do that in one small book, when the whole Scripture, every jot and tittle of it, is on our side?"[45] This book is the heartbeat of the Reformation, which was more than a battle for justification by faith. It was a declaration of the sovereignty of God's grace in salvation.

## APPEAL TO THE GERMAN NOBILITY

In 1520, Luther wrote this work calling on the German nobility to reform the church because the papacy and church councils had failed to do so. He argued that the pope and the priesthood had built walls to protect themselves from reform, indicting the claims of the Roman Catholic leaders that they alone could interpret Scripture. Rome claimed that the church had authority over civil affairs, but Luther insisted that the pope should not interfere in such matters. Moreover, he maintained the priesthood of the believer, the idea that all Christians are priests of God with direct access to the throne of grace and able to interpret Scripture themselves.

## BABYLONIAN CAPTIVITY OF THE CHURCH

Also in 1520, Luther penned this piece attacking the seven sacraments of the Roman Catholic Church. Just as the Babylonians carried the Jews away from Jerusalem into captivity, so the papacy had carried Christians in Europe away from the Scriptures, he said. Luther recognized only baptism and the Lord's Supper as valid sacraments, whereas Rome had added five more. Further, Luther opposed Rome for withholding Communion from the laity and for teaching that the Mass is a sacrifice offered to God.

## The Freedom of a Christian

Yet again in 1520, Luther wrote this work that attacked Rome's view of salvation, maintaining that justification is by faith alone. It is not by good works that we become righteous, he said, but only by personal faith in Christ. In short, faith is the root of justification and good works are its fruit. The former is the means; the latter is the result. Faith is a matter of the inner person, Luther claimed, and good works deal with the outer person. Further, he maintained that a Christian is not under the tyranny of the pope, but under the lordship of Christ: "A Christian is a perfectly free lord of all, subject to none. A Christian is a perfectly dutiful servant of all, subject to all."[46]

## Luther's Bible

Luther began the work of translating the Bible into the German language while hiding in the Wartburg Castle. Making use of Erasmus's edition of the Greek New Testament, he completed his German translation of the New Testament in less than a year. The Old Testament translation was a sizeable task that he would complete in 1534. This project made the Scriptures available to the common person in Germany. Further, it helped shape the German language into its modern form.

## Short Catechism

In 1529, Luther penned his Short Catechism, a series of questions and answers about the Ten Commandments, the Apostles' Creed, the Lord's Prayer, and other critical areas of theology. "In the catechism," Luther said, "we have a very exact, direct, and short way to the whole Christian religion. For God Himself gave the ten commandments, Christ Himself penned and taught the Lord's prayer, the Holy Ghost brought together the articles of faith. These three pieces are set down so excellently, that never could anything have been better. . . . The catechism is the most complete and best doctrine, and therefore should continually be preached; all public sermons should be grounded and built thereupon."[47] Schaff remarks that "the Little Catechism, which is his best, bears the stamp of his religious genius, and is, next to his translation of the Bible, his most useful and enduring work."[48] This catechism plainly demonstrates Luther's towering intellect and his theological prowess in a succinct manner.

## REFORMATION HYMNS

Luther composed some 125 hymns for the church. In 1524, he published the first German hymnbook, containing only eight hymns, but subsequent editions added many more. Without question, his most famous hymn remains "A Mighty Fortress Is Our God," which he wrote in 1527, the year the Black Plague swept through Germany. In the midst of this soul-crushing experience, in which he personally witnessed the loss of countless lives, Luther wrote this renowned hymn based on Psalm 46. He found strength by contemplating God as a protective stronghold.

# LUTHER'S THEOLOGY

In his teaching of Scripture, Luther gave evidence of a strong adherence to the doctrines of grace. The main drift of medieval theology was toward a weakening of Augustine's strict predestinarian stance, but Luther led a charge to reverse this tendency. This is especially apparent in *The Bondage of the Will*. In this work, Luther asserted the captivity of the human will in spiritual matters, which makes fallen man entirely dependent on sovereign grace. Luther adamantly defended the doctrines of original sin, total depravity, sovereign election, and irresistible grace, both in *The Bondage of the Will* and other works. He declared that although man is entirely responsible to obey the gospel, he is unable to do so apart from sovereign grace.

**Doctrine in Focus:**

## DIVINE SOVEREIGNTY

Luther held firmly to the absolute sovereignty of God over all things. He writes: "He is God, and for His will there is no cause or reason that can be laid down as a rule or measure for it, since there is nothing equal or superior to it, but it is itself the rule of all things. For if there were any rule or standard for it, either as cause or reason, it could no longer be the will of God."[49] The divine will is supreme over all things. Nothing equals it or surpasses it. Thus, no one can thwart God's purposes. Elsewhere Luther says, "God is dependable—His predestination cannot fail, and no one can withstand Him."⁵⁰ God is sovereign over all, Luther asserts, and able to do all that pleases Him. Furthermore, Luther states, "The will of God is immutable and infallible, and it governs our mutable will, as Boethius sings: 'Remaining fixed, you make all things move.'"⁵¹ The will of God governs even the will of man.

Luther spoke frequently of God's secret will, but he was clear that God is sovereign, whether He reveals His purposes or not. He writes: "God does many things that He does not disclose to us in His Word; He also wills many things which He does not disclose Himself as willing in His Word. Thus He does not will the death of a sinner, according to His Word; but He wills it according to that inscrutable will of His."⁵² Elsewhere he adds: "The hidden will of God cannot be searched out by man. . . . We have enough to learn about the humanity of Christ, in whom the Father revealed Himself."⁵³ He also says: "If it is predestined, it will happen. But it has not been given to us to know what is predestined. Much rather, we are forbidden to know what has been predestined."⁵⁴ Luther clearly understood that God is actively reigning over His creation in ways that are often beyond human understanding.

God's sovereign will must be believed even though it cannot be entirely understood, Luther declared. He writes, "You who are listening to me now should remember that I have taught that one should not inquire into the predestination of the hidden God but should be satisfied with what is revealed through the calling and through the ministry of the Word."⁵⁵ In short, God's sovereign foreordination of all things is a subject into which man should not probe, but should be content with what He has revealed.

**Doctrine in Focus:**
RADICAL DEPRAVITY

Luther followed in the footsteps of Augustine, Gottschalk, and Anselm. His understanding of the doctrines of sin and depravity, alongside those of grace and election, was in keeping with these forerunners, but he, as well as the other Reformers, provided a more exact description and systematic explanation of the relationship between Adam's sin and that of the rest of the human race. With his thoroughly biblical understanding, Luther believed that original sin "is a hereditary depravity and corruption of the human nature."⁵⁶ Luther grasped, as did all the Reformers, that human nature is infected with sin inherited from Adam and that man is completely incapable of doing any spiritual good. He felt that this doctrine was critically important but was too often misunderstood. Luther says: "It is a great teaching, to know and understand what original sin is . . . all the universities together have not understood what original sin is."[57] The German Reformer recovered the Augustinian view of sin and proclaimed it to the masses.

Luther recognized that Adam's one act of disobedience resulted in the fall and defilement of mankind. He writes, "Through his sin Adam destroyed us and made us enemies of God who are liable to God's wrath and judgment and worthy of eternal death . . . I feel and confess that I am a sinner on account of the transgression of Adam."[58] He saw ample evidence of man's fallenness both in Scripture and in day-to-day life. He says: "How shall a man be able to govern himself in a God-pleasing manner when he knows nothing of God, is born and conceived in sin (Ps. 51:5), as we all are, and is by nature a child of wrath (Eph. 2:3) and an enemy of God? . . . Why should we poor, miserable people desire to boast loudly of great comfort, help, and counsel against the judgments of God, the wrath of God, and eternal death, when every day and every hour we experience in ourselves and in others that even in trivial, bodily needs we can neither counsel and help ourselves nor seek comfort?"[59] The sin of Adam corrupted the entire race.

Adam's sin, Luther asserted, resulted in the defilement of every human soul. Everyone enters this world already plagued by the poison of sin. He writes:

> As soon as they had eaten of the forbidden tree and sinned, their con-created righteousness fell away and perished. Then evil lusts began to arise and grow in them, and they became inclined to pride, unchasteness, wantonness of the flesh, and to all sins, as we now are. For as Adam and Eve were after the transgression, so all their descendants are. For just as Adam had a flesh poisoned with sin, so also all his descendants, born of him, have flesh inclined to all evil. And the sin that was in the parents is also born in all their descendants.[60]

Expanding on this idea that original sin is passed down from parent to child at the moment of conception, Luther writes: "Through his disobedience and transgression of the divine commandment Adam fell into sin, which polluted his body and soul, so that he was full of sin, wrath, and ungraciousness. This misery and abominable corruption he transmitted to his descendants, that is, to the entire human race. Just as Adam fell into sin and became subject to death, so we all who descended from him must bear sin, sorrows of all kinds, and death, sin's penalty, simply because we were born from the sinful flesh which was Adam's since the Fall."[61] In short, every child conceived in the womb inherits a sin nature.

In expositing Psalm 51:5, Luther showed the cause-and-effect relationship between original sin and actual sin. He says: "We are not sinners because we commit this or that sin, but we commit them because we are sinners first. That is, a bad tree and bad seed also bring forth bad fruit, and from a bad root only a bad tree can grow."[62] Original corruption is the root of all sins. Or, put another way, the sin nature is the root and individual acts of sin are the fruit.

In one colorful illustration, Luther compared the sin nature to a beard. He says: "The original sin in a man is like his beard, which, though shaved off today so that a man is very smooth around his mouth, yet grows again by tomorrow morning. As long as a man lives, such growth of the hair and the beard does not stop. . . . Just so original sin remains in us and bestirs itself as long as we live, but we must resist it and always cut off its hair."[63] The corruption within human beings is not permanently eradicated until they are glorified, but it must be battled.

Every aspect of human nature, Luther contended, is corrupted by sin. He asserts that "the Sacred Scripture . . . declares explicitly that nature is corrupt, meaning that the entirety of man is wicked and evil."[64] In other words, "[We] are infected with the poison of original sin from the soles of our feet to the crowns of our heads."[65] Elsewhere Luther writes, "Original sin really means that human nature has completely fallen; that the intellect has become darkened, so that we no longer know God and His will and no longer perceive the works of God; furthermore, that the will is so extraordinarily depraved, so that we do not trust the mercy of God and we do not fear God but . . . follow the desire and the impulses of the flesh."[66] He goes on to say: "Original sin . . . it is not only a lack of a certain quality in the will, nor even only a lack of light in the mind or of power in the memory, but particularly it is a total lack of uprightness and of the power of all the faculties both of body and soul and of the whole inner and outer man. On top of all this, it is a propensity toward evil. It is a nausea toward the good, a loathing of light and wisdom, and a delight in error and darkness, a flight from and an abomination of all good works, a pursuit of evil."[67] Luther's biblical diagnosis is that man's nature is bent toward sin constantly.

Regarding the mind, Luther taught that sin distorts man's reasoning in spiritual matters. He writes: "When [false teachers] say that by the dictates of right reason they can elicit and perform the good, what is this but to deny that our nature is corrupted by sin? . . . Human reason as well as the will has been blinded and turned away from the good and the true."[68] Concerning the will, Luther said that sin has utterly destroyed the freedom of man's will. He says, "We are so impetuously foolish and evil that we often sin against our own advantage and are our own worst enemies."[69] He adds, "Our will, especially when it is evil, cannot of itself do good."[70]

The worst effect of sin, Luther affirmed, is the way in which it blinds man to his need and helplessness. He writes, "Our nature is so corrupt and we are so inclined to presumption and security in prosperous times that it would be impossible for us to stand if the Holy Spirit did not change our hearts."[71] Man, he said, cannot even understand the way in which God provides justification. He says, "For human nature, corrupt and blinded by the blemish of original sin, is not able to imagine or conceive of any justification above and beyond works."[72] The unconverted mind, he said, can understand only a works righteousness to gain acceptance with God. The thought of a grace-based righteousness is incomprehensible to the carnal mind.

Luther summarizes the full effects of radical corruption in this manner: "Scripture . . . represents man as one who is not only bound, wretched, captive, sick, and dead, but in addition to his other miseries is afflicted, through the agency of Satan his prince, with this misery of blindness, so that he believes himself to be free, happy, unfettered, able, well, and alive."[73] Man is so depraved that he cannot even know the depths of his defilement.

**Doctrine in Focus:**

## Sovereign Election

Luther was also deeply convinced of the truth of the unconditional election of God. He believed that before time began, God chose out of fallen humanity those whom He would save. He affirms, "He ordains by His own counsel which and what sort of persons He wills to be recipients and partakers of His preached and offered mercy."[74] He adds:

> All things take place according to God's election. Jacob was loved by God because he had been elected, and he obtained mercy because it thus pleased God from eternity, just as also He said to Moses: "I will show mercy, etc." (Ex. 33:19). . . . It is solely because of a merciful

God that anyone is chosen or is righteous, inasmuch as all men are equally a part of the mass of perdition and no one is righteous before God unless he receives mercy . . . that everything depends on a merciful God and not on someone's will is evident and proved by the fact that in order that God might show this to be the case and that man might know that it is not due to his own running but to the mercy of God, that he wills and runs.[75]

Luther saw many examples of God's election in Scripture. He writes: "He demonstrates His election by the fact that He permits many people to live a good life from their birth and to do great good deeds, and yet they are not saved; again He permits many people to do great evil, and yet they are suddenly converted and saved. Examples of this are Saul and Manasseh. Likewise Judas the betrayer and the thief on the cross, and many other cases of harlots and open sinners."[76] He understood that God's choices are not man's choices.

Paul's epistle to the Romans was Luther's lecture focus early in his teaching career, and it was in that book that he discovered the truth of justification by faith alone. Not surprisingly, he turned often to this highly doctrinal book to argue the case for sovereign election. In teaching on Romans 8:28, Luther explains, "The term 'purpose' in this passage means God's predestination or free election and deliberation, or counsel."[77] This, he says, is illustrated "in the following chapter on the basis of the two stories of Isaac and Ishmael, and likewise of Jacob and Esau, [in which] the apostle shows that nothing except election distinguished the men, as he expressly says (Rom. 9:8ff)."[78] Luther believed that God had every right to choose some men for salvation but to pass over others.

Luther also addressed the doctrine of election in his introduction to his commentary on Romans, affirming that if not for God's election of some to receive salvation, no one would be saved:

In chapters 9, 10, and 11 he teaches of God's eternal predestination—out of which originally proceeds who shall believe or not, who can or cannot get rid of sin—in order that our salvation may be taken entirely out of our hands and put in the hand of God alone. And this too is utterly necessary. For we are so weak and uncertain that if it depended on us, not even a single person would be saved; the devil would surely overpower us all. But since God is dependable—His predestination cannot fail, and no one can withstand Him—we still have hope in the face of sin.[79]

Luther made this same point when commenting specifically on Romans 9:16, saying: "Concerning the statement, 'It depends not upon man's will or exertion, but upon God's mercy,' I respond: . . . 'You must despair, give God the glory, and confess that you did not start it.' When I was a monk I depended on such willing and exertion, but the longer [I worked at it] the farther away I got. What I have now I have not from exertion but from God. So in this passage Paul was saying everything against presumption, so that we may say, 'Lord, whatever [good] there is in us exists by Your grace.'"[80] It is clear that Luther believed that salvation depends on the determinative will of God, not the will of man.

That thought prompted Luther to rejoice that God's election puts the outcome of salvation entirely in His hands. Luther says, "God has taken my salvation out of my hands into His, making it depend on His choice and not mine, and has promised to save me, not by my own work or exertion but by His grace and mercy."[81] Fallen man can never choose to believe on Christ due to the deadening effects of original sin. But by His electing love, God makes salvation certain for His elect.

Luther insisted that the doctrine of election should be preached because it humbles man, thus preparing the unconverted soul for the gospel. He says: "It is thus for the sake of the elect that these things are published, in order that being humbled and brought back to nothingness by this means they may be saved. The rest resist this humiliation, indeed they condemn this teaching of self-despair, wishing for something, however little, to be left for them to do themselves; so they remain secretly proud and enemies of the grace of God. This, I say, is one reason, namely, that the godly, being humbled, may recognize, call upon, and receive the grace of God."[82] Commenting elsewhere on the humbling effect of this doctrine, he writes:

No man can be thoroughly humbled until he knows that his salvation is utterly beyond his own powers, devices, endeavors, will, and works, and depends entirely on the choice, will, and work of another, namely, of God alone. For as long as he is persuaded that he himself can do even the least thing toward his salvation, he retains some self-confidence and does not altogether despair of himself, and therefore he is not humbled before God, but presumes that there is—or at least hopes or desires that there may be—some place, time, and work for him, by which he may at length attain to salvation. But when a man has no doubt that everything depends on the will of God, then he completely despairs of himself and chooses nothing for himself, but waits for God to work; then he has come close to grace, and can be saved.[83]

When a man is thus brought to the end of himself and receives God's salvation as a gift, Luther said, the doctrine of God's election becomes beautiful and sweet. He affirms, "The matter of predestination and election . . . is not as deep a subject as is commonly thought, but rather is a wonderfully sweet thing for those who have the Spirit."[84] Elsewhere he adds, "This will is not to be inquired into, but reverently adored, as by far the most awe-inspiring secret of the Divine Majesty, reserved for Himself."[85] The doctrine of sovereign election should instill awe and reverence in a believer's heart.

Luther concluded that the doctrine of election is "very strong wine and the most complete meal, solid food for those who are perfect, that is, the most excellent theology."[86] However, "he who has not denied himself and learned to subject his questions to the will of God and hold them down will always keep asking why God wills this and does that, and he will never find the reason."[87] The unconverted heart will always reject this teaching. One must be taught by God in order to receive it.

**Doctrine in Focus:**

### DEFINITE ATONEMENT

There is disagreement as to what Luther believed about the extent of the atonement. On occasion, Luther spoke of the atonement as limited and particular. He writes, "Christ did not die for all absolutely."[88] Elsewhere he says, "For in an absolute sense Christ did not die for all, because He says: 'This is My blood which is poured out for you' and 'for many'—He does not say: for all—'for the forgiveness of sins' (Mark 14:24, Matt. 26:28)."[89] Here Luther appears to be arguing for a definite atonement exclusively for the elect.

Other selections from Luther's writings also seem to indicate belief in a particular atonement. In explaining 1 Timothy 4:12, Luther observed a clear distinction in Christ's saving work. He writes: "'He is the Savior of all men, especially of those who believe.' This passage clearly distinguishes between 'all men' and 'those who believe.' The latter He saves eternally, but not the former. Accordingly, when we make a distinction of salvation between faithful and faithless people, we must draw from those passages this conclusion, that Paul here refers to general salvation. That is, God saves all the faithful, but He does not save the faithless in the same way."[90] The context of this statement shows that Luther was thinking about the difference between common grace and saving grace. Luther recognized that the nonelect enjoy temporal, nonsaving benefits from the death of Christ. But Christ's death was redemptive only for those who believe, namely, the elect. Luther likewise states:

> In the first place, He [Christ] did not make a testament for all, because "He disinherits some," as He says in John 17:9: "I am praying for them, not for the world." Likewise in John 17:20: "I do not pray for these only, but also for those who are to believe in Me through their word." Likewise because He did not say "for all" but "which will be shed for many" (Mark 14:24; Matt. 26:28). And here (Heb. 9:15) we read: "So that those who are called may receive the promised eternal salvation." But this touches on the subject of predestination, which is either too difficult or too harsh for our feeble intellect to be able to grasp. Therefore, to speak rather humbly, He left the legacy only to those who fear His name and believe in Him.[91]

Here Luther acknowledged that Christ's sacrifice was not for all, but for those given to Him by the Father.

Regarding Luther's understanding of the specific intent of the atonement, Timothy George writes, "Luther restricted the scope of the atonement to the elect."[92] Still, it must be acknowledged that at times Luther seemed to speak of a universal atonement, and most Luther scholars agree that he taught a universal atonement in most if not all of his writings.[93] A possible solution is put forward by Raymond Blacketer in his essay "Definite Atonement in Historical Perspective," where he notes that "while the Lutheran confessional tradition would ultimately endorse universal atonement, Luther himself reflects the tradition of Augustinian particularism."[94] In the end, we must conclude that while Luther was clear in his teaching on most aspects of sovereign grace, his true beliefs on the doctrine of definite atonement remain uncertain.

**Doctrine in Focus:**

IRRESISTIBLE CALL

In contrast with his position on the atonement, Luther clearly believed strongly in the effectual nature of the sovereign call of God that draws the elect to faith in Christ. With his strong understanding of human depravity, Luther recognized that God must overcome the spiritual deadness and stubborn resistance of sinful men if any are to believe unto eternal life. He writes: "But what do the words 'The Father must draw you' mean? . . . Outwardly He [the Father] draws by means of Christ's Word, and inwardly through the Holy Spirit. Christ ascribes these works to the Father in order to distract us from our reason and human wisdom, and to impress upon us that we must view His Word not as the word of a mere man but as the Word of the Father. For He declares: 'Everyone who has heard and learned from the Father comes to Me.'"[95] Here Luther affirmed that conversion is entirely the work of God, not man alone or man in cooperation with God. As he says elsewhere, "Faith is not our work; for I am drawn to Christ, whom I neither feel nor see."[96] He clearly saw that God must draw the elect to Christ and work faith in them.

Expanding on the means by which God "draws" sinners to Himself, Luther focused on the role of the Spirit. He writes: "The ungodly does not 'come', even when he hears the word, unless the Father draws and teaches him inwardly; which He does by shedding abroad His Spirit. When that happens, there follows a 'drawing' other than that which is outward; Christ is then displayed by the enlightening of the Spirit, and by it man is rapt to Christ with the sweetest rapture, he being passive while God speaks, teaches and draws, rather than seeking or running himself."[97] Through the Holy Spirit, the Father works regeneration and belief.

Luther contended that the one who believes in Christ does so because he is eternally predestined and personally called by God to do so. He states, "If you believe, you are called; if you are called, you surely are also predestinated."[98] He adds, "Without the Holy Spirit and without grace man can do nothing but sin and so goes on endlessly from sin to sin."[99] Salvation cannot happen unless God acts on the dead sinner.

The will of the natural man, Luther insisted, cannot choose to come to God to accept the offer of salvation. He writes:

To say: man does not seek God, is the same as saying: man cannot seek God, as you may hence gather: If there were potency or power in man to will good, the movement of Divine omnipotence would not suffer it to remain inactive or keep holiday. . . . Paul's whole aim is to make grace necessary to all men, and if they could initiate something by themselves, they would not need grace . . . "free-will" is utterly laid low, and nothing good or upright is left to man; for he is declared to be unrighteous, ignorant of God, a despiser of God, turned away from Him and unprofitable in His sight. . . . Here is unbelief, disobedience, sacrilege, blasphemy towards God, cruelty and mercilessness towards one's neighbor, and love of self in all the things of God and of man! Here you have the glory and potency of "free-will"![100]

Luther was adamant on this impotency of the will. In explaining John 6:44, he says: "When Christ says in John 6: 'No man can come to Me, except My Father which hath sent Me draw him' (v. 44), what does He leave to 'free-will'? . . . Here, indeed, He declares, not only that the works and efforts of 'free-will' are unavailing, but that even the very word of the gospel (of which He is here speaking) is heard in vain, unless the Father Himself speaks within, and teaches, and draws. 'No man, no man can come,' He says, and what He is talking about is your 'power whereby man can make some endeavour towards Christ.' In things that pertain to salvation, He asserts that power to be null."[101] No man has the power to believe the gospel on his own.

With this thought in mind, Luther was quick to refute those who held that man contributes to his salvation. He says: "Granted that they attribute very little to 'free will,' yet they teach that we are able to obtain righteousness and grace by that 'very little.'"[102] Luther believed man contributes nothing to his salvation, not even "very little."

Luther described the radical change that comes over the human will when God issues His saving call. He writes: "If God works in us, the will is changed, and being gently breathed upon by the Spirit of God, it again wills and acts from pure willingness and inclination and of its own accord, not from compulsion, so that it cannot be turned another way by any opposition, nor be overcome or compelled even by the gates of hell, but it goes on willing and delighting in and loving the good, just as before it willed and delighted in and loved evil."[103] Elsewhere he adds: "The will does nothing. It is rather the substance in which the Holy Spirit works also in those who resist, as in Paul. But working on the will of him who resists He moves the will to consent."[104] When God changes a sinner's heart, that person no longer hates and resents God. He now wants God and joyfully accepts His offer of salvation.

In the end, Luther had no doubts that salvation is God's work from beginning to end. He writes: "We are people who have been born, not fashioned by man, but 'begotten.' This is not our work. As little as a child contributes to its being born, so little do we contribute to our being spiritually born. God is the Father . . . the 'Word of Truth' is the mother."[105] No one contributes to his natural birth. Neither, Luther reasoned, does anyone contribute to his supernatural birth.

**Doctrine in Focus:**

## Preserving Grace

Luther affirmed that God's sovereign grace preserves the salvation of the elect. He writes: "When you have Him as your Shepherd, you will surely not want. Yes, you already have what you shall have—eternal life. Nor will you ever perish. Nor shall any power be so great and mighty that it could snatch you out of His hand. Of that you can be sure. For this Shepherd's voice will surely not lead you astray."[106] Similarly, in expounding John 10, Luther paraphrased the words of Christ as the words of His sheep, saying: "I shall never perish, neither shall any man snatch me out of His hand; I shall have eternal life (John 10:28). And He will keep this promise, no matter what happens to me."[107] Luther was confident about the eternal preservation of every believer. He understood that none of the elect can be snatched out of the Father's hand.

While explaining 1 John 2:19, Luther affirmed that perseverance is a mark of those who are truly saved. He says, "The Day will reveal those who have been of us and have been born of the Gospel of truth, and vice versa. 'For if they had been of us, they would have continued with us.'"[108] Luther knew that all who are in Christ will never lose their salvation. Conversely, those who profess Christ but later apostatize reveal that they are not numbered among the elect.

Despite living amid many dangers in this world, the elect are held secure by God. Luther notes: "He saves us . . . and exposes His elect to as many rapacious forces as are mentioned here, all of which are striving to pull the elect down into damnation so that they might be lost, in order to show that He saves us not by our own merits, but purely by His own election and immutable will, in the very face of so many rapacious and terrifying adversaries who try in vain to harm us."[109] The key words here are "in vain"—nothing can separate God and His children. Expanding on this idea elsewhere, Luther writes: "God exposes His saints to so many evils, which are all like grasping hands, and yet He does not lose His saints. In this way He shows sufficiently clearly the firmness of His election, that it cannot be hindered by any creature, although He leads every creature up against it."[110] Election makes God's people eternally secure, because He completes what He begins.

**Doctrine in Focus:**
### Divine Reprobation

Luther ardently upheld God's sovereign choice in salvation as well as its biblical corollary—reprobation. George notes, "Luther did not shrink from a doctrine of absolute, double predestination."[111] Against the objection that such a view turns God into an arbitrary ogre, Luther answered—with Paul—that "God wills it so, and in so willing He is not evil. For all things are of Him, as the clay is the potter's. Therefore He gives commands that the elect might fulfill them and the reprobate be enmeshed in them, so that He might show both His anger and His mercy. Then 'the prudence of the flesh' says: 'It is harsh and wretched that God should seek His glory in my misery.' Note how the voice of the flesh is always saying 'my,' 'my'; get rid of this 'my' and rather say: 'Glory to Thee, O Lord!' And then you will be saved."[112] Luther believed that men ought to submit to the biblical teaching of election and reprobation as the wise plan of God. To be sure, Luther was convinced that no one who examines the Scriptures can escape this truth. Luther affirmed both that God brings some to salvation and that He wills the destruction of the nonelect.

# LAYING THE GROUNDWORK

Luther was the divinely appointed man who set all of Germany—and, eventually, Europe and the world—ablaze for the glory of God. To be sure, his legacy was far-reaching and his influence long-lasting. This German Reformer was the unquestioned leader of the Protestant movement, and it was upon his broad shoulders that men such as Zwingli, Tyndale, Bullinger, and Calvin stood. With Luther's groundwork laid, these noble men, armed with the Word of God, contended for the biblical truth that salvation is by grace *alone* through faith *alone* in Christ *alone* to the glory of God *alone*!

The church today stands in dire need of valiant spiritual leaders like Luther. Never has the need been greater for such men to appear on the scene. We live in a day in which "Ichabod" is written across the lintels of many churches, for the glory of God has departed from them (1 Sam. 4:21). Our withering pulpits beg for such stalwarts of the faith. Our languishing churches await such heralds of the gospel. But only God can give faithful men to the church. Writing more than one hundred years ago, Charles Spurgeon said:

> We want again Luthers, Calvins, Bunyans, Whitefields, men fit to mark eras, whose names breathe terror in our foemen's ears. We have dire need of such. Whence will they come to us? They are the gifts of Jesus Christ to the church, and will come in due time. He has power to give us back again a golden age of preachers, and when the good old truth is once more preached by men whose lips are touched as with a live coal from off the altar, this shall be the instrument in the hand of the Spirit for bringing about a great and thorough revival of religion in the land.[113]

May God grant to His church modern-day Luthers, each with a mallet in hand and a Wittenberg door before him, to bring about a new Reformation in this day.

NOTES

1  Martin Luther, *Luther's Works, Vol. 33*, American Edition, eds. Jaroslav Jan Pelikan, Hilton C. Oswald, and Helmut T. Lehmann (St. Louis: Concordia, 2002), 62.

2  Philip Schaff, *History of the Christian Church, Vol. VII: Modern Christianity—The German Reformation* (1910; repr., Grand Rapids: Eerdmans, 1980), 1.

3  W. Robert Godfrey, *Reformation Sketches* (Phillipsburg, N.J.: P&R, 2003), xiv.

4  T. M. Lindsay, *The Reformation: A Handbook* (Edinburgh: Banner of Truth, 2006), xi.

5  Stephen Nichols, *The Reformation: How a Monk and a Mallet Changed the World* (Wheaton: Crossway, 2007), 17.

6  René Pache, *The Inspiration and Authority of Scripture*, trans. Helen I. Needham (Chicago: Moody, 1969), 132.

7  James Montgomery Boice, *Whatever Happened to the Gospel of Grace? Recovering the Doctrines That Shook the World* (Wheaton: Crossway, 2001), 32.

8  Schaff, *History of the Christian Church, Vol. VII*, 17.

9  Nichols, *The Reformation*, 25.

10 Earle E. Cairns, *Christianity Through the Centuries: A History of the Christian Church*, 3rd Ed. (Grand Rapids: Zondervan, 1996), 288.

11 Paul Althaus, *The Theology of Martin Luther*, trans. Robert C. Schultz (Philadelphia: Fortress, 1966), vi.

12 Jonathan Hill, *The History of Christian Thought* (Downers Grove, Ill.: InterVarsity, 2003), 181.

13 Tony Lane, *A Concise History of Christian Thought* (Grand Rapids: Baker Academic, 2006), 148.

14 Hill, *The History of Christian Thought*, 181.

15 Justo L. González, *The Story of Christianity: Vol. 2: The Reformation to the Present Day* (Peabody, Mass.: Prince, 1984), 14.

16 R. Stipperich, "Martin Luther," in *Introduction to the History of Christianity*, ed. Tim Dowley (Minneapolis: Fortress, 2002), 368.

17 Luther, cited in E. G. Rupp and Benjamin Drewery, eds., *Martin Luther* (London: Edward Arnold, 1970), 2.

18 Luther, *Luther's Works, Vol. 24*, American Edition, 24.

19 Luther, *Luther's Works, Vol. 12*, American Edition, 273.

20 Bruce L. Shelley, *Church History in Plain Language*, 2nd Ed. (Nashville: Thomas Nelson, 1995), 238.

21 Luther, cited in Barbara A. Somervill, *Martin Luther: Father of the Reformation* (Minneapolis: Compass Point Books, 2006), 36.

22 Shelley, *Church History in Plain Language*, 240.

23 Luther, *Luther's Works, Vol. 31*, American Edition, 25, 27–28, 31.

24 Schaff, *History of the Christian Church, Vol. VII*, 156.

25 Luther, *Luther's Works, Vol. 34*, American Edition, 337.

26 "The event that led to Luther's new understanding of justification is called 'the tower experience,' because he once stated that it happened in the tower of the monastery. Although Luther described it as a critical turning point in his theological development, scholars are divided over when it occurred and what actually took place. In the preface to the first volume of his collected Latin works, written in 1545, Luther stated that the experience occurred while he was giving his second lectures on the Psalms, which would place it in 1518. Historians have long questioned Luther's dating, maintaining that his memory may well have been faulty since his account of the experience was written almost thirty years after the event, and they generally prefer to date it somewhere between 1513 and 1515. Recently it has become more common to accept Luther's dating." Rudolph W. Heinze, *Reform and Conflict: From the Medieval World to the Wars of Religion, A.D. 1350–1648* (Grand Rapids: Baker, 2005), 78.

27 Luther, *Luther's Works, Vol. 34*, American Edition, 336–337.

28 Luther, cited in Roland H. Bainton, *Here I Stand: A Life of Martin Luther* (New York: Abingdon Press, 1950), 116–117.

29 Pope Leo, *Exsurge Domine*, as cited in R. C. Sproul, *The Holiness of God* (1985; repr., Wheaton: Tyndale, 1998), 81.

30 Pope Leo, *Exsurge Domine*, as cited in Shelley, *Church History in Plain Language*, 237.

31 Pope Leo, *Exsurge Domine*, as cited in Shelley, 237.

32 Thomas Lindsay, *Martin Luther: The Man Who Started the Reformation* (Ross-shire, Scotland: Christian Focus, 2004), 91.

33 Luther, *Luther's Works, Vol. 32*, American Edition, 113.

34 Luther, *Luther's Works, Vol. 51*, American Edition, 77.

35 Luther, *Luther's Works, Vol. 33*, American Edition, 294.

36 Luther, *Luther's Works, Vol. 33*, American Edition, 65–66.

37 Luther, cited in Martin Brecht, *Martin Luther, Vol. I*, trans. James L. Schaaf (Minneapolis: Fortress, 1985–1993), 230.

38 Heinze, *Reform and Conflict*, 106.

39 Nichols, *The Reformation*, 25.

40 Katherine Luther, cited in Martin E. Marty, *Martin Luther: A Life* (New York: Penguin Group, 2008), 188.

41 Curt Daniel, *The History and Theology of Calvinism* (Dallas: Scholarly Reprints, 1993), 18.

42 Timothy George, *Theology of the Reformers* (Nashville: Broadman, 1988), 51.

43 Luther, *Luther's Works, Vol. 9*, German Edition. 65, as cited in George, *Theology of the Reformers*, 57.

44 J. I. Packer, "Historical and Theological Introduction," in Martin Luther, *The Bondage of the Will* (Grand Rapids: Revell, 2000), 40–41.

45 Luther, *Luther's Works, Vol. 33*, American Edition, 246–247.

46 Luther, *Luther's Works, Vol. 31*, American Edition, 344, 349, 368.

47 Martin Luther, *Table Talk*, trans. William Hazlitt (Ross-shire, Scotland: Christian Focus, 2003), 212.

48 Schaff, *History of the Christian Church, Vol. VII*, 89.

49 Luther, *Luther's Works, Vol. 33*, American Edition, 181.

50 Luther, *Luther's Works, Vol. 35*, American Edition, 378.

51 Luther, *Luther's Works, Vol. 33*, American Edition, 39.

52 Luther, *Luther's Works, Vol. 33*, American Edition, 140.

53 Luther, *Luther's Works, Vol. 54*, American Edition, 385.

54 Luther, *Luther's Works, Vol. 43*, American Edition, 236.

55 Luther, *Luther's Works, Vol. 5*, American Edition, 550.

56 Louis Berkhof, *The History of Christian Doctrines* (1937; repr., Edinburgh: Banner of Truth, 2002), 147.

57 Luther, *Luther's Works, Vol. 34*, American Edition, 165.

58 Luther, *Luther's Works, Vol. 26*, American Edition, 179.

59 Luther, *Luther's Works, Vol. 12*, American Edition, 154.

60 Luther, *What Luther Says*, compiled by Ewald M. Plass (St. Louis: Concordia, 1959), 1296–1297.

61 Luther, *Luther's Works, Vol. 22*, American Edition, 138.

62 Luther, *Luther's Works, Vol. 12*, American Edition, 348.

63 Luther, *What Luther Says*, 1302–1303.

64 Luther, *Luther's Works, Vol. 2*, American Edition, 126.

65 Luther, *Luther's Works, Vol. 1*, American Edition, 163.

66 Luther, *Luther's Works, Vol. 1*, American Edition, 114.

67 Luther, *Luther's Works, Vol. 25*, American Edition, 299.

68 Luther, *Luther's Works, Vol. 12*, American Edition, 342.

69 Luther, *Luther's Works, Vol. 6*, American Edition, 344.

70 Luther, *Luther's Works, Vol. 33*, American Edition, 39.

71 Luther, *Luther's Works, Vol. 12*, American Edition, 82.

72 Luther, *Luther's Works, Vol. 34*, American Edition, 151.

73  Luther, *Luther's Works, Vol. 33*, American Edition, 131.

74  Luther, *Luther's Works, Vol. 33*, American Edition, 139.

75  Luther, *Luther's Works, Vol. 25*, American Edition, 391.

76  Luther, *Luther's Works, Vol. 25*, American Edition, 374–375.

77  Luther, *Luther's Works, Vol. 25*, American Edition, 373–374.

78  Luther, *Luther's Works, Vol. 25*, American Edition, 374.

79  Luther, *Luther's Works, Vol. 35*, American Edition, 378.

80  Luther, *Luther's Works, Vol. 54*, American Edition, 88.

81  Luther, *Luther's Works, Vol. 33*, American Edition, 298.

82  Luther, *Luther's Works, Vol. 33*, American Edition, 62.

83  Luther, *Luther's Works, Vol. 33*, American Edition, 62.

84  Luther, *Luther's Works, Vol. 25*, American Edition, 371.

85  Luther, *Luther's Works, Vol. 33*, American Edition, 139.

86  Luther, *Luther's Works, Vol. 25*, American Edition, 389.

87  Luther, *Luther's Works, Vol. 25*, American Edition, 375.

88  Luther, *Luther's Works, Vol. 25*, American Edition, 376.

89  Luther, *Luther's Works, Vol. 25*, American Edition, 376.

90  Luther, *Luther's Works, Vol. 28*, American Edition, 261.

91  Luther, *Luther's Works, Vol. 29*, American Edition, 214.

92  George, *Theology of the Reformers*, 77.

93  Daniel, *The History and Theology of Calvinism*, 77.

94  Raymond A. Blacketer, "Definite Atonement in Historical Perspective," in *The Glory of the Atonement*, eds. Charles E. Hill and Frank A. James, III (Downers Grove, Ill.: InterVarsity, 2004), 313.

95  Luther, *Luther's Works, Vol. 36*, American Edition, 41.

96  Luther, *Luther's Works, Vol. 23*, American Edition, 23.

97  Luther, *The Bondage of the Will*, 311.

98  Luther, *What Luther Says*, 455–456.

99  Luther, *Luther's Works, Vol. 2*, American Edition, 40.

100  Luther, *The Bondage of the Will*, 281–282.

101  Luther, *The Bondage of the Will*, 310–311.

102  Luther, *What Luther Says*, 345.

103  Luther, *Luther's Works, Vol. 33*, American Edition, 65.

104  Luther, *What Luther Says*, 347.

105  Luther, *What Luther Says*, 347.

106  Luther, *Luther's Works, Vol. 12*, American Edition, 158.

107  Luther, *Luther's Works, Vol. 12*, American Edition, 159.

108  Luther, *Luther's Works, Vol. 30*, American Edition, 254.

109  Luther, *Luther's Works, Vol. 25*, American Edition, 371.

110  Luther, *Luther's Works, Vol. 25*, American Edition, 374.

111  George, *Theology of the Reformers*, 77.

112  Luther, *Luther's Works, Vol. 25*, American Edition, 376.

113  Charles Spurgeon, *Autobiography, Vol. 1: The Early Years, 1834–1859*, comp. Susannah Spurgeon and Joseph Harrald (Edinburgh: Banner of Truth, 1962), v.

# CHAPTER TWENTY
## STUDY QUESTIONS

1. Who were the Reformers? What were the key components to their message of reform? What effect did their commitment to Scripture have on the doctrines of grace?

2. Describe Martin Luther as a monk. How might his experience in the monastery have influenced his later belief in justification by faith alone? According to Scripture, what is the relationship of faith and works? What Bible passages can you cite concerning righteousness by faith versus righteousness by works?

3. Comment on the corruption of the sixteenth-century Roman Catholic Church. What were indulgences? What was Luther's response to the selling of indulgences?

4. Define *sola Scriptura*. Why was acceptance of this truth essential in order for reform to take place? In what way did this stance differ from the teachings of Rome? What effect did *sola Scriptura* have on the development of the doctrines of grace?

5. Summarize Luther's position on man's will. What event sparked the writing of his *magnum opus* in 1524? How does the helplessness of man's will promote monergistic regeneration? According to Luther, what role does man play in salvation?

6. Define Luther's doctrine of radical depravity. How were Luther's understandings of original sin and total depravity in agreement with those of the Church Fathers? In what way did Luther advance the doctrine of original sin farther than his predecessors?

7. To what extent did Luther hold to a definite atonement? Did the German Reformer believe that Christ died exclusively for His elect or for the entire world? What scriptural passages does Luther point to in affirming his position?

8. According to Luther, if man's will is in complete bondage to sin, how does one come to Christ? What does Scripture mean when it says that God "draws" men to Himself?

*W*e agree with Paul that predestination is the free disposition of God concerning us, independent of any consideration of our works, good or bad.[1]

*I* would that the word "free-will" had never been invented; neither is it in the Scripture, and might better be called self-will, which is of no use.[2]

–Ulrich Zwingli

# ZURICH REVOLUTIONARY

## SWISS REFORMER: ULRICH ZWINGLI

W hile Reformation fires were spreading throughout Germany, similar sparks were igniting in Switzerland. Nestled in the Alps, this loosely confederated nation was to play the pivotal role in the historic events of the Protestant movement. If a reformation is measured by its end rather than by its beginning, the Swiss reform movement was even more far-reaching than that which was birthed in Wittenberg.[3] What caught fire in Switzerland soon extended to France, England, Scotland, Hungary, and Holland. Even parts of Germany adopted the teaching of the Swiss Reformers more fully than that of Martin Luther and Philip Melanchthon.

The widespread impact of the Swiss Reformation was the result of several factors. First, Switzerland was a nation comprised of self-governing republics known as cantons; it had no monarchy such as France or England possessed. These cantons joined together in 1291, when they signed a treaty of mutual defense against the Austrians. However, each canton retained significant autonomy, including the choice of which faith to follow. Each Swiss province was a *reichfrie*—a free state—governed by its own city council, free to choose its own religion. Thus, each Swiss republic could decide whether to follow the papacy of Rome or the teachings of the Reformers.

Furthermore, many of the leading Swiss cities became centers for the advancement of humanism, an intellectual movement based chiefly on a return to the original sources in literature. Whether it was the study of Roman and Greek manuscripts from the classical period or the study of the Latin and

Greek manuscripts of the Church Fathers, the humanist motto was *ad fontes*—
"to the sources." Applying this approach to the Bible, the Swiss Reformers
went back to the Scriptures in the original languages, especially Greek for the
New Testament, seeking to recover the purity and vitality of the apostolic age.[4]
This became the prevailing approach in the leading schools and universities
in Switzerland. The University of Basel, for example, was where Erasmus, the
leading humanist of the day, edited his Greek New Testament.

Finally, the Reformation flourished in Switzerland because the country
was a refuge for many believers fleeing persecution in their homelands. The
Huguenots of France and exiles from Scotland and England escaped to safety
in Switzerland. There they sat under biblical preaching by Swiss teachers with
strong Reformed convictions. When the political climates changed in their
native lands, these persecuted believers returned home and took with them
the teaching of the Swiss Reformers. By this gathering and dispersal, the Swiss
Reformation spread farther and wider than that of even Germany.

## LUTHERAN AND REFORMED MOVEMENTS

In many regards, the two major branches of the Reformation in Europe—the
Lutheran movement in Germany and the Reformed movement in Switzerland—were much alike. Both were founded on the absolute authority of
Scripture alone—*sola Scriptura*—in opposition to the tradition and leadership of Rome. The difference lay in the application of biblical truth to the
church. At this point, the Swiss Reformers broke further from the Roman
Catholic Church than did the Lutherans. This is to say, the Swiss leaders were
more strict than the Germans in their interpretation and application of Scripture. Luther, for example, felt that the church could practice whatever was not
contrary to the Bible, allowing for a smaller departure from the practices of
Rome. With this understanding, the German Reformers first tried to reform
the church from *within*. But the Swiss Reformers, including Ulrich Zwingli,
Heinrich Bullinger, and John Calvin, chose to pursue only what is set forth in
Scripture. The result was a more decisive break with Rome, an effort to bring
reform from *outside* the Catholic Church.

Another contrast between the German and Swiss movements had to do
with their chief emphases. Luther made justification by faith the article on
which the church stands or falls. But the Swiss Reformers—who certainly
preached this cardinal doctrine—were zealous for a more all-encompassing
truth, namely, the sovereign grace of God in man's salvation. Philip Schaff

writes: "The Swiss theology proceeds from God's grace to man's needs; the Lutheran, from man's need to God's grace."[5] Consequently, Zwingli and Calvin subordinated every doctrine to the eternal predestination of God in sovereign grace. Luther clearly believed in the sovereignty of God in salvation and treated it as a part of the gospel of grace. But the Swiss Reformers treated God's sovereignty as the first principle of Christian thought and emphasized it more prominently. In this sense, the Swiss had a higher trajectory than the Germans in their preaching and writing. While the Lutherans stressed *sola fide* ("faith alone"), the Swiss Reformers stressed *soli Deo gloria* ("glory to God alone") more than even *sola gratia* ("grace alone"). Grace, they stressed, is the highest means to the ultimate end of God's glory.

## A COMPANY OF SWISS REFORMERS

Among the leading Swiss Reformers were Zwingli (1484–1531) and Bullinger (1504–1575) in Zurich, Johannes Oecolampadius (1482–1531) in Basel, Berthold Haller (1492–1536) in Berne, William Farel (1489–1565) in Neuchâtel, Pierre Viret (1511–1571) in Lausanne, and Calvin (1509–1564) and Theodore Beza (1519–1605) in Geneva. These men heralded God's sovereignty in providence and salvation. The first of them to take his stand in the long line of godly men was Zwingli.

# ULRICH ZWINGLI

Other than Luther, Bullinger, and Calvin, the most important early Reformer was Ulrich Zwingli.[6] A first-generation Reformer, he is regarded as the founder of Swiss Protestantism.[7] Furthermore, history remembers him as "the first Reformed theologian."[8] Though Calvin would later surpass Zwingli as a theologian, he would stand squarely on Zwingli's broad shoulders.

Less than two months after Luther came into the world, Zwingli was born on January 1, 1484, in Wildhaus, a small village in the eastern part of modern-day Switzerland, forty miles from Zurich. His father, Ulrich Sr., had risen from peasant stock to become an upper-middle-class man of means, a successful farmer and shepherd, as well as the chief magistrate for the district. This prosperity allowed him to provide his son with an excellent education. He presided over a home where typical Swiss values were inculcated in young Ulrich: sturdy independence, strong patriotism, zeal for religion, and real interest in scholarship.[9]

The elder Ulrich early recognized the intellectual abilities of his son and sent him to his uncle, a former priest, to learn reading and writing. Thanks to his prosperity, Zwingli's father was able to provide his son with further education. In 1494, he sent the ten-year-old Ulrich to the equivalent of high school at Basel, where he studied Latin, dialectic, and music. He made such rapid progress that his father transferred him to Berne in 1496 or 1497, where he continued his studies under a noted humanist, Heinrich Woeflin. Here Zwingli was given significant exposure to the ideas and Scholastic methods of the Renaissance. His talents were noted by the Dominican monks, who tried to recruit him to their order, but Zwingli's father did not want his son to become a friar.

## Universities of Vienna and Basel

In 1498, Zwingli's father sent him to the University of Vienna, which had become a center of classical learning as Scholasticism was displaced by humanist studies. There he studied philosophy, astronomy, physics, and ancient classics. In 1502, he enrolled at the University of Basel and received a fine humanist education. In class, he came under the influence of Thomas Wyttenbach, professor of theology, and began to be aware of abuses in the church. He also taught Latin as he pursued further classical studies. He received his bachelor's (1504) and master's (1506) degrees from the school.

Zwingli was ordained to the priesthood in the Roman Catholic Church and immediately purchased a pastorate at Glarus, his boyhood church. Paying money to a prince for a church position was a common practice prior to the Reformation. His time was spent preaching, teaching, and pastoring. He also devoted himself to much private study, teaching himself Greek and studying the Church Fathers and the ancient classics. He became enamored with the pagan philosophers and poets of old. Most significantly, he began reading the humanist writings of Erasmus and was profoundly impressed with his scholarship and piety. This sparked a highly prized correspondence with Erasmus.

During his service in Glarus, from 1506 to 1516, Zwingli twice served as chaplain to bands of young Swiss mercenaries. Swiss soldiers for hire were in great demand across Europe and were a major source of income for Swiss cantons. Even the pope had Swiss guards around him. But this practice cost the lives of many of the best Swiss young men. As a chaplain, Zwingli witnessed many of them fighting each other, Swiss killing Swiss on foreign soil for foreign rulers. He was forced to administer the last rites countless times.

The Battle of Marignano (1515) took nearly ten thousand Swiss lives. Zwingli came to deplore the evils of this system and began to preach against it.

His final year at Glarus proved to be pivotal. It was at this time that Zwingli came to an evangelical understanding of the Scriptures. Erasmus published his Greek New Testament in that year, and Zwingli devoured it; it is said he memorized Paul's epistles in the original language. This occurred a little more than a year before Luther nailed his Ninety-five Theses to the Wittenberg Castle Church door. Thanks to his study of the Scriptures, with no knowledge of Luther's ideas, Zwingli began to preach the same message Luther would soon proclaim. He wrote: "Before anyone in the area had ever heard of Luther, I began to preach the gospel of Christ in 1516. . . . I started preaching the gospel before I had even heard Luther's name. . . . Luther, whose name I did not know for at least another two years, had definitely not instructed me. I followed holy Scripture alone."[10]

## POPULAR PREACHER AT EINSIEDELN

Because of political pressures and his sermons against mercenary fighting, Zwingli was forced to leave Glarus in 1516. He served as a priest at the Benedictine monastery of Einsiedeln until 1518. Einsiedeln was a resort city that was known for its shrine to the Virgin Mary. This shrine attracted large numbers of pilgrims from all parts of Switzerland and beyond. This wider audience heard Zwingli preach, which expanded his reputation and influence.

Einsiedeln was smaller than Glarus, so his duties were lighter. That afforded him more time for the study of Scripture and the Church Fathers. He read the works of Ambrose, Jerome, Chrysostom, and Augustine, as well as the writings of Erasmus. Further, he copied by hand Erasmus's Greek New Testament. As he distinguished himself as a popular preacher, he also began attacking some of the abuses of the church, specifically the sale of indulgences, and his preaching began to take on a stronger evangelical tone. However, Zwingli did not yet see the need for changes in what the church believed. Rather, he felt reform should be primarily institutional and moral. Also, he remained more dependent on the Church Fathers than the Scriptures in his teaching. He was not yet ready for the work of reform.

In December 1518, Zwingli's growing influence secured for him the office of "people's priest" at the Grossmünster (Great Cathedral) at Zurich. This pastorate was a significant position. Zwingli immediately broke from the normal practice of preaching according to the church calendar. Instead, he announced he would preach sequentially through whole books of the Bible. On January 1, 1519, his thirty-fifth birthday, Zwingli began a series of expository sermons through Matthew that were drawn from his exegesis of the Greek text. He continued this consecutive style until he had preached through the entire New Testament. This ambitious project took six years and prepared the ground for the work of reform that was to follow.

In autumn 1519, Zurich suffered an outbreak of the plague. Two thousand of its seven thousand citizens died. Zwingli chose to stay in the city to care for the sick and dying. In the process, he himself contracted the disease and nearly died. His three-month recovery taught him much about trusting God. This personal sacrifice also increased his popularity with the people.

## INTRODUCING REFORM

As Zwingli preached through the Bible, he expounded the truths he encountered in the text, even if they differed from the historical tradition of the church. This kind of direct preaching was not without challenges. In 1522, some of his parishioners defied the church's rule about eating meat during Lent. Zwingli supported their practice based on the biblical truths of Christian liberty. He saw such restrictions as man-made. That same year, he composed the first of his many Reformation writings, which circulated his ideas throughout Switzerland.

In November 1522, Zwingli began to work with other religious leaders and the city council to bring about major reforms in the church and state. In January 1523, he wrote *Sixty-seven Theses*, in which he rejected many medieval beliefs, such as forced fasting, clerical celibacy, purgatory, the Mass, and priestly mediation. Further, he began to question the use of images in the church. In June 1524, the city of Zurich, following his lead, ruled that all religious images were to be removed from churches. Also in 1524, Zwingli took yet another step of reform—he married Anna Reinhard, a widow. All of this appears to have happened before Zwingli ever heard of Luther. This was truly an independent work of God.

By 1525, the Reformation movement in Zurich had gained significant traction. On April 14, 1525, the Mass was officially abolished and Protestant worship services were begun in and around Zurich. Zwingli chose to implement only what was taught in Scripture. Anything that had no explicit Scriptural support was rejected. The words of Scripture were read and preached in the language of the people. The entire congregation, not merely the clergy, received both bread and wine in a simple Communion service. The minister wore robes like those found in lecture halls rather than at Catholic altars. The veneration of Mary and saints was forbidden, indulgences were banned, and prayers for the dead were stopped. The break with Rome was complete.

## ANABAPTISTS: RADICAL REFORMERS

Zwingli also entered into controversy with a new group known as the Anabaptists or Rebaptizers, a more radical reform movement that began in Zurich in 1523. Though Zwingli had made great changes, he had not gone far enough for these believers. For the Anabaptists, the issue of baptizing believers only was secondary to separation from the Roman Catholic Church. The Anabaptists sought an entire reconstruction of the church that was akin to a revolution.

Zwingli saw the Anabaptist proposals as radical excess. In response to the Anabaptist demands for the immediate overhaul of church and society, he urged moderation and patience in the transition from Rome. He counseled that the Anabaptists must bear with the weaker brethren who were gradually accepting the teaching of the Reformers. However, this approach only caused the conflict between Zwingli and the radicals to widen.

An order by the magistrates of Zurich for all infants in the city to be baptized proved too explosive. The Anabaptists responded by marching through the streets of Zurich in loud protests. Rather than baptizing their infants, they baptized each other by pouring or immersion in 1525. They also rejected Zwingli's affirmation of the city council's authority over church affairs and advocated total separation of church and state.

The Anabaptist leaders were arrested and charged with revolutionary teaching. Some were put to death by drowning. It is not known whether Zwingli consented to the death sentences, but he did not oppose them.[11]

## THE LORD'S SUPPER CONTROVERSY

Meanwhile, a controversy began brewing between Zwingli and Luther over the Lord's Supper. Luther held to consubstantiation, the belief that the body and blood of Christ were present in, through, or under the elements. There is, he contended, a real presence of Christ in the elements, though he differed from the Roman Catholic teaching of transubstantiation, which holds that the elements change into the body and blood of Christ when blessed by the priest during Mass. Zwingli adopted the position that the Lord's Supper is mainly a memorial of Christ's death—a symbolic remembrance.

In an attempt to bring unity to the Reformed movement, the Marburg Colloquy was convened in October 1529. The two Reformers appeared face to face, along with Martin Bucer, Melanchthon, Oecolampadius, and other Protestant leaders. They agreed in principle to fourteen of the fifteen items put before them: the church-state relationship, infant baptism, the historical continuity of the church, and more. But no agreement could be reached regarding the Lord's Supper. Luther said that "Zwingli was a 'very good man,' yet of a 'different spirit,' and hence refused to accept his hand of fellowship offered to him with tears."[12] To colleagues, Luther commented of Zwingli and his supporters, "I suppose God has blinded them."[13]

In one of the strange ironies of history, Zwingli, who earlier had opposed the practice of using mercenaries in war, died on the battlefield in 1531. An escalating conflict between Protestants and Catholics had cantons in arms, and a war soon broke out. The city of Zurich went to battle to defend itself against five invading Catholic cantons from the south. Zwingli accompanied Zurich's army into battle as a field chaplain. Clad in armor and armed with a battle-ax, he was severely wounded on October 11, 1531. When enemy soldiers found him lying wounded, they killed him. The southern forces then subjected his corpse to disgraceful treatment.[14] They quartered him, hacked his remains to pieces, and burned them, then mixed his ashes with dung and scattered them abroad.

Today, prominently displayed at the Water Church in Zurich, is a statue of Zwingli. He is standing with a Bible in one hand and a sword in the other. The statue represents Zwingli in his towering influence over the Swiss Reformation, strong and resolute. Though his Zurich ministry was relatively short, he accomplished much. Through his heroic stand for the truth, Zwingli reformed the church in Zurich and led the way for other Reformers to follow.

# ZWINGLI'S WRITINGS

Zwingli's extensive literary labors were primarily in defense of the teaching of the Swiss Reformation. The theological challenges and conflicts of his day dictated what he wrote. Thus, most of his writings were polemic in nature. Through these works, Zwingli left a lasting mark on the Reformation.

## THE CLARITY AND CERTAINTY OF GOD'S WORD

In this work, published in 1522, Zwingli set forth the fundamental Reformed position on the full and final authority of Scripture. He argued for the perspicuity of Scripture, the supernatural capacity of the Bible to interpret itself lucidly and unambivalently in all matters of importance. He affirmed that the Bible is powerful, certain, and clear.[15] He wrote that the Author of Scripture, the Holy Spirit, illumines believers and enables them to see what God's Word truly says. Zwingli therefore concluded that the church does not need a self-proclaimed infallible interpreter such as the pope. Rather, believers simply need the Spirit's inner enlightenment, which enables them to perceive the truth.

## COMMENTARY ON TRUE AND FALSE RELIGION

Written in 1525, Zwingli's *Commentary on True and False Religion* was a systematic theology that had a considerable impact on Protestantism. This book is regarded as more mature and consistent than his other works. Moreover, it remains the chief source of information as to his theological system.[16] Here Zwingli writes that the Roman Catholic system of works-salvation is false, being built on religious superstition and human tradition. True religion, he contended, must be derived from the Bible alone. In this work, Zwingli renounced the Mass, reduced the number of sacraments from seven to two, rejected the teaching of purgatory, and repudiated the office of pope, calling him the Antichrist.

## ON PROVIDENCE

Zwingli argued in this work that the providence of God is absolute. God is the ultimate cause of every action or event in nature and history. At the same time, he denied that God is morally responsible for the sinful acts of men. While affirming that God is the ultimate cause of these acts, he denied that God is the direct author of sin. In the mystery of providence, Zwingli was clear to say that though divine providence is absolute, sin is derived from man, not God.

# ZWINGLI'S THEOLOGY

As the first Reformed theologian, Zwingli affirmed many of the basic elements of Augustinian theology. His theology was a magnificent first attempt to state Christian doctrine in a consistent evangelical form.[17] Two great doctrines were foundational in Zwingli's theology: the supremacy of the Scriptures and the sovereignty of God in His providence and His electing grace.[18] He held to the supreme authority of God over everything, most notably in the salvation of chosen individuals. Zwingli's theology was truly God-centered.

**Doctrine in Focus:**

DIVINE SOVEREIGNTY

Zwingli's entire theology was shaped by his sense of the sovereignty of God.[19] Timothy George notes: "Zwingli, like Luther before him, affirmed the sovereignty of God in creation and salvation. Indeed, his doctrines of providence and predestination were, if anything, even more clearly delineated than those of the Wittenberg reformer."[20] G. W. Bromiley adds that Zwingli placed a "tremendous stress upon divine sovereignty in his teaching. . . . The unifying factor in Zwingli's theology was the overwhelming emphasis upon the divine sovereignty. . . . He found it necessary both to include the fall of man in the providential ordering of the universe and also to assert a rigid predestination both to life and perdition. . . . He had a fine sense of the fact that God's providence must in some way include all events within the sphere of its operation."[21]

Zwingli asserted that God rules as an absolute Sovereign on His throne. He writes, "As it belongs to the legislator or prince to dispose according to what is right and good, so it belongs to the sovereignty of God to dispose according to his own nature, as that is goodness."[22] He also taught that God disposes people as His sovereign will dictates, saying: "He orders His vessels, that is, us men, as He will. . . . He can make His creation whole, or destroy it, as He will."[23] All things are in the hands of the sovereign God, he believed.

What is more, Zwingli maintained that the doctrine of providence is inseparably connected with God's predestination. He saw the one producing the other. He says, "Providence is, so to speak, the mother of predestination."[24] Again he writes, "Predestination, which one may also call foreordination, springs from providence, and is, indeed, itself providence."[25] Explaining his meaning, Zwingli adds: "I defined Providence as the rule over and direction of all things in the universe. For if anything were guided by its own power or insight, just so far would the wisdom and power of our Deity be deficient."[26] Thus, he reasoned that since God is sovereign, nothing else can have the power of self-determination. God is the primary cause of everything that happens.

God foreordained all things by His eternal decree, Zwingli believed. However, he acknowledged that few theologians are ready to confess this truth. He writes: "Why do we not confess, that everything is so governed and ordered by the providence of God, that nothing happens apart from His will or command? We are over-cautious; for we are afraid lest we be compelled to confess that God is the author of evil also."[27] Zwingli was not hesitant to proclaim the sovereignty of God because he knew from Scripture that while God's decree permits evil, He is not its direct cause.

This hesitancy to recognize God's guiding hand arises when mysterious providences occur, Zwingli said. He writes, "When things happen, of which we do not know the cause or the end, we are unwilling to recognize therein God's providence, which freely makes use of us, and indeed, of all things."[28] Believers, he thought, should accept the clear teaching of Scripture concerning God's sovereignty, even if it is not entirely understood.

Zwingli saw God's foreknowledge not as passive foresight but as active, causative foreordination. He states, "His wisdom . . . knows all things even before they exist, His knowledge comprehends all things, His foresight regulates all things."[29] With infinite wisdom and omniscience, God regulates all creation. In doing so, He causes everything to work together for the good of the elect. Zwingli says, "God uses for good both good and evil, though with this difference, that with the elect He turns everything to good, even their evil deeds, but not so with those who are rejected."[30] God's sovereign control is for His glory and for the good of His chosen ones.

Zwingli insisted that, in one way or another, whether directly or through secondary causes, everything that comes to pass is from God. He writes: "Everything that happens with regard to man, whether it concerns his body or his soul, comes from God, the real and sole cause; and even the work of sin comes from none other than God; although it is not sin for Him."[31] All things, whether events or human beings, are ultimately from God. He says: "Nothing is hidden from Him, nothing unknown to Him, nothing beyond His reach, nothing disobedient to Him. Hence not even the mosquito has its sharp sting and musical hum without God's wisdom, knowledge, and foresight."[32] Simply put, Zwingli saw that God is God.

**Doctrine in Focus:**
### Radical Depravity
In his teaching on human sinfulness, Zwingli focused more on the manifestations of it than the causes of it. Bromiley notes: "His Augustinian theology was tempered always by his humanistic training and impulses. In this connection

it is significant that Zwingli had no very pronounced doctrine of original sin, or at any rate original guilt."[33] Others argue that he held a fundamentally biblical view of sin,[34] and he did refer to the doctrine of original sin from time to time.

Zwingli taught that Adam's fall brought about man's slavery to sin and death. He writes: "Adam turned away from the light and guidance of the Spirit of God, and turned to himself, and trusting in his own counsel he thought to become great and like God. Through this sin he brought himself and us under the dominion or slavery of the law of sin and of bitter death."[35] He adds: "It would have been right and reasonable for God to have our first parents destroyed. But in His mercy God changed this death sentence into the condition wherein he whom God might have killed was made into a slave. And neither he nor his offspring could alter this condition, for a slave can only beget a slave; so by that deadly bite he plunged the whole of his posterity into slavery."[36] Adam became a slave; therefore, all of his descendants are born into slavery. Zwingli says, "original sin is innate in all who are born of the desire of man and woman; and I know that we are by nature children of wrath."[37]

Zwingli sometimes spoke of humanity's sin problem as a disease contracted from Adam. He says: "Original sin . . . is really, therefore, a sickness and a state. It is a sickness, because just as [Adam] fell through self-love, so do we; it is a state, because just as he became a slave, and subject to death, so we are born as slaves and children of wrath and subject to death."[38] At other times, he spoke of people as dead in sin. He writes: "They who have been born of one dead are themselves also dead. The dead Adam could not generate one free from death."[39] Elsewhere he adds, "The death which consists of sin is the parent of physical death."[40] Sin is spiritual death, which causes people to die physically.

Original sin, Zwingli maintained, is the cause of evil in the nature of all people. The result, he says, is that "nothing good comes from man."[41] He adds, "The mind of man is evil, and his spirit is evil from the moment his life begins, because he is flesh."[42] Expanding on the mental effects of sin, Zwingli says, "Man is called 'flesh,' because by disposition his mind is set only on what is carnal and deadly."[43] However, Zwingli said, man's will also is plagued by evil. He notes: "The will of the flesh, that is, of our broken human nature, struggles constantly against God. If God bids us die, or suffer, or be patient, then we all know well how sweet that seems to us! It all springs from the sinful weakness of man's first fall and his self-centeredness."[44] Zwingli saw that the mind and will of all men are governed by sin.

Zwingli emphasized the terrible effects that result from this control of the human mind and will. All people, he said, are subjected to moral inability. He writes, "By nature we are as incapable as was Adam of doing anything that is either right or good."[45] The key word here is *incapable*. Zwingli believed that original sin had rendered every person unable to please God. He adds: "We are evil by nature"[46] and "Our flesh . . . is evil by its very nature and character."[47] He also spoke of "the wretched state of fallen man, in which he is continually taken up with love and concern for himself."[48] He took up this theme of self-love elsewhere, writing: "The sin which dwells in us is nothing other than the defectiveness of our corrupt flesh, which because of its self-love is filled with constant longings that are in opposition to the Spirit. For the Spirit seeks the common good, whereas the flesh seeks its own."[49]

In one colorful illustration, Zwingli compared the sin nature to a Trojan horse. He writes: "Self-love contrives and hatches everything. It is the sickness or defectiveness from which all evils come, as though from a Trojan horse."[50] Zwingli clearly saw that man's problem lies within him.

This internal sinfulness, Zwingli affirmed, is the source of all actual sins. He notes: "The word 'sin' is taken to mean something like this: the weakness of our broken nature, which is always inciting us to the temptations of the flesh, and which can therefore fittingly be called 'the irreparable breach' . . . thus sin is this sinful breach, from which the various sins grow like branches. Therefore adultery, whoremongering, gluttony, avarice, arrogance, envy, ill-will, discord and murder are the fruit and the branches of this sinful weakness, which Paul also calls 'the flesh' in Galatians 5:19 and many other places, for these gullies spring from our broken flesh as a fount."[51] He understood that the sinful nature produces a gusher of sinful acts.

**Doctrine in Focus:**

## SOVEREIGN ELECTION

Zwingli taught the "unconditional predestination of God to salvation."[52] Schaff notes that he saw God's sovereign election as the true source of salvation: "Zwingli traced salvation exclusively to the sovereign grace of God."[53] In short, Zwingli plainly taught that God's election is determinative, and he boldly asserted God's freedom to choose those who would be His people in time and eternity.

Bromiley provides an accurate picture of the broad impact Zwingli's doctrine of election had upon his entire theology:

> Zwingli could not possibly explain predestination as a mere foreknowledge of belief or unbelief; on the contrary, it is a free determination of the divine will concerning those who are to be saved. This determination is the true source of all the redemptive activity of God, for in fulfillment of it God provides everything which is necessary for the salvation of His elect.[54]

> It was the same doctrine of the divine sovereignty in election and grace which determined Zwingli's understanding of the Church. The true Church which the New Testament describes as the body or bride of Christ is not at all co-terminous with that visible organization or complex of organizations which is its outward expression in the world. In its strictest and most proper sense the Church is the whole company of the elect or redeemed as called out from every age and country. And it is to this Church that the traditional notes apply. . . . To this inward Church of the elect Zwingli applied the term "invisible." By this he did not mean that the Church finds no external expression in the world, but that membership of it cannot be known merely by the external tests which can be applied by man. The election of God remains always the secret of God and of those who know the inward work of the Spirit. . . . The body of the elect as Zwingli envisaged it was not a small and exclusive company but a wide assemblage from every age and race and culture, probably including all children who died in infancy.[55]

Zwingli defined election as "the free disposition of God's will concerning those who are to be saved."[56] Thus, God is unconstrained in His choice of whom to save. Zwingli adds, "In the predestination of men to salvation, it is the will of God that is the prime force, but His wisdom, goodness, and righteousness and other attributes assist."[57] Elsewhere he says, "It is election which saves us, and it is wholly free."[58] Finally he notes, "Election is a free, sovereign and authoritative disposition of the will of God concerning those who are saved."[59] God's choice is His alone, guided by all His attributes.

Zwingli taught that the choices God made in eternity past are irreversible. He writes: "God's election stands fast and remains sure. For those whom He chose before the foundation of the world, He chose in such a manner, that He chose them for Himself through His son."[60] He adds, "The election of God stands firm and immovable."[61] The eternal will of God is unalterable within the present and throughout eternity future.

Finally, Zwingli affirmed that the faith that God requires in justification is derived from the sovereign election of God. He writes: "When one ascribes the gaining of eternal salvation to faith, one is ascribing to the consequence, to the seal, that which originally belongs to the title-deed itself. . . . One ascribes justification and salvation to faith, when they really come from the election and grace of God. Yet faith does follow election, in the sense that those who have it know it by this seal and pledge that they are elect."[62] This is to say, faith is a necessary consequence of election, not its originating cause. Thus, faith proceeds from election, not election from faith.

The act of believing does not number a person among the elect, Zwingli said. Long before a person believes, Zwingli contended, he was chosen by God in eternity past. He writes, "Those who are elect from eternity are surely elect before they believe."[63] The act of believing only reveals that one is a member of God's elect. In fact, many such elect have not yet believed. Zwingli says, "Many are elect, who do not yet have faith."[64] Many chosen individuals are yet to come to faith in Christ, but they surely will at the appointed time.

**Doctrine in Focus:**
DEFINITE ATONEMENT

Zwingli had little to say about the extent of Christ's atonement. However, in one place in his writings he declared that sovereign election is inseparably connected with the death of Christ. He explains, "Election . . . belongs to His goodness to have chosen whom He will, and it belongs to His justice to adopt the elect as His children and to bind them to Himself through His Son, whom He gave for a sacrifice to render satisfaction to divine justice for us."[65] This is a clear affirmation that the death of Christ was intended to save those who had been chosen by God. Thus, while it was not a major aspect of his teaching, Zwingli apparently held to the doctrine of definite atonement.

**Doctrine in Focus:**
IRRESISTIBLE CALL

Zwingli clearly believed that saving faith does not originate within fallen man. To the contrary, the capacity to trust in Christ must come from God Himself.

Bromiley writes: "The sole causality of God necessarily involved for Zwingli a rigorous doctrine of the divine predestination and election, for all that is good in man derives from God, and faith itself is possible only where God Himself has sovereignly decreed to give it."[66] Putting it even more plainly, Bromiley writes that Zwingli taught that "even faith itself is a direct work of God by the Holy Spirit."[67]

Zwingli affirmed this point unreservedly. He writes: "All men do not have faith; it comes solely from God. For Paul ascribes it to the Holy Spirit, from whom he received it. For those who are earthly mind earthly things; but those who have been born again from above mind heavenly things. Just leave man to himself! Whence will he obtain or acquire faith for himself, when he considers and seeks only earthly things? Thus faith is the gift of God alone."[68] This affirmation shows that Zwingli held that no man can believe apart from the effectual call of God's Spirit.

With great care, Zwingli explained the cause-and-effect relationship between election and faith. He writes, "Election is not the consequence of faith, but faith is the consequence of election."[69] This statement certainly denies the notion that election is based on divine foresight, that God merely looked ahead through time to see who would trust Christ and, in response to their actions, elected them to salvation. Instead, Zwingli saw election as preceding faith. He writes, "If election had not gone before like the blossom, faith could never have followed."[70] He adds, "Faith is given to those who are chosen and ordained to eternal life; but in such a way that election has precedence, and faith follows election as a symbol."[71] Simply put, the elect receive the gift of faith.

**Doctrine in Focus:**

PRESERVING GRACE

Zwingli also held to the eternal security of the believer. He states, "Faith is so efficacious, prompt and lively a medicine that whoever drinks it is safe and secure."[72] Though the elect may become temporarily ensnared in sin, Zwingli taught that they remain secure in grace. He says: "Even if one of the elect should fall into such horrible sins as are contrived by the impious and the reprobate; for the elect these are a cause for rising up again, whereas for the reprobate they are a cause for despair. David, Paul, Magdalene, the thief and others bear witness to this"[73] The elect of God can never fall away from saving grace.

Moreover, Zwingli said, believers may have assurance of their election and salvation. The fact that they have believed in Christ is a clear indication that they have been eternally ordained by God to eternal life: "Believers know that they are elect; for those who believe are ordained to eternal life."[74] He adds, "Those who believe know themselves to be elect; for those who believe are elect."[75] Zwingli's logic is impeccable—those who believe may be assured that they will never fall away, for their ability to believe shows they are elect, and election is unto eternal life.

More than this logic-based assurance, Zwingli taught, the indwelling Holy Spirit gives assurance to the believer that his faith is real and he is truly saved. He writes: "Nobody except the believer himself knows whether he truly believes. But he is certain that he is elect. For he has the Spirit as a pledge . . . the Spirit cannot deceive"[76] The Spirit gives an internal assurance about a believer's eternal state.

**Doctrine in Focus:**
### DIVINE REPROBATION
Zwingli believed that those who hear and reject the gospel in unbelief are predestined to condemnation.[77] He asserts, "As election is granted to those who are to be saved, one should not speak of election with regard to those who will be lost; the will of God does indeed ordain concerning them, but only to repel, reject and repudiate them, in order that they may be an example of His justice."[78] Zwingli distinguished between vessels of wrath prepared for destruction and vessels of mercy prepared for life (Rom. 9:22–23). God sovereignly grants mercy to the elect, but justice to the nonelect. He assigned the direct responsibility for unbelief not to God but to the individual sinner. Thus, God remains absolutely just in the eternal destiny of the nonelect.

# ONE PLANTS, ANOTHER WATERS

Because of his death at a relatively early age, Zwingli's theological thought did not have time to mature. He also never had the opportunity to record his thoughts in an organized, solidly Reformed theology. In the providence of God, the strategic work of developing Reformed theology in Switzerland would be carried out by Bullinger and Calvin, and further spread throughout Europe. But they built on the theological foundation for the Swiss Reformation that Zwingli had laid.

To be sure, God strategically works in His church through the unfolding succession of a long line of godly men. So it is that one plants and another waters. Ultimately, however, it is God who causes the growth. Thus, each man must know his place in God's vineyard. Each servant must recognize that God has sovereignly placed him in the field according to His perfect wisdom. Every spiritual leader must accept his God-appointed role. God determines where each man serves, when he serves, and for how long.

From a human perspective, Zwingli suffered what may seem to be a premature death. But in the economy of God, he passed from the scene precisely at the appointed hour. Likewise, Bullinger and Calvin appeared at the time ordained by God to carry on the work Zwingli had begun. So it is that each man performs his God-given task within his God-given time.

Where has the Lord assigned you to serve Him? What is your unique role? What is His calling on your life? Are you laying a foundation for others to build upon? Are you one to start a new work for God? Or are you building on the work of another? Every person has his own gift and divinely appointed place to serve God in this day. Everyone has his own time in history to carry out the Lord's assignment. May we all be faithful to do what God has entrusted us to do.

NOTES

1  Ulrich Zwingli, *Huldreich Zwingli's Werke, Vol. IV*, eds. Melchior Schuler and Johannes Schulthess (Zurich: F. Schulthess, 1828–42), 114, cited in Gottfried W. Locher, *Zwingli's Thought: New Perspectives* (Leiden: Brill, 1981), 130n32.

2  Ulrich Zwingli, *Huldreich Zwingli's Samtliche Werke: Einzig Vollstandige Ausgabe Der Werke Zwinglis, Vol. XXIV*, ed. Emil Egli, *Corpus Reformatorum, Vols. 88–101* (Zurich: Theologischer Verlag, 1982), 146, cited in Frank Hugh Foster, "Zwingli's Theology, Philosophy, and Ethics," in Samuel Macauley Jackson, *Huldreich Zwingli: The Reformer of German Switzerland* (New York: Putnam, 1901), 368.

3  T. M. Lindsay, *The Reformation: A Handbook* (Edinburgh: Banner of Truth, 2006), 59.

4  Philip Schaff, *History of the Christian Church, Vol. VII: Modern Christianity—The German Reformation* (1910; repr., Grand Rapids: Eerdmans, 1980), 19.

5  Philip Schaff, *History of the Christian Church, Vol. VIII: Modern Christianity: The Swiss Reformation* (1910; repr., Grand Rapids: Eerdmans, 1984), 10.

6  Mark Noll, "Ulrich Zwingli," in *Evangelical Dictionary of Theology*, 2nd Ed., ed. Walter A. Elwell (Grand Rapids: Baker, 2001), 1311.

7  Tony Lane, *A Concise History of Christian Thought* (Grand Rapids: Baker Academic, 2006), 169.

8 Gottfried Locher, "The Message and Impact of Huldrych Zwingli: The Significance for His Time," in *Prophet, Pastor, Protestant: The Work of Huldrych Zwingli After Five Hundred Years*, eds. E. J. Furcha and H. Wayne Pipkin (Eugene, Ore.: Pickwick, 1984), 111.

9 G. W. Bromiley, ed., "General Introduction," *Zwingli and Bullinger: Library of Christian Classics, Vol. XXIV* (Philadelphia: Westminster Press, 1963), 13.

10 Zwingli, cited in *The European Reformations Sourcebook*, 6.12, ed. Carter Lindberg (Malden, Mass.: Blackwell, 2000), 112.

11 Schaff, *History of the Christian Church, Vol. VIII*, 82.

12 Schaff, *History of the Christian Church, Vol. VIII*, 87.

13 Luther, cited in Heiko Oberman, *Luther: Man Between God and the Devil*, trans. Eileen Walliser-Scharzbart (New York: Doubleday, 1992), 120.

14 J. H. Merle d'Aubigné, *History of the Reformation of the Sixteenth Century*, trans. H. White (Harrisonburg, Va.: Sprinkle, 2003), 457–458.

15 Stephen Nichols, *The Reformation: How a Monk and a Mallet Changed the World* (Wheaton: Crossway, 2007), 47.

16 Foster, "Zwingli's Theology, Philosophy, and Ethics," in *Huldreich Zwingli*, 370.

17 Bromiley, "General Introduction," *Zwingli and Bullinger*, 38

18 Bromiley, "General Introduction," *Zwingli and Bullinger*, 31.

19 W. P. Stephens, *The Theology of Huldrych Zwingli* (Oxford: Clarendon, 1986), 86.

20 Timothy George, *Theology of the Reformers* (Nashville: Broadman, 1988), 122.

21 Bromiley, "General Introduction," *Zwingli and Bullinger*, 34, 37–38.

22 Zwingli, *Huldreich Zwingli's Werke, Vol. IV*, 113, cited in Locher, *Zwingli's Thought*, 131n34.

23 Zwingli, *Samtliche Werke, Vol. II*, 180, cited in Locher, *Zwingli's Thought*, 139.

24 Zwingli, *Huldreich Zwingli's Werke, Vol. III*, 842, cited in Locher, *Zwingli's Thought*, 124.

25 Zwingli, *Samtliche Werke, Vol. III*, 843, cited in Locher, *Zwingli's Thought*, 208n295.

26 Ulrich Zwingli, "On the Providence of God," in *On Providence and Other Essays*, eds. Samuel Jackson and William John Hinke (Durham, N.C.: Labyrinth, 1983), 130.

27 Zwingli, *Samtliche Werke, Vol. III*, 842, cited in Locher, *Zwingli's Thought*, 206n286.

28 Zwingli, *Samtliche Werke, Vol. III*, 843, cited in Locher, *Zwingli's Thought*, 206n286.

29 Zwingli, *Huldreich Zwingli's Werke, Vol. III*, 66, cited in Stephens, *The Theology of Huldrych Zwingli*, 91.

30 Zwingli, *Huldreich Zwingli's Werke, Vol. IV*, 137, cited in Locher, *Zwingli's Thought*, 124–25.

31 Zwingli, *Huldreich Zwingli's Werke, Vol. IV*, 125, cited in Locher, *Zwingli's Thought*, 206n287.

32 Zwingli, *Huldreich Zwingli's Werke, Vol. III*, 66, cited in Stephens, *The Theology of Huldrych Zwingli*, 91.

33 Bromiley, "General Introduction," *Zwingli and Bullinger*, 38.

34 Stephens, *The Theology of Huldrych Zwingli*, 146–47.

35 Zwingli, *Samtliche Werke, Vol. II*, 38, cited in Locher, *Zwingli's Thought*, 204n275.

36 Zwingli, *Huldreich Zwingli's Werke, Vol. IV*, 6, cited in Locher, *Zwingli's Thought*, 204–205n279.

37 Zwingli, *Huldreich Zwingli's Werke, Vol. IV*, 7, cited in Locher, *Zwingli's Thought*, 204n278.

38 Zwingli, *Huldreich Zwingli's Werke, Vol. IV*, 6, cited in Locher, *Zwingli's Thought*, 205n279.

39 Zwingli, *Huldreich Zwingli's Werke, Vol. III*, 169; Foster, "Zwingli's Theology, Philosophy, and Ethics," in *Huldreich Swingli*, 377.

40 Zwingli, *Samtliche Werke, Vol. III*, 657, cited in Locher, *Zwingli's Thought*, 204n277.

41 Zwingli, *Samtliche Werke, Vol. II*, 177, cited in Locher, *Zwingli's Thought*, 203n272.

42 Zwingli, *Samtliche Werke, Vol. III*, 659, cited in Locher, *Zwingli's Thought*, 203n273.

43 Zwingli, *Samtliche Werke, Vol. III*, 660, cited in Locher, *Zwingli's Thought*, 203n273.

44 Zwingli, *Samtliche Werke, Vol. II*, 633, cited in Locher, *Zwingli's Thought*, 203–204n275.

45 Zwingli, *Samtliche Werke, Vol. II*, 632, cited in Locher, *Zwingli's Thought*, 203n272.

46 Zwingli, *Samtliche Werke, Vol. II*, 186, cited in Locher, *Zwingli's Thought*, 140.

47 Zwingli, *Samtliche Werke, Vol. II*, 98, cited in Locher, *Zwingli's Thought*, 203n272.

48 Zwingli, *Samtliche Werke, Vol. III*, 662, cited in Locher, *Zwingli's Thought*, 204n275.

49 Zwingli, *Samtliche Werke, Vol. V*, 377, cited in Locher, *Zwingli's Thought*, 204n276.

50 Zwingli, *Samtliche Werke, Vol. V*, 377, cited in Locher, *Zwingli's Thought*, 204n276.

51 Zwingli, *Samtliche Werke, Vol. II*, 44, 235, cited in Locher, *Zwingli's Thought*, 202n270.

52 Earle E. Cairns, *Christianity Through the Centuries: A History of the Christian Church*, 3rd Ed. (1954; repr., Grand Rapids: Zondervan, 1996), 297.

53 Schaff, *History of the Christian Church, Vol. VIII*, 96.

54 Bromiley, "General Introduction," *Zwingli and Bullinger*, 33–34.

55 Bromiley, "General Introduction," *Zwingli and Bullinger*, 35, 38.

56 Zwingli, *Huldreich Zwingli's Werke, Vol. IV*, 113, cited in Locher, *Zwingli's Thought*, 130.

57 Zwingli, *Huldreich Zwingli's Werke, Vol. IV*, 114–15, cited in Locher, *Zwingli's Thought*, 131n38.

58 Zwingli, *Huldreich Zwingli's Werke, Vol. IV*, 123, cited in Locher, *Zwingli's Thought*, 138n75.

59 Zwingli, *Huldreich Zwingli's Werke, Vol. IV*, 115, cited in Locher, *Zwingli's Thought*, 130n30.

60 Zwingli, *Huldreich Zwingli's Werke, Vol. IV*, 5, 6, cited in Locher, *Zwingli's Thought*, 133.

61 Zwingli, *Huldreich Zwingli's Werke, Vol. IV*, 140, cited in Locher, *Zwingli's Thought*, 140.

62 Zwingli, *Huldreich Zwingli's Werke, Vol. IV*, 124, cited in Locher, *Zwingli's Thought*, 138n75.

63 Zwingli, *Huldreich Zwingli's Werke, Vol. IV*, 7, cited in Locher, *Zwingli's Thought*, 137n70.

64 Zwingli, *Huldreich Zwingli's Werke, Vol. IV*, 8, cited in Locher, *Zwingli's Thought*, 137n70.

65 Zwingli, *Huldreich Zwingli's Werke, Vol. IV*, 5, 6, cited in Locher, *Zwingli's Thought*, 133–134.

66 Bromiley, "General Introduction," *Zwingli and Bullinger*, 33.

67 Bromiley, "General Introduction," *Zwingli and Bullinger*, 34.

68 Zwingli, *Huldreich Zwingli's Werke, Vol. IV*, 121; Locher, *Zwingli's Thought*, 138n74.

69 Zwingli, *Huldreich Zwingli's Werke, Vol. IV*, 7, cited in Locher, *Zwingli's Thought*, 136–137.

70 Zwingli, *Huldreich Zwingli's Werke, Vol. IV*, 124, cited in Locher, *Zwingli's Thought*, 137.

71 Zwingli, *Huldreich Zwingli's Werke, Vol. IV*, 121, cited in Locher, *Zwingli's Thought*, 138n75.

72 Zwingli, *Huldreich Zwingli's Werke, Vol. IV*, 121, cited in Locher, *Zwingli's Thought*, 137n67.

73 Zwingli, *Huldreich Zwingli's Werke, Vol. IV*, 140, cited in Locher, *Zwingli's Thought*, 125n16.

74 Zwingli, *Huldreich Zwingli's Werke, Vol. IV*, 123, cited in Locher, *Zwingli's Thought*, 209n296.

75 Zwingli, *Huldreich Zwingli's Werke, Vol. IV*, 123, cited in Locher, *Zwingli's Thought*, 139.

76 Zwingli, *Huldreich Zwingli's Werke, Vol. IV*, 8, cited in Locher, *Zwingli's Thought*, 139n77.

77 Cairns, *Christianity Through the Centuries*, 297.

78 Zwingli, *Huldreich Zwingli's Werke, Vol. IV*, 115, cited in Locher, *Zwingli's Thought*, 129n26.

# CHAPTER TWENTY-ONE
## STUDY QUESTIONS

1.  Why was the fact that Switzerland was a confederation of autonomous republics crucial in the spread of Reformation teaching there? How was this governmental structure different from other countries at the time, such as France and England?

2.  What impact did humanism have on the Protestant movement? What was its influence on Swiss reform?

3.  Explain how the German Lutheran movement was akin to its Swiss Reformed counterpart. How were the two different? What doctrinal stress did the Swiss Reformers bring to the Protestant Reformation in the sixteenth century?

4.  Comment on Ulrich Zwingli's preaching at Glarus, Einsiedeln, and Zurich. What specifically was revolutionary about his preaching in Zurich? What were the effects of his consecutive preaching through the Bible? How should this truth affect preaching today?

5.  Who were the Anabaptists? Explain their view of baptism. What relationship did the Anabaptists believe the church should have with the state?

6.  Describe Zwingli's view of God's sovereignty. According to Zwingli, what is the relationship between providence and predestination?

7.  Summarize Zwingli's understanding of radical depravity. In what way was his view of original sin different, or less emphasized, as compared with the other Protestant Reformers? What reason can you provide for this difference?

8.  What did Zwingli assert is the relationship between sovereign election and particular redemption? For whom did Christ die?

$W$hen Christ is . . . preached . . . the hearts
of them which are elect and chosen, begin to
wax soft and melt at the bounteous mercy
of God.[1]

–William Tyndale

# PRINCE OF TRANSLATORS

## ENGLISH REFORMER: WILLIAM TYNDALE

T he Reformation battle cry of *sola Scriptura* was so powerful that it shook the thrones of kings and turned Europe upside down. This confessional affirmation, Latin for "Scripture alone," was a declaration that the Bible is the sole and ultimate authority for Christians. As such, Scripture takes precedence over all church traditions, decisions of ecclesiastical councils, human wisdom, secular learning, and even the teachings of the pope himself. The Reformers affirmed that Scripture is the highest authority and final arbitrator. Because of this tenet of their faith, the Reformers believed that everyone ought to be able to read the Word in his own language.

The German Reformer Martin Luther spearheaded the drive to restore the Bible to the place of highest authority in the church. He asserted that the ministry of God's Word must always be the centerpiece of Christian worship: "Therefore, when God's Word is not preached, one had better neither sing nor read, or even come together. . . . We can spare everything except the Word."[2] Luther maintained that a church where the Word of God is not preached and taught is no church at all: "The only perpetual and infallible mark of the church was always the Word."[3] Thus, Scripture must have primacy in the church: "The Word comes first," Luther said, "and with the Word the Spirit breathes upon my heart so that I believe."[4] Where the Word is honored, Luther affirmed, the Spirit brings life.

## DARKNESS COVERS ENGLAND

As the Reformers held up the Word of God and taught it, supernatural light began to dawn over the European continent. Such light was especially needful in England. Knowledge of the Scriptures had all but vanished from the British Isles. The Bible was available only in Latin and only to priests, but it was neither taught nor even understood. Although there were some twenty thousand priests in England, it was said that most could not translate a simple clause of the Lord's Prayer from Latin into English.[5]

More than a century earlier, John Wycliffe had attempted to relieve this darkness by translating the Bible into English and distributing copies by the Lollards, the preachers he sent out. But the church had brutally suppressed Wycliffe's efforts. Only a few hand-copied Wycliffe Bibles were available, and it could be fatal to possess one. In 1401, Parliament passed the *de Haeretico Comburendo*—"the burning of heretics"—which made it a crime to own or produce an English translation of the Bible and stipulated that those who did would be burned at the stake. In 1408, Thomas Arundel, the archbishop of Canterbury, wrote the *Constitutions of Oxford*, forbidding any translation of the Bible into English unless authorized by the bishops. Arundel wrote: "It is a dangerous thing . . . to translate the text of the Holy Scripture out of one tongue into another, for in the translation the same sense is not always easily kept. . . . We therefore decree and ordain, that no man hereafter, by his own authority translate any text of the Scripture into English or any other tongue. . . . No man can read any such book . . . in part or in whole."[6] The unlawful teaching of the Bible in English was considered a crime punishable by death. In 1519, seven Lollards were burned at the stake for teaching their children the Lord's Prayer in English. A night of deep darkness covered England.

## THE SPREADING FIRE

However, the Reformation fires that were igniting in places such as Wittenberg and Zurich could not be kept out. Soon, sparks began to drift across the English Channel. By 1520, Luther's works were being read and discussed by scholars in the university cities of Oxford and Cambridge. Desiderius Erasmus's Greek New Testament with his companion Latin translation, which he had completed in 1516, one year before Luther posted his Ninety-five Theses, were proving to be of great value to scholars. However, it was of no use to the common Englishman, who could not read the ancient languages. If the

Reformation was to come to England, the Bible must be made available in the English language for the people to read.

In this dark hour, God raised up a man who possessed the linguistic skills and steadfast devotion to translate the Bible into English. He was a remarkable scholar and linguist, being proficient in eight languages—Hebrew, Greek, Latin, Italian, Spanish, English, German, and French. Further, he possessed an ability to work with the sounds, rhythms, and senses of the English language. In order to do his translation work, he was willing to endure a forced exile from England and to live underground as a wanted fugitive for the last twelve years of his life. He paid the ultimate price by suffering a martyr's death to give his countrymen the New Testament and half of the Old Testament in English, translated from the original Greek and Hebrew, then printed. This remarkable Reformer was the most significant of the early English Protestants, and like others in the long line of godly men, he was steeped in the doctrines of grace. His name was William Tyndale.

## WILLIAM TYNDALE

Tyndale (ca. 1494–1536) made an enormous contribution to the Reformation in England. Many would say that by translating the Bible into English and overseeing its publication[7] that he made *the* contribution. One biographer, Brian Edwards, states that not only was Tyndale "the heart of the Reformation in England," he "*was* the Reformation in England."[8] Reformation historian J. H. Merle d'Aubigné calls him "the mighty mainspring of the English Reformation."[9] Because of his powerful use of the English language in his Bible, this Reformer has been called "the father of modern English"[10] and "a prophet of the English language."[11] His translation made him "the true father of the English Bible."[12] In recognition of his enduring influence, he has been called "the first of the Puritans, or, at least their grandfather."[13] John Foxe went so far as to call him "the Apostle of England."[14] There is no doubt that by his monumental work, Tyndale changed the course of English history and Western civilization.

Tyndale was born sometime in the early 1490s, most likely in 1494. The place of his birth was in Gloucestershire, in rural western England, close to the Welsh border. His predecessors had migrated to the Gloucestershire area earlier in the fifteenth century, when they became landowners. He was born into an industrious and important family of well-to-do yeoman farmers. The Tyndales were successful people in one of England's most prosperous counties,

452 PILLARS OF GRACE

having the means to send William to Oxford. Their extended family in the area included wealthy merchants, landowners, and local officials.

William had at least two brothers, Edward and John. Eventually, both brothers joined the cause of the Reformation. John was fined for possessing and distributing Bibles. Edward left a number of Reformed books in his will, likewise a crime. Little else is known about William's early years.

In 1506, William, age twelve, entered Magdalen School, the equivalent of a preparatory grammar school located inside Magdalen College at Oxford University. He was to spend approximately ten years at Oxford, from 1506 to 1516.[15] After two years at Magdalen School, Tyndale entered Magdalen College, where he learned grammar, arithmetic, geometry, astronomy, music, rhetoric, logic, and philosophy. He also made rapid progress in languages under the finest classical scholars in England. He earned a bachelor's degree in 1512 and a master's degree in 1515. Before leaving Oxford, Tyndale was ordained into the priesthood, though he never entered monastic orders.

It was only in the late stage of his time at Oxford that Tyndale was allowed to study theology. However, it was useless, speculative theology. He later expressed his disappointment in being shielded from the Bible: "In the universities, they have ordained that no man shall look on the Scripture until he be noselled [nursed] in heathen learning eight or nine years, and armed with false principles with which he is clean shut out of the understanding of the Scripture. . . . [T]he Scripture is locked up with . . . false expositions, and with false principles of natural philosophy."[16]

## CAMBRIDGE AND THE WHITE HORSE INN

Tyndale next went to study at Cambridge University, where it is believed he took a degree.[17] Many of Luther's works were being circulated among the instructors and students, creating great excitement on the campus. Cambridge was becoming the university of future Reformers and even martyrs. In this environment, Tyndale embraced the core truths of the Protestant movement.

In 1520, just three years after Luther had posted his Ninety-five Theses, a small group of Cambridge scholars began meeting regularly to discuss this "new" theology. They gathered at a pub on the campus of King's College called the White Horse Inn. As they debated the ideas of the German Reformer, this group became known as "little Germany." The group included many future leaders in the Reformed movement, including Robert Barnes, Nicholas Ridley, Hugh Latimer, Miles Coverdale, Thomas Cranmer, Thomas Bilney, Robert

Clark, John Frith, John Lambert, and, many believe, Tyndale.[18] Bilney was responsible for bringing most of them to the White Horse Inn, having come to faith in Christ through reading Erasmus's Greek New Testament.[19] Of this group, two became archbishops, seven became bishops, and nine became Protestant martyrs—Barnes, Ridley, Latimer, Cranmer, Bilney, Clark, Frith, Lambert, and Tyndale.

In 1521, Tyndale felt he needed to step away from the academic atmosphere in order to give more careful thought to the truths of the Reformation. He also wanted time to study and digest the Greek New Testament. So he took a job back in Gloucestershire, working for the wealthy family of Sir John Walsh at Little Sodbury, less than a dozen miles from his birthplace. Tyndale served as the tutor for the children and possibly as the chaplain for the family and secretary for Sir John. He also preached regularly in the little church of St. Adeline. During this time, he realized that England would never be evangelized using Latin Bibles. He came to see that "it was impossible to establish the lay people in any truth, except the Scripture were laid before their eyes in their mother tongue."[20] As he traveled about the region, it became known that his beliefs were becoming distinctly Luther-like. Around 1522, he was called before John Bell, the chancellor of the diocese of Worcester, and warned about his controversial views. No formal charges were made, but this incident was a foretaste of what was to come.

Local priests often came to dine at the Walsh manor, and Tyndale witnessed firsthand the appalling ignorance of the Roman clergy. During one meal, he fell into a heated argument with a Catholic clergyman, the latter asserting, "We had better be without God's laws than the pope's."[21] Tyndale boldly responded: "I defy the pope and all his laws." He then added these famous words: "If God spare my life ere many years, I will cause a boy that driveth the plough, shall know more of the Scripture than thou dost."[22] In saying this, Tyndale was echoing Erasmus's words in the preface to his Greek New Testament: "I would to God that the plowman would sing a text of the Scripture at his plow and that the weaver would hum them to the tune of his shuttle."[23] From this point forward, the ambitious task of translating the Bible into English was Tyndale's driving mission.

## To London with a Plan

In 1523, Tyndale traveled to London to seek official authorization for a translation project. He arranged to meet the bishop of London, Cuthbert Tunstall, a well-known classicist who had worked with Erasmus in compiling his Greek New Testament. Tyndale felt Tunstall would be open to his translation project, but he was met with resistance. Tunstall was determined to resist the spread of Luther's ideas, fearing an upheaval in England such as had occurred in Germany after the release in 1522 of Luther's German Bible. Tunstall knew that an English Bible, accessible to the people, would promote Reformed teachings and challenge the Catholic Church.

This stonewalling by Tunstall only deepened Tyndale's convictions. He knew England desperately needed a Bible that the common man could read. However, he was not certain how to do it—or where. Meanwhile, he preached numerous times, mostly at St. Dunstan's Church in west London. A wealthy cloth merchant, Humphrey Monmouth, heard him preach and became his patron. This financial backing allowed Tyndale to remain in London for a year, long enough to develop a plan. If he was to accomplish this translation project, he realized that "there was no place to do it in all England."[24] Opposed by the English church, Tyndale conceded that he must leave the country to undertake this work.

In April 1524, Tyndale, about age thirty, sailed to the Continent to launch his translation and publishing work. He was doing so without the king's consent—a clear breach of English law. Tyndale would live in exile from England for the final twelve years of his life, a fugitive and outlaw.

After arriving in Hamburg, Germany, it appears that Tyndale first journeyed to Wittenberg to be under the influence of Luther,[25] who had thrown off the last vestiges of popish authority.[26] Here Tyndale began the work of translating the New Testament from Greek into English.

In August 1525, Tyndale traveled to Cologne, where he completed his first translation of the New Testament. At that time, Cologne was the most populous town in Germany. In this bustling city, Tyndale found a printer, Peter Quentell, to publish his translation. He wanted the secrecy of the printing to be guarded at all costs, but the news about the project leaked when one of the print workers drank too much wine and spoke openly of the endeavor. A bitter opponent of the Reformation, John Cochlaeus, overheard and immediately arranged for a raid on the press. However, Tyndale was forewarned; he gathered the printed leaves after only ten pages had been run and escaped into the night. Leaving Catholic-entrenched Cologne, he fled up the Rhine to the more Protestant-friendly city of Worms.

## The First Printed English New Testament

In 1526, Tyndale was living in Worms, the city where Luther had been tried for heresy in 1521. After his refusal to recant his beliefs, Luther had become something of a folk hero in Worms, and the Reformation had made inroads there. Tyndale found a printer, Peter Schoeffer, who agreed to complete the printing of his English New Testament. This was the first portion of the Scriptures to be translated into English from the Greek and to be mechanically printed. Some six thousand copies were printed in clear, common English. Over the next eight years, two revised editions followed.

In spring 1526, Tyndale began to smuggle his English New Testaments into England in bales of cotton. In Antwerp, English merchants shipped them to England, where German Lutheran cloth merchants received them. Once past the royal agents, these forbidden New Testaments were picked up by the Christian Brethren, a secret Protestant society, and taken around England to various cities, universities, and monasteries. They were sold to eager merchants, students, tailors, weavers, bricklayers, and peasants alike, all hungry to read God's Word. Each one cost three shillings two pence—a week's wages for a skilled laborer. But demand quickly outstripped supply.

By the summer of 1526, this underground circulation of Tyndale's New Testament was known to church officials. Both the archbishop of Canterbury and the bishop of London were enraged. They attempted to destroy all the copies of Tyndale's New Testament that they could find and declared it a serious crime to buy, sell, or even handle it. Bishop Tunstall even preached a scathing sermon against Tyndale's New Testament at St. Paul's Cathedral in London and ceremonially burned copies of this "unauthorized" book. But these actions failed to stop the spread of Tyndale's translation. Demand only increased.

## Tyndale's New Testament Burned

William Warham, the archbishop of Canterbury, designed an ingenious plan to stop the spread of Tyndale's translation in 1527. He decided to purchase the remaining copies of Tyndale's New Testament and then destroy them. However, the money from the sales enabled Tyndale to produce a revised second edition. Warham unintentionally financed a better, more accurate edition with a larger print run.

In May 1528, Tyndale published his first major theological work, *The*

*Parable of the Wicked Mammon.* It focused on the heart of the gospel, the theme of justification by faith alone. Because of the decisive steps that were being taken in England to stop his work, Tyndale disguised his whereabouts by putting the name of a nonexistent printer, "Hans Luft," on the title page, along with a false place of publishing, "Marburg." The book actually was printed by John Hoochstraton at Antwerp, a major European center for printing.

On June 18, 1528, the archbishop of York, Cardinal Thomas Wolsey, dispatched three agents to the Continent to search aggressively for Tyndale. Wolsey also ordered John Hacket—the English ambassador to the Low Countries (the Netherlands)—to demand that the regent of the Low Countries authorize the arrest of Tyndale. But Tyndale withdrew to Marburg for safety. While hiding there, Tyndale wrote his second theological title, *The Obedience of a Christian Man,* which proved to be his most powerful and influential work. Like *The Parable of the Wicked Mammon,* it was published in Antwerp to confuse those looking for him. Hacket eventually reported that Tyndale could not be found. It would be seven years before his pursuers would track him down.

## TRANSLATING THE PENTATEUCH

In September 1528, another attempt was launched to track Tyndale down. John West, a friar, was dispatched from England to the Continent to apprehend the fugitive and bring him back. West landed at Antwerp, dressed in civilian attire, and began hunting for Tyndale. He scoured the cities and interrogated printers. In the meantime, a Cologne senator, Hermann Rinck, was buying and destroying all the Tyndale New Testaments he could find. Sensing the pressure, Tyndale remained in Marburg. He spent the time teaching himself Hebrew, a language that had not been taught in the English universities when Tyndale was a student. With this new skill, Tyndale began translating the Pentateuch from Hebrew into English. He also worked on revising his New Testament.

In 1529, Tyndale moved from Marburg to Antwerp. This thriving city offered him good printing, sympathetic fellow Englishmen, and a direct supply route to England. Under this new cover, he completed his translation of the five books of Moses, but he felt the danger was too great to stay in this large city. He realized that the Pentateuch must be printed elsewhere. So Tyndale boarded a ship to sail to the mouth of the Elbe River in Germany and then to Hamburg. But a severe storm struck the ship and it was wrecked off the coast of Holland. Tragically, his books, writings, and the Pentateuch translation were lost at sea. He had to start the work from scratch.

Tyndale eventually made his way to Hamburg. There he was received into the home of the von Emersons, a family with strong sympathies for the Reformation. In this house, Tyndale was reunited with Coverdale, a former classmate at Cambridge. Coverdale eventually would complete the translation project begun by Tyndale in the Coverdale Bible. In this protective environment, Tyndale undertook the laborious effort of retranslating the Pentateuch from the Hebrew language. This task, carried out with Coverdale's help, took from March to December 1529.

That same year, Sir Thomas More, a devout and intelligent Roman Catholic who was lord chancellor of England, was commissioned by King Henry VIII and the church to launch a bitter attack against Tyndale's arguments and to discredit his character. The result was *A Dialogue Concerning Heresies*, a vicious assault on Tyndale. More called him "the captain of English heretics," "a hell-hound in the kennel of the devil," "a new Judas," "worse than Sodom and Gomorrah," "an idolater and devil-worshipper," and "a beast out of whose brutish beastly mouth cometh a filthy foam."[27] More maintained that the only true church is the Roman Catholic Church, which, he claimed, speaks infallibly. Thus, anyone opposing the teaching of Rome must be a heretic. But Tyndale contended that true faith comes from the teachings of Scripture alone. Anything else, he said, is of the spirit of the Antichrist.

In January 1530, the five books of Moses in English were printed by Hoochstraton in Antwerp, again with a title page that said "Hans Luft at Marburg." These well-made little books were smuggled into England and distributed.

Tyndale's ambitious plan was to complete the translation of the Old Testament. He had received helpful feedback and input on his New Testament, which he planned to incorporate into the next edition. He also continued to write original works. In late 1530, he published *The Practice of Prelates*, a strong polemic against the clergy that documented the corrupt relationship between the English crown and the Roman papacy.

## An Offer for Tyndale

In November 1530, Thomas Cromwell, a counselor to Henry, tried another strategy to sway Tyndale. He commissioned Stephen Vaughan, an English merchant who was sympathetic to the Reformation, to find Tyndale. On behalf of the king, Vaughan was instructed to offer Tyndale a salary and safe passage back to England. When he arrived on the Continent, Vaughan sent three letters to Tyndale, each addressed to a different city—Frankfurt, Hamburg, and Marburg. Tyndale replied, and a series of secret meetings took place in Antwerp in April 1531. However, Tyndale feared that the king would break his promise of safe passage, ending the translation work. Similar promises of safety had been made and broken to John Hus and Luther. Therefore, Tyndale told Vaughan that he would return on only one condition—the king must have the Bible translated into the English language by someone else. If the king would do that, Tyndale said, he would return to England, never translate again, and offer his life unto death to the king if need be.

On June 19, Vaughan wrote back to Cromwell from Antwerp these simple words: "I find him [Tyndale] always singing one note."[28] In other words, Tyndale would not change his tune.[29] He would not promise to stop writing books or return to England until the king had commissioned a Bible in the English language.[30] So Vaughan returned to England without Tyndale.

Cromwell next turned to a more aggressive strategy. A new emissary, Sir Thomas Elyot, was dispatched to the Continent. But he was not sent to persuade Tyndale. Rather, he was commissioned to apprehend him and bring him back to the king. But this effort also yielded nothing. Elyot returned to England without the heretic in hand.

In 1531, Tyndale wrote his *Answer unto Sir Thomas More's Dialogue*. Tyndale defended his translation of certain crucial passages of the Bible that More had singled out for their potential to lead believers from Catholic theology. Tyndale said that Scripture is lucid, clear enough to be understood without church leadership or dogmatic tradition. More responded in 1532 and 1533 with a six-volume work, *Confutation of Tyndale's Answer*. In these tomes, More alleged that Tyndale was a traitor to England and a heretic to the church. At nearly a half-million words, it was the most imposing of More's polemical works. *Confutation* was a frontal assault on virtually every line of Tyndale's works and a statement of Roman Catholic positions. But despite this attack, the Reformation continued to spread across Europe and England.

## Undercover in Antwerp

In early 1534, Tyndale moved into a house in Antwerp as the guest of Thomas Poyntz, a wealthy English merchant who was, according to Tyndale biographer

David Daniell, "a good, shrewd, friend and loyal sympathiser."[31] Poyntz took Tyndale into his protection and even provided him with a stipend. John Rogers, the chaplain of the English House, a lodging for English merchants in Antwerp, also became a friend of Tyndale and a supporter of Reformed truths. Later, he would produce his own English Bible, the Matthew's Bible (1537), containing Tyndale's New Testament with only minor changes. It would become the most influential of all the early printed English Bibles.

Feeling secure, Tyndale set about the work of completing the revision of his New Testament translation, which Daniell calls "the glory of his life's work."[32] This second edition contained some four thousand changes and corrections from the 1526 edition. These edits were the result of suggestions Tyndale had received and the result of his own study. Further, Tyndale placed a short prologue before each book except Acts and Revelation, and he added cross references and marginal notes. Tyndale's Hebrew was now as good as his Greek, which allowed him to work masterfully on the next part of his Old Testament translation, Joshua through 2 Chronicles.

Back in England, a certain Harry Phillips had been given a large sum of money by his father to pay a man in London. But Phillips gambled the money away. An unknown high official in the church—probably the bishop of London, John Stokesley—was made aware of Phillips' plight and offered him a large sum of money to travel to the Continent and find Tyndale. In his desperation, Phillips accepted the offer. He arrived in Antwerp in early summer 1535 and began to make the necessary contacts among the English merchants. When he found Tyndale, he deviously established his friendship and won Tyndale's trust. Then, one day he lured Tyndale into a narrow passage, where soldiers arrested him. After twelve years as a fugitive, Tyndale was captured.

Poyntz's home was then raided and a number of Tyndale's possessions were removed. However, his bulky manuscript translation of Joshua to 2 Chronicles somehow survived the raid. In all likelihood it was in the possession of Rogers, who eventually printed it in the Matthew's Bible.

## Imprisoned in Vilvoorde

Tyndale was taken to the castle of Vilvoorde six miles north of Brussels. There he was imprisoned behind its imposing moat, seven towers, three drawbridges, and massive walls. Shivering in the dungeon of this castle-prison, Tyndale languished for nearly a year and a half as preparations were made for his trial.

During this time, he wrote another treatise, *Faith Alone Justifies before God*, to defend his chief doctrinal belief.

In the harsh winter of 1535, Tyndale wrote a final letter to the marquis of Bergen, requesting "a warmer cap; for I suffer greatly from cold . . . a warmer coat . . . a piece of cloth too to patch my leggings. My overcoat is worn out; my shirts are also worn out." Further, he asked for "a lamp in the evening; it is indeed wearisome sitting alone in the dark . . . permit me to have the Hebrew Bible, Hebrew grammar, and Hebrew dictionary, that I may pass the time in that study."[33] These months were "a long dying leading to dying."[34] Foxe writes that Tyndale "was affecting his very . . . enemies," because, during the time of his imprisonment "it is said, he converted his keeper, the keeper's daughter, and others of his household."[35]

In August 1536, Tyndale at last stood trial. A long list of charges was drawn up against him and he was condemned as a heretic. His offenses included believing that justification is by faith alone, that human traditions cannot bind the conscience, that the human will is bound by sin, that there is no purgatory, and that neither Mary nor the saints pray for Christians and Christians should not pray to them.

That same day, Tyndale was excommunicated from the priesthood in a public service. In such ceremonies, the priest typically was brought before a large gathering in his priestly robes and forced to kneel. His hands were scraped with a knife or sharp glass to symbolize the removal of the anointing of the priesthood. The bread and wine of the Mass were then placed into his hands and removed. Finally, he was stripped of his priest's vestments and reclothed as a layman.

After this humiliating ceremony, Tyndale was handed over to the secular powers for punishment. The death sentence was then pronounced. Back in his dungeon, a steady stream of priests and monks came to his cell to harass him and call on him to recant.

### "Lord, Open the King of England's Eyes"

Tyndale was executed on October 6, 1536. A large crowd gathered at the southern gate of the town, held back by a barricade. In the circular space, two beams were raised in the form of a cross. At the top was a strong iron chain. Brush, straw, and logs were piled at the base. At a set time, the procurer-general, who was the emperor's attorney, sat down with the other officials. The crowd parted as the guards brought Tyndale out.

Tyndale was allowed a moment to pray and then was urged one last time to recant. When he refused, the guards tied his feet to the bottom of the cross and fastened the chain around his neck. The brush, straw, and logs were packed around him, and gunpowder was added. It probably was at this moment that Tyndale cried his famous last words: "Lord, open the king of England's eyes."[36]

When the procurer-general gave the signal, the executioner quickly tightened the noose, strangling Tyndale. The procurer-general then handed a lighted wax torch to the executioner, who lit the brush and straw. The gunpowder then exploded, blowing up Tyndale's corpse. What remained of the limply hanging burnt body then fell into the glowing fire.[37]

# TYNDALE'S WRITINGS

Tyndale's abilities as a Bible translator were remarkable. But his work went beyond his Bible. Iain Murray notes, "Tyndale's work was wider than that of a translator only: he was a reformer."[38] In this capacity, he wrote a number of theological works that were important to the Reformation. "Tyndale's theological writings," N. R. Needham writes, "are the most important of any produced by the English Reformers during Henry VIII's reign."[39] An overview of Tyndale's works reveals the magnitude of his contribution.

## TYNDALE'S BIBLE

Tyndale's translation of the English Bible was his literary masterpiece. Working from Erasmus's Greek text and consulting the Latin Vulgate and Luther's German version, Tyndale produced an original rendering of the entire New Testament. He subsequently translated the first half of the Old Testament from the Hebrew, Genesis through 2 Chronicles, as well as Jonah. Tyndale's translation would prove to be so fundamentally correct and generally readable that it would form the foundation for all early English New Testaments, including the Great Bible (1539), the Geneva Bible (1560), the Bishop's Bible (1568), and the King James Version (1611). Ninety percent of the New Testament in the King James Version is Tyndale's work, and 75 percent of the entire Bible.

By this work, Tyndale shaped the English language itself. In the sixteenth century, there was no generally accepted right or wrong way of spelling in English. Tyndale's own name, for example, was spelled in many different ways:

Tyntaell, Tandeloo, Tendalle, and the like. But many of Tyndale's spelling choices became a permanent part of the English language.

Also, Tyndale's translation was rendered in a beautiful prose style. Far from the stilted medieval approach, it was plain, readable, and straight-forward, yet with beautiful words and phrases. It was truly a book for the common people. Tyndale did away with Catholic terms and used words such as *congregation* rather than *church*; *senior* and later *elder* in place of *priest*; *repent* for *do penance*; and *acknowledge* in place of *confess*. These changes drastically undercut the sacramental system Rome had built in the previous thousand years. Tyndale also coined new English words, such as *Jehovah*, *Passover*, *atonement*, and *scapegoat*. Further, he originated such now-familiar phrases as "lead us not into temptation but deliver us from evil," "knock and it shall be opened unto you," "twinkling of an eye," "a moment in time," "seek and you shall find," "judge not that you not be judged," "let there be light," "the powers that be," "my brother's keeper," "the salt of the earth," "a law unto themselves," "filthy lucre," "it came to pass," "gave up the ghost," "the signs of the times," "the spirit is willing," "live and move and have our being," and "fight the good fight." Tyndale's phrases became staples of the English language. It is said that Tyndale made a language for England at a time when English was trying to find its own form.[40]

Tyndale also included lists of key words in his Pentateuch. He thus was the pioneer of English lexicography, as no English dictionary existed at that time. He also wrote prologues to all the books of the New Testament except Acts and Revelation, and to the Pentateuch and Genesis. Further, he wrote marginal notes to his New Testament to explain the meaning of the text. This Bible was the chief vehicle for promoting Reformation truth in England.

### THE PARABLE OF THE WICKED MAMMON

The first of Tyndale's theological works, *The Parable of the Wicked Mammon* (1528), proved to be his best known. Written with a strong Augustinian emphasis, it was a passionate exposition and sound defense of the doctrine of justification by faith alone, the truth that we are made righteous before God solely through faith in Christ. Murray defines the central message of this work in this way: "Faith, wrought by the Spirit, unites the sinner to Christ."[41] Of justification, Tyndale writes: "Christ is thine, and all His deeds are thy deeds. Christ is in thee, and thou in Him, knit together inseparably. Neither canst thou be damned, except Christ be damned with thee: neither can Christ be saved, except thou be saved with Him."[42] In this work, Tyndale drew heavily on Luther, simply translating him in places.

### THE OBEDIENCE OF A CHRISTIAN MAN

*The Obedience of a Christian Man* (1528) was the largest of Tyndale's theological works. It is regarded as a major theological treatise.[43] This work answered the charge that Tyndale preached rebellion against secular rulers, specifically the king. He declared that civil authorities—whether kings, parents, husbands, masters, or landlords—should be obeyed by those under them, but everyone must give his ultimate loyalty to God. The king is the highest human authority, but God is yet higher. This work also indicted the corruptions of England's bishops.

### THE PRACTICE OF PRELATES

In *The Practice of Prelates* (1530), Tyndale outlined the corruption in the hierarchy of the established church. He gave a historical overview of the rise of the false system of church hierarchy and prelacy. In particular, he denounced Henry VIII's divorce from Catherine of Aragon on the grounds that it was unscriptural, and he argued that the divorce rendered the king spiritually unfit to lead the nation. Tyndale speculated that the royal divorce was a plot by Cardinal Wolsey to draw Henry into the entanglement of the papal courts. The king was so enraged that he asked Holy Roman Emperor Charles V to have Tyndale arrested and returned to England.

## TYNDALE'S THEOLOGY

Tyndale did not merely translate the Bible; he was concerned for its proper interpretation. As a Reformer, he was committed to sound doctrine, including the doctrines of grace. Reformed truths, such as the bondage of the human will and the sovereign exercise of God's will, impressed on him by Luther's writings, were a major influence on his understanding of Scripture. From 1529 onward, Swiss Protestant theology, from Ulrich Zwingli and others, also exercised a growing influence on him. Edwards writes: "Tyndale . . . knew that the cause of the corrupt state of the Church was its corrupt doctrine, and until the doctrine of the Church was corrected, the abuses would continue. On this turned the whole issue of the Reformation. The evangelical reformers were forced out of the Church of Rome, not because they could not accept the corrupt practices, but because they early discovered that the corrupt doctrines could never be changed."[44] Thus, it was Tyndale's high doctrines of sovereign grace that fueled his relentless drive in life and ministry.

**Doctrine in Focus:**

DIVINE SOVEREIGNTY

Tyndale believed God is sovereign in His reign over all things. Daniell notes: "Tyndale was more than a mildly theological thinker. He is at last being understood as, theologically as well as linguistically, well ahead of his time. For him, as decades later for Calvin . . . the overriding message of the New Testament is the sovereignty of God. Everything is contained in that. It must never, as he wrote, be lost from sight. . . . For Tyndale, God is, above all, sovereign, active in the individual and in history."[45] This view of divine sovereignty formed the foundation of Tyndale's God-centered beliefs.

In advising the best way to read the Scriptures, Tyndale writes, "First note with strong faith the power of God, in creating all of nought."[46] This was an affirmation that God created everything *ex nihilo*, out of nothing. Further, he asserted that God possesses the supreme right to do with His creation as He pleases, saying, "God has power over all His creatures of right, to do with them what He will, or to make of every one of them as He wills."[47] He strongly denied that any external constraints can force God to act. He writes, "God is free, and no further bound than He bindeth Himself."[48] The only restraints on God are His own holy character and perfect will. He freely acts in history, doing whatsoever He determines to do.

Even the greatest of men, kings and governors, are subject to God's supreme will, Tyndale said. He notes, "God [has] all tyrants in His hand, and letteth them not do whatsoever they would, but as much only as He appointeth them to do."[49] He adds: "As God maketh the king head over his realm, even so giveth he him commandment to execute the laws upon all men indifferently. For the law is God's, and not the king's. The king is but a servant, to execute the law of God. . . . God hath made governors in the world . . . they have received their offices of God, to minister and to do service."[50] God sovereignly raises up one ruler and lowers another, but these divinely appointed leaders do only as He directs them to do.

Tyndale saw his life as subject to divine sovereignty when he said that he would continue in his ministry "if it be God's will that I shall further labour in His harvest."[51] He knew himself to be under the overruling sovereign providence of God.

## Doctrine in Focus:
### RADICAL CORRUPTION

Tyndale was strongly convinced of the biblical doctrine of total depravity. On this issue, he stood shoulder to shoulder with the other Reformers and, more important, with Scripture itself.

He affirmed that the sin of Adam brought about the ruin of the human race. He writes, "The fall of Adam has made us heirs of the vengeance and wrath of God, and heirs of eternal damnation; and has brought us into captivity and bondage under the devil."[52] When Adam sinned, Tyndale held, all mankind sinned in him, and hence became subject to God's judgment.

Furthermore, he said, the "poison" of original sin, the sinful nature inherited from Adam, infects all men from the moment of conception. He says: "As a serpent, yet young, or yet unbrought forth, is full of poison, and cannot afterward (when the time is come, and occasion given) but bring forth the fruits thereof; and as an adder, a toad, or a snake, is hated of man, not for the evil that it has done, but for the poison that is in it, and hurt which it cannot but do: so are we hated of God, for that natural poison, which is conceived and born with us, before we do any outward evil."[53] Even before a person commits any actual sin, he is justly under God's wrath because of the inward inclination of his heart. Tyndale adds, "Our nature cannot but sin, if occasions be given, except that God of His special grace keep us back."[54] Fallen human beings cannot overcome their sinful natures. Commenting more extensively on this sinful inclination, Tyndale notes:

By nature, through the fall of Adam, are we the children of wrath, heirs of the vengeance of God by birth, yea, and from our conception. And we have our fellowship with damned devils, under the power of darkness and rule of Satan, while we are yet in our mother's wombs; and though we do not show the fruits of sin [as soon as we are born,] yet we are full of the natural poison, whereof all sinful deeds spring, and cannot but sin outwards, (be we never so young,) [as soon as we are able to work,] if occasion be given: for our nature is to do sin, as is the nature of a serpent to sting.[55]

Man's inherent sinfulness, Tyndale said, is expressed in every way imaginable. He writes: "With what poison, deadly, and venomous hate hates a man his enemy! With how great malice of mind, inwardly, do we slay and murder! With what violence and rage, yea, and with how fervent list commit we advoutry, fornication, and such like uncleaness! With what pleasure and dedication, inwardly, serves a glutton his belly! With what diligence deceive we! How busily we seek the things of this world!"[56] He adds: "Of nature we are evil, therefore we both think and do evil, and are under vengeance under the law, convict to eternal damnation by the law, and are contrary to the will of God in all our will."[57] Fallen man, Tyndale believed, is bound by his corrupted nature to pursue sin.

So great is radical corruption, Tyndale maintained, the natural man can do nothing to please God. He states: "Whatsoever we do, think, or imagine, is abominable in the sight of God. [For we can refer nothing unto the honor of God; neither is His law, or will, written in our members or in our hearts: neither is there any more power in us to follow the will of God, than in a stone to ascend upward of his own self.]"[58] Elsewhere he says, "The text is plain: we were stone dead, and without life or power to do or consent to good."[59] Putting it more simply, he writes, "It is not possible for a natural man to consent to the law."[60] Tyndale affirmed that sinful man is so debilitated by the fall of Adam he is entirely unable to honor God or obey Him.

Tyndale maintained that man is so depraved he cannot see his need for grace. He writes, "We are as it were asleep in so deep blindness, that we can neither see nor feel what misery, thraldom, and wretchedness we are in."[61] Blind in his spiritual deadness, fallen man is unconscious of his desperate need for Christ.

Tyndale also taught that the fallen human race is in bondage to Satan to do his bidding. He writes: "The devil is our lord, and our ruler, our head, our governor, our prince, yea, and our god. And our will is locked and knit faster unto the will of the devil, than could a hundred thousand chains bind a man unto a post."[62] With their wills held captive by Satan, the lost eagerly follow his lead. Tyndale adds: "The law and will of the devil is written as well in our hearts as in our members, and we run headlong after the devil with full zeal, and the whole swing of all the power we have; as a stone cast up into the air comes down naturally of his own self, with all the violence and swing of his own weight."[63] Clearly he understood unbelieving humans to be under Satan's tyrannical reign.

In short, Tyndale maintained that mankind deserves eternal damnation. He says: "We are all sinners without exception. And the Scripture witnesses that we are damnable sinners, and that our nature is to sin: which corrupt and poisoned nature, though it be begun to be healed, yet it is never thorough whole until the hour of death."[64] Tyndale had a clear understanding of the condition of the human race, and as John Piper notes, "This view of human sinfulness set the stage for Tyndale's grasp of the glory of God's sovereign grace in the gospel."[65] The terrible bondage to sin in which human beings are naturally held absolutely necessitates electing grace.

**Doctrine in Focus:**

## Sovereign Election

Tyndale was firmly convinced that God, acting in eternal, unconditional love, chose a people out of fallen humanity to be His own possession. He says, "Predestination . . . and salvation are clean taken out of our hands, and put in the hands of God only . . . for we are so weak and so uncertain, that if it stood in us, there would of a truth be no man saved; the devil, no doubt, would deceive us."[66] Salvation is impossible apart from divine election. Furthermore, it was not based on any supposed foreseen choice of God by man. Tyndale writes, "God chose them [the elect] first, and they not God."[67] Again, he asserted that God made this distinguishing choice at His own pleasure, writing, "In Christ God chose us, and elected us before the beginning of the world, created us anew by the word of the gospel, and put His Spirit in us, . . . that we should do good works."[68] All saving grace is traced back to this first cause, the sovereign choice of God unto salvation.

Putting it another way, Tyndale affirmed that election is an expression of God's mercy. The Roman Catholic Church, he said, maintained that "a man's free will is the cause why God chooses one and not another, contrary to all Scripture. [However,] Paul said that it comes not from the will, nor of deed, but of the mercy of God."[69] Here Tyndale affirmed that Roman Catholics believe in the free will of man, but Protestants affirm the sovereign will of God. Moreover, Tyndale said, God chose to love His elect for His own glory and for their good. He writes: "The end of all things shall be unto His glory and the profit of the elect."[70] God did not choose His elect to reward them, but to bless them undeservedly and to glorify His name through the demonstration of His mercy and love.

In agreement with Scripture, Tyndale affirmed that the Father chose His elect as a gift for His Son, who would redeem them in the proper time. He states, "You are chosen for Christ's sake to the inheritance of eternal life."[71] Elsewhere he adds: "God is ever fatherly minded toward the elect members of His church. He loved them, before the world began, in Christ."[72] In yet another place he writes, "In Christ God loved us, His elect and chosen, before the world began, and reserved us unto the knowledge of his Son and of His holy gospel."[73] The elect were chosen by God before time to know Christ and be His prized possession.

Tyndale acknowledged that not all those who are in the professing church are of the elect. He understood that many are called to salvation, but only those who are chosen by God form the true church. He writes, "There shall be in the church a fleshy seed of Abraham and a spiritual; a Cain and an Abel; an Ishmael and an Isaac; an Esau and a Jacob; as I have said, a worker and a believer; a great multitude of them that be called, and a small flock of them that be elect and chosen."[74] The true church is comprised of the total number of the believing elect.

Though many contend that election is a dangerous doctrine that is to be feared, Tyndale contended that it emboldens the preacher and ensures the success of gospel preaching. He explains, "When Christ is . . . preached . . . the hearts of them which are elect and chosen, begin to wax soft and melt at the bounteous mercy of God."[75] God's sovereign election undergirds the success of the gospel enterprise. Those who are chosen for eternal life will respond when the gospel is proclaimed, but if no one is chosen, it is theoretically possible that no one will be saved.

Tyndale believed that sovereign election is a mystery that must be accepted and believed by faith. He says:

Why doth God open one man's eyes and not another's? Paul (Rom. 9) forbiddeth to ask why; for it is too deep for man's capacity. God we see is honoured thereby, and His mercy set out and the more seen in the vessels of mercy. But the popish can suffer God to have no secret, hid to Himself. They have searched to come to the bottom of His bottomless wisdom: and because they cannot attain to that secret, and be too proud to let it alone, and to grant themselves ignorant, with the apostle, that knew no other than God's glory in the elect; they go and set up free-will with the heathen philosophers, and say that a man's free-will is the cause why God chooseth one and not another, contrary unto all the scripture.[76]

By these stirring words, Tyndale affirmed that sovereign election glorifies God, humbles man, and honors Scripture.

**Doctrine in Focus:**

IRRESISTIBLE CALL

Tyndale believed that divine election is inseparably linked to the irresistible call of the Spirit. All whom the Father has chosen, he maintained, are divinely brought to saving faith in Christ. This is a work God must do because man is dead in his sin and cannot choose to believe the gospel. Before anyone can believe, Tyndale writes, "the Spirit must first come, and wake him out of his sleep with the thunder of the law, and fear Him, and show him his miserable estate and wretchedness; and make him abhor and hate himself, and to desire help; and then comfort him again with the pleasant rain of the gospel."[77] Elsewhere he restates this work of the Spirit in these terms: "Note now the order: first God gives me light to see the goodness and righteousness of the law, and my own sin and unrighteousness; out of which knowledge springs repentance. . . . Then the same Spirit works in my heart trust and confidence, to believe the mercy of God and His truth, that He will do as He has promised; which belief saves me."[78] The sovereign work of the Spirit brings the elect sinner to faith in Christ.

This spiritual awakening is known as regeneration or the new birth. It is, Tyndale said, a sovereign work of God in the spiritually dead soul of the lost sinner. He writes, "We are, in . . . our second birth, God's workmanship and creation in Christ; so that, as he which is yet unmade has no life or power to work, no more had we, till we were made again in Christ."[79] Tyndale strongly denied that the sinner has anything to do with his regeneration, writing, "The will has no operation at all in the working of faith in my soul, no more than the child has in the begetting of his father: for Paul said, 'It is the gift of God,' and not of us."[80] Just as a child does not cause the conception of his father or even of himself, an unsaved person does not initiate his salvation. That work is done upon him by the Spirit of God.

When a sinner is regenerated by the Spirit, Tyndale taught, he then believes on Christ through faith. This faith does not arise from within the sinner. Rather, it is a gift of God. Tyndale says, "True faith is . . . the gift of God; and is given to sinners, after the law has passed upon them, and has brought their consciences unto the brim of desperation and sorrows of hell."[81] Elsewhere he writes, "Faith springs not of man's fantasy, neither is it in any man's power to obtain it; but it is altogether the pure gift of God poured into us freely, without all manner doing of us, without deserving and merits, yea, and without seeking for us; and is . . . God's gift and grace, purchased through Christ."[82] He described saving faith as "mighty in operation, full of virtue, and ever working; which also renews a man, and begets him afresh, altering him, changing him, and turning him altogether into a new creature and conversation."[83] The gift of faith works a great change in those to whom it is given.

Tyndale maintained that God bestows the gift of saving faith on the elect. He writes, "Of the whole multitude of the nature of man, whom God has chosen, and to whom He has appointed mercy and grace in Christ, to them sends He His Spirit; which opens their eyes, shows them their misery, and brings them unto the knowledge of themselves; so that they hate and abhor themselves."[84] He adds, "When His word is preached, faith roots herself in the hearts of the elect; and as faith enters, and the word of God is believed, the power of God looses the heart from captivity and bondage under sin."[85] The Spirit regenerates God's elect, enabling them to hear the Word and believe it. The result is that they are set free from captivity to sin.

Tyndale held that it is an evil thing to teach that man has free will to believe in Christ. He states: "Is it not a froward and perverse blindness, to teach how a man can do nothing of his own self; and yet presumptuously take upon them the greatest and highest work of God, even to make faith in themselves of their own power, and of their own false imagination and thoughts."[86] To say that fallen man has the ability in himself to believe, Tyndale stated, is perverse and presumptuous. Such a doctrine denies the teaching of Scripture and robs God of His glory. He advises: "Beware of the leaven that says, we have power in our free-will, before the preaching of the gospel, to deserve grace, to keep the law of congruity, or God to be unrighteous. . . . And when they say our deeds with grace deserve heaven, say thou with Paul, (Romans 6) that 'everlasting life is the gift of God through Jesus Christ our Lord.'"[87] For Tyndale, it was essential that believers keep this truth before their eyes—that salvation is the gift of God, not something they earn or deserve.

**Doctrine in Focus:**

## Preserving Grace

Tyndale affirmed that no elect believer will lose his salvation. All who truly repent and trust Christ will never fall from grace. He says, "God's elect cannot so fall that they rise not again, because that the mercy of God ever waits upon them, to deliver them from evil, as the care of a kind father waits upon his son to warn him and to keep him from occasions, and to call him back again if he be gone too far."[88] Believers who stumble and fall in life will be upheld by the sustaining grace of God, Tyndale believed. Elsewhere he writes, "Life eternal and all good things are promised unto faith and belief; so that he that believes on Christ shall be safe."[89] Believers are safe from condemnation. They are delivered from the wrath of God that is to come.

Tyndale also asserted that believers may have assurance of their salvation. He believed that a converted sinner "feels so great mercy, love, and kindness in God, that he is sure in himself how that it is not possible that God should forsake him, or withdraw his mercy and love from him; and boldly cries out with Paul, saying, 'Who shall separate us from the love that God loved us withal?'"[90] Tyndale was convinced from Scripture that believers can rest in the knowledge that God will never forsake one of His own.

# A FLOWING RIVER OF TRUTH

God ultimately answered Tyndale's dying prayer. In the year he was martyred, 1536, two English Bibles—unknown to Tyndale—were already circulating in England. Both of these works were predominately drawn from Tyndale's translation. The first of these Bibles was the product of Coverdale; it was known simply as the Coverdale Bible. The second English translation had come from Rogers; this version was known as the Matthew's Bible.

Less than a year after Tyndale's death, Cranmer, who had become archbishop of Canterbury, and Cromwell persuaded Henry VIII to officially approve the publication of an English Bible. When Henry saw the Coverdale Bible, he emphatically proclaimed, "If there be no heresies in it, then let it be spread abroad among all the people!"[91] In September 1538, the king issued a decree that a copy of the Bible in English and in Latin should be placed in every church in England. The permissible copies of the Bible were the Coverdale Bible and the Matthew's Bible.

D'Aubigné writes that after Tyndale's death, the flow of English Bibles into England was "like a mighty river continually bearing new waters to the sea."[92] As these printed English Bibles became accessible to the common man in England, Tyndale's plowman was, at last, reading, discussing, living, and proclaiming the truths of the Bible among his relatives and friends.

Almost five hundred years later, the river of Scripture continues to flow mightily across the face of the globe. The Bible is readily available in many lands and is being translated into new languages each year. Now it is up to us to drink deeply of this river of life. As the current of truth surges forward in this hour, may the truths of God's Word inundate our hearts and the swells of sovereign grace flood our minds. May there be a renewed commitment to the simplicity and sufficiency of this blood-stained book. And may the eyes of the church be opened to behold the glorious, soul-saving gospel and, specifically, the life-changing doctrines of sovereign grace.

NOTES

1   William Tyndale, *A Pathway into the Holy Scripture*, in *Works of William Tyndale, Vol. 1*, ed. Henry Walter (1849 and 1850; repr., Edinburgh: Banner of Truth, 2010), 19.

2   Martin Luther, *Concerning the Order of Public Worship*, in *Luther's Works, Vol. 53: Liturgy and Hymns*, 11, eds. Jaroslav Jan Pelikan, Hilton C. Oswald, and Helmut T. Lehmann (Philadelphia: Fortress, 1965), 14.

3   Luther, cited in Stephen Nichols, *Martin Luther: A Guided Tour of His Life and Thought* (Phillipsburg, N.J.: P&R, 2003), 196.

4   Martin Luther, *Table Talk*, 42, in *Luther's Works, Vol. 54: Table Talk*, eds. Jaroslav Jan Pelikan, Hilton C. Oswald, and Helmut T. Lehmann (Philadelphia: Fortress, 1967), 63.

5   Robert Demaus and Richard Lovett, *William Tyndale: A Biography* (London: The Religious Tract Society, 1886), 28.

6   Thomas Arundel, cited in Brian Moynahan, *God's Bestseller: William Tyndale, Thomas More, and the Writing of the English Bible—A Story of Martyrdom and Betrayal* (New York: St. Martin's, 2002), 1.

7   N. R. Needham, *2,000 Years of Christ's Power, Part Three: Renaissance and Reformation* (London: Grace Publications, 2004), 378.

8   Brian H. Edwards, *God's Outlaw: The Story of William Tyndale and the English Bible* (Darlington, England: Evangelical Press, 1999), 170.

9   J. H. Merle d'Aubigné, *The Reformation in England, Vol. 1* (1853; repr., Edinburgh: Banner of Truth, 1994), 167.

10  Needham, *2,000 Years of Christ's Power, Part Three*, 379.

11 Robert Sheehan, "William Tyndale's Legacy," *The Banner of Truth*, Issue 557, February 2010, 29.

12 Sir Frederick Kenyon, *Our Bible and the Ancient Manuscripts* (Whitefish, Mont.: Kessinger, 2007), 211, 217.

13 Sheehan, "William Tyndale's Legacy," 24.

14 John Foxe, *Foxe's Book of Martyrs* (Nashville: Thomas Nelson, 2000), 114.

15 David Daniell, *William Tyndale: A Biography* (New Haven, Conn.: Yale University Press, 1994), 38.

16 William Tyndale, *Expositions and Notes on Sundry Portions of the Holy Scriptures, Together with the Practice of Prelates*, in *Works of William Tyndale, Vol. 2*, ed. Henry Walter (1849 and 1850; repr., Edinburgh: Banner of Truth, 2010), 1.291.

17 The time Tyndale spent at Cambridge may have been "short or longer, between 1517 and 1521." Daniell, *William Tyndale*, 49.

18 Some historians assert that Tyndale was probably at the White Horse Inn. Those include Brian H. Edwards and S. M. Houghton. Others, including David Daniell, feel that Tyndale was not present.

19 Bilney testified: "It is Jesus Christ who saves, and not the church. I see it all, my vigils, my fasts, my pilgrimages, my purchases of mass and indulgences were destroying instead of saving me. All these efforts were, as St. Augustine says, a hasty running out of the right way." Thomas Bilney, cited in J. H. Merle d'Aubigné, *History of the Reformation of the Sixteenth Century, Vol. 5* (Edinburgh: Oliver & Boyd, 1853), 218.

20 Demaus and Lovett, *William Tyndale*, 71.

21 Foxe, *Foxe's Book of Martyrs*, 77.

22 Foxe, *Foxe's Book of Martyrs*, 77, cited in Daniell, *William Tyndale*, 79.

23 Robert G. Clouse, "Erasmus," in *New International Dictionary of the Christian Church*, gen. ed. J. D. Douglas (Grand Rapids: Zondervan, 1978), 350.

24 William Tyndale, *Preface to the Five Books of Moses*, in *Works of William Tyndale, Vol. 1*, 396.

25 Tony Lane writes: "It appears that he first went to Wittenberg to study. Contemporaries such as Thomas More refer to his time there. There is also an entry in the matriculation register for 27 May 1524 reading 'Guillelmus Daltici Ex Anglia'. If the final 'ci' is a copyist's error for 'n' we have an anagram of 'Tindal' with the two syllables reversed." Tony Lane, "William Tyndale," in *Biographical Dictionary of Evangelicals* (Downers Grove, Ill.: InterVarsity, 2003), 678.

26 "William Tyndale," in *Cyclopedia of Biblical, Theological, and Ecclesiastical Literature, Vol. X*, eds. John McClintock and James Strong (Grand Rapids: Baker, 1981), 607.

27 Thomas More, cited in Needham, *2,000 Years of Christ's Power, Vol. Three*, 381.

28 Stephen Vaughan, cited in Daniell, *William Tyndale*, 217.

29 Daniell, *William Tyndale*, 213.

30 Daniell, *William Tyndale*, 217.

31 Daniell, *William Tyndale*, 361.

32 Daniell, *William Tyndale*, 316.

33 William Tyndale, cited in J. F. Mozley, *William Tyndale* (1937; repr., London: Greenwood, 1971), 333–335.

34 John Piper, *Filling Up the Afflictions of Christ: The Cost of Bringing the Gospel to the Nations in the Lives of William Tyndale, Adoniram Judson, and John Paton* (Wheaton: Crossway, 2009), 50.

35 Foxe, *Foxe's Book of Martyrs*, 127.

36 Tyndale, cited in Foxe, *Foxe's Book of Martyrs*, 83.

37 This scene has been reconstructed by David Daniell from similar capital punishments at the time of Tyndale. Daniell, *William Tyndale*, 383.

38 Iain Murray, "The Light That Scattered Roman Darkness," *The Banner of Truth Magazine*, Issue 560, May 2010, 18.

39 Needham, *2,000 Years of Christ's Power, Part Three*, 381.

40 Daniell, *William Tyndale*, 3.

41 Murray, "The Light That Scattered Roman Darkness," 18.

42 Tyndale, *The Parable of the Wicked Mammon*, in *Works of William Tyndale, Vol. 1*, 79.

43 D. F. Payne, "William Tyndale," in *New International Dictionary of the Christian Church*, 990.

44 Edwards, *God's Outlaw*, 70.

45 David Daniell, "Introduction," in William Tyndale, *Selected Writings*, ed. David Daniell (New York: Routledge, 2003), viii–ix.

46 Tyndale, *Works of William Tyndale, Vol. 1*, 400.

47 Tyndale, *Works of William Tyndale, Vol. 1*, 89.

48 Tyndale, *Works of William Tyndale, Vol. 1*, 316.

49 Tyndale, *Works of William Tyndale, Vol. 1*, 140.

50 Tyndale, *Works of William Tyndale, Vol. 1*, 334.

51 Tyndale, *Works of William Tyndale, Vol. 1*, 397.

52 Tyndale, *Works of William Tyndale, Vol. 1*, 17.

53 Tyndale, *Works of William Tyndale, Vol. 1*, 14.

54 Tyndale, *Works of William Tyndale, Vol. 2*, 1.151.

55 Tyndale, *Works of William Tyndale, Vol. 1*, 14.

56 Tyndale, *Works of William Tyndale, Vol. 1*, 17.

57 Tyndale, *Works of William Tyndale, Vol. 1*, 14.

58 Tyndale, *Works of William Tyndale, Vol. 1*, 17–18.

59 Tyndale, *Works of William Tyndale, Vol. 2*, 1.199.

60 Tyndale, *Works of William Tyndale, Vol. 1*, 18.

61 Tyndale, *Works of William Tyndale, Vol. 1*, 18.

62 Tyndale, *Works of William Tyndale, Vol. 1*, 17.

63 Tyndale, *Works of William Tyndale, Vol. 1*, 17.

64 Tyndale, *Works of William Tyndale, Vol. 2*, 1.150.

65 Piper, *Filling Up the Afflictions of Christ*, 39.

66 Tyndale, *Works of William Tyndale, Vol. 1*, 505.

67 Tyndale, *Works of William Tyndale, Vol. 2*, 2.35.

68 Tyndale, *Works of William Tyndale, Vol. 1*, 77.

69 Tyndale, *Works of William Tyndale, Vol. 2*, 2.191–92.

70 Tyndale, *Works of William Tyndale, Vol. 2*, 1.171.

71 Tyndale, *Works of William Tyndale, Vol. 1*, 49.

72 Tyndale, *Works of William Tyndale, Vol. 2*, 2.111.

73 Tyndale, *Works of William Tyndale, Vol. 1*, 14.

74 Tyndale, *Works of William Tyndale, Vol. 2*, 2.107.

75 Tyndale, *Works of William Tyndale, Vol. 1*, 19.

76 Tyndale, *An Answer to Sir Thomas More's Dialogue* (Parker Soc. Reprint, 1850), 191, cited in Iain Murray, *The Forgotten Spurgeon* (Edinburgh: Banner of Truth, 1972), 8–9.

77 Tyndale, *Works of William Tyndale, Vol. 1*, 498.

78 Tyndale, *Works of William Tyndale, Vol. 2*, 2.195–96.

79 Tyndale, *Works of William Tyndale, Vol. 2*, 1.200.

80 Tyndale, *Works of William Tyndale, Vol. 2*, 2.140.

81 Tyndale, *Works of William Tyndale, Vol. 1*, 12–13.

82 Tyndale, *Works of William Tyndale, Vol. 1*, 53.

83 Tyndale, *Works of William Tyndale, Vol. 1*, 53.

84 Tyndale, *Works of William Tyndale, Vol. 1*, 89.

85 Tyndale, *Works of William Tyndale, Vol. 1*, 54.

86 Tyndale, *Works of William Tyndale, Vol. 1*, 56.

87 Tyndale, *Works of William Tyndale, Vol. 1*, 466.

88 Tyndale, *Works of William Tyndale, Vol. 2*, 2.36.

89 Tyndale, *Works of William Tyndale, Vol. 1*, 65.

90 Tyndale, *Works of William Tyndale, Vol. 1*, 22.

91 William J. McRae, *A Book to Die For: A Practical Study Guide on How our Bible Came to Us* (Toronto, Ont.: Clements, 2002), xiv, as cited in Tony Lane, "A Man For All People: Introducing William Tyndale," *Christian History*, Vol. VI, no. 4, issue 16, 6–9.

92 J. H. Merle d'Aubigné, *The Reformation in England, Vol. 2* (1866–1878; repr., Edinburgh: Banner of Truth, 1994), 348.

# CHAPTER TWENTY-TWO
# STUDY QUESTIONS

1. Trace the spread of Reformation flames across Europe in the sixteenth century. What foundational stance served as the primary catalyst for the Protestant movement? In what way was this position influential?

2. Describe William Tyndale's education at Oxford and Cambridge. What was the White Horse Inn? Explain its importance to the Reformed movement in England.

3. Summarize Tyndale's efforts to translate the Bible into English. What prompted him to undertake such a daunting project? What opposition did he face? What lexicographic innovations did Tyndale make in his translation?

4. Comment on Tyndale's theological writings. How did these writings compare with his *magnum opus*, that is, the English Bible? In what ways were they similar to the writings of the Church Fathers?

5. What was foundational to all of Tyndale's theological beliefs? How did this belief influence his thinking on the doctrines of grace? How should this truth impact your life and belief in the doctrines of grace?

6. According to Tyndale, what is the nature of mankind? What effect did the fall of Adam have on man's nature? To what extent is man able to contribute to his salvation?

7. Define God's sovereign election. What is the purpose of election? When did God's election occur? According to Tyndale, how should this truth affect gospel preaching?

8. What is regeneration? Does anything precede our rebirth? List several biblical passages that speak to one's need to be born again.

*If* you ask me whether you are elected to life, or predestinate to death . . . I answer simply out of the Scripture. . . . If you have communion or fellowship with Christ, you are predestinate to life . . . but if you be a stranger from Christ, howsoever otherwise you seem to flourish in virtues, you are predestinate to death.[1]

*The* fiction of the Pelagians is false, whereby they affirm that we are born without vice: it is false, that the voluntary action only, and not the corruption or depravation which is not yet burst forth to the deed, is sin.[2]

–Heinrich Bullinger

# Chapter Twenty-Three

# COVENANT THEOLOGIAN

## SWISS REFORMER: HEINRICH BULLINGER

A s the Reformers exposited the Scriptures in their lofty pulpits and expounded them in their voluminous writings, the truths of sovereign grace were brought to the forefront. These doctrines were radically different from the corrupt teachings of the Roman Catholic Church. Rome's false gospel caused much confusion among the common people in the church. Thus, from the earliest days of the Reformation, the leaders of the Protestant movement found it necessary to define the truths they believed. They did so by means of theologically precise documents known as confessions of faith. In the first fifty years of the Reformation—from Martin Luther's posting of his Ninety-five Theses on October 31, 1517, until the publication of the Heidelberg Catechism in 1566—at least fifty confessional documents were written.

These statements of Reformed teaching served several purposes. First, they defined precisely what the Protestant churches believed, demonstrating their essential agreement with historical orthodox Christianity. Second, the Reformed confessions clearly distinguished the true gospel of God's free grace from the works-based, indulgence-selling, sacerdotal religion of the Roman Catholic Church. Thus, they delineated the major fault lines separating the biblical teachings of the Reformers from the religious traditions of Rome. Third, these statements of belief served as rallying points for Reformed churches. With such written standards, true doctrinal unity could be built on common core beliefs drawn from Scripture. Fourth, these articles of faith served as teaching tools for imparting the church's doctrines to congregations and to future generations. Rightly used, these statements stimulated deeper study of the Bible and anchored the Reformed churches in the Word.

## CONFESSIONS IN SWITZERLAND

The churches of Switzerland played the lead role in composing these initial Reformed confessions. The first was the Sixty-Seven Theses (1523), a confession prepared by the Swiss Reformer of Zurich, Ulrich Zwingli (1484–1531). This brief theological summary was written for a public debate between Zwingli and Roman Catholic leaders known as the First Zurich Disputation. Subsequently, Zwingli drafted his Short Christian Instruction (1523), a document, addressed to the Zurich clergy, declaring that images, statues, and the Mass are contrary to the Word of God. The city council of Zurich immediately endorsed this statement, making it binding on the city's clergy and churches. The Swiss city of Berne followed suit with the Ten Theses of Berne (1528), drafted by Berthold Haller (1492–1536) and Franz Kolb (1465–1535), and revised by Zwingli. This confession solidified the Reformed movement in Berne, likewise abolishing the Mass, icons, and altars from its churches.

William Farel (1489–1565), the fiery, red-haired Reformer, wrote his Summary in 1529. This was the initial statement of his Reformed beliefs before he went to Geneva. This was followed by the Berne Synod (1532), a strong reaffirmation of Reformation truth in Berne. At this time, Basel was becoming a hotbed of evangelical teaching, and the First Confession of Basel (1534) was adopted there. When Lausanne joined the Reformed movement, it adopted the Lausanne Articles (1536) for all the churches of the city.

That same year, the First Helvetic Confession was written by Heinrich Bullinger with other Reformers; it was the first national standard binding together the Reformed churches of Switzerland. Also in 1536, John Calvin went to Geneva, where he wrote the Geneva Confession (1536–1537) and his Catechism (1537) to instruct the faithful in that newly Reformed Swiss city. When the Geneva Bible (1560) was translated, it included the Confession of Faith, a clear statement of Reformed belief as taught by Calvin. Likewise, Theodore Beza wrote his Confession (1560) in Geneva, an abbreviated summary of Reformed doctrine that followed the outline of the Apostles' Creed.

## THE SECOND HELVETIC CONFESSION

The most widely accepted confession of faith that came out of the Swiss Reformation—second only to the German-produced Heidelberg Catechism

(1566) among all Reformation confessions—was the Second Helvetic Confession (1566). This document was drafted by Bullinger, an industrious preacher and gifted theologian who became Zwingli's successor in Zurich. Bullinger had co-authored the First Helvetic Confession, but the Second Helvetic Confession was his work alone. Bullinger played an indispensible role in the Reformation by writing these formal statements of the Reformed faith, as well as through his powerful preaching and prolific writings, in which he gave the truths of sovereign grace a prominent place.

# HEINRICH BULLINGER

Bullinger (1504–1575) is regarded as the most influential second-generation Reformer.[3] As the heir to Zwingli in Zurich, he consolidated and continued the Swiss Reformation that his predecessor had started. Philip Schaff writes that Bullinger was "a man of firm faith, courage, moderation, patience, and endurance . . . [who was] providentially equipped" to preserve and advance the truth in a difficult time in history.[4] During his forty-four years as the chief minister in Zurich, Bullinger's literary output exceeded that of Luther, Calvin, and Zwingli combined.[5] He was of monumental importance in the spread of Reformed teaching throughout the Reformation.[6] So far-reaching was Bullinger's influence throughout continental Europe and England that Beza called him "the common shepherd of all Christian churches."[7]

Bullinger was born on July 18, 1504, in the tiny Swiss town of Bremgarten, ten miles west of Zurich. His father, also named Heinrich, was the local parish priest, who lived in a common-law marriage with Anna Wiederkehr. This practice was officially forbidden by the Roman Catholic hierarchy, but Bullinger's father had received permission to enter into such a relationship by agreeing to pay his bishop a yearly tribute. The younger Heinrich was the fifth child born of this illegitimate, yet tolerated, wedlock. The marriage between Bullinger's parents was eventually formalized in 1529, when the elder Bullinger joined the Reformed movement.

Young Heinrich's father groomed him for the priesthood from a very early age. At age twelve, he was sent to the monastic school at Emmerich, known as the School of the Brethren of the Common Life. This school was a citadel of the *via antique*, the "old way" of learning that was stressed by the theologians of the High Middle Ages, such as Thomas Aquinas (1225–1274) and John Duns Scotus (ca. 1265–1308). There, Bullinger received an advanced education in humanistic principles, especially Latin. At the same time, he came under the influence of the *devotio moderna*, the "modern devotion," a medieval emphasis on the Eucharist and the deep spiritual life. Augustine and Bernard were among the earlier leaders of this pietistic movement, and it had been revived by Thomas á Kempis in his book *The Imitation of Christ.* Bullinger was attracted to this movement's stress on meditation and the search for a personal spiritual experience with God. Also at this time, Bullinger began displaying a remarkable aptitude for scholarship.

## THE UNIVERSITY OF COLOGNE

Three years later, in 1519, Bullinger proceeded to the University of Cologne, where he began studying traditional Scholastic theology. Cologne was the largest city in Germany, and Roman Catholicism was deeply entrenched there—papal superstitions ran high in the city and German mystics gathered there in large numbers. Aquinas and Scotus had taught there earlier, and their Scholastic influence remained firmly embedded in Cologne. But Bullinger was convinced of the humanist approach. In his studies, he pursued the writings of the Church Fathers, especially Ambrose, Chrysostom, and Augustine. Their insistence on the priority of Scripture moved him to study the Bible for himself. Such a pursuit, he later admitted, was unknown to most of his fellow students.

While at Cologne, Bullinger was exposed to the teaching of the leading humanist of the day, Desiderius Erasmus of Rotterdam (ca. 1466–1536). Erasmus had elevated the Scriptures over Aristotelian logic and sought to reform the church through humanistic scholarship and the moral teachings of Christ. But it was Luther's works that most challenged Bullinger's thinking. Luther's books were being burned in Cologne, which only piqued Bullinger's interest in their content. Soon his mind was captured by Luther's ideas. He also studied Philip Melanchthon's *Loci communes* (1521), the first systematic treatment of Lutheran theology. In it, Melanchthon treated the Reformed hallmark doctrines of the bondage of the will and justification by faith alone. This work further impacted Bullinger. Seeds of reform were being sown in his mind. At age seventeen, he embraced the pivotal truth that justification is by faith alone in Christ alone. Amid this personal transformation, Bullinger gained his master's degree.

In 1522, Bullinger returned home to Bremgarten a new man. He continued his persistent study of Scripture along with his reading of the Church

Fathers, Luther, and Melanchthon. The next year, he became the head teacher of the school at the Cistercian convent at Kappel. From 1523 to 1529, he instructed the monks from the New Testament and introduced Reformed teaching. Under his influence, Protestant worship replaced the Mass. Further, many monks became Reformed ministers.

Bullinger took a five-month leave of absence in 1527 and made a trip to Zurich. This journey proved to be life-changing for him. He attended lectures by Zwingli and met the Swiss Reformer, starting a relationship that would have a profound effect on him and the future of the Swiss Reformation. He was appointed to accompany Zwingli to the Disputation in Berne, which opened on January 7, 1528. On this occasion, the Ten Theses of Berne was presented and subscribed. Through all this, Bullinger was given a privileged inside look at Reformation workings. Subsequently, Bullinger made an annual journey to Zurich to discuss theology with Zwingli. Through this close association, Zwingli became aware of Bullinger's abilities in the Scriptures. Though neither knew it at the time, Bullinger was being prepared to become Zwingli's successor.

## Pastoring at Hausen and Bremgarten

Later in 1528, Bullinger became the part-time pastor of the village church at Hausen, near Kappel. He preached his first sermon on June 21, beginning an appointment that would allow him to develop his pulpit gifts. The following year, Heinrich Sr. publicly declared his commitment to Reformed teaching and started to reform his parish at Bremgarten. However, the elder Bullinger was forced to resign his position because of the resistance of his parishioners. In an unusual turn of events, the younger Bullinger succeeded his father as pastor of the church. He continued the biblical reform his father had begun and became known as the Reformer of Bremgarten.

Yearning for a wife, Bullinger traveled to the former Dominican convent at Oetenbach in 1529, having heard that the nuns had become Reformed. The nunnery had disbanded, but two women had stayed to establish a Protestant witness. One was Anna Adischwyler, a devoted believer. Bullinger asked her to become his wife and she accepted. Through the years, they had eleven children of their own and adopted others. Remarkably, all six of their sons became Protestant ministers.

For the next two years, Bullinger helped spread Reformed teaching through his pulpit and the beginning of his prolific writing ministry. At this time, he began his long series of commentaries on the books of the New Testament.

With the growing entrenchment of Protestant beliefs in Switzerland, Roman Catholic resistance soon arose. Five Catholic cantons (states), alarmed at the rise of Protestantism in Zurich, declared war on this Reformed stronghold in October 1531. No Protestant canton offered Zurich any support. On October 11, at the Battle of Kappel, the Protestants were ambushed and Zwingli, serving as a military chaplain, was killed. Zurich was forced to accept unfavorable terms of peace. Some regions of Switzerland, including Bremgarten, reverted to Catholicism.

Bullinger, a recognized Protestant leader, was threatened with the scaffold at Bremgarten. He fled to Zurich, where, three days later, he was prevailed upon to preach in Zwingli's empty pulpit. So powerful was Bullinger's preaching that the people exclaimed he must be the second coming of Zwingli. Oswald Myconius, a follower of Zwingli, said, "Like the phoenix, he [Zwingli] has risen from the ashes."[8] It was vitally important for the Swiss churches that Zwingli be replaced by a man of the same Reformed convictions and abounding energy in the Lord's work. In Bullinger, they found such a man.

## CHIEF MINISTER OF ZURICH

Six weeks later, on December 9, 1531, Bullinger, only twenty-seven years old, was unanimously elected by the Council of Zurich and the citizens to succeed Zwingli. After the council agreed to guarantee the clergy's freedom to preach on all aspects of life in the city, Bullinger accepted the position. He became the *antistes*—the "chief minister"—of the city. In so doing, he assumed the leadership of the Reformed movement in German-speaking Switzerland. On December 23, he took the pulpit of the Grossmünster, a position he held for forty-four years until his death in 1575. In this role, Bullinger presided over the other churches of the cantonal synod as a sort of "Reformed bishop." He was also responsible for the reform of the school system.

Bullinger was a tireless preacher. For the first ten years of his ministry in Zurich, he preached six or seven times a week. After 1542, he preached twice a week, on Sundays and Fridays, which allowed him to devote himself to a rigorous writing schedule. Bullinger followed Zwingli in the *lectio continua* method of preaching, moving verse by verse through whole books of Scripture. His expository sermons were biblical, simple, clear, and practical. In all, it is estimated that Bullinger preached in Zurich between seven thousand and seventy-five hundred sermons. These expositions became the basis for his commentaries, which covered much of the Bible.

Bullinger was also a big-hearted pastor. His house was open to widows, orphans, strangers, exiles, and persecuted brethren. He freely bestowed food, clothing, and money on those in need. Bullinger even secured a pension for Zwingli's widow and educated Zwingli's children with his own sons and daughters. He was a devoted pastor who produced one of the first Protestant books for comforting the sick and dying. Many of the persecuted believers of England escaped Mary Tudor's reign of terror in Zurich, finding refuge in Bullinger's open arms. Upon their return home, these refugees became leading English Puritans.

A man of considerable theological abilities, Bullinger helped co-author the First Helvetic Confession (1536) and played a key role in the *Consensus Tigurinus* (1549). The former was the first national Swiss confession; the latter was an attempt by Calvin and Bullinger to rectify Protestant disagreements over the Lord's Supper. During the discussions over this document, Bullinger invited Calvin to Zurich for face-to-face talks. Calvin accepted the invitation. On May 20, 1549, he and Farel journeyed to Zurich, where they met with Bullinger. Calvin and Bullinger reached an agreement regarding the sacraments that united the Reformed efforts in Geneva and Zurich. By these confessional documents, Bullinger helped galvanize Switzerland during the beginning of its Reformation period. He combated the Lutheran doctrine of consubstantiation in the Lord's Supper and refuted Anabaptist teaching on baptism. However, he remained open-minded toward the various radical movements.

Throughout this time, Bullinger was consulted by English royalty, including Edward VI (1550) and Elizabeth I (1566). He viewed the leaders of the Church of England as fellow Reformed churchmen as they struggled against Rome. Portions of his book *Decades* were dedicated to Edward VI and Lady Jane Grey. On a broader scale, he maintained correspondence with Reformed leaders all over the Protestant world, including Philip of Hesse. His wise and balanced counsel gave much-needed direction to many in the Reformed movement.

In Bullinger's closing years, he suffered the tragic deaths of his wife, Anna, and several of their daughters. Their lives were taken in outbreaks of the plague in 1564 and 1565. Bullinger himself became severely ill during the second outbreak. Though he survived the outbreak, his health remained poor, and he died on September 17, 1575, after four decades of tireless and effective ministry. He left behind a rich legacy in the truths of sovereign grace that helped give theological and ecclesiastical order to the Reformation.

# BULLINGER'S WRITINGS

As noted above, Bullinger produced more Christian writings than Luther, Calvin, and Zwingli combined. He began writing ten years before Calvin took up his pen in Geneva to defend the Reformed faith and continued eleven years after Calvin's death. Bullinger's influence on Calvin's *Institutes of the Christian Religion* is clear, especially the 1550 version. Calvin often simply reworded Bullinger, incorporating many of his themes, scriptural proofs, and biblical examples.[9] In all, Bullinger wrote 124 books and thousands of tracts and letters. These works initially were in greater demand than Calvin's, though the Genevan's popularity was to grow immensely. The flow of Bullinger's works from the printing press of his colleague and friend Christopher Froschauer seemingly never stopped.

### FIRST HELVETIC CONFESSION

Bullinger was a co-author of this Reformed doctrinal statement, signed in 1536, that became the first creedal standard of the Swiss Reformed churches. Co-authored with Myconius, Simon Grynaeus, Leo Juda, and Kaspar Megander, it was an attempt to reconcile Lutheran and Zwinglian views throughout Switzerland before the spread of Calvinism. Consisting of twenty-seven articles, this confession was aimed primarily at the German-speaking Swiss cantons in the north. The statement on the Lord's Supper made it unacceptable to the Lutherans, though it was accepted by the Swiss Zwinglian churches, which eventually merged with the Calvinist movement.

### COMMENTARIES ON THE BIBLE

Over the course of his ministry, Bullinger wrote a commentary on every book of the New Testament except the Revelation of the apostle John. Almost all of these commentaries arose from his exegetical work and expository preaching in Zurich.

## THE DECADES

This work, which is the most famous of the hundreds of treatises and manuscripts Bullinger wrote, is comprised of fifty lengthy sermons, five series of ten sermons each.[10] Published from 1549 to 1551, it dealt with the major tenets of Christian doctrine. Included in *The Decades* was an exposition of the Ten Commandments, a commentary on the Apostles' Creed, and writings on the sacraments. The first sermons dealt with the giving of Scripture as God's all-sufficient revelation to all people for their salvation and sanctification. These expositions on Christian doctrine were translated into English in 1577 and were adopted as a standard textbook for English clergy who had not obtained a master's degree. This work was also soon translated into Dutch and French.

## SECOND HELVETIC CONFESSION

Bullinger's crowning confessional achievement came in 1566 with the Second Helvetic Confession. Written thirty years after the First Helvetic Confession, it became one of the most influential Reformed confessions. Bullinger wrote the text of this confession in 1561, but it was not circulated until Frederick III, elector of the Palatinate, requested a Reformed confession similar to what the Lutherans had in the Augsburg Confession. While the First Helvetic Confession was accepted only within Switzerland, this second confession was accepted internationally, finding wide approval in Calvinistic churches in Switzerland, France, Scotland, Hungary, Poland, the Netherlands, and Germany.

## OTHER WRITINGS

Bullinger also penned major studies on providence, justification, and the nature of the Scriptures. His other works include *On the Only and Eternal Covenant* (1534), *The Old Faith* (1537), *On the Authority of Holy Scripture* (1538), *On the Origin of Errors* (1539), *A True Confession* (1545), and *The Christian Religion* (1556). Moreover, he is regarded as "a passionate historian, and a good one" who "relentlessly pursued historical documents."[11] To this end, Bullinger, a "deeply reflective"[12] historian, composed his "mature work," *History of the Reformation*, 1519–1532.[13] Unfortunately, this seminal work remained unpublished until 1838, when it was first put into print as two volumes, a part of his larger work, *History of the Venerable Swiss Confederation*. In addition, Bullinger wrote doctrinal treatises and polemical works primarily against Anabaptists and Lutherans. The *Zurich Letters* (1542, 1545) contain his correspondence with leaders in England.

## BULLINGER'S THEOLOGY

Comparing Bullinger with Zwingli as a theologian, G. W. Bromiley writes: "The doctrinal discussions of Bullinger are more impressive than those of Zwingli. For one thing they are much better arranged, and the thought moves with a logic which is lacking in the more hurried compositions of Zwingli. . . . Bullinger looks upon the whole and is able to treat his theme . . . comprehensively. . . . Bullinger brings to bear perhaps a greater weight of scholarship. . . . Bullinger's arguments as a whole present a much more solid appearance than the acute but not always convincing reasoning of Zwingli."[14] Simply put, Bullinger advanced beyond the theological abilities of his mentor, Zwingli, and the Reformation was the better for it.

Bullinger was strongly committed to the doctrines of grace. Cornelis P. Venema writes, "Bullinger undoubtedly embraced the principal teaching of historic Augustinianism: salvation is based upon God's unconditional election of His own in Christ, not upon human working or merit of any kind."[15]

However, there is some question as to how thoroughgoing was Bullinger's adherence to the doctrine of predestination. Robert Walton states, "He accommodated his own moderate Augustinian doctrine of predestination to the more rigorous one advanced by Calvin."[16] Others believe that Bullinger's position was as strong as the Genevan Reformer's. James T. Dennison writes: "The observation that Bullinger is less severe on the divine decrees than Calvin is belied by chapter X [of the Second Helvetic Confession]—every bit as Calvinistic as Calvin's own doctrine of the *decretum horrible*. In sum, Bullinger's Second Helvetic Confession is systematic Reformed/Calvinistic theology."[17]

**Doctrine in Focus:**
DIVINE SOVEREIGNTY
Bullinger affirmed the sovereignty of God over all the works of His hands. He believed that God eternally decreed all that comes to pass. He writes, "For God, who has appointed everything to its end, has also ordained the beginning and the means by which we must attain unto the end."[18] God, he held, is executing His eternal purpose in the daily affairs of providence. Bullinger says, "We believe that all things, both in heaven and in earth and

in all creatures, are sustained and governed by the providence of this wise, eternal, and omnipotent God."[19] By upholding the doctrine of providence, Bullinger maintained a high view of God's sovereign control over all people, events, and destinies.

Bullinger noted that fallen human beings deny God's sovereign control over His creation. He states, "The heathens ascribe things to blind fortune and uncertain chance."[20] But with biblical perspective, he asserted that God orders all things with specific design and purpose. Bullinger says, "If God comprehends that which contains all things, and all things and the whole does consist of parts and particulars; then shall His care reach consequently even to every part and particular, whose providence has reached already to the very whole."[21] God oversees all people and events such that each small part of creation and history fits perfectly into His overall purpose. There is no part of the universe that escapes God's sovereignty.

**Doctrine in Focus:**

## RADICAL CORRUPTION

Firmly grounded in Scripture, Bullinger emphasized the doctrine of original sin, the teaching that the consequences of Adam's one transgression are imputed to the entire human race, so that each person inherits a sinful nature at the point of conception. The result is the total depravity of mankind. Bullinger writes, "Original sin . . . comes from the first beginning, being derived from our first parents into us all by lineal descent and continual course from one to another; for we bring it with us in our nature from our mother's womb into this life."[22] He adds, "All we which do descend from his [Adam's] impure seed are born infected with the contagious poison of sin."[23] Bullinger clearly saw the effect of Adam's sin on his descendants.

In defining this inner depravity, Bullinger writes, "Original sin is the inheritably descending naughtiness or corruption of our nature, which does first make us endangered to the wrath of God, and then brings forth in us those works which the Scripture calls the works of the flesh."[24] Elsewhere he adds, "Original sin is neither a deed, nor a word, nor a thought; but a disease, a vice, a depravation, I say, of judgment and concupiscence; or a corruption of the whole man, that is, of the understanding, will, and all the power of man; out of which at last do flow all evil thoughts, naughty words, and wicked deeds."[25] In short, original sin is the inward corruption that all people inherit from Adam.

All people without exception are infected with such depravity, Bullinger taught. He writes, "Original sin is born together with us, that is, that all men are born sinners into the world."[26] This means that original sin is even in infants. Bullinger says, "The first effect of original sin is this, that it brings wrath, death, and damnation upon very infants, and so consequently upon all mankind."[27] Elsewhere he notes, "For even very babes give manifest tokens of evident depravation so soon as they once begin to be able to do anything; yea, before they can perfectly sound any one syllable of a whole word."[28] Again he writes, "Infants do bring damnation with them into this world even from their mother's wombs; because they bring with them a corrupt nature: and therefore they perish not by any others,' but by their own, fault and naughtiness."[29] This, Bullinger said, explains why even babies suffer in this world. He writes, "Since all the inclination, disposition, and desire of our nature, even in a child but one day old, is repugnant to the pureness and will of God, which is only good; no man therefore is punished for his father, but every one for his own iniquity: and calamities fall even on the youngest babes, whom we see to be touched with many afflictions by the holy and just judgment of the most just God."[30] All people, regardless of age or seeming innocence, Bullinger insisted, are morally corrupt.

Because of this corruption, Bullinger said, all people are under the condemnation of God. He writes, "Original sin makes us the sons of wrath."[31] He adds, "We are all for our original corruption made subject to death and utter damnation"[32] and "Sin makes all men subject to the curse of God."[33] Adam was condemned by God for his transgression, and so are his descendants.

Bullinger was careful to distinguish between man's sin nature and the actual sins that nature drives him to commit. He writes: "Sin is the natural corruption of mankind, and the action which arises of it contrary to the law of God, whose wrath, that is, both death and sundry punishments, it brings upon us."[34] He adds, "Sin is not only a voluntary action, but also an hereditary corruption or depravation that comes by inheritance."[35] This inward corruption produces outward acts of rebellion against God. Bullinger states, "We define actual sin to be an action, or work, or fruit, of our corrupt and naughty nature, expressing itself in thoughts, words, and works against the law of God, and thereby deserving the wrath of God."[36] In other words, "The cause of actual sin is known to be the very corruption of mankind."[37] By these statements, Bullinger showed he understood that original sin leads to actual sins.

Bullinger likewise taught that the total depravity of human nature results in moral inability. He says, "There is in us no power or ability to do any good: for we are slow, sluggish, and heavy to goodness."[38] He contended that the mind, affections, and will of fallen man cannot please God, saying: "All our understanding is dull, blunt, gross, and altogether blind in heavenly things. Our judgment in divine matters is perverse and frivolous."[39] He adds, "Our whole mind is apt and ready to errors, to fables, and our own destruction: and when as our judgments are nothing but mere folly, yet do we prefer them far above God's wisdom, which we esteem but foolishness in comparison of our own conceits and corrupt imaginations."[40] As for the will, "Our whole will is led captive by concupiscence, which, as a root envenomed with poison, infects all that is in man, and does incline, draw on, and drive men to things carnal, forbidden, and contrary to God, to the end that he may greedily pursue them, put his delight in them, and content himself with them."[41] Fallen man, left to himself, cannot choose God, Christ, or the gospel—only sin.

Bullinger understood that his Augustinian stance was in direct opposition to Pelagian doctrine, with its denial of original sin. He writes, "The fiction of the Pelagians is false, whereby they affirm that we are born without vice: it is false, that the voluntary action only, and not the corruption or depravation which is not yet burst forth to the deed, is sin."[42] He adds, "We, which condemn both Pelagius and Pelagians, do affirm both those things which they deny; to wit, that infants are born in original sin, and therefore that the sanctification of Christ is necessary unto them, without which they are not saved."[43] Consequently, the Augustinian position alone, he saw, magnifies God's grace. He writes, "If there be no original sin, there be no grace."[44] Because he understood the depths of man's depravity, he saw clearly that God must act if man is to be saved.

**Doctrine in Focus:**

## SOVEREIGN ELECTION

Bullinger possessed equally strong convictions on unconditional election. Venema writes, "Together with Augustine, Calvin, Luther, Zwingli, Vermigli, Zanchius and the mainstream tradition of reformational theology at the time, Bullinger was as vigorous an advocate of sovereign election as anyone."[45] This predestinarian stance can be clearly seen in the Second Helvetic Confession: "God has from the beginning freely, and of His mere grace, without any respect of men, predestinated or elected the saints, whom He will save in

Christ . . . though not for any merit of ours, yet not without a means, but in Christ, and for Christ, did God choose us."[46] This is a strong and plain affirmation of God's election of His people.

Bullinger used various terms in describing God's election, including *predestination* and *fore-appointed*. He writes, "The predestination of God is the eternal decree of God, whereby He has ordained either to save or destroy men; a most certain end of life and death being appointed unto them."[47] Elsewhere he says, "God by His eternal and unchangeable counsel has fore-appointed who are to be saved and who are to be condemned."[48] These theological terms all point to one truth—that God determined who would and would not be saved before time began.

This divine choice was not based on any inherent goodness in the ones chosen or on any foreseen faith in them. Bullinger declares, "God's predestination is not stayed or stirred with any worthiness or unworthiness of ours; but of the mere grace and mercy of God the Father, it respects Christ alone."[49] Again he writes, "Therefore, though not for any merit of ours, yet not without a means, but in Christ, and for Christ, did God choose us."[50] He adds, "For they are wrong, that think those that are to be saved to life are predestinate of God for the merit's sake, or good works, which God did foresee in them."[51] Finally he writes, "The cause of God's love to us-wards must of necessity be not in us, nor in any other thing beside God."[52] God chose to love His elect not for what He saw in them, but simply because He chose to love them.

Saving faith in Christ, Bullinger stated, is the visible mark of the elect. He says: "If you ask me whether you are elected to life, or predestinate to death . . . I answer simply out of the Scripture. . . . If you have communion or fellowship with Christ, you are predestinate to life . . . but if you be a stranger from Christ, howsoever otherwise you seem to flourish in virtues, you are predestinate to death."[53] This is to say, those who have believed on Christ should have great assurance that they are numbered among God's elect. Bullinger further states, "Faith . . . is a most assured sign that you are elected."[54] In other words, he is saying that only the elect come to faith in Christ. Such faith brings true assurance and confirmation of one's election.

Bullinger knew that the elect are a small minority within the larger community of the church. He says, "God knows who are His, and now and then mention is made of the small number of the elect."[55] This minority, Bullinger insisted, comprises the true church. He writes, "This inward and invisible church of God may be well named the elect spouse of Christ, only known unto God, who alone knows who are His."[56] That even a "small number" is chosen to be a part of the true church is a staggering indication of divine mercy.

## Doctrine in Focus:
### IRRESISTIBLE CALL

Bullinger understood the inseparable connection between sovereign election and the irresistible call of the elect to Christ. All the elect come to faith in Christ because God Himself brings it to pass. Regarding Bullinger's position on this doctrine, Venema writes: "Only the monergism of sovereign electing grace can redress the situation of fallen man whose will, though free from any external compulsion to evil, has no capacity to perform what is good. . . . The condition of the human will *post lapsum* requires divine monergism in the accomplishment of salvation. . . . There is, accordingly, no place for any form of synergism in Bullinger's thought."[57] Bullinger saw that in his depraved condition, man can do nothing to save himself; it is all of God. This is clearly seen in his affirmation that "the only cause of our salvation [is] the mere and only grace of God, which is received by faith in Christ."[58] The conversion of the sinner is accomplished by sovereign grace.

Thus, Bullinger taught that sinners cannot come to Christ apart from the irresistible call of God. He states, "Unless we be drawn by the heavenly Father, we cannot believe."[59] God carries out this drawing in myriad ways, Bullinger taught, saying: "God verily drew Paul violently, but He does not draw all unto Him by the hair. There are also other ways of drawing, by which God draws man unto Him."[60] He also laid out some of the steps by which God draws His elect. He writes, "God . . . does then draw you, when He preaches unto you the gospel by His servants; when He touches your heart; when He stirs you to prayer, whereby you may call and cry for His grace and assistance, His enlightening and drawing."[61] Bullinger believed that sinners call on the Lord only when He calls them to Himself.

Because they are spiritually dead, sinners need to be made alive before they can respond to Christ. This work, which is called regeneration or the new birth, is performed on sinners by the Holy Spirit. Bullinger explains, "The second birth is wrought by the means of the Holy Ghost, which, being from heaven poured into our hearts, does bring us to the knowledge of ourselves, so that we may easily perceive, assuredly know, and sensibly feel, that in our flesh there is not life, no integrity, or righteousness at all; and so consequently, that no man is saved by his own strengths or merits."[62] The Holy Spirit produces the new birth, not the lost sinner.

Saving faith, Bullinger maintained, is essential for salvation. He writes, "Christ is received by faith, and not by works."[63] Elsewhere he adds, "Faith alone, whereby we believe in Christ, who was lift up for the remission of our sins, and in whom alone our life and sure salvation does assuredly consist, is the only thing that quickens us which are already dying by the envenomed sting of Satan, which is sin."[64] Bullinger wholeheartedly affirmed the Reformation motto *sola fide*, or "faith alone."

However, faith is not something man contributes to his salvation. Rather, it is a gift God grants to the elect. Bullinger says, "Faith is the mere gift of God because God alone of His power gives it to His elect according to measure; and that when, to whom, and how much He will; and that by His Holy Spirit."[65] Elsewhere he writes, "Faith is God's gift in the heart of man, which God alone does search and know."[66] No one can believe on Christ for salvation unless God bestows faith on him or her.

**Doctrine in Focus:**
## Preserving Grace

Bullinger was confident that those chosen in Christ have a certain end in eternity. None who are chosen by God will fall away from a state of grace. Bullinger writes, "The saints are chosen in Christ by God unto a sure end."[67] None of the elect will ever perish.

Bullinger further contends that salvation is entirely of divine grace. He asserts, "Grace . . . does call, justify, save, or glorify the faithful: so that we must make our account, that the whole work of our salvation and all the virtues of the godly do proceed of the only grace of God alone."[68] Again he says, "The grace of God . . . is the favor and good-will of the eternal Godhead, wherewith He according to His incomprehensible goodness does embrace, call, justify, and save men freely for Christ His sake, our Lord and Savior."[69] The entirety of salvation is of God, he says: "We are saved freely or by the grace of God . . . we are saved by the love of God . . . we are saved through the mercy of God."[70] In short, Bullinger believed that everything in salvation—from regeneration to preservation—ultimately depends on God, not man.

**Doctrine in Focus:**

## DIVINE REPROBATION

While Zwingli taught that God elected some to salvation and chose others to reprobation, Bullinger held that God ordained some to eternal life and merely passed by others, passively allowing the reprobation of the nonelect rather than actively causing it. In addressing this point, Bullinger writes, "When the Lord calls man and he resists, making himself unworthy of the kingdom of heaven, He does then permit him unto himself: that is, He leaves man unto his own corrupt nature, according unto which the heart of man is stony."[71]

According to this view of reprobation, God withdraws His saving influence from those whom He chooses to pass over. Bullinger maintains, "God is said to blind men's eyes, so often as He does revoke, or take away, the contemned light of His truth and sincerity, leaving them that delight in darkness to walk and stick in their darkness still."[72] God abandons the nonelect to their sinful choices. Bullinger adds, "The withdrawing of God's grace is the hardening of man's heart; and when we are left unto ourselves, then are we hardened."[73] Thus, the hearts of men become ever more opposed to God when He withdraws His grace.

Bullinger further asserted that the reprobate do not believe because they choose not to believe. He writes: "There is a defection of apostasy: in the which, through hatred of faith or religion, atheists or godless men, of mere ungodliness and contempt of God . . . fall away from the sound and catholic faith, and finally from the fellowship of the faithful."[74] When this type of falling away happens, no blame can be assigned to God. Bullinger affirms that God is righteous and just in the eternal punishment of the reprobate: "The Lord does punish sinners justly; for He is Himself a most just judge."[75] Man always remains responsible for his sinful choices, so God is wholly just in His judgments.

# THE TORCH IS PASSED

In the flow of church history, it has been common for one to ignite a fire while another fans its flames. So it was with Zwingli and Bullinger in Zurich, and so it was again with Bullinger and all of Switzerland.

Upon Bullinger's death, Reformation flames were rapidly spreading across Switzerland. Zurich, once the main hub of the Swiss Reformation, was giving way to other cities, such as Berne and Basel, as influential centers of Reformed thought. But it was Geneva that would make the most profound and long-lasting impact for the Protestant movement. This shift in influence was brought about by the ministry of the great Reformer, John Calvin, who carried out his work of expository genius and exegetical prowess in Geneva. In a sense, Bullinger had taken the torch of Swiss reform from Zwingli and, in due time, passed it to Calvin.

In the same way, the torch of Reformed truth has been passed down through the centuries to the church today. Has your soul been inflamed with these truths from the pages of Scripture? Has your heart been ignited by these God-honoring doctrines that shook the world in the sixteenth century? Will you uphold the light of this truth in the midst of this dark and sinful generation? Will you earnestly advance the biblical teaching of God's sovereign grace in salvation?

May God set our hearts ablaze with a restored commitment to sound doctrine. May He give us a renewed devotion to the lofty truths of the doctrines of grace. And as He does so, may there be a new reformation in this day, all for His glory and for the good of His church.

## Notes

1   Heinrich Bullinger, *The Decades of Henry Bullinger, Vol. 2*, ed. Thomas Harding (1852; repr., Grand Rapids: Reformation Heritage, 2004), 187.

2   Heinrich Bullinger, *The Decades of Henry Bullinger, Vol. 1*, ed. Thomas Harding (1852; repr., Grand Rapids: Reformation Heritage, 2004), 388.

3   "Heinrich Bullinger," in *The Oxford Dictionary of the Christian Church*, 3rd Ed., ed. E. A. Livingstone (Oxford: Oxford University Press, 1997), 250.

4   Philip Schaff, *History of the Christian Church, Vol. VIII: Modern Christianity: The Swiss Reformation* (1910; repr., Grand Rapids: Eerdmans, 1984), 205.

5   George Ella, "Henry Bullinger (1504–1575): Shepherd of the Churches," in Bullinger, *The Decades of Henry Bullinger, Vol. 1*, x.

6   Bruce Gordon, "Heinrich Bullinger," in *The Reformation Theologians: An Introduction to Theology in the Early Modern Period*, ed. Carter Lindberg (Oxford: Blackwell, 2002), 170.

7   Theodore Beza, cited in Schaff, *History of the Christian Church, Vol. VIII*, 207.

8   Oswald Myconius, cited in J. H. Merle d'Aubigné, *History of the Reformation in the Sixteenth Century, Vol. 3* (Glasgow: W. G. Blackie, 1847), 514.

9   George Ella, "The Importance of Henry Bullinger," in Bullinger, *The Decades of Henry Bullinger, Vol. 1*, xiii.

10 Joel R. Beeke, "Henry Bullinger's Decades," in Bullinger, *The Decades of Henry Bullinger, Vol. 1*, lxxiii.

11 Gordon, "Heinrich Bullinger," in *The Reformation Theologians*, 180.

12 Gordon, "Heinrich Bullinger," in *The Reformation Theologians*, 181.

13 Gordon, "Heinrich Bullinger," in *The Reformation Theologians*, 180.

14 G. W. Bromiley, ed., "General Introduction," *Zwingli and Bullinger: Library of Christian Classics, Volume XXIV* (Philadelphia: Westminster, 1963), 45–46.

15 Cornelis P. Venema, *Heinrich Bullinger and the Doctrine of Predestination* (Grand Rapids: Baker Academic, 2002), 87.

16 Robert C. Walton, "Johann Heinrich Bullinger," in *New International Dictionary of the Christian Church*, gen. ed. J. D. Douglas (Grand Rapids: Zondervan, 1978), 166.

17 James T. Dennison Jr., introduction to the Second Helvetic Confession, in *Reformed Confessions of the 16th and 17th Centuries in English Translations, Vol. 2*, compiled and ed. James T. Dennison Jr. (Grand Rapids: Reformation Heritage, 2010), 810.

18 Bullinger, the Second Helvetic Confession, in *Reformed Confessions of the 16th and 17th Centuries in English Translations, Vol. 2*, 819.

19 Bullinger, the Second Helvetic Confession, in *Reformed Confessions of the 16th and 17th Centuries in English Translations, Vol. 2*, 818.

20 Bullinger, the Second Helvetic Confession, in *Reformed Confessions of the 16th and 17th Centuries in English Translations, Vol. 2*, 819.

21 Bullinger, *The Decades of Henry Bullinger, Vol. 2*, 194.

22 Bullinger, *The Decades of Henry Bullinger, Vol. 1*, 384.

23 Bullinger, *The Decades of Henry Bullinger, Vol. 1*, 394.

24 Bullinger, *The Decades of Henry Bullinger, Vol. 1*, 385.

25 Bullinger, *The Decades of Henry Bullinger, Vol. 1*, 385.

26 Bullinger, *The Decades of Henry Bullinger, Vol. 1*, 386.

27 Bullinger, *The Decades of Henry Bullinger, Vol. 1*, 395.

28 Bullinger, *The Decades of Henry Bullinger, Vol. 1*, 393.

29 Bullinger, *The Decades of Henry Bullinger, Vol. 1*, 396.

30 Bullinger, *The Decades of Henry Bullinger, Vol. 1*, 389.

31 Bullinger, *The Decades of Henry Bullinger, Vol. 1*, 396.

32 Bullinger, *The Decades of Henry Bullinger, Vol. 1*, 396.

33 Bullinger, *The Decades of Henry Bullinger, Vol. 1*, 395.

34 Bullinger, *The Decades of Henry Bullinger, Vol. 1*, 360.

35 Bullinger, *The Decades of Henry Bullinger, Vol. 1*, 389.

36 Bullinger, *The Decades of Henry Bullinger, Vol. 1*, 403.

37 Bullinger, *The Decades of Henry Bullinger, Vol. 1*, 404.

38 Bullinger, *The Decades of Henry Bullinger, Vol. 1*, 394.

39 Bullinger, *The Decades of Henry Bullinger, Vol. 1*, 393.

40 Bullinger, *The Decades of Henry Bullinger, Vol. 1*, 393.

41 Bullinger, *The Decades of Henry Bullinger, Vol. 1*, 393–394.

42 Bullinger, *The Decades of Henry Bullinger, Vol. 1*, 388.

43 Bullinger, *The Decades of Henry Bullinger, Vol. 2*, 376.

44 Bullinger, *The Decades of Henry Bullinger, Vol. 1*, 400.

45 Venema, *Heinrich Bullinger and the Doctrine of Predestination*, 87.

46 Bullinger, the Second Helvetic Confession, in *Reformed Confessions of the 16th and 17th Centuries in English Translations, Vol. 2*, 825.

47 Bullinger, *The Decades of Henry Bullinger, Vol. 2*, 185.

48 Bullinger, *The Decades of Henry Bullinger, Vol. 2*, 186.

49 Bullinger, *The Decades of Henry Bullinger, Vol. 2*, 187–188.

50 Bullinger, the Second Helvetic Confession, in *Reformed Confessions of the 16th and 17th Centuries in English Translations, Vol. 2*, 825.

51 Bullinger, *The Decades of Henry Bullinger, Vol. 2*, 188.

52 Bullinger, *The Decades of Henry Bullinger, Vol. 2*, 7.

53 Bullinger, *The Decades of Henry Bullinger, Vol. 2*, 187.

54 Bullinger, *The Decades of Henry Bullinger, Vol. 2*, 187.

55 Bullinger, the Second Helvetic Confession, in *Reformed Confessions of the 16th and 17th Centuries in English Translations, Vol. 2*, 825.

56 Bullinger, *The Decades of Henry Bullinger, Vol. 2*, 7.

57 Venema, *Heinrich Bullinger and the Doctrine of Predestination*, 95, 102, 103.

58 Bullinger, *The Decades of Henry Bullinger, Vol. 2*, 38.

59 Bullinger, *The Decades of Henry Bullinger, Vol. 2*, 190.

60 Bullinger, *The Decades of Henry Bullinger, Vol. 2*, 190.

61 Bullinger, *The Decades of Henry Bullinger, Vol. 2*, 190.

62 Bullinger, *The Decades of Henry Bullinger, Vol. 2*, 37.

63 Bullinger, *The Decades of Henry Bullinger, Vol. 2*, 37.

64 Bullinger, *The Decades of Henry Bullinger, Vol. 2*, 38.

65 Bullinger, the Second Helvetic Confession, in *Reformed Confessions of the 16th and 17th Centuries in English Translations, Vol. 2*, 841.

66 Bullinger, *The Decades of Henry Bullinger, Vol. 1*, 363.

67 Bullinger, the Second Helvetic Confession, in *Reformed Confessions of the 16th and 17th Centuries in English Translations, Vol. 2*, 825.

68 Bullinger, *The Decades of Henry Bullinger, Vol. 2*, 9.

69 Bullinger, *The Decades of Henry Bullinger, Vol. 2*, 11.

70 Bullinger, *The Decades of Henry Bullinger, Vol. 2*, 12.

71 Bullinger, *The Decades of Henry Bullinger, Vol. 1*, 381.

72 Bullinger, *The Decades of Henry Bullinger, Vol. 1*, 380.

73 Bullinger, *The Decades of Henry Bullinger, Vol. 1*, 381.

74 Bullinger, *The Decades of Henry Bullinger, Vol. 2*, 77.

75 Bullinger, *The Decades of Henry Bullinger, Vol. 1*, 427.

# CHAPTER TWENTY-THREE
## STUDY QUESTIONS

1. Comment on the confessions of faith that were written in Switzerland. What role did these statements play in the Swiss Reformation? What significance should creeds have in the life of the church today?

2. Describe Heinrich Bullinger's upbringing. What aspects of his youth were influential in his spiritual development? Who proved to be of greatest influence in his later years?

3. Summarize Bullinger's preaching at Hausen, Bremgarten, and Zurich. How long did his pastorate in Zurich last? What effect did his long tenure have upon his preaching and writing?

4. In what ways can Bullinger be classified as one of the leading Reformation historians? Explain his particular contributions to the Swiss confederation. To what extent did these and his other works impact surrounding nations?

5. Compare Bullinger's theological beliefs with those of his predecessor in Zurich, Ulrich Zwingli. In what ways were they similar? In what ways were they different?

6. Define the doctrine of providence. How is providence related to the sovereignty of God in creation? In salvation?

7. Explain Bullinger's view of original sin. Did his position show an increased development in the church's understanding of this doctrine? If so, how?

8. Comment on Bullinger's belief in divine reprobation. How did Bullinger view the relationship between sovereign election and human responsibility? What does it mean to say that God passes over the nonelect?

*W*hen God elects one and rejects another, it
is owing not to any respect to the individual,
but entirely to His own mercy which is free to
display and exert itself when and where He
pleases . . . in order to humble the pride of
the flesh.[1]

*S*ince God places your salvation in Himself
alone, why should you descend to yourself?
Since He assigns you His own mercy alone,
why will you recur to your own merits?[2]

–John Calvin

# THEOLOGIAN FOR THE AGES

## SWISS REFORMER: JOHN CALVIN

W hen Martin Luther nailed his Ninety-five Theses to the Castle Church door in Wittenberg, Germany, in 1517, an eight-year-old French boy was standing in the shadows of obscurity, being groomed for the Catholic priesthood in northeast France. That boy would become, arguably, the most important theologian in the history of the church. Furthermore, Luther's mantle as leader of the Reformation would eventually fall on his shoulders, and he would greatly advance the Protestant movement Luther had begun. His name was John Calvin.

Though the two Reformers never met, they greatly admired one another's works. Luther praised Calvin's early writings, stating, "[His] books I have perused with singular pleasure."[3] Calvin, in turn, addressed Luther, twenty-five years his elder, as his "most respected father" and "a remarkable apostle of Christ, through whose work and ministry, most of all, the purity of the gospel has been restored in our time."[4] In fact, Luther may have helped bring Calvin to faith in Christ through his treatises *The Freedom of a Christian* and *The Babylonian Captivity of the Christian Church.*[5]

Despite this mutual esteem, the two Reformers were as different as night and day. Luther was fiery, spontaneous, and explosive, while Calvin was more careful, pensive, and systematic. Luther has been likened to a bull, stubborn and strong-headed, whereas Calvin has been compared to an owl, wise and calculating.[6] Luther was passionate, dynamic, and prone to exaggeration.[7] Calvin was a logical systematizer, quiet, and thoughtful, with a far more stable character.[8]

## SPEAKING WITH ONE VOICE

Even with these starkly different temperaments, Luther and Calvin spoke with one voice in essential matters of theology. This was especially true with regard to the sovereignty of God in saving grace. Both men insisted on *sola Scriptura*, "Scripture alone," as the sole basis of Christian doctrine and duty in the church. Both were committed to the other four solas—*sola gratia, sola fide, solus Christus,* and *soli Deo gloria*—asserting that salvation is by grace alone through faith alone in Christ alone for the glory of God alone. More specifically, both men taught the essential truths of the doctrines of grace. Both believed and broadcast the right of God to act as He pleases with whom He pleases in the salvation of undeserving sinners. Both were strict predestinarians of the Augustinian stripe. In short, these two magisterial Reformers were champions of the God-exalting truths of sovereign grace.

Calvin, however, went further than Luther in advancing these doctrines. He took the central tenets of the Reformation and fashioned them into a comprehensive body of divinity. "From the disparate, disorganized heritage of Luther and Zwingli," Jonathan Hill writes, "[Calvin] forged a systematic version of the Christian faith and life that still profoundly influences modern Western society."[9] Whereas Luther emphasized justification by faith, Calvin took aim at a higher target, underscoring the glory of God in the display of His sovereignty in the world, both in salvation and in providence. Both Reformers were correct in their teachings in these areas, but Calvin gave a more comprehensive explanation of the many facets of the doctrines of grace.

## BRINGING ORDER TO IDEAS

Martyn Lloyd-Jones contrasts the two Reformers in this way: "Luther was a volcano, spewing out fiery ideas in all directions without much pattern or system. But ideas cannot live and last without a body, and the great need of the Protestant movement in the last days of Luther was for a theologian with the ability to arrange and to express the new faith within a system. That person was Calvin. . . . It was he who saved Protestantism by giving it a body of theology with his *Institutes*; and it is from this that the faith and the theology of most of the Protestant churches have sprung."[10]

R. C. Sproul explains the roles these titans played as follows:

Luther, being a brilliant student of language, brought to the theological table an uncanny ability to provide vignettes of insight into particular questions of truth. But Luther was not a systematician by nature, and so he could not be the theologian of theologians. He never developed a full-orbed systematic theology for the instruction of the church. That task in the sixteenth century was left to the genius of the Genevan theologian John Calvin. Calvin brought to the study of theology a passion for biblical truth and a coherent understanding of the Word of God. Of all of the thinkers of the sixteenth century, Calvin was most noted for his ability to provide a systematic theological understanding of Christian truth.[11]

"Calvin's great achievement," Timothy George likewise argues, "was to take the classic insights of the Reformation (*sola gratia, sole fide, sola Scriptura*) and give them a clear, systematic exposition, which neither Luther nor Zwingli ever did. . . . From Geneva they took on a life of their own and developed into a new international theology, extending from Poland and Hungary in the East to the Netherlands, Scotland, England (Puritanism), and eventually to New England in the West."[12] William Cunningham adds, "Calvin was by far the greatest of the Reformers with respect to the talents he possessed, the influence he exerted, and the services he rendered in the establishment and diffusion of important truth."[13]

Thus, it was Calvin, a second-generation Reformer, who brought order to the Reformed ideas that were emerging and fashioned them into a seamless tapestry of thought, a systematic whole that was exegetical, logical, and sound. It is no exaggeration to say he was the architect of Reformed theology.

# JOHN CALVIN

Calvin (1509–1564) is easily the most important Protestant theologian of all time[14] and remains one of the truly great men who have lived.[15] A world-class theologian, a renowned teacher, an ecclesiastical statesman, and a valiant Reformer, Calvin is seen by many as the greatest influence on the church since the first century. Apart from the biblical authors themselves, Calvin stands as the most influential minister of the Word the world has ever seen. Philip Melanchthon revered him as the most able interpreter of Scripture in the church, and therefore labeled him simply "the theologian."[16] And Charles Spurgeon said that Calvin "propounded truth more clearly than any other man that ever breathed, knew more of Scripture, and explained it more clearly."[17]

Calvin was born on July 10, 1509, to Gerard and Jeanne Cauvin in the French cathedral city of Noyon, some sixty miles north of Paris. Gerard was a notary, or financial administrator, for the Roman Catholic bishop of the Noyon diocese and, thus, a member of the professional class. When John was eleven, Gerard used his influence to gain a chaplaincy for his son at the Noyon Cathedral. At age fourteen, John entered the leading educational institution of Europe, the University of Paris, to study theology in preparation for the priesthood. There, he was immersed in the principles of the Renaissance, humanism, and scholarship. A serious and remarkably learned young man, he graduated with a master's degree (1528), having received the finest education of the day in the study of Latin, literature, logic, theology, rhetoric, and philosophy.

Upon Calvin's graduation, his father attempted to gain two more appointments for him in the Roman Catholic Church. But Gerard fell into a conflict with the bishop of Noyon, and this falling-out with the church caused him to redirect his brilliant son to the study of law at the universities of Orléans (1528) and later Bourges (1529). Calvin learned Greek and sharpened his skills in analytical thinking and persuasive argument, skills he would use with great effect in the pulpit in Geneva. But when Gerard unexpectedly died (1531), Calvin, twenty-one years old, moved back to Paris to pursue his great love, the study of classical literature. He would later return to Bourges, where he completed his legal studies and received his law degree in 1532.

## Suddenly Converted

While he was a student at the University of Orléans, Calvin encountered some of the early reform ideas through Luther's writings, which were widely discussed in academic circles. It is possible that he came to a deeper understanding of evangelical truth through his Greek teacher, Melchior Wolmar. Subsequently, Calvin was converted to Christ. With that, a champion for the cause of the Reformation entered the camp.

Calvin recorded a testimony of his conversion in the preface to his *Commentary on the Book of Psalms* (1557):

To this pursuit [of the study of law] I endeavored faithfully to apply myself, in obedience to the will of my father; but God, by the secret guidance of His providence, at length gave a different direction to my course. At first, since I was too obstinately devoted to the superstitions of popery to be easily extricated from so profound an abyss of mire, God by a sudden conversion subdued and brought my mind to a teachable frame, which was more hardened in such matters than might have been expected from one at my early period of life. Having thus received some taste and knowledge of true godliness, I was immediately inflamed with so intense a desire to make progress therein, that although I did not altogether leave off other studies, I yet pursued them with less ardor.[18]

Calvin saw himself like the unsuspecting Saul of Tarsus on the Damascus Road, dramatically converted by sovereign grace. In that moment, God conquered his proud heart and subdued his will. The young Frenchman's intellect was enlightened by the Holy Spirit. Immediately he lost much of his interest in the study of law and became consumed with the spiritual truths of God's Word. Soon, people began to gather around Calvin to be taught the truth.

In November 1533, Nicolas Cop, rector of the University of Paris and a friend of Calvin, preached the opening address of the winter term at the university. The message was a plea for reformation on the basis of the New Testament and a bold attack on the Scholastic theologians of the day. Cop encountered strong resistance to his expressed "Luther-like" views. Calvin is believed to have collaborated with Cop on the address, as a copy of the manuscript exists in Calvin's handwriting.[19] As a result, Calvin was forced to flee Paris before he could be arrested.

Calvin withdrew to the estate of Louis du Tillet, a well-to-do man who was sympathetic to the Reformation cause. There, Calvin had the opportunity to spend five months in du Tillet's extensive theological library. He read the Bible along with the writings of the Church Fathers, most notably Augustine. By hard work, genius, and grace, Calvin was becoming a self-taught theologian of no small stature.

## Writing the *Institutes*

In 1534, Calvin moved to Basel, Switzerland, which had become a Protestant stronghold, in order to study in solitude. Calvin writes, "Being of a disposition somewhat unpolished and bashful, which led me always to love the shade and retirement, I then began to seek some secluded corner where I might be withdrawn from the public view."[20] In Basel, Calvin penned the first edition of what would become his theological masterpiece and the single most important book written during the Reformation, the *Institutes of the Christian Religion*. In it, he outlined the fundamentals of the Protestant faith and presented a compelling argument for the Reformed interpretation of Scripture. In a preface addressed to the king of France, Francis I, he called for tolerance toward French Protestants, who were being persecuted. Amazingly, Calvin began this work at age twenty-five, only one year after his conversion. It was published when he was twenty-six.

In 1536, Calvin decided to move to Strasbourg, in southwest Germany, to further his studies as a quiet scholar. But a war between Francis I and Charles V, the Holy Roman emperor, prevented him from taking the most direct route. Calvin was forced to detour to Geneva, where he intended to spend only one night. But when he entered the city, he was immediately recognized as the young author of the *Institutes*. Those sympathetic to the Reformation took him to meet William Farel, who had led the Protestant movement in Geneva for ten years.

Geneva had recently voted to leave the Roman Catholic Church and become a Reformation city, but it was in dire need of a teacher who could articulate Reformed truths. The fiery Farel challenged Calvin to take up the task; when Calvin hesitated, Farel resorted to an imprecatory threat. Calvin reports it this way:

> Farel, who burned with an extraordinary zeal to advance the gospel, immediately strained every nerve to detain me. And after having learned that my heart was set upon devoting myself to private studies, for which I wished to keep myself free from other pursuits, and finding that he gained nothing by entreaties, he proceeded to utter an imprecation that God would curse my retirement, and the tranquility of the studies which I sought, if I should withdraw and refuse to give assistance, when the necessity was so urgent. By this imprecation I was so stricken with terror, that I desisted from the journey which I had undertaken.[21]

Calvin began his ministry in Geneva as a lecturer, then as a pastor. Along with Farel, he began the task of bringing the life and practice of the church into accord with the teaching of Scripture. Among the reforms he implemented was the exercise of church discipline at the Communion table. This did not sit well with prominent Geneva citizens, many of whom were living sinful lives. This crisis reached the boiling point on Easter Sunday, April 23, 1538, when Calvin refused to administer Communion to certain leading people who were living in open sin. The tensions grew so great that Calvin and Farel were forced to leave Geneva.

## EXILED TO STRASBOURG

Calvin withdrew to Strasbourg, where he had intended to go two years earlier. His purpose was to escape from the public eye. But Strasbourg's chief Reformer, Martin Bucer, insisted that Calvin must continue in public pulpit ministry and threatened him much as Farel had earlier. Yielding to Bucer, Calvin became the pastor of nearly five hundred Protestant refugees from France. He writes: "Alarmed by the example of Jonas which he set before me, I still continued in the work of teaching. And although I always continued like myself, studiously avoiding celebrity; yet I was carried, I know not how, as it were by force to the Imperial assemblies, where, willing or unwilling, I was under the necessity of appearing before the eyes of many."[22]

However, this theologian-in-exile was also given time and freedom to write in Strasbourg. Calvin wrote his *Commentaries on the Epistle of Paul the Apostle to the Romans* and enlarged his *Institutes*, translating it into French. At this same time, he wrote what has been hailed as the greatest apologetic for the Reformation, *A Reply to Sadoleto*. After Calvin's departure from Geneva, Cardinal Jacopo Sadoleto had written an open letter to the people of the city, inviting them to return to the Roman Catholic Church. The city fathers appealed to Calvin to respond, which he did with his *Reply*, a compelling defense of the glory of God in the gospel of grace. Also during his time in Strasbourg, he married Idelette de Bure, a widow with two children, who brought him much happiness.

After Calvin had spent three happy years in Strasbourg, the city fathers of Geneva wrote to ask him to return as their pastor. In his absence, the religious and political situation had deteriorated. But Calvin had no intention of returning. In a letter to Farel on March 29, 1540, he said, "Rather would I submit to death a hundred times than to that cross, on which one had to perish daily a thousand times over."[23] But Calvin eventually changed his mind, despite the many dangers he knew awaited him in Geneva. On March 1, 1541, Calvin wrote to Pierre Viret: "There is no place under heaven of which I can have a greater dread, not because I have hated it, but because I see so many difficulties presented in that quarter which I do feel myself far from being equal to surmount. Whenever the recollection of former times recurs to my mind, I cannot but shudder throughout with heartfelt alarm at the thought, that I may be forced to expose myself a second time to these sort of contests."[24]

Despite these fears, Calvin *did* return to Geneva, fully surrendered to the will of God. Most representative of this consecration to the Lord is Calvin's personal seal—a hand holding a heart. The motto beneath reads: "My heart I give Thee, Lord, eagerly and earnestly."[25] Calvin saw his life in Christ entirely and willingly given to God. Therefore, he bowed to what he believed to be God's will and returned to his pastorate in Switzerland.

## THE RETURN TO GENEVA

Calvin arrived in Geneva on September 13, 1541, after an absence of three and a half years. In his first sermon, he resumed his exposition of Scripture at the next verse after the last one he had covered before being exiled. This continuation was intended as a bold statement that verse-by-verse preaching of the Word would hold the primary place in his ministry. James Montgomery Boice writes: "Calvin had no weapon but the Bible. From the very first, his emphasis had been on Bible teaching. Calvin preached from the Bible every day, and under the power of that preaching the city began to be transformed. As the people of Geneva acquired knowledge of God's Word and were changed by it, the city became, as John Knox called it later, a New Jerusalem."[26]

Intent on fostering reform, Calvin issued an ultimatum to the Genevan church:

> If you desire to have me for your pastor, correct the disorder of your lives. If you have with sincerity recalled me from my exile, banish the crimes and debaucheries which prevail among you. . . . I consider the principal enemies of the gospel to be, not the pontiff of Rome, nor heretics, nor seducers, nor tyrants but bad Christians. . . . Of what use is a dead faith without good works? Of what importance is even truth itself, where a wicked life belies it and actions make words blush? Either command me to abandon a second time your town and let me go and soften the bitterness of my afflictions in a new exile, or let the severity of the laws reign in the church. Re-establish there pure discipline.[27]

Calvin's second Genevan pastorate had two periods. The first was the years of opposition (1541–1555), when he endured much resistance and difficulty. The opposition began to manifest itself in the form of the Patriots, the oldest, most influential families of Geneva. They disliked Calvin in large measure because he was a foreigner. He was not allowed to become a citizen of Geneva until 1559, twenty-three years after his arrival. He also faced the resistance of the Libertines, people within Geneva who were antinomians, living in open sin and immorality. But most demanding by far was the ordeal caused by Michael Servetus in 1553. This known heretic was burned at the stake by the city fathers after Calvin had been called as an expert witness. In other trials during this time, Calvin's son, Jacques, died only two weeks after his birth in 1542, and Calvin's wife, Idelette, died in 1549 after only nine years of marriage. Calvin said Jacques' death was "a severe wound, but our Father knows what is best for His children."[28] He not only preached divine sovereignty, he submitted to it.

This draining opposition finally subsided and the last nine years of Calvin's life (1555–1564) could be described as the years of support. At long last, Calvin gained the support of the city fathers. With this backing, he established the Geneva Academy in 1559, based on the example he had seen in Strasbourg. The academy had a private school for elementary instruction and a public school offering more advanced studies in biblical languages and theology to train ministers, lawyers, and doctors. Also in 1559, the fifth and final edition of the *Institutes* was released. In 1560, the Geneva Bible was released, an English translation that was the first Bible with theological notes in the margins. This monumental work, produced by men under Calvin's teaching, presented a worldview of the sovereignty of God over all creation.

Calvin dispatched French-speaking pastors, whom he had trained for the gospel ministry, from Geneva to other French-speaking provinces in Europe. Most went to France, where the Reformed movement grew to encompass about one-tenth of the population. Eventually, thirteen hundred Geneva-trained missionaries went to France. By 1560, more than a hundred underground churches had been planted in France by men sent out from Geneva. By 1562, the number of churches had multiplied to as many as 2,150, with more than 3 million members.[29] The membership of some of the churches numbered in the thousands. This growth produced a Huguenot church that almost overcame the Catholic Counter-Reformation in France. Further, Geneva-trained missionaries planted churches in Italy, Hungary, Poland, Germany, the Netherlands, England, Scotland, and the Rhineland—even Brazil.

## A Farewell Address

In early 1564, Calvin became seriously ill. He preached for the last time from the pulpit of Saint Peter's Cathedral on Sunday, February 6. By April, it was obvious that he did not have long to live. Calvin, age fifty-four, faced death as he had faced the pulpit—with great resolution. The strength of his faith, built on the sovereignty of God, appears in his last will and testament. On April 25, 1564, Calvin dictated the following words:

> In the name of God, I John Calvin, minister of the word of God in the Church of Geneva, feeling myself reduced so low by diverse maladies, that I cannot but think that it is the will of God to withdraw me shortly from this world, have advised to make and set down in writing my testament and declaration of my last will in form, as follows: In the first place, I render thanks to God, not only because he has had compassion on me, His poor creature, to draw me out of the abyss of idolatry in which I was plunged, in order to bring me to the light of His gospel and make me a partaker of the doctrine of salvation, of which I was altogether unworthy, and continuing His mercy He has supported me amid so many sins and short-comings, which were such that I well deserved to be rejected by Him a hundred thousand times—but what is more, He has so far extended His mercy towards me as to make use of me and of my labour, to convey and announce the truth of His gospel; protesting that it is my wish to live and die in this faith which He has bestowed on me, having no other hope nor refuge except in His gratuitous adoption, upon which all my salvation is founded; embracing the grace which He has given me in our Lord Jesus Christ, and accepting the merits of His death and passion, in order that by this means all my sins may be buried; and praying Him so to wash and cleanse me by the blood of this great Redeemer, which has been shed for us poor sinners, that I may appear before His face, bearing as it were His image.[30]

Three days later, on April 28, 1654, Calvin called his fellow ministers to his bedchamber and issued his farewell address to them. He cautioned them that the battles of the Reformation were not over, but only beginning: "You will have troubles when God shall have called me away; for though I am nothing, yet know I well that I have prevented three thousand tumults that would have broken out in Geneva. But take courage and fortify yourselves, for God will make use of this church and will maintain it, and assures you that He will protect it."[31] With that, he passed the torch from his feeble hands to theirs.

Calvin died on May 27, 1564, in the arms of Theodore Beza, his successor. Calvin's last words—"How long, O Lord?"—were the very words of Scripture (Pss. 79:5; 89:46). He died quoting the Bible he had so long preached. Appropriately, this humble servant was buried in a common cemetery in an unmarked grave—at his own request.

Looking back on Calvin's life, Beza concluded, "Having been a spectator of his conduct for sixteen years . . . I can now declare, that in him all men may see a most beautiful example of the Christian character, an example which it is as easy to slander as it is difficult to imitate."[32]

# CALVIN'S WRITINGS

Calvin was one of the most gifted and prolific writers in the history of the church. Tony Lane notes, "His output would have been remarkable for a full-time scholar—yet Calvin fitted it into a schedule that would have exhausted two lesser men. . . . He is the only writer ever to belong without question both to the first rank of theologians *and* to the first rank of commentators."[33] Calvin's collected writings fill fifty-nine large volumes of the 101-volume set known as the *Corpus Reformatorum*, the collected works of the Reformation. Calvin's other works fill another twelve volumes in the *Supplementa Calviniana*. That is a total of seventy-one encyclopedic volumes, which Calvin produced in only twenty-eight years of publishing, an average of more than two large volumes per year. In his most prolific years, Calvin was generating half a million words annually. On average, he wrote about a thousand pages a year—all of it sound theology. Calvin stands as the premier example of the pastor-scholar in church history.

## *INSTITUTES OF THE CHRISTIAN RELIGION*
The first major theological work that Calvin published was the *Institutes*. It became the centerpiece of his vast theological legacy, his most important, best-known, and most influential work. The *Institutes* was a clear statement of the doctrinal standards of the Reformation. The first edition was published in 1536 as a primer on biblical teaching; it contained 111 pages in six large chapters. Over the years, Calvin expanded the *Institutes* through five editions,

enlarging it from eighty-five thousand to four hundred and fifty thousand words. Calvin's thesis was that the Protestant Reformation was consistently biblical and not a novelty. The *Institutes* was a reliable restatement of the orthodox teaching of the prophets and apostles, as well as the Church Fathers.

## Biblical Commentaries

Calvin wrote commentaries on most of the books of the Bible. They fill forty-five large volumes of more than four hundred pages each. They were usually based on his lectures. His commentaries covered twenty-four of the thirty-nine books in the Old Testament, including Genesis to Joshua, Psalms, and all of the prophets except Ezekiel 21–48. Further, he wrote commentaries on all of the New Testament except 2 and 3 John and Revelation. In all, he covered about 75 percent of the Bible in this, his largest literary undertaking. The commentaries are expositional, exegetical, insightful, warm, pastoral, and powerful.

## Sermons

Calvin preached some four thousand expository sermons during his years in Geneva. Beginning in 1549, a professional stenographer took down his sermons word for word. These expositions were protracted series in which Calvin moved verse by verse through entire books in the Bible, often taking more than a year to do so. During his Genevan pastorate, Calvin preached through Genesis (123 sermons), Deuteronomy (200), Judges (a short series), 1 Samuel (107), 2 Samuel (87), 1 Kings (various sermons), Job (159), individual psalms (72), Psalm 119 (22), Isaiah (353), Jeremiah (91), Lamentations (25), Ezekiel (175), Daniel (47), Hosea (65), Joel (17), Amos (43), Obadiah (5), Jonah (6), Micah (28), Nahum (not recorded), Zephaniah (17), a harmony of the Gospels (65 sermons, concluding when he died), Acts (189), 1 Corinthians (110), 2 Corinthians (66), Galatians (43), Ephesians (48), 1 and 2 Thessalonians (46), 1 Timothy (55), 2 Timothy (31), and Titus (17).[34] This kind of exposition gave breadth to Calvin's preaching.

## Letters, Treatises, Catechisms

Calvin's most underrated writings were his letters. Approximately four thousand of them have been published, comprising eleven large volumes in the *Corpus Reformatorum*. The tone of each letter fits the occasion, most being warm expressions of compassion. Calvin wrote many treatises, including several on the sovereignty of God. One was titled *A Treatise on the Eternal Predestination of God* (1552). Another was *A Defense of the Secret Providence of God* (1558). Yet another, mentioned earlier, was his response to the open letter of Cardinal Sadoleto, titled *Reply by John Calvin to Letter by Cardinal Sadoleto to the Senate and People of Geneva*[35] (1541). Calvin also authored the Genevan Catechism in 1537, the first confession for the Genevan church. After his return from exile in Strasbourg in 1541, he produced another catechism that had sharper phrases more easily learned. This catechism was adopted by the French Reformed Church and was translated and used as the Scottish church's catechism until the Westminster Shorter Catechism (1648). Calvin also wrote two short confessions of faith. One was the Gallic Confession, which became the main confession for the French Reformed Church. The other was the *Consensus Tigurinus*, written with Heinrich Bullinger, uniting the two branches of the Swiss Reformation.

### ECCLESIASTICAL ORDINANCES OF THE CHURCH

Calvin wrote the *Ecclesiastical Ordinances* upon his return to Geneva to begin his second pastorate there (1541). It became the foundational guide for sixteenth-century Reformed churches. It returned the church to its biblical design and apostolic simplicity. The *Ecclesiastical Ordinances* established the three marks of the church: (1) the ministry of the Word and prayer; (2) the faithful administration of the sacraments; and (3) church discipline.

# CALVIN'S THEOLOGY

Calvin's theology was drawn from the deep wells of Scripture. Earle Cairns writes: "Although Calvin's theology has an emphasis similar to that of Augustine, Calvin owes his system to his study of the Scriptures rather than to Augustine. Like other Reformers, he went from the Bible to Augustine to seek the support of that prince of the Fathers rather than going from Augustine to the Bible and the doctrines of the Reformation."[36] But because Calvin was first and foremost an exegete of Scripture, his doctrine was distinctively Augustinian. Although the five points of Calvinism would not be officially stated until the Synod of Dort (1618–1619), Calvin clearly taught the contours of these doctrines.

514 PILLARS OF GRACE

**Doctrine in Focus:**

DIVINE SOVEREIGNTY

The foundation of Calvin's theology was the sovereignty of God. He taught that God is the cause and the end, both the Creator and Controller of all things.[37] Intensely theocentric, Calvin placed God and His glory at the center of life and experience. Benjamin B. Warfield writes: "Here we have the secret of Calvin's greatness. . . . No man ever had a profounder view of God than he."[38] Articulating this high view of God, Calvin asserts, "God is the disposer and ruler of all things,—that from the remotest eternity, according to His own wisdom, He decreed what He was to do, and now by His power executes what He decreed."[39] God formed all of creation and planned all of history, and is ruling over all things and all events.

Calvin was adamant about God's rightful place as Lord over all. He asserts, "We maintain, that by His providence, not heaven and earth and inanimate creatures only, but also the counsels and wills of men are so governed as to move exactly in the course which He has destined."[40] He believed that, by the free exercise of His will, God foreordained all that comes to pass, and this implies that nothing happens by chance. He says: "You will say, does nothing happen fortuitously, nothing contingently? I answer, it was a true saying of Basil the Great, that *fortune* and *chance* are heathen terms; the meaning of which ought not to occupy pious minds. For if all success is blessing from God, and calamity and adversity are His curse, there is no place left in human affairs for fortune and chance."[41] Elsewhere he adds, "If God is the judge of the world, fortune has no place in its government."[42] He also says, "We are not afflicted by chance, but through the infallible providence of God."[43] Again he writes, "Everything done in the world is according to His decree."[44] Calvin was convinced that nothing happens randomly, but all things are ordered by divine design.

All living things, even the Devil, are under God's authority, Calvin declared. He writes, "Thus, for the good and safety of His people, He overrules all the creatures, even the devil himself who, we see, does not attempt anything against Job without His permission and command."[45] He adds, "Whatever men or Satan himself devise, God holds the helm, and makes all their efforts contribute to the execution of His judgments."[46] All creatures are but instruments for God's purposes.

Whatever God sovereignly decrees, Calvin taught, is holy and perfect. He says: "The will of God is the supreme rule of righteousness, so that everything which He wills must be held to be righteous by the mere fact of His willing it. Therefore, when it is asked why the Lord did so, we must answer, because He pleased."[47] He insisted that God's sovereign choice in salvation is not dependent on divine foresight, saying, "The foreknowledge of God, which Paul mentions, is not a bare prescience, as some unwise persons absurdly imagine, but the adoption by which He had always distinguished His children from the reprobate."[48] Thus, Calvin maintained that all that comes to pass is due to God's active sovereignty and providence.

Calvin held that God's sovereign rule over all of creation is a vitally important truth. He insists, "The most important truth of all [is] that God governs the world by His providence."[49] Elsewhere he adds, "Nothing is more useful than a knowledge of this doctrine."[50] Far from an academic doctrine with little practicality, the truth of the sovereignty of God brings all other truths into focus.

**Doctrine in Focus:**

## RADICAL DEPRAVITY

Calvin strongly asserted the biblical doctrine of total depravity, which states the effects of original sin on the human race. All mankind, he declared, is afflicted with the inward corruption of Adam's sin. John MacArthur writes: "It is impossible to overstate the importance of the doctrine of total depravity in Calvin's theology. It is the starting point and the logical linchpin for both anthropology and soteriology in the Calvinist system."[51]

Calvin was clear as to the extent and the origins of human sinfulness. He writes, "All the parts of the soul were possessed by sin, ever since Adam revolted from the fountain of righteousness."[52] He affirmed that Adam's sin also affected his descendants, writing, "[Adam] not only brought disaster and ruin upon himself, but also plunged our nature into like destruction."[53] Adam's one act of disobedience, Calvin says, "infected his whole seed."[54] Because of Adam's sin, he writes, "We have all sinned; for we are all imbued with natural corruption, and so are become sinful and wicked."[55] Calvin likened the transmission of the Adamic nature to a bad root that leads to bad fruit. He states: "When [Adam] was divested, his nature was left naked and destitute, that he having been defiled by sin, the pollution extends to all his seed. Thus, from a corrupt root corrupt branches proceeding, transmit their corruption to the saplings which spring from them."[56] No man and no part of man is excluded from the effects of the fall.

This means that even infants are inwardly corrupt, Calvin understood. He writes, "Their [infants'] whole nature is, as it were, a seed-bed of sin, and therefore cannot but be odious and abominable to God."[57] Every human being enters the world defiled by sin. Calvin notes, "The impurity of parents is transmitted to their children, so that all, without exception, are originally depraved."[58] This transmission of depravity from parent to child happens at the moment of conception, he explains: "We are not corrupted by acquired wickedness, but bring an innate corruption from the very womb."[59] Calvin adds: "[We are] born into the world with the seed of every iniquity. . . . The Bible . . . clearly asserts that we are born in sin, and that it exists within us as a disease fixed in our nature."[60] Summing up this truth, Calvin writes: "All of us, therefore, descending from an impure seed, come into the world tainted with the contagion of sin. Nay, before we behold the light of the sun we are in God's sight defiled and polluted."[61] No one is born "innocent"; all people are depraved from conception.

Calvin grasped that original sin leaves all people guilty before God and also produces actual sinful actions. He writes, "Original sin, then, may be defined as a hereditary corruption and depravity of our nature, extending to all the parts of the soul, which first makes us obnoxious to the wrath of God, and then produces in us works which in Scripture are termed works of the flesh."[62] Elsewhere he states, "The natural depravity which we bring, from our mother's womb, though it brings not forth immediately its own fruits, is yet sin before God, and deserves his vengeance: and this is that sin which they call original."[63] Because of original sin, all people stand condemned before God even before they commit an actual transgression.

Depravity is indeed "total," Calvin taught—the mind, affections, and will are ruined by original sin. Calvin says, "Corruption does not dwell in one part only, but . . . no part is free from its deadly taint."[64] In Calvin's thinking, "The whole man, from the crown of the head to the sole of the foot, is so deluged, as it were, that no part remains exempt from sin, and, therefore, everything which proceeds from him is imputed as sin."[65] Elsewhere he adds, "Sin has seized both on the mind and heart."[66] No part of man's nature is free from the taint of sin.

The result of total depravity is moral inability, Calvin said. Man can only sin; he cannot do any truly good works on his own. Calvin writes, "The Holy Spirit teaches us in Scripture, that our mind is smitten with so much blindness, that the affections of our heart are so depraved and perverted, that our whole nature is so vitiated, that we can do nothing but sin, until He forms a new will within us."[67] Illustrating the change that must occur in man's soul, he adds, "[We] are born lions, tigers, wolves and bears, until the Spirit of Christ tames us, and from wild and savage beasts forms us to be mild sheep."[68] Man is responsible for this inability, Calvin says: "Our inability to [resist sin] is our own fault. If lust, in which sin has its dominion, so enthralls us, that we are not free to obey our Father, there is no ground for pleading necessity as a defense, since this evil necessity is within, and must be imputed to ourselves."[69] This moral inability amounts to slavery. Calvin writes:

> Man is a slave of sin. . . . Man's spirit is so alienated from the justice of God that man conceives, covets, and undertakes nothing that is not evil, perverse, iniquitous, and soiled. Because the heart, totally imbued with the poison of sin, can emit nothing but the fruits of sin. Yet one must not infer therefrom that man sins as constrained by violent necessity. For, man sins with the consent of a very prompt and inclined will. But because man, by the corruption of his affections, very strongly keeps hating the whole righteousness of God and, on the other hand, is fervent in all kinds of evil, it is said that he has not the free power of choosing between good and evil—which is called free will.[70]

The result of human depravity, Calvin maintained, is divine judgment and eternal punishment. He writes, "By Adam's sin we are not condemned through imputation alone, as though we were punished only for the sin of another; but we suffer his punishment, because we also ourselves are guilty; for as our nature is vitiated in him, it is regarded by God as having committed sin."[71] The entire human race is condemned before God, helpless to save itself.

**Doctrine in Focus:**
## Sovereign Election

Calvin taught that, ultimately, the determinative factor in any person's salvation is the choice of God. This is the doctrine of predestination. Calvin writes: "By predestination we mean the eternal decree of God, by which He determined with Himself whatever He wished to happen with regard to every man. All are not created on equal terms, but some are preordained to eternal life, others to eternal damnation; and, accordingly, as each has been created for one or other of these ends, we say that he has been predestinated to life or to death."[72] With Scripture, Calvin affirmed that God's election of individual sinners occurred before time began. He writes, "God, it is true, wrote the names of His children in the Book of Life before the creation of the world."[73] By the exercise of His will in eternity past, God determined every man's eternal destiny.

The reasons for God's choices in election lie within His holy character, Calvin declared. He writes, "God has a sufficiently just reason for electing and for reprobating, in His own will."[74] He also states, "Inasmuch as God elects some and passes by others, the cause is not to be found in anything else but in His own purpose."[75] Elsewhere he adds, "God has no other book than His eternal counsel, in which He has predestinated us to salvation by adopting us for His children."[76] He also says, "By the word *chosen*, God calls us back to the consideration of His own free will."[77] God had reasons for each choice He made, though He has not chosen to disclose those reasons.

Expanding on this theme, Calvin writes, "God by His eternal and immutable counsel determined once for all those whom it was His pleasure one day to admit to salvation, and those whom, on the other hand, it was His pleasure to doom to destruction."[78] Again he affirms, "Among men some perish, some obtain salvation; but the cause of this depends on the secret will of God."[79] He adds, "The difference which exists between the elect and the rest of the world . . . [is] referred to the mere good pleasure of God."[80] Calvin maintains, "God . . . predestined according to the good pleasure of His will."[81] God's choices are for His own pleasure.

Calvin had no doubt, however, that the reasons for election had nothing to do with those whom God chose. He writes, "When Paul declares that we were chosen in Christ before the foundation of the world (Eph. 1:4), he certainly shows that no regard is had to our own worth . . . we were in Christ adopted unto the heavenly inheritance, because in ourselves we were incapable of such excellence."[82] He also notes, "By saying they were elected before the foundation of the world, [Paul] takes away all reference to worth."[83] Because this is so, Calvin taught, election was not based on anything good that God foresaw in man. Calvin notes: "If you say that He [God] foresaw they would be holy, and therefore elected them, you invert the order of Paul. You may, therefore, safely infer, if He elected us that we might be holy, He did not elect us because He foresaw that we would be holy."[84] Calvin reasons: "For when it is said that believers were elected that they might be holy, it is at the same time intimated that the holiness which was to be in them has its origin in election. And how can it be consistently said, that things derived from election are the cause of election?"[85] He adds, "If election precedes that divine grace by which we are made fit to obtain immortal life, what can God find in us to induce Him to elect us?"[86] Calvin understood from Scripture that nothing in man prompted God's choice.

Calvin was convinced that God owes salvation to none. The entire world stands condemned before Him, with no claim on His grace. That God chooses any to be saved is awe-inspiring evidence of His grace. Calvin explains, "We assert that, with respect to the elect, this plan was founded upon his freely given mercy, without regard to human worth; but by his just and irreprehensible but incomprehensible judgment he has barred the door of life to those whom he has given over to damnation."[87] God's choice of guilty sinners reveals matchless grace.

Calvin declared that God's choice was motivated by His love. He says, "When we come to election, mercy alone everywhere appears."[88] Calvin understood that election was merciful because it was the extension of God's grace to His enemies. He writes, "He chooses from among His enemies those whose hearts He bends to the love of Him."[89] Calvin adds that God's choice is the ultimate privilege, saying, "The grace which God displays towards His chosen is not extended to all men in common, but is a privilege by which He distinguishes a few from the great mass of mankind."[90] Election, Calvin understood, is incontrovertible proof of God's love.

Because God is not under obligation to sinful man, Calvin said, He is free to bestow His grace as He pleases. He notes, "God has always been at liberty to bestow His grace on whom He would."[91] In other words, God is unconstrained in the free exercise of His electing grace. Calvin writes, "God saves whom He wills of His mere good pleasure, and does not pay a debt, a debt which never can be due . . . there being no other means of humbling us as we ought, or making us feel how much we are bound to Him."[92] God, the sovereign Creator and King of all, is completely free to do as He pleases with His creatures.

What is more, Calvin saw that election is the cause of saving faith, not the result of it. He succinctly states, "Election is . . . the parent of faith."[93] Elsewhere he asserts that election precedes and produces faith: "We are believers, because we have been elected."[94] He adds, "The fruit of adoption does not exist in all the children of the flesh, for [God's] secret election precedes [adoption]."[95] Election is the fountain from which every spiritual blessing flows.

Calvin maintained that the doctrine of sovereign election should be freely preached, for to withhold this truth is to withhold the full counsel of God. He states, "Everything, therefore delivered in Scripture on the subject of predestination, we must beware of keeping from the faithful, lest we seem either maliciously to deprive them of the blessing of God, or to accuse and scoff at the Spirit, as having divulged what ought on any account to be suppressed."[96] Furthermore, Calvin believed that withholding this doctrine would dishonor God. He writes, "Whoever, therefore, throws obloquy on the doctrine of predestination, openly brings a charge against God, as having inconsiderately allowed something to escape from Him which is injurious to the Church."[97] By contrast, he said, teaching the doctrine of election helps believers understand God's grace and mercy. He states, "We shall never feel persuaded as we ought that our salvation flows from the free mercy of God as its fountain, until we are made acquainted with His eternal election."[98] He adds, "Ignorance of this principle detracts from the glory of God, and impairs true humility . . . those who would extinguish it . . . pluck up humility by the very roots."[99] Simply put, Calvin believed that manifold benefits flow from the teaching of the truth of election in the church.

**Doctrine in Focus:**

### Definite Atonement

What Calvin taught regarding the extent of the atonement, Robert Peterson notes, "has been the matter of considerable debate."[100] Some scholars hold that Calvin taught a universal atonement.[101] Others assert that he set forth particular redemption.[102] Calvin admittedly often appears ambiguous in discussing the extent of the atonement. Nevertheless, he did make clear and direct statements that support a definite atonement. It can be said that this position is "a logical extension of Calvin's thought."[103]

To this end, Timothy George states that Calvin's teaching on the extent of the atonement must be seen in light of his strong views on predestination: "Predestination is particular in that it pertains to individuals and not to groups of people. . . . With respect to the atonement, this means that Christ died not for everyone indiscriminately, but only for the elect."[104] John Murray likewise writes: "Election is fundamental to Calvin's thinking, and election implies differentiation at the fountain of the whole process of salvation. The evidence indicates that Calvin did not discount this differentiation at the point of Christ's expiatory offering."[105]

In the *Institutes*, Calvin writes, "The doctrine of salvation, which is said to be set apart for the sons of the Church only, is abused when it is represented as effectually available to all."[106] This is an affirmation of definite atonement. Elsewhere, the Reformer maintained that Christ did not offer a sacrifice for those who die in unbelief. With unmistakable language, he writes, "I should like to know how the wicked can eat the flesh of Christ which was not crucified for them, and how they can drink the blood which was not shed to expiate their sins."[107] By these words, Calvin strongly asserted that Christ did not die for the nonelect, but exclusively for those chosen by the Father and entrusted to Him.

Calvin's comments on 1 John 2:2 are particularly important to this point. This verse reads, "He [Christ] is the propitiation for our sins, and not for ours only but also for the sins of the whole world." In exegeting this text, Calvin focuses on the clause "and not for ours only," explaining:

[John] added this for the sake of amplifying, in order that the faithful might be assured that the expiation made by Christ, extends to all who by faith embrace the gospel. Here a question may be raised, how have the sins of the whole world been expiated? I pass by the dotages of the fanatics, who under this pretense extend salvation to all the reprobate, and therefore to Satan himself. Such a monstrous thing deserves no refutation. They who seek to avoid this absurdity, have said that Christ suffered sufficiently for the whole world, but efficiently only for the elect. This solution has commonly prevailed in the schools. Though then I allow that what has been said is true, yet I deny that it is suitable to this passage; for the design of John was no other than to make this benefit common to the whole church. Then under the word *all* or whole, he does not include the reprobate, but designates those who should believe as well as those who were then scattered through various parts of the world. For then is really made evident, as it is meet, the grace of Christ, when it is declared to be the only true salvation of the world.[108]

Addressing Calvin's comments on this pivotal passage, George notes, "While Calvin is sometimes said to have denied the doctrine of limited atonement, this passage [1 John 2:2], among others, is proof to the contrary: Under the word 'all' he does not include the reprobate."[109] Murray writes, "This is an explicit statement to the effect that the reprobate are not included in the propitiation and that 'the whole world' refers to all throughout the world who are the partakers of salvation without distinction of race, or clime, or time."[110] He adds:

> [Calvin] is simply recognizing what every exegete must reckon with, that a universal term does not always imply distributive universalism. It is surely significant that if there are any texts which offered Calvin the opportunity to set forth the doctrine of universal atonement they are 1 John 2.2; 1 Timothy 2.4, 6. But it is in connection with these passages that he is careful to distinguish between distributive universalism and ethnic universalism. . . . Since Calvin is explicit at these points on the distinction between individuals distributively considered and individuals without distinction of race or class, we are not only justified but required to reckon with that distinction in numerous other passages where, in connection with the vicarious sacrifice of Christ, he uses universal terms. We must also bear in mind that Calvin's jealousy for the proclamation of the gospel of reconciliation to all without exception is not in the least incompatible with his exclusion of the reprobate from the scope of the expiation wrought by Christ. Calvin is indeed aware of the tension that arises for us when we consider that the gospel is to be proclaimed to all without exception and yet that God has secretly predestined the reprobate to death. But this tension is not that between universal atonement and the degree of reprobation. It is the tension between the secret will of purpose and the proclaimed will for us, a tension with which Calvin deals at great length at various places.[111]

Murray's point is clear: Calvin did not contend that Christ's sacrifice was for "all" in the sense of every person, including the reprobate. Rather, Christ's death was specifically for all His elect, or all kinds or classes of men (1 Tim. 2:4; Titus 2:11).[112]

Numerous comments by Calvin support Murray's conclusion. In his commentary on 1 Timothy 2:5, Calvin writes, "The universal term *all* must always be referred to classes of men, and not to persons; as if he had said, that not only Jews, but Gentiles also, not only persons of humble rank, but princes also, were redeemed by the death of Christ."[113] Commenting on 1 Timothy 2:4, he writes: "There is no people and no rank in the world that is excluded from salvation; because God wishes that the gospel should be proclaimed to all without exception. . . . The present discourse relates to classes of men, and not to individual persons."[114] He goes on to say:

> Hence we see the childish folly of those who represent this passage to be opposed to predestination. "If God," say they, "wishes all men indiscriminately to be saved, it is false that some are predestinated by His eternal purpose to salvation, and others to perdition." They might have had some ground for saying this, if Paul were speaking here about individual men; although even then we should not have wanted the means of replying to their argument; for, although the will of God ought not to be judged from His secret decrees, when He reveals them to us by outward signs, yet it does not therefore follow that He has not determined with Himself what He intends to do as to every individual man.[115]

Moreover, commenting on Titus 2:11, Calvin states: "That [salvation] is common to all men is expressly testified by [Paul] on account of the slaves of whom he had spoken. Yet he does not mean individual men, but rather describes individual classes, or various ranks of life."[116] Elsewhere he affirms, "As to the word *all*, it must be limited to the elect."[117] He maintains, "The word *all*, which [John] employs, must be understood to refer to the children of God, who belong to his flock."[118] He also says, "We are commanded to pray for all . . . [but] the prayers which we offer for all are still limited to the elect of God."[119] Calvin understood these scriptural uses of the word *all* not to refer to all people in a universal sense, but to all kinds or classes of people. In other words, he distinguished *all* to mean all the elect of God. It was for these Christ died.

Pulling together the various arguments concerning Calvin's position on the atonement, Roger Nicole presents a cohesive case that Calvin held to a definite atonement. He establishes the following points: (1) Calvin strongly held to a specific eternal purpose of God; therefore, it is incongruous to conclude that Calvin, at the same time, espoused an indefinite, hypothetical, general redemption; (2) Calvin repeatedly stressed that God's election is ultimate; therefore, to assume that he held to a universal redemption, which would be more inclusive than the extent of divine election, would be inconsistent; (3) Calvin believed that the cross purchased repentance and faith for the elect; this means that Jesus' death did not merely make sinners savable, but actually saved the elect; (4) Calvin often joined together both the benefits that come only to the elect with reference to the intent of the death of Christ (Rom. 4:25); in this, Calvin repeatedly used "we" when referring to the elect and the redeemed; (5) Calvin closely united the priestly, intercessory work of Christ on the cross with His present, intercessory work in heaven (John 17:9); both intercessions, the Reformer claimed, are directed toward the same group, namely, the elect; and (6) Calvin often viewed texts usually taken to mean God's universal saving intent to be of a particular, limited nature (Ezek. 18:32; John 3:16; 2 Peter 3:9).[120]

Moreover, Nicole writes: (7) Calvin said that universal expressions in connection with the atonement are intended to place special emphasis on the indiscriminate call of the gospel (2 Peter 3:9); (8) Calvin pointed out that many passages directly teach that Christ came to save His people (Matt. 1:21), His sheep (John 10:15), His church (Acts 20:28; Eph. 5:23–26), and "us" (Titus 2:14); he also understood the particular extent of the cross to be taught in John 11:52 and Hebrews 2:9; (9) Calvin stated that unbelievers who observe the Lord's Supper should have no assurance that Christ died for them; (10) Calvin stressed that Scripture addresses the atonement as an accomplishment that actually changes the relationship between God and sinners; the cross does not provide a mere potential blessing that is ineffective, depending on something the sinner must do; (11) Calvin would not have ignored the fact that if the atonement is universal, no one will be punished in hell; (12) Calvin stressed the unity of saving purpose among the Father, Son, and Spirit, while a universal atonement fractures the persons of the Trinity in Their saving efforts; (13) Reformed contemporaries of Calvin, such as Peter Martyr Vermigli, Beza, and William Ames, clearly taught particular redemption, but they were never conscious of differing with Calvin, nor he with them.[121] In addition, Nicole observes that Calvin understood the "all" passages to refer, as noted, to all kinds or classes of men (1 Tim. 2:4; Titus 2:11).[122] He also notes that Calvin believed that many "world" passages transcend nationalistic Israel and should be seen to include elect Gentiles (John 1:29; 1 John 2:2).[123]

When all these citations and arguments are considered, it is reasonable to conclude that Calvin held to definite atonement. This position was to be more carefully defined and developed by his successor, Beza, and by the Synod of Dort and the Westminster Assembly.

**Doctrine in Focus:**

## IRRESISTIBLE CALL

Calvin taught that more is required to bring a person to faith in Christ than the external offer of the gospel. God also must issue an internal call by which He draws His elect to Himself. With this in mind, Calvin writes, "The external call alone would be insufficient, did not God effectually draw to Himself those whom He has called."[124] He adds, "Though our heavenly Father inviteth all men unto the faith by the external voice of man, yet doth He not call effectually by His Spirit any save those whom He hath determined to save."[125] What is more, he states, "There is this difference in the calling of God, that He invites all indiscriminately by His word, whereas He inwardly calls the elect alone (John 6:37)."[126] Calvin was emphatic that the gospel is to be preached to all, but that only the elect are drawn to Christ. He says, "The gospel is preached indiscriminately to the elect and the reprobate; but the elect alone come to Christ, because they have been 'taught by God.'"[127] This is to say, the gospel is an open invitation to all, yet it is only those chosen by God who inevitably accept this summons by the Holy Spirit.

Moreover, Calvin understood that God must first call individual sinners before they will turn to Him in faith. He says: "No one will dedicate himself to God till he be drawn by His goodness, and embrace Him with all his heart. He must therefore call us to Him before we call upon Him."[128] God works in a special way in the elect, Calvin taught, so that they believe the gospel. He adds, "The effectual cause of faith is not the perspicacity of our mind, but the calling of God."[129] Thus, it is through God's efficacious grace that His elect are granted faith by which to trust Him.

Calvin maintained that divine election leads to God's irresistible call, resulting in faith. He says: "We are near [God], not as having anticipated His grace, and come to Him of ourselves, but because, in His condescension, He has stretched out His hand as far as hell itself, to reach us. . . . He first elects us, and then testifies His love by calling us."[130] Furthermore, Calvin affirmed that God brings all of those He has chosen to faith in Christ. He writes, "Christ brings none to the Father, but those given Him by the Father; and this donation, as we know, depends on eternal election."[131] The elect, he adds, are regenerated by the Spirit: "[God] declares His election when He regenerates

His elect by His Holy Spirit and thus inscribes them with a certain mark, while they prove the reality of their sonship by the whole course of their lives, and confirm their own adoption."[132] In regeneration, Calvin writes, "The one thing which distinguishes His elect from the Reprobate is, that . . . He presents the former with new eyes . . . and inclines their hearts to obey His word."[133] Using a similar metaphor, Calvin says, "God prepares His elect for hearing, and gives them ears for that purpose."[134] Calvin thus affirmed that God grants the faith by which the elect see the truth, hear the gospel, and believe in Christ.

Calvin spoke clearly on this matter when commenting on John 6:44, which reads: "No one can come to me unless the Father who sent me draws him. And I will raise him up on the last day." He writes: "We ought not to wonder if many refuse to embrace the Gospel; because no man will ever of himself be able to come to Christ, but God must first approach him by His Spirit; and hence it follows that all are not *drawn*, but that God bestows this grace on those whom He has elected. True, indeed, as to the kind of *drawing*, it is not violent, so as to compel men by external force; but still it is a powerful impulse of the Holy Spirit, which makes men willing who formerly were unwilling and reluctant."[135] Here Calvin again emphasized that God initiates the sovereign work of regeneration and that not all people are drawn to Christ, only the elect. Not even one of the elect can come to Christ unless God acts first. This is because all men are dead in sin and can do nothing to move toward Christ. God must overcome man's stubborn resistance.

Because of man's sinfulness, Calvin believed, no one will turn to God in his own power, but must be changed by God. Only then, he said, will a man trust in Christ. He writes: "It is entirely the work of grace and a benefit conferred by it that our heart is changed from a stony one to one of flesh, that our will is made new, and that we, created anew in heart and mind, at length will what we ought to will."[136] The new birth, he said, is not a work that is part God and part man, but entirely a monergistic work of sovereign grace.

Calvin gave careful attention to the cause-and-effect relationship between God's grace and man's will. He writes: "The human will is of itself evil and therefore needs transformation and renewal so that it may begin to be good, but that grace itself is not merely a tool which can help someone if he is pleased to stretch out his hand to [take] it. That is, [God] does not merely offer it, leaving [to man] the choice between receiving it and rejecting it, but He steers the mind to choose what is right, He moves the will also effectively to obedience, He arouses and advances the endeavor until the actual completion of the work is attained."[137] For Calvin, sovereign grace is the cause and saving faith is the result.

**Doctrine in Focus:**

PRESERVING GRACE

Calvin emphatically taught that none of God's elect lose their salvation. He writes, "Not one of those whom Christ has once ingrafted into His body will He ever permit to perish, for in securing their salvation, He will perform what He has promised; that is, exert a divine power greater than all."[138] He adds, "[The elect differ] in no respect from others, except in being protected by the special mercy of God from rushing down the precipice of eternal death. . . . That they go not to the most desperate extremes of impiety, is not owing to any innate goodness of theirs, but because the eye of God watches over them, and His hand is extended for their preservation."[139] Man's best intentions, he said, would falter were it not for God's perseverance in His elect. He writes, "Both will and effort would immediately fail in us, were He not to add His gift of perseverance."[140] Believers are kept secure by the power of God. No power is greater than that which belongs to God. Therefore, no power can overrule God's power to preserve His people in grace.

Calvin saw that divine election inevitably leads to divine preservation. He writes, "The permanency of our salvation does not depend on us, but on the secret election of God."[141] What God predetermined in eternity past cannot be undone in time or in eternity future. Calvin adds, "He vouchsafes to the elect alone, the living root of faith, that they may persevere even to the end."[142] Election is the root and perseverance is the sure fruit. Indeed, Calvin said, God *must* accomplish the final preservation of the elect. He states, "Redemption would be incomplete, if He did not by continual advances carry us forward to the ultimate end of salvation."[143] Simply put, Calvin writes, "The perseverance of faith . . . flows from election."[144]

This perseverance, Calvin understood, is accomplished by the indwelling Holy Spirit. He writes, "The Holy Spirit not only originates faith, but increases it by degrees, till He conducts us by it all the way to the heavenly kingdom."[145] The Spirit never ceases to uphold and maintain true faith in the elect. Calvin explains, "We persevere in piety only insofar as God is present to sustain us by His hand, and confirm us in perseverance by the agency of His Spirit."[146] It is the work of the Spirit to enable the elect to persevere.

In the final analysis, Calvin affirmed, those who continue in the faith do so because God enables them to do so. He writes, "All our progress and perseverance are from God."[147] Looking at it another way, perseverance is God's grace at work in the elect. Calvin states simply, "Perseverance [is] God's singular gift."[148] Salvation, from start to finish, is all of grace.

**Doctrine in Focus:**
## DIVINE REPROBATION

Calvin also taught the doctrine of reprobation, the theological truth that God not only chooses those who will be saved but those who will not be saved. He states plainly, "There could be no election without its opposite reprobation."[149] He adds, "God . . . claims to Himself alone the difference between the elect and the reprobate"[150] and "God by His secret counsel chooses whom He will while He rejects others."[151] Furthermore, Calvin says, "Some are preordained to eternal life, others to eternal damnation; and, accordingly, as each has been created for one or other of these ends, we say that he has been predestinated to life or to death."[152] In these statements we see a robust affirmation of double predestination, the doctrine that God actively determines who will be saved and who will be condemned.

Calvin taught that the reasons behind reprobation lie with God. He says, "Those, therefore, whom God passes by He reprobates, and that for no other cause but because He is pleased to exclude them from the inheritance which He predestines to His children."[153] This is the only way to understand the strange story of Jacob and Esau, one of whom God loved and the other He hated (Rom. 9:13). Calvin notes: "Both having been at the same time in the womb of their mother, there was something very strange in the change by which the honor of the birthright was transferred to Jacob, and yet Paul declares that the change was an attestation to the election of the one and the reprobation of the other. . . . The adoption of Jacob proceeded not on works but on the calling of God. . . . The only thing to be considered is what pleased God, not what men furnished of themselves."[154] God chooses His elect and His reprobate just as He pleases, without regard for works, family status, or any other external factor.

Calvin challenged those who rejected the doctrine of reprobation, explaining that they were denying the clear teaching of Scripture. This doctrine, he declared, is biblical. He writes, "Scripture clearly proves this much, that God by His eternal and immutable counsel determined once for all those whom it was His pleasure one day to admit to salvation, and those whom, on the other hand, it was His pleasure to doom to destruction."[155] Elsewhere he asks: "How will those who refuse to admit that any are reprobated by God explain the following words of Christ? 'Every plant which my heavenly Father has not planted shall be rooted up,' (Mt. 15:13). They are plainly told that all whom the heavenly Father has not been pleased to plant as sacred trees in His garden, are doomed and devoted to destruction."[156] Those individuals God has not planted—that is, regenerated and drawn to faith in Christ—are destined to be uprooted and given over to eternal destruction.

Calvin anticipated the inevitable offense that the teaching of reprobation brings. He states: "The decree, I admit, is dreadful; and yet it is impossible to deny that God foreknew what the end of man was to be before He made him, and foreknew, because He had so ordained by His decree."[157] The word Calvin uses here, *dreadful*, means "awe-inspiring" or even "terrifying." Calvin also asserted that the doctrine of reprobation reveals God's justice. He says: "Since God inflicts due punishment on those whom He reprobates, and bestows unmerited favor on those whom He calls, He is free from every accusation; just as it belongs to the creditor to forgive the debt to one, and exact it of another. The Lord therefore may show favor to whom He will, because He is merciful; not show it to all, because He is a just judge. In giving to some what they do not merit, He shows His free favor; in not giving to all, He declares what all deserve."[158] In other words, God is merciful in that He gives grace to any. All deserve His wrath and condemnation as a result of sin. Nevertheless, God sovereignly bestows His grace on a chosen few and renders divine judgment on the rest. The question is not, "Why did God not choose everyone?" for all deserve hell. The more accurate question is, "Why did God choose any?"

Calvin maintained that reprobation does not absolve man of his responsibility before God. With pointed words, he writes, "It is not without cause the vessels of wrath are said to be fitted for destruction, and that God is said to have prepared the vessels of mercy, because in this way the praise of salvation is claimed for God, whereas the blame of perdition is thrown upon those who of their own accord bring it upon themselves."[159] In other words, those whom God passes over have only themselves to blame for their sinful choices against Him.

For this reason, Calvin explained, the reprobate receive the full measure of divine justice. He writes, "God acts as a Father towards His elect, and as a judge towards the reprobate."[160] In other words, "The weight of God's wrath lies on the reprobate."[161] This means that they will receive eternal destruction. Calvin says, "The reprobate will be delivered over into eternal fire with their bodies . . . the instruments of perpetrating evil."[162] This determination can never be altered; the destiny of the reprobate is fixed. Calvin writes, "There is no hope of repentance to the reprobate."[163] God's choices are set.

Nevertheless, Calvin insisted that believers should pray for the salvation of all people. He writes: "It does not belong to us to determine before the time who the reprobate and the irreclaimable are. . . . We ought to pray for all without exception."[164] God, he said, answers all prayers according to His sovereign will. He notes: "The prayers which we offer for all are still limited to the elect of God. . . . We leave to the judgment of God those whom He knows to be reprobate."[165] In addition, Calvin urges, "We ought not rashly to conclude that anyone has brought on himself the judgment of eternal death."[166] God alone knows who is elect or reprobate.

# GOD-EXALTING, WORLD-IMPACTING

Calvin's legacy has extended around the world and across the years. The Genevan Reformer left a standard of sound doctrine for the church that endures to this day. At the heart of his teaching were the God-exalting truths of the doctrines of grace. This is to say, Calvin preached the majestic glory of an awesome and transcendent God who sovereignly rules over all. He was emphatically God-centered in His understanding of divine truth. By this conviction, Calvin, alongside the other Reformers, restored the truth of the sovereignty of God to its rightful place in the life of the church.

Furthermore, Calvin maintained that everything in life—every decision, every activity, every duty—must be done to the glory of God. In Calvin's worldview, the glory of God is the *summum bonum*, the highest good. Calvin sought to make God's glory the chief aim and ultimate end in everything, and he pursued this lofty goal with a steadfast commitment. In his estimation, the glory of God is nowhere more radiantly displayed than in the sovereign choice and eternal salvation of God's elect, those purchased by Christ, regenerated by the Spirit, and preserved throughout all the ages to come.

From Clement of Rome to Calvin of Geneva, these transcendent truths of sovereign grace endured through the centuries. What is more, these doctrinal convictions served to undergird the church from the first through the sixteenth century. The heroic men who developed, taught, and championed these grand truths proved themselves to be true pillars of sovereign grace. May the Lord give to His church today a new generation of believers who, like the pillars of old, possess a singular vision for God's supreme majesty. May our sovereign God raise up new pillars of grace to join the long line of godly men who have stood for truth throughout the first fifteen centuries of church history. May such valiant servants be used by God to build His church with the gold, silver, and precious stones of the priceless doctrines of grace.

*Soli Deo gloria!*

Notes

1   John Calvin, *Institutes of the Christian Religion*, trans. Henry Beveridge (Grand Rapids: Eerdmans, 1989), 3.23.10.

2   Calvin, *Institutes of the Christian Religion*, 3.22.6.

3   Martin Luther, from a letter to Martin Bucer, October 14, 1539, as cited in Philip Schaff, *History of the Christian Church, Vol. VIII: Modern Christianity: The Swiss Reformation* (1910; repr., Grand Rapids: Eerdmans, 1984), 272.

4   John Calvin, cited in Donald K. McKim, ed., *The Cambridge Companion to Martin Luther* (Cambridge: Cambridge University Press, 2003), xvi.

5   Randall C. Zachman, "John Calvin (1509–1564)," in *The Reformation Theologians: An Introduction to Theology in the Early Modern Period*, ed. Carter Lindberg (Malden, Mass.: Blackwell, 2002), 185.

6   Curt Daniel, *The History and Theology of Calvinism* (Dallas: Scholarly Reprints, 1993), 25.

7   Jonathan Hill, *The History of Christian Thought* (Downers Grove, Ill.: InterVarsity, 2003), 198.

8   Hill, *The History of Christian Thought*, 198.

9   Hill, *The History of Christian Thought*, 194.

10  Martyn Lloyd-Jones, *Puritans* (Edinburgh: Banner of Truth, 1996), 222.

11  R. C. Sproul, "The Theologian," *Tabletalk*, July 2009, Vol. 33: Number 76, 6.

12  Timothy George, *Theology of the Reformers* (Nashville: Broadman, 1988), 166.

13  William Cunningham, *The Reformers and the Theology of the Reformation* (1866; repr., Edinburgh: Banner of Truth, 1967), 292.

14  Hill, *The History of Christian Thought*, 194.

15  Daniel, *The History and Theology of Calvinism*, 24.

16  J. H. Merle d'Aubigné, *History of the Reformation in Europe in the Time of Calvin, Vol. 7* (1880; repr., Harrisonburg, Va.: Sprinkle, 2000), 82.

17  C. H. Spurgeon, "Laus Deo," *The Metropolitan Tabernacle Pulpit: Sermons Preached by C. H. Spurgeon, Vol. 10* (Pasadena, Texas: Pilgrim, 1976), 310.

18  John Calvin, *Commentary on the Book of Psalms*, trans. James Anderson (Grand Rapids: Baker, 2003), 1:xl–xli.

19 Alister McGrath, *Christianity's Dangerous Idea: The Protestant Revolution—A History from the Sixteenth Century to the Twenty-First* (New York: HarperOne, 2007), 88.

20 Calvin, *Commentary on the Book of Psalms*, 1:xli.

21 Calvin, *Commentary on the Book of Psalms*, 1:xlii–xliii.

22 Calvin, *Commentary on the Book of Psalms*, 1:xliii.

23 John Calvin, *Tracts and Letters, Vol. 4: Letters, Part I, 1528–1545*, ed. Jules Bonnet, trans. David Constable (Edinburgh: Banner of Truth, 2009), 175.

24 Calvin, *Tracts and Letters, Vol. 4*, 231.

25 Gordon J. Spykman, *Reformational Theology: A New Paradigm for Doing Theology* (Grand Rapids: Eerdmans, 1992), 217.

26 James Montgomery Boice, *Whatever Happened to the Gospel of Grace? Rediscovering the Doctrines that Shook the World* (Wheaton: Crossway, 2001), 83–84.

27 Calvin, cited in Theodore Beza, *Life of Calvin* (Milwaukie, Ore.: Back Home Industries, 1996), 25–26.

28 Calvin, cited in John T. McNeill, *The History and Character of Calvinism* (Oxford: Oxford University Press, 1954), 157.

29 Alister E. McGrath, *A Life of John Calvin* (Malden, Mass.: Blackwell, 1990), 196–202.

30 John Calvin, *Tracts and Letters, Vol. 7: Letters, Part 4, 1559–1564*, ed. Jules Bonnet, trans. Marcus Robert Gilchrist (Edinburgh: Banner of Truth, 2009), 365–366.

31 Calvin, *Tracts and Letters, Vol. 7*, 375.

32 Theodore Beza, *Life of Calvin*, cited in John Calvin, *Tracts and Letters, Vol. 1: Tracts, Part 1, 1559–1564*, ed. and trans. Henry Beveridge (Edinburgh: Banner of Truth, 2009), c.

33 Tony Lane, *A Concise History of Christian Thought* (Grand Rapids: Baker Academic, 2006), 176.

34 Steven J. Lawson, *The Expository Genius of John Calvin* (Lake Mary, Fla.: Reformation Trust, 2007), 32–34.

35 Calvin, *Tracts and Letters, Vol. 1*, 25–68.

36 Earle E. Cairns, *Christianity Through the Centuries: A History of the Christian Church*, 3rd Ed. (Grand Rapids: Zondervan, 1996), 303.

37 Daniel, *The History and Theology of Calvinism*, 28.

38 Benjamin B. Warfield, "John Calvin: The Man and His Work," in *Calvin and Calvinism* (Grand Rapids: Baker, 2000), 24.

39 Calvin, *Institutes of the Christian Religion*, 1.16.8.

40 Calvin, *Institutes of the Christian Religion*, 1.16.8.

41 Calvin, *Institutes of the Christian Religion*, 1.16.8.

42 John Calvin, *Commentary on the Book of the Prophet Daniel*, trans. Thomas Myers (Grand Rapids: Baker, 2003), 2:173 (Dan. 9:14).

43 John Calvin, *Commentaries on the Catholic Epistles*, trans. John Owen (Grand Rapids: Baker, 2003), 40 (1 Peter 1:11).

44 Calvin, *Institutes of the Christian Religion*, 1.16.3.

45 Calvin, *Institutes of the Christian Religion*, 1.17.7.

46 Calvin, *Institutes of the Christian Religion*, 1.18.1.

47 Calvin, *Institutes of the Christian Religion*, 3.23.2.

48 John Calvin, *Commentaries on the Epistle of Paul the Apostle to the Romans*, trans. and ed. John Owen (Grand Rapids: Baker, 2003), 317 (Rom. 8:29), cited in John Murray, *Calvin on Scripture and Divine Sovereignty* (Grand Rapids: Baker, 1978), 58.

49 Calvin, *Commentary on the Book of Psalms*, 2:249 (Ps. 49:14).

50 Calvin, *Institutes of the Christian Religion*, 1.17.3.

51 John MacArthur, "Man's Radical Corruption," in *John Calvin: A Heart For Devotion, Doctrine & Doxology*, ed. Burk Parsons (Orlando, Fla.: Reformation Trust, 2008), 133.

52 Calvin, *Institutes of the Christian Religion*, 2.1.9.

53 Calvin, *Institutes of the Christian Religion*, 2.1.6.

54 Calvin, *Institutes of the Christian Religion*, 2.1.6.

55 Calvin, *Commentaries on the Epistle of Paul the Apostle to the Romans*, 201 (Rom. 5:12).

56 Calvin, *Institutes of the Christian Religion*, 2.1.7.

57 Calvin, *Institutes of the Christian Religion*, 2.1.8.

58 Calvin, *Institutes of the Christian Religion*, 2.1.6.

59 Calvin, *Institutes of the Christian Religion*, 2.1.5.

60 Calvin, *Commentary on the Book of Psalms*, 2:290 (Ps. 51:5).

61 Calvin, *Institutes of the Christian Religion*, 2.1.5.

62 Calvin, *Institutes of the Christian Religion*, 2.1.8.

63 Calvin, *Commentaries on the Epistle of Paul the Apostle to the Romans*, 200 (Rom. 5:12).

64 Calvin, *Institutes of the Christian Religion*, 2.1.9.

65 Calvin, *Institutes of the Christian Religion*, 2.1.9.

66 Calvin, *Institutes of the Christian Religion*, 2.1.9.

67 Calvin, *Commentaries on the Catholic Epistles*, xvii (1 Peter, dedication).

68 John Calvin, *Commentary on the Gospel According to John*, trans. William Pringle (Grand Rapids: Baker, 2003), 1:399 (John 10:8).

69 Calvin, *Institutes of the Christian Religion*, 2.8.2.

70 John Calvin, *Instruction in Faith*, trans. Paul Fuhrmann (Philadelphia: Westminster Press, 1949), 22.

71 Calvin, *Commentaries on the Epistle of Paul the Apostle to the Romans*, 210 (Rom. 5:17).

72 Calvin, *Institutes of the Christian Religion*, 3.21.5.

73 Calvin, *Commentary on the Book of Psalms*, 3:403 (Ps. 87:6).

74 Calvin, *Commentaries on the Epistle of Paul the Apostle to the Romans*, 350 (Rom. 9:11).

75 Calvin, *Commentaries on the Epistle of Paul the Apostle to the Romans*, 354 (Rom. 9:14).

76 John Calvin, *Commentary on the Book of the Prophet Isaiah*, trans. William Pringle (Grand Rapids: Baker, 2003), 1:155 (Isa. 4:3).

77 Calvin, *Commentary on the Book of Psalms*, 3:433 (Ps. 89:19).

78 Calvin, *Institutes of the Christian Religion*, 3.21.7.

79 John Calvin, *Commentaries on the Book of Genesis*, trans. John King (Grand Rapids: Baker, 2003), 2:47 (Gen. 25:23).

80 Calvin, *Commentary on the Book of Psalms*, 2:154 (Ps. 44:3).

81 Calvin, *Institutes of the Christian Religion*, 3.22.2.

82 Calvin, *Institutes of the Christian Religion*, 3.22.1.

83 Calvin, *Institutes of the Christian Religion*, 3.22.2.

84 Calvin, *Institutes of the Christian Religion*, 3.22.3.

85 Calvin, *Institutes of the Christian Religion*, 3.22.3.

86 Calvin, *Institutes of the Christian Religion*, 3.22.1.

87 Calvin, *Institutes of the Christian Religion*, 3.21.7.

88 Calvin, *Institutes of the Christian Religion*, 3.24.1.

89  Calvin, *Commentary on the Gospel According to John*, 2:97 (John 14:22).

90  Calvin, *Commentary on the Book of Psalms*, 2:210 (Ps. 47:4).

91  Calvin, *Institutes of the Christian Religion*, 3.22.1.

92  Calvin, *Institutes of the Christian Religion*, 3.21.1.

93  Calvin, *Institutes of the Christian Religion*, 3.22.10.

94  John Calvin, *Commentaries on the Twelve Minor Prophets*, trans. John Owen (Grand Rapids: Baker, 2003), 5:480 (Mal. 1:2–6).

95  Calvin, *Commentaries on the Epistle of Paul the Apostle to the Romans*, 410 (Rom. 11:2).

96  Calvin, *Institutes of the Christian Religion*, 3.21.3.

97  Calvin, *Institutes of the Christian Religion*, 3.21.4.

98  Calvin, *Institutes of the Christian Religion*, 3.21.1.

99  Calvin, *Institutes of the Christian Religion*, 3.21.1.

100  Robert A. Peterson, "Calvin on Christ's Saving Work," in *Theological Guide to Calvin's Institutes*, eds. David W. Hall and Peter A. Lillback (Phillipsburg, N.J.: P&R, 2008), 246.

101  James B. Torrance, "The Incarnation and Limited Atonement, *EQ*, 55, 1983, 82–94; M. Charles Bell, *Calvin and Scottish Theology: the Doctrine of Assurance* (Edinburgh: Handsel, 1985), 13–40; [Curt D.] Daniel, *op. cit* ["HyperCalvinism and John Gill" (University of Edinburgh: PhD thesis, 1983)], 777–829.

102  Paul Helm, *Calvin and the Calvinists* (Edinburgh, Banner of Truth, 1982); "Calvin and the Covenants: Unity and Continuity," *EQ*, 55, 1983, 65–81; W. Robert Godfrey, "Reformed Thought on the Extent of the Atonement to 1618," *Westminster Theological Journal*, 37, 1975, 137–138.

103  Peterson, "Calvin on Christ's Saving Work," in *Theological Guide to Calvin's Institutes*, 247.

104  George, *Theology of the Reformers*, 233.

105  John Murray, Review of Paul Van Burren, "Christ in Our Place," *Westminster Theological Journal*, November 1959, 59; also found in *Collected Writings of John Murray, Vol. 4* (Edinburgh: Banner of Truth, 1976–82), 313.

106  Calvin, *Institutes of the Christian Religion*, 3.22.10.

107  John Calvin, *Calvin: Theological Treatises*, ed. J. K. S. Reid (Louisville: Westminster John Knox, 2000), 285.

108  Calvin, *Commentaries on the Catholic Epistles*, 172–173 (1 John 2:2).

109  George, *Theology of the Reformers*, 222n112.

110  John Murray, "Calvin on the Extent of the Atonement," *Banner of Truth Magazine*, Issue 234, March 1983, 21.

111  Murray, "Calvin on the Extent of the Atonement," *Banner of Truth Magazine*, 22; also found in *Collected Writings of John Murray, Vol. 4*, 313.

112  Roger Nicole, "John Calvin's View of the Extent of the Atonement," in *Standing Forth: Collected Writings of Roger Nicole* (Ross-shire, Scotland: Mentor, 2002), 298–300.

113  John Calvin, *Commentaries on the Epistles to Timothy, Titus, and Philemon*, trans. by Rev. William Pringle (Grand Rapids: Baker, 2003), 57 (1 Tim. 2:5).

114  Calvin, *Commentaries on the Epistles to Timothy, Titus, and Philemon*, 54–55 (1 Tim. 2:4).

115  Calvin, *Commentaries on the Epistles to Timothy, Titus, and Philemon*, 54 (1 Tim. 2:4).

116  Calvin, *Commentaries on the Epistles to Timothy, Titus, and Philemon*, 318 (Titus 2:11).

117  Calvin, *Commentary on the Gospel According to John*, 1:258 (John 6:45).

118  Calvin, *Commentary on the Gospel According to John*, 2:37 (John 12:32).

119 Calvin, *Commentary on the Gospel According to John*, 2:172 (John 17:9).

120 Nicole, "John Calvin's View of the Extent of the Atonement," in *Standing Forth*, 283–312.

121 Nicole, "John Calvin's View of the Extent of the Atonement," in *Standing Forth*, 283–312.

122 Nicole, "John Calvin's View of the Extent of the Atonement," in *Standing Forth*, 298–300.

123 Nicole, "John Calvin's View of the Extent of the Atonement," in *Standing Forth*, 298–300.

124 Calvin, *Commentary on the Book of Psalms*, 3:322 (Ps. 81:11).

125 John Calvin, *Commentary upon the Acts of the Apostles*, trans. Henry Beveridge (Grand Rapids: Baker, 2003), 1:556 (Acts 13:48).

126 John Calvin, *Tracts and Letters, Vol. 3: Tracts, Part 3*, ed. and trans. Henry Beveridge (1851; repr., Edinburgh: Banner of Truth, 2009), 155–56.

127 Calvin, *Commentary on the Book of the Prophet Isaiah*, 4:146 (Isa. 54:13).

128 Calvin, *Commentary on the Book of the Prophet Isaiah*, 2:74 (Isa. 19:20).

129 Calvin, *Commentaries on the Catholic Epistles*, 369 (2 Peter 1:3).

130 Calvin, *Commentary on the Book of Psalms*, 2:457 (Ps. 65:4).

131 John Calvin, *Commentaries on the Epistle of Paul the Apostle to the Hebrews*, trans. John Owen (Grand Rapids: Baker, 2003), 70 (Heb. 2:13).

132 Calvin, *Commentary on the Book of the Prophet Daniel*, 2:372 (Dan. 12:1).

133 Calvin, *Tracts and Letters, Vol. 3, Tracts, Part 3*, 253.

134 John Calvin, *Commentaries on the Prophet Ezekiel*, trans. Thomas Myers (Grand Rapids: Baker, 2003), 1:139 (Ezek. 3:10–11).

135 Calvin, *Commentary on the Gospel According to John*, 1:257 (John 6:44). Emphasis in original.

136 John Calvin, *The Bondage and Liberation of the Will: A Defence of the Orthodox Doctrine of Human Choice Against Pighius*, ed. A. N. S. Lane, trans. G. I. Davies (Grand Rapids: Baker, 1996), 114.

137 Calvin, *The Bondage and Liberation of the Will*, 114.

138 Calvin, *Institutes of the Christian Religion*, 3.22.7.

139 Calvin, *Institutes of the Christian Religion*, 3.24.10.

140 Calvin, *Commentaries on the Twelve Minor Prophets*, 4:346 (Hag. 1:14).

141 John Calvin, *Commentary on a Harmony of the Evangelists*, trans. William Pringle (Grand Rapids: Baker, 2003), 3:141 (Matt. 24:24).

142 Calvin, *Institutes of the Christian Religion*, 3.2.11.

143 Calvin, *Institutes of the Christian Religion*, 2.16.1.

144 Calvin, *Commentaries on the Epistle of Paul the Apostle to the Romans*, 432 (Rom. 11:22).

145 Calvin, *Institutes of the Christian Religion*, 3.2.33.

146 John Calvin, *Commentaries on the Book of Joshua*, trans. Henry Beveridge (Grand Rapids: Baker, 2003), 261 (Josh. 22:30).

147 Calvin, *Commentaries on the Catholic Epistles*, 373 (2 Peter 1:5).

148 Calvin, *Commentaries on the Prophet Ezekiel*, 1:380 (Ezek. 11:19–20).

149 Calvin, *Institutes of the Christian Religion*, 3.23.1.

150 Calvin, *Commentaries on the Prophet Ezekiel*, 2:250 (Ezek. 18:24).

151 Calvin, *Institutes of the Christian Religion*, 3.21.7.

152 Calvin, *Institutes of the Christian Religion*, 3.21.5.

153 Calvin, *Institutes of the Christian Religion*, 3.23.1.

154 Calvin, *Institutes of the Christian Religion*, 3.22.4.

155 Calvin, *Institutes of the Christian Religion*, 3.21.7.

156 Calvin, *Institutes of the Christian Religion*, 3.23.1.

157 Calvin, *Institutes of the Christian Religion*, 3.23.7.

158 Calvin, *Institutes of the Christian Religion*, 3.23.11.

159 Calvin, *Institutes of the Christian Religion*, 3.23.1.

160 John Calvin, *Commentaries on the Book of the Prophet Jeremiah and the Lamentations*, trans John Owen (Grand Rapids: Baker, 2003), 2:66 (Jer. 10:25).

161 Calvin, *Commentary on the Book of the Prophet Isaiah*, 2:385 (Isa. 30:32).

162 Calvin, *Commentaries on the Book of Genesis*, 1:166 (Gen. 3:14).

163 Calvin, *Commentaries on the Prophet Ezekiel*, 1:404 (Ezek. 12:15).

164 Calvin, *Commentaries on the Book of the Prophet Jeremiah and the Lamentations*, 3:43 (Jer. 20:12).

165 Calvin, *Commentary on the Gospel According to John*, 2:172–173 (John 17:9).

166 Calvin, *Commentaries on the Catholic Epistles*, 270 (1 John 5:16).

# CHAPTER TWENTY-FOUR
## STUDY QUESTIONS

1. Comment on the two great Protestant Reformers, Martin Luther and John Calvin. In what ways were they alike? How did they differ?

2. List the five *solas* of the sixteenth-century Reformation. What do these Reformation slogans mean? What impact did they have in the development of the doctrines of grace? What Scripture passages can be cited for each position?

3. What was arguably Calvin's greatest theological writing for the church? What was the occasion and purpose for the writing of this masterpiece? How many editions were there? How was each revision different?

4. Summarize Calvin's pastorate at Geneva. Under what circumstances was Calvin forced into exile at Strasbourg? What was remarkable about his return three and one half years later? What are some benefits to expository preaching?

5. Describe Calvin's compositional output (theological treatises, letters, commentaries, and sermons).

6. What was the relationship between Calvin's theology and Augustinianism? Between Calvin's theology and Calvinism?

7. Comment on the development of the church's understanding of the extent of Christ's atonement by the sixteenth century. Explain the importance of this subject for Calvin's exegetical study of various passages of Scripture.

8. Define the effectual call of God. How does God's internal call differ from the external gospel invitation that is preached? Why is God's effectual call to His elect said to be irresistible?

Afterword

# AN UNEXPECTED
# CONTINUITY

C ontinuity and discontinuity are the themes of historical debate. If history revealed only unbroken continuity, the discipline would be of
little value. On the other hand, if history revealed only discontinuity, the discipline would be incomprehensible.

We can understand the present only in terms of the past, but that often
means present-day debates are directed toward contentious arguments over
the past. This is true when it comes to the history of ideas, the history of
law, the history of peoples, and, of course, the history of theology within the
Christian tradition.

Thus, a work of historical theology is always an argument. A totally objective history of doctrine is an impossibility. As G. W. Bromiley once remarked,
such a work "lies beyond the limits of human possibility."[1] Nevertheless, the
historian of doctrine works by documenting the arguments and by marshaling
materials for that documentation.

In *Pillars of Grace*, Dr. Steven J. Lawson has argued for an unexpected
continuity in the teaching of the Church Fathers, the medieval theologians,
and the Reformers on the reality and operations of God's saving grace. The
freshness of his argument is evident in the fact that most evangelicals tend to
think of the Fathers primarily in terms of the christological and Trinitarian
controversies that marked the first centuries of the church. The evangelical temptation is to be thankful for the establishment and articulation of
orthodoxy on those central issues, but to assume that, with rare exceptions
(Augustine chief among them), the Fathers have little to say to us concerning
grace and the gift of salvation.

This would be a major mistake and a costly confusion. In this important book, Dr. Lawson has documented the teachings of many of the most important theologians, churchmen, and Christian thinkers of these centuries, showing that these men did indeed have much to say about God's saving grace—and much that will be of great encouragement to evangelicals today.

This is Dr. Lawson's great concern in this book and series—to encourage us to see continuity in the affirmation of God's gracious act of salvation and God's sovereignty over the entire economy of salvation from beginning to end. He has accomplished this very well. Left to other authors and other books is the story of other continuities and the inevitable discontinuities that accompany and rival them. What makes this book so important is the fact that it draws attention to a vital continuity where American evangelicals so often assume the opposite.

The standard evangelical summary of history argues that the New Testament and the apostles clearly understood that sinners are justified by grace alone through faith alone in Christ alone, but that this simple gospel of grace was quickly lost in the midst of early church controversies and the rise of Roman Catholicism as the religion of the empire. The church was then plunged into the Dark Ages of the medieval era and the light dawned only when the Reformation began and the gospel of God's sheer grace was recovered and reaffirmed by the Reformers and their heirs.

This history, we must note, is not wrong—it is just not all there is to the story. Indeed, when the Reformers asserted doctrines as central as justification by faith, they argued for the essential *continuity* of their beliefs with those of the apostles, many of the Fathers, and select medieval authorities.

Thus, Martin Luther always referenced Augustine with high honor, often speaking of him as "the blessed Augustine." In Calvin's magisterial *Institutes of the Christian Religion*, Augustine is cited more frequently than any other authority, except for the Bible. Second only to Augustine in frequency of citation is Bernard of Clairvaux. Readers of *Pillars of Grace* will understand why this is so, having read Dr. Lawson's treatment of both Augustine and Bernard in these pages.

*Pillars of Grace* represents a theological expedition into the *terra incognita* of the evangelical imagination when it comes to the history of theology. Those who have read this volume must now be humbled by the knowledge that God preserved His gospel in these centuries and raised up faithful men to teach and defend that gospel. Armed with that knowledge, readers can now see the Reformation in its proper light—as the reassertion of the faith "once for all delivered to the saints" (Jude 3).

—*R. Albert Mohler Jr.*
Louisville, Kentucky
September 2010

NOTE

1   G. W. Bromiley, *Historical Theology: An Introduction* (Grand Rapids: Eerdmans, 1978), xxi.

# SCRIPTURE INDEX

# SUBJECT INDEX

Calvinism, 1, 19–20, 331, 486, 513
Calvin, John, 5, 10, 19–20, 37, 228, 276,
    277, 286, 340, 396, 428, 429, 485,
    500, 501–30
  and Anselm, 304
  on Augustine, 214, 216, 540
  on Bernard, 30–31, 318, 325
  on Church Fathers, 117
  on Cyprian, 128, 134
  as father of Reformation, 360
  influenced by Bradwardine, 351
  influenced by Wycliffe, 365
  influence from Luther, 501
  influence of Bullinger, 486
  on Lord's Supper, 403
  on monastic theology, 29
  on sovereign grace, 35–36
Cambridge, 31, 32, 35, 339, 340, 450, 452
cannibalism, Christians accused of, 61,
    76, 94
Cappadocia, 163, 181
Cappadocian Fathers, 25–26, 127, 163,
    164–65, 181, 196, 197
Carolingian Renaissance, 276
Carthage, 24, 112, 130, 131, 217
Cassian, John, 29, 228, 256
catechism, 220
Cathari, 217
Catherine of Aragon, 463
causative cooperation, 27
Cause of God Against the Pelagians
    (Bradwardine), 342, 343–44, 346
Charlemagne, 276
Charles V, 401, 463, 506
chastity, 29
Christendom, 295, 317, 404
Christian Brethren, 455
Christian liberty, 406, 432
Chrysostom, John, 63, 64, 431, 482
church, 136
  Ambrose on, 200

Augustine on, 28, 34, 229
  Hus on, 386
  unity of, 384
church and state, 196, 207
church discipline, 506–7
Church Fathers, 5–7, 10, 16, 19–20, 32,
    36, 37, 52, 482, 505
church government, 37
church history, 3–6, 37–38
circumcision, 67
Cistercian order, 318, 319–20, 321, 322
Citeaux, 318, 320–21
City of God (Augustine), 231
civil magistrate, 394–95, 463
Clairvaux, 320, 322
Clarity and Certainty of God's Word
    (Zwingli), 435
Clark, Robert, 452–53
Clement of Alexandria, 25, 111
Clement of Rome, 5, 10, 22, 23, 37, 44,
    49–56, 530
Cletus, 50
cloud of witnesses, 11
Cluny, 318, 323
Cochlaeus, John, 454
Coelestius, 227
Cologne, 482
Columbus, Christopher, 393
Commentary on True and False Religion
    (Zwingli), 435
Concerning the Lapsed (Cyprian), 132
Confessions (Augustine), 217, 221, 224,
    230, 236
confessions, 479
Conrad of Waldhausen, 375
Consensus Tigurinus, 485, 513
Constantine, 145, 146–47, 148, 163,
    195–96
Constantinople, 184–85
Constantinople Creed, 180, 185
Constantius, 148–49

Phillips, Harry, 459
*Philocalia*, 167, 182
Photinians, 180, 204
Piper, John, 467
Plato, 75, 78, 87n31
Platonic Academy, 166, 182
Platonism, 47, 75, 79, 91
Pneumatomachians, 26, 164, 167, 169, 180
Polycarp, 22, 49, 66, 93
polytheism, 48
pope, as the Antichrist, 361
*posse non peccare*, 234
*posse peccare*, 234
Pothinus, 93, 94
poverty, 29, 320
Poyntz, Thomas, 458–59
*Practice of Prelates* (Tyndale), 463
predestination, 4, 5, 28, 32, 47, 99, 429,
    436, 520. *See also* double predesti-
    nation; election
  and atonement, 520
  Augustine on, 232
  Bullinger on, 488, 492
  Calvin on, 517
  and Church Fathers, 52
  from eternity, 238
  as foreknowledge, 29
  as foresight, 30
  progress of doctrine of, 45
  as twofold, 30
  unto damnation, 30
  unto salvation, 30
  Zwingli on, 440
*Predestination of the Saints* (Augustine), 232
Pre-Reformers, 10, 20, 21, 32–33, 350,
    358–59, 376
preserving grace, 5, 16
  Ambrose on, 205–6
  Anselm on, 310
  Apostolic Fathers on, 51
  Athanasius on, 155–56
  Augustine on, 243–45

Basil on, 173
Bradwardine on, 349
Bullinger on, 494
Calvin on, 527–28
Clement on, 55
Cyprian on, 136–38
Hus on, 385–86
Ignatius on, 68
Isidore on, 266
Luther on, 418–19
Tertullian on, 119
Tyndale on, 471
Wycliffe on, 368–69
Zwingli on, 442–43
priesthood of the believer, 405
printing press, 394
Priscius, 78
progressive justification, 28
prophets, Old Testament, 11, 79
*Proslogion* (Anselm), 299, 302
Prosper of Aquitaine, 29, 256–57, 344
Protestants
  and Augustine, 213
  on church history, 6
  and Patristics, 7
Protestant theology, 213
providence, 97, 233, 435, 436, 515
Ptolemaeus, 95
Puritans, 276, 485
Purvey, John, 364

*quadrivium*, 276
Quentell, Peter, 454

radical depravity, 5, 16, 28
  Ambrose on, 203
  Anselm on, 305–7
  Apostolic Fathers on, 51
  Athanasius on, 152–53
  Augustine on, 234–36
  Basil on, 170–71
  Bernard on, 326–28

# ABOUT THE AUTHOR

D r. Steven J. Lawson is the senior pastor of Christ Fellowship Baptist Church in Mobile, Alabama, a teaching fellow of Ligonier Ministries, and a council member and executive staff member of the Alliance of Confessing Evangelicals.

He is a graduate of Texas Tech University (BBA), Dallas Theological Seminary (ThM), and Reformed Theological Seminary (DMin).

Dr. Lawson is the author of sixteen books, his most recent being *The Unwavering Resolve of Jonathan Edwards* and *The Expository Genius of John Calvin*, both in the Long Line of Godly Men Profiles series from Reformation Trust Publishing, for which he serves as series editor. His other titles include *Foundations of Grace, Famine in the Land*, and a two-volume commentary on the Psalms. His books have been translated into various languages around the world, including Russian, Portuguese, Spanish, and Indonesian.

He has contributed articles to *Bibliotheca Sacra, The Southern Baptist Journal of Theology, Faith and Mission, Decision* magazine, *Discipleship Journal*, and *Tabletalk*, among other journals and periodicals.

The focus of Dr. Lawson's ministry is the verse-by-verse exposition of the Bible. His pulpit ministry takes him around the world and to many conferences in the United States, including the annual Ligonier Ministries National Conference and Pastors Conference in Orlando, Florida; the Shepherd's Conference and Resolved, sponsored by Grace Community Church in Sun Valley, California; and the Philadelphia Conference on Reformed Theology.

He is president of New Reformation, a ministry designed to bring about biblical reformation in the church. He serves on the Executive Board of The Master's Seminary and College and teaches in the doctor of ministry programs at The Master's Seminary and the Ligonier Academy of Biblical and Theological Studies.

Dr. Lawson and his wife, Anne, have three sons and a daughter.